STERNE

STERNE

MEMOIRS OF MR. LAURENCE STERNE

THE LIFE & OPINIONS OF TRISTRAM SHANDY

A SENTIMENTAL JOURNEY

SELECTED SERMONS AND LETTERS

Edited by

DOUGLAS GRANT

HARVARD UNIVERSITY PRESS
CAMBRIDGE MASSACHUSETTS

SBN 674-56525-8
1970 Importation
PRINTED IN GREAT BRITAIN

CONTENTS

CONTENTS

INTRODUCTION

THE ANCIENT MARINER—the type of all successful fabulists—with a glance of his brilliant eye, drew aside the unwilling Wedding Guest to listen to his story. Laurence Sterne is the Mariner among novelists. He takes no notice of the public; he will not throw his message upon its impatient waters; but he collects from here and there a few to whom he will tell his tale. He makes his way up to us where we are standing in the crowd and compels us, with a nudge and a nod, to follow him to some secluded spot where he can conveniently and frankly pour out his whole heart. He is intimate with us from the start; he assumes a familiar and confidential air which at once disarms us of the critical hostility that tempers our attitude towards a writer who, adopting the character of "author," addresses us as "the public"; and he insinuates under this screen much that we would not otherwise tolerate. He fully uses the advantage he has thus gained, and, even when we are most restless under his digressions, galled by his sallies, and annoyed by his foolery, we cannot break away. We are the victims of a *tête-à-tête*. We are fascinated by the secrets he parades, sympathetic to the tears he freely sheds, caught in the sentimentality he spins, and continually amused by his antics and jokes. We are, in brief, before we know it, what he wishes us to be, intimate with him. He relies, and his skill depends, upon this intimacy.

His style is determined by his intention to have it all out with us alone. He does not confront us with rhetoric, nor conduct us down lengthening periods, but addresses us in the easy tones of a graceful conversationalist. He writes English as it is spoken; each fluent sentence catches the cadence, rhythm, inflections, and hesitations of the voice; and to further this end he devises his own notation. He softens the formality of conventional prose by inserting the Shandean *dash*—a simple mark which has a world of significance. It suggests all those conversational subtleties which are for ever beyond the reach of printed words; it is the pause which emphasises a point, or allows an insinuation to strike home, or anticipates a sudden change in tone; it is the nod, wink,

[7]

grimace, shrug, and hundred other slight movements which accompany and trick out speech; it is the very breath—the intimacy—of his style. He must not be read as though he were an ordinary author. We cannot casually put out on his sentences and trust that a strong current will drift us to a meaning at the end; nor can we accelerate on as if there was only a straight road ahead and nothing of interest to the right or left; we must follow closely and carefully behind him, stopping when he stops, straying off the track where he strays, if we are to appreciate him. He leaves unsaid and implies so much, that to have read only each word is to have read only half his work. His exclamation in praise of 'the insensible, MORE or LESS' can be used to describe his own style: 'Just heaven! how does the *Poco piu* and the *Poco meno* of the *Italian* artists;————the insensible, MORE or LESS, determine the precise line of beauty in the sentence, as well as in the statue! How do the slight touches of the chisel, the pencil, the pen, the fiddle-stick, *et cætera*,————give the true swell, which gives the true pleasure! O my countrymen!————be nice;———— be cautious in your language;————and never, O! never let it be forgotten upon what small particles your eloquence and your fame depend.'

His themes are as intimate as his style. He is not concerned with general rights and wrongs as they can be shown in the lives and deaths of the great as they brave and go down in humanity's maëlstrom. He is preoccupied with the domestic whirlpool which, threatening only to duck and not to drown, involves in its limited confusion man and wife, flirtatious maid-servant and eccentric relation, and all those other characters who mark out the family circle; and he is diverted by the small passions, vagaries, senti-ments, jests, and gossip which the whirlpool sets in motion. He places his scenes within doors—within the scope of ordinary hearts—and he never ambles more than a mile or two down the narrow lane that leads from the front garden to the main road. Within doors is his proper province, and in countless small ways he makes us feel as closely as if we had spent our lives in its rooms the very spirit of the house. When we close *Tristram Shandy*, we can still smell in our nostrils the smoky warmth of the parlour where we have watched and listened to Uncle Toby and Walter Shandy at odds or in agreement; we know which door creaks on its hinges, and why it does so; we can visualise where the pale face of the grandfather clock at the head of the stairs glimmers through the darkness; and, were we driven to it by a broken bell-pull, we could make our way safely to the kitchen downstairs. Whose lands adjoin the garden, which village lies at the lane's end, and what cities beyond, we are never told, nor do we care to ask; we are as contented as an eighteenth-century squire to dismiss the world's progress and to busy ourselves only with adventures at home. The adventures are the slight happenings which have always agitated domestic scenes. A birth, a journey, a fall from a horse, a whimsy, a disagreement, and a reconciliation are the incidents which he describes, but his style, his nice perception of character, his humour, and his imagination so invest these trivialities, that they appear to have greater significance than the grand events out-of-doors. Certainly, these small inside occurrences bulk larger in life than the outside events, and by choosing to tell their story, he showed that he thoroughly understood the truth of the adage, *multum in parvo*.

A Sentimental Journey carries a promise in its title to take us farther afield—to walk us up mountains, to sail us down rivers, and to stand us wondering before the ruins of the ancient world —but, in fact, we never really leave home. We spend the journey in rooms, and our attention is so taken up by what goes on within those small spaces that we forget we have come to see the mountains, palaces, cathedrals, and the foreignness outside. What happens to us might have happened just as easily at Shandy Hall. We are journeying in search of sentiments, and since their home is the heart, and it is the same heart that beats in France as in England, we must expect that they will be little different from those we already know. *A Sentimental Journey* might be appropriately sub-titled, *home-thoughts abroad*. Whatever their place of origin, however, the sentiments are never common-place. The 'insensible, MORE or LESS' of his style allows him to refine his sentiments to a pure essence which he then stoppers within the vial of a slight experience; the beat of a beautiful *grisette's* pulse, the trill of a caged starling, or the action of offering a pinch of snuff, are so charged with sentiment that they touch the heart more nearly, and stay in the memory longer, than the ecstatic loves and poignant deaths upon which so much literary talent has been expended.

His characters are as skilfully and as intimately drawn as his scenes. Charles Lamb, with his unerring eye for quality, spoke of 'those Shandean lights and shades,' and it is by the artful disposal of lights and shades, by fine touches laid on here and there with marvellous exactitude, that Sterne builds up his characters.

There are perhaps no more real characters in English fiction than his, and he succeeds in realising them so absolutely by never sparing us the smallest trick of speech and gesture, or point of personal appearance, which reflects in some way their personalities. He describes them rather in the same way as the *pointilliste* painters interpret a landscape—by building the whole out of minute particulars; and just as the dabbled surface of their pictures at first conceals their skill, so his apparently haphazard relation of facts and incidents disguises the tact and artfulness with which they are introduced. His range of characters is, of course, very limited. He disregards the world over the garden wall and nobody comes through the gate except by invitation; if an Ophelia or a Clarissa Harlowe tried to enter there would be havoc among the sentiments; but he selects the company within so happily, that there are few collections of characters which are brought more clearly before our imaginations.

His humour is of a piece with his characterisation. It is not of the cosmic kind which Thomas Carlyle so thunderously praised; it is not the laughter of the gods but the chuckling of ordinary men. It is, however, of remarkable variety. It ranges from mere foolery to pure comedy; it includes the practical joke of inserting a marbled page in order to trip up the reader, and the glorious scene in which Uncle Toby and the Widow Wadman are brought together in the summer-house; and it effortlessly burns or glimmers on from page to page. His wit, too, is no less constant, and it can make the most improbable subject sparkle and delight. George Saintsbury pointed out long ago, that the flaw in Sterne's humour is his frequent sniggering. His prurience has been commented on enough, and he does not need to be excused or belaboured again. There is a cess-pool outside Shandy Hall and a whiff sometimes spoils the pleasantries within; but the prevailing wind does not blow from that quarter and the air is usually fresh.

A choice of his *Sermons* has been included in this volume because they throw light upon his genius and its development. They are, considered as sermons, poor stuff. They are devised to beguile us into sentimental reflections rather than to disturb our complacency; the least hardened sinner would not turn a hair at their tone; and an undercurrent of facetiousness troubles the affectation of solemnity and sincerity which the preacher concedes to his office. They are, however, beautifully written, and the source of his style. He was middle-aged when he began to write

Tristram Shandy. His character was already fixed, his ideas were sorted out, and his style had been largely formed by the composition of sermons. He had learnt from this practice how to make his prose exactly echo his speech, how to trick out his thoughts in familiar dress, how to insinuate a message, and how to play up to an audience. When he turned his attention to secular subjects, so much more suitable to his character, he simply addressed the public in the intimate and disarming manner which he had for so long used in the pulpit.

The selection from his letters show how little his epistolary and his literary styles differ: he treats both his readers and his correspondents in the same intimate manner. And they also provide some commentary upon his two great books and upon his personality. Naturally, this selected commentary is biassed; the best letters have been chosen; and he appears at the end in a much more favourable light than he really deserves. Byron's jest, that Sterne "preferred whining over a dead ass to relieving a living mother," may be based upon ignorance of Sterne's actual relations with his mother, but it neatly points out a side of his character which this volume will hardly discover. Our attitude towards him will always be a curious mixture of pity and affection, admiration and contempt; we shall never succeed in reconciling the author of *A Sentimental Journey* with the maudlin scribbler of *The Journal to Eliza*; but the Wedding Guest, although he disliked much about the Ancient Mariner, had to listen to his story to the end.

DOUGLAS GRANT

CHRONOLOGICAL TABLE

1713

(*24 November*) Laurence Sterne born at Clonmel, in Tipperary, where his father, Ensign Roger Sterne, was stationed with the Thirty-Fourth Regiment of Foot.

1713-1723

Lived in various garrison towns in England and Ireland.

1723-1731

Pupil at a school near Halifax.

1731

(*March*) Death of his father while on service in Jamaica, leaving a widow and children provided with a pension of twenty pounds a year.

1731-1733

Lived on the bounty of his cousin Richard Sterne of Elvington near Halifax.

1733

(*6 July*) Admitted a sizar and, later, elected an exhibitioner of Jesus College, Cambridge.

1737

(*January*) Graduated B.A. proceeding M.A. in July, 1740.

(*March*) Ordained deacon and licensed to serve the curacy of St. Ives near Huntingdon.

1738

(*20 August*) Ordained priest and, four days later, collated to the vicarage of Sutton-in-the-Forest near York.

[13]

1741

(*12 January*) Preferred to the prebend of Givendale in York Cathedral.

(*30 March*) Married Elizabeth Lumley, a small heiress and a member of a good county family, who died in January, 1773, in France.

1742

(*5 January*) Resigned the prebend of Givendale for the wealthier stall of North Newbald.

1743

(*13 March*) Preferred to the living of Stillington, a parish adjoining Sutton-in-the-Forest.

(*July*) Published in *The Gentleman's Magazine, The Unknown World. Verses occasioned by hearing a Pass-Bell.*

1747

(*July*) Published *The Case of Elijah and the Widow of Zarephath considered. A Charity Sermon.*

(*1 December*) Birth of a daughter, Lydia, who married Alexandre de Medalle at Albi, near Toulouse, on 28 April, 1772, and died in France sometime between 1775 and 1783.

1750

(*August*) Published *The Abuses of Conscience: set forth in a Sermon, preached in the Cathedral Church of St. Peter's, York.* This sermon was later included in *Tristram Shandy*, Vol. II.

1759

(*January*) Published *A Political Romance*—later re-named *The History of a Good Warm Watch-Coat*—a satire upon ecclesiastical politics in York.

(*January–June*) Composition of *The Life and Opinions of Tristram Shandy, Gentleman,* Vols. I and II.

(*December*) Publication at York of *Tristram Shandy,* Vols. I and II.

1760

(*1 January*) Publication at London of *Tristram Shandy*, Vols. I and II.

(*March*) Arrived in London to enjoy in person his great literary success, and acclaimed and fêted by society. Nominated by Lord Fauconberg to the living of Coxwold in Yorkshire.

(*May*) Published *The Sermons of Mr. Yorick*, Vols. I and II. Returned from London to settle at Coxwold.

(*June–November*) Composition of *Tristram Shandy*, Vols. III and IV.

(*December*) Arrived in London to see Vols. III and IV through the press.

1761

(*28 January*) Publication of *Tristram Shandy*, Vols. III and IV.

(*June*) Returned from London to Coxwold.

(*July–October*) Composition of *Tristram Shandy*, Vols. V and VI.

(*November*) Arrived in London to see Vols. V and VI through the press.

(*21 December*) Publication of *Tristram Shandy*, Vols. V and VI.

1762

(*January*) Travelled to Paris to recuperate from a serious illness.

(*January–June*) Acclaimed and fêted by Parisian society.

(*July*) Travelled to Toulouse in company with his wife and daughter, who had joined him at Paris.

1762-1764

Domiciled in the south of France.

1764

(*June*) Returned to England alone leaving his wife and daughter, at their request, in France.

(*October–November*) Completion of *Tristram Shandy*, Vols. VII and VIII, which he had begun in France.

(*December*) Arrived in London to see Vols. VII and VIII through the press.

1765

(*22 January*) Publication of *Tristram Shandy*, Vols. VII and VIII.

(*April*) Returned from London to Coxwold.

(*April–October*) Composition of *Sermons*, Vols. III and IV.

(*October*) Arrived in London and compelled by ill-health to set out on a tour through France and Italy.

1766

(*22 January*) Publication of *The Sermons of Mr. Yorick*, Vols. III and IV.

(*May*) Returned from abroad to Coxwold.

(*July–November*) Composition of *Tristram Shandy*, Vol. IX.

1767

(*January*) Arrived in London to see Vol. IX through the press. Publication of *Tristram Shandy*, Vol. IX. Met for the first time, and fell in love with, Mrs. Elizabeth Draper—the *Eliza* of *A Sentimental Journey*—who was on a visit to England from India.

(*April*) Mrs. Draper sailed for India after agreeing to his suggestion that they should both keep intimate journals during their separation.

(*May*) Returned from London to Coxwold.

(*June–November*) Composition of *A Sentimental Journey* and of *The Journal to Eliza* (first published 1904).

1768

(*January*) Arrived in London to see *A Sentimental Journey* through the press.

(*24 February*) Publication of *A Sentimental Journey*.

(*18 March*) Died in his lodgings at 3 Old Bond Street.

(*22 March*) Buried in the burial ground of St. George's, Hanover Square.

MEMOIRS

OF THE LIFE AND FAMILY

OF THE LATE

Rev. Mr. Laurence Sterne

This essay in autobiography was written by Sterne in 1767, and was first published by his daughter, Lydia de Medalle, in *Letters of the late Rev. Mr. Laurence Sterne, To his most intimate Friends*, 1775.

MEMOIRS

OF THE LIFE AND FAMILY OF THE LATE

Rev. Mr. Laurence Sterne

ROGER STERNE, (grandson to Archbishop Sterne) Lieutenant in Handaside's regiment, was married to Agnes Hebert, widow of a captain of a good family: her family name was (I believe) Nuttle—though, upon recollection, that was the name of her father-in-law, who was a noted sutler in Flanders, in Queen Ann's wars, where my father married his wife's daughter (N.B. he was in debt to him) which was in September 25, 1711, Old Stile.—This Nuttle had a son by my grandmother— a fine person of a man but a graceless whelp—what became of him I know not.—The family (if any left), live now at Clonmel in the south of Ireland, at which town I was born November 24th, 1713, a few days after my mother arrived from Dunkirk.—My birth-day was ominous to my poor father, who was, the day after our arrival, with many other brave officers, broke, and sent adrift into the wide world with a wife and two children—the elder of which was Mary; she was born in Lisle in French Flanders, July the tenth, one thousand seven hundred and twelve, New Stile.—This child was most unfortunate—she married one Weemans in Dublin—who used her most unmercifully—spent his substance, became a bankrupt, and left my poor sister to shift for herself,—which she was able to do but for a few months, for she went to a friend's house in the country, and died of a broken heart. She was a most beautiful woman—of a fine figure, and deserved a better fate.—The regiment, in which my father served, being broke, he left Ireland as soon as I was able to be carried, with the rest of his family, and came to the family seat at Elvington, near York, where his mother lived. She was daughter to Sir Roger Jaques, and an heiress. There we sojourned for about ten months, when the regiment was established, and our household decamped with bag and baggage for Dublin— within a month of our arrival, my father left us, being ordered to Exeter, where, in a sad winter, my mother and her two children followed him, travelling from Liverpool by land to Plymouth. (Melancholy description of this journey not necessary to be transmitted here). In twelve months we were all sent back to

Dublin.—My mother, with three of us, (for she laid in at Plymouth of a boy, Joram), took ship at Bristol, for Ireland, and had a narrow escape from being cast away by a leak springing up in the vessel.—At length, after many perils, and struggles, we got to Dublin.—There my father took a large house, furnished it, and in a year and a half's time spent a great deal of money.—In the year one thousand seven hundred and nineteen, all unhing'd again; the regiment was ordered, with many others, to the Isle of Wight, in order to embark for Spain in the Vigo expedition. We accompanied the regiment, and was driven into Milford Haven, but landed at Bristol, from thence by land to Plymouth again, and to the Isle of Wight—where I remember we stayed encamped some time before the embarkation of the troops—(in this expedition from Bristol to Hampshire we lost poor Joram—a pretty boy, four years old, of the small-pox), my mother, sister, and myself, remained at the Isle of Wight during the Vigo Expedition, and until the regiment had got back to Wicklow in Ireland, from whence my father sent for us.—We had poor Joram's loss supplied during our stay in the Isle of Wight, by the birth of a girl, Anne, born September the twenty-third, one thousand seven hundred and nineteen.—This pretty blossom fell at the age of three years, in the Barracks of Dublin—she was, as I well remember, of a fine delicate frame, not made to last long, as were most of my father's babes.—We embarked for Dublin, and had all been cast away by a most violent storm; but through the intercessions of my mother, the captain was prevailed upon to turn back into Wales, where we stayed a month, and at length got into Dublin, and travelled by land to Wicklow, where my father had for some Weeks given us over for lost.— We lived in the barracks at Wicklow, one year, (one thousand seven hundred and twenty) when Devijeher (so called after Colonel Devijeher,) was born; from thence we decamped to stay half a year with Mr. Fetherston, a clergyman, about seven miles from Wicklow, who being a relation of my mother's, invited us to his parsonage at Animo.—It was in this parish, during our stay, that I had that wonderful escape in falling through a mill-race whilst the mill was going, and of being taken up unhurt—the story is incredible, but known for truth in all that part of Ireland—where hundreds of the common people flocked to see me.—From hence we followed the regiment to Dublin, where we lay in the barracks a year.—In this year, one thousand seven hundred and twenty-one, I learned to write, &c.—The

regiment, ordered in twenty-two, to Carrickfergus in the north
of Ireland; we all decamped, but got no further than Drogheda,
thence ordered to Mullengar, forty miles west, where by Providence we stumbled upon a kind relation, a collateral descendant
from Archbishop Sterne, who took us all to his castle and kindly
entreated us for a year—and sent us to the regiment at Carrickfergus, loaded with kindnesses, &c.—a most rueful and tedious
journey had we all, in March, to Carrickfergus, where we
arrived in six or seven days—little Devijeher here died, he was
three years old—He had been left behind at nurse at a farmhouse
near Wicklow, but was fetch'd to us by my father the summer
after—another child sent to fill his place, Susan; this babe too
left us behind in this weary journey—The autumn of that year,
or the spring afterwards, (I forget which) my father got leave of
his colonel to fix me at school—which he did near Halifax, with
an able master; with whom I staid some time, 'till by God's care
of me my cousin Sterne, of Elvington, became a father to me, and
sent me to the university, &c., &c. To pursue the thread of our
story, my father's regiment was the year after ordered to London-
derry, where another sister was brought forth, Catherine, still
living, but most unhappily estranged from me by my uncle's
wickedness, and her own folly—from this station the regiment
was sent to defend Gibraltar, at the seige, where my father was
run through the body by Captain Phillips, in a duel, (the quarrel
begun about a goose) with much difficulty he survived—tho'
with an impaired constitution, which was not able to withstand
the hardships it was put to—for he was sent to Jamaica, where
he soon fell by the country fever, which took away his senses
first, and made a child of him, and then, in a month or two,
walking about continually without complaining, till the moment
he sat down in an arm chair, and breathed his last—which was
at Port Antonio, on the north of the island.—My father was
a little smart man—active to the last degree, in all exercises—
most patient of fatigue and disappointments, of which it pleased
God to give him full measure—he was in his temper somewhat
rapid, and hasty—but of a kindly, sweet disposition, void of all
design; and so innocent in his own intentions, that he suspected
no one; so that you might have cheated him ten times in a day, if
nine had not been sufficient for your purpose—my poor father
died in March 1731—I remained at Halifax 'till about the latter
end of that year, and cannot omit mentioning this anecdote of
myself, and school-master—He had had the ceiling of the school-

room new white-washed—the ladder remained there—I one unlucky day mounted it, and wrote with a brush in large capital letters, LAU. STERNE, for which the usher severely whipped me. My master was very much hurt at this, and said, before me, that never should that name be effaced, for I was a boy of genius, and he was sure I should come to preferment—this expression made me forget the stripes I had received—In the year thirty-two my cousin sent me to the university, where I staid some time. 'Twas there that I commenced a friendship with Mr. H[all,] which has been most lasting on both sides—I then came to York, and my uncle got me the living of Sutton—and at York I became acquainted with your mother, and courted her for two years— she owned she liked me, but thought herself not rich enough, or me too poor, to be joined together—she went to her sister's in S[taffordshire], and I wrote to her often—I believe then she was partly determined to have me, but would not say so—at her return she fell into a consumption—and one evening that I was sitting by her with an almost broken heart to see her so ill, she said, "my dear Lawrey, I can never be yours, for I verily believe I have not long to live—but I have left you every shilling of my fortune;" —upon that she shewed me her will—this generosity over-powered me.—It pleased God that she recovered, and I married her in the year 1741. My uncle and myself were then upon very good terms, for he soon got me the Prebendary of York—but he quarrelled with me afterwards, because I would not write paragraphs in the newspapers—though he was a party-man, I was not, and detested such dirty work: thinking it beneath me —from that period, he became my bitterest enemy.—By my wife's means I got the living of Stillington—a friend of her's in the south had promised her, that if she married a clergyman in Yorkshire, when the living became vacant, he would make her a compliment of it. I remained near twenty years at Sutton, doing duty at both places—I had then very good health.— Books, painting, fiddling, and shooting were my amusements; as to the 'Squire of the parish, I cannot say we were upon a very friendly footing—but at Stillington, the family of the C[roft]s shewed us every kindness—'twas most truly agreeable to be within a mile and a half of an amiable family, who were ever cordial friends—In the year 1760, I took a house at York for your mother and yourself, and went up to London to publish my two first volumes of Shandy. In that year Lord F[auconberg] presented me with the curacy of Coxwold—a sweet retirement in comparison of Sutton. In sixty-two I went to France before the peace was concluded, and you both followed me.—I left you both in France, and in two years after I went to Italy for the recovery of my health—and when I called upon you, I tried to engage your mother to return to England, with me—she and yourself are at length come—and I have had the inexpressible joy of seeing my girl every thing I wished her.

I have set down these particulars relating to my family, and self, for my Lydia, in case hereafter she might have a curiosity, or a kinder motive to know them.

THE

Life and Opinions

OF

TRISTRAM SHANDY

Gentleman

Ταράσσει τους Ἀνθρώπους οὐ τὰ Πράγματα,
ἀλλὰ τὰ περὶ τῶν Πραγμάτων, Δόγματα.

The text of the present edition of *The Life and Opinions of Tristram Shandy, Gentleman,* is that of the first editions of the nine Volumes. The Dedication, "To the Right Honourable Mr. Pitt", first appeared in the second edition of Vol. I. Because publication of the work was spread over a number of years, typographical conventions—particularly the use of *italics*—changed in the last three Volumes; but, except for the rationalisation of typography and the correction of obvious misprints, the present text exactly follows the first editions. The "practical jokes"—the black and marbled pages, &c.—have also been inserted. (For details of the composition and publication of *Tristram Shandy* see Chronological Table.)

VOLUME I

Mr. PITT

SIR,

NEVER poor Wight of a Dedicator had less hopes from his Dedication, than I have from this of mine; for it is written in a bye corner of the kingdom, and in a retired thatch'd house, where I live in a constant endeavour to fence against the infirmities of ill health, and other evils of life, by mirth; being firmly persuaded that every time a man smiles,—but much more so, when he laughs, that it adds something to this Fragment of Life.

I humbly beg, Sir, that you will honour this book by taking it——(not under your Protection;——it must protect itself, but)—into the country with you; where, if I am ever told, it has made you smile, or can conceive it has beguiled you of one moment's pain——I shall think myself as happy as a minister of state;——perhaps much happier than any one (one only excepted) that I have ever read or heard of.

I am, great Sir,
(*and what is more to your Honour,*)
I am, good Sir,
Your Well-wisher,
and most humble Fellow-Subject,

THE AUTHOR.

THE LIFE AND OPINIONS OF

TRISTRAM SHANDY

GENTLEMAN

CHAPTER I

I WISH either my father or my mother, or indeed both of
them, as they were in duty both equally bound to it, had
minded what they were about when they begot me; had they
duly consider'd how much depended upon what they were then
doing;—that not only the production of a rational Being was
concern'd in it, but that possibly the happy formation and
temperature of his body, perhaps his genius and the very cast of
his mind;—and, for aught they knew to the contrary, even the
fortunes of his whole house might take their turn from the
humours and dispositions which were then uppermost:——Had
they duly weighed and considered all this, and proceeded
accordingly,——I am verily persuaded I should have made
a quite different figure in the world, from that, in which the reader
is likely to see me.—Believe me, good folks, this is not so
inconsiderable a thing as many of you may think it;—you have
all, I dare say, heard of the animal spirits, as how they are
transfused from father to son, &c. &c.—and a great deal to that
purpose:—Well, you may take my word, that nine parts in ten
of a man's sense or his nonsense, his successes and miscarriages
in this world depend upon their motions and activity, and the
different tracks and trains you put them into; so that when they
are once set a-going, whether right or wrong, 'tis not a halfpenny matter,—away they go cluttering like hey-go-mad; and
by treading the same steps over and over again, they presently
make a road of it, as plain and as smooth as a garden-walk,
which, when they are once used to, the Devil himself sometimes
shall not be able to drive them off it.

   Pray, my dear, quoth my mother, *have you not forgot to wind
up the clock?*——*Good G—*! cried my father, making an exclamation, but taking care to moderate his voice at the same time,——
*Did ever woman, since the creation of the world, interrupt a man
with such a silly question?* Pray, what was your father saying?——
Nothing.

CHAPTER II

THEN, positively, there is nothing in the question, that I can see, either good or bad.——Then let me tell you, Sir, it was a very unseasonable question at least,——because it scattered and dispersed the animal spirits, whose business it was to have escorted and gone hand-in-hand with the *HOMUN-CULUS*, and conducted him safe to the place destined for his reception.

The HOMUNCULUS, Sir, in however low and ludicrous a light he may appear, in this age of levity, to the eye of folly or prejudice; —to the eye of reason in scientifick research, he stands confess'd —a BEING guarded and circumscribed with rights:——The minutest philosophers, who, by the bye, have the most enlarged understandings, (their souls being inversely as their enquiries) shew us incontestably, That the HOMUNCULUS is created by the same hand,—engender'd in the same course of nature,—endowed with the same loco-motive powers and faculties with us:——That he consists, as we do, of skin, hair, fat, flesh, veins, arteries, ligaments, nerves, cartilages, bones, marrow, brains, glands, genitals, humours, and articulations;——is a Being of as much activity, ——and, in all senses of the word, as much and as truly our fellow-creature as my Lord Chancellor of *England.*—He may be benefited, he may be injured,—he may obtain redress;—in a word, he has all the claims and rights of humanity, which *Tully, Puffendorff,* or the best ethick writers allow to arise out of that state and relation.

Now, dear Sir, what if any accident had befallen him in his way alone?——or that, thro' terror of it, natural to so young a traveller, my little gentleman had got to his journey's end miserably spent;——his muscular strength and virility worn down to a thread;—his own animal spirits ruffled beyond description,— and that in this sad disorder'd state of nerves, he had laid down a prey to sudden starts, or a series of melancholy dreams and fancies for nine long, long months together.——I tremble to think what a foundation had been laid for a thousand weaknesses both of body and mind, which no skill of the physician or the philosopher could ever afterwards have set thoroughly to rights.

CHAPTER III

TO MY uncle Mr. *Toby Shandy* do I stand indebted for the preceding anecdote, to whom my father, who was an excellent natural philosopher, and much given to close reasoning upon the smallest matters, had oft, and heavily complain'd of the injury; but once more particularly, as my uncle *Toby* well remember'd, upon his observing a most unaccountable obliquity, (as he call'd it) in my manner of setting up my top, and justifying the principles upon which I had done it,—the old gentleman shook his head, and in a tone more expressive by half of sorrow than reproach,—he said his heart all along foreboded, and he saw it verified in this, and from a thousand other observations he had made upon me, That I should neither think nor act like any other man's child:——*But alas!* continued he, shaking his head a second time, and wiping away a tear which was trickling down his cheeks, *My Tristram's misfortunes began nine months before ever he came into the world.*

——My mother, who was sitting by, look'd up,—but she knew no more than her backside what my father meant,—but my uncle, Mr. *Toby Shandy*, who had been often informed of the affair,—understood him very well.

CHAPTER IV

I KNOW there are readers in the world, as well as many other good people in it, who are no readers at all,—who find themselves ill at ease, unless they are let into the whole secret from first to last, of every thing which concerns you.

It is in pure compliance with this humour of theirs, and from a backwardness in my nature to disappoint any one soul living, that I have been so very particular already. As my life and opinions are likely to make some noise in the world, and, if I conjecture right, will take in all ranks, professions, and denominations of men whatever,—be no less read than the *Pilgrim's Progress* itself—and, in the end, prove the very thing which *Montaigne* dreaded his Essays should turn out, that is, a book for a parlour-window;—I find it necessary to consult every one a little in his turn; and therefore must beg pardon for going on a little further in the same way: For which cause, right

glad I am, that I have begun the history of myself in the way
I have done; and that I am able to go on tracing every thing in it,
as *Horace* says, *ab Ovo*.

Horace, I know, does not recommend this fashion altogether:
But that gentleman is speaking only of an epic poem or a tragedy;
—(I forget which,)—besides, if it was not so, I should beg Mr.
Horace's pardon;—for in writing what I have set about, I shall
confine myself neither to his rules, nor to any man's rules that
ever lived.

To such, however, as do not choose to go so far back into these
things, I can give no better advice, than that they skip over the
remaining part of this Chapter; for I declare before hand, 'tis
wrote only for the curious and inquisitive.
—————————————Shut the door.—————————————
I was begot in the night, betwixt the first *Sunday* and the first
Monday in the month of *March*, in the year of our Lord one
thousand seven hundred and eighteen. I am positive I was.—
But how I came to be so very particular in my account of a thing
which happened before I was born, is owing to another small
anecdote known only in our own family, but now made publick
for the better clearing up this point.

My father, you must know, who was originally a *Turky* merchant, but had left off business for some years, in order to retire
to, and die upon, his paternal estate in the county of ————,
was, I believe, one of the most regular men in every thing he did,
whether 'twas matter of business, or matter of amusement, that
ever lived. As a small specimen of this extreme exactness of his,
to which he was in truth a slave,—he had made it a rule for many
years of his life,—on the first *Sunday night* of every month
throughout the whole year,—as certain as ever the *Sunday night*
came,——to wind up a large house-clock which we had standing
upon the back-stairs head, with his own hands:—And being
somewhere between fifty and sixty years of age, at the time I have
been speaking of,—he had likewise gradually brought some other
little family concernments to the same period, in order, as he
would often say to my uncle *Toby*, to get them all out of the
way at one time, and be no more plagued and pester'd with them
the rest of the month.

It was attended but with one misfortune, which, in a great
measure, fell upon myself, and the effects of which I fear I shall
carry with me to my grave; namely, that from an unhappy
association of ideas which have no connection in nature, it so

fell out at length, that my poor mother could never hear the said clock wound up,—but the thoughts of some other things unavoidably popp'd into her head,—& *vice versâ*:—Which strange combination of ideas, the sagacious *Locke*, who certainly understood the nature of these things better than most men, affirms to have produced more wry actions than all other sources of prejudice whatsoever.

But this by the bye.

Now it appears, by a memorandum in my father's pocket-book, which now lies upon the table, "That on *Lady-Day*, which was on the 25th of the same month in which I date my geniture,— my father set out upon his journey to *London* with my eldest brother *Bobby*, to fix him at *Westminster* school;" and, as it appears from the same authority, "That he did not get down to his wife and family till the *second week* in *May* following,"—it brings the thing almost to a certainty. However, what follows in the beginning of the next chapter puts it beyond all possibility of doubt.

————But pray, Sir, What was your father doing all *December*,—*January*, and *February?*——Why, Madam,—he was all that time afflicted with a Sciatica.

CHAPTER V

O N THE fifth day of *November*, 1718, which to the æra fixed on, was as near nine kalendar months as any husband could in reason have expected,—was I *Tristram Shandy*, Gentleman, brought forth into this scurvy and disasterous world of ours.—I wish I had been born in the Moon, or in any of the planets, (except *Jupiter* or *Saturn*, because I never could bear cold weather) for it could not well have fared worse with me in any of them (tho' I will not answer for *Venus*) than it has in this vile, dirty planet of ours,—which o' my conscience, with reverence be it spoken, I take to be made up of the shreds and clippings of the rest;——not but the planet is well enough, provided a man could be born in it to a great title or to a great estate; or could any how contrive to be called up to publick charges, and employments of dignity or power;—but that is not my case;——and therefore every man will speak of the fair as his own market has gone in it;—for which cause I affirm it over again to be one of the vilest worlds that ever was made;—for I can truly say, that from the first hour I drew my breath in it, to this, that I can now scarce draw it at all, for an asthma I got in scating against the wind in *Flanders*;—I have been the continual sport of what the world calls Fortune; and though I will not wrong her by saying, She has ever made me feel the weight of any great or signal evil; —yet with all the good temper in the world, I affirm it of her, that in every stage of my life, and at every turn and corner where she could get fairly at me, the ungracious Duchess has pelted me with a set of as pitiful misadventures and cross accidents as ever small HERO sustained.

CHAPTER VI

IN THE beginning of the last chapter, I informed you exactly *when* I was born;—but I did not inform you, *how*. *No*; that particular was reserved entirely for a chapter by itself;— besides, Sir, as you and I are in a manner perfect strangers to each other, it would not have been proper to have let you into too many circumstances relating to myself all at once.—You must have a little patience. I have undertaken, you see, to write not only my life, but my opinions also; hoping and expecting that your knowledge of my character, and of what kind of a mortal I am, by the one, would give you a better relish for the other: As you proceed further with me, the slight acquaintance which is now beginning betwixt us, will grow into familiarity; and that, unless one of us is in fault, will terminate in friendship. ——*O diem præclarum!*——then nothing which has touched me will be thought trifling in its nature, or tedious in its telling. Therefore, my dear friend and companion, if you should think me somewhat sparing of my narrative on my first setting out, —bear with me,—and let me go on, and tell my story my own way:——Or, if I should seem now and then to trifle upon the road,——or should sometimes put on a fool's cap with a bell to it, for a moment or two as we pass along,—don't fly off,—but rather courteously give me credit for a little more wisdom than appears upon my outside;—and as we jog on, either laugh with me, or at me, or in short, do any thing,—only keep your temper.

CHAPTER VII

I N THE same village where my father and my mother dwelt, dwelt also a thin, upright, motherly, notable, good old body of a midwife, who with the help of a little plain good sense, and some years full employment in her business, in which she had all along trusted little to her own efforts, and a great deal to those of dame nature,—had acquired, in her way, no small degree of reputation in the world;—by which word *world*, need I in this place inform your worship, that I would be understood to mean no more of it, than a small circle described upon the circle of the great world, of four *English* miles diameter, or thereabouts, of which the cottage where the good old woman lived, is supposed to be the centre.——She had been left, it seems, a widow in great distress, with three or four small children, in her forty-seventh year; and as she was at that time a person of decent carriage,—grave deportment,——a woman moreover of few words, and withall an object of compassion, whose distress and silence under it called out the louder for a friendly lift: The wife of the parson of the parish was touched with pity; and having often lamented an inconvenience, to which her husband's flock had for many years been exposed, inasmuch, as there was no such thing as a midwife, of any kind or degree to be got at, let the case have been never so urgent, within less than six or seven long miles riding; which said seven long miles in dark nights and dismal roads, the country thereabouts being nothing but a deep clay, was almost equal to fourteen; and that in effect was sometimes next to having no midwife at all; it came into her head, that it would be doing as seasonable a kindness to the whole parish, as to the poor creature herself, to get her a little instructed in some of the plain principles of the business, in order to set her up in it. As no woman thereabouts was better qualified to execute the plan she had formed than herself, the Gentlewoman very charitably undertook it; and having great influence over the female part of the parish, she found no difficulty in effecting it to the utmost of her wishes. In truth, the parson join'd his interest with his wife's in the whole affair; and in order to do things as they should be, and give the poor soul as good a title by law to practise, as his wife had given by institution,—— he chearfully paid the fees for the ordinary's licence himself, amounting in the whole, to the sum of eighteen shillings and four-pence; so that, betwixt them both, the good woman was fully invested in the real and corporal possession of her office, together with all its *rights, members, and appurtenances whatsoever.*

These last words, you must know, were not according to the old form in which such licences, faculties, and powers usually ran, which in like cases had heretofore been granted to the sisterhood. But it was according to a neat *Formula* of *Didius* his own devising, who having a particular turn for taking to pieces, and new framing over again, all kind of instruments in that way, not only hit upon this dainty amendment, but coax'd many of the old licensed matrons in the neighbourhood, to open their faculties afresh, in order to have this whim-wham of his inserted.

I own I never could envy *Didius* in these kinds of fancies of his: —But every man to his own taste.—Did not Dr. *Kunastrokius,* that great man, at his leisure hours, take the greatest delight imaginable in combing of asses tails, and plucking the dead hairs out with his teeth, though he had tweezers always in his pocket? Nay, if you come to that, Sir have not the wisest of men in all ages, not excepting *Solomon* himself,—have they not had their HOBBY-HORSES;—their running-horses,—their coins and their cockle-shells, their drums and their trumpets, their fiddles, their pallats,——their maggots and their butterflies?—and so long as a man rides his HOBBY-HORSE peaceably and quietly along the King's highway, and neither compels you or me to get up behind him,——pray, Sir, what have either you or I to do with it?

CHAPTER VIII

—**D**E GUSTIBUS NON EST DISPUTANDUM;—that is, there is no disputing against HOBBY-HORSES; and, for my part, I seldom do; nor could I with any sort of grace, had I been an enemy to them at the bottom; for happening, at certain intervals and changes of the Moon, to be both fiddler and painter, according as the fly stings:—Be it known to you, that I keep a couple of pads myself, upon which, in their turns, (nor do I care who knows it) I frequently ride out and take the air;—tho' sometimes, to my shame be it spoken, I take somewhat longer journies than what a wise man would think altogether right.—But the truth is,—I am not a wise man;——and besides am a mortal of so little consequence in the world, it is not much matter what I do; so I seldom fret or fume at all about it: Nor does it much disturb my rest when I see such great Lords and tall Personages as hereafter follow;—such, for instance, as my Lord A, B, C, D, E, F, G, H, I, K, L, M, N, O, P, Q, and so on, all of a row, mounted upon their several horses;—some with large stirrups, getting on in a more grave and sober pace;——others on the contrary, tuck'd up to their very chins, with whips across their mouths, scouring and scampering it away like so many little party-colour'd devils astride a mortgage,—and as if some of them were resolved to break their necks.—So much the better—say I to myself;—for in case the worst should happen, the world will make a shift to do excellently well without them;—and for the rest,——why,——God speed them,——e'en let them ride on without opposition from me; for were their lordships unhorsed this very night,——'tis ten to one but that many of them would be worse mounted by one half before to-morrow morning.

Not one of these instances therefore can be said to break in upon my rest.—But there is an instance, which I own puts me off my guard, and that is, when I see one born for great actions, and, what is still more for his honour, whose nature ever inclines him to good ones;——when I behold such a one, my Lord, like yourself, whose principles and conduct are as generous and noble as his blood, and whom, for that reason, a corrupt world cannot spare one moment;—when I see such a one, my Lord, mounted, though it is but for a minute beyond the time which my love to my country has prescribed to him, and my zeal for his glory wishes,—then, my Lord, I cease to be a philosopher, and in the first transport of an honest impatience, I wish the HOBBY-HORSE, with all his fraternity, at the Devil.

My Lord,

I MAINTAIN this to be a dedication, notwithstanding its singularity in the three great essentials of matter, form and place: I beg, therefore, you will accept it as such, and that you will permit me to lay it, with the most respectful humility, at your Lordship's feet,—when you are upon them,—which you can be when you please;—and that is, my Lord, whenever there is occasion for it, and I will add, to the best purposes too. I have the honour to be,

My Lord,
Your Lordship's most obedient,
and most devoted,
and most humble servant,
TRISTRAM SHANDY.

[37]

CHAPTER IX

I SOLEMNLY declare to all mankind, that the above dedication was made for no one Prince, Prelate, Pope, or Potentate, —Duke, Marquis, Earl, Viscount, or Baron of this, or any other Realm in Christendom;——nor has it yet been hawk'd about, or offered publickly or privately, directly or indirectly, to any one person or personage, great or small; but is honestly a true Virgin-Dedication untried on, upon any soul living.

I labour this point so particularly, merely to remove any offence or objection which might arise against it from the manner in which I propose to make the most of it;—which is the putting it up fairly to publick sale; which I now do.

——Every author has a way of his own, in bringing his points to bear;—for my own part, as I hate chaffering and higgling for a few guineas in a dark entry;—I resolved within myself, from the very beginning, to deal squarely and openly with your Great Folks in this affair, and try whether I should not come off the better by it.

If therefore there is any one Duke, Marquis, Earl, Viscount, or Baron, in these his Majesty's dominions, who stands in need of a tight, genteel dedication, and whom the above will suit, (for by the bye, unless it suits in some degree, I will not part with it) ——it is much at his service for fifty guineas;——which I am positive is twenty guineas less than it ought to be afforded for, by any man of genius.

My Lord, if you examine it over again, it is far from being a gross piece of daubing, as some dedications are. The design, your Lordship sees, is good, the colouring transparent,—the drawing not amiss,—or to speak more like a man of science,—and measure my piece in the painter's scale, divided into 20,—I believe, my Lord, the out-lines will turn out as 12,—the composition as 9,—the colouring as 6,—the expression 13 and a half,—and the design,—if I may be allowed, my Lord, to understand my own *design*, and supposing absolute perfection in designing, to be as 20,—I think it cannot well fall short of 19. Besides all this,—there is keeping in it, and the dark strokes in the HOBBY-HORSE, (which is a secondary figure, and a kind of back-ground to the whole) give great force to the principal lights in your own figure, and make it come off wonderfully;——and besides, there is an air of originality in the *tout ensemble*.

Be pleased, my good Lord, to order the sum to be paid into

the hands of Mr. *Dodsley*, for the benefit of the author; and in the next edition care shall be taken that this chapter be expunged, and your Lordship's titles, distinctions, arms, and good actions, be placed at the front of the preceding chapter: All which, from the words, *De gustibus non est disputandum*, and whatever else in this book relates to HOBBY-HORSES, but no more, shall stand dedicated to your Lordship.—The rest I dedicate to the MOON, who, by the bye, of all the PATRONS or MATRONS I can think of, has most power to set my book a-going, and make the world run mad after it.

    Bright Goddess,
If thou art not too busy with CANDID and Miss CUNEGUND's affairs,—take *Tristram Shandy*'s under thy protection also.

CHAPTER X

WHATEVER degree of small merit, the act of benignity in favour of the midwife, might justly claim, or in whom that claim truly rested,—at first sight seems not very material to this history;——certain however it was, that the gentlewoman, the parson's wife, did run away at that time with the whole of it: And yet, for my life, I cannot help thinking but that the parson himself, tho' he had not the good fortune to hit upon the design first,—yet, as he heartily concurred in it the moment it was laid before him, and as heartily parted with his money to carry it into execution, had a claim to some share of it,
  if not to a full half of whatever honour was due to it.

The world at that time was pleased to determine the matter otherwise.

Lay down the book, and I will allow you half a day to give a probable guess at the grounds of this procedure.

Be it known then, that, for about five years before the date of the midwife's licence, of which you have had so circumstantial an account,—the parson we have to do with, had made himself a country-talk by a breach of all decorum, which he had committed against himself, his station, and his office;——and that was in never appearing better, or otherwise mounted, than upon a lean, sorry, jack-ass of a horse, value about one pound fifteen shillings; who, to shorten all description of him, was full brother to *Rosinante*, as far as similitude congenial could make him; for he answered his description to a hair-breadth in every thing,—except that I do not remember 'tis any where said, that *Rosinante* was broken winded; and that, moreover, *Rosinante*, as is the happiness of most *Spanish* horses, fat or lean,—was undoubtedly a horse at all points.

I know very well that the HERO'S horse was a horse of chaste deportment, which may have given grounds for a contrary opinion: But it is as certain at the same time, that *Rosinante*'s continency (as may be demonstrated from the adventure of the *Yanguesian* carriers) proceeded from no bodily defect or cause whatsoever, but from the temperance and orderly current of his blood.—And let me tell you, Madam, there is a great deal of very good chastity in the world, in behalf of which you could not say more for your life.

Let that be as it may, as my purpose is to do exact justice to every creature brought upon the stage of this dramatic work,—I could not stifle this distinction in favour of Don *Quixote*'s horse;——in all other points the parson's horse, I say, was just such another,—for he was as lean, and as lank, and as sorry a jade, as HUMILITY herself could have bestrided.

In the estimation of here and there a man of weak judgment, it was greatly in the parson's power to have helped the figure of this horse of his,—for he was master of a very handsome demi-peak'd saddle, quilted on the seat with green plush, garnished with a double row of silver-headed studs, and a double pair of shining brass stirrups, with a housing altogether suitable, of grey superfine cloth, with an edging of black lace, terminating in a deep, black, silk fringe, *poudré d'or*,—all which he had purchased in the pride and prime of his life, together with a grand embossed bridle, ornamented at all points as it should be.——But not caring to banter his beast, he had hung all these up behind his study door;—and, in lieu of them, had seriously befitted him with just such a bridle and such a saddle, as the figure and value of such a steed might well and truly deserve.

In the several sallies about his parish, and in the neighbouring visits to the gentry who lived around him,——you will easily comprehend, that the parson, so appointed, would both hear and see enough to keep his philosophy from rusting. To speak the truth, he never could enter a village, but he caught the attention of both old and young.——Labour stood still as he pass'd, —the bucket hung suspended in the middle of the well,——the spinning-wheel forgot its round,—even chuck-farthing and shuffle-cap themselves stood gaping till he had got out of sight; and as his movement was not of the quickest, he had generally time

[40]

enough upon his hands to make his observations,—to hear the groans of the serious,——and the laughter of the light-hearted;—all which he bore with excellent tranquillity.—His character was, ——he loved a jest in his heart—and as he saw himself in the true point of ridicule, he would say, he could not be angry with others for seeing him in a light, in which he so strongly saw himself: So that to his friends, who knew his foible was not the love of money, and who therefore made the less scruple in bantering the extravagance of his humour,—instead of giving the true cause,——he chose rather to join in the laugh against himself; and as he never carried one single ounce of flesh upon his own bones, being altogether as spare a figure as his beast,—he would sometimes insist upon it, that the horse was as good as the rider deserved;—that they were, centaur-like,—both of a piece. At other times, and in other moods, when his spirits were above the temptation of false wit,—he would say, he found himself going off fast in a consumption; and, with great gravity, would pretend, he could not bear the sight of a fat horse without a dejection of heart, and a sensible alteration in his pulse; and that he had made choice of the lean one he rode upon, not only to keep himself in countenance, but in spirits.

At different times he would give fifty humorous and opposite reasons for riding a meek-spirited jade of a broken-winded horse, preferably to one of mettle;—for on such a one he could sit mechanically, and meditate as delightfully *de vanitate mundi et fugâ sæculi*, as with the advantage of a death's head before him; —that, in all other exercitations, he could spend his time, as he rode slowly along,——to as much account as in his study;—— that he could draw up an argument in his sermon,—or a hole in his breeches, as steadily on the one as in the other;—that brisk trotting and slow argumentation, like wit and judgment, were two incompatible movements.— But that, upon his steed—he could unite and reconcile every thing,—he could compose his sermon,—he could compose his cough,—and, in case nature gave a call that way, he could likewise compose himself to sleep.—In short, the parson upon such encounters would assign any cause, but the true cause,—and he withheld the true one, only out of a nicety of temper, because he thought it did honour to him.

But the truth of the story was as follows: In the first years of this gentleman's life, and about the time when the superb saddle and bridle were purchased by him, it had been his manner, or vanity, or call it what you will,——to run into the opposite extream.—In the language of the county where he dwelt, he was said to have loved a good horse, and generally had one of the best in the whole parish standing in his stable always ready for saddling; and as the nearest midwife, as I told you, did not live nearer to the village than seven miles, and in a vile country,—— it so fell out that the poor gentleman was scarce a whole week together without some piteous application for his beast; and as he was not an unkind-hearted man, and every case was more pressing and more distressful than the last,—as much as he loved his beast, he had never a heart to refuse him; the upshot of which was generally this, that his horse was either clapp'd, or spavin'd, or greaz'd;—or he was twitter-bon'd, or broken-winded, or something, in short, or other had befallen him which would let him carry no flesh;—so that he had every nine or ten months a bad horse to get rid of,—and a good horse to purchase in his stead.

What the loss in such a balance might amount to, *communibus annis*, I would leave to a special jury of sufferers in the same traffick, to determine;—but let it be what it would, the honest gentleman bore it for many years without a murmur, till at length, by repeated ill accidents of the kind, he found it necessary to take the thing under consideration; and upon weighing the whole, and summing it up in his mind, he found it not only disproportion'd to his other expences, but withall so heavy an article in itself, as to disable him from any other act of generosity in his parish: Besides this he considered, that, with half the sum thus galloped away, he could do ten times as much good;——and what still weighed more with him than all other considerations put together, was this, that it confined all his charity into one particular channel, and where, as he fancied, it was the least wanted, namely to the child-bearing· and child-getting part of his parish; reserving nothing for the impotent,—nothing for the aged,—nothing for the many comfortless scenes he was hourly called forth to visit, where poverty, and sickness, and affliction dwelt together.

For these reasons he resolved to discontinue the expence; and there appeared but two possible ways to extricate him clearly out of it;—and these were, either to make it an irrevocable law never more to lend his steed upon any application whatever,—or else be content to ride the last poor devil, such as they had made him, with all his aches and infirmities, to the very end of the chapter.

As he dreaded his own constancy in the first,——he very chearfully betook himself to the second; and tho' he could very well have explain'd it, as I said, to his honour,—yet, for that very reason, he had a spirit above it; choosing rather to bear the contempt of his enemies, and the laughter of his friends, than undergo the pain of telling a story, which might seem a panegyric upon himself.

I have the highest idea of the spiritual and refined sentiments of this reverend gentleman, from this single stroke in his character, which I think comes up to any of the honest refinements of the peerless knight of *La Mancha*, whom, by the bye, with all his follies, I love more, and would actually have gone further to have paid a visit to, than the greatest hero of antiquity.

But this is not the moral of my story: The thing I had in view was to shew the temper of the world in the whole of this affair. —For you must know, that so long as this explanation would have done the parson credit,—the devil a soul could find it out,— I suppose his enemies would not, and that his friends could not. ——But no sooner did he bestir himself in behalf of the midwife, and pay the expences of the ordinary's licence to set her up,— but the whole secret came out; every horse he had lost, and two horses more than ever he had lost, with all the circumstances of their destruction, were known and distinctly remembered.—The story ran like wild-fire.—"The parson had a returning fit of pride which had just seized him; and he was going to be well mounted once again in his life; and if it was so, 'twas plain as the sun at noon-day, he would pocket the expence of the licence, ten times told the very first year:——So that every body was left to judge what were his views in this act of charity."

What were his views in this, and in every other action of his life,—or rather what were the opinions which floated in the brains of other people concerning it, was a thought which too much floated in his own, and too often broke in upon his rest, when he should have been sound asleep.

About ten years ago this gentleman had the good fortune to be made entirely easy upon that score,—it being just so long since he left his parish,——and the whole world at the same time behind him,—and stands accountable to a judge of whom he will have no cause to complain.

But there is a fatality attends the actions of some men: Order them as they will, they pass thro' a certain medium which so twists and refracts them from their true directions————that, with all the titles to praise which a rectitude of heart can give, the doers of them are nevertheless forced to live and die without it.

Of the truth of which this gentleman was a painful example.
——But to know by what means this came to pass,—and to make
that knowledge of use to you, I insist upon it that you read the
two following chapters, which contain such a sketch of his life
and conversation, as will carry its moral along with it.—When this
is done, if nothing stops us in our way, we will go on with the
midwife.

CHAPTER XI

YORICK was this parson's name, and what is very remarkable in it, (as appears from a most ancient account of
the family, wrote upon strong vellum, and now in perfect
preservation) it had been exactly so spelt for near,——I was
within an ace of saying nine hundred years;——but I would not
shake my credit in telling an improbable truth, however indisputable in itself;——and therefore I shall content myself with only
saying—It had been exactly so spelt, without the least variation
or transposition of a single letter, for I do not know how long;
which is more than I would venture to say of one half of the best
surnames in the kingdom; which in a course of years, have
generally undergone as many chops and changes as their owners.
—Has this been owing to the pride, or to the shame of the
respective proprietors?—In honest truth, I think, sometimes to
the one, and sometimes to the other, just as the temptation has
wrought. But a villainous affair it is, and will one day so blend
and confound us all together, that no one shall be able to stand
up and swear, "That his own great grandfather was the man who
did either this or that."

This evil had been sufficiently fenced against by the prudent
care of the *Yorick*'s family, and their religious preservation of
these records I quote, which do further inform us, That the family
was originally of *Danish* extraction, and had been transplanted
into *England* as early as in the reign of *Horwendillus*, king of
Denmark, in whose court it seems, an ancestor of this Mr.
Yorick's, and from whom he was lineally descended, held a considerable post to the day of his death. Of what nature this considerable post was, this record saith not;—it only adds, That, for
near two centuries, it had been totally abolished as altogether
unnecessary, not only in that court, but in every other court of
the Christian world.

It has often come into my head, that this post could be no

other than that of the king's chief Jester;—and that *Hamlet*'s *Yorick*, in our *Shakespeare*, many of whose plays, you know, are founded upon authenticated facts,—was certainly the very man.

I have not the time to look into *Saxo-Grammaticus*'s *Danish* history, to know the certainty of this;—but if you have leisure, and can easily get at the book, you may do it full as well yourself.

I had just time, in my travels through *Denmark* with Mr. *Noddy*'s eldest son, whom, in the year 1741, I accompanied as governor, riding along with him at a prodigious rate thro' most parts of *Europe*, and of which original journey perform'd by us two, a most delectable narrative will be given in the progress of this work. I had just time, I say, and that was all, to prove the truth of an observation made by a long sojourner in that country;——namely, "That nature was neither very lavish, nor was she very stingy in her gifts of genius and capacity to its inhabitants;—but, like a discreet parent, was moderately kind to them all; observing such an equal tenor in the distribution of her favours, as to bring them, in those points, pretty near to a level with each other; so that you will meet with few instances in that kingdom of refin'd parts; but a great deal of good plain houshold understanding amongst all ranks of people, of which every body has a share;" which is, I think, very right.

With us, you see, the case is quite different;—we are all ups and downs in this matter;—you are a great genius;—or 'tis fifty to one, Sir, you are a great dunce and a blockhead;—not that there is a total want of intermediate steps,—no,—we are not so irregular as that comes to;—but the two extremes are more common, and in a greater degree in this unsettled island, where nature, in her gifts and dispositions of this kind, is most whimsical and capricious; fortune herself not being more so in the bequest of her goods and chattels than she.

This is all that ever stagger'd my faith in regard to *Yorick*'s extraction, who, by what I can remember of him, and by all the accounts I could ever get of him, seemed not to have had one single drop of *Danish* blood in his whole crasis; in nine hundred years, it might possibly have all run out:——I will not philosophize one moment with you about it; for happen how it would, the fact was this:—That instead of that cold phlegm and exact regularity of sense and humours, you would have look'd for, in one so extracted;—he was, on the contrary, as mercurial and sublimated a composition,—as heteroclite a creature in all his declensions;——with as much life and whim, and *gaité de cœur* about him, as the kindliest climate could have engendered and put together. With all this sail, poor *Yorick* carried not one ounce of ballast; he was utterly unpractised in the world; and, at the age of twenty-six, knew just about as well how to steer his course in it, as a romping, unsuspicious girl of thirteen: So that upon his first setting out, the brisk gale of his spirits, as you will imagine, ran him foul ten times in a day of some body's tackling; and as the grave and more slow-paced were oftenest in his way, ——you may likewise imagine, 'twas with such he had generally the ill luck to get the most entangled. For aught I know there might be some mixture of unlucky wit at the bottom of such *Fracas:*—For, to speak the truth, *Yorick* had an invincible dislike and opposition in his nature to gravity;——not to gravity as such;——for where gravity was wanted, he would be the most grave and serious of mortal men for days and weeks together;— but he was an enemy to the affectation of it, and declared open war against it, only as it appeared a cloak for ignorance, or for folly; and then, whenever it fell in his way, however sheltered and protected, he seldom gave it much quarter.

Sometimes, in his wild way of talking, he would say, That gravity was an errant scoundrel, and he would add,—of the most dangerous kind too,—because a sly one; and that, he verily believed, more honest, well-meaning people were bubbled out of their goods and money by it in one twelve-month, than by pocket-picking and shop-lifting in seven. In the naked temper which a merry heart discovered, he would say, There was no danger,—but to itself;—whereas the very essence of gravity was design, and consequently deceit;—'twas a taught trick to gain credit of the world for more sense and knowledge than a man was worth; and that, with all its pretensions,—it was no better, but often worse, than what a *French* wit had long ago defined it,— *viz. A mysterious carriage of the body to cover the defects of the mind;*—which definition of gravity, *Yorick*, with great imprudence, would say, deserved to be wrote in letters of gold.

But, in plain truth, he was a man unhackneyed and unpractised in the world, and was altogether as indiscreet and foolish on every other subject of discourse where policy is wont to impress restraint. *Yorick* had no impression but one, and that was what arose from the nature of the deed spoken of; which impression he would usually translate into plain *English* without any peri- phrasis,——and too oft without much distinction of either per- sonage, time, or place;—so that when mention was made of

[46]

a pitiful or an ungenerous proceeding,—he never gave himself
a moment's time to reflect who was the Hero of the piece,——
what his station,——or how far he had power to hurt him hereafter;—but if it was a dirty action,——without more ado,——
The man was a dirty fellow,—and so on:—And as his comments
had usually the ill fate to be terminated either in a *bon mot*, or to
be enliven'd throughout with some drollery or humour of
expression, it gave wings to *Yorick*'s indiscretion. In a word, tho'
he never sought, yet, at the same time, as he seldom shun'd
occasions of saying what came uppermost, and without much
ceremony;——he had but too many temptations in life, of
scattering his wit and his humour,—his gibes and his jests about
him.——They were not lost for want of gathering.

What were the consequences, and what was *Yorick*'s catastrophe thereupon, you will read in the next chapter.

CHAPTER XII

THE *Mortgager* and *Mortgagée* differ the one from the
other, not more in length of purse, than the *Jester* and
Jestée do, in that of memory. But in this the comparison
between them runs, as the scholiasts call it, upon all-four; which,
by the bye, is upon one or two legs more, than some of the best
of *Homer*'s can pretend to;——namely, That the one raises
a sum, and the other a laugh at your expence, and think no
more about it. Interest, however, still runs on in both cases;—
the periodical or accidental payments of it, just serving to keep
the memory of the affair alive; till, at length, in some evil hour,
—pop comes the creditor upon each, and by demanding principal
upon the spot, together with full interest to the very day, makes
them both feel the full extent of their obligations.

As the reader (for I hate your *ifs*) has a thorough knowledge
of human nature, I need not say more to satisfy him, that my
Hero could not go on at this rate without some slight experience
of these incidental mementos. To speak the truth, he had
wantonly involved himself in a multitude of small book-debts
of this stamp, which, notwithstanding *Eugenius*'s frequent advice,
he too much disregarded; thinking, that as not one of them was
contracted thro' any malignancy;—but, on the contrary, from
an honesty of mind, and a mere jocundity of humour, they would
all of them be cross'd out in course.

Eugenius would never admit this; and would often tell him, that one day or other he would certainly be reckoned with; and he would often add, in an accent of sorrowful apprehension,—to the uttermost mite. To which *Yorick*, with his usual carelessness of heart, would as often answer with a pshaw!—and if the subject was started in the fields,—with a hop, skip, and a jump, at the end of it; but if close pent up in the social chimney corner, where the culprit was barricado'd in, with a table and a couple of arm chairs, and could not so readily fly off in a tangent,—*Eugenius* would then go on with his lecture upon discretion, in words to this purpose, though somewhat better put together.

Trust me, dear *Yorick*, this unwary pleasantry of thine will sooner or later bring thee into scrapes and difficulties, which no after-wit can extricate thee out of.——In these sallies, too oft, I see, it happens, that a person laugh'd at, considers himself in the light of a person injured, with all the rights of such a situation belonging to him; and when thou viewest him in that light too, and reckons up his friends, his family, his kindred, and allies,—— and musters up with them the many recruits which will list under him from a sense of common danger;—'tis no extravagant arithmetic to say, that for every ten jokes,—thou hast got an hundred enemies; and till thou hast gone on, and raised a swarm of wasps about thine ears, and art half stung to death by them, thou wilt never be convinced it is so.

I cannot suspect it in the man whom I esteem, that there is the least spur from spleen or malevolence of intent in these sallies. ——I believe and know them to be truly honest and sportive:— But consider, my dear lad, the fools cannot distinguish this,— and that knaves will not; and thou knowest not what it is, either to provoke the one, or to make merry with the other,—whenever they associate for mutual defence, depend upon it, they will carry on the war in such a manner against thee, my dear friend, as to make thee heartily sick of it and of thy life too.

Revenge from some baneful corner shall level a tale of dishonour at thee, which no innocence of heart or integrity of conduct shall set right.——The fortunes of thy house shall totter,— thy character, which led the way to them, shall bleed on every side of it,—thy faith questioned,—thy works belied,—thy wit forgotten,—thy learning trampled on. To wind up the last scene of thy tragedy, CRUELTY and COWARDICE, twin ruffians, hired and set on by MALICE in the dark, shall strike together at all thy infirmities and mistakes:—The best of us, my dear lad, lie open

[48]

there,—and trust me,—trust me, *Yorick, when to gratify a private appetite, it is once resolved upon, that an innocent and an helpless creature shall be sacrificed, 'tis an easy matter to pick up sticks enow from any thicket where it has strayed, to make a fire to offer it up with.*

Yorick scarce ever heard this sad vatication of his destiny read over to him, but with a tear stealing from his eye, and a promissory look attending it, that he was resolved, for the time to come, to ride his tit with more sobriety.——But, alas, too late!—a grand confederacy, with * * * * * and * * * * * at the head of it, was form'd before the first prediction of it.—The whole plan of the attack, just as *Eugenius* had foreboded, was put in execution all at once,—with so little mercy on the side of the allies,—and so little suspicion in *Yorick*, of what was carrying on against him,—that when he thought, good easy man! full surely preferment was o'ripening,—they had smote his root, and then he fell, as many a worthy man had fallen before him.

Yorick, however, fought it out with all imaginable gallantry for some time; till over-power'd by numbers, and worn out at length by the calamities of the war,—but more so, by the ungenerous manner in which it was carried on,—he threw down the sword; and though he kept up his spirits in appearance to the last, he died, nevertheless, as was generally thought, quite broken-hearted.

What inclined *Eugenius* to the same opinion, was as follows:

A few hours before *Yorick* breath'd his last, *Eugenius* stept in with an intent to take his last sight and last farewell of him: Upon his drawing *Yorick*'s curtain, and asking how he felt himself, *Yorick*, looking up in his face, took hold of his hand,—and, after thanking him for the many tokens of his friendship to him, for which, he said, if it was their fate to meet hereafter,—he would thank him again and again.—He told him, he was within a few hours of giving his enemies the slip for ever.—I hope not, answered *Eugenius*, with tears trickling down his cheeks, and with the tenderest tone that ever man spoke,—I hope not *Yorick*, said he.—*Yorick* replied, with a look up, and a gentle squeeze of *Eugenius*'s hand, and that was all,—but it cut *Eugenius* to his heart.—Come,—come, *Yorick*, quoth *Eugenius*, wiping his eyes, and summoning up the man within him,—my dear lad, be comforted,—let not all thy spirits and fortitude forsake thee at this crisis when thou most wants them;——who knows what resources are in store, and what the power of God may yet do for .

thee?——*Yorick* laid his hand upon his heart, and gently shook his head;—for my part, continued *Eugenius*, crying bitterly as he uttered the words,—I declare I know not, *Yorick*, how to part with thee,——and would gladly flatter my hopes, added *Eugenius*, chearing up his voice, that there is still enough left of thee to make a bishop,—and that I may live to see it.——I beseech thee, *Eugenius*, quoth *Yorick*, taking off his night-cap as well as he could with his left-hand,——his right being still grasped closed in that of *Eugenius*,——I beseech thee to take a view of my head. —I see nothing that ails it, replied *Eugenius*. Then, alas! my friend, said *Yorick*, let me tell you, that 'tis so bruised and mis-shapen'd with the blows which * * * * * and * * * * *, and some others have so unhandsomely given me in the dark, that I might say with *Sancho Pança*, that should I recover, and "Mitres thereupon be suffer'd to rain down from heaven as thick as hail, not one of 'em would fit it."——*Yorick*'s last breath was hanging upon his trembling lips ready to depart as he uttered this;—yet still it was uttered with something of a *Cervantick* tone;—and as he spoke it, *Eugenius* could perceive a stream of lambent fire lighted up for a moment in his eyes;— faint picture of those flashes of his spirit, (which as *Shakespeare* said of his ancestor) were wont to set the table in a roar!

Eugenius was convinced from this, that the heart of his friend was broke; he squeez'd his hand,——and then walked softly out of the room, weeping as he walk'd. *Yorick* followed *Eugenius* with his eyes to the door,—he then closed them,—and never opened them more.

He lies buried in a corner of his church-yard, in the parish of ———, under a plain marble slab, which his friend *Eugenius*, by leave of his executors, laid upon his grave, with no more than these three words of inscription serving both for his epitaph and elegy.

> Alas, poor YORICK!

Ten times in a day has *Yorick*'s ghost the consolation to hear his monumental inscription read over with such a variety of plaintive tones, as denote a general pity and esteem for him;—— a foot-way crossing the church-yard close by the side of his grave,—not a passenger goes by without stopping to cast a look upon it,——and sighing as he walks on,

Alas, poor YORICK!

CHAPTER XIII

IT IS so long since the reader of this rhapsodical work has been parted from the midwife, that it is high time to mention her again to him, merely to put him in mind that there is such a body still in the world, and whom, upon the best judgment I can form upon my own plan at present,—I am going to introduce to him for good and all: But as fresh matter may be started, and much unexpected business fall out betwixt the reader and myself, which may require immediate dispatch;——'twas right to take care that the poor woman should not be lost in the mean time;—because when she is wanted we can no way do without her.

I think I told you that this good woman was a person of no small note and consequence throughout our whole village and township;—that her fame had spread itself to the very out-edge and circumference of that circle of importance, of which kind every soul living, whether he has a shirt to his back or no,—— has one surrounding him;—which said circle, by the way, when-ever 'tis said that such a one is of great weight and importance in the *world*,——I desire may be enlarged or contracted in your worship's fancy, in a compound-ratio of the station, profession, knowledge, abilities, height and depth (measuring both ways) of the personage brought before you.

In the present case, if I remember, I fixed it at about four or five miles, which not only comprehended the whole parish, but extended itself to two or three of the adjacent hamlets in the skirts of the next parish; which made a considerable thing of it. I must add, That she was, moreover, very well looked on at one large grange-house and some other odd houses and farms within two or three miles, as I said, from the smoke of her own chimney: ——But I must here, once for all, inform you, that all this will be more exactly delineated and explain'd in a map, now in the hands of the engraver, which, with many other pieces and develop-ments to this work, will be added to the end of the twentieth volume,—not to swell the work,—I detest the thought of such a thing;——but by way of commentary, scholium, illustration, and key to such passages, incidents, or inuendos as shall be thought to be either of private interpretation, or of dark or doubtful meaning after my life and my opinions shall have been read over, (now don't forget the meaning of the word) by all the *world*;—which, betwixt you and me, and in spite of all the gentlemen reviewers in *Great-Britain*, and of all that their worships shall undertake to write or say to the contrary,——— I am determined shall be the case.———I need not tell your worship, that all this is spoke in confidence.

CHAPTER XIV

UPON looking into my mother's marriage settlement, in order to satisfy myself and reader in a point necessary to be clear'd up, before we could proceed any further in this history;—I had the good fortune to pop upon the very thing I wanted before I had read a day and a half straight forwards,— it might have taken me up a month;—which shews plainly, that when a man sits down to write a history,—tho' it be but the history of *Jack Hickathrift* or *Tom Thumb*, he knows no more than his heels what lets and confounded hinderances he is to meet with in his way,—or what a dance he may be led, by one excursion or another, before all is over. Could a historiographer drive on his history, as a muleteer drives on his mule,—straight forward;———for instance, from *Rome* all the way to *Loretto*, without ever once turning his head aside either to the right hand or to the left,—he might venture to foretell you to an hour when he should get to his journey's end;———but the thing is, morally speaking, impossible: For, if he is a man of the least spirit, he will have fifty deviations from a straight line to make with this or that party as he goes along, which he can no ways avoid. He will have views and prospects to himself perpetually soliciting his eye, which he can no more help standing still to look at than he can fly; he will moreover have various

Accounts to reconcile:

Anecdotes to pick up:

Inscriptions to make out:

Stories to weave in:

Traditions to sift:

Personages to call upon:

Panegyricks to paste up at this door:

Pasquinades at that:———All which both the man and his mule are quite exempt from. To sum up all; there are archives at every stage to be look'd into, and rolls, records, documents, and endless genealogies, which justice ever and anon calls him back to stay the reading of:—In short, there is no end of it;——for my own part, I declare I have been at it these six weeks, making all the speed I possibly could,—and am not yet born:—I have just been able, and that's all, to tell you *when* it happen'd, but not *how*; —so that you see the thing is yet far from being accomplished.

These unforeseen stoppages, which I own I had no conception of when I first set out;—but which, I am convinced now, will rather increase than diminish as I advance,—have struck out a hint which I am resolved to follow;—and that is,—not to be in a hurry;—but to go on leisurely, writing and publishing two volumes of my life every year;——which, if I am suffered to go on quietly, and can make a tolerable bargain with my bookseller, I shall continue to do as long as I live.

CHAPTER XV

THE article in my mother's marriage settlement, which I told the reader I was at the pains to search for, and which, now that I have found it, I think proper to lay before him,—is so much more fully express'd in the deed itself, than ever I can pretend to do it, that it would be barbarity to take it out of the lawyer's hand:—It is as follows.

"And this Indenture further witnesseth, That the said *Walter Shandy*, merchant, in consideration of the said intended marriage to be had, and, by God's blessing, to be well and truly solemnized and consummated between the said *Walter Shandy* and *Elizabeth Mollineux* aforesaid, and divers other good and valuable causes and considerations him thereunto specially moving,—doth grant, covenant, condescend, consent, conclude, bargain, and fully agree to and with *John Dixon*, and *James Turner*, Esqrs; the above-named trustees, *&c. &c.*—to wit,—That in case it should hereafter so fall out, chance, happen, or otherwise come to pass, —That the said *Walter Shandy*, merchant, shall have left off business before the time or times, that the said *Elizabeth Mollineux* shall, according to the course of nature, or otherwise, have left off bearing and bringing forth children;—and that, in consequence of the said *Walter Shandy* having so left off business, shall, in despight, and against the free-will, consent, and good-liking of the said *Elizabeth Mollineux*,—make a departure from the city of *London*, in order to retire to, and dwell upon, his estate at *Shandy-Hall*, in the county of ——, or at any other country-seat, castle, hall, mansion-house, messuage or grainge-house, now purchased, or hereafter to be purchased, or upon any part or parcel thereof:—That then, and as often as the said *Elizabeth Mollineux* shall happen to be enceint with child or children severally and lawfully begot, or to be begotten, upon the body of the said *Elizabeth Mollineux* during her said coverture,—he the said *Walter Shandy* shall, at his own proper cost and charges, and out of his own proper monies, upon good and reasonable notice, which is hereby agreed to be within six weeks of her the said *Elizabeth Mollineux*'s full reckoning, or time of supposed and computed delivery,—pay, or cause to be paid, the sum of one hundred and twenty pounds of good and lawful money, to *John Dixon* and *James Turner*, Esqrs.; or assigns,—upon TRUST and confidence, and for and unto the use and uses, intent, end, and purpose following:—𝔗𝔥𝔞𝔱 𝔦𝔰 𝔱𝔬 𝔰𝔞𝔶,—That the said sum of one hundred and twenty pounds shall be paid into the hands of the said *Elizabeth Mollineux*, or to be otherwise applied by them the said trustees, for the well and truly hiring of one coach, with able and sufficient horses, to carry and convey the body of the said *Elizabeth Mollineux* and the child or children which she shall be then and there enceint and pregnant with,—unto the city of *London*; and for the further paying and defraying of all other incidental costs, charges, and expences whatsoever,—in and about, and for, and relating to her said intended delivery and lying-in, in the said city or suburbs thereof. And that the said *Elizabeth Mollineux* shall and may, from time to time, and at all such time and times as are here convenanted and agreed upon,—peaceably and quietly hire the said coach and horses, and have free ingress, egress, and regress throughout her journey, in and from the said coach, according to the tenor, true intent, and meaning of these presents, without any let, suit, trouble, disturbance, molestation, discharge, hinderance, forfeiture, eviction, vexation, interruption, or incumberance whatsoever.—And that it shall moreover be lawful to and for the said *Elizabeth Mollineux*, from time to time, and as oft or often as she shall well and truly be advanced in her said pregnancy, to the time heretofore stipulated and agreed upon,—to live and reside in such place or places, and in such family or families, and with such relations, friends, and other persons within the said city of *London*, as she, at her own will and pleasure, notwithstanding her present coverture, and as if she was a *femme sole* and unmarried,—shall

[56]

think fit.—*And this Indenture further witnesseth*, That for the more effectually carrying of the said covenant into execution, the said *Walter Shandy*, merchant, doth hereby grant, bargain, sell, release, and confirm unto the said *John Dixon*, and *James Turner*, Esqrs; their heirs, executors, and assigns, in their actual possession, now being by virtue of an indenture of bargain and sale for a year to them the said *John Dixon* and *James Turner*, Esqrs; by him the said *Walter Shandy*, merchant, thereof made; which said bargain and sale for a year, bears date the day next before the date of these presents, and by force and virtue of the statute for transferring of uses into possession,———*All* that the manor and lordship of *Shandy* in the county of ———, with all the rights, members, and appurtenances thereof; and all and every the messuages, houses, buildings, barns, stables, orchards, gardens, backsides, tofts, crofts, garths, cottages, lands, meadows, feedings, pastures, marshes, commons, woods, underwoods, drains, fisheries, waters, and water-courses;—together with all rents, reversions, services, annuities, fee-farms, knights fees, views, of frank-pledge, escheats, reliefs, mines, quarries, goods and chattels of felons and fugitives, felons of themselves, and put in exigent, deodands, free warrens, and all other royalties and seignories, rights and jurisdictions, privileges and hereditaments whatsoever.
———*And also* the advowson, donation, presentation and free disposition of the rectory or parsonage of *Shandy* aforesaid, and all and every the tenths, tythes, glebe-lands"———In three words, ———"My mother was to lay in, (if she chose it) in *London*."

But in order to put a stop to the practice of any unfair play on the part of my mother, which a marriage article of this nature too manifestly opened a door to, and which indeed had never been thought of at all, but for my uncle *Toby Shandy*;—a clause was added in security of my father, which was this:—"That in case my mother hereafter should, at any time put my father to the trouble and expence of a *London* journey upon false cries and tokens;———that for every such instance she should forfeit all the right and title which the covenant gave her to the next turn;——— but to no more,—and so on, *toties quoties*, in as effectual a manner, as if such a covenant betwixt them had not been made."

—This, by the way, was no more than what was reasonable;— and yet, as reasonable as it was, I have ever thought it hard that the whole weight of the article should have fallen entirely, as it did, upon myself.

But I was begot and born to misfortunes;—for my poor mother, whether it was wind or water,—or a compound of both,—or neither;—or whether it was simply the mere swell of imagination and fancy in her;—or how far a strong wish and desire to have it so, might mislead her judgment;—in short, whether she was deceived or deceiving in this matter, it no way becomes me to decide. The fact was this, That, in the latter end of *September* 1717, which was the year before I was born, my mother having carried my father up to town much against the grain,—he peremptorily insisted upon the clause;—so that I was doom'd, by marriage articles, to have my nose squeez'd as flat to my face, as if the destinies had actually spun me without one.

How this event came about,—and what a train of vexatious disappointments, in one stage or other of my life, have pursued me from the mere loss, or rather compression, of this one single member,—shall be laid before the reader all in due time.

CHAPTER XVI

MY FATHER, as any body may naturally imagine, came down with my mother into the country, in but a pettish kind of a humour. The first twenty or five-and-twenty miles he did nothing in the world but fret and teaze himself, and indeed my mother too, about the cursed expence, which he said might every shilling of it have been saved;—then what vexed him more than every thing else was the provoking time of the year, ——which, as I told you, was towards the end of *September*, when his wall-fruit and green gages especially, in which he was very curious, were just ready for pulling:—"Had he been whistled up to *London*, upon a *Tom Fool*'s errand in any other month of the whole year, he should not have said three words about it."

For the next two whole stages, no subject would go down, but the heavy blow he had sustain'd from the loss of a son, whom it seems he had fully reckon'd upon in his mind, and register'd down in his pocket-book, as a second staff for his old age, in case *Bobby* should fail him. "The disappointment of this, he said, was ten times more to a wise man than all the money which the journey, &c. had cost him, put together,—rot the hundred and twenty pounds,——he did not mind it a rush."

From *Stilton*, all the way to *Grantham*, nothing in the whole affair provoked him so much as the condolences of his friends, and the foolish figure they should both make at church the first *Sunday*;——of which, in the satirical vehemence of his wit, now sharpen'd a little by vexation, he would give so many humorous and provoking descriptions,—and place his rib and self in so many tormenting lights and attitudes in the face of the whole congregation;—that my mother declared, these two stages were so truly tragi-comical, that she did nothing but laugh and cry in a breath, from one end to the other of them all the way.

From *Grantham*, till they had cross'd the *Trent*, my father was out of all kind of patience at the vile trick and imposition which he fancied my mother had put upon him in this affair.—"Certainly," he would say to himself, over and over again, "the woman could not be deceived herself;——if she could,—— what weakness!"——tormenting word! which led his imagination a thorny dance, and, before all was over, play'd the duce and all with him;——for sure as ever the word *weakness* was uttered, and struck full upon his brain,—so sure it set him upon running divisions upon how many kinds of weaknesses there were;— that there was such a thing as weakness of the body,——as well as weakness of the mind,—and then he would do nothing but syllogize within himself for a stage or two together, How far the cause of all these vexations might, or might not, have arisen out of himself.

In short, he had so many little subjects of disquietude springing out of this one affair, all fretting successively in his mind as they rose up in it, that my mother, whatever was her journey up, had but an uneasy journey of it down.——In a word, as she complained to my uncle *Toby*, he would have tired out the patience of any flesh alive.

CHAPTER XVII

THOUGH my father travelled homewards as I told you, in none of the best of moods,—pshawing and pishing all the way down,—yet he had the complaisance to keep the worst part of the story still to himself;—which was the resolution he had taken of doing himself the justice, which my uncle *Toby*'s clause in the marriage settlement empowered him; nor was it till the very night in which I was begot, which was thirteen months after, that she had the least intimation of his design;—when my father, happening, as you remember, to be a little chagrin'd and out of temper,——took occasion as they lay chatting gravely in bed afterwards, talking over what was to come,——to let her know that she must accommodate herself as well as she could to the bargain made between them in their marriage deeds; which was to lye-in of her next child in the country to balance the last year's journey.

My father was a gentleman of many virtues,—but he had a strong spice of that in his temper which might, or might not, add to the number.—'Tis known by the name of perseverance in a good cause,—and of obstinacy in a bad one: Of this my mother had so much knowledge, that she knew 'twas to no purpose to make any remonstrance,—so she e'en resolved to sit down quietly, and make the most of it.

CHAPTER XVIII

AS THE point was that night agreed, or rather determin'd, that my mother should lye-in of me in the country, she took her measures accordingly; for which purpose, when she was three days, or thereabouts, gone with child, she began to cast her eyes upon the midwife, whom you have so often heard me mention; and before the week was well got round, as the famous Dr. *Maningham* was not to be had, she had come to a final determination in her mind,——notwithstanding there was a scientifick operator within so near a call as eight miles of us, and who, moreover, had expressly wrote a five shillings book upon the subject of midwifery, in which he had exposed, not only the blunders of the sisterhood itself,——but had likewise superadded many curious improvements for the quicker extraction of the fœtus in cross births, and some other cases of danger which belay us in getting into the world; notwithstanding all this, my mother, I say, was absolutely determined to trust her life and mine with it, into no soul's hand but this old woman's only.—Now this I like;—when we cannot get at the very thing we wish, ——never to take up with the next best in degree to it;—no; that's pitiful beyond description;—it is no more than a week from this very day, in which I am now writing this book for the edification of the world;—which is *March* 9, 1759,——that my dear,

dear *Jenny*, observing I look'd a little grave, as she stood cheapening a silk of five-and-twenty shillings a yard,—told the mercer, she was sorry she had given him so much trouble;—and immediately went and bought herself a yard-wide stuff of ten-pence a yard. —'Tis the duplication of one and the same greatness of soul; only what lessen'd the honour of it somewhat, in my mother's case, was, that she could not heroine it into so violent and hazardous an extream, as one in her situation might have wished, because the old midwife had really some little claim to be depended upon,—as much, at least, as success could give her; having, in the course of her practice of near twenty years in the parish, brought every mother's son of them into the world without any one slip or accident which could fairly be laid to her account.

These facts, tho' they had their weight, yet did not altogether satisfy some few scruples and uneasinesses which hung upon my father's spirits in relation to his choice.—To say nothing of the natural workings of humanity and justice,—or of the yearnings of parental and connubial love, all which prompted him to leave as little to hazard as possible in a case of this kind;——he felt himself concern'd in a particular manner, that all should go right in the present case;—from the accumulated sorrow he lay open to, should any evil betide his wife and child in lying-in at *Shandy-Hall*.——He knew the world judged by events, and would add to his afflictions in such a misfortune, by loading him with the whole blame of it.——"Alas o'day;—had Mrs. *Shandy*, poor gentlewoman! had but her wish in going up to town just to lye-in and come down again;—which, they say, she begg'd and pray'd for upon her bare knees,——and which, in my opinion, considering the fortune which Mr. *Shandy* got with her,—was no such mighty matter to have complied with, the lady and her babe might both of 'em have been alive at this hour."

This exclamation, my father knew was unanswerable;—and yet, it was not merely to shelter himself,—nor was it altogether for the care of his offspring and wife that he seemed so extremely anxious about this point;—my father had extensive views of things,——and stood moreover, as he thought, deeply concern'd in it for the publick good, from the dread he entertained of the bad uses an ill-fated instance might be put to.

He was very sensible that all political writers upon the subject had unanimously agreed and lamented, from the beginning of Queen *Elizabeth*'s reign down to his own time, that the current of men and money towards the metropolis, upon one frivolous

errand or another,—set in so strong,—as to become dangerous to
our civil rights;—tho', by the bye,——a *current* was not the
image he took most delight in,—a *distemper* was here his favourite
metaphor, and he would run it down into a perfect allegory, by
maintaining it was identically the same in the body national as in
the body natural, where blood and spirits were driven up into
the head faster than they could find their ways down;——
a stoppage of circulation must ensue, which was death in both
cases.

There was little danger, he would say, of losing our liberties by
French politicks or *French* invasions;——nor was he so much in
pain of a consumption from the mass of corrupted matter and
ulcerated humours in our constitution,—which he hoped was not
so bad as it was imagined;—but he verily feared, that in some
violent push, we should go off, all at once, in a state-apoplexy;
—and then he would say, *The Lord have mercy upon us all.*

My father was never able to give the history of this distemper,
—without the remedy along with it.

"Was I an absolute prince," he would say, pulling up his
breeches with both his hands, as he rose from his arm-chair,
"I would appoint able judges, at every avenue of my metropolis,
who should take cognizance of every fool's business who came
there;—and if, upon a fair and candid hearing, it appeared not
of weight sufficient to leave his own home, and come up, bag and
baggage, with his wife and children, farmers sons, &c. &c. at his
backside, they should be all sent back, from constable to constable, like vagrants as they were, to the place of their legal
settlements. By this means I shall take care, that my metropolis
totter'd not thro' its own weight;—that the head be no longer too
big for the body;—that the extreams, now wasted and pin'd in,
be restored to their due share of nourishment, and regain, with
it, their natural strength and beauty:—I would effectually provide, That the meadows and corn-fields, of my dominions, should
laugh and sing;—that good chear and hospitality flourish once
more;—and that such weight and influence be put thereby into
the hands of the Squirality of my kingdom, as should counterpoise what I perceive my Nobility are now taking from them.

"Why are there so few palaces and gentlemen's seats," he
would ask, with some emotion, as he walked a-cross the room,
"throughout so many delicious provinces in *France?* Whence is
it that the few remaining *Chateaus* amongst them are so dismantled,—so unfurnished, and in so ruinous and desolate a con-

dition?—Because, Sir," (he would say) "in that kingdom no man has any country-interest to support;—the little interest of any kind, which any man has any where in it, is concentrated in the court, and the looks of the Grand Monarch; by the sun-shine of whose countenance, or the clouds which pass a-cross it, every *French* man lives or dies."

Another political reason which prompted my father so strongly to guard against the least evil accident in my mother's lying-in in the country,——was, That any such instance would infallibly throw a balance of power, too great already, into the weaker vessels of the gentry, in his own, or higher stations;——which, with the many other usurped rights which that part of the constitution was hourly establishing,—would, in the end, prove fatal to the monarchical system of domestick government established in the first creation of things by God.

In this point he was entirely of Sir *Robert Filmer's* opinion, That the plans and institutions of the greatest monarchies in the eastern parts of the world, were, originally, all stolen from that admirable pattern and prototype of this houshold and paternal power;—which, for a century, he said, and more, had gradually been degenerating away into a mix'd government;——the form of which, however desirable in great combinations of the species, ——was very troublesome in small ones,—and seldom produced any thing, that he saw, but sorrow and confusion.

For all these reasons, private and publick, put together,— my father was for having the man-midwife by all means,—my mother by no means. My father begg'd and intreated, she would for once recede from her prerogative in this matter, and suffer him to choose for her;—my mother, on the contrary, insisted upon her privilege in this matter, to choose for herself,—and have no mortal's help but the old woman's.—What could my father do? He was almost at his wit's end;——talked it over with her in all moods;—placed his arguments in all lights;—argued the matter with her like a christian,—like a heathen,—like a husband, —like a father,—like a patriot,—like a man:—My mother answered every thing only like a woman; which was a little hard upon her;—for as she could not assume and fight it out behind such a variety of characters,—'twas no fair match;—'twas seven to one.—What could my mother do?——She had the advantage (otherwise she had been certainly overpowered) of a small reinforcement of chagrin personal at the bottom which bore her up, and enabled her to dispute the affair with my father with so equal an advantage,——that both sides sung *Te Deum.* In a word, my mother was to have the old woman,—and the operator was to have licence to drink a bottle of wine with my father and my uncle *Toby Shandy* in the back parlour,—for which he was to be paid five guineas.

I must beg leave, before I finish this chapter, to enter a caveat in the breast of my fair reader;—and it is this:——Not to take it absolutely for granted from an unguarded word or two which I have dropp'd in it,——"That I am a married man."—I own the tender appellation of my dear, dear *Jenny*,—with some other strokes of conjugal knowledge, interspersed here and there, might, naturally enough, have misled the most candid judge in the world into such a determination against me.—All I plead for, in this case, Madam, is strict justice, and that you do so much of it, to me as well as to yourself,—as not to prejudge or receive such an impression of me, till you have better evidence, than I am positive, at present, can be produced against me:—Not that I can be so vain or unreasonable, Madam, as to desire you should therefore think, that my dear, dear *Jenny* is my kept mistress; —no,—that would be flattering my character in the other extream, and giving it an air of freedom, which, perhaps, it has no kind of right to. All I contend for, is the utter impossibility for some volumes that you, or the most penetrating spirit upon earth, should know how this matter really stands.—It is not impossible, but that my dear, dear *Jenny!* tender as the appellation is, may be my child.—Consider,—I was born in the year eighteen.—Nor is there any thing unnatural or extravagant in the supposition, that my dear *Jenny* may be my friend.——Friend!—My friend.— Surely, Madam, a friendship between the two sexes may subsist, and be supported without——Fy! Mr. *Shandy*:—Without any thing, Madam, but that tender and delicious sentiment, which ever mixes in friendship, where there is a difference of sex. Let me intreat you to study the pure and sentimental parts of the best *French* Romances;——it will really, Madam, astonish you to see with what a variety of chaste expression this delicious sentiment, which I have the honour to speak of, is dress'd out.

CHAPTER XIX

I WOULD sooner undertake to explain the hardest problem in Geometry, than pretend to account for it, that a gentleman of my father's great good sense,——knowing, as the reader must have observed him, and curious too, in philosophy,—wise also in political reasoning,—and in polemical (as he will find) no way ignorant,—could be capable of entertaining a notion in his head, so out of the common track,—that I fear the reader, when I come to mention it to him, if he is the least of a cholerick temper, will immediately throw the book by; if mercurial, he will laugh most heartily at it;—and if he is of a grave and saturnine cast, he will, at first sight, absolutely condemn as fanciful and extravagant; and that was in respect to the choice and imposition of Christian names, on which he thought a great deal more depended than what superficial minds were capable of conceiving.

His opinion, in this matter, was, That there was a strange kind of magick bias, which good or bad names, as he called them, irresistibly impress'd upon our characters and conduct.

The Hero of *Cervantes* argued not the point with more seriousness,——nor had he more faith,   or more to say on the powers of Necromancy in dishonouring his deeds,—or on DULCINEA's name, in shedding lustre upon them, than my father had on those of TRISMEGISTUS or ARCHIMEDES, on the one hand, —or of NYKY and SIMKIN on the other. How many CÆSARS and POMPEYS, he would say, by mere inspiration of the names, have been render'd worthy of them? And how many, he would add, are there, who might have done exceeding well in the world, had not their characters and spirits been totally depress'd and NICODEMUS'D into nothing.

I see plainly, Sir, by your looks, (or as the case happen'd) my father would say,—that you do not heartily subscribe to this opinion of mine,—which, to those, he would add, who have not carefully sifted it to the bottom,—I own has an air more of fancy than of solid reasoning in it;——and yet, my dear Sir, if I may presume to know your character, I am morally assured, I should hazard little in stating a case to you,—not as a party in the dispute,—but as a judge, and trusting my appeal upon it to your own good sense and candid disquisition in this matter;——you are a person free from as many narrow prejudices of education as most men;—and, if I may presume to penetrate further into you,—of a liberality of genius above bearing down an opinion, merely because it wants friends. Your son! —your dear son,—from whose sweet and open temper you have so much to expect.—Your BILLY, Sir!—would you, for the world, have called him JUDAS?—Would you my dear Sir, he would say, laying his hand upon your breast, with the genteelest address,— and in that soft and irresistible *piano* of voice, which the nature of the *argumentum ad hominem* absolutely requires,—Would you, Sir, if a *Jew* of a godfather had proposed the name for your child, and offered you his purse along with it, would you have consented to such a desecration of him?—O my God! he would say, looking up, if I know your temper right, Sir,—you are incapable of it;—— you would have trampled upon the offer;—you would have thrown the temptation at the tempter's head with abhorrence.

Your greatness of mind in this action, which I admire, with that generous contempt of money which you shew me in the whole transaction, is really noble;—and what renders it more so, is the principle of it;—the workings of a parent's love upon the truth and conviction of this very hypothesis, namely, That was your son called JUDAS,—the sordid and treacherous idea, so inseparable from the name, would have accompanied him thro' life like his shadow, and, in the end, made a miser and a rascal of him, in spight, Sir, of your example.

I never knew a man able to answer this argument.——But, indeed, to speak of my father as he was;—he was certainly irresistible, both in his orations and disputations;—he was born an orator;—Θεοδιδακτος.—Persuasion hung upon his lips, and the elements of Logick and Rhetorick were so blended up in him,—and, withall, he had so shrewd a guess at the weaknesses and passions of his respondent,——that NATURE might have stood up and said,—"This man is eloquent." In short, whether he was on the weak or the strong side of the question, 'twas hazardous in either case to attack him.—And yet, 'tis strange, he had never read *Cicero* nor *Quintilian de Oratore*, nor *Isocrates*, nor *Aristotle*, nor *Longinus* amongst the antients;——nor *Vossius*, nor *Skioppius*, nor *Ramus*, nor *Farnaby* amongst the moderns;— and what is more astonishing, he had never in his whole life the least light or spark of subtilty struck into his mind, by one single lecture upon *Crackenthorp* or *Burgersdicius*, or any *Dutch* logician or commentator;—he knew not so much as in what the difference of an argument *ad ignorantiam*, and an argument *ad hominem* consisted; so that I well remember, when he went up

[66]

along with me to enter my name at *Jesus College* in * * * *,—it was a matter of just wonder with my worthy tutor, and two or three fellows of that learned society,—that a man who knew not so much as the names of his tools, should be able to work after that fashion with 'em.

To work with them in the best manner he could, was what my father was, however, perpetually forced upon;——for he had a thousand little sceptical notions of the comick kind to defend, ——most of which notions, I verily believe, at first enter'd upon the footing of mere whims, and of a *vive la Bagatelle*; and as such he would make merry with them for half an hour or so, and having sharpen'd his wit upon 'em, dismiss them till another day.

I mention this, not only as matter of hypothesis or conjecture upon the progress and establishment of my father's many odd opinions,—but as a warning to the learned reader against the indiscreet reception of such guests, who, after a free and undisturbed enterance, for some years, into our brains,—at length claim a kind of settlement there,——working sometimes like yeast;—but more generally after the manner of the gentle passion, beginning in jest,—but ending in downright earnest.

Whether this was the case of the singularity of my father's notions,—or that his judgment, at length, became the dupe of his wit;—or how far, in many of his notions, he might, tho' odd, be absolutely right;——the reader, as he comes at them, shall decide. All that I maintain here, is, that in this one, of the influence of Christian names, however it gained footing, he was serious; he was all uniformity;—he was systematical, and, like all systematick reasoners, he would move both heaven and earth, and twist and torture every thing in nature to support his hypothesis. In a word, I repeat it over again;—he was serious;—and, in consequence of it, he would lose all kind of patience whenever he saw people, especially of condition, who should have known better, ——as careless and as indifferent about the name they imposed upon their child,—or more so, than in the choice of *Ponto* or *Cupid* for their puppy-dog.

This, he would say, look'd ill;—and had, moreover, this particular aggravation in it, *viz.* That when once a vile name was wrongfully or injudiciously given, 'twas not like the case of a man's character, which, when wrong'd, might hereafter be clear'd;——and, possibly, sometime or other, if not in the man's life, at least after his death,—be, somehow or other, set to rights with the world: But the injury of this, he would say, could never be undone;—nay, he doubted even whether an act of parliament could reach it:——He knew as well as you, that the legislator assum'd a power over surnames;—but for very strong reasons, which he could give, it had never yet adventured, he would say, to go a step further.

It was observable, that tho' my father, in consequence of this opinion, had, as I have told you, the strongest likings and dislikings towards certain names;—that there were still numbers of names which hung so equally in the balance before him, that they were absolutely indifferent to him. *Jack*, *Dick*, and *Tom* were of this class: These my father call'd neutral names;—affirming of them, without a satyr, That there had been as many knaves and fools, at least, as wise and good men, since the world began, who had indifferently borne them;—so that like equal forces acting against each other in contrary directions, he thought they mutually destroyed each others effects; for which reason, he would often declare, He would not give a cherry-stone to choose amongst them. *Bob*, which was my brother's name, was another of these neutral kinds of Christian names, which operated very little either way; and as my father happen'd to be at *Epsom*, when it was given him,—he would oft times thank heaven it was no worse. *Andrew* was something like a negative quantity in Algebra with him;—'twas worse, he said, than nothing.—*William* stood pretty high:—*Numps* again was low with him;—and *Nick*, he said, was the DEVIL.

But, of all the names in the universe, he had the most unconquerable aversion for TRISTRAM;—he had the lowest and most contemptible opinion of it of any thing in the world,—thinking it could possibly produce nothing in *rerum naturâ*, but what was extreamly mean and pitiful: So that in the midst of a dispute on the subject, in which, by the bye, he was frequently involved,—— he would sometimes break off in a sudden and spirited EPIPHONEMA, or rather EROTESIS, raised a third, and sometimes a full fifth, above the key of the discourse,——and demand it categorically of his antagonist, Whether he would take upon him to say, he had ever remember'd,——whether he had ever read,— or even whether he had ever heard tell of a man, call'd *Tristram*, performing any thing great or worth recording?—No,—he would say,—TRISTRAM!—The thing is impossible.

What could be wanting in my father but to have wrote a book to publish this notion of his to the world? Little boots it to the subtle speculatist to stand single in his opinions,—unless he gives

them proper vent:—It was the identical thing which my father did;
—for in the year sixteen, which was two years before I was born,
he was at the pains of writing an express DISSERTATION simply
upon the word *Tristram*,—shewing the world, with great candour
and modesty, the grounds of his great abhorrence to the name.

When this story is compared with the title-page,—Will not the
gentle reader pity my father from his soul?—to see an orderly and
well-disposed gentleman, who tho' singular,—yet inoffensive in
his notions,—so played upon in them by cross purposes;——to
look down upon the stage, and see him baffled and overthrown
in all his little systems and wishes; to behold a train of events
perpetually falling out against him, and in so critical and cruel
a way, as if they had purposedly been plann'd and pointed
against him, merely to insult his speculations.——In a word, to
behold such a one, in his old age, ill-fitted for troubles, ten times
in a day suffering sorrow;—ten times in a day calling the child
of his prayers TRISTRAM!——Melancholy dissyllable of sound!
which, to his ears, was unison to *Nicompoop*, and every name
vituperative under heaven.——By his ashes! I swear it,—if ever
malignant spirit took pleasure, or busied itself by traversing the
purposes of mortal man,—it must have been here;—and if it was
not necessary I should be born before I was christened, I would
this moment give the reader an account of it.

CHAPTER XX

—HOW COULD you, Madam, be so inattentive in reading
the last chapter? I told you in it, *That my mother was
not a papist.*——Papist! You told me no such thing,
Sir. Madam, I beg leave to repeat it over again, That I told you as
plain, at least, as words, by direct inference, could tell you such
a thing.—Then, Sir, I must have miss'd a page.—No, Madam,—
you have not miss'd a word.——Then I was asleep, Sir.—My
pride, Madam, cannot allow you that refuge.——Then, I declare,
I know nothing at all about the matter.—That, Madam, is the
very fault I lay to your charge; and as a punishment for it, I do
insist upon it, that you immediately turn back, that is, as soon as
you get to the next full stop, and read the whole chapter over
again.

I have imposed this penance upon the lady, neither out of
wantonness or cruelty; but from the best of motives; and therefore shall make her no apology for it when she returns back:—

'Tis to rebuke a vicious taste which has crept into thousands besides herself,—of reading straight forwards, more in quest of the adventures, than of the deep erudition and knowledge which a book of this cast, if read over as it should be, would infallibly impart with them.——The mind should be accustomed to make wise reflections, and draw curious conclusions as it goes along; the habitude of which made *Pliny* the younger affirm, "That he never read a book so bad, but he drew some profit from it." The stories of *Greece* and *Rome*, run over without this turn and application,—do less service, I affirm it, than the history of *Parismus* and *Parismenus*, or of the Seven Champions of *England*, read with it

——But here comes my fair Lady. Have you read over again the chapter, Madam, as I desired you?—You have: And did you not observe the passage, upon the second reading, which admits the inference?——Not a word like it! Then, Madam, be pleased to ponder well the last line but one of the chapter, where I take upon me to say, "It was *necessary* I should be born before I was christen'd." Had my mother, Madam, been a Papist, that consequence did not follow*.

It is a terrible misfortune for this same book of mine, but more so to the Republick of Letters;—so that my own is quite swallowed up in the consideration of it,—that this self-same vile pruriency for fresh adventures in all things, has got so strongly into our habit and humours,—and so wholly intent are we upon satisfying the impatience of our concupiscence that way,—that nothing but the gross and more carnal parts of a composition will go down:—The subtle hints and sly communications of science fly off, like spirits, upwards;——the heavy moral escapes downwards; and both the one and the other are as much lost to the world, as if they were still left in the bottom of the ink-horn.

---

* The *Romish* Rituals direct the baptizing of the child, in cases of danger, *before* it is born;—but upon this proviso, That some part or other of the child's body be seen by the baptizer:——But the Doctors of the *Sorbonne*, by a deliberation held amongst them, *April* 10, 1733,—have enlarged the powers of the midwives, by determining, That tho' no part of the child's body should appear,——that baptism shall, nevertheless, be administered to it by injection, *par le moyen d'une petite Canulle.*—Anglicé *a squirt.*—'Tis very strange that St. *Thomas Aquinas*, who had so good a mechanical head, both for tying and untying the knots of school divinity,—should, after so much pains bestowed upon this,—give up the point at last, as a second *La chose impossible*,—"Infantes in maternis uteris existentes (quoth St. *Thomas*) baptizari possunt *nullo modo*."—O *Thomas! Thomas!*

If the reader has the curiosity to see the question upon baptism, *by injection*, as presented to the Doctors of the *Sorbonne*,—with their consultation thereupon, it is as follows.

I wish the male-reader has not pass'd by many a one, as quaint and curious as this one, in which the female-reader has been detected. I wish it may have its effects;—and that all good people, both male and female, from her example, may be taught to think as well as read.

MÉMOIRE presenté à Messieurs les Docteurs de SORBONNE.*

*U*N *CHIRURGIEN Accoucheur, represente à Messieurs les Docteurs de* Sorbonne, *qu'il y a des cas, quoique, trés rares, où une mere ne sçauroit accoucher, & même où l'enfant est tellement renfermé dans le sein de sa mere, qu'il ne fait paroître aucune partie de son corps, ce qui seroit un cas, suivant les Rituels, de lui conférer, du moins sous condition, le baptême. Le Chirurgien, qui consulte, prétend, par le moyen d'une* petite canulle, *de pouvoir baptiser immediatement l'enfant, sans faire aucun tort à la mere. ——Il demand si ce moyen, qu'il vient de proposer, est permis & légitime, & s'il peut s'en servir dans le cas qu'il vient d' exposer.*

RESPONSE

*L*E *CONSEIL estime, que la question proposée souffre de grandes difficulties. Les Théologiens posent d'un coté pour principe, que le baptême, qui est une naissance spirituelle, suppose une premiere naissance; il faut être né dans le monde, pour renaître en* Jesus Christ, *comme ils l'enseignent. S.* Thomas, 3 part. quæst. 88. artic. 11. *suit cette doctrine comme une verité constante; l'on ne peut, dit ce S. Docteur, baptiser les enfans qui sont renfermés dans le sein de leurs Meres, & S.* Thomas *est fondé sur ce, que les enfans ne sont point nés, & ne peuvent être comptés parmi les autres hommes; d'où il conclud, qu'ils ne peuvent être l'object d'une action extérieure, pour recevoir par leur ministére, les sacremens nécessaires au salut:* Pueri in maternis uteris existentes, nondum prodierunt in lucem ut cum aliis hominibus vitam ducant; unde non possunt subjici actioni humanæ, ut per eorum ministerium sacramenta recipiant ad salutem. *Les rituels ordonnent dans la pratique ce que les théologiens ont établi sur les mêmes matiéres, & ils deffendent tous d'une maniére uniforme, de baptiser les enfans qui sont renfermés dans le sein de leurs meres, s'ils ne font paroître quelque partie de leurs corps. Le concours des théologiens, & des rituels, qui sont les régles des diocéses, paroît former une autorité qui termine la question presente; cependant le conseil de conscience considerant d'un coté, que le raisonnement des théo-*

* Vide Deventer. Paris Edit. 4to, 1734, p. 366.

logiens est uniquement fondé sur une raison de convenance, & que la deffense des rituels, suppose que l'on ne peut baptiser immediatement les enfans ainsi renfermés dans le sein de leurs meres, ce qui est contre la supposition presente; & d'un autre côté, considerant que les mêmes théologiens enseignent, que l'on peut risquer les sacremens que Jesus Christ *a établis comme des moyens faciles, mais nécessaires pour sanctifier les hommes; & d'ailleurs estimant, que les enfans renfermés dans le sein de leurs meres, pourroient être capables de salut, parcequ'ils sont capables de damnation;—pour ces considerations, & en égard à l'exposé, suivant lequel on assure avoir trouvé un moyen certain de baptiser ces enfans ainsi renfermés, sans faire aucun tort à la mere, le Conseil estime que l'on pourroit se servir du moyen proposé, dans la confiance qu'il a, que Dieu n'a point laissé ces sortes d'enfans sans aucuns secours, & supposant, comme il est exposé, que le moyen dont il s'agit est propre à leur procurer le baptême; cependant comme il s'agiroit, en autorisant la pratique proposée, de changer une regle universellement établie, le Conseil croit que celui qui consulte doit s'addresser à son évêque, & à qui il appartient de juger de l'utilité, & du danger du moyen proposé, & comme, sous le bon plaisir de l'evêque, le conseil estime qu'il faudroit recourir au Pape, qui a le droit d'expliquer les régles de l'eglise, & d'y déroger dans le cas, ou la loi ne sçauroit obliger, quelque sage & quelque utile que paroisse la maniére de baptiser dont il s'agit, le conseil ne pourroit l'approuver sans le concours de ces deux autorités. On conseile au moins à celui qui consulte, de s'addresser à son evêque, & de lui faire part de la presente décision, afin que, si le prelat entre dans les raisons sur lesquelles les docteurs soussignés s'appuyent, il puisse être autorisé dans le cas de nécessité, au il risqueroit trop d'attendre que la permission fût demandée & accordée d'employer le moyen, qu'il propose si avantageux au salut de l'enfant. Au reste le conseil, en estimant que l'on pourroit s'en servir, croit cependant, que si les enfans dont il s'agit, venoient au monde, contre l'esperance de ceux qui se seroient servis du même moyen, il seroit nécessaire de les baptiser* sous condition, *& en cela le conseil se conformé a tous les rituels, qui en autorisant le baptême d'un enfant qui fait paroître quelque partie de son corps, enjoignent néantmoins, & ordonnent de le baptiser* sous condition, *s'il vient heureusement au monde.*

Déliberé en *Sorbonne*, le 10 *Avril*, 1733.

A. LE MOYNE,
L. DE ROMIGNY,
DE MARCILLY.

Mr. *Tristram Shandy*'s compliments to Messirs. *Le Moyne, De Romigny*, and *De Marcilly*, hopes they all rested well the night after so tiresome a consultation.—He begs to know, whether, after the ceremony of marriage, and before that of consummation, the baptizing all the HOMUNCULI at once, slap-dash, by *injection*, would not be a shorter and safer cut still; on condition, as above, That if the HOMUNCULI do well and come safe into the world after this, that each and every of them shall be baptized again (*sous condition.*)——And provided, in the second place, That the thing can be done, which Mr. *Shandy* apprehends it may, *par le moyen d'une* petite canulle, and *sans faire aucun tort à le père.*

CHAPTER XXI

—I WONDER what's all that noise, and running backwards and forwards for, above stairs, quoth my father, addressing himself, after an hour and a half's silence, to my uncle *Toby*, ——who you must know, was sitting on the opposite side of the fire, smoking his social pipe all the time, in mute contemplation of a new pair of black plush-breeches which he had got on:—What can they be doing brother?—quoth my father,—we can scarce hear ourselves talk.

I think, replied my uncle *Toby*, taking his pipe from his mouth, and striking the head of it two or three times upon the nail of his left thumb, as he began his sentence,——I think, says he:—— But to enter rightly into my uncle *Toby*'s sentiments upon this matter, you must l↑ made to enter first a little into his character, the out-lines of which I shall just give you, and then the dialogue between him and my father will go on as well again.

—Pray what was that man's name,—for I write in such a hurry, I have no time to recollect or look for it,——who first made the observation, "That there was great inconstancy in our air and climate?" Whoever he was, 'twas a just and good observation in him.—But the corollary drawn from it, namely, "That it is this which has furnished us with such a variety of odd and whimsical characters;"—that was not his;—it was found out by another man, at least a century and a half after him:—Then again,—that this copious store-house of original materials, is the true and natural cause that our Comedies are so much better than those of *France*, or any others that either have, or can be

[73]

wrote upon the Continent;——that discovery was not fully made till about the middle of king *William*'s reign,—when the great *Dryden*, in writing one of his long prefaces, (if I mistake not) most fortunately hit upon it. Indeed towards the latter end of queen *Anne*, the great *Addison* began to patronize the notion, and more fully explained it to the world in one or two of his Spectators; —but the discovery was not his.—Then, fourthly and lastly, that this strange irregularity in our climate, producing so strange an irregularity in our characters,——doth thereby, in some sort, make us amends, by giving us somewhat to make us merry with when the weather will not suffer us to go out of doors,—that observation is my own;—and was struck out by me this very rainy day, *March* 26, 1759, and betwixt the hours of nine and ten in the morning.

Thus,—thus my fellow-labourers and associates in this great harvest of our learning, now ripening before our eyes; thus it is, by slow steps of casual increase, that our knowledge physical, metaphysical, physiological, polemical, nautical, mathematical, ænigmatical, technical, biographical, romantical, chemical, and obstetrical, with fifty other branches of it, (most of 'em ending, as these do, in *ical*) have, for these two last centuries and more, gradually been creeping upwards towards that 'Ακμὴ of their perfections, from which, if we may form a conjecture from the advances of these last seven years, we cannot possibly be far off.

When that happens, it is to be hoped, it will put an end to all kind of writings whatsoever;—the want of all kind of writing will put an end to all kind of reading;—and that in time, *As war begets poverty, poverty peace,*——must, in course, put an end to all kind of knowledge,—and then——we shall have all to begin over again; or, in other words, be exactly where we started.

——Happy! thrice happy Times! I only wish that the æra of my begetting, as well as the mode and manner of it, had been a little alter'd,—or that it could have been put off with any convenience to my father or mother, for some twenty or five-and-twenty years longer, when a man in the literary world might have stood some chance.——

But I forgot my uncle *Toby*, whom all this while we have left knocking the ashes out of his tobacco pipe.

His humour was of that particular species, which does honour to our atmosphere; and I should have made no scruple of ranking him amongst one of the first-rate productions of it, had not there appear'd too many strong lines in it of a family-likeness,

[74]

which shewed that he derived the singularity of his temper more from blood, than either wind or water, or any modifications or combinations of them whatever: And I have, therefore, oft times wondered, that my father, tho' I believe he had his reasons for it, upon his observing some tokens of excentricity in my course when I was a boy,—should never once endeavour to account for them in this way; for all the SHANDY FAMILY were of an original character throughout:——I mean the males,—the females had no character at all,—except, indeed, my great aunt DINAH, who, about sixty years ago, was married and got with child by the coachman, for which my father, according to his hypothesis of Christian names, would often say, She might thank her godfathers and godmothers.

It will seem very strange,——and I would as soon think of dropping a riddle in the reader's way, which is not my interest to do, as set him upon guessing how it could come to pass, that an event of this kind, so many years after it had happened, should be reserved for the interruption of the peace and unity, which otherwise so cordially subsisted, between my father and my uncle *Toby.* One would have thought, that the whole force of the misfortune should have spent and wasted itself in the family at first, —as is generally the case:—But nothing ever wrought with our family after the ordinary way. Possibly at the very time this happened, it might have something else to afflict it; and as afflictions are sent down for our good, and that as this had never done the SHANDY FAMILY any good at all, it might lye waiting till apt times and circumstances should give it an opportunity to discharge its office.————Observe, I determine nothing upon this. ————My way is ever to point out to the curious, different tracts of investigation, to come at the first springs of the events I tell;— not with a pedantic *Fescue,*—or in the decisive Manner of *Tacitus,* who outwits himself and his reader;—but with the officious humility of a heart devoted to the assistance merely of the inquisitive;—to them I write,——and by them I shall be read,—— if any such reading as this could be supposed to hold out so long, to the very end of the world.

Why this cause of sorrow, therefore, was thus reserved for my father and uncle, is undetermined by me. But how and in what direction it exerted itself, so as to become the cause of dissatisfaction between them, after it began to operate, is what I am able to explain with great exactness, and is as follows:

My uncle TOBY SHANDY, Madam, was a gentleman, who, with

the virtues which usually constitute the character of a man of honour and rectitude,—possessed one in a very eminent degree, which is seldom or never put into the catalogue; and that was a most extream and unparallel'd modesty of nature;——tho' I correct the word nature, for this reason, that I may not prejudge a point which must shortly come to a hearing; and that is, Whether this modesty of his was natural or acquir'd.——Which ever way my uncle *Toby* came by it, 'twas nevertheless modesty in the truest sense of it; and that is, Madam, not in regard to words, for he was so unhappy as to have very little choice in them,—but to things;——and this kind of modesty so possess'd him, and it arose to such a height in him, as almost to equal, if such a thing could be, even the modesty of a woman: That female nicety, Madam, and inward cleanliness of mind and fancy, in your sex, which makes you so much the awe of ours.

You will imagine, Madam, that my uncle *Toby* had contracted all this from this very source;—that he had spent a great part of his time in converse with your sex; and that from a thorough knowledge of you, and the force of imitation which such fair examples render irresistible,—he had acquired this amiable turn of mind.

I wish I could say so,—for unless it was with his sister-in-law, my father's wife and my mother,——my uncle *Toby* scarce exchanged three words with the sex in as many years;——no, he got it, Madam, by a blow.—A blow!—Yes, Madam, it was owing to a blow from a stone, broke off by a ball from the parapet of a horn-work at the siege of *Namur*, which struck full upon my uncle *Toby*'s groin.—Which way could that effect it? The story of that, Madam, is long and interesting;—but it would be running my history all upon heaps to give it you here.——'Tis for an episode hereafter; and every circumstance relating to it in its proper place, shall be faithfully laid before you:—'Till then, it is not in my power to give further light into this matter, or say more than what I have said already,——That my uncle *Toby* was a gentleman of unparallel'd modesty, which happening to be somewhat subtilized and rarified by the constant heat of a little family-pride,——they both so wrought together within him, that he could never bear to hear the affair of my aunt DINAH touch'd upon, but with the greatest emotion.——The least hint of it was enough to make the blood fly into his face; but when my father enlarged upon the story in mixed companies, which the illustration of his hypothesis frequently obliged him to do,—the unfortunate blight of one of the fairest branches of the family, would set my uncle *Toby*'s honour and modesty o'bleeding; and he would often take my father aside, in the greatest concern imaginable, to expostulate and tell him, he would give him any thing in the world, only to let the story rest.

My father, I believe, had the truest love and tenderness for my uncle *Toby*, that ever one brother bore towards another, and would have done any thing in nature, which one brother in reason could have desir'd of another, to have made my uncle *Toby*'s heart easy in this, or any other point. But this lay out of his power.

——My father, as I told you, was a philosopher in grain,—speculative,—systematical;—and my aunt *Dinah*'s affair was a matter of as much consequence to him, as the retrogradation of the planets to *Copernicus*:—The backslidings of *Venus* in her orbit fortified the *Copernican* system, call'd so after his name; and the backslidings of my aunt *Dinah* in her orbit, did the same service in establishing my father's system, which, I trust, will for ever hereafter be call'd the *Shandean System*, after his.

In any other family dishonour, my father, I believe, had as nice a sense of shame as any man whatever;——and neither he, nor, I dare say, *Copernicus*, would have divulged the affair in either case, or have taken the least notice of it to the world, but for the obligations they owed, as they thought, to truth.—*Amicus Plato*, my father would say, construing the words to my uncle *Toby*, as he went along, *Amicus Plato*; that is, DINAH was my aunt;—*sed magis amica veritas*——but TRUTH is my sister.

This contrariety of humours betwixt my father and my uncle, was the source of many a fraternal squabble. The one could not bear to hear the tale of family disgrace recorded,——and the other would scarce ever let a day pass to an end without some hint at it.

For God's sake, my uncle *Toby* would cry,——and for my sake, and for all our sakes my dear brother *Shandy*,—do let this story of our aunt's and her ashes sleep in peace;——how can you,—— how can you have so little feeling and compassion for the character of our family:——What is the character of a family to an hypothesis? my father would reply.——Nay, if you come to that—what is the life of a family:——The life of a family! —my uncle *Toby* would say, throwing himself back in his arm-chair, and lifting up his hands, his eyes, and one leg.——Yes the life,——my father would say, maintaining his point. How many thousands of 'em are there every year that come cast away, (in all civilized countries at least)——and consider'd as nothing but common air, in competition of an hypothesis. In my plain sense of things, my uncle *Toby*, would answer,——every such instance is downright MURDER, let who will commit it.——There lies your mistake, my father would reply;——for, in *Foro Scientiæ* there is no such thing as MURDER,——'tis only DEATH, brother.

My uncle *Toby* would never offer to answer this by any other kind of argument, than that of whistling half a dozen bars of *Lillabullero*.——You must know it was the usual channel thro' which his passions got vent, when any thing shocked or surprised him;——but especially when any thing, which he deem'd very absurd, was offer'd.

As not one of our logical writers, nor any of the commentators upon them, that I remember, have thought proper to give a name to this particular species of argument,—I here take the liberty to do it myself, for two reasons. First, That, in order to prevent all confusion in disputes, it may stand as much distinguished for ever, from every other species of argument,——as the *Argumentum ad Verecundiam, ex Absurdo, ex Fortiori*, or any other argument whatsoever:—And, secondly, That it may be said by my children's children, when my head is laid to rest,——that their learn'd grand-father's head had been busied to as much purpose once, as other people's:—That he had invented a name,— and generously thrown it into the TREASURY of the *Ars Logica*, for one of the most unanswerable arguments in the whole science. And if the end of disputation is more to silence than convince,—they may add, if they please, to one of the best arguments too.

I do therefore, by these presents, strictly order and command, That it be known and distinguished by the name and title of the *Argumentum Fistulatorium*, and no other;—and that it rank hereafter with the *Argumentum Baculinum*, and the *Argumentum ad Crumenam*, and for ever hereafter be treated of in the same chapter.

As for the *Argumentum Tripodium*, which is never used but by the woman against the man;—and the *Argumentum ad Rem*, which, contrarywise, is made use of by the man only against the woman:—As these two are enough in conscience for one lecture; ——and, moreover, as the one is the best answer to the other,— let them likewise be kept apart, and be treated of in a place by themselves.

CHAPTER XXII

THE learned Bishop *Hall*, I mean the famous Dr. *Joseph Hall*, who was Bishop of *Exeter*, in King *James* the first's reign, tells us in one of his *Decads*, at the end of his divine art of meditation, imprinted at *London*, in the year 1610, by *John Beal*, dwelling in *Aldergate-street*, "That it is an abominable thing for a man to commend himself;"—and I really think it is so.

And yet, on the other hand, when a thing is executed in a masterly kind of a fashion, which thing is not likely to be found out;—I think it is full as abominable, that a man should lose the honour of it, and go out of the world with the conceit of it rotting in his head.

This is precisely my situation.

For in this long digression which I was accidentally led into, as in all my digressions (one only excepted) there is a masterstroke of digressive skill, the merit of which has all along, I fear, been overlooked by my reader,—not for want of penetration in him,—but because 'tis an excellence seldom looked for, or expected indeed, in a digression;—and it is this: That tho' my digressions are all fair, as you observe,—and that I fly off from what I am about, as far and as often too as any writer in *Great-Britain*; yet I constantly take care to order affairs so, that my main business does not stand still in my absence.

I was just going, for example, to have given you the great outlines of my uncle *Toby*'s most whimsical character;—when my aunt *Dinah* and the coachman came a-cross us, and led us a vagary some millions of miles into the very heart of the planetary system: Notwithstanding all this you perceive that the drawing of my uncle *Toby*'s character went on gently all the time;—not the great contours of it,—that was impossible,—but some familiar strokes and faint designations of it, were here and there touch'd in, as we went along, so that you are much better acquainted with my uncle *Toby* now than you was before.

By this contrivance the machinery of my work is of a species by itself; two contrary motions are introduced into it, and reconciled, which were thought to be at variance with each other. In a word, my work is digressive, and it is progressive too,—and at the same time.

This, Sir, is a very different story from that of the earth's moving round her axis, in her diurnal rotation, with her progress in her elliptick orbit which brings about the year, and constitutes that variety and vicissitude of seasons we enjoy;—though I own it suggested the thought,—as I believe the greatest of our boasted improvements and discoveries have come from some such trifling hints.

Digressions, incontestably, are the sun-shine;——they are the life, the soul of reading;—take them out of this book for instance, —you might as well take the book along with them;—one cold eternal winter would reign in every page of it; restore them to the writer;——he steps forth like a bridegroom,—bids All hail; brings in variety, and forbids the appetite to fail.

All the dexterity is in the good cookery and management of them, so as to be not only for the advantage of the reader, but also of the author, whose distress, in this matter, is truly pitiable: For, if he begins a digression,—from that moment, I observe, his whole work stands stock still;—and if he goes on with his main work,——then there is an end of his digression.

——This is vile work.—For which reason, from the beginning of this, you see, I have constructed the main work and the adventitious parts of it with such intersections, and have so complicated and involved the digressive and progressive movements, one wheel within another, that the whole machine, in general, has been kept a-going;—and, what's more, it shall be kept a-going these forty years, if it pleases the fountain of health to bless me so long with life and good spirits.

CHAPTER XXIII

I HAVE a strong propensity in me to begin this chapter very nonsensically, and I will not balk my fancy.—Accordingly I set off thus.

If the fixture of *Momus*'s glass, in the human breast, according to the proposed emendation of that arch-critick, had taken place, ——first, This foolish consequence would certainly have followed,—That the very wisest and the very gravest of us all, in one coin or other, must have paid window-money every day of our lives.

And, secondly, That had the said glass been there set up, nothing more would have been wanting, in order to have taken a man's character, but to have taken a chair and gone softly, as you would to a dioptrical bee-hive, and look'd in,—view'd the soul stark naked;—observ'd all her motions,—her machinations; —traced all her maggots from their first engendering to their crawling forth;—watched her loose in her frisks, her gambols, her capricios; and after some notice of her more solemn deportment, consequent upon such frisks, &c.——then taken your pen and ink and set down nothing but what you had seen, and could have sworn to:—But this is an advantage not to be had by the biographer in this planet, in the planet *Mercury* (belike) it may be so, if not better still for him;——for there the intense heat of the country, which is proved by computators, from its vicinity to the sun, to be more than equal to that of red hot iron,—must, I think, long ago have vitrified the bodies of the inhabitants, (as the efficient cause) to suit them for the climate (which is the final cause); so that, betwixt them both, all the tenements of their souls, from top to bottom, may be nothing else, for aught the soundest philosophy can shew to the contrary, but one fine transparent body of clear glass (bating the umbilical knot);—so, that till the inhabitants grow old and tolerably wrinkled, whereby the rays of light, in passing through them, become so monstrously refracted,——or return reflected from their surfaces in such transverse lines to the eye, that a man cannot be seen thro';—his soul might as well, unless, for more ceremony,—or the trifling advantage which the umbilical point gave her,—might, upon all other accounts, I say, as well play the fool out o'doors as in her own house.

But this, as I said above, is not the case of the inhabitants of this earth;—our minds shine not through the body, but are wrapt up here in a dark covering of uncrystalized flesh and blood; so that if we would come to the specifick characters of them, we must go some other way to work.

Many, in good truth, are the ways which human wit has been forced to take to do this thing with exactness.

Some, for instance, draw all their characters with wind instruments.—*Virgil* takes notice of that way in the affair of *Dido* and *Æneas*;—but it is as fallacious as the breath of fame;— and, moreover, bespeaks a narrow genius. I am not ignorant that the *Italians* pretend to a mathematical exactness in their designations of one particular sort of character among them, from the *forte* or *piano* of a certain wind instrument they use,—which they say is infallible.—I dare not mention the name of the instrument in this place;—'tis sufficient we have it amongst us,—but never think of making a drawing by it;—this is ænigmatical, and

[81]

intended to be so, at least, *ad populum*:—And therefore I beg, Madam, when you come here, that you read on as fast as you can, and never stop to make any inquiry about it.

There are others again, who will draw a man's character from no other helps in the world, but merely from his evacuations;—but this often gives a very incorrect out-line,—unless, indeed, you take a sketch of his repletions too; and by correcting one drawing from the other, compound one good figure out of them both.

I should have no objection to this method, but that I think it must smell too strong of the lamp,—and be render'd still more operose, by forcing you to have an eye to the rest of his *Non-Naturals*.——Why the most natural actions of a man's life should be call'd his Non-Naturals,—is another question.

There are others, fourthly, who disdain every one of these expedients;—not from any fertility of his own, but from the various ways of doing it, which they have borrowed from the honourable devices which the Pentagraphic Brethren* of the brush have shewn in taking copies.—These, you must know, are your great historians.

One of these you will see drawing a full-length character *against the light*;—that's illiberal,—dishonest,—and hard upon the character of the man who sits.

Others, to mend the matter, will make a drawing of you in the *Camera*;—that is most unfair of all,—because, *there* you are sure to be represented in some of your most ridiculous attitudes.

To avoid all and every one of these errors, in giving you my uncle *Toby*'s character, I am determined to draw it by no mechanical help whatever;——nor shall my pencil be guided by any one wind instrument which ever was blown upon, either on this, or on the other side of the *Alps*;—nor will I consider either his repletions or his discharges,—or touch upon his Non-Naturals; —but, in a word, I will draw my uncle *Toby*'s character from his HOBBY-HORSE.

---

* Pentagraph, an instrument to copy prints and pictures mechanically, and in any proportion.

CHAPTER XXIV

IF I WAS not morally sure that the reader must be out of all patience for my uncle *Toby*'s character,——I would here previously have convinced him, that there is no instrument so fit to draw such a thing with, as that which I have pitch'd upon.

A man and his HOBBY-HORSE, tho' I cannot say that they act and re-act exactly after the same manner in which the soul and body do upon each other: Yet doubtless there is a communication between them of some kind, and my opinion rather is, that there is something in it more of the manner of electrified bodies,—and that by means of the heated parts of the rider, which come immediately into contact with the back of the HOBBY-HORSE.—By long journies and much friction, it so happens that the body of the rider is at length fill'd as full of HOBBY-HORSICAL matter as it can hold;——so that if you are able to give but a clear description of the nature of the one, you may form a pretty exact notion of the genius and character of the other.

Now the HOBBY-HORSE which my uncle *Toby* always rode upon, was, in my opinion, an HOBBY-HORSE well worth giving a description of, if it was only upon the score of his great singularity; for you might have travelled from *York* to *Dover*, ——from *Dover* to *Penzance* in *Cornwall*, and from *Penzance* to *York* back again, and not have seen such another upon the road; or if you had seen such a one, whatever haste you had been in, you must infallibly have stopp'd to have taken a view of him. Indeed, the gait and figure of him was so strange, and so utterly unlike was he, from his head to his tail, to any one of the whole species, that it was now and then made a matter of dispute,——whether he was really a HOBBY-HORSE or no: But as the Philosopher would use no other argument to the sceptic, who disputed with him against the reality of motion, save that of rising up upon his legs, and walking a-cross the room;—so would my uncle *Toby* use no other argument to prove his HOBBY-HORSE was a HOBBY-HORSE indeed, but by getting upon his back and riding him about;—leaving the world after that to determine the point as it thought fit.

In good truth, my uncle *Toby* mounted him with so much pleasure, and he carried my uncle *Toby* so well,——that he troubled his head very little with what the world either said or thought about it.

It is now high time, however, that I give you a description of him:—But to go on regularly, I only beg you will give me leave to acquaint you first, how my uncle *Toby* came by him.

CHAPTER XXV

THE wound in my uncle *Toby*'s groin, which he received at the siege of *Namur*, rendering him unfit for the service, it was thought expedient he should return to *England*, in order, if possible, to be set to rights.

He was four years totally confined,—part of it to his bed, and all of it to his room; and in the course of his cure, which was all that time in hand, suffer'd unspeakable miseries,—owing to a succession of exfoliations from the *os pubis*, and the outward edge of that part of the *coxendix* called the *os illeum*,——both which bones were dismally crush'd, as much by the irregularity of the stone, which I told you was broke off the parapet,—as by its size,—(though it was pretty large) which inclined the surgeon all along to think, that the great injury which it had done my uncle *Toby*'s groin, was more owing to the gravity of the stone itself, than to the projectile force of it,—which he would often tell him was a great happiness.

My father at that time was just beginning business in *London*, and had taken a house;—and as the truest friendship and cordiality subsisted between the two brothers,—and that my father thought my uncle *Toby* could no where be so well nursed and taken care of as in his own house,——he assign'd him the very best apartment in it.—And what was a much more sincere mark of his affection still, he would never suffer a friend or an acquaintance to step into the house on any occasion, but he would take him by the hand, and lead him up stairs to see his brother *Toby*, and chat an hour by his bed-side.

The history of a soldier's wound beguiles the pain of it;—my uncle's visiters at least thought so, and in their daily calls upon him, from the courtesy arising out of that belief, they would frequently turn the discourse to that subject,—and from that subject the discourse would generally roll on to the siege itself.

These conversations were infinitely kind; and my uncle *Toby* received great relief from them, and would have received much more, but that they brought him into some unforeseen perplexities, which, for three months together, retarded his cure greatly; and if he had not hit upon an expedient to extricate himself out of them, I verily believe they would have laid him in his grave.

What these perplexities of my uncle *Toby* were,——'tis impossible for you to guess;—if you could,—I should blush; not as a relation,—not as a man,—nor even as a woman,—but I should blush as an author; inasmuch as I set no small store by myself upon this very account, that my reader has never yet been able to guess at any thing. And in this, Sir, I am of so nice and singular a humour, that if I thought you was able to form the least judgment or probable conjecture to yourself, of what was to come in the next page,—I would tear it out of my book.

END of the FIRST VOLUME.

VOLUME II

CHAPTER I

I HAVE begun a new book, on purpose that I might have room enough to explain the nature of the perplexities in which my uncle *Toby* was involved, from the many discourses and interrogations about the siege of *Namur*, where he received his wound.

I must remind the reader, in case he has read the history of King *William*'s wars,—but if he has not,—I then inform him, that one of the most memorable attacks in that siege, was that which was made by the *English* and *Dutch* upon the point of the advanced counterscarp, before the gate of *St. Nicolas*, which inclosed the great sluice or water-stop, where the *English* were terribly exposed to the shot of the counter-guard and demi-bastion of *St. Roch:* The issue of which hot dispute, in three words, was this; That the *Dutch* lodged themselves upon the counter-guard,—and that the *English* made themselves masters of the covered way before *St. Nicolas*'s *gate*, notwithstanding the gallantry of the *French* officers, who exposed themselves upon the glacis sword in hand.

As this was the principal attack of which my uncle *Toby* was an eye-witness at *Namur*,——the army of the besiegers being cut off, by the confluence of the *Maes* and *Sambre*, from seeing much of each other's operations,—my uncle *Toby* was generally more eloquent and particular in his account of it; and the many perplexities he was in, arose out of the almost insurmountable difficulties he found in telling his story intelligibly, and giving such clear ideas of the differences and distinctions between the scarp and counterscarp,——the glacis and covered way,——the half-moon and ravelin,——as to make his company fully comprehend where and what he was about.

Writers themselves are too apt to confound these terms;——so that you will the less wonder, if in his endeavours to explain them, and in opposition to many misconceptions, that my uncle *Toby* did oft times puzzle his visiters, and sometimes himself too.

To speak the truth, unless the company my father led up stairs were tolerably clear-headed, or my uncle *Toby* was in one of his best explanatory moods, 'twas a difficult thing, do what he could, to keep the discourse free from obscurity.

What rendered the account of this affair the more intricate to

[89]

my uncle *Toby*, was this,—that in the attack of the counterscarp before the gate of *St. Nicolas*, extending itself from the bank of the *Maes*, quite up to the great water-stop;—the ground was cut and cross-cut with such a multitude of dykes, drains, rivulets, and sluices, on all sides,—and he would get so sadly bewildered and set fast amongst them, that frequently he could neither get backwards or forwards to save his life; and was oft times obliged to give up the attack upon that very account only.

These perplexing rebuffs gave my uncle *Toby Shandy* more perturbations than you would imagine; and as my father's kindness to him was continually dragging up fresh friends and fresh inquirers,—he had but a very uneasy task of it.

No doubt my uncle *Toby* had great command of himself,—and could guard appearances, I believe, as well as most men;—yet any one may imagine, that when he could not retreat out of the ravelin without getting into the half-moon, or get out of the covered way without falling down the counterscarp, nor cross the dyke without danger of slipping into the ditch, but that he must have fretted and fumed inwardly:—He did so;—and these little and hourly vexations, which may seem trifling and of no account to the man who has not read *Hippocrates*, yet, whoever has read *Hippocrates*, or Dr. *James Mackenzie*, and has considered well the effects which the passions and affections of the mind have upon the digestion,—(Why not of a wound as well as of a dinner?) ——may easily conceive what sharp paroxisms and exacerbations of his wound my uncle *Toby* must have undergone upon that score only.

—My uncle *Toby* could not philosophize upon it;—'twas enough he felt it was so,—and having sustained the pain and sorrows of it for three months together, he was resolved some way or other to extricate himself.

He was one morning lying upon his back in his bed, the anguish and nature of the wound upon his groin suffering him to lye in no other position, when a thought came into his head, that if he could purchase such a thing, and have it pasted down upon a board, as a large map of the fortifications of the town and citadel of *Namur*, with its environs, it might be a means of giving him ease.—I take notice of his desire to have the environs along with the town and citadel, for this reason,—because my uncle *Toby*'s wound was got in one of the traverses, about thirty toises from the returning angle of the trench, opposite to the salient angle of the demi-bastion of *St. Roch*;—so that he was pretty confident he could stick a pin upon the identical spot of ground where he was standing in when the stone struck him.

All this succeeded to his wishes, and not only freed him from a world of sad explanations, but, in the end, it prov'd the happy means, as you will read, of procuring my uncle *Toby* his HOBBY-HORSE.

CHAPTER II

THERE is nothing so foolish, when you are at the expence of making an entertainment of this kind, as to order things so badly, as to let your criticks and gentry of refined taste run it down: Nor is there any thing so likely to make them do it, as that of leaving them out of the party, or, what is full as offensive, of bestowing your attention upon the rest of your guests in so particular a way, as if there was no such thing as a critick (by occupation) at table.

———I guard against both; for, in the first place, I have left half a dozen places purposely open for them;—and, in the next place, I pay them all court,—Gentlemen, I kiss your hands, I protest no company could give me half the pleasure,—by my soul I am glad to see you,——I beg only you will make no strangers of yourselves, but sit down without any ceremony, and fall on heartily.

I said I had left six places, and I was upon the point of carrying my complaisance so far, as to have left a seventh open for them,—and in this very spot I stand on; but being told by a critick, (tho' not by occupation,—but by nature) that I had acquitted myself well enough, I shall fill it up directly, hoping, in the mean time, that I shall be able to make a great deal of more room next year.

———How, in the name of wonder! could your uncle *Toby*, who, it seems, was a military man, and whom you have represented as no fool,—be at the same time such a confused, pudding-headed, muddle-headed fellow, as—Go look.

So, Sir Critick, I could have replied; but I scorn it.———
'Tis language unurbane,—and only befitting the man who cannot give clear and satisfactory accounts of things, or dive deep enough into the first causes of human ignorance and confusion. It is moreover the reply valiant,—and therefore I reject it; for tho' it might have suited my uncle *Toby*'s character as a soldier excellently well,—and had he not accustomed himself, in such

attacks, to whistle the *Lillabullero*,—as he wanted no courage, 'tis the very answer he would have given; yet it would by no means have done for me. You see as plain as can be, that I write as a man of erudition;—that even my similes, my allusions, my illustrations, my metaphors, are erudite,—and that I must sustain my character properly, and contrast it properly too,—else what would become of me? Why, Sir, I should be undone;——at this very moment that I am going here to fill up one place against a critick, —I should have made an opening for a couple.

————Therefore I answer thus:

Pray, Sir, in all the reading which you have ever read, did you ever read such a book as *Locke*'s Essay upon the Human Understanding?————Don't answer me rashly,—because many, I know, quote the book, who have not read it,—and many have read it who understand it not:—If either of these is your case, as I write to instruct, I will tell you in three words what the book is.—It is a history.—A history! of who? what? where? when? Don't hurry yourself.——It is a history-book, Sir, (which may possibly recommend it to the world) of what passes in a man's own mind; and if you will say so much of the book, and no more, believe me, you will cut no contemptible figure in a metaphysic circle.

But this by the way.

Now if you will venture to go along with me, and look down into the bottom of this matter, it will be found that the cause of obscurity and confusion, in the mind of man, is threefold.

Dull organs, dear Sir, in the first place. Secondly, slight and transient impressions made by objects when the said organs are not dull. And thirdly, a memory like unto a sieve, not able to retain what it has received.—Call down *Dolly* your chambermaid, and I will give you my cap and bell along with it, if I make not this matter so plain that *Dolly* herself shall understand it as well as *Malbranch*.——When *Dolly* has indited her epistle to *Robin*, and has thrust her arm into the bottom of her pocket hanging by her right-side;——take that opportunity to recollect that the organs and faculties of perception, can, by nothing in this world, be so aptly typified and explained as by that one thing which *Dolly*'s hand is in search of.—Your organs are not so dull that I should inform you,—'tis an inch, Sir, of red seal-wax.

When this is melted and dropped upon the letter, if *Dolly* fumbles too long for her thimble, till the wax is over hardened, it will not receive the mark of her thimble from the usual impulse which was wont to imprint it. Very well: If *Dolly*'s wax, for want of better, is bees-wax, or of a temper too soft,—tho' it may receive,—it will not hold the impression, how hard soever *Dolly* thrusts against it; and last of all, supposing the wax good, and eke the thimble, but applied thereto in careless haste, as her Mistress rings the bell;————in any one of these three cases, the print, left by the thimble, will be as unlike the prototype as a brass-jack.

Now you must understand that not one of these was the true cause of the confusion in my uncle *Toby*'s discourse; and it is for that very reason I enlarge upon them so long, after the manner of great physiologists,—to shew the world what it did *not* arise from.

What it did arise from, I have hinted above, and a fertile source of obscurity it is,—and ever will be,—and that is the unsteady uses of words which have perplexed the clearest and most exalted understandings.

It is ten to one (at *Arthur*'s) whether you have ever read the literary histories of past ages;—if you have,—what terrible battles, 'yclept logomachies, have they occasioned and perpetuated with so much gall and ink-shed,—that a good-natured man cannot read the accounts of them without tears in his eyes.

Gentle critick! when thou hast weigh'd all this, and consider'd within thyself how much of thy own knowledge, discourse, and conversation has been pestered and disordered, at one time or other, by this, and this only:————What a pudder and racket in COUNCILS about οὐσία and ὑπόστασις; and in the SCHOOLS of the learned about power and about spirit;—about essences, and about quintessences;————about substances, and about space:———— What confusion in greater THEATRES from words of little meaning, and as indeterminate a sense;—when thou considerest this, thou wilt not wonder at my uncle *Toby*'s perplexities,—thou wilt drop a tear of pity upon his scarp and his counterscarp;—his glacis and his covered-way; his ravelin and his half-moon: 'Twas not by ideas,————by heaven! his life was put in jeopardy by words.

CHAPTER III

WHEN my uncle *Toby* got his map of *Namur* to his mind, he began immediately to apply himself, and with the utmost diligence, to the study of it; for nothing being of more importance to him than his recovery, and his recovery depending, as you have read, upon the passions and affections of his mind, it behoved him to take the nicest care to make himself so far master of his subject, as to be able to talk upon it without emotion.

In a fortnight's close and painful application, which, by the bye, did my uncle *Toby*'s wound, upon his groin, no good,—he was enabled, by the help of some marginal documents at the feet of the elephant, together with *Gobesius*'s military architecture and pyroballogy, translated from the *Flemish*, to form his discourse with passable perspicuity; and before he was two full months gone,—he was right eloquent upon it, and could make not only the attack of the advanced counterscarp with great order;—— but having, by that time, gone much deeper into the art, than what his first motive made necessary,—my uncle *Toby* was able to cross the *Maes* and *Sambre*; make diversions as far as *Vauban*'s line, the abbey of *Salsines*, &c. and give his visitors as distinct a history of each of their attacks, as of that of the gate of *St. Nicolas*, where he had the honour to receive his wound.

But the desire of knowledge, like the thirst of riches, increases ever with the acquisition of it. The more my uncle *Toby* pored over his map, the more he took a liking to it;—by the same process and electrical assimilation, as I told you, thro' which I ween the souls of connoisseurs themselves, by long friction and incumbition, have the happiness, at length, to get all be-virtu'd,—be-pictur'd,—be-butterflied, and be-fiddled.

The more my uncle *Toby* drank of this sweet fountain of science, the greater was the heat and impatience of his thirst, so that, before the first year of his confinement had well gone round, there was scarce a fortified town in *Italy* or *Flanders*, of which, by one means or other, he had not procured a plan, reading over as he got them, and carefully collating therewith the histories of their sieges, their demolitions, their improvements, and new works, all which he would read with that intense application and delight, that he would forget himself, his wound, his confinement, his dinner.

In the second year my uncle *Toby* purchased *Ramelli* and *Cataneo*, translated from the *Italian*;—likewise *Stevinus*, *Marolis*, the Chevalier *de Ville*, *Lorini*, *Cochorn*, *Sheeter*, the Count *de Pagan*, the Marshal *Vauban*, Mons. *Blondel*, with almost as many more books of military architecture, as Don *Quixote* was found to have of chivalry, when the curate and barber invaded his library.

Towards the beginning of the third year, which was in *August*, ninety-nine, my uncle *Toby* found it necessary to understand a little of projectiles:—And having judged it best to draw his knowledge from the fountain head, he began with *N. Tartaglia*, who it seems was the first man who detected the imposition of a cannon-ball's doing all that mischief under the notion of a right line.—This *N. Tartaglia* proved to my uncle *Toby* to be an impossible thing,

————Endless is the Search of Truth!

No sooner was my uncle *Toby* satisfied which road the cannon-ball did not go, but he was insensibly led on, and resolved in his mind to enquire and find out which road the ball did go: For which purpose he was obliged to set off afresh with old *Maltus*, and studied him devoutly.—He proceeded next to *Gallileo* and *Torricellius*, wherein, by certain geometrical rules, infallibly laid down, he found the precise path to be a PARABOLA,—or else an HYPERBOLA,—and that the parameter, or *latus rectum*, of the conic section of the said path, was to the quantity and amplitude in a direct *ratio*, as the whole line to the sine of double the angle of incidence, form'd by the breech upon an horizontal plane;—and that the semi-parameter,————stop! my dear uncle *Toby*,—stop!—go not one foot further into this thorny and bewilder'd track,—intricate are the steps! intricate are the mazes of this labyrinth! intricate are the troubles which the pursuit of this bewitching phantom KNOWLEDGE, will bring upon thee.—O my uncle; fly—fly—fly from it as from a serpent.—Is it fit, good natur'd man! thou shouldest sit up, with the wound upon thy groin, whole nights baking thy blood with hectic watchings?—Alas! 'twill exasperate thy symptoms,—check thy perspirations,—evaporate thy spirits,—waste thy animal strength,—dry up thy radical moisture,—bring thee into a costive habit of body, impair thy health,—and hasten all the infirmities of thy old age. —O my uncle! my uncle *Toby*.

CHAPTER IV

I WOULD not give a groat for that man's knowledge in pen-craft, who does not understand this,—That the best plain narrative in the world, tack'd very close to the last spirited apostrophe to my uncle *Toby*—would have felt both cold and vapid upon the reader's palate;—therefore I forthwith put an end to the chapter,—though I was in the middle of my story.

————Writers of my stamp have one principle in common with painters. Where an exact copying makes our pictures less striking, we choose the less evil; deeming it even more pardonable to trespass against truth, than beauty. This is to be understood *cum grano salis*; but be it as it will,—as the parallel is made more for the sake of letting the apostrophe cool, than any thing else,—'tis not very material whether upon any other score the reader approves of it or not.

In the latter end of the third year, uncle *Toby* perceiving that the parameter and semi-parameter of the conic section, angered his wound, he left off the study of projectiles in a kind of a huff, and betook himself to the practical part of fortification only; the pleasure of which, like a spring held back, returned upon him with redoubled force.

It was in this year that my uncle began to break in upon the daily regularity of a clean shirt,——to dismiss his barber unshaven,——and to allow his surgeon scarce time sufficient to dress his wound, concerning himself so little about it, as not to ask him once in seven times dressing how it went on: When, lo!—all of a sudden, for the change was as quick as lightening, he began to sigh heavily for his recovery,—complain'd to my father, grew impatient with the surgeon; and one morning as he heard his foot coming up stairs, he shut up his books, and thrust aside his instruments, in order to expostulate with him upon the protraction of his cure, which, he told him, might surely have been accomplished at least by that time:—He dwelt long upon the miseries he had undergone, and the sorrows of his four years melancholy imprisonment;—adding, that had it not been for the kind looks, and fraternal chearings of the best of brothers,—he had long since sunk under his misfortunes.—My father was by: My uncle *Toby*'s eloquence brought tears into his eyes;—'twas unexpected—My uncle *Toby*, by nature, was not eloquent;——it had the greater effect.—The surgeon was confounded;—not that there wanted grounds for such, or greater, marks of impatience,—but 'twas unexpected too; in the four years he had attended him, he had never seen any thing like it in my uncle *Toby*'s carriage;—he had never once dropp'd one fretful or discontented word;—he had been all patience,—all submission.

—We lose the right of complaining sometimes by forbearing it;——but we oftener treble the force:—The surgeon was astonished;—but much more so, when he heard my uncle *Toby* go on, and peremptorily insist upon his healing up the wound directly,———or sending for Monsieur *Ronjat*, the King's Serjeant-Surgeon, to do it for him.

The desire of life and health is implanted in man's nature;—the love of liberty and enlargement is a sister-passion to it: These my uncle *Toby* had in common with his species;—and either of them had been sufficient to account for his earnest desire to get well and out of doors;—but I have told you before that nothing wrought with our family after the common way;—and from the time and manner in which this eager desire shewed itself in the present case, the penetrating reader will suspect there was some other cause or crotchet for it in my uncle *Toby*'s head:—There was so, and 'tis the subject of the next chapter to set forth what that cause and crotchet was. I own, when that's done, 'twill be time to return back to the parlour fire-side, where we left my uncle *Toby* in the middle of his sentence.

CHAPTER V

WHEN a man gives himself up to the government of a ruling passion,———or, in other words, when his HOBBY-HORSE grows head-strong,———farewell cool reason and fair discretion!

My uncle *Toby*'s wound was near well, and as soon as the surgeon recovered his surprize, and could get leave to say as much—he told him, 'twas just beginning to incarnate; and that if no fresh exfoliation happened, which there was no sign of,—it would be dried up in five or six weeks. The sound of as many olympiads twelve hours before, would have convey'd an idea of shorter duration to my uncle *Toby*'s mind.—The succession of his ideas was now rapid,—he broil'd with impatience to put his design in execution;—and so, without consulting farther with any soul living,—which, by the bye, I think is right, when you are pre-determined to take no one soul's advice,—he privately ordered *Trim*, his man, to pack up a bundle of lint and dressings, and hire a chariot and four to be at the door exactly by twelve o'clock that day, when he knew my father would be upon 'Change—So leaving a bank-note upon the table for the surgeon's care of him, and a letter of tender thanks for his brother's—he pack'd up his maps, his books of fortification, his instruments, &c. and, by the help of a crutch on one side, and *Trim* on the other,———my uncle *Toby* embarked for *Shandy-Hall*.

The reason, or rather the rise, of this sudden demigration, was as follows:

The table in my uncle *Toby*'s room, and at which, the night before this change happened, he was sitting with his maps, *&c,* about him,—being somewhat of the smallest, for that infinity of great and small instruments of knowledge which usually lay crouded upon it—he had the accident, in reaching over for his tobacco-box, to throw down his compasses, and in stooping to take the compasses up, with his sleeve he threw down his case of instruments and snuffers;—and as the dice took a run against him, in his endeavouring to catch the snuffers in falling,—he thrust Monsieur *Blondel* off the table and Count *de Pagan* o'top of him.

'Twas to no purpose for a man, lame as my uncle *Toby* was, to think of redressing all these evils by himself,—he rung his bell for his man *Trim*;—*Trim*, quoth my uncle *Toby*, pri'thee see what confusion I have here been making.—I must have some better contrivance, *Trim.*—Can'st not thou take my rule and measure the length and breadth of this table, and then go and bespeak me one as big again?—Yes, an' please your Honour, replied *Trim*, making a bow; but I hope your Honour will be soon well enough to get down to your country-seat, where,—as your Honour takes so much pleasure in fortification, we could manage this matter to a T.

I must here inform you, that this servant of my uncle *Toby*'s, who went by the name of *Trim*, had been a Corporal in my uncle's own company,——his real name was *James Butler*,—but having got the nick-name of *Trim* in the regiment, my uncle *Toby*, unless when he happened to be very angry with him, would never call him by any other name.

The poor fellow had been disabled for the service, by a wound on his left-knee by a musket-bullet, at the battle of *Landen*, which was two years before the affair of *Namur*;—and as the fellow was well beloved in the regiment, and a handy fellow into the bargain, my uncle *Toby* took him for his servant, and of excellent use was he, attending my uncle *Toby* in the camp and in his quarters as valet, groom, barber, cook, sempster, and nurse; and indeed, from first to last, waited upon him and served him with great fidelity and affection.

My uncle *Toby* loved the man in return, and what attached him more to him still, was the similitude of their knowledge:—For Corporal *Trim*, (for so, for the future, I shall call him) by four

years occasional attention to his Master's discourse upon fortified towns, and the advantage of prying and peeping continually
into his Master's plans, &c. exclusive and besides what he gained
HOBBY-HORSICALLY, as a body-servant, *Non Hobby-Horsical
per se*;——had become no mean proficient in the science; and
was thought, by the cook and chamber-maid, to know as much
of the nature of strong-holds as my uncle *Toby* himself.

I have but one more stroke to give to finish Corporal *Trim*'s
character,—and it is the only dark line in it.——The fellow loved
to advise,—or rather to hear himself talk; his carriage, however,
was so perfectly respectful, 'twas easy to keep him silent when
you had him so; but set his tongue a-going;—you had no hold of
him;—he was voluble;—the eternal interlardings of *your Honour*,
with the respectfulness of Corporal *Trim*'s manner, interceding so
strong in behalf of his elocution,—that tho' you might have been
incommoded,—you could not well be angry. My uncle *Toby* was
seldom either the one or the other with him,—or, at least, this
fault, in *Trim*, broke no squares with 'em. My uncle *Toby*, as
I said, loved the man;—and besides, as he ever looked upon
a faithful servant,—but as an humble friend,—he could not bear
to stop his mouth.—Such was Corporal *Trim*.

If I durst presume, continued *Trim*, to give your Honour my
advice, and speak my opinion in this matter—Thou art welcome,
Trim, quoth my uncle *Toby*,—speak,—speak what thou thinkest
upon the subject, man, without fear. Why then, replied *Trim*, (not
hanging his ears and scratching his head like a country lout, but)
stroking his hair back from his forehead, and standing erect as
before his division.——I think, quoth *Trim*, advancing his left,
which was his lame leg, a little forwards,—and pointing with his
right hand open towards a map of *Dunkirk*, which was pinn'd
against the hangings,—I think, quoth Corporal *Trim*, with humble
submission to your Honour's better judgment,—that these
ravelins, bastions, curtins, and horn-works make but a poor, contemptible, fiddle-faddle piece of work of it here upon paper, compared to what your Honour and I could make of it, were we in
the country by ourselves, and had but a rood, or a rood and a half
of ground to do what we pleased with: As summer is coming on,
continued *Trim*, your Honour might sit out of doors, and give
me the nography——(Call it ichnography, quoth my uncle.)—of
the town or citadel, your Honour was pleased to sit down before,
—and I will be shot by your Honour upon the glacis of it, if I did
not fortify it to your Honour's mind.—I dare say thou would'st,

Trim, quoth my uncle.—For if your Honour, continued the Corporal, could but mark me the polygon, with its exact lines and angles——That I could do very well, quoth my uncle.—— I would begin with the fossé, and if your Honour could tell me the proper depth and breadth—I can to a hair's breadth, *Trim*, replied my uncle.—I would throw out the earth upon this hand towards the town for the scarp,—and on that hand towards the campaign for the counterscarp.—Very right, *Trim*, quoth my uncle *Toby*.— And when I had sloped them to your mind,—an' please your Honour, I would face the glacis, as the finest fortifications are done in *Flanders*, with sods,—and as your Honour knows they should be,——and I would make the walls and parapets with sods too.—The best engineers call them gazons, *Trim*, said my uncle *Toby*.—Whether they are gazons or sods, is not much matter, replied *Trim*, your Honour knows they are ten times beyond a facing either of brick or stone.——I know they are, *Trim*, in some respects,—quoth my uncle *Toby*, nodding his head;—for a cannon-ball enters into the gazon right onwards, without bringing any rubbish down with it, which might fill the fossé, (as was the case at *St. Nicolas*'s *Gate*) and facilitate the passage over it.

Your Honour understands these matters, replied Corporal *Trim*, better than any officer in his Majesty's service;—but would your Honour please to let the bespeaking of the table alone, and let us but go into the country, I would work under your Honour's directions like a horse, and make fortifications for you something like a tansy, with all their batteries, saps, ditches, and palisadoes, that it should be worth all the world's riding twenty miles to go and see it.

My uncle *Toby* blushed as red as scarlet as *Trim* went on;—but it was not a blush of guilt,—of modesty,—or of anger;—it was a blush of joy;—he was fired with Corporal *Trim*'s project and description.—*Trim*! said my uncle *Toby*, thou hast said enough.— We might begin the campaign, continued *Trim*, on the very day that his Majesty and the Allies take the field, and demolish them town by town as fast as——*Trim*, quoth my uncle *Toby*, say no more.—Your Honour, continued *Trim*, might sit in your arm-chair (pointing to it) this fine weather, giving me your orders, and I would——Say no more, *Trim*, quoth my uncle *Toby*.—— Besides, your Honour would get not only pleasure and good pastime,—but good air, and good exercise, and good health,—and your Honour's wound would be well in a month. Thou hast said enough, *Trim*,—quoth my uncle *Toby* (putting his hand into his breeches-pocket)——I like thy project mightily.—And if your Honour pleases, I'll, this moment, go and buy a pioneer's spade to take down with us, and I'll bespeak a shovel and a pick-ax, and a couple of——Say no more, *Trim*, quoth my uncle *Toby*, leaping up upon one leg, quite overcome with rapture,——and thrusting a guinea into *Trim*'s hand,——*Trim*, said my uncle *Toby*, say no more;—but go down, *Trim*, this moment, my lad, and bring up my supper this instant.

Trim ran down and brought up his Master's supper,—to no purpose:——*Trim*'s plan of operation ran so in my uncle *Toby*'s head, he could not taste it.—*Trim*, quoth my uncle *Toby*, get me to bed.—'Twas all one.— Corporal *Trim*'s description had fired his imagination,—my uncle *Toby* could not shut his eyes.—The more he consider'd it, the more bewitching the scene appeared to him;—so that, two full hours before day-light, he had come to a final determination, and had concerted the whole plan of his and Corporal *Trim*'s decampment.

My uncle *Toby* had a little neat country-house of his own, in the village where my father's estate lay at *Shandy*, which had been left him by an old uncle, with a small estate of about one hundred pounds a year. Behind this house, and contiguous to it, was a kitchen-garden of about half an acre;—and at the bottom of the garden, and cut off from it by a tall yew hedge, was a bowling-green, containing just about as much ground as Corporal *Trim* wished for;—so that as *Trim* uttered the words, "A rood and a half of ground to do what they would with,"——this identical bowling-green instantly presented itself, and became curiously painted all at once, upon the retina of my uncle *Toby*'s fancy; ——which was the physical cause of making him change colour, or at least of heightening his blush to that immoderate degree I spoke of.

Never did lover post down to a belov'd mistress with more heat and expectation, than my uncle *Toby* did, to enjoy this self-same thing in private;—I say in private;——for it was sheltered from the house, as I told you, by a tall yew hedge, and was covered on the other three sides, from mortal sight, by rough holly and thickset flowering shrubs;—so that the idea of not being seen, did not a little contribute to the idea of pleasure pre-conceived in my uncle *Toby*'s mind.——Vain thought! however thick it was planted about,——or private soever it might seem,— to think, dear uncle *Toby*, of enjoying a thing which took up a whole rood and a half of ground,—and not have it known!

How my uncle *Toby* and Corporal *Trim* managed this matter, —with the history of their campaigns, which were no way barren of events,——may make no uninteresting under-plot in the epitasis and working up of this drama.—At present the scene must drop,—and change for the parlour fire-side.

CHAPTER VI

—WHAT can they be doing, brother? said my father.—I think, replied my uncle *Toby*,—taking, as I told you, his pipe from his mouth, and striking the ashes out of it as he began his sentence;—I think, replied he,—it would not be amiss, brother, if we rung the bell.

Pray, what's all that racket over our heads, *Obadiah?*—quoth my father;—my brother and I can scarce hear ourselves speak.

Sir, answer'd *Obadiah*, making a bow towards his left-shoulder, —my Mistress is taken very badly—And where's *Susannah* running down the garden there, as if they were going to ravish her? ——Sir, she is running the shortest cut into the town, replied *Obadiah*, to fetch the old midwife.——Then saddle a horse, quoth my father, and do you go directly for Dr. *Slop*, the man-midwife, with all our services,—and let him know your Mistress is fallen into labour,—and that I desire he will return with you with all speed.

It is very strange, says my father, addressing himself to my uncle *Toby*, as *Obadiah* shut the door,——as there is so expert an operator as Dr. *Slop* so near—that my wife should persist to the very last in this obstinate humour of hers, in trusting the life of my child, who has had one misfortune already, to the ignorance of an old woman;——and not only the life of my child, brother, —but her own life, and with it the lives of all the children I might, peradventure, have begot out of her hereafter.

Mayhap, brother, replied my uncle *Toby*, my sister does it to save the expence:—A pudding's end,—replied my father,——the doctor must be paid the same for inaction as action,—if not better,—to keep him in temper.

————Then it can be out of nothing in the whole world, quoth my uncle *Toby*, in the simplicity of his heart,—but MODESTY.—My sister, I dare say, added he, does not care to let a man come so near her * * * *. I will not say whether my

[102]

uncle *Toby* had compleated the sentence or not;————'tis for his advantage to suppose he had,————as, I think, he could have added no ONE WORD which would have improved it.

If, on the contrary, my uncle *Toby* had not fully arrived at his period's end,—then the world stands indebted to the sudden snapping of my father's tobacco-pipe, for one of the neatest examples of that ornamental figure in oratory, which Rhetoricians stile the *Aposiopesis.*—Just heaven! how does the *Poco piu* and the *Poco meno* of the *Italian* artists;—the insensible, more or less, determine the precise line of beauty in the sentence, as well as in the statue! How do the slight touches of the chisel, the pencil, the pen, the fiddle-stick, *et cætera,*—give the true swell, which gives the true pleasure!—O my countrymen!—be nice;—be cautious of your language;————and never, O! never let it be forgotten upon what small particles your eloquence and your fame depend.

————"My sister, mayhap," quoth my uncle *Toby*, "does not choose to let a man come so near her * * * *." Make this dash,—'tis an Aposiopesis.—Take the dash away, and write *Backside,*————'tis Bawdy.—Scratch Backside out, and put *Cover'd-way* in,—'tis a Metaphor;—and, I dare say, as fortification ran so much in my uncle *Toby's* head, that if he had been left to have added one word to the sentence,—that word was it.

But whether that was the case or not the case;—or whether the snapping of my father's tobacco-pipe so critically, happened thro' accident or anger,—will be seen in due time.

CHAPTER VII

THO' my father was a good natural philosopher,————yet he was something of a moral philosopher too; for which reason, when his tobacco-pipe snapp'd short in the middle,————he had nothing to do,—as such,—but to have taken hold of the two pieces, and thrown them gently upon the back of the fire.—He did no such thing;—he threw them with all the violence in the world;—and, to give the action still more emphasis,—he started up upon both his legs to do it.

This look'd something like heat;————and the manner of his reply to what my uncle *Toby* was saying, prov'd it was so.

—"Not choose," quoth my father, (repeating my uncle *Toby*'s words) "to let a man come so near her————" By heaven, brother

Toby! you would try the patience of a *Job*;—and I think I have the plagues of one already, without it.——Why?—Where?—Wherein?——Wherefore?—Upon what account, replied my uncle *Toby*, in the utmost astonishment.——To think, said my father, of a man living to your age, brother, and knowing so little about women!——I know nothing at all about them,——replied my uncle *Toby*; and I think, continued he, that the shock I received the year after the demolition of *Dunkirk*, in my affair with widow *Wadman*;—which shock you know I should not have received, but from my total ignorance of the sex,—has given me just cause to say, That I neither know, nor do pretend to know, any thing about 'em, or their concerns either.——Methinks, brother, replied my father, you might, at least, know so much as the right end of a woman from the wrong.

It is said in *Aristotle*'s *Master-Piece*, "That when a man doth think of any thing which is past,—he looketh down upon the ground;—but that when he thinketh of something that is to come, he looketh up towards the heavens."

My uncle *Toby*, I suppose, thought of neither,—for he look'd horizontally.——Right end, quoth my uncle *Toby*, muttering the two words low to himself, and fixing his two eyes insensibly as he muttered them, upon a small crevice, formed by a bad joint in the chimney-piece.——Right end of a woman!——I declare, quoth my uncle, I know no more which it is than the man in the moon;—and if I was to think, continued my uncle *Toby*, (keeping his eye still fix'd upon the bad joint) this month together, I am sure I should not be able to find it out.

Then, brother *Toby*, replied my father, I will tell you.

Every thing in this world, continued my father (filling a fresh pipe)—every thing in this earthly world, my dear brother *Toby*, has two handles.—Not always, quoth my uncle *Toby*.—At least, replied my father, every one has two hands,——which comes to the same thing,——Now, if a man was to sit down coolly, and consider within himself the make, the shape, the construction, com-at-ability, and convenience of all the parts which constitute the whole of that animal, call'd Woman, and compare them analogically—I never understood rightly the meaning of that word,——quoth my uncle *Toby*.——ANALOGY, replied my father, is the certain relation and agreement, which different——Here a devil of a rap at the door snapp'd my father's definition (like his tobacco-pipe) in two,—and, at the same time, crushed the head of as notable and curious a dissertation as ever was engendered in the womb of speculation;—it was some months before my father could get an opportunity to be safely deliver'd of it:—And, at this hour, it is a thing full as problematical as the subject of the dissertation itself,—(considering the confusion and distresses of our domestick misadventures, which are now coming thick one upon the back of another) whether I shall be able to find a place for it in the third volume or not.

CHAPTER VIII

I T IS about an hour and a half's tolerable good reading since my uncle *Toby* rung the bell, when *Obadiah* was ordered to saddle a horse, and go for Dr. *Slop* the man-midwife;——so that no one can say, with reason, that I have not allowed *Obadiah* time enough, poetically speaking, and considering the emergency too, both to go and come;————tho', morally and truly speaking, the man, perhaps, has scarce had time to get on his boots.

If the hypercritick will go upon this; and is resolved after all to take a pendulum, and measure the true distance betwixt the ringing of the bell, and the rap at the door;——and, after finding it to be no more than two minutes, thirteen seconds, and three fifths,——should take upon him to insult over me for such a breach in the unity, or rather probability, of time;—I would remind him, that the idea of duration and of its simple modes, is got merely from the train and succession of our ideas,—and is the true scholastic pendulum,——and by which, as a scholar, I will be tried in this matter,——abjuring and detesting the jurisdiction of all other pendulums whatever.

I would, therefore, desire him to consider that it is but poor eight miles from *Shandy-Hall* to Dr. *Slop*, the man-midwife's house;—and that whilst *Obadiah* has been going those said miles and back, I have brought my uncle *Toby* from *Namur*, quite across all *Flanders*, into *England:*—That I have had him ill upon my hands near four years;—and have since travelled him and Corporal *Trim*, in a chariot and four, a journey of near two hundred miles down into *Yorkshire*;—all which put together, must have prepared the reader's imagination for the entrance of Dr. *Slop* upon the stage,—as much, at least, (I hope) as a dance, a song, or a concerto between the acts.

If my hypercritick is intractable, alledging, that two minutes and thirteen seconds are no more than two minutes and thirteen seconds,———when I have said all I can about them;———and that this plea, tho' it might save me dramatically, will damn me biographically, rendering my book, from this very moment, a profess'd ROMANCE, which, before, was a book apocryphal:—— If I am thus pressed—I then put an end to the whole objection and controversy about it all at once,—by acquainting him, that *Obadiah* had not got above threescore yards from the stable-yard before he met with Dr. *Slop*;—and indeed he gave a dirty proof that he had met with him, and was within an ace of giving a tragical one too.

Imagine to yourself;—but this had better begin a new chapter.

CHAPTER IX

I MAGINE to yourself a little, squat, uncourtly figure of a Doctor *Slop*, of about four feet and a half perpendicular height, with a breadth of back, and a sesquipedality of belly, which might have done honour to a serjeant in the horse-guards.

Such were the out-lines of Dr. *Slop*'s figure, which,——if you have read *Hogarth*'s analysis of beauty, and if you have not, I wish you would;—you must know, may as certainly be caracatur'd, and convey'd to the mind by three strokes as three hundred.

Imagine such a one,—for such, I say, were the out-lines of Dr. *Slop*'s figure, coming slowly along, foot by foot, waddling thro' the dirt upon the vertebræ of a little diminutive pony, of a pretty colour;——but of strength,——alack!——scarce able to have made an amble of it, under such a fardel, had the roads been in an ambling condition.——They were not.——Imagine to yourself, *Obadiah* mounted upon a strong monster of a coach-horse, prick'd into a full gallop, and making all practicable speed the adverse way.

Pray, Sir, let me interest you a moment in this description.

Had Dr. *Slop* beheld *Obadiah* a mile off, posting in a narrow lane directly towards him, at that monstrous rate,——splashing and plunging like a devil thro' thick and thin, as he approach'd, would not such a phænomenon, with such a vortex of mud and water moving along with it, round its axis,——have been a subject of juster apprehension to Dr *Slop* in his situation,

than the *worst* of *Whiston*'s comets?—To say nothing of the
NUCLEUS; that is, of *Obadiah* and the coach-horse.————In my
idea, the vortex alone of 'em was enough to have involved and
carried, if not the Doctor, at least the Doctor's pony quite away
with it. What then do you think must the terror and hydrophobia
of Dr. *Slop* have been, when you read (which you are just going to
do) that he was advancing thus warily along towards *Shandy-Hall*,
and had approach'd to within sixty yards of it, and within five
yards of a sudden turn, made by an acute angle of the garden wall,
——and in the dirtiest part of a dirty lane,——when *Obadiah*
and his coach-horse turned the corner, rapid, furious,——pop,—
full upon him!——Nothing, I think, in nature, can be supposed
more terrible than such a Rencounter,——so imprompt! so ill
prepared to stand the shock of it as Dr. *Slop* was!

What could Dr. *Slop* do? He cross'd himself ✝ ——Pugh!——
but the Doctor, Sir, was a Papist.—No matter; he had better have
kept hold of the pummel. He had so; nay, as it happen'd, he
had better have done nothing at all;—for in crossing himself he
let go his whip,——and in attempting to save his whip betwixt his
knee and his saddle's skirt, as it slipp'd, he lost his stirrup,—in
losing which he lost his seat;——and in the multitude of all these
losses (which, by the bye, shews what little advantage there is in
crossing) the unfortunate Doctor lost his presence of mind. So
that, without waiting for *Obadiah*'s onset, he left his pony to its
destiny, tumbling off it diagonally, something in the stile and
manner of a pack of wool, and without any other consequence
from the fall, save that of being left (as it would have been) with
the broadest part of him sunk about twelve inches deep in the
mire.

Obadiah pull'd off his cap twice to Dr. *Slop*; —once as he was
falling,—and then again when he saw him seated.—Ill-timed
complaisance;——had not the fellow better have stopp'd his
horse, and got off and help'd him?——Sir, he did all that his
situation would allow;—but the MOMENTUM of the coach-horse
was so great, that *Obadiah* could not do it all at once; —he rode
in a circle three times round Dr. *Slop*, before he could fully
accomplish it any how;—and at the last, when he did stop his
beast, 'twas done with such an explosion of mud that *Obadiah*
had better have been a league off. In short, never was a Dr. *Slop*
so beluted, and so transubstantiated, since that affair came into
fashion.

CHAPTER X

WHEN Dr. *Slop* entered the back-parlour, where my father and my uncle *Toby* were discoursing upon the nature of women,——it was hard to determine whether Dr. *Slop*'s figure, or Dr. *Slop*'s presence, occasioned more surprize to them; for as the accident happened so near the house, as not to make it worth while for *Obadiah* to remount him,——*Obadiah* had led him in as he was, *unwiped, unappointed, unanealed*, with all his stains and blotches on him.——He stood like *Hamlet*'s ghost, motionless and speechless, for a full minute and a half, at the parlour door (*Obadiah* still holding his hand) with all the majesty of mud. His hinder parts, upon which he had received his fall, totally besmear'd,——and in every other part of him, blotched over in such a manner with *Obadiah*'s explosion, that you would have sworn (without mental reservation) that every grain of it had taken effect.

Here was a fair opportunity for my uncle *Toby* to have triumphed over my father in his turn;——for no mortal, who had beheld Dr. *Slop* in that pickle, could have dissented from so much, at least, of my uncle *Toby*'s opinion, "That mayhap his sister might not care to let such a Dr. *Slop* come so near her * * * *." But it was the *Argumentum ad hominem*; and if my uncle *Toby* was not very expert at it, you may think, he might not care to use it.——No; the reason was,——'twas not his nature to insult.

Dr. *Slop*'s presence, at that time, was no less problematical than the mode of it; tho', it is certain, one moment's reflection in my father might have solved it; for he had apprized Dr. *Slop* but the week before, that my mother was at her full reckoning; and as the doctor had heard nothing since, 'twas natural and very political too in him, to have taken a ride to *Shandy-Hall*, as he did, merely to see how matters went on.

But my father's mind took unfortunately a wrong turn in the investigation; running, like the hypercritick's, altogether upon the ringing of the bell and the rap upon the door,——measuring their distance,——and keeping his mind so intent upon the operation, as to have power to think of nothing else,——common-place infirmity of the greatest mathematicians! working with might and main at the demonstration, and so wasting all their strength upon it, that they have none left in them to draw the corollary, to do good with.

The ringing of the bell and the rap upon the door, struck likewise

strong upon the sensorium of my uncle *Toby*,—but it excited
a very different train of thoughts;—the two irreconcileable pulsations instantly brought *Stevinus*, the great engineer, along with
them, into my uncle *Toby*'s mind:—What business *Stevinus* had
in this affair,—is the greatest problem of all;—it shall be solved,
—but not in the next chapter.

CHAPTER XI

WRITING, when properly managed, (as you may be sure
I think mine is) is but a different name for conversation:
As no one, who knows what he is about in good company,
would venture to talk all;—so no author, who understands the
just boundaries of decorum and good breeding, would presume
to think all: The truest respect which you can pay to the reader's
understanding, is to halve this matter amicably, and leave him
something to imagine, in his turn, as well as yourself.

For my own part, I am eternally paying him compliments of
this kind, and do all that lies in my power to keep his imagination
as busy as my own.

'Tis his turn now;—I have given an ample description of Dr.
Slop's sad overthrow, and of his sad appearance in the back parlour;——his imagination must now go on with it for a while.

Let the reader imagine then, that Dr. *Slop* has told his tale;——
and in what words, and with what aggravations his fancy chooses:
—Let him suppose, that *Obadiah* has told his tale also, and with
such rueful looks of affected concern, as he thinks will best contrast the two figures as they stand by each other:—Let him imagine,
that my father has stepp'd up stairs to see my mother:—And,
to conclude this work of imagination,—let him imagine the doctor wash'd,——rubb'd down,——condoled with,—felicitated,—
got into a pair of *Obadiah*'s pumps, stepping forwards towards the
door, upon the very point of entring upon action.

Truce!—truce, good Dr. *Slop*!—stay thy obstetrick hand;—
return it safe into thy bosom to keep it warm;—little dost thou
know what obstacles—little dost thou think what hidden causes
retard its operation!—Hast thou, Dr. *Slop*,—hast thou been
intrusted with the secret articles of this solemn treaty which has
brought thee into this place?—Art though aware that, at this
instant, a daughter of *Lucina* is put obstetrically over thy head?

Alas!—'tis too true.—Besides, great son of *Pilumnus*! what canst thou do?——Thou hast come forth unarm'd;—thou hast left thy *tire tête*,—thy new-invented *forceps*,—thy *crochet*,—thy *squirt*, and all thy instruments of salvation and deliverance behind thee. ——By heaven! at this moment they are hanging up in a green bays bag, betwixt thy two pistols, at thy bed's head!—Ring;—call;—send *Obadiah* back upon the coach-horse to bring them with all speed.

—Make great haste, *Obadiah*, quoth my father, and I'll give thee a crown;—and, quoth my uncle *Toby*, I'll give him another.

CHAPTER XII

YOUR sudden and unexpected arrival, quoth my uncle *Toby*, addressing himself to Dr. *Slop*, (all three of them sitting down to the fire together, as my uncle *Toby* began to speak)—instantly brought the great *Stevinus* into my head, who, you must know, is a favourite author with me.——Then, added, my father, making use of the argument *Ad Crumenam*, ——I will lay twenty guineas to a single crown piece, (which will serve to give away to *Obadiah* when he gets back) that this same *Stevinus* was some engineer or other,—or has wrote something or other, either directly or indirectly, upon the science of fortification.

He has so,—replied my uncle *Toby*—I knew it, said my father; —tho', for the soul of me, I cannot see what kind of connection there can be betwixt Dr. *Slop*'s sudden coming, and a discourse upon fortification;—yet I fear'd it.—Talk of what we will, brother,—or let the occasion be never so foreign or unfit for the subject,—you are sure to bring it in: I would not, brother *Toby*, continued my father,—I declare I would not have my head so full of curtins and horn-works.——That, I dare say, you would not, quoth Dr. *Slop*, interrupting him, and laughing most immoderately at his pun.

Dennis the critick could not detest and abhor a pun, or the insinuation of a pun, more cordially than my father;——he would grow testy upon it at any time;—but to be broke in upon by one, in a serious discourse, was as bad, he would say, as a fillip upon the nose;—he saw no difference.

Sir, quoth my uncle *Toby*, addressing himself to Dr. *Slop*,—— the curtins my brother *Shandy* mentions here, have nothing to do with bed-steads;—tho', I know, *Du Cange* says, "That bed-curtains, in all probability, have taken their name from them;" —nor have the horn-works, he speaks of, any thing in the world to do with the horn-works of cuckoldom:—But the *curtin*, Sir, is the word we use in fortification, for that part of the wall or rampart which lies between the two bastions and joins them.— Besiegers seldom offer to carry on their attacks directly against the curtin, for this reason, because they are so well *flanked*; ('Tis the case of other curtins, quoth Dr. *Slop*, laughing.) however, continued my uncle *Toby*, to make them sure, we generally choose to place ravelins before them, taking care only to extend them beyond the fossé or ditch:—The common men, who know very little of fortification, confound the ravelin and the half-moon together,—tho' they are very different things;—not in their figure or construction, for we make them exactly alike in all points;— for they always consist of two faces, making a salient angle, with the gorges, not straight, but in form of a crescent.—Where then lies the difference? (quoth my father, a little testily.)—In their situations, answered my uncle *Toby:*—For when a ravelin, brother, stands before the curtin, it is a ravelin; and when a ravelin stands before a bastion, then the ravelin is not a ravelin;—it is a half-moon;—a half-moon likewise is a half-moon, and no more, so long as it stands before its bastion;—but was it to change place, and get before the curtin, 'would be no longer a half-moon; a half-moon, in that case, is not a half-moon;—'tis no more than a ravelin.—I think, quoth my father, that the noble science of defence has its weak sides,—as well as others.

—As for the horn-works (high! ho! sigh'd my father) which, continued my uncle *Toby*, my brother was speaking of, they are a very considerable part of an outwork;—they are called by the *French* engineers, *Ouvrage à corne*, and we generally make them to cover such places as we suspect to be weaker than the rest;— 'tis form'd by two epaulments or demi-bastions,—they are very pretty, and if you will take a walk, I'll engage to shew you one well worth your trouble.——I own, continued my uncle *Toby*, when we crown them,—they are much stronger, but then they are very expensive, and take up a great deal of ground; so that, in my opinion, they are most of use to cover or defend the head of a camp; otherwise the double tenaille——By the mother who bore us!——brother *Toby*, quoth my father, not able to hold out any longer,—you would provoke a saint;—here have you got us, I know not how, not only souse into the middle of the old subject again:—But so full is your head of these confounded works, that tho' my wife is this moment in the pains of labour,—and you hear her cry out,—yet nothing will serve you but to carry off the man-midwife.————*Accoucheur*,—if you please, quoth Dr. *Slop*.— With all my heart, replied my father, I don't care what they call you,———but I wish the whole science of fortification, with all its inventors, at the Devil;—it has been the death of thousands,——— and it will be mine in the end.—I would not, I would not, brother *Toby*, have my brains so full of saps, mines, blinds, gabions, palisadoes, ravelins, half-moons, and such trumpery, to be pro-prietor of *Namur*, and of all the towns in *Flanders* with it.

My uncle *Toby* was a man patient of injuries;—not from want of courage,—I have told you in the fifth chapter of this second book, "That he was a man of courage:"—And will add here, that where just occasions presented, or called it forth,—I know no man under whose arm I would sooner have taken shelter; nor did this arise from any insensibility or obtuseness of his intellectual parts;—for he felt this insult of my father's as feelingly as a man could do;—but he was of a peaceful, placid nature,—no jarring element in it—all was mix'd up so kindly within him; my uncle *Toby* had scarce a heart to retaliate upon a fly.

—Go—says he, one day at dinner, to an over-grown one which had buzz'd about his nose, and tormented him cruelly all dinner-time,— and which, after infinite attempts, he had caught at last, as it flew by him;———I'll not hurt thee, says my uncle *Toby*, rising from his chair, and going across the room, with the fly in his hand,———I'll not hurt a hair of thy head:—Go, says he, lifting up the sash, and opening his hand as he spoke, to let it escape;— go, poor Devil, get thee gone, why should I hurt thee?———This world surely is wide enough to hold both thee and me.

I was but ten years old when this happened;———but whether it was, that the action itself was more in unison to my nerves at that age of pity, which instantly set my whole frame into one vibration of most pleasureable sensation;—or how far the manner and ex-pression of it might go towards it;———or in what degree, or by what secret magick,———a tone of voice and harmony of movement, attuned by mercy, might find a passage to my heart, I know not; —this I know, that the lesson of universal good-will then taught and imprinted by my uncle *Toby*, has never since been worn out of my mind: And tho' I would not depreciate what the study of the *Literæ humaniores*, at the university, have done for me in that respect, or discredit the other helps of an expensive education bestowed upon me, both at home and abroad since;—yet I often think that I owe one half of my philanthropy to that one accidental impression.

☞ This is to serve for parents and governors instead of a whole volume upon the subject.

I could not give the reader this stroke in my uncle *Toby*'s picture, by the instrument with which I drew the other parts of it,——— that taking in no more than the mere HOBBY-HORSICAL likeness; ⸺this is a part of his moral character. My father, in this patient endurance of wrongs, which I mention, was very different, as the reader must long ago have noted; he had a much more acute and quick sensibility of nature, attended with a little soreness of temper; tho' this never transported him to any thing which looked like malignancy;———yet, in the little rubs and vexations of life, 'twas apt to shew itself in a drollish and witty kind of peevishness: ———He was, however, frank and generous in his nature; ———at all times open to conviction; and in the little ebullitions of this subacid humour towards others, but particularly towards my uncle *Toby*, whom he truly loved;———he would feel more pain, ten times told (except in the affair of my aunt *Dinah*, or where an hypothesis was concerned) than what he ever gave.

The characters of the two brothers, in this view of them, reflected light upon each other, and appear'd with great advantage in this affair which arose about *Stevinus*.

I need not tell the reader, if he keep a HOBBY-HORSE,—that a man's HOBBY-HORSE is as tender a part as he has about him; and that these unprovoked strokes, at my uncle *Toby*'s could not be unfelt by him.———No;———as I said above, my uncle *Toby* did feel them, and very sensibly too.

Pray, Sir, what said he?———How did he behave?———Oh, Sir! ———it was great: For as soon as my father had done insulting his HOBBY-HORSE,———he turned his head, without the least emotion, from Dr. *Slop*, to whom he was addressing his discourse, and look'd up into my father's face, with a countenance spread over with so much good nature;———so placid;———so fraternal;———so inexpressibly tender towards him;———it penetrated my father to his heart: He rose up hastily from his chair, and seizing hold of both my uncle *Toby*'s hands as he spoke:———Brother *Toby*, said he,———I beg thy pardon;———forgive, I pray thee, this rash humour which my mother gave me.———My dear, dear brother, answer'd my uncle *Toby*, rising up by my father's help, say no more about it;———you are heartily welcome, had it been ten times as

[113]

much, brother. But 'tis ungenerous, replied my father, to hurt any man;——a brother worse;——but to hurt a brother of such gentle manners,—so unprovoking,—and so unresenting;—'tis base:—By heaven, 'tis cowardly.——You are heartily welcome, brother, quoth my uncle *Toby*,——had it been fifty times as much.——Besides, what have I to do, my dear *Toby*, cried my father, either with your amusements or your pleasures, unless it was in my power (which it is not) to increase their measure?

—Brother *Shandy*, answer'd my uncle *Toby*, looking wistfully in his face,——you are much mistaken in this point;——for you do increase my pleasure very much, in begetting children for the *Shandy* family at your time of life.——But, by that, Sir, quoth Dr. *Slop*, Mr. *Shandy* increases his own.————Not a jot, quoth my father.

CHAPTER XIII

MY BROTHER, does it, quoth my uncle *Toby*, out of *principle*.——In a family-way, I suppose, quoth Dr. *Slop*. —Pshaw!—said my father,—'tis not worth talking of.

CHAPTER XIV

AT THE end of the last chapter, my father and my uncle *Toby* were left both standing, like *Brutus* and *Cassius* at the close of the scene making up their accounts.

As my father spoke the three last words,—he sat down;—my uncle *Toby* exactly followed his example, only, that before he took his chair, he rung the bell, to order Corporal *Trim*, who was in waiting, to step home for *Stevinus*;——my uncle *Toby*'s house being no farther off than the opposite side of the way.

Some men would have dropp'd the subject of *Stevinus*;—but my uncle *Toby* had no resentment in his heart, and he went on with the subject, to shew my father that he had none.

Your sudden appearance, Dr. *Slop*, quoth my uncle, resuming the discourse, instantly brought *Stevinus* into my head. (My father, you may be sure, did not offer to lay any more wagers upon *Stevinus*'s head)——Because, continued my uncle *Toby*, the celebrated sailing chariot, which belonged to Prince *Maurice*, and was of such wonderful contrivance and velocity, as to carry half a dozen people thirty *German* miles, in I don't know how few minutes,——was invented by *Stevinus*, that great mathematician and engineer.

You might have spared your servant the trouble, quoth Dr. *Slop* (as the fellow is lame) of going for *Stevinus*'s account of it, because, in my return from *Leyden* thro' the *Hague*, I walked as far as *Schevling*, which is two long miles, on purpose to take a view of it.

—That's nothing, replied my uncle *Toby*, to what the learned *Peireskius* did, who walked a matter of five hundred miles, reckoning from *Paris* to *Schevling*, and from *Schevling* to *Paris* back again, in order to see it,—and nothing else.

Some men cannot bear to be out-gone.

The more fool *Peireskius*, replied Dr. *Slop*. But mark, 'twas out of no contempt of *Peireskius* at all;——but that *Peireskius*'s indefatigable labour in trudging so far on foot out of love for the sciences, reduced the exploit of Dr. *Slop*, in that affair, to nothing; —the more fool *Peireskius*, said he again:—Why so?—replied my father, taking his brother's part, not only to make reparation as fast as he could for the insult he had given him, which sat still upon my father's mind;—but partly, that my father began really to interest himself in the discourse.—Why so? said he. Why is *Peireskius* or any man else, to be abused for an appetite for that, or any other morsel of sound knowledge? For, notwithstanding I know nothing of the chariot in question, continued he, the inventer of it must have had a very mechanical head; and tho' I cannot guess upon what principles of philosophy he has atchiev'd it;——yet certainly his machine has been constructed upon solid ones, be they what they will, or it could not have answer'd at the rate my brother mentions.

It answered, replied my uncle *Toby* as well, if not better; for, as *Peireskius* elegantly expresses it, speaking of the velocity of its motion, *Tam citus erat, quam erat ventus*; which, unless I have forgot my Latin, is, that it was as swift as the wind itself.

But pray, Dr. *Slop*, quoth my father, interrupting my uncle (tho' not without begging pardon for it, at the same time) upon what principles was this self-same chariot set a-going?—Upon very pretty principles to be sure, replied Dr. *Slop*;——and I have often wondered, continued he, evading the question, why none of our Gentry, who live upon large plains like this of ours,— (especially they whose wives are not past child-bearing) attempt nothing of this kind; for it would not only be infinitely expeditious upon sudden calls, to which the sex is subject,—if the wind only served,——but would be excellent good husbandry to make use of the winds, which cost nothing, and which eat nothing, rather than horses, which (the Devil take 'em) both cost and eat a great deal.

For that very reason, replied my father, "Because they cost nothing, and because they eat nothing,"—the scheme is bad;—— it is the consumption of our products, as well as the manufactures of them, which gives bread to the hungry, circulates trade,— brings in money, and supports the value of our lands;—and tho', I own, if I was a Prince, I would generously recompense the scientific head which brought forth such contrivances;—yet I would as peremptorily suppress the use of them.

My father here had got into his element,——and was going on as prosperously with his dissertation upon trade, as my uncle *Toby* had before, upon his of fortification;——but, to the loss of much sound knowledge, the destinies in the morning had decreed that no dissertation of any kind should be spun by my father that day;——for as he opened his mouth to begin the next sentence,

CHAPTER XV

IN POPP'D Corporal *Trim* with *Stevinus:*——But 'twas too late,——all the discourse had been exhausted without him, and was running into a new channel.

—You may take the book home again, *Trim*, said my uncle *Toby*, nodding to him.

But pri'thee, Corporal, quoth my father, drolling,——look first into it, and see if thou canst spy aught of a sailing chariot in it.

Corporal *Trim*, by being in the service, had learned to obey, ——and not to remonstrate;——so taking the book to a side-table, and running over the leaves; An' please your Honour, said *Trim*, I can see no such thing;—however, continued the Corporal, drolling a little in his turn, I'll make sure work of it, an' please your Honour;—so taking hold of the two covers of the book, one in each hand, and letting the leaves fall down, as he bent the covers back, he gave the book a good sound shake.

There is something fallen out, however, said *Trim*, an' please your Honour; but it is not a chariot, or any thing like one:—

Pri'thee, Corporal, said my father, smiling, what is it then?——
I think, answered *Trim*, stooping to take it up,——'tis more like
a sermon,——for it begins with a text of scripture, and the chapter and verse;——and then goes on, not as a chariot,—but like
a sermon directly.

The company smiled.

I cannot conceive how it is possible, quoth my uncle *Toby*, for
such a thing as a sermon to have got into my *Stevinus*.

I think 'tis a sermon, replied *Trim*;—but if it please your
Honours, as it is a fair hand, I will read you a page;—for *Trim*,
you must know, loved to hear himself read almost as well as talk.

I have ever a strong propensity, said my father, to look into
things which cross my way, by such strange fatalities as these;—
and as we have nothing better to do, at least till *Obadiah* gets
back, I should be obliged to you, brother, if Dr. *Slop* has no
objection to it, to order the Corporal to give us a page or two of it,
—if he is as able to do it, as he seems willing. An' please your
Honour, quoth *Trim*, I officiated two whole campaigns, in
Flanders, as Clerk to the Chaplain of the Regiment.—He can read
it, quoth my uncle *Toby*, as well as I can.—*Trim*, I assure you, was
the best scholar in my company, and should have had the next
Halberd, but for the poor fellow's misfortune. Corporal *Trim* laid
his hand upon his heart, and made an humble bow to his Master;
—then laying down his hat upon the floor, and taking up the
sermon in his left-hand, in order to have his right at liberty,—he
advanced, nothing doubting, into the middle of the room, where
he could best see, and be best seen by, his audience.

CHAPTER XVI

—IF YOU have any objection,—said my father, addressing himself to Dr. *Slop*. Not in the least, replied Dr. *Slop*;—for it
does not appear on which side of the question it is wrote;
——it may be a composition of a divine of our church, as well as
yours,—so that we run equal risks.——'Tis wrote upon neither
side, quoth *Trim*, for 'tis only upon *Conscience*, an' please your
Honours.

Trim's reason put his audience into good humour,—all but
Dr. *Slop*, who, turning his head about towards *Trim*, look'd
a little angry.

Begin, *Trim*,——and read distinctly, quoth my father.—I will, an' please your Honour, replied the Corporal, making a bow, and bespeaking attention with a slight movement of his right-hand.

CHAPTER XVII

BUT BEFORE the Corporal begins, I must first give you a description of his attitude;——otherwise he will naturally stand represented, by your imagination, in an uneasy posture,—stiff,—perpendicular,—dividing the weight of his body equally upon both legs;—his eye fixed, as if on duty;—his look determined,—clinching the sermon in his left-hand, like his firelock.—In a word, you would be apt to paint *Trim*, as if he was standing in his platoon ready for action.——His attitude was as unlike all this as you can conceive.

He stood before them with his body swayed, and bent forwards just so far, as to make an angle of 85 degrees and a half upon the plain of the horizon;——which sound orators, to whom I address this, know very well, to be the true persuasive angle of incidence;—in any other angle you may talk and preach;—'tis certain;—and it is done every day;—but with what effect,— I leave the world to judge!

The necessity of this precise angle of 85 degrees and a half to a mathematical exactness,—does it not shew us, by the way,— how the arts and sciences mutually befriend each other?

How the duce Corporal *Trim*, who knew not so much as an acute angle from an obtuse one, came to hit it so exactly;——or whether it was chance or nature, or good sense or imitation, &c. shall be commented upon in that part of this cyclopædia of arts and sciences, where the instrumental parts of the eloquence of the senate, the pulpit, the bar, the coffee-house, the bed-chamber, and fire-side, fall under consideration.

He stood,——for I repeat it, to take the picture of him in at one view, with his body swayed, and somewhat bent forwards,—his right-leg firm under him, sustaining seven-eighths of his whole weight,—the foot of his left-leg, the defect of which was no disadvantage to his attitude, advanced a little,—not laterally, nor forwards, but in a line betwixt them;—his knee bent, but that not violently,—but so as to fall within the limits of the line of beauty;

[118]

—and I add, of the line of science too;—for consider, it had one eighth part of his body to bear up;—so that in this case the position of the leg is determined,—because the foot could be no farther advanced, or the knee more bent, than what would allow him, mechanically, to receive an eighth part of his whole weight under it, and to carry it too.

☛ This I recommend to painters;—need I add,—to orators? —I think not; for, unless they practise it,—they must fall upon their noses.

So much for Corporal *Trim*'s body and legs.—He held the sermon loosely,—not carelessly, in his left-hand, raised something above his stomach, and detached a little from his breast;——his right-arm falling negligently by his side, as nature and the laws of gravity ordered it,—but with the palm of it open and turned towards his audience, ready to aid the sentiment, in case it stood in need.

Corporal *Trim*'s eyes and the muscles of his face were in full harmony with the other parts of him;—he looked frank,—unconstrained,—something assured,——but not bordering upon assurance.

Let not the critick ask how Corporal *Trim* could come by all this;—I've told him it shall be explained;—but so he stood before my father, my uncle *Toby*, and Dr. *Slop*,—so swayed his body, so contrasted his limbs, and with such an oratorical sweep throughout the whole figure,—a statuary might have modell'd from it;—nay, I doubt whether the oldest Fellow of a College,—or the *Hebrew* Professor himself, could have much mended it.

Trim made a bow, and read as follows:

THE SERMON

HEBREWS XIII 18

——*For we* trust *we have a good Conscience.*——

"TRUST!—Trust we have a good conscience!"

[Certainly, *Trim*, quoth my father, interrupting him, you give that sentence a very improper accent; for you curl up your nose, man, and read it with such a sneering tone, as if the Parson was going to abuse the Apostle.

He is, an' please your Honour, replied *Trim*. Pugh! said my father, smiling.

Sir, quoth Dr. *Slop*, *Trim* is certainly in the right; for the writer (who I perceive is a Protestant) by the snappish manner in which he takes up the Apostle, is certainly going to abuse him,—if this treatment of him has not done it already. But from whence, replied my father, have you concluded so soon, Dr. *Slop*, that the writer is of our Church?—for aught I can see yet,—he may be of any Church.——Because, answered Dr. *Slop*, if he was of ours, ——he durst no more take such a licence,—than a bear by his beard:——If, in our communion, Sir, a man was to insult an Apostle,——a saint,——or even the paring of a saint's nail,—he would have his eyes scratched out.——What, by the saint? quoth my uncle *Toby*. No, replied Dr. *Slop*,—he would have an old house over his head. Pray is the Inquisition an antient building, answered my uncle *Toby*, or is it a modern one?—I know nothing of architecture, replied Dr. *Slop*.——An' please your Honours, quoth *Trim*, the Inquisition is the vilest——Pri'thee spare thy description, *Trim*, I hate the very name of it, said my father.—No matter for that, answered Dr. *Slop*,—it has its uses; for tho' I'm no great advocate for it, yet in such a case as this, he would soon be taught better manners; and I can tell him, if he went on at that rate, would be flung into the Inquisition for his pains. God help him then, quoth my uncle *Toby*. Amen, added *Trim*; for heaven above knows, I have a poor brother who has been fourteen years a captive in it.—I never heard one word of it before, said my uncle *Toby*, hastily:—How came he there, *Trim*?——O, Sir! the story will make your heart bleed,—as it has made mine a thousand times;——but it is too long to be told now;——your Honour shall hear it from first to last some day when I am working besides you in our fortifications;——but the short of the story is this:—That my brother *Tom* went over a servant to *Lisbon*,—and then married a *Jew*'s widow, who kept a small shop, and sold sausages, which, somehow or other, was the cause of his being taken in the middle of the night out of his bed, where he was lying with his wife and two small children, and carried directly to the Inquisition, where, God help him, continued *Trim*, fetching a sigh from the bottom of his heart,—the poor honest lad lies confined at this hour;——he was as honest a soul, added *Trim*, (pulling out his handkerchief) as ever blood warm'd.——

——The tears trickled down *Trim*'s cheeks faster than he could well wipe them away:—A dead silence in the room ensued for some minutes.——Certain proof of pity!

Come, *Trim*, quoth my father, after he saw the poor fellow's

grief had got a little vent,—read on,—and put this melancholy
story out of thy head:—I grieve that I interrupted thee;—but
pri'thee begin the sermon again;—for if the first sentence in it is
matter of abuse, as thou sayest, I have a great desire to know what
kind of provocation the Apostle has given.

Corporal *Trim* wiped his face, and returning his handkerchief
into his pocket, and, making a bow as he did it,—he began again.]

THE SERMON

HEBREWS XIII 18

——*For we* trust *we have a good Conscience.*——

"TRUST! trust we have a good conscience! Surely if there
is any thing in this life which a man may depend upon,
and to the knowledge of which he is capable of arriving upon
the most indisputable evidence, it must be this very thing,—
whether he has a good conscience or no."

[I am positive I am right, quoth Dr. *Slop.*]

"If a man thinks at all, he cannot well be a stranger to the true
state of this account;—he must be privy to his own thoughts and
desires;——he must remember his past pursuits, and know certainly the true springs and motives which, in general, have governed the actions of his life."

[I defy him, without an assistant, quoth Dr. *Slop.*]

"In other matters we may be deceived by false appearances;
and, as the Wise Man complains, *hardly do we guess aright at the
things that are upon the earth, and with labour do we find the things
that are before us.* But here the mind has all the evidence and facts
within herself;—is conscious of the web she has wove;—knows its
texture and fineness, and the exact share which every passion has
had in working upon the several designs which virtue or vice has
plann'd before her."

[The language is good, and I declare *Trim* reads very well,
quoth my father.]

"Now,—as conscience is nothing else but the knowledge which
the mind has within herself of this; and the judgment, either of
approbation or censure, which it unavoidably makes upon the
successive actions of our lives; 'tis plain you will say, from the
very terms of the proposition,—whenever this inward testimony
goes against a man, and he stands self-accused,—that he must

necessarily be a guilty man.—And, on the contrary, when the report is favourable on his side, and his heart condemns him not;——that it is not a matter of *trust*, as the Apostle intimates,—but a matter of *certainty* and fact, that the conscience is good, and that the man must be good also."

[Then the Apostle is altogether in the wrong, I suppose, quoth Dr. *Slop*, and the Protestant divine is in the right. Sir, have patience, replied my father, for I think it will presently appear that St. *Paul* and the Protestant divine are both of an opinion.—As nearly so, quoth Dr. *Slop*, as East is to West;—but this, continued he, lifting both hands, comes from the liberty of the press.

It is no more, at the worst, replied my uncle *Toby*, than the liberty of the pulpit; for it does not appear that the sermon is printed, or ever likely to be.

Go on, *Trim*, quoth my father.]

"At first sight this may seem to be a true state of the case; and I make no doubt but the knowledge of right and wrong is so truly impressed upon the mind of man,—that did no such thing ever happen, as that the conscience of a man, by long habits of sin, might (as the scripture assures it may) insensibly become hard;——and, like some tender parts of his body, by much stress and continual hard usage, lose, by degrees, that nice sense and perception with which God and nature endow'd it:—Did this never happen;—or was it certain that self-love could never hang the least bias upon the judgment;—or that the little interests below, could rise up and perplex the faculties of our upper regions, and encompass them about with clouds and thick darkness:——Could no such thing as favour and affection enter this sacred COURT:—Did WIT disdain to take a bribe in it;—or was asham'd to shew its face as an advocate for an unwarrantable enjoyment:—Or, lastly, were we assured, that INTEREST stood always unconcern'd whilst the cause was hearing,—and that passion never got into the judgment-seat, and pronounc'd sentence in the stead of reason, which is supposed always to preside and determine upon the case:——Was this truly so, as the objection must suppose;—no doubt then, the religious and moral state of a man would be exactly what he himself esteem'd it;—and the guilt or innocence of every man's life could be known, in general, by no better measure, than the degrees of his own approbation and censure.

"I own, in one case, whenever a man's conscience does accuse him, (as it seldom errs on that side) that he is guilty; and unless in melancholy and hypocondriack cases, we may safely pronounce upon it, that there is always sufficient grounds for the accusation.

"But the converse of the proposition will not hold true — namely, that whenever there is guilt, the conscience must accuse; and if it does not, that a man is therefore innocent.—This is not fact:——So that the common consolation which some good christian or other is hourly administering to himself,——that he thanks God his mind does not misgive him; and that, consequently, he has a good conscience, because he has a quiet one,—is fallacious;—and as current as the inference is, and as infallible as the rule appears at first sight, yet, when you look nearer to it, and try the truth of this rule upon plain facts,—you see it liable to so much error from a false application;—the principle upon which it goes so often perverted;——the whole force of it lost, and sometimes so vilely cast away, that it is painful to produce the common examples from human life which confirm the account.

"A man shall be vicious and utterly debauched in his principles; —exceptionable in his conduct to the world; shall live shameless, in the open commission of a sin which no reason or pretence can justify;——a sin, by which, contrary to all the workings of humanity, he shall ruin for ever the deluded partner of his guilt;— rob her of her best dowry; and not only cover her own head with dishonour,—but involve a whole virtuous family in shame and sorrow for her sake.—Surely, you will think conscience must lead such a man a troublesome Life;—he can have no rest night or day from its reproaches.

"Alas! CONSCIENCE had something else to do, all this time, than break in upon him; as *Elijah* reproached the God *Baal,*—— this domestick God *was either talking, or pursuing, or was in a journey, or peradventure he slept and could not be awoke.*

"Perhaps HE was gone out in company with HONOUR to fight a duel;—to pay off some debt at play;——or dirty annuity, the bargain of his lust: Perhaps CONSCIENCE all this time was engaged at home, talking loud against petty larceny, and executing vengeance upon some such puny crimes as his fortune and rank in life secured him against all temptation of committing; so that he lives as merrily," [if he was of our church tho', quoth Dr. *Slop,* he could not]—"sleeps as soundly in his bed;—and at last meets death as unconcernedly;—perhaps much more so than a much better man."

[All this is impossible with us, quoth Dr. *Slop,* turning to my father,—the case could not happen in our Church.——It happens in ours, however, replied my father, but too often.—I own, quoth Dr. *Slop*, (struck a little with my father's frank acknowledgement)—that a man in the *Romish* Church may live as badly;——but then he cannot easily die so.——'Tis little matter, replied my father, with an air of indifference,——how a rascal dies.—— I mean, answered Dr. *Slop*, he would be denied the benefits of the last sacraments.——Pray how many have you in all, said my uncle *Toby*,—for I always forget?——Seven, answered Dr. *Slop*.— Humph!——said my uncle *Toby*;——tho' not accented as a note of acquiescence,——but as an interjection of that particular species of surprize, when a man, in looking into a drawer, finds more of a thing than he expected.—Humph! replied my uncle *Toby*. Dr. *Slop*, who had an ear, understood my uncle *Toby* as well as if he had wrote a whole volume against the seven sacraments.——Humph! replied Dr. *Slop*, (stating my uncle *Toby*'s argument over again to him)——Why, Sir, are there not seven cardinal virtues?——Seven mortal sins?——Seven golden candlesticks?——Seven heavens?——'Tis more than I know, replied my uncle *Toby*.——Are there not seven wonders of the world?——Seven days of the creation?——Seven planets?——Seven plagues?——That there are, quoth my father, with a most affected gravity. But pri'thee, continued he, go on with the rest of thy characters, *Trim*.]

"Another is sordid, unmerciful," (here *Trim* waved his right-hand) "a strait-hearted, selfish wretch, incapable either of private friendship or publick spirit. Take notice how he passes by the widow and orphan in their distress, and sees all the miseries incident to human life without a sigh or a prayer."

[An' please your Honours, cried *Trim*, I think this a viler man than the other.]

"Shall not conscience rise up and sting him on such occasions; —No; thank God there is no occasion; *I pay every man his own; —I have no fornication to answer to my conscience;——no faithless vows or promises to make up;——I have debauched no man's wife or child; thank God, I am not as other men, adulterers, unjust, or even as this libertine, who stands before me.*

"A third is crafty and designing in his nature. View his whole life;—'tis nothing but a cunning contexture of dark arts and unequitable subterfuges, basely to defeat the true intent of all laws,—plain dealing and the safe enjoyment of our several properties.——You will see such a one working out a frame of little designs upon the ignorance and perplexities of the poor and needy man;——shall raise a fortune upon the inexperience of a youth, or the unsuspecting temper of his friend, who would have trusted him with his life.

"When old age comes on, and repentance calls him to look back upon this black account, and state it over again with his conscience,——CONSCIENCE looks into the STATUTES at LARGE; —finds no express law broken by what he has done;—perceives no penalty or forfeiture of goods and chattels incurred;—sees no scourge waving over his head, or prison opening his gates upon him:—What is there to affright his conscience?——Conscience has got safely entrenched behind the Letter of the Law; sits there invulnerable, fortified with 𝕮𝖆𝖘𝖊𝖘 and 𝕽𝖊𝖕𝖔𝖗𝖙𝖘 so strongly on all sides;——that it is not preaching can dispossess it of its hold."

[Here Corporal *Trim* and my uncle *Toby* exchanged looks with each other.—Aye,—aye, *Trim*! quoth my uncle *Toby*, shaking his head,——these are but sorry fortifications, *Trim*.——O! very poor work, answered *Trim,* to what your Honour and I make of it.——The character of this last man, said Dr. *Slop*, interrupting *Trim*, is more detestable than all the rest;——and seems to have been taken from some pettifogging Lawyer amongst you:——Amongst us, a man's conscience could not possibly continue so long *blinded*;——three times in a year, at least, he must go to confession. Will that restore it to sight, quoth my uncle *Toby*?——Go on, *Trim*, quoth my father, or *Obadiah* will have got back before thou hast got to the end of thy sermon;—— 'tis a very short one, replied *Trim*.—I wish it was longer, quoth my uncle *Toby*, for I like it hugely.——*Trim* went on.]

"A fourth man shall want even this refuge;——shall break through all this ceremony of slow chicane;——scorns the doubtful workings of secret plots and cautious trains to bring about his purpose:——See the bare-faced villain, how he cheats, lies, perjures, robs, murders,——Horrid!——But indeed much better was not to be expected, in the present case——the poor man was in the dark!—his priest had got the keeping of his conscience; ——and all he would let him know of it, was, That he must believe in the Pope;——go to Mass;—cross himself;—tell his beads;——be a good Catholick, and that this, in all conscience, was enough to carry him to heaven. What;——if he perjures!— Why;—he had a mental reservation in it.—But if he is so wicked and abandoned a wretch as you represent him;——if he robs,—— if he stabs,—will not conscience, on every such act, receive a wound itself?—Aye,—but the man has carried it to confession;

[125]

————the wound digests there, and will do well enough, and in a short time be quite healed up by absolution. O Popery! what hast thou to answer for?————when, not content with the too many natural and fatal ways, thro' which the heart of man is every day thus treacherous to itself above all things;————thou hast wilfully set open this wide gate of deceit before the face of this unwary traveller, too apt, God knows, to go astray of himself; and confidently speak peace to himself, when there is no peace.

"Of this the common instances which I have drawn out of life, are too notorious to require much evidence. If any man doubts the reality of them, or thinks it impossible for a man to be such a bubble to himself,————I must refer him a moment to his own reflections, and will then venture to trust my appeal with his own heart.

"Let him consider in how different a degree of detestation, numbers of wicked actions stand *there*, tho' equally bad and vicious in their own natures;—he will soon find that such of them as strong inclination and custom have prompted him to commit, are generally dress'd out and painted with all the false beauties, which a soft and a flattering hand can give them;————and that the others, to which he feels no propensity, appear, at once, naked and deformed, surrounded with all the true circumstances of folly and dishonour.

"When *David* surprized *Saul* sleeping in the Cave, and cut off the skirt of his robe,————we read his heart smote him for what he had done:————But in the matter of *Uriah*, where a faithful and gallant servant, whom he ought to have loved and honoured, fell to make way for his lust,————where conscience had so much greater reason to take the alarm, his heart smote him not. A whole year had almost passed from the first commission of that crime, to the time *Nathan* was sent to reprove him; and we read not once of the least sorrow or compunction of heart which he testified, during all that time, for what he had done.

"Thus conscience, this once able monitor,————placed on high as a judge within us, and intended by our maker as a just and equitable one too,————by an unhappy train of causes and impediments, takes often such imperfect cognizance of what passes,———— does its office so negligently,————sometimes so corruptly,———— that it is not to be trusted alone; and therefore we find there is a necessity, an absolute necessity of joining another principle with it, to aid, if not govern, its determinations.

"So that if you would form a just judgment of what is of

[126]

infinite importance to you not to be misled in,——namely, in
what degree of real merit you stand either as an honest man, an
useful citizen, a faithful subject to your King, or a good servant
to your God,—call in religion and morality.—Look,—What is
written in the law of God?——How readest thou?——Consult
calm reason and the unchangeable obligations of justice and truth;
—what say they?

"Let CONSCIENCE determine the matter upon these reports;—
and then if thy heart condemns thee not, which is the case the
Apostle supposes,—the rule will be infallible;" [Here Dr. *Slop*
fell asleep] "*thou wilt have confidence towards God*;—that is, have
just grounds to believe the judgment thou hast past upon thyself, is the judgment of God; and nothing else but an anti-
cipation of that righteous sentence which will be pronounced
upon thee hereafter by that Being, to whom thou art finally to
give an account of thy actions.

"*Blessed is the man*, indeed then, as the author of the book of
Ecclesiasticus expresses it, *who is not prick'd with the multitude of
his sins: Blessed is the man whose heart hath not condemned him;
whether he be rich, or whether he be poor, if he have a good heart*
(a heart thus guided and informed) *he shall at all times rejoice in
a cheurful countenance; his mind shall tell him more than seven
watch-men that sit above upon a tower on high.*"————[A tower
has no strength, quoth my uncle *Toby*, unless 'tis flank'd.] "In
the darkest doubts it shall conduct him safer than a thousand
casuists, and give the state he lives in a better security for his
behaviour than all the clauses and restrictions put together, which
law-makers are forced to multiply:——*Forced*, I say, as things
stand; human laws not being a matter of original choice, but of
pure necessity, brought in to fence against the mischievous effects
of those consciences which are no law unto themselves; well
intending, by the many provisions made,——that in all such
corrupt and misguided cases, where principles and the checks of
conscience will not make us upright,——to supply their force,
and, by the terrors of gaols and halters, oblige us to it."

[I see plainly, said my father, that this sermon has been composed to be preach'd at the Temple,——or at some Assize.——
I like the reasoning,——and am sorry that Dr. *Slop* has fallen
asleep before the time of his conviction;——for it is now clear,
that the Parson, as I thought at first, never insulted St. *Paul* in the
least;——nor has there been, brother, the least difference between
them.——A great matter, if they had differed, replied my uncle

Toby,——the best friends in the world may differ sometimes.——
True,—brother *Toby*, quoth my father, shaking hands with him,
—we'll fill our pipes, brother, and then *Trim* shall go on.

Well,—what dost thou think of it? said my father, speaking to
Corporal *Trim*, as he reach'd his tobacco-box.

I think, answered the Corporal, that the seven watch-men upon
the tower, who, I suppose, are all centinels there,——are more,
an' please your Honour, than were necessary;—and, to go on at
that rate, would harrass a regiment all to pieces, which a commanding officer, who loves his men, will never do, if he can help
it; because two centinels, added the Corporal, are as good as
twenty.—I have been a commanding officer myself in the *Corps
de Garde* a hundred times, continued *Trim*, rising an inch higher
in his figure, as he spoke,—and all the time I had the honour to
serve his Majesty King *William*, in relieving the most considerable
posts, I never left more than two in my life.—Very right, *Trim*,
quoth my uncle *Toby*;——but you do not consider, *Trim*, that
the towers, in *Solomon*'s days, were not such things as our bastions, flanked and defended by other works;—this, *Trim*, was an
invention since *Solomon*'s death; nor had they horn-works, or
ravelins before the curtin, in his time;—or such a fossé as we
make with a cuvette in the middle of it, and with cover'd-ways
and counterscarps pallisadoed along it, to guard against a *Coup
de main:*—So that the seven men upon the tower were a party,
I dare say, from the *Corps de Garde*, set there, not only to look
out, but to defend it.—They could be no more, an' please your
Honour, than a Corporal's Guard.—My father smiled inwardly,
—but not outwardly;—the subject between my uncle *Toby* and
Corporal *Trim* being rather too serious, considering what had
happened, to make a jest of:—So putting his pipe into his mouth,
which he had just lighted,—he contented himself with ordering
Trim to read on. He read on as follows:]

"To have the fear of God before our eyes, and, in our mutual
dealings with each other, to govern our actions by the eternal
measures of right and wrong:—The first of these will comprehend
the duties of religion;—the second, those of morality, which are
so inseparably connected together, that you cannot divide these
two *tables*, even in imagination (tho' the attempt is often made in
practice) without breaking and mutually destroying them both.

"I said the attempt is often made, and so it is;——there being
nothing more common than to see a man who has no sense at all
of religion,—and indeed has so much honesty as to pretend to none,

who would take it as the bitterest affront, should you but hint at a suspicion of his moral character,—or imagine he was not conscientiously just and scrupulous to the uttermost mite.

"When there is some appearance that it is so,—tho' one is unwilling even to suspect the appearance of so amiable a virtue as moral honesty, yet were we to look into the grounds of it, in the present case, I am persuaded we should find little reason to envy such a one the honour of his motive.

"Let him declaim as pompously as he chooses upon the subject, it will be found to rest upon no better foundation than either his interest, his pride, his ease, or some such little and changeable passion as will give us but small dependence upon his actions in matters of great stress.

"I will illustrate this by an example.

"I know the banker I deal with, or the physician I usually call in," [There is no need, cried Dr. *Slop*, (waking) to call in any physician in this case] "to be neither of them men of much religion: I hear them make a jest of it every day, and treat all its sanctions with so much scorn, as to put the matter past doubt. Well;—notwithstanding this, I put my fortune into the hands of the one;—and, what is dearer still to me, I trust my life to the honest skill of the other.

"Now, let me examine what is my reason for this great confidence.——Why, in the first place, I believe there is no probability that either of them will employ the power I put into their hands to my disadvantage;—I consider that honesty serves the purposes of this life:—I know their success in the world depends upon the fairness of their characters.——In a word,—I'm persuaded that they cannot hurt me, without hurting themselves more.

"But put it otherwise, namely, that interest lay, for once, on the other side; that a case should happen, wherein the one, without stain to his reputation, could secrete my fortune, and leave me naked in the world;—or that the other could send me out of it, and enjoy an estate by my death, without dishonour to himself or his art:—In this case, what hold have I of either of them?— Religion, the strongest of all motives, is out of the question:— Interest, the next most powerful motive in the world, is strongly against me:—What have I left to cast into the opposite scale to balance this temptation?—Alas! I have nothing,—nothing but what is lighter than a bubble—I must lay at the mercy of HONOUR, or some such capricious principle.—Strait security for two of my most valuable blessings!—my property and my life.

"As, therefore, we can have no dependence upon morality without religion;—so, on the other hand, there is nothing better to be expected from religion without morality;—nevertheless, 'tis no prodigy to see a man whose real moral character stands very low, who yet entertains the highest notion of himself, in the light of a religious man.

"He shall not only be covetous, revengeful, implacable,—— but even wanting in points of common honesty; yet, inasmuch as he talks aloud against the infidelity of the age,——is zealous for some points of religion,——goes twice a day to church,—— attends the sacraments,——and amuses himself with a few instru- mental parts of religion,——shall cheat his conscience into a judg- ment that, for this, he is a religious man, and has discharged truly his duty to God: And you will find that such a man, thro' force of this delusion, generally looks down with spiritual pride upon every other man who has less affectation of piety,—tho', per- haps, ten times more moral honesty than himself.

"*This likewise is a sore evil under the sun;* and I believe there is no one mistaken principle, which, for its time, has wrought more serious mischiefs.—For a general proof of this,—examine the history of the *Romish* church;"—[Well, what can you make of that, cried Dr. *Slop*?]—"see what scenes of cruelty, murders, rapines, blood-shed," [They may thank their own obstinacy, cried Dr. *Slop*] "have all been sanctified by a religion not strictly governed by morality.

"In how many kingdoms of the world," [Here *Trim* kept wav- ing his right-hand from the sermon to the extent of his arm, returning it backwards and forwards to the conclusion of the Paragraph.]

"In how many kingdoms of the world has the crusading sword of this misguided saint-errant spared neither age, or merit, or sex, or condition?—and, as he fought under the banners of a religion which set him loose from justice and humanity, he shewed none; mercilessly trampled upon both,——heard neither the cries of the unfortunate, nor pitied their distresses."

[I have been in many a battle, an' please your Honour, quoth *Trim*, sighing, but never in so melancholy a one as this.—I would not have drawn a tricker in it against these poor souls,——to have been made a general officer.——Why, what do you under- stand of the affair? said Dr. *Slop*, looking towards *Trim* with something more contempt than the Corporal's honest heart deserved.—What do you know, friend, about this battle you talk of?——I know, replied *Trim*, that I never refused quarter in my life to any man who cried out for it;—but to a woman or a child, continued *Trim*, before I would level my musket at them, I would lose my life a thousand times.——Here's a crown for thee, *Trim*, to drink with *Obadiah* to-night, quoth my uncle *Toby*, and I'll give *Obadiah* another too.—God bless your Honour, replied *Trim*,—I had rather these poor women and children had it.—— Thou art an honest fellow, quoth my uncle *Toby*.——My father nodded his head,——as much as to say,——and so he is.——

But pri'thee, *Trim*, said my father, make an end,—for I see thou hast but a leaf or two left.]

Corporal *Trim* read on.

"If the testimony of past centuries in this matter is not sufficient, —consider at this instant, how the votaries of that religion are every day thinking to do service and honour to God, by actions which are a dishonour and scandal to themselves.

"To be convinced of this, go with me for a moment into the prisons of the inquisition." [God help my poor brother *Tom*.]— "Behold *Religion*, with *Mercy* and *Justice* chained down under her feet,—there sitting ghastly upon a black tribunal, propp'd up with racks and instruments of torment. Hark!—hark! what a piteous groan!" [Here *Trim*'s face turned as pale as ashes] "See the melancholy wretch who uttered it,"—[Here the tears began to trickle down] "just brought forth to undergo the anguish of a mock trial, and endure the utmost pains that a studied system of cruelty has been able to invent."—[D—n them all, quoth *Trim*, his colour returning into his face as red as blood.]—"Behold this helpless victim delivered up to his tormentors,—his body so wasted with sorrow and confinement."——[Oh! 'tis my brother, cried poor *Trim* in a most passionate exclamation, dropping the sermon upon the ground, and clapping his hands together— I fear 'tis poor *Tom*. My father's and my uncle *Toby*'s hearts yearn'd with sympathy for the poor fellow's distress,—even *Slop* himself acknowledged pity for him.—Why, *Trim*, said my father, this is not a history,—'tis a sermon thou art reading;—pri'thee begin the sentence again.]—"Behold this helpless victim deliver'd up to his tormentors,—his body so wasted with sorrow and confinement, you will see every nerve and muscle as it suffers.

"Observe the last movement of that horrid engine!" [I would rather face a cannon, quoth *Trim*, stamping.]——"See what convulsions it has thrown him into!——Consider the nature of the posture in which he now lies stretched,—what exquisite tortures

he endures by it!"——[I hope 'tis not in *Portugal*.]—"'Tis all
nature can bear! Good God! see how it keeps his weary soul
hanging upon his trembling lips!" [I would not read another line
of it, quoth *Trim*, for all this world;—I fear, an' please your
Honours, all this is in *Portugal*, where my poor brother *Tom* is.
I tell thee, *Trim*, again, quoth my father, 'tis not an historical
account,—'tis a description.—'Tis only a description, honest
man, quoth *Slop*, there's not a word of truth in it.—That's
another story, replied my father.—However, as *Trim* reads it with
so much concern,—'tis cruelty to force him to go on with it.—
Give me hold of the sermon, *Trim*,—I'll finish it for thee, and
thou may'st go. I must stay and hear it too, replied *Trim*, if your
Honour will allow me;—tho' I would not read it myself for
a Colonel's pay.——Poor *Trim*! quoth my uncle *Toby*. My father
went on.]—

"—Consider the nature of the posture in which he now lies
stretch'd,—what exquisite torture he endures by it!—'Tis all
nature can bear!—Good God! See how it keeps his weary soul
hanging upon his trembling lips,—willing to take its leave,——
but not suffered to depart!——Behold the unhappy wretch led
back to his cell!" [Then, thank God, however, quoth *Trim*, they
have not killed him]—"See him dragged out of it again to meet
the flames, and the insults in his last agonies, which this principle,
——this principle, that there can be religion without mercy, has
prepared for him." [Then, thank God,—he is dead, quoth *Trim*,—
he is out of his pain,—and they have done their worst at him.—
O Sirs!——Hold your peace, *Trim*, said my father, going on with
the sermon, lest *Trim* should incense Dr. *Slop*,—we shall never
have done at this rate.]

"The surest way to try the merit of any disputed notion is, to
trace down the consequences such a notion has produced, and
compare them with the spirit of Christianity;—'tis the short and
decisive rule which our Saviour hath left us, for these and such-
like cases, and it is worth a thousand arguments,—*By their fruits
ye shall know them*.

"I will add no farther to the length of this sermon, than, by
two or three short and independent rules deducible from it.

"*First*, Whenever a man talks loudly against religion, always
suspect that it is not his reason, but his passions which have got
the better of his CREED. A bad life and a good belief are disagreeable and troublesome neighbours, and where they separate,
depend upon it, 'tis for no other cause but quietness sake.

"*Secondly*, When a man, thus represented, tells you in any particular instance,—That such a thing goes *against* his conscience,—always believe he means exactly the same thing, as when he tells you such a thing goes *against* his stomach;—a present want of appetite being generally the true cause of both.

"In a word,—trust that man in nothing, who has not a CONSCIENCE in every thing.

"And, in your own case, remember this plain distinction, a mistake in which has ruined thousands,——that your conscience is not a law:—No, God and reason made the law, and have placed conscience within you to determine;—not like an *Asiatick* Cadi, according to the ebbs and flows of his own passions,—but like a *British* judge in this land of liberty and good sense, who makes no new law, but faithfully declares that law which he knows already written."

F I N I S

Thou hast read the sermon extremely well, *Trim*, quoth my father.—If he had spared his comments, replied Dr. *Slop*, he would have read it much better. I should have read it ten times better, Sir, answered *Trim*, but that my heart was so full.—That was the very reason, *Trim*, replied my father, which has made thee read the sermon as well as thou hast done; and if the clergy of our church, continued my father, addressing himself to Dr. *Slop*, would take part in what they deliver, as deeply as this poor fellow has done,—as their compositions are fine, (I deny it, quoth Dr. *Slop*) I maintain it, that the eloquence of our pulpits, with such subjects to inflame it,—would be a model for the whole world:—But, alas! continued my father, and I own it, Sir, with sorrow, that, like *French* politicians in this respect, what they gain in the cabinet they lose in the field.——'Twere a pity, quoth my uncle, that this should be lost. I like the sermon well, replied my father,——'tis dramatic,——and there is something in that way of writing, when skilfully managed, which catches the attention.

——We preach much in that way with us, said Dr. *Slop*.—— I know that very well, said my father,—but in a tone and manner which disgusted Dr. *Slop*, full as much as his assent, simply, could have pleased him.——But in this, added Dr. *Slop*, a little piqued, ——our sermons have greatly the advantage, that we never introduce any character into them below a patriarch or a patriarch's wife, or a martyr or a saint.—There are some very bad characters

[133]

in this, however, said my father, and I do not think the sermon a jot the worse for 'em.——But pray, quoth my uncle *Toby*,—who's can this be?—How could it get into my *Stevinus*? A man must be as great a conjurer as *Stevinus*, said my father, to resolve the second question:—The first, I think, is not so difficult;—for unless my judgment greatly decives me,—I know the author, for 'tis wrote, certainly, by the parson of the parish.

The similitude of the stile and manner of it, with those my father constantly had heard preached in his parish-church, was the ground of his conjecture,————proving it as strongly, as an argument *à priori* could prove such a thing to a philosophic mind, That it was *Yorick*'s and no one's else:————It was proved to be so *à posteriori*, the day after, when *Yorick* sent a servant to my uncle *Toby*'s house to enquire after it.

It seems that *Yorick*, who was inquisitive after all kinds of knowledge, had borrowed *Stevinus* of my uncle *Toby*, and had carelessly popp'd his sermon, as soon as he had made it, into the middle of *Stevinus*; and, by an act of forgetfulness, to which he was ever subject, he had sent *Stevinus* home, and his sermon to keep him company.

Ill-fated sermon! Thou was lost, after this recovery of thee, a second time, dropp'd thro' an unsuspected fissure in thy master's pocket, down into a treacherous and a tatter'd lining,—trod deep into the dirt by the left hind foot of his Rosinante, inhumanly stepping upon thee as thou falledst;—buried ten days in the mire, —raised up out of it by a beggar, sold for a halfpenny to a parish-clerk,—transferred to his parson,—lost for ever to thy own, the remainder of his days,—nor restored to his restless MANES till this very moment, that I tell the world the story.

Can the reader believe, that this sermon of *Yorick*'s was preached at an assize, in the cathedral of *York*, before a thousand witnesses, ready to give oath of it, by a certain prebendary of that church, and actually printed by him when he had done,——and within so short a space as two years and three months after *Yorick*'s death.— *Yorick*, indeed, was never better served in his life!——but it was a little hard to male-treat him after, and plunder him after he was laid in his grave.

However, as the gentleman who did it was in perfect charity with *Yorick*,—and, in conscious justice, printed but a few copies to give away;—and that, I am told he could moreover have made as good a one himself, had he thought fit,—I declare I would not have published this anecdote to the world;—nor do I publish it with an intent to hurt his character and advancement in the church;—I leave that to others;—but I find myself impelled by two reasons, which I cannot withstand.

The first is, That, in doing justice, I may give rest to *Yorick*'s ghost;—which, as the country people,—and some others, believe, ——*still walks.*

The second reason is, That, by laying open this story to the world, I gain an opportunity of informing it,—That in case the character of parson *Yorick*, and this sample of his sermons is liked,—there are now in the possession of the *Shandy* family, as many as will make a handsome volume, at the world's service, ————and much good may they do it.

CHAPTER XVIII

OBADIAH gain'd the two crowns without dispute; for he came in jingling, with all the instruments in the green bays bag we spoke of, slung across his body, just as Corporal *Trim* went out of the room.

It is now proper, I think, quoth Dr. *Slop*, (clearing up his looks) as we are in a condition to be of some service to Mrs. *Shandy*, to send up stairs to know how she goes on.

I have ordered, answered my father, the old midwife to come down to us upon the least difficulty;——for you must know, Dr. *Slop*, continued my father, with a perplexed kind of a smile upon his countenance, that by express treaty, solemnly ratified between me and my wife, you are no more than an auxiliary in this affair,—and not so much as that,——unless the lean old mother of a midwife above stairs cannot do without you.—— Women have their particular fancies, and in points of this nature, continued my father, where they bear the whole burden, and suffer so much acute pain for the advantage of our families, and the good of the species,—they claim a right of deciding, *en Soveraines*, in whose hands, and in what fashion, they chuse to undergo it.

They are in the right of it,—quoth my uncle *Toby*. But, Sir, replied Dr. *Slop*, not taking notice of my uncle *Toby*'s opinion, but turning to my father,—they had better govern in other points; —and a father of a family, who wished its perpetuity, in my opinion, had better exchange this prerogative with them, and give up some other rights in lieu of it.—I know not, quoth my father, answering a little too testily, to be quite dispassionate in what he said,—I know not, quoth he, what we have left to give up, in lieu of who shall bring our children into the world,—unless that,—of who shall beget them.——One would almost give up any thing, replied Dr. *Slop*.——I beg your pardon,—answered my uncle *Toby*.——Sir, replied Dr. *Slop*, it would astonish you to know what Improvements we have made of late years in all branches of obstetrical knowledge, but particularly in that one single point of the safe and expeditious extraction of the *fœtus*,——which has received such lights, that, for my part (holding up his hands) I declare I wonder how the world has——I wish, quoth my uncle *Toby*, you had seen what prodigious armies we had in *Flanders*.

CHAPTER XIX

I HAVE dropp'd the curtain over this scene for a minute,—— to remind you of one thing,——and to inform you of another.

What I have to inform you, comes, I own, a little out of its due course;—for it should have been told a hundred and fifty pages ago, but that I foresaw then 'twould come in pat hereafter, and be of more advantage here than elsewhere.——Writers had need look before them to keep up the spirit and connection of what they have in hand.

When these two things are done,—the curtain shall be drawn up again, and my uncle *Toby*, my father, and Dr. *Slop* shall go on with their discourse, without any more interruption.

First, then, the matter which I have to remind you of, is this; ——that from the specimens of singularity in my father's notions in the point of Christian-names, and that other point previous thereto,—you was led, I think, into an opinion, (and I am sure I said as much) that my father was a gentleman altogether as odd and whimsical in fifty other opinions. In truth, there was not a stage in the life of man, from the very first act of his begetting, ——down to the lean and slipper'd pantaloon in his second childishness, but he had some favourite notion to himself, springing out of it, as sceptical, and as far out of the high-way of thinking, as these two which have been explained.

[136]

—Mr. *Shandy*, my father, Sir, would see nothing in the light in which others placed it;——he placed things in his own light;—he would weigh nothing in common scales;—no,—he was too refined a researcher to lay open to so gross an imposition.—To come at the exact weight of things in the scientific steel-yard, the fulcrum, he would say, should be almost invisible, to avoid all friction from popular tenets;—without this the minutiæ of philosophy, which should always turn the balance, will have no weight at all. Knowledge, like matter, he would affirm was divisible *in infinitum*;—that the grains and scruples were as much a part of it, as the gravitation of the whole world.—In a word, he would say, error was error,—no matter where it fell,——whether in a fraction,—or a pound,—'twas alike fatal to truth, and she was kept down at the bottom of her well as inevitably by a mistake in the dust of a butterfly's wing,—as in the disk of the sun, the moon, and all the stars of heaven put together.

He would often lament that it was for want of considering this properly, and of applying it skilfully to civil matters, as well as to speculative truths, that so many things in this world were out of joint;—that the political arch was giving way;—and that the very foundations of our excellent constitution in church and state, were so sapp'd as estimators had reported.

You cry out, he would say, we are a ruined, undone people.—Why? he would ask, making use of the sorites or syllogism of *Zeno* and *Chrysippus*, without knowing it belonged to them.—Why? why are we a ruined people?—Because we are corrupted.—Whence is it, dear Sir, that we are corrupted?—Because we are needy;—our poverty, and not our wills, consent.—And wherefore, he would add,—are we needy?—From the neglect, he would answer, of our pence and our halfpence:—Our bank notes, Sir, our guineas,—nay our shillings take care of themselves.

'Tis the same, he would say, throughout the whole circle of the sciences;——the great, the established points of them, are not to be broke in upon.—The laws of nature will defend themselves;—but error—(he would add, looking earnestly at my mother)—error, Sir, creeps in thro' the minute holes, and small crevices, which human nature leaves unguarded.

This turn of thinking in my father, is what I had to remind you of:—The point you are to be informed of, and which I have reserved for this place, is as follows:

Amongst the many and excellent reasons, with which my father had urged my mother to accept of Dr. *Slop*'s assistance preferably to that of the old woman,——there was one of a very singular nature; which, when he had done arguing the matter with her as a Christian, and came to argue it over again with her as a philosopher, he had put his whole strength to, depending indeed upon it as his sheet anchor.——It failed him; tho' from no defect in the argument itself; but that, do what he could, he was not able for his soul to make her comprehend the drift of it.—Cursed luck!—said he to himself, one afternoon, as he walk'd out of the room, after he had been stating it for an hour and a half to her, to no manner of purpose;—cursed luck! said he, biting his lip as he shut the door,—for a man to be master of one of the finest chains of reasoning in nature,—and have a wife at the same time with such a head-piece, that he cannot hang up a single inference within side of it, to save his soul from destruction.

This argument, tho' it was intirely lost upon my mother,—had more weight with him, than all his other arguments joined together:—I will therefore endeavour to do it justice,—and set it forth with all the perspicuity I am master of.

My father set out upon the strength of these two following axioms:

First, That an ounce of a man's own wit, was worth a tun of other people's; and,

Secondly, (Which, by the bye, was the ground-work of the first axiom,—tho' it comes last)—That every man's wit must come from every man's own soul,—and no other body's.

Now, as it was plain to my father, that all souls were by nature equal,—and that the great difference between the most acute and the most obtuse understanding,——was from no original sharpness or bluntness of one thinking substance above or below another,—but arose merely from the lucky or unlucky organization of the body, in that part where the soul principally took up her residence,——he had made it the subject of his inquiry to find out the identical place.

Now, from the best accounts he had been able to get of this matter, he was satisfied it could not be where *Des Cartes* had fixed it, upon the top of the *pineal* gland of the brain; which, as he philosophised, form'd a cushion for her about the size of a marrow pea; tho' to speak the truth, as so many nerves did terminate all in that one place,—'twas no bad conjecture;——and my father had certainly fallen with that great philosopher plumb into the center of the mistake, had it not been for my uncle *Toby*, who rescued him out of it, by a story he told him of a *Walloon* Officer at the battle of *Landen*, who had one part of his brain shot away by a musket-ball,——and another part of it taken out after by a *French* surgeon; and, after all, recovered, and did his duty very well without it.

If death, said my father, reasoning with himself, is nothing but the separation of the soul from the body;—and if it is true that people can walk about and do their business without brains,—then certes the soul does not inhabit there. Q.E.D.

As for that certain very thin, subtle and very fragrant juice which *Coglionissimo Borri*, the great *Milaneze* physician, affirms, in a letter to *Bartholine*, to have discovered in the cellulæ of the occipital parts of the cerebellum, and which he likewise affirms to be the principal seat of the reasonable soul (for, you must know, in these latter and more enlightened ages, there are two souls in every man living,—the one, according to the great *Metheglingius*, being called the *Animus*, the other the *Anima*);—as for this opinion, I say, of *Borri*,—my father could never subscribe to it by any means; the very idea of so noble, so refined, so immaterial, and so exalted a being as the *Anima*, or even the *Animus*, taking up her residence, and sitting dabbling, like a tad-pole, all day long, both summer and winter, in a puddle,—or in a liquid of any kind, how thick or thin soever, he would say, shock'd his imagination; he would scarce give the doctrine a hearing.

What, therefore, seem'd the least liable to objections of any, was, that the chief sensorium, or head-quarters of the soul, and to which place all intelligences were referred, and from whence all her mandates were issued,—was in, or near, the cerebellum,—or rather some-where about the *medulla oblongata,* wherein it was generally agreed by *Dutch* anatomists, that all the minute nerves from all the organs of the seven senses concentered, like streets and winding alleys, into a square.

So far there was nothing singular in my father's opinion,—he had the best of philosophers, of all ages and climates, to go along with him.—But here he took a road of his own, setting up another *Shandean* hypothesis upon these corner-stones they had laid for him;—and which said hypothesis equally stood its ground; whether the subtilty and fineness of the soul depended upon the temperature and clearness of the said liquor, or of the finer net-work and texture in the cerebellum itself; which opinion he favoured.

He maintained, that next to the due care to be taken in the act of propagation of each individual, which required all the thought in the world, as it laid the foundation of this incomprehensible contexture in which wit, memory, fancy, eloquence, and what is usually meant by the name of good natural parts, do consist;—that next to this and his Christian-name, which were the two original and most efficacious causes of all;—that the third cause, or rather what logicians call the *Causa sine quâ non*, and without which all that was done was of no manner of significance,—was the preservation of this delicate and fine-spun web, from the havock which was generally made in it by the violent compression and crush which the head was made to undergo, by the nonsensical method of bringing us into the world by that part foremost.

——This requires explanation.

My father, who dipp'd into all kinds of books, upon looking into *Lithopædus Senonesis de Partu difficili* *, published by *Adrianus Smelvogt*, had found out, That the lax and pliable state of a child's head in parturition, the bones of the cranium having no sutures at that time, was such,——that by force of the woman's efforts, which, in strong labour-pains, was equal, upon an average, to a weight of 470 pounds averdupois acting perpendicularly upon it;——it so happened that, in 49 instances out of 50, the said head was compressed and moulded into the shape of an oblong conical piece of dough, such as a pastry-cook generally rolls up in order to make a pye of.——Good God! cried my father, what havock and destruction must this make in the infinitely fine and tender texture of the cerebellum!——Or if there is such a juice as *Borri* pretends,——is it not enough to make the clearest liquor in the world both feculent and mothery?

But how great was his apprehension, when he farther understood, that this force acting upon the very vertex of the head, not only injured the brain itself or cerebrum,—but that it necessarily squeez'd and propell'd the cerebrum towards the cerebellum, which was the immediate seat of the understanding.——Angels and Ministers of grace defend us! cried my father,—can any soul withstand this shock?—No wonder the intellectual web is so rent and tatter'd as we see it; and that so many of our best heads are

---

* The author is here twice mistaken;——for *Lithopædus* should be wrote thus, *Lithopædii Senonensis Icon*. The second mistake is, that this *Lithopædus* is not an author, but a drawing of a petrified child. The account of this, published by *Albosius*, 1580, may be seen at the end of *Cordæus's* works in *Spachius*. Mr. *Tristram Shandy* has been led into this error, either from seeing *Lithopædus's* name of late in a catalogue of learned writers in Dr.———, or by mistaking *Lithopædus* for *Trinecavellius*,——from the too great similitude of the names.

no better than a puzzled skein of silk,—all perplexity,—all confusion within side.

But when my father read on, and was let into the secret, that when a child was turn'd topsy-turvy, which was easy for an operator to do, and was extracted by the feet;—that instead of the cerebrum being propell'd towards the cerebellum, the cerebellum, on the contrary, was propell'd simply towards the cerebrum where it could do no manner of hurt:——By heavens! cried he, the world is in a conspiracy to drive out what little wit God has given us,—and the professors of the obstetrick art are listed into the same conspiracy.—What is it to me which end of my son comes foremost into the world, provided all goes right after, and his cerebellum escapes uncrushed?

It is the nature of an hypothesis, when once a man has conceived it, that it assimilates every thing to itself, as proper nourishment; and, from the first moment of your begetting it, it generally grows the stronger by every thing you see, hear, read, or understand. This is of great use.

When my father was gone with this about a month, there was scarce a phænomenon of stupidity or of genius, which he could not readily solve by it;—it accounted for the eldest son being the greatest blockhead in the family.—Poor Devil, he would say,—he made way for the capacity of his younger brothers.—It unriddled the observation of drivellers and monstrous heads,—shewing, *a priori*, it could not be otherwise,—unless * * * * I don't know what. It wonderfully explain'd and accounted for the acumen of the *Asiatick* genius, and that sprightlier turn, and a more penetrating intuition of minds, in warmer climates; not from the loose and common-place solution of a clearer sky, and a more perpetual sun-shine, &c.—which, for aught he knew, might as well rarify and dilute the faculties of the soul into nothing, by one extreme,—as they are condensed in colder climates by the other;—but he trac'd the affair up to its spring-head;—shew'd that, in warmer climates, nature had laid a lighter tax upon the fairest parts of the creation;—their pleasures more;—the necessity of their pains less, insomuch that the pressure and resistance upon the vertex was so slight, that the whole organization of the cerebellum was preserved;—nay, he did not believe, in natural births, that so much as a single thread of the net-work was broke or displaced,—so that the soul might just act as she liked.

When my father had got so far,—what a blaze of light did the accounts of the *Cæsarean* section, and of the towering geniuses who had come safe into the world by it, cast upon this hypothesis? Here you see, he would say, there was no injury done to the sensorium;—no pressure of the head against the pelvis;—no propulsion of the cerebrum towards the cerebellum, either by the *os pubis* on this side, or the *os coxcygis* on that;——and, pray, what were the happy consequences? Why, Sir, your *Julius Cæsar*, who gave the operation a name;—and your *Hermes Trismegistus*, who was born so before ever the operation had a name;—your *Scipio Africanus;* your *Manlius Torquatus;* our *Edward* the sixth, —who, had he lived, would have done the same honour to the hypothesis:—These, and many more, who figur'd high in the annals of fame,—all came *side-way*, Sir, into the world.

This incision of the *abdomen* and *uterus*, ran for six weeks together in my father's head;—he had read, and was satisfied, that wounds in the *epigastrium*, and those in the *matrix*, were not mortal;—so that the belly of the mother might be opened extremely well to give a passage to the child.—He mentioned the thing one afternoon to my mother,—merely as a matter of fact;—but seeing her turn as pale as ashes at the very mention of it, as much as the operation flattered his hopes,—he thought it as well to say no more of it,—contenting himself with admiring—what he thought was to no purpose to propose.

This was my father Mr. *Shandy*'s hypothesis; concerning which I have only to add, that my brother *Bobby* did as great honour to it (whatever he did to the family) as any one of the great heroes we spoke of:—For happening not only to be christen'd, as I told you, but to be born too, when my father was at *Epsom*,——being moreover my mother's *first* child,—coming into the world with his head *foremost*,—and turning out afterwards a lad of wonderful slow parts,—my father spelt all these together into his opinion; and as he had failed at one end,—he was determined to try the other.

This was not to be expected from one of the sisterhood, who are not easily to be put out of their way,—and was therefore one of my father's great reasons in favour of a man of science, whom he could better deal with.

Of all men in the world, Dr. *Slop* was the fittest for my father's purpose;—for tho' his new-invented forceps was the armour he had proved, and what he maintained, to be the safest instrument of deliverance,—yet, it seems, he had scattered a word or two in his book, in favour of the very thing which ran in my father's fancy;—tho' not with a view to the soul's good in extracting by the feet, as was my father's system,—but for reasons merely obstetrical.

This will account for the coalition betwixt my father and Dr. *Slop*, in the ensuing discourse, which went a little hard against my uncle *Toby*.—In what manner a plain man, with nothing but common sense, could bear up against two such allies in science,—is hard to conceive.—You may conjecture upon it, if you please, —and whilst your imagination is in motion, you may encourage it to go on, and discover by what causes and effects in nature it could come to pass, that my uncle *Toby* got his modesty by the wound he received upon his groin.—You may raise a system to account for the loss of my nose by marriage articles,—and shew the world how it could happen, that I should have the misfortune to be called TRISTRAM, in opposition to my father's hypothesis, and the wish of the whole family, God-fathers and God-mothers not excepted.—These, with fifty other points left yet unravelled, you may endeavour to solve if you have time;—but I tell you beforehand it will be in vain,—for not the sage *Alquise*, the magician in Don *Belianis* of *Greece*, nor the no less famous *Urganda*, the sorceress his wife, (were they alive) could pretend to come within a league of the truth.

The reader will be content to wait for a full explanation of these matters till the next year,—when a series of things will be laid open which he little expects.

END of the SECOND VOLUME.

VOLUME III

Multitudinis imperitæ non formido judicia; meis tamen, rogo, parcant opusculis——in quibus fuit propositi semper, u jocis ad seria, a seriis vicissim ad jocos transire.

JOAN. SARESBERIENSIS,
Episcopus Lugdun.

CHAPTER I

—"I WISH, Dr. *Slop*," quoth my uncle *Toby* (repeating his wish for Dr. *Slop* a second time, and with a degree of more zeal and earnestness in his manner of wishing, than he had wished it at first*)——"*I wish*, Dr. *Slop*," quoth my uncle *Toby*, "*you had seen what prodigious armies we had in Flanders*."

My uncle *Toby*'s wish did Dr. *Slop* a disservice which his heart never intended any man,——Sir, it confounded him—and thereby putting his ideas first into confusion, and then to flight, he could not rally them again for the soul of him.

In all disputes,——male or female,——whether for honour, for profit or for love,—it makes no difference in the case;—nothing is more dangerous, madam, than a wish coming sideways in this unexpected manner upon a man: the safest way in general to take off the force of the wish, is, for the party wished at, instantly to get up upon his legs—and wish the *wisher* something in return, of pretty near the same value,——so balancing the account upon the spot, you stand as you were—nay sometimes gain the advantage of the attack by it.

This will be fully illustrated to the world in my chapter of wishes.——

Dr. *Slop* did not understand the nature of this defence;——he was puzzled with it, and it put an entire stop to the dispute for four minutes and a half;——five had been fatal to it:—my father saw the danger——the dispute was one of the most interesting disputes in the world, "Whether the child of his prayers and endeavours should be born without a head or with one:"—— he waited to the last moment to allow Dr. *Slop*, in whose behalf the wish was made, his right of returning it; but perceiving, I say, that he was confounded, and continued looking with that perplexed vacuity of eye which puzzled souls generally stare with, ——first in my uncle *Toby*'s face——then in his——then up—— then down——then east——east and by east, and so on,—— coasting it along by the plinth of the wainscot till he had got to the opposite point of the compass,—and that he had actually begun to count the brass nails upon the arm of his chair——my father thought there was no time to be lost with my uncle *Toby*, so took up the discourse as follows.

* Vid. Vol. II, p. 136.

[146]

CHAPTER II

—"WHAT prodigious armies you had in *Flanders*!"——
Brother *Toby*, replied my father, taking his wig
from off his head with his right hand, and with his
left pulling out a striped *India* handkerchief from his right coat
pocket, in order to rub his head, as he argued the point with my
uncle *Toby*.——

——Now, in this I think my father was much to blame; and
I will give you my reasons for it.

Matters of no more seeming consequence in themselves than,
"*Whether my father should have taken off his wig with his right
hand or with his left*,"——have divided the greatest kingdoms,
and made the crowns of the monarchs who governed them, to
totter upon their heads.—But need I tell you, Sir, that the circumstances with which every thing in this world is begirt, give
every thing in this world its size and shape;——and by tightening
it, or relaxing it, this way or that, make the thing to be, what it is
—great—little—good—bad——indifferent or not indifferent,
just as the case happens.

As my father's *India* handkerchief was in his right coat pocket,
he should by no means have suffered his right hand to have got
engaged: on the contrary, instead of taking off his wig with it, as
he did, he ought to have committed that entirely to the left; and
then, when the natural exigency my father was under of rubbing
his head, call'd out for his handkerchief, he would have had
nothing in the world to have done, but to have put his right hand
into his right coat pocket and taken it out;—which he might have
done without any violence, or the least ungraceful twist in any
one tendon or muscle of his whole body.

In this case, (unless indeed, my father had been resolved to
make a fool of himself by holding the wig stiff in his left hand—
or by making some nonsensical angle or other at his elbow joint,
or armpit)—his whole attitude had been easy—natural—unforced:
Reynolds himself, as great and gracefully as he paints, might have
painted him as he sat.

Now, as my father managed this matter,——consider what
a devil of a figure my father made of himself.

—In the latter end of Queen *Anne*'s reign, and in the beginning
of the reign of King *George* the first—"*Coat pockets were cut
very low down in the skirt.*"——I need say no more——the

father of mischief, had he been hammering at it a month, could not have contrived a worse fashion for one in my father's situation.

CHAPTER III

I T WAS not an easy matter in any king's reign, (unless you were as lean a subject as myself) to have forced your hand diagonally, quite across your whole body, so as to gain the bottom of your opposite coat-pocket.—In the year, one thousand seven hundred and eighteen, when this happened, it was extremely difficult; so that when my uncle *Toby* discovered the transverse zig-zaggery of my father's approaches towards it, it instantly brought into his mind those he had done duty in, before the gate of St. *Nicolas*;——the idea of which drew off his attention so entirely from the subject in debate, that he had got his right hand to the bell to ring up *Trim*, to go and fetch his map of *Namur*, and his compasses and sector along with it, to measure the returning angles of the traverses of that attack,—but particularly of that one, where he received his wound upon his groin.

My father knit his brows, and as he knit them, all the blood in his body seemed to rush up into his face——my uncle *Toby* dismounted immediately.

—I did not apprehend your uncle *Toby* was o' horseback.——

CHAPTER IV

A MAN'S body and his mind, with the utmost reverence to both I speak it, are exactly like a jerkin, and a jerkin's lining;—rumple the one—you rumple the other. There is one certain exception however in this case, and that is, when you are so fortunate a fellow, as to have had your jerkin made of a gum-taffeta, and the body-lining to it, of a sarcenet or thin persian.

Zeno, Cleanthes, Diogenes Babylonius, Dyonisius Heracleotes, Antipater, Panætius and *Possidonius* amongst the *Greeks*;— *Cato* and *Varro* and *Seneca* amongst the *Romans*;—*Pantenus* and *Clemens Alexandrinus* and *Montaigne* amongst the Christians; and a score and a half of good honest, unthinking, *Shandean* people as ever lived, whose names I can't recollect,—all pretended that their jerkins were made after this fashion,——you might have rumpled and crumpled, and doubled and creased, and fretted and fridged the outsides of them all to pieces;—in short, you might have played the very devil with them, and at the same time, not one of the insides of 'em would have been one button the worse, for all you had done to them.

I believe in my conscience that mine is made up somewhat after this sort:—for never poor jerkin has been tickled off, at such a rate as it has been these last nine months together,——and yet I declare the lining to it,——as far as I am a judge of the matter, it is not a three-penny piece the worse;—pell mell, helter skelter, ding dong, cut and thrust, back stroke and fore stroke, side way and long way, have they been trimming it for me:—had there been the least gumminess in my lining,——by heaven! it had all of it long ago been fray'd and fretted to a thread.

—You Messrs. the monthly Reviewers!——how could you cut and slash my jerkin as you did?——how did you know, but you would cut my lining too?

Heartily and from my soul, to the protection of that Being who will injure none of us, do I recommend you and your affairs,—— so God bless you;—only next month, if any one of you should gnash his teeth, and storm and rage at me, as some of you did last MAY, (in which I remember the weather was very hot)— don't be exasperated, if I pass it by again with good temper,—— being determined as long as I live or write (which in my case means the same thing) never to give the honest gentleman a worse word or a worse wish, than my uncle *Toby* gave the fly which buzz'd about his nose all *dinner time*,   —"Go,——go poor devil," quoth he, "——get thee gone,——why should I hurt thee? This world is surely wide enough to hold both thee and me."

CHAPTER V

ANY MAN, madam, reasoning upwards, and observing the prodigious suffusion of blood in my father's countenance, —by means of which, (as all the blood in his body seemed to rush up into his face, as I told you) he must have redden'd, pictorically and scientintically speaking, six whole tints and a half, if not a full octave above his natural colour:——any man, madam, but my uncle *Toby*, who had observed this, together with the violent knitting of my father's brows, and the extravagant contortion of his body during the whole affair,—would have concluded my father in a rage; and taking that for granted,——had he been a lover of such kind of concord as arises from two such instruments being put into exact tune,—he would instantly have skrew'd up his, to the same pitch; ——and then the devil and all had broke loose—the whole piece, madam, must have been played off like the sixth of Avison Scarlatti—*con furia*,—like mad. ——Grant me patience!——What has *con furia*,——*con strepito*, ——or any other hurlyburly word whatever to do with harmony?

Any man, I say, madam, but my uncle *Toby*, the benignity of whose heart interpreted every motion of the body in the kindest sense the motion would admit of, would have concluded my father angry and blamed him too. My uncle *Toby* blamed nothing but the taylor who cut the pocket-hole;——so sitting still, till my father had got his handkerchief out of it, and looking all the time up in his face with inexpressible good will—my father at length went on as follows.

CHAPTER VI

—"WHAT prodigious armies you had in *Flanders*!" ——Brother *Toby*, quoth my father, I do believe thee to be as honest a man, and with as good and as upright a heart as ever God created;——nor is it thy fault, if all the children which have been, may, can, shall, will or ought to be begotten, come with their heads foremost into the world:—but believe me, dear *Toby*, the accidents which unavoidably way-lay them, not only in the article of our begetting 'em,—though these in my opinion, are well worth considering,——but the dangers and difficulties our children are beset with, after they are got forth into the world, are enow,—little need is there to expose them to unnecessary ones in their passage to it.——Are these dangers, quoth my uncle *Toby*, laying his hand upon my father's knee, and looking up seriously in his face for an answer,——are these dangers greater now o' days, brother, than in times past? Brother *Toby*, answered my father, if a child was but fairly begot, and born alive, and healthy, and the mother did well after it,—— our forefathers never looked further.——My uncle *Toby* instantly withdrew his hand from off my father's knee, reclined his body gently back in his chair, raised his head till he could just see the cornish of the room, and then directing the buccinatory muscles along his cheeks, and the orbicular muscles around his lips to do their duty—he whistled *Lillabullero*.

CHAPTER VII

WHILST my uncle *Toby* was whistling Lillabullero to my father,—Dr. *Slop* was stamping, and cursing and damning at *Obadiah* at a most dreadful rate;——it would have done your heart good, and cured you, Sir, for ever, of the vile sin of swearing to have heard him.—I am determined therefore to relate the whole affair to you.

When Dr. *Slop*'s maid delivered the green bays bag, with her master's instruments in it, to *Obadiah*, she very sensibly exhorted him to put his head and one arm through the strings, and ride with it slung across his body: so undoing the bow-knot, to lengthen the strings for him, without any more ado, she helped him on with it. However, as this, in some measure, unguarded the mouth of the bag, lest any thing should bolt out in galloping back at the speed *Obadiah* threatened, they consulted to take it off again; and in the great care and caution of their hearts, they had taken the two strings and tied them close (pursing up the mouth of the bag first) with half a dozen hard knots, each of which, *Obadiah*, to make all safe, had twitched and drawn together with all the strength of his body.

This answered all that *Obadiah* and the maid intended; but was no remedy against some evils which neither he or she foresaw. The instruments, it seems, as tight as the bag was tied above, had so much room to play in it, towards the bottom, (the shape of the bag being conical) that *Obadiah* could not make a trot of it, but with such a terrible jingle, what with the *tire-tête, forceps* and *squirt*, as would have been enough, had *Hymen* been taking a jaunt that way, to have frightened him out of the country; but when *Obadiah* accelerated this motion, and from a plain trot assayed to prick his coach-horse into a full gallop—by heaven! Sir,—the jingle was incredible.

As *Obadiah* had a wife and three children—the turpitude of fornication, and the many other political ill consequences of this jingling, never once entered his brain,——he had however his objection, which came home to himself, and weighed with him, as it has oft-times done with the greatest patriots.——"*The poor fellow, Sir, was not able to hear himself whistle.*"

CHAPTER VIII

AS *Obadiah* loved wind musick preferably to all the instrumental musick he carried with him,—he very considerately set his imagination to work, to contrive and to invent by what means he should put himself in a condition of enjoying it.

In all distresses (except musical) where small cords are wanted, ——nothing is so apt to enter a man's head, as his hat-band:——the philosophy of this is so near the surface—I scorn to enter into it.

As *Obadiah*'s was a mix'd case,——mark, Sirs,—I say, a mix'd case; for it was obstretical,—*scrip*-tical,—squirtical, papistical,—and as far as the coach-horse was concerned in it,—caball-istical—and only partly musical;—*Obadiah* made no scruple of availing himself of the first expedient which offered;—so taking hold of the bag and instruments, and griping them hard together with one hand, and with the finger and thumb of the other, putting the end of the hat-band betwixt his teeth, and then slipping his hand down to the middle of it,—he tied and cross-tied them all fast together from one end to the other (as you would cord a trunk) with such a multiplicity of round-abouts and intricate cross turns, with a hard knot at every intersection or point where the strings met,—that Dr. *Slop* must have had three fifths of *Job*'s patience at least to have unloosed them.—I think in my conscience, that had NATURE been in one of her nimble moods, and in humour for such a contest——and she and Dr. *Slop* both fairly started together—there is no man living who had seen the bag with all that *Obadiah* had done to it,—and known likewise, the great speed the goddess can make when she thinks proper, who would have had the least doubt remaining in his mind——which of the two would have carried off the prize. My mother, madam, had been delivered sooner than the green bag infallibly—at least by twenty *knots*.——Sport of small accidents, *Tristram Shandy*! that thou art, and ever will be! had that trial been made for thee, and it was fifty to one but it had,——thy affairs had not been so depress'd—(at least by the depression of thy nose) as they have been; nor had the fortunes of thy house and the occasions of making them, which have so often presented themselves in the course of thy life, to thee, been so often, so vexatiously, so tamely, so irrecoverably abandoned—as thou hast been forced to leave them!—but 'tis over,—all but the account of 'em, which cannot be given to the curious till I am got out into the world.

CHAPTER IX

GREAT wits jump: for the moment Dr. *Slop* cast his eyes upon his bag (which he had not done till the dispute with my uncle *Toby* about midwifery put him in mind of it)—the very same thought occurred.——'Tis God's mercy, quoth he, (to himself) that Mrs. *Shandy* has had so bad a time of it,—else she might have been brought to bed seven times told, before one half of these knots could have got untied.——But here, you must distinguish——the thought floated only in Dr. *Slop*'s mind, without sail or ballast to it, as a simple proposition; millions of which, as your worship knows, are every day swimming quietly in the middle of the thin juice of a man's understanding, without being carried backwards or forwards, till some little gusts of passion or interest drive them to one side.

A sudden trampling in the room above, near my mother's bed, did the proposition the very service I am speaking of. By all that's unfortunate, quoth Dr. *Slop*, unless I make haste, the thing will actually befall me as it is.

CHAPTER X

IN THE case of *knots*,——by which, in the first place, I would not be understood to mean slip-knots,——because in the course of my life and opinions,——my opinions concerning them will come in more properly when I mention the catastrophe of my great uncle Mr. *Hammond Shandy*,——a little man,——but of high fancy:——he rushed into the duke of *Monmouth*'s affair:——nor, secondly, in this place, do I mean that particular species of knots, called bow-knots;——there is so little address, or skill, or patience, required in the unloosing them, that they are below my giving any opinion at all about them.——But by the knots I am speaking of, may it please your reverences to believe, that I mean good, honest, devilish tight, hard knots, made *bona fide*, as *Obadiah* made his;—in which there is no quibbling provision made by the duplication and return of the two ends of the strings through the annulus or noose made by the second *implication* of them—to get them slipp'd and undone by————I hope you apprehend me.

In the case of these *knots* then, and of the several obstructions, which, may it please your reverences, such knots cast in our way in getting through life——every hasty man can whip out his penknife and cut through them.——'Tis wrong. Believe me, Sirs, the most virtuous way, and which both reason and conscience dictate —is to take our teeth or our fingers to them.——Dr. *Slop* had lost his teeth—his favourite instrument, by extracting in a wrong direction, or by some misapplication of it, unfortunately slipping, he had formerly in a hard labour, knock'd out three of the best of them, with the handle of it:—he tried his fingers—alas! the nails of his fingers and thumbs were cut close.—The deuce take it! I can make nothing of it either way, cried Dr. *Slop*.—The trampling over head near my mother's bed side increased.—Pox take the fellow! I shall never get the knots untied as long as I live. —My mother gave a groan—Lend me your penknife—I must e'en cut the knots at last——pugh!—psha!—Lord! I have cut my thumb quite across to the very bone——curse the fellow ——if there was not another man midwife within fifty miles—I am undone for this bout——I wish the scoundrel hang'd——I wish he was shot——I wish all the devils in hell had him for a blockhead——

My father had a great respect for *Obadiah*, and could not bear to hear him disposed of in such a manner——he had moreover some little respect for himself——and could as ill bear with the indignity offer'd to himself in it.

Had Dr. *Slop* cut any part about him, but his thumb——my father had pass'd it by——his prudence had triumphed: as it was, he was determined to have his revenge.

Small curses, Dr. *Slop*, upon great occasions, quoth my father, (condoling with him first upon the accident) are but so much waste of our strength and soul's health to no manner of purpose. —I own it, replied Dr. *Slop*.— They are like sparrow shot, quoth

my uncle *Toby*, (suspending his whistling) fired against a bastion.
——They serve, continued my father, to stir the humours—but
carry off none of their acrimony:—for my own part, I seldom
swear or curse at all——I hold it bad—but if I fall into it, by surprize, I generally retain so much presence of mind (right, quoth
my uncle *Toby*) as to make it answer my purpose—that is, I swear
on, till I find myself easy. A wise and a just man however would
always endeavour to proportion the vent given to these humours,
not only to the degree of them stirring within himself—but to the
size and ill intent of the offence upon which they are to fall.——
"*Injuries come only from the heart*,"——quoth my uncle *Toby*.
For this reason, continued my father, with the most *Cervantick*
gravity, I have the greatest veneration in the world for that gentleman, who, in distrust of his own discretion in this point, sat down
and composed (that is at his leisure) fit forms of swearing suitable
to all cases, from the lowest to the highest provocations which
could possibly happen to him,—which forms being well consider'd
by him, and such moreover as he could stand to, he kept them
ever by him on the chimney piece, within his reach, ready for
use.——I never apprehended, replied Dr. *Slop*, that such a thing
was ever thought of,——much less executed. I beg your pardon—
answered my father; I was reading, though not using, one of them
to my brother *Toby* this morning, whilst he pour'd out the tea—
'tis here upon the shelf over my head;——but if I remember right,
'tis too violent for a cut of the thumb.——Not at all, quoth Dr.
Slop—the devil take the fellow.—Then answered my father, 'Tis
much at your service, Dr. *Slop*——on condition you will read it
aloud;——so rising up and reaching down a form of excommunication of the church of *Rome*, a copy of which, my father (who
was curious in his collections) had procured out of the leger-book
of the church of *Rochester*, writ by ERNULPHUS the bishop—with
a most affected seriousness of look and voice, which might have
cajoled ERNULPHUS himself,—he put it into Dr. *Slop*'s hands.—
Dr. *Slop* wrapt his thumb up in the corner of his handkerchief,
and with a wry face, though without any suspicion, read aloud,
as follows,—my uncle *Toby* whistling *Lillabullero*, as loud as he
could, all the time.

Textus de Ecclesiâ Roffensi, per Ernulfum Episcopum.

CAP. XXV

EXCOMMUNICATIO

EX auctoritate Dei omnipotentis, Patris, et Filij, et Spiritus Sancti, et sanctorum canonum, sanctæque et intemeratæ Virginis Dei genetricis Mariæ,

———Atque omnium cœlestium virtutum, angelorum, archangelorum, thronorum, dominationum, potestatuum, cherubin ac seraphin, & sanctorum patriarchum, prophetarum, & omnium apostolorum et evangelistarum, & sanctorum innocentum, qui in conspectu Agni soli digni inventi sunt canticum cantare novum, et sanctorum martyrum, et sanctorum confessorum, et sanctarum virginum, atque omnium simul sanctorum et electorum Dei,—Excommunicamus, et

   vel os s *vel* os   s
anathematizamus hunc furem, vel hunc malefactorem, N. N. et a liminibus sanctæ Dei ecclesiæ sequestramus et æternis suppliciis

  vel i   n
excruciandus, mancipetur, cum Dathan et Abiram, et cum his qui dixerunt Domino Deo, Recede à nobis, scientiam viarum tuarum nolumus: et sicut aquâ ignis extinguitur, sic extinguatur

  vel eorum   n
lucerna ejus in secula seculorum nisi respuerit, et ad satisfac-

   n
tionem venerit. Amen.

    os
 Maledicat illum Deus Pater qui hominem creavit. Maledicat

 os   os
illum Dei Filius qui pro homine passus est. Maledicat illum

                    os
Spiritus Sanctus qui in baptismo effusus est. Maledicat illum

As the genuineness of the consultation of the *Sorbonne* upon the question of baptism, was doubted by some, and denied by others,——'twas thought proper to print the original of this excommunication; for the copy of which Mr. *Shandy* returns thanks to the chapter clerk of the dean and chapter of *Rochester*.

CHAPTER XI

"BY THE authority of God Almighty, the Father, Son, and Holy Ghost, and of the holy canons, and of the undefiled Virgin *Mary*, mother and patroness of our Saviour." I think there is no necessity, quoth Dr. *Slop*, dropping the paper down to his knee, and addressing himself to my father,——as you have read it over, Sir, so lately, to read it aloud;—and as Captain *Shandy* seems to have no great inclination to hear it,——I may as well read it to myself. That's contrary to treaty, replied my father,—besides, there is something so whimsical, especially in the latter part of it, I should grieve to lose the pleasure of a second reading. Dr. *Slop* did not altogether like it,—but my uncle *Toby* offering at that instant to give over whistling, and read it himself to them;——Dr. *Slop* thought he might as well read it under the cover of my uncle *Toby*'s whistling,—as suffer my uncle *Toby* to read it alone;—so raising up the paper to his face, and holding it quite parallel to it, in order to hide his chagrin,— he read it aloud as follows,——my uncle *Toby* whistling Lillabullero, though not quite so loud as before.

"By the authority of God Almighty, the Father, Son, and Holy Ghost, and of the undefiled Virgin *Mary*, mother and patroness of our Saviour, and of all the celestial virtues, angels, archangels, thrones, dominions, powers, cherubins and seraphins, and of all the holy patriarchs, prophets, and of all the apostles and evangelists, and of the holy innocents, who in the sight of the holy Lamb, are found worthy to sing the new song of the holy martyrs and holy confessors, and of the holy virgins, and of all the saints together, with the holy and elect of God.——May he," (*Obadiah*) "be damn'd," (for tying these knots.)——"We excommunicate, and anathematise him, and from the thresholds of the holy church of God Almighty we sequester him, that he may be tormented, disposed and delivered over with *Dathan* and *Abiram*, and with those who say unto the Lord God, Depart from us, we desire none of thy ways. And as fire is quenched with water, so let the light of him be put out for evermore, unless it shall repent him" (*Obadiah*, of the knots which he has tied) "and make satisfaction" (for them.) Amen.

"May the Father who created man, curse him.—May the Son who suffered for us, curse him.——May the Holy Ghost who was given to us in baptism, curse him" (*Obadiah*.)—"May the holy

[157]

sancta crux, quam Christus pro nostrâ salute hostem triumphans, ascendit.

os
Maledicat illum sancta Dei genetrix et perpetua Virgo Maria.

os
Maledicat illum sanctus Michael, animarum susceptor sacrarum.

os
Maledicant illum omnes angeli et archangeli, principatus et potestates, omnisque militia cœlestis.

os
Maledicat illum patriarcharum et prophetarum laudabilis numerus. Maledicat illum sanctus Johannes præcursor et Baptista Christi, et sanctus Petrus, et sanctus Paulus, atque sanctus Andreas, omnesque Christi apostoli, simul et cæteri discipuli, quatuor quoque evangelistæ, qui sua prædicatione mundum
os
universum converterunt. Maledicat illum cuneus martyrum et confessorum mirificus, qui Deo bonis operibus placitus inventus est.

os
Maledicant illum sacrarum virginum chori, quæ mundi vana causa honoris Christi respuenda contempserunt. Maledicant
os
illum omnes sancti qui ab initio mundi usque in finem seculi Deo dilecti inveniuntur.

os
Maledicant illum cœli et terra, et omnia sancta in eis manentia.
i   n   n
Maledictus sit ubicunque fuerit, sive in domo, sive in agro, sive in viâ, sive in semitâ, sive in silvâ, sive in aquâ, sive in ecclesiâ.
i   n
Maledictus sit vivendo, moriendo,———   ——   ——   ——
—   ——   ——   ——   —— manducando, bibendo, esuriendo, sitiendo, jejunando, dormitando, dormiendo, vigilando, ambulando, stando, sedendo, jacendo, operando, quiescendo, mingendo, cacando, flebotomando.
i   n
Maledictus sit in totis viribus corporis.
i   n
Maledictus sit intus et exterius.
i   n   n   i
Maledictus sit in capillis; maledictus sit in cerebro. Maledictus
n
sit in vertice, in temporibus, in fronte, in auriculis, in superciliis, in òculis, in genis, in maxillis, in naribus, in dentibus, mordacibus, in labris sive molibus, in labiis, in guttere, in humeris, in harnis,

cross which Christ, for our salvation triumphing over his enemies, ascended,—curse him.

"May the holy and eternal *Virgin Mary*, mother of God, curse him.—May St. *Michael* the advocate of holy souls, curse him.—May all the angels and archangels, principalities and powers, and all the heavenly armies, curse him." [Our armies swore terribly in *Flanders*, cried my uncle *Toby*,—but nothing to this.—For my own part, I could not have a heart to curse my dog so.]

"May St. John the præ-cursor, and St. John the Baptist, and St. Peter and St. Paul, and St. Andrew, and all other Christ's apostles, together curse him. And may the rest of his disciples and four evangelists, who by their preaching converted the universal world,—and may the holy and wonderful company of martyrs and confessors, who by their holy works are found pleasing to God Almighty, curse him" (*Obadiah*.)

"May the holy choir of the holy virgins, who for the honour of Christ have despised the things of the world, damn him.—May all the saints who from the beginning of the world to everlasting ages are found to be beloved of God, damn him.—May the heavens and earth, and all the holy things remaining therein, damn him," (*Obadiah*) "or her," (or whoever else had a hand in tying these knots.)

"May he" (*Obadiah*) "be damn'd wherever he be,—whether in the house or the stables, the garden or the field, or the highway, or in the path, or in the wood, or in the water, or in the church. —May he be cursed in living, in dying." [Here my uncle *Toby* taking the advantage of a *minim* in the second barr of his tune, kept whistling one continual note to the end of the sentence—— Dr. *Slop* with his division of curses moving under him, like a running bass all the way.] "May he be cursed in eating and drinking, in being hungry, in being thirsty, in fasting, in sleeping, in slumbering, in walking, in standing, in sitting, in lying, in working, in resting, in pissing, in shitting, and in blood-letting.

"May he" (*Obadiah*) "be cursed in all the faculties of his body!

"May he be cursed inwardly and outwardly!—May he be cursed in the hair of his head!—May he be cursed in his brains, and in his vertex," (that is a sad curse, quoth my father) "in his temples, in his forehead, in his ears, in his eye-brows, in his cheeks, in his jaw-bones, in his nostrils, in his foreteeth and grinders, in his lips, in his throat, in his shoulders, in his wrists, in his arms, in his hands, in his fingers!

in brachiis, in manubus, in digitis, in pectore, in corde, et in omnibus interioribus stomacho tenus, in renibus, in inguinibus, in femore, in genitalibus, in coxis, in genubus, in cruribus, in pedibus, et in unguibus.

Maledictus sit in totis compagibus membrorum, a vertice capitis, usque ad plantam pedis——non sit in eo sanitas.

Maledicat illum Christus Filius Dei vivi toto suæ majestatis imperio——

——et insurgat adversus illum cœlum cum omnibus virtutibus quæ in eo moventur ad *damnandum* eum, nisi penituerit et ad satisfactionem venerit. Amen. Fiat, fiat. Amen.

"May he be damn'd in his mouth, in his breast, in his heart and purtenance, down to the very stomach.

"May he be cursed in his reins, and in his groin," (God in heaven forbid, quoth my uncle *Toby*)—"in his thighs, in his genitals," (my father shook his head) " and in his hips, and in his knees, his legs, and feet, and toe-nails.

"May he be cursed in all the joints and articulations of his members, from the top of his head to the soal of his foot, may there be no soundness in him.

"May the Son of the living God, with all the glory of his Majesty"——[Here my uncle *Toby*, throwing back his head, gave a monstrous, long, loud Whew—w—w—— something betwixt the interjectional whistle of *Hey day*! and the word itself.——

—By the golden beard of *Jupiter*—(and of *Juno*, if her majesty wore one)—and by the beards of the rest of your heathen worships, which by the bye was no small number, since what with the beards of your celestial gods, and gods aerial and acquatick,—to say nothing of the beards of town-gods and country-gods, or of the celestial goddesses your wives, or of the infernal goddesses your whores and concubines, (that is in case they wore 'em)——all which beards, as *Varro* tells me, upon his word and honour, when mustered up together, made no less than thirty thousand effective beards upon the pagan establishment;——every beard of which claimed the rights and privileges of being stroked and sworn by,— by all these beards together then,——I vow and protest, that of the two bad cassocks I am worth in the world, I would have given the better of them, as freely as ever *Cid Hamet* offered his,——only to have stood by, and heard my uncle *Toby*'s accompanyment.]

——"Curse him,"—— continued Dr. *Slop*,——"and may heaven with all the powers which move therein, rise up against him, curse and damn him" (*Obadiah*) "unless he repent and make satisfaction. Amen. So be it,—so be it. Amen."

I declare, quoth my uncle *Toby*, my heart would not let me curse the devil himself with so much bitterness.——He is the father of curses, replied Dr. *Slop*.——So am not I, replied my uncle.——But he is cursed, and damn'd already, to all eternity, ——replied Dr. *Slop*.

I am sorry for it, quoth my uncle *Toby*.

Dr. *Slop* drew up his mouth, and was just beginning to return my uncle *Toby* the compliment of his Whu—u—u——or interjectional whistle,——when the door hastily opening in the next chapter but one——put an end to the affair.

[161]

CHAPTER XII

NOW don't let us give ourselves a parcel of airs, and pretend that the oaths we make free with in this land of liberty of ours are our own; and because we have the spirit to swear them,——imagine that we have had the wit to invent them too.

I'll undertake this moment to prove it to any man in the world, except to a connoisseur;——though I declare I object only to a connoisseur in swearing,—as I would do to a connoisseur in painting, &c. &c. the whole set of 'em are so hung round and *befetish'd* with the bobs and trinkets of criticism,——or to drop my metaphor, which by the bye is a pity,——for I have fetch'd it as far as from the coast of *Guinea*;——their heads, Sir, are stuck so full of rules and compasses, and have that eternal propensity to apply them upon all occasions, that a work of genius had better go to the devil at once, than stand to be prick'd and tortured to death by 'em.

——And how did *Garrick* speak the soliloquy last night?—Oh, against all rule, my Lord,—most ungrammatically! betwixt the substantive and the adjective, which should agree together in *number*, *case* and *gender*, he made a breach thus,—stopping, as if the point wanted settling;——and betwixt the nominative case, which your lordship knows should govern the verb, he suspended his voice in the epilogue a dozen times, three seconds and three fifths by a stop-watch, my Lord, each time.——Admirable grammarian!——But in suspending his voice——was the sense suspended likewise? Did no expression of attitude or countenance fill up the chasm?—Was the eye silent? Did you narrowly look?—I look'd only at the stop-watch, my Lord.——Excellent observer!

And what of this new book the whole world makes such a rout about?—Oh! 'tis out of all plumb, my Lord,——quite an irregular thing!—not one of the angles at the four corners was a right angle.—I had my rule and compasses, &c. my Lord, in my pocket.——Excellent critic!

—And for the epick poem, your lordship bid me look at;—upon taking the length, breadth, height, and depth of it, and trying them at home upon an exact scale of *Bossu*'s,—'tis out, my Lord, in every one of its dimensions.——Admirable connoisseur!

—And did you step in, to take a look at the grand picture, in your way back.——'Tis a melancholy daub! my Lord; not one

principle of the *pyramid* in any one group!——and what a price!
——for there is nothing of the colouring of *Titian*,——the expression of *Rubens*,——the grace of *Raphael*,——the purity of *Dominichino*,—the *corregiescity* of *Corregio*,—the learning of *Poussin*,—the airs of *Guido*,—the taste of the *Carrachis*,—or the grand contour of *Angelo*.——Grant me patience, just heaven!——Of all the cants which are canted in this canting world,——though the cant of hypocrites may be the worst,—the cant of criticism is the most tormenting!

I would go fifty miles on foot, for I have not a horse worth riding on, to kiss the hand of that man whose generous heart will give up the reins of his imagination into his author's hands,——be pleased he knows not why, and cares not wherefore.

Great *Apollo*! if thou art in a giving humour,——give me,——I ask no more, but one stroke of native humour, with a single spark of thy own fire along with it,——and send *Mercury*, with the *rules and compasses*, if he can be spared, with my compliments to——no matter.

Now to any one else I will undertake to prove, that all the oaths and imprecations which we have been puffing off upon the world for these two hundred and fifty years last past as originals,——except St. *Paul*'s *thumb*,——God's *flesh and* God's *fish*, which were oaths monarchical, and, considering who made them, not much amiss; and as kings oaths, 'tis not much matter whether they were fish or flesh;——else, I say, there is not an oath, or at least a curse amongst them, which has not been copied over and over again out of *Ernulphus*, a thousand times: but, like all other copies, how infinitely short of the force and spirit of the original!—It is thought to be no bad oath,——and by itself passes very well——"G—d *damn you*."——Set it beside *Ernulphus's*—— "God Almighty the Father damn you,—God the Son damn you,—God the Holy Ghost damn you,"—you see 'tis nothing.——There is an orientality in his, we cannot rise up to: besides, he is more copious in his invention,——possess'd more of the excellencies of a swearer,——had such a thorough knowledge of the human frame, its membranes, nerves, ligaments, knittings of the joints, and articulations,—that when *Ernulphus* cursed,—no part escaped him.—'Tis true, there is something of a *hardness* in his manner,—and, as in *Michael Angelo*, a want of *grace*,——but then there is such a greatness of *gusto*!—

My father, who generally look'd upon every thing in a light very different from all mankind, would, after all, never allow this to be an original.——He consider'd rather *Ernulphus*'s anathema, as an institute of swearing, in which, as he suspected, upon the decline of *swearing* in some milder pontificate, *Ernulphus*, by order of the succeeding pope, had with great learning and diligence collected together all the laws of it;——for the same reason that *Justinian*, in the decline of the empire, had ordered his chancellor *Tribonian* to collect the *Roman* or civil laws all together into one code or digest,—lest, through the rust of time,—and the fatality of all things committed to oral tradition—they should be lost to the world for ever.

For this reason my father would oft-times affirm, there was not an oath, from the great and tremendous oath of *William* the Conqueror, (*By the splendour of God*) down to the lowest oath of a scavenger, (*Damn your eyes*) which was not to be found in *Ernulphus*.——In short, he would add,—I defy a man to swear *out* of it.

The hypothesis is, like most of my father's, singular and ingenious too;——nor have I any objection to it, but that it overturns my own.

CHAPTER XIII

—**B**LESS my soul!——my poor mistress is ready to faint,—— and her pains are gone,——and the drops are done,—— and the bottle of julap is broke,——and the nurse has cut her arm,——(and I, my thumb, cried Dr. *Slop*) and the child is where it was, continued *Susannah*,——and the midwife has fallen backwards upon the edge of the fender, and bruised her hip as black as your hat.——I'll look at it, quoth Dr. *Slop*.——There is no need of that, replied *Susannah*,——you had better look at my mistress,——but the midwife would gladly first give you an account how things are, so desires you would go up stairs and speak to her this moment.

Human nature is the same in all professions.

The midwife had just before been put over Dr. *Slop*'s head.— He had not digested it.—No, replied Dr. *Slop*, 'twould be full as proper, if the midwife came down to me.—I like subordination, quoth my uncle *Toby*,—and but for it, after the reduction of *Lisle*, I know not what might have become of the garrison of *Ghent*, in the mutiny for bread, in the year Ten.——Nor, replied Dr. *Slop*, (parodying my uncle *Toby*'s hobby-horsical reflection, though full as hobby-horsically himself)—do I know, Captain *Shandy*, what might have become of the garrison above stairs, in the mutiny and confusion I find all things are in at present, but for the subordination of fingers and thumbs to * * * * * * ——the application of which, Sir, under this accident of mine, comes in so *a propos*, that without it, the cut upon my thumb might have been felt by the *Shandy* family, as long as the *Shandy* family had a name.

CHAPTER XIV

LET US go back to the * * * * * *——in the last chapter. It is a singular stroke of eloquence (at least it was so, when eloquence flourished at *Athens* and *Rome*, and would be so now, did orators wear mantles) not to mention the name of a thing, when you had the thing about you, *in petto*, ready to produce, pop, in the place you want it. A scar, an axe, a sword, a pink'd-doublet, a rusty helmet, a pound and a half of pot-ashes in an urn, or a three-halfpenny pickle pot,——but above all, a tender infant royally accoutred.—Tho' if it was too young, and the oration as long as *Tully*'s second *Philippick*,——it must certainly have beshit the orator's mantle.——And then again, if too old,—it must have been unwieldy and incommodious to his action,—so as to make him lose by his child almost as much as he could gain by it.—Otherwise, when a state orator has hit the precise age to a minute,—hid his **BAMBINO** in his mantle so cunningly that no mortal could smell it,—and produced it so critically, that no soul could say, it came in by head and shoulders,——Oh, Sirs! it has done wonders.——It has open'd the sluices, and turn'd the brains, and shook the principles, and unhinged the politicks of half a nation.

These feats however are not to be done, except in those states and times, I say, where orators wore mantles,—and pretty large ones too, my brethren, with some twenty or five and twenty yards of good purple, superfine, marketable cloth in them,——with large flowing folds and doubles, and in a great stile of design. ————All which plainly shews, may it please your worships, that the decay of eloquence, and the little good service it does at present, both within and without doors, is owing to nothing else in the world, but short coats, and the disuse of *trunk-hose*.———— We can conceal nothing under ours, Madam, worth shewing.

CHAPTER XV

D R. *SLOP* was within an ace of being an exception to all this argumentation: for happening to have his green bays bag upon his knees, when he began to parody my uncle *Toby*,——'twas as good as the best mantle in the world to him: for which purpose, when he foresaw the sentence would end in his new invented *forceps*, he thrust his hand into the bag in order to have them ready to clap in, where your reverences took so much notice of the * * * * * *, which had he managed,—my uncle *Toby* had certainly been overthrown: the sentence and the argument in that case jumping closely in one point, so like the two lines which form the salient angle of a raveline,—Dr. *Slop* would never have given them up;——and my uncle *Toby* would as soon thought of flying, as taking them by force: but Dr. *Slop* fumbled so vilely in pulling them out, it took off the whole effect, and what was a ten times worse evil (for they seldom come alone in this life) in pulling out his *forceps*, his *forceps* unfortunately drew out the *squirt* along with it.

When a proposition can be taken in two senses,——'tis a law in disputation, That the respondent may reply to which of the two he pleases, or finds most convenient for him.——This threw the advantage of the argument quite on my uncle *Toby*'s side.—— "Good God!" cried my uncle *Toby*, "*are children brought into the world with a squirt?*"

CHAPTER XVI

-U PON my honour, Sir, you have tore every bit of the skin quite off the back of both my hands with your forceps, cried my uncle *Toby*,—and you have crush'd all my knuckles into the bargain with them, to a jelly. 'Tis your own fault, said Dr. *Slop*,——you should have clinch'd your two fists together into the form of a child's head, as I told you, and sat firm.——I did so, answered my uncle *Toby*,——Then the points of my forceps have not been sufficiently arm'd, or the rivet wants closing—or else the cut on my thumb has made me a little auk-ward,——or possibly—'Tis well, quoth my father, interrupting the detail of possibilities,——that the experiment was not first made upon my child's head piece.——It would not have been a cherry stone the worse, answered Dr. *Slop*. I maintain it, said my uncle *Toby*, it would have broke the cerebellum, (unless indeed the skull had been as hard as a granado) and turned it all into a perfect posset. Pshaw! replied Dr. *Slop*, a child's head is naturally as soft as the pap of an apple,——the sutures give way, ——and besides, I could have extracted by the feet after.——Not you, said she.—I rather wish you would begin that way, quoth my father.

Pray do, added my uncle *Toby*.

CHAPTER XVII

— AND PRAY, good woman, after all, will you take upon you to say, it may not be the child's hip, as well as the child's head?——'Tis most certainly the head, replied the midwife. Because, continued Dr. *Slop*, (turning to my father) as positive as these old ladies generally are,——'tis a point very difficult to know,—and yet of the greatest consequence to be known;——because, Sir, if the hip is mistaken for the head,— there is a possibility (if it is a boy) that the forceps *.

——What the possibility was, Dr. *Slop* whispered very low to my father, and then to my uncle *Toby*.——There is no such danger, continued he, with the head.—No, in truth, quoth my father,——but when your possibility has taken place at the hip, ——you may as well take off the head too.

——It is morally impossible the reader should understand this, ——'tis enough Dr. *Slop* understood it;——so taking the green bays bag in his hand, with the help of *Obadiah*'s pumps, he tripp'd pretty nimbly, for a man of his size, across the room to the door, ——and from the door was shown the way, by the good old midwife, to my mother's apartment.

CHAPTER XVIII

I T IS two hours, and ten minutes,—and no more,——cried my father, looking at his watch, since Dr. *Slop* and *Obadiah* arrived,——and I know not how it happens, brother *Toby*, ——but to my imagination it seems almost an age.

——Here——pray, Sir, take hold of my cap,—nay, take the bell along with it, and my pantoufles too.——

[167]

Now, Sir, they are all at your service; and I freely make you a present of 'em, on condition, you give me all your attention to this chapter.

Though my father said, "*he knew not how it happen'd,*"——yet he knew very well, how it happen'd;——and at the instant he spoke it, was pre-determined in his mind, to give my uncle *Toby* a clear account of the matter by a metaphysical dissertation upon the subject of *duration and its simple modes*, in order to shew my uncle *Toby*, by what mechanism and mensurations in the brain it came to pass, that the rapid succession of their ideas, and the eternal scampering of discourse from one thing to another, since Dr. *Slop* had come into the room, had lengthened out so short a period, to so inconceivable an extent.——"I know not how it happens,"——cried my father,——"but it seems an age."

—'Tis owing, entirely, quoth my uncle *Toby*, to the succession of our ideas.

My father, who had an itch in common with all philosophers, of reasoning upon every thing which happened, and accounting for it too,——proposed infinite pleasure to himself in this, of the succession of ideas, and had not the least apprehension of having it snatch'd out of his hands by my uncle *Toby*, who (honest man!) generally took every thing as it happened;——and who, of all men in the world, troubled his brain the least with abstruse thinking;—the ideas of time and space,——or how we came by those ideas,——or of what stuff they were made,—or whether they were born with us,——or we pick'd them up afterwards as we went along,—or whether we did it in frocks,—or not till we had got into breeches,—with a thousand other inquiries and disputes about INFINITY, PRESCIENCE, LIBERTY, NECESSITY, and so forth, upon whose desperate and unconquerable theories, so many fine heads have been turned and crack'd,—never did my uncle *Toby*'s the least injury at all; my father knew it,—and was no less surprised, than he was disappointed with my uncle's fortuitous solution.

Do you understand the theory of that affair? replied my father.

Not I, quoth my uncle.

——But you have some ideas, said my father, of what you talk about.——

No more than my horse, replied my uncle *Toby*.

Gracious heaven! cried my father, looking upwards, and clasping his two hands together,—there is a worth in thy honest ignorance, brother *Toby*,—'twere almost a pity to exchange it for a knowledge.————But I'll tell thee.————

To understand what *time* is aright, without which we never can comprehend *infinity*, insomuch as one is a portion of the other,————we ought seriously to sit down and consider what idea it is we have of *duration*, so as to give a satisfactory account, how we came by it.—What is that to any body? quoth my uncle *Toby*. * *For if you will turn your eyes inwards upon your mind*, continued my father, *and observe attentively, you will perceive, brother, that whilst you and I are talking together, and thinking and smoking our pipes: or whilst we receive successively ideas in our minds, we know that we do exist, and so we estimate the existence, or the continuation of the existence of ourselves, or any thing else commensurate to the succession of any ideas in our minds, the duration of ourselves, or any such other thing co-existing with our thinking,————and so according to that preconceived*—You puzzle me to death, cried my uncle *Toby*.—

————'Tis owing to this, replied my father, that in our computations of *time*, we are so used to minutes, hours, weeks, and months,————and of clocks (I wish there was not a clock in the kingdom) to measure out their several portions to us, and to those who belong to us,————that 'twill be well, if in time to come, the *succession of our ideas* be of any use or service to us at all.

Now, whether we observe it or no, continued my father, in every sound man's head, there is a regular succession of ideas of one sort or other, which follow each other in train just like———— A train of artillery? said my uncle *Toby*.—A train of a fiddle stick!—quoth my father,—which follow and succeed one another in our minds at certain distances, just like the images in the inside of a lanthorn turned round by the heat of a candle.—I declare, quoth my uncle *Toby*, mine are like a smoak-jack.————Then, brother *Toby*, I have nothing more to say to you upon the subject, said my father.

* Vid. Locke.

[169]

CHAPTER XIX

—WHAT a conjuncture was here lost!——My father in one of his best explanatory moods,—in eager pursuit of a metaphysic point into the very regions where clouds and thick darkness would soon have encompassed it about;———my uncle *Toby* in one of the finest dispositions for it in the world;—his head like a smoak-jack;——the funnel unswept, and the ideas whirling round and round about in it, all obfuscated and darkened over with fuliginous matter!——By the tomb stone of *Lucian*——if it is in being,——if not, why then, by his ashes! by the ashes of my dear *Rabelais*, and dearer *Cervantes*, ——my father and my uncle *Toby*'s discourse upon TIME and ETERNITY,—was a discourse devoutly to be wished for! and the petulancy of my father's humour in putting a stop to it, as he did, was a robbery of the *Ontologic treasury*, of such a jewel, as no coalition of great occasions and great men, are ever likely to restore to it again.

CHAPTER XX

THO' MY father persisted in not going on with the discourse, —yet he could not get my uncle *Toby*'s smoak-jack out of his head,—piqued as he was at first with it;——there was something in the comparison at the bottom, which hit his fancy; for which purpose resting his elbow upon the table, and reclining the right side of his head upon the palm of his hand,—but looking first stedfastly in the fire,——he began to commune with himself and philosophize about it: but his spirits being wore out with the fatigues of investigating new tracts, and the constant exertion of his faculties upon that variety of subjects which had taken their turn in the discourse,—the idea of the smoak-jack soon turned all his ideas upside down,—so that he fell asleep almost before he knew what he was about.

As for my uncle *Toby*, his smoak-jack had not made a dozen revolutions, before he fell asleep also.——Peace be with them both.——Dr. *Slop* is engaged with the midwife, and my mother above stairs.—*Trim* is busy in turning an old pair of jack-boots into a couple of mortars to be employed in the siege of *Messina* next summer,——and is this instant boring the touch holes with the point of a hot poker.——All my heroes are off my hands;—— 'tis the first time I have had a moment to spare,—and I'll make use of it, and write my preface.

THE AUTHOR'S PREFACE

N O, I'LL not say a word about it,—here it is;——in publishing it,——I have appealed to the world,——and to the world I leave it;——it must speak for itself.

All I know of the matter is,—when I sat down, my intent was to write a good book; and as far as the tenuity of my understanding would hold out,—a wise, aye, and a discreet,——taking care only, as I went along, to put into it all the wit and the judgment (be it more or less) which the great Author and Bestower of them had thought fit originally to give me,——so that, as your worships see,—'tis just as God pleases.

Now, *Agalastes* (speaking dispraisingly) sayeth, That there may be some wit in it, for aught he knows,——but no judgment at all. And *Triptolemus* and *Phutatorius* agreeing thereto, ask, How is it possible there should? for that wit and judgment in this world never go together; inasmuch as they are two operations differing from each other as wide as east is from west.—So, says *Locke*,— so are farting and hickuping, say I. But in answer to this, *Didius* the great church lawyer, in his code *de fartandi et illustrandi fallaciis*, doth maintain and make fully appear, That an illustration is no argument,—nor do I maintain the wiping of a looking-glass clean, to be a syllogism;—but you all, may it please your worships, see the better for it,——so that the main good these things do, is only to clarify the understanding, previous to the application of the argument itself, in order to free it from any little motes, or specks of opacular matter, which, if left swimming therein, might hinder a conception and spoil all.

Now, my dear Anti-Shandeans, and thrice able critics, and fellow-labourers, (for to you I write this Preface)——and to you, most subtle statesmen and discreet doctors (do—pull off your beards) renowned for gravity and wisdom;—*Monopolos* my politician,—*Didius*, my counsel; *Kysarcius*, my friend;— *Phutatorius*, my guide;—*Gastripheres*, the preserver of my life;

[171]

Somnolentius, the balm and repose of it,—not forgetting all others as well sleeping as waking, ecclesiastical as civil, whom for brevity, but out of no resentment to you, I lump all together.
————Believe me, right worthy,

My most zealous wish and fervent prayer in your behalf, and in my own too, in case the thing is not done already for us,——is, that the great gifts and endowments both of wit and judgment, with every thing which usually goes along with them,————such as memory, fancy, genius, eloquence, quick parts, and what not, may this precious moment without stint or measure, let or hinderance, be poured down warm as each of us could bear it,—scum and sediment an' all; (for I would not have a drop lost) into these veral receptacles, cells, cellules, domiciles, dormitories, refectories, and spare places of our brains,—in such sort, that they might continue to be injected and tunn'd into, according to the true intent and meaning of my wish, until every vessel of them, both great and small, be so replenished, saturated and fill'd up therewith, that no more, would it save a man's life, could possibly be got either in or out.

Bless us!—what noble work we should make!——how should I tickle it off!——and what spirits should I find myself in, to be writing away for such readers!—and you,—just heaven!——with what raptures would you sit and read,——but oh!——'tis too much,——I am sick,——I faint away deliciously at the thoughts of it!——'tis more than nature can bear!——lay hold of me,—I am giddy,—I am stone blind,——I'm dying,——I am gone.—— Help! Help! Help!—But hold,—I grow something better again, for I am beginning to foresee, when this is over, that as we shall all of us continue to be great wits,—we should never agree amongst ourselves, one day to an end:——there would be so much satire and sarcasm,——scoffing and flouting, with raillying and reparteeing of it,——thrusting and parrying in one corner or another,——there would be nothing but mischief amongst us.—Chaste stars! what biting and scratching, and what a racket and a clatter we should make, what with breaking of heads, and rapping of knuckles, and hitting of sore places,——there would be no such thing as living for us.

But then again, as we should all of us be men of great judgment, we should make up matters as fast as ever they went wrong; and though we should abominate each other, ten times worse than so many devils or devilesses, we should nevertheless, my dear creatures, be all courtesy and kindness,——milk and honey,——'twould be a second land of promise,——a paradise upon earth, if there was such a thing to be had,—so that upon the whole we should have done well enough.

All I fret and fume at, and what most distresses my invention at present, is how to bring the point itself to bear; for as your worships well know, that of these heavenly emanations of *wit* and *judgment*, which I have so bountifully wished both for your worships and myself,—there is but a certain *quantum* stored up for us all, for the use and behoof of the whole race of mankind; and such small *modicums* of 'em are only sent forth into this wide world, circulating here and there in one by corner or another,— and in such narrow streams, and at such prodigious intervals from each other, that one would wonder how it holds out, or could be sufficient for the wants and emergencies of so many great states, and populous empires.

Indeed there is one thing to be considered, that in *Nova Zembla*, *North Lapland*, and in all those cold and dreary tracts of the globe, which lie more directly under the artick and antartick circles,—— where the whole province of a man's concernments lies for near nine months together, within the narrow compass of his cave,——where the spirits are compressed almost to nothing, ——and where the passions of a man, with every thing which belongs to them, are as frigid as the zone itself;—there the least quantity of *judgment* imaginable does the business,—and of *wit*, —there is a total and an absolute saving,—for as not one spark is wanted,—so not one spark is given. Angels and ministers of grace defend us! What a dismal thing would it have been to have governed a kingdom, to have fought a battle, or made a treaty, or run a match, or wrote a book, or got a child, or held a provincial chapter there, with so *plentiful a lack* of wit and judgment about us! for mercy's sake! let us think no more about it, but travel on as fast as we can southwards into *Norway*,——crossing over *Swedeland*, if you please, through the small triangular province of *Angermania* to the lake of *Bothnia*; coasting along it through east and west *Bothnia*, down to *Carelia*, and so on, through all those states and provinces which border upon the far side of the *Gulf* of *Finland*, and the north east of the *Baltick*, up to *Petersbourg*, and just stepping into *Ingria*;—— then stretching over directly from thence through the north parts of the *Russian* empire—leaving *Siberia* a little upon the left hand till we get into the very heart of *Russian* and *Asiatick Tartary*.

[173]

Now throughout this long tour which I have led you, you observe the good people are better off by far, than in the polar countries which we have just left:—for if you hold your hand over your eyes, and look very attentively, you may perceive some small glimmerings (as it were) of wit, with a comfortable provision of good plain *houshold* judgment, which, taking the quality and quantity of it together, they make a very good shift with,—and had they more of either the one or the other, it would destroy the proper ballance betwixt them, and I am satisfied moreover they would want occasions to put them to use.

Now, Sir, if I conduct you home again into this warmer and more luxuriant island, where you perceive the spring tide of our blood and humours runs high,—where we have more ambition, and pride, and envy, and lechery, and other whoreson passions upon our hands to govern and subject to reason,—the *height* of our wit and the *depth* of our judgment, you see, are exactly proportioned to the *length* and *breadth* of our necessities,—and accordingly, we have them sent down amongst us in such a flowing kind of decent and creditable plenty, that no one thinks he has any cause to complain.

It must however be confessed on this head, that, as our air blows hot and cold,——wet and dry, ten times in a day, we have them in no regular and settled way;——so that sometimes for near half a century together, there shall be very little wit or judgment, either to be seen or heard of amongst us:——the small channels of them shall seem quite dried up,—then all of a sudden the sluices shall break out, and take a fit of running again like fury,—you would think they would never stop:——and then it is, that in writing and fighting, and twenty other gallant things, we drive all the world before us.

It is by these observations, and a wary reasoning by analogy in that kind of argumentative process, which *Suidas* calls *dialectick induction*,—that I draw and set up this position as most true and veritable.

That of these two luminaries, so much of their irradiations are suffered from time to time to shine down upon us; as he, whose infinite wisdom which dispenses every thing in exact weight and measure, knows will just serve to light us on our way in this night of our obscurity; so that your reverences and worships now find out, nor is it a moment longer in my power to conceal it from you, That the fervent wish in your behalf with which I set out, was no more than the first insinuating *How d'ye* of a caressing prefacer stifling his reader, as a lover sometimes does a coy mistress, into silence. For alas! could this effusion of light have been as easily procured, as the exordium wished it—I tremble to think how many thousands for it, of benighted travellers (in the learned sciences at least) must have groped and blundered on in the dark, all the nights of their lives,—running their heads against posts, and knocking out their brains without ever getting to their journies end;——some falling with their noses perpendicularly into stinks, —others horizontally with their tails into kennels. Here one half of a learned profession tilting full butt against the other half of it, and then tumbling and rolling one over the other in the dirt like hogs.——Here the brethren, of another profession, who should have run in opposition to each other, flying on the contrary like a flock of wild geese, all in a row the same way.—What confusion! —what mistakes!—fiddlers and painters judging by their eyes and ears,—admirable!—trusting to the passions excited in an air sung, or a story painted to the heart,——instead of measuring them by a quadrant.

In the foreground of this picture, a *statesman* turning the political wheel, like a brute, the wrong way round—*against* the stream of corruption,—by heaven!—instead of *with* it.

In this corner, a son of the divine *Esculapius*, writing a book against pre-destination; perhaps worse,—feeling his patient's pulse, instead of his apothecary's—a brother of the faculty in the back ground upon his knees in tears,—drawing the curtains of a mangled victim to beg his forgiveness;—offering a fee,—instead of taking one.

In that spacious HALL, a coalition of the gown, from all the barrs of it, driving a damn'd, dirty, vexatious cause before them, with all their might and main, the wrong way;——kicking it *out* of the great doors, instead of, *in*,——and with such fury in their looks, and such a degree of inveteracy in their manner of kicking it, as if the laws had been originally made for the peace and preservation of mankind:—perhaps a more enormous mistake committed by them still,—a litigated point fairly hung up;——for instance, Whether *John o'Nokes* his nose, could stand in *Tom o'Stiles* his face, without a trespass, or not,—rashly determined by them in five and twenty minutes, which, with the cautious pro's and con's required in so intricate a proceeding, might have taken up as many months,—and if carried upon on a military plan, as your honours know, an ACTION should be, with all the stratagems practicable therein,—such as feints,—forced marches,—surprizes,

—ambuscades,—mask-batteries, and a thousand other strokes of generalship which consist in catechising at all advantages on both sides,——might reasonably have lasted them as many years, finding food and raiment all that term for a centumvirate of the profession.

As for the clergy————No——If I say a word against them, I'll be shot.—I have no desire,—and besides, if I had,——I durst not for my soul touch upon the subject,——with such weak nerves and spirits, and in the condition I am in at present, 'twould be as much as my life was worth, to deject and contrist myself with so sad and melancholy an account,—and therefore, 'tis safer to draw a curtain across, and hasten from it, as fast as I can, to the main and principal point I have undertaken to clear up,——and that is, How it comes to pass, that your men of least *wit* are reported to be men of most *judgment*.——But mark,— I say, *reported to be*,——for it is no more, my dear Sirs, than a report, and which like twenty others taken up every day upon trust, I maintain to be a vile and a malicious report into the bargain.

This by the help of the observations already premised, and I hope already weighed and perpended by your reverences and worships, I shall forthwith make appear.

I hate set dissertations,——and above all things in the world, 'tis one of the silliest things in one of them, to darken your hypothesis by placing a number of tall, opake words, one before another, in a right line, betwixt your own and your readers conception,——when in all likelihood, if you had looked about, you might have seen something standing, or hanging up, which would have cleared the point at once,—"for what hinderance, hurt, or harm doth the laudable desire of knowledge bring to any man, if even from a sot, a pot, a fool, a stool, a winter-mittain, a truckle for a pully, the lid of a goldsmith's crucible, an oyl bottle, an old slipper, or a cane chair,"——I am this moment sitting upon one. Will you give me leave to illustrate this affair of wit and judgment, by the two knobs on the top of the back of it,——they are fasten'd on, you see, with two pegs stuck slightly into two gimletholes, and will place what I have to say in so clear a light, as to let you see through the drift and meaning of my whole preface, as plainly as if every point and particle of it was made up of sun beams.

I enter now directly upon the point.

——Here stands *wit*,——and there stands *judgment*, close

beside it, just like the two knobs I'm speaking of, upon the back of this self same chair on which I am sitting.

——You see, they are the highest and most ornamental parts of its *frame*,——as wit and judgment are of *ours*,——and like them too, indubitably both made and fitted to go together, in order, as we say in all such cases of duplicated embellishments, ——*to answer one another.*

Now for the sake of an experiment, and for the clearer illustrating this matter,—let us for a moment, take off one of these two curious ornaments (I care not which) from the point or pinacle of the chair it now stands on;——nay, don't laugh at it.——But did you ever see in the whole course of your lives such a ridiculous business as this has made of it?——Why, 'tis as miserable a sight as a sow with one ear; and there is just as much sense and symmetry in the one, as in the other:—do,—pray, get off your seats, only to take a view of it.——Now would any man who valued his character a straw, have turned a piece of work out of his hand in such a condition?——nay, lay your hands upon your hearts, and answer this plain question, Whether this one single knob which now stands here like a blockhead by itself, can serve any purpose upon earth, but to put one in mind of the want of the other;—— and let me further ask, in case the chair was your own, if you would not in your consciences think, rather than be as it is, that it would be ten times better without any knob at all.

Now these two knobs——or top ornaments of the mind of man, which crown the whole entablature,—being, as I said, wit and judgment, which of all others, as I have proved it, are the most needful,—the most priz'd,——the most calamitous to be without, and consequently the hardest to come at,——for all these reasons put together, there is not a mortal amongst us, so destitute of a love of good fame or feeding,——or so ignorant of what will do him good therein,—who does not wish and stedfastly resolve in his own mind, to be, or to be thought at least master of the one or the other, and indeed of both of them, if the thing seems any way feasible, or likely to be brought to pass.

Now your graver gentry having little or no kind of chance in aiming at the one,—unless they laid hold of the other,——pray what do you think would become of them?—Why, Sirs, in spight of all their *gravities*, they must e'en have been contented to have gone with their insides naked:—this was not to be borne, but by an effort of philosophy not to be supposed in the case we are upon,——so that no one could well have been angry with them, had they been satisfied with what little they could have snatched up and secreted under their cloaks and great perrywigs, had they not raised a *hue* and *cry* at the same time against the lawful owners.

I need not tell your worships, that this was done with so much cunning and artifice,—that the great *Locke*, who was seldom out-witted by false sounds,——was nevertheless bubbled here. The cry, it seems, was so deep and solemn a one, and what with the help of great wigs, grave faces, and other implements of deceit, was rendered so general a one against the *poor wits* in this matter, that the philosopher himself was deceived by it,—it was his glory to free the world from the lumber of a thousand vulgar errors;——but this was not of the number; so that instead of sitting down cooly, as such a philosopher should have done, to have examined the matter of fact before he philosophised upon it;—— on the contrary, he took the fact for granted, and so joined in with the cry, and halloo'd it as boisterously as the rest.

This has been made the *Magna Charta* of stupidity ever since,— but your reverences plainly see, it has been obtained in such a manner, that the title to it is not worth a groat;——which by the bye is one of the many and vile impositions which gravity and grave folks have to answer for hereafter.

As for great wigs, upon which I may be thought to have spoken my mind too freely,——I beg leave to qualify whatever has been unguardedly said to their dispraise or prejudice, by one general declaration——That I have no abhorrence whatever, nor do I detest and abjure either great wigs or long beards,——any further than when I see they are bespoke and let grow on purpose to carry on this self-same imposture—for any purpose,—peace be with them!—☞ mark only,—I write not for them.

CHAPTER XXI

EVERY day for at least ten years together did my father resolve to have it mended,——'tis not mended yet;——no family but ours would have borne with it an hour,—and what is most astonishing, there was not a subject in the world upon which my father was so eloquent, as upon that of door-hinges.——And yet at the same time, he was certainly one of the greatest bubbles to them, I think, that history can produce:

his rhetoric and conduct were at perpetual handy-cuffs.——
Never did the parlour-door open—but his philosophy or his
principles fell a victim to it;——three drops of oyl with a feather,
and a smart stroke of a hammer, had saved his honour for ever.

——Inconsistent soul that man is!—languishing under
wounds, which he has the power to heal!—his whole life a contradiction to his knowledge!—his reason, that precious gift of God
to him—(instead of pouring in oyl) serving but to sharpen his
sensibilities,——to multiply his pains and render him more
melancholy and uneasy under them!—poor unhappy creature,
that he should do so!——are not the necessary causes of misery
in this life enow, but he must add voluntary ones to his stock of
sorrow;——struggle against evils which cannot be avoided, and
submit to others, which a tenth part of the trouble they create
him, would remove from his heart for ever?

By all that is good and virtuous! if there are three drops of oy
to be got, and a hammer to be found within ten miles of *Shandy-
Hall,*—the parlour-door hinge shall be mended this reign.

CHAPTER XXII

WHEN corporal *Trim* had brought his two mortars to bear,
he was delighted with his handy-work above measure;
and knowing what a pleasure it would be to his master
to see them, he was not able to resist the desire he had of carrying
them directly into his parlour.

Now next to the moral lesson I had in view in mentioning the
affair of *hinges,* I had a speculative consideration arising out of
it, and it is this.

Had the parlour-door open'd and turn'd upon its hinges, as
a door should do———

—Or for example, as cleverly as our government has been
turning upon its hinges,——(that is, in case things have all along
gone well with your worship,—otherwise I give up my simile)—
in this case, I say, there had been no danger either to master or
man, in corporal *Trim*'s peeping in: the moment, he had beheld
my father and my uncle *Toby* fast asleep,——the respectfulness
of his carriage was such, he would have retired as silent as death,
and left them both in their armchairs, dreaming as happy as he
had found them: but the thing was, morally speaking, so very

impracticable, that for the many years in which this hinge was suffered to be out of order, and amongst the hourly grievances my father submitted to upon its account,—this was one; that he never folded his arms to take his nap after dinner, but the thoughts of being unavoidably awakened by the first person who should open the door, was always uppermost in his imagination, and so incessantly stepp'd in betwixt him and the first balmy presage of his repose, as to rob him, as he often declared, of the whole sweets of it.

When things move upon bad hinges, an' please your lordships, *how can it be otherwise?*

Pray what's the matter? Who is there? cried my father, waking, the moment the door began to creak.——I wish the smith would give a peep at that confounded hinge.——'Tis nothing, an' please your honour, said *Trim*, but two mortars I am bringing in.—— They shan't make a clatter with them here, cried my father hastily.——If Dr. *Slop* has any drugs to pound, let him do it in the kitchen.——May it please your honour, cried *Trim*,—they are two mortar-pieces for a siege next summer, which I have been making out of a pair of jack-boots, which *Obadiah* told me your honour had left off wearing.——By heaven! cried my father, springing out of his chair, as he swore,—I have not one appointment belonging to me, which I set so much store by, as I do by these jack-boots,——they were our great-grandfather's, brother *Toby*,——they were *hereditary*. Then I fear, quoth my uncle *Toby*, *Trim* has cut off the entail.——I have only cut off the tops, an' please your honour, cried *Trim*.—I hate *perpetuities* as much as any man alive, cried my father,——but these jack-boots, continued he, (smiling, though very angry at the same time) have been in the family, brother, ever since the civil wars;——Sir *Roger Shandy* wore them at the battle of *Marston-Moor*.—I declare I would not have taken ten pounds for them.——I'll pay you the money, brother *Shandy*, quoth my uncle *Toby*, looking at the two mortars with infinite pleasure, and putting his hand into his breeches-pocket, as he viewed them.——I'll pay you the ten pounds this moment with all my heart and soul.——

Brother *Toby*, replied my father, altering his tone, you care not what money you dissipate and throw away, provided, continued he, 'tis but upon a SIEGE.—Have I not a hundred and twenty pounds a year, besides my half-pay? cried my uncle *Toby*.—— What is that, replied my father, hastily,—to ten pounds for a pair of jack-boots?——twelve guineas for your *pontoons*;——half as

[180]

much for your *Dutch*-draw-bridge;—to say nothing of the train of little brass-artillery you bespoke last week, with twenty other preparations for the siege of *Messina*; believe me, dear brother *Toby*, continued my father, taking him kindly by the hand,—these military operations of yours are above your strength;—you mean well, brother,—but they carry you into greater expences than you were first aware of,——and take my word,——dear *Toby*, they will in the end quite ruin your fortune, and make a beggar of you. ——What signifies it if they do, brother, replied my uncle *Toby*, so long as we know 'tis for the good of the nation.—

My father could not help smiling for his soul;—his anger at the worst was never more than a spark,—and the zeal and simplicity of *Trim*,——and the generous (tho' hobby-horsical) gallantry of my uncle *Toby*, brought him into perfect good humour with them in an instant.

Generous souls!—God prosper you both, and your mortar-pieces too, quoth my father to himself!

CHAPTER XXIII

ALL IS quiet and hush, cried my father, at least above stairs, —I hear not one foot stirring.——Prithee, *Trim*, who is in the kitchen? There is no one soul in the kitchen, answered *Trim*, making a low bow as he spoke, except Dr. *Slop*.——Confusion! cried my father, (getting up upon his legs a second time) ——not one single thing has gone right this day! had I faith in astrology, brother, (which by the bye, my father had) I would have sworn some retrograde planet was hanging over this unfortunate house of mine, and turning every individual thing in it out of its place.——Why, I thought Dr. *Slop* had been above stairs with my wife, and so said you.—What can the fellow be puzzling about in the kitchen?——He is busy, an' please your honour, replied *Trim*, in making a bridge.——'Tis very obliging in him, quoth my uncle *Toby*;——pray give my humble service to Dr. *Slop*, *Trim*, and tell him I thank him heartily.

You must know, my uncle *Toby* mistook the bridge as widely as my father mistook the mortars;——but to understand how my uncle *Toby* could mistake the bridge,—I fear I must give you an exact account of the road which led to it;——or to drop my metaphor, (for there is nothing more dishonest in an historian,

[181]

than the use of one,)——in order to conceive the probability of this error in my uncle *Toby* aright, I must give you some account of an adventure of *Trim*'s though much against my will. I say much against my will, only because the story, in one sense, is certainly out of its place here; for by right it should come in, either amongst the ancedotes of my uncle *Toby*'s amours with widow *Wadman*, in which corporal *Trim* was no mean actor,—or else in the middle of his and my uncle *Toby*'s campaigns on the bowling green,——for it will do very well in either place;——but then if I reserve it for either of those parts of my story,—I ruin the story I'm upon,—and if I tell it here—I anticipate matters, and ruin it there.

—What would your worships have me to do in this case?

—Tell it, Mr. *Shandy*, by all means.——You are a fool, *Tristram*, if you do.

O ye powers! (for powers ye are, and great ones too)—which enable mortal man to tell a story worth the hearing,—that kindly shew him, where he is to begin it,—and where he is to end it,—what he is to put into it,—and what he is to leave 'out,—how much of it he is to cast into shade,—and whereabouts he is to throw his light!——Ye, who preside over this vast empire of biographical free-booters, and see how many scrapes and plunges your subjects hourly fall into;—will you do one thing?

I beg and beseech you, (in case you will do nothing better for us) that wherever, in any part of your dominions it so falls out, that three several roads meet in one point, as they have done just here,—that at least you set up a guide-post, in the center of them, in mere charity to direct an uncertain devil which of the three he is to take.

CHAPTER XXIV

THO' THE shock my uncle *Toby* received the year after the demolition of *Dunkirk*, in his affair with widow *Wadman*, had fixed him in a resolution, never more to think of the sex,——or of aught which belonged to it;—yet corporal *Trim* had made no such bargain with himself. Indeed in my uncle *Toby*'s case there was a strange and unaccountable concurrence of circumstances which insensibly drew him in, to lay siege to that fair and strong citadel.——In *Trim*'s case there was a concurrence of

nothing in the world, but of him and *Bridget* in the kitchen;——
though in truth, the love and veneration he bore his master was
such, and so fond was he of imitating him in all he did, that had
my uncle *Toby* employed his time and genius in tagging of points,
——I am persuaded the honest corporal would have laid down
his arms, and followed his example with pleasure. When therefore
my uncle *Toby* sat down before the mistress,—corporal *Trim*
incontinently took ground before the maid.

Now, my dear friend *Garrick*, whom I have so much cause to
esteem and honour,—(why, or wherefore, 'tis no matter)—can
it escape your penetration,—I defy it,—that so many play-wrights,
and opificers of chit chat have ever since been working upon
Trim's and my uncle *Toby*'s pattern.—I care not what *Aristotle*,
or *Pacuvius*, or *Bossu*, or *Ricaboni* say,—(though I never read one
of them)——there is not a greater difference between a single-
horse chair and madam *Pompadour*'s *vis à vis*, than betwixt a
single amour, and an amour thus nobly doubled, and going upon
all four, prancing throughout a grand drama.—Sir, a simple,
single, silly affair of that kind,—— is quite lost in five acts;——
but that is neither here or there.

After a series of attacks and repulses in a course of nine months
on my uncle *Toby*'s quarter, a most minute account of every particular of which shall be given in its proper place, my uncle *Toby*,
honest man! found it necessary to draw off his forces, and raise
the siege somewhat indignantly.

Corporal *Trim*, as I said, had made no such bargain either with
himself——or with any one else,——the fidelity however of his
heart not suffering him to go into a house which his master had
forsaken with disgust,——he contented himself with turning his
part of the siege into a blockade;——that is, he kept others off,——
for though he never after went to the house, yet he never met
Bridget in the village, but he would either nod or wink, or smile,
or look kindly at her,—or (as circumstances directed), he would
shake her by the hand,——or ask her lovingly how she did,——
or would give her a ribban,——and now and then, though never
but when it could be done with decorum, would give *Bridget* a——

Precisely in this situation, did these things stand for five years;
that is, from the demolition of *Dunkirk* in the year 13, to the
latter end of my uncle *Toby*'s campaign in the year 18, which was
about six or seven weeks before the time I'm speaking of.—When
Trim, as his custom was, after he had put my uncle *Toby* to bed,
going down one moon-shiny night to see that every thing was

right at his fortifications,——in the lane separated from the bowling-green with flowering shrubs and holly,—he espied his *Bridget*.

As the corporal thought there was nothing in the world so well worth shewing as the glorious works which he and my uncle *Toby* had made, *Trim* courteously and gallantly took her by the hand, and led her in: this was not done so privately, but that the foulmouth'd trumpet of Fame carried it from ear to ear, till at length it reached my father's, with this untoward circumstance along with it, that my uncle *Toby*'s curious draw-bridge, constructed and painted after the *Dutch* fashion, and which went quite across the ditch,—was broke down, and some how or other crush'd all to pieces that very night.

My father, as you have observed, had no great esteem for my uncle *Toby*'s hobby-horse,—he thought it the most ridiculous horse that ever gentleman mounted; and indeed unless my uncle *Toby* vexed him about it, could never think of it once, without smiling at it,——so that it never could get lame or happen any mischance, but it tickled my father's imagination beyond measure; but this being an accident much more to his humour than any one which had yet befall'n it, it proved an inexhaustible fund of entertainment to him.——Well,——but dear *Toby*! my father would say, do tell us seriously how this affair of the bridge happened.——How can you teaze me so much about it? my uncle *Toby* would reply,—I have told it you twenty times, word for word as *Trim* told it me.—Prithee, how was it then, corporal? my father would cry, turning to *Trim*.—It was a mere misfortune, an' please your honour,——I was shewing Mrs. *Bridget* our fortifications, and in going too near the edge of the fossè, I unfortunately slip'd in.——Very well *Trim*! my father would cry,—(smiling mysteriously, and giving a nod,——but without interrupting him)——and being link'd fast, an' please your honour, arm in arm with Mrs. *Bridget*, I dragg'd her after me, by means of which she fell backwards soss against the bridge,—— and *Trim*'s foot, (my uncle *Toby* would cry, taking the story out of his mouth) getting into the cuvette, he tumbled full against the bridge too.—It was a thousand to one, my uncle *Toby* would add, that the poor fellow did not break his leg.—Ay truly! my father would say,——a limb is soon broke, brother *Toby*, in such encounters.——And so, an' please your honour, the bridge, which your honour knows was a very slight one, was broke down betwixt us, and splintered all to pieces.

At other times, but especially when my uncle *Toby* was so unfortunate as to say a syllable about cannóns, bombs or petards, ——my father would exhaust all the stores of his eloquence (which indeed were very great) in a panegyric upon the BATTER-ING-RAMS of the ancients,—the VINEA which *Alexander* made use of at the siege of *Tyre*.——He would tell my uncle *Toby* of the CATAPULTÆ of the *Syrians* which threw such monstrous stones so many hundred feet, and shook the strongest bulwarks from their very foundation;—he would go on and describe the wonderful mechanism of the BALLISTA, which *Marcellinus* makes so much rout about,—the terrible effects of the PYRABOLI,—which cast fire,—the danger of the TEREBRA and SCORPIO, which cast javelins.—But what are these, he would say, to the destructive machinery of corporal *Trim*?—Believe me, brother *Toby*, no bridge, or bastion, or sally port, that ever was constructed in this world, can hold out against such artillery.

My uncle *Toby* would never attempt any defence against the force of this ridicule, but that of redoubling the vehemence of smoking his pipe; in doing which, he raised so dense a vapour one night after supper, that it set my father, who was a little phthisical, into a suffocating fit of violent coughing: my uncle *Toby* leap'd up without feeling the pain upon his groin,—and, with infinite pity, stood beside his brother's chair, tapping his back with one hand, and holding his head with the other, and from time to time wiping his eyes with a clean cambrick handker-chief, which he pull'd out of his pocket.——The affectionate and endearing manner in which my uncle *Toby* did these little offices, ——cut my father thro' his reins, for the pain he had just been giving him.——May my brains be knock'd out with a battering ram or a catapulta, I care not which, quoth my father to himself, ——if ever I insult this worthy soul more.

CHAPTER XXV

THE draw-bridge being held irreparable, *Trim* was ordered directly to set about another,——but not upon the same model; for cardinal *Alberoni*'s intrigues at that time being discovered, and my uncle *Toby* rightly foreseeing that a flame would inevitably break out betwixt *Spain* and the Empire, and that the operations of the ensuing campaign must in all likelihood be either in *Naples* or *Sicily*,——he determined upon an *Italian* bridge,—(my uncle *Toby*, by the bye, was not far out in his conjectures)——but my father, who was infinitely the better politician, and took the lead as far of my uncle *Toby* in the cabinet, as my uncle *Toby* took it of him in the field,—convinced him, that if the King of *Spain* and the Emperor went together by the ears, that *England* and *France* and *Holland* must, by force of their pre-engagements, all enter the lists too;——and if so, he would say, the combatants, brother *Toby*, as sure as we are alive, will fall to it again, pell-mell, upon the old prize-fighting stage of *Flanders*;——then what will you do with your *Italian* bridge?

——We will go on with it then, upon the old model, cried my uncle *Toby*.

When corporal *Trim* had about half finished it in that stile,—— my uncle *Toby* found out a capital defect in it, which he had never thoroughly considered before. It turned, it seems, upon hinges at both ends of it, opening in the middle, one half of which turning to one side of the fossè, and the other, to the other; the advantage of which was this, that by dividing the weight of the bridge into two equal portions, it impowered my uncle *Toby* to raise it up or let it down with the end of his crutch, and with one hand, which, as his garrison was weak, was as much as he could well spare,— but the disadvantages of such a construction were insurmountable, ——for by this means, he would say, I leave one half of my bridge in my enemy's possession,——and pray of what use is the other?

The natural remedy for this, was no doubt to have his bridge fast only at one end with hinges, so that the whole might be lifted up together, and stand bolt upright,——but that was rejected for the reason given above.

For a whole week after he was determined in his mind to have one of that particular construction which is made to draw back horizontally, to hinder a passage; and to thrust forwards again to gain a passage,——of which sorts your worships might have seen three famous ones at *Spires* before its destruction,—and one now at *Brisac*, if I mistake not;——but my father advising my uncle *Toby*, with great earnestness, to have nothing more to do with thrusting bridges,—and my uncle foreseeing moreover that it would but perpetuate the memory of the corporal's misfortune, ——he changed his mind for that of the marquis *d'Hôpital*'s invention, which the younger *Bernouilli* has so well and learnedly described, as your worships may see,—*Act. Erud. Lips.* an. 1695, —to these a lead weight is an eternal balance, and keeps watch as well as a couple of centinels, inasmuch as the construction of them was a curve-line approximating to a cycloid,——if not a cycloid itself.

My uncle *Toby* understood the nature of a parabola as well as any man in *England*,—but was not quite such a master of the cycloid;—he talked however about it every day;——the bridge went not forwards.——We'll ask somebody about it, cried my uncle *Toby* to *Trim*.

CHAPTER XXVI

WHEN *Trim* came in and told my father, that Dr. *Slop* was in the kitchen, and busy in making a bridge,—my uncle *Toby*,—the affair of the jack-boots having just then raised a train of military ideas in his brain,——took it instantly for granted that Dr. *Slop* was making a model of the marquis *d'Hôpital*'s bridge.——'Tis very obliging in him, quoth my uncle *Toby*;—pray give my humble service to Dr. *Slop*, *Trim*, and tell him I thank him heartily.

Had my uncle *Toby*'s head been a *Savoyard*'s box, and my father peeping in all the time at one end of it,——it could not have given him a more distinct conception of the operations in my uncle *Toby*'s imagination, than what he had; so notwithstanding the catapulta and battering-ram, and his bitter imprecation about them, he was just beginning to triumph——

When *Trim*'s answer, in an instant, tore the laurel from his brows, and twisted it to pieces.

CHAPTER XXVII

—THIS unfortunate draw-bridge of yours, quoth my father— God bless your honour, cried *Trim*, 'tis a bridge for master's nose.——In bringing him into the world with his vile instruments, he has crush'd his nose, *Susannah* says, as flat as a pancake to his face, and he is making a false bridge with a piece of cotton and a thin piece of whalebone out of *Susannah*'s stays, to raise it up.

——Lead me, brother *Toby*, cried my father, to my room this instant.

CHAPTER XXVIII

FROM the first moment I sat down to write my life for the amusement of the world, and my opinions for its instruction, has a cloud insensibly been gathering over my father.——A tide of little evils and distresses has been setting in against him.——Not one thing, as he observed himself, has gone right: and now is the storm thicken'd, and going to break, and pour down full upon his head.

I enter upon this part of my story in the most pensive and melancholy frame of mind, that ever sympathetic breast was touched with.———My nerves relax as I tell it.———Every line I write, I feel an abatement of the quickness of my pulse, and of that careless alacrity with it, which every day of my life prompts me to say and write a thousand things I should not.——And this moment that I last dipp'd my pen into my ink, I could not help taking notice what a cautious air of sad composure and solemnity there appear'd in my manner of doing it.——Lord! how different from the rash jerks, and hare-brain'd squirts thou art wont, *Tristram*! to transact it with in other humours,——dropping thy pen,—spurting thy ink about thy table and thy books,——as if thy pen and thy ink, thy books and thy furniture cost thee nothing.

CHAPTER XXIX

—I WON'T go about to argue the point with you,—'tis so,—and I am persuaded of it, madam, as much as can be, "That both man and woman bear pain or sorrow, (and, for aught I know, pleasure too) best in a horizontal position."

The moment my father got up into his chamber, he threw himself prostrate across his bed in the wildest disorder imaginable, but at the same time, in the most lamentable attitude of a man borne down with sorrows, that ever the eye of pity dropp'd a tear for.——The palm of his right hand, as he fell upon the bed, receiving his forehead, and covering the greatest part of both his eyes, gently sunk down with his head (his elbow giving way backwards) till his nose touch'd the quilt;——his left arm hung insensible over the side of the bed, his knuckles reclining upon the handle of the chamber pot, which peep'd out beyond the valance,

—his right leg (his left being drawn up towards his body) hung half over the side of the bed, the edge of it pressing upon his shin-bone.——He felt it not. A fix'd, inflexible sorrow took possession of every line of his face.—He sigh'd once,—heaved his breast often,—but uttered not a word.

An old set-stitch'd chair, valanced and fringed around with party-colour'd worsted bobs, stood at the bed's head, opposite to the side where my father's head reclined.——My uncle *Toby* sat him down in it.

Before an affliction is digested,——consolation ever comes too soon;——and after it is digested,—it comes too late: so that you see, madam, there is but a mark between these two, as fine almost as a hair, for a comforter to take aim at: my uncle *Toby* was always either on this side, or on that of it, and would often say, He believed in his heart, he could as soon hit the longitude; for this reason, when he sat down in the chair, he drew the curtain a little forwards, and having a tear at every one's service,—he pull'd out a cambrick handkerchief,——gave a low sigh,——but held his peace.

CHAPTER XXX

—"ALL IS NOT GAIN *that is got into the purse.*"——So that notwithstanding my father had the happiness of reading the oddest books in the universe, and had moreover, in himself, the oddest way of thinking, that ever man in it was bless'd with, yet it had this drawback upon him after all, ——that it laid him open to some of the oddest and most whimsical distresses; of which this particular one which he sunk under at present is as strong an example as can be given.

No doubt, the breaking down of the bridge of a child's nose, by the edge of a pair of forceps,—however scientifically applied, ——would vex any man in the world, who was at so much pains in begetting a child, as my father was,——yet it will not account for the extravagance of his affliction, or will it justify the unchristian manner he abandoned and surrender'd himself up to it.

To explain this, I must leave him upon the bed for half an hour,——and my good uncle *Toby* in his old fringed chair sitting beside him.

CHAPTER XXXI

—I THINK it a very unreasonable demand,——cried my great grandfather, twisting up the paper, and throwing it upon the table.——By this account, madam, you have but two thousand pounds fortune, and not a shilling more,——and you insist upon having three hundred pounds a year jointure for it.——

—"Because," replied my great grandmother, "you have little or no nose, Sir."——

Now, before I venture to make use of the word *Nose* a second time,—to avoid all confusion in what will be said upon it, in this interesting part of my story, it may not be amiss to explain my own meaning, and define, with all possible exactness and precision, what I would willingly be understood to mean by the term: being of opinion, that 'tis owing to the negligence and perverseness of writers, in despising this precaution, and to nothing else, ——That all the polemical writings in divinity, are not as clear and demonstrative as those upon *a Will o' the Wisp*, or any other sound part of philosophy, and natural pursuit; in order to which, what have you to do, before you set out, unless you intend to go puzzling on to the day of judgment,——but to give the world a good definition, and stand to it, of the main word you have most occasion for,—changing it, Sir, as you would a guinea, into small coin?—which done,—let the father of confusion puzzle you, if he can; or put a different idea either into your head, or your reader's head, if he knows how.

In books of strict morality and close reasoning, such as this I am engaged in,—the neglect is inexcusable; and heaven is witness, how the world has revenged itself upon me for leaving so many openings to equivocal strictures,—and for depending so much as I have done, all along, upon the cleanliness of my reader's imaginations.

——Here are two senses, cried *Eugenius*, as we walk'd along, pointing with the fore finger of his right hand to the word *Crevice*, in the fifty-second page of the second volume of this book of books,—here are two senses,——quoth he.—And here are two roads, replied I, turning short upon him,——a dirty and a clean one,——which shall we take?——The clean,—by all means, replied *Eugenius*. *Eugenius*, said I, stepping before him, and laying my hand upon his breast,——to define—is to distrust.—Thus I triumph'd over *Eugenius*; but I triumph'd over him as I always do, like a fool.——'Tis my comfort however, I am not an obstinate one; therefore

I define a nose, as follows,——intreating only beforehand, and beseeching my readers, both male and female, of what age, complexion, and condition soever, for the love of God and their own souls, to guard against the temptations and suggestions of the devil, and suffer him by no art or wile to put any other ideas into their minds, than what I put into my definition.——For by the word *Nose*, throughout all this long chapter of noses, and in every other part of my work, where the word *Nose* occurs,—I declare, by that word I mean a Nose, and nothing more, or less.

CHAPTER XXXII

—"**B**ECAUSE," quoth my great grandmother, repeating the words again,—"you have little or no nose, Sir"—— S'death! cried my great grandfather, clapping his hand upon his nose,—'tis not so small as that comes to;—'tis a full inch longer than my father's.——Now, my great grandfather's nose was for all the world like unto the noses of all the men, women, and children, whom *Pantagruel* found dwelling upon the island of ENNASIN.——By the way, if you would know the strange way of getting a-kin amongst so flat-nosed a people,——you must read the book;—find it out yourself, you never can.——

——'Twas shaped, Sir, like an ace of clubs.

——'Tis a full inch, continued my great grandfather, pressing up the ridge of his nose with his finger and thumb; and repeating his assertion,——'tis a full inch longer, madam, than my father's —.You must mean your uncle's, replied my great grandmother.

——My great grandfather was convinced.—He untwisted the paper, and signed the article.

CHAPTER XXXIII

—**W**HAT an unconscionable jointure, my dear, do we pay out of this small estate of ours, quoth my grandmother to my grandfather.

My father, replied my grandfather, had no more nose, my dear, saving the mark, than there is upon the back of my hand.——

[191]

——Now, you must know, that my great grandmother out-
lived my grandfather twelve years; so that my father had the
jointure to pay, a hundred and fifty pounds half yearly—(on
Michaelmas and *Lady day*)—during all that time.

No man discharged pecuniary obligations with a better grace
than my father.——And as far as the hundred pounds went, he
would fling it upon the table, guinea by guinea, with that spirited
jerk of an honest welcome, which generous souls, and generous
souls only, are able to fling down money: but as soon as ever he
enter'd upon the odd fifty,—he generally gave a loud *Hem*!—
rubb'd the side of his nose leisurely with the flat part of his fore
finger,—inserted his hand cautiously betwixt his head and the cawl
of his wig,—look'd at both sides of every guinea, as he parted
with it,—and seldom could get to the end of the fifty pounds,
without pulling out his handkerchief, and wiping his temples.

Defend me, gracious heaven! from those persecuting spirits
who make no allowances for these workings within us.—Never,—
O never may I lay down in their tents, who cannot relax the
engine, and feel pity for the force of education, and the prevalence
of opinions long derived from ancestors!

For three generations at least, this *tenet* in favour of long noses
had gradually been taking root in our family.——Tradition was
all along on its side, and Interest was every half year stepping
in to strengthen it; so that the whimsicality of my father's brain
was far from having the whole honour of this, as it had of almost
all his other strange notions.—For in a great measure he might
be said to have suck'd this in with his mother's milk. He did his
part however.——If education planted the mistake, (in case it
was one) my father watered it, and ripened it to perfection.

He would often declare, in speaking his thoughts upon the
subject, that he did not conceive how the greatest family in
England could stand it out against an uninterrupted succession
of six or seven short noses.—And for the contrary reason, he
would generally add, That it must be one of the greatest problems
in civil life, where the same number of long and jolly noses, following one another in a direct line, did not raise and hoist it up
into the best vacancies in the kingdom.——He would often boast
that the *Shandy* family rank'd very high in king *Harry* the VIIIth's
time, but owed its rise to no state engine,—he would say,—but to
that only;—but that, like other families, he would add,—it had
felt the turn of the wheel, and had never recovered the blow of
my great grandfather's nose.——It was an ace of clubs indeed,

he would cry, shaking his head,——and as vile a one for an unfortunate family, as ever turn'd up trumps.

——Fair and softly, gentle reader!——where is thy fancy carrying thee?——If there is truth in man, by my great grandfather's nose, I mean the external organ of smelling, or that part of man which stands prominent in his face, and—which painters say, in good jolly noses and well-proportioned faces, should comprehend a full third,—that is, measuring downwards from the setting on of the hair.——

——What a life of it has an author, at this pass!

CHAPTER XXXIV

I T IS a singular blessing, that nature has form'd the mind of man with the same happy backwardness and renitency against conviction, which is observed in old dogs,——"of not learning new tricks."

What a shuttlecock of a fellow would the greatest philosopher that ever existed, be whisk'd into at once, did he read such books, and observe such facts, and think such thoughts, as would eternally be making him change sides!

Now, my father, as I told you last year, detested all this.—He pick'd up an opinion, Sir, as a man in a state of nature picks up an apple.—It becomes his own,—and if he is a man of spirit, he would lose his life rather than give it up.——

I am aware that *Didius* the great civilian, will contest this point; and cry out against me, Whence comes this man's right to this apple? *ex confesso*, he will say,——things were in a state of nature.—The apple, as much *Frank*'s apple, as *John*'s. Pray, Mr. *Shandy*, what patent has he to shew for it? and how did it begin to be his? was it, when he set his heart upon it? or when he gather'd it? or when he chew'd it? or when he roasted it? or when he peel'd? or when he brought it home? or when he digested? ——or when he——?——. For 'tis plain, Sir, if the first picking up of the apple, made it not his,——that no subsequent act could.

Brother *Didius*, *Tribonius* will answer,—(now *Tribonius* the civilian and church lawyer's beard being three inches and half and three eighths longer than *Didius* his beard,—I'm glad he takes up the cudgels for me, so I give myself no further trouble about the answer.)—Brother *Didius*, *Tribonius* will say, it is a decreed case, as you may find it in the fragments of *Gregorius* and *Hermogenes*'s codes, and in all the codes from *Justinian*'s down to the codes of *Louis* and *Des Eaux*,—That the sweat of a man's brows, and the exsudations of a man's brains, are as much a man's own property, as the breeches upon his backside;——which said exsudations, &c. being dropp'd upon the said apple by the labour of finding it, and picking it up; and being moreover indissolubly wasted, and as indissolubly annex'd by the picker up, to the thing pick'd up, carried home, roasted, peel'd, eaten, digested, and so on;——'tis evident that the gatherer of the apple, in so doing, has mix'd up something which was his own, with the apple which was not his own, by which means he has acquired a property;—or, in other words, the apple is *John*'s apple.

By the same learned chain of reasoning my father stood up for all his opinions: he had spared no pains in picking them up, and the more they lay out of the common way, the better still was his title.——No mortal claim'd them: they had cost him moreover as much labour in cooking and digesting as in the case above, so that they might well and truely be said to be his own goods and chattles.——Accordingly he held fast by 'em, both by teeth and claws,——would fly to whatever he could lay his hands on,—— and, in a word, would intrench and fortify them round with as many circumvallations and breast-works, as my uncle *Toby* would a citadel.

There was one plaguy rub in the way of this,——the scarcity of materials to make any thing of a defence with, in case of a smart attack; inasmuch as few men of great genius had exercised their parts in writing books upon the subject of great noses: by the trotting of my lean horse, the thing is incredible! and I am quite lost in my understanding when I am considering what a treasure of precious time and talents together has been wasted upon worse subjects,——and how many millions of books in all languages, and in all possible types and bindings, have been fabricated upon points not half so much tending to the unity and peace-making of the world. What was to be had, however, he set the greater store by; and though my father would oft-times sport with my uncle *Toby*'s library,——which, by the bye, was ridiculous enough,—yet at the very same time he did it, he collected every book and treatise which had been systematically wrote upon noses, with as much care as my honest uncle *Toby* had done those upon military architecture.——'Tis true, a much less table would have held them,—but that was not thy transgression, my dear uncle.—

Here,——but why here,——rather than in any other part of my story,——I am not able to tell;——but here it is,——my heart stops me to pay to thee, my dear uncle *Toby*, once for all, the tribute I owe thy goodness.—Here let me thrust my chair aside, and kneel down upon the ground, whilst I am pouring forth the warmest sentiments of love for thee, and veneration for the excellency of thy character, that ever virtue and nature kindled in a nephew's bosom.——Peace and comfort rest for evermore upon thy head!—Thou envied'st no man's comforts,——insulted'st no man's opinions.——Thou blackened'st no man's character,——devoured'st no man's bread: gently with faithful *Trim* behind thee, didst thou amble round the little circle of thy pleasures, jostling no creature in thy way;——for each one's service, thou hadst a tear,——for each man's need, thou hadst a shilling.

Whilst I am worth one, to pay a weeder,——thy path from thy door to thy bowling green shall never be grown up.——Whilst there is a rood and a half of land in the *Shandy* family, thy fortifications, my dear uncle *Toby*, shall never be demolish'd.

CHAPTER XXXV

MY FATHER'S collection was not great, but to make amends, it was curious; and consequently, he was some time in making it; he had the great good fortune however to set off well, in getting *Bruscambille*'s prologue upon long noses, almost for nothing,—for he gave no more for *Bruscambille* than three half crowns; owing indeed to the strong fancy which the stall-man saw my father had for the book the moment he laid his hands upon it.——There are not three *Bruscambilles* in *Christendom*,——said the stall-man, except what are chain'd up in the libraries of the curious. My father flung down the money as quick as lightening,—took *Bruscambille* into his bosom,——hyed home from *Piccadilly* to *Coleman*-street with it, as he would have hyed home with a treasure, without taking his hand once off from *Bruscambille* all the way.

To those who do not yet know of which gender *Bruscambille* is,—inasmuch as a prologue upon long noses might easily be done by either,——'twill be no objection against the simile,—to say, That when my father got home, he solaced himself with *Bruscam-*

bille after the manner, in which, 'tis ten to one, your worship solaced yourself with your first mistress,——that is, from morning even unto night: which by the bye, how delightful soever it may prove to the inamorato,—is of little, or no entertainment at all, to by-standers.—Take notice, I go no farther with the simile,—my father's eye was greater than his appetite,—his zeal greater than his knowledge,——he cool'd——his affections became divided,——he got hold of *Prignitz*,—purchased *Scroderus*, *Andrea Parœus*, *Bouchet*'s Evening Conferences, and above all, the great and learned *Hafen Slawkenbergius*; of which, as I shall have much to say by and bye,——I will say nothing now.

CHAPTER XXXVI

OF ALL the tracts my father was at the pains to procure and study in support of his hypothesis, there was not any one wherein he felt a more cruel disappointment at first, than in the celebrated dialogue between *Pamphagus* and *Cocles*, written by the chaste pen of the great and venerable *Erasmus*, upon the various uses and seasonable applications of long noses. ——Now don't let Satan, my dear girl, in this chapter, take advantage of any one spot of rising-ground to get astride of your imagination, if you can any ways help it; or if he is so nimble as to slip on,——let me beg of you, like an unback'd filly, *to frisk it, to squirt it, to jump it, to rear it, to bound it,—and to kick it, with long kicks and short kicks*, till like *Tickletoby*'s mare, you break a strap or a crupper, and throw his worship into the dirt.—— You need not kill him.——

——And pray who was *Tickletoby*'s mare?—'tis just as discreditable and unscholar-like a question, Sir, as to have asked what year (*ab urb. con.*) the second Punic war broke out.—Who was *Tickletoby*'s mare!—Read, read, read, read, my unlearned reader! read,—or by the knowledge of the great saint *Paraleipomenon*—I tell you before-hand, you had better throw down the book at once; for without *much reading*, by which your reverence knows, I mean *much knowledge*, you will no more be able to penetrate the moral of the next marbled page (motly emblem of my work!) than the world with all its sagacity has been able to unraval the many opinions, transactions and truths which still lie mystically hid under the dark veil of the black one.

CHAPTER XXXVII

"*NIHIL ME PÆNITET HUJUS NASI*," quoth *Pamphagus*;—that is,——"My nose has been the making of me."——"*Nec est cur pœniteat*," replies *Cocles*; that is, "How the duce should such a nose fail?"

The doctrine, you see, was laid down by *Erasmus*, as my father wished it, with the utmost plainness; but my father's disappointment was, in finding nothing more from so able a pen, but the bare fact itself; without any of that speculative subtilty or ambidexterity of argumentation upon it, which heaven had bestow'd upon man on purpose to investigate truth and fight for her on all sides.——My father pish'd and pugh'd at first most terribly,—'tis worth something to have a good name. As the dialogue was of *Erasmus*, my father soon came to himself, and read it over and over again with great application, studying every word and every syllable of it thro' and thro' in its most strict and literal interpretation,—he could still make nothing of it, that way. Mayhaps there is more meant, than is said in it, quoth my father.—Learned men, brother *Toby*, don't write dialogues upon long noses for nothing.——I'll study the mystic and the allegoric sense,——here is some room to turn a man's self in, brother.

My father read on.——

Now, I find it needful to inform your reverences and worships, that besides the many nautical uses of long noses enumerated by *Erasmus*, the dialogist affirmeth that a long nose is not without its domestic conveniences also, for that in a case of distress,—and for want of a pair of bellows, it will do excellently well, *ad excitandum focum*, (to stir up the fire.)

Nature had been prodigal in her gifts to my father beyond measure, and had sown the seeds of verbal criticism as deep within him, as she had done the seeds of all other knowledge,—so that he had got out his penknife, and was trying experiments upon the sentence, to see if he could not scratch some better sense into it.—I've got within a single letter, brother *Toby*, cried my father, of *Erasmus* his mystic meaning.—You are near enough, brother, replied my uncle, in all conscience.——Pshaw! cried my father, scratching on,—I might as well be seven miles off.—I've done it,——said my father, snapping his fingers.—See, my dear brother *Toby*, how I have mended the sense.—But you have marr'd a

word, replied my uncle *Toby*.—My father put on his spectacles,—
bit his lip,—and tore out the leaf in a passion.

CHAPTER XXXVIII

O SLAWKENBERGIUS! thou faithful analyzer of my
Disgrázias,——thou sad foreteller of so many of the
whips and short turns, which in one stage or other of my
life have come slap upon me from the shortness of my nose, and
no other cause, that I am conscious of.——Tell me, *Slawkenbergius*! what secret impulse was it? what intonation of voice?
whence came it? how did it sound in thy ears?—art thou sure
thou heard'st it?—which first cried out to thee,—go,—go,
Slawkenbergius! dedicate the labours of thy life,—neglect thy
pastimes,—call forth all the powers and faculties of thy nature,
——macerate thyself in the service of mankind, and write a grand
FOLIO for them, upon the subject of their noses.

How the communication was conveyed into *Slawkenbergius*'s
sensorium,——so that *Slawkenbergius* should know whose finger
touch'd the key,——and whose hand it was that blew the bellows,
——as *Hafen Slawkenbergius* has been dead and laid in his
grave above fourscore and ten years,——we can only raise
conjectures.

Slawkenbergius was play'd upon, for aught I know, like one of
Whitfield's disciples,——that is, with such a distinct intelligence,
Sir, of which of the two *masters* it was, that had been practising
upon his *instrument*,——as to make all reasoning upon it needless.

——For in the account which *Hafen Slawkenbergius* gives the
world of his motives and occasions for writing, and spending so
many years of his life upon this one work.—Towards the end of
his prologomena, which by the bye should have come first,——
but the bookbinder has most injudiciously placed it betwixt the
analitical contents of the book, and the book itself,——he informs
his reader, that ever since he had arrived at the age of discern-
ment, and was able to sit down coolly, and consider within himself the true state and condition of man, and distinguish the main
end and design of his being;——or,——to shorten my translation, for *Slawkenbergius*'s book is in *Latin*, and not a little prolix
in this passage,——ever since I understood, quoth *Slawkenbergius*,

[200]

any thing,——or rather *what was what*,——and could perceive
that the point of long noses had been too loosely handled by all
who had gone before;——have I, *Slawkenbergius*, felt a strong
impulse, with a mighty and an unresistible call within me, to gird
up myself to this undertaking.

And to do justice to *Slawkenbergius*, he has entered the list
with a stronger lance, and taken a much larger career in it, than
any one man who had ever entered it before him,——and indeed,
in many respects, deserves to be *en-nich'd* as a prototype for all
writers, of voluminous works at least, to model their books by,
——for he has taken in, Sir, the whole subject,—examined every
part of it, *dialectically*,—then brought it into full day; dilucidating
it with all the light which either the collision of his own natural
parts could strike,—or the profoundest knowledge of the sciences
had impowered him to cast upon it,——collating, collecting and
compiling,—begging, borrowing, and stealing, as he went along,
all that had been wrote or wrangled thereupon in the schools and
porticos of the learned: so that *Slawkenbergius* his book may
properly be considered, not only as a model,—but as a thorough-
stitch'd DIGEST and regular institute of *noses*; comprehending in
it, all that is, or can be needful to be known about them.

For this cause it is, that I forbear to speak of so many (otherwise) valuable books and treatises of my father's collecting, wrote
either, plump upon noses,—or collaterally touching them;——
such for instance as *Prignitz*, now lying upon the table before me,
who with infinite learning, and from the most candid and scholar-
like examination of above four thousand different skulls, in upwards of twenty charnel houses in *Silesia*, which he had rum-
maged,—has informed us, that the mensuration and configuration
of the osseous or boney parts of human noses, in any *given* tract
of country, except *Crim Tartary*, where they are all crush'd down
by the thumb, so that no judgment can be formed upon them,——
are much nearer alike, than the world imagines;——the difference
amongst them, being, he says, a mere trifle, not worth taking
notice of,——but that the size and jollity of every individual nose,
and by which one nose ranks above another, and bears a higher
price, is owing to the cartilagenous and muscular parts of it, into
whose ducts and sinuses the blood and animal spirits being
impell'd, and driven by the warmth and force of the imagination,
which is but a step from it, (bating the case of ideots, whom
Prignitz, who had lived many years in *Turky*, supposes under the
more immediate tutelage of heaven)——it so happens, and ever

[201]

must, says *Prignitz*, that the excellency of the nose is in a direct arithmetical proportion to the excellency of the wearer's fancy.

It is for the same reason, that is, because 'tis all comprehended in *Slawkenbergius*, that I say nothing likewise of *Scroderus* (*Andrea*) who all the world knows, set himself to oppugn *Prignitz* with great violence,——proving it in his own way, first *logically*, and then by a series of stubborn facts, "That so far was *Prignitz* from the truth, in affirming that the fancy begat the nose, that on the contrary,—the nose begat the fancy."

—The learned suspected *Scroderus*, of an indecent sophism in this,—and *Prignitz* cried out aloud in the dispute, that *Scroderus* had shifted the idea upon him,—but *Scroderus* went on, maintaining his thesis.——

My father was just balancing within himself, which of the two sides he should take in this affair; when *Ambrose Parœus* decided it in a moment, and by over-throwing the systems, both of *Prignitz* and *Scroderus*, drove my father out of both sides of the controversy at once.

Be witness——

I don't acquaint the learned reader,—in saying it, I mention it only to shew the learned, I know the fact myself.——

That this *Ambrose Parœus* was chief surgeon and nose-mender to *Francis* the ninth of *France*, and in high credit with him and the two preceding, or succeeding kings (I know not which)—and that except in the slip he made in his story of *Taliacotius*'s noses, and his manner of setting them on,——was esteemed by the whole college of physicians at that time, as more knowing in matters of noses, than any one who had ever taken them in hand.

Now *Ambrose Parœus* convinced my father, that the true and efficient cause of what had engaged so much the attention of the world, and upon which *Prignitz* and *Scroderus* had wasted so much learning and fine parts,—was neither this nor that,——but that the length and goodness of the nose was owing simply to the softness and flaccidity in the nurse's breast,——as the flatness and shortness of *puisne* noses was, to the firmness and elastic repulsion of the same organ of nutrition in the hale and lively, —which, tho' happy for the woman, was the undoing of the child, inasmuch as his nose was so snubb'd, so rebuff'd, so rebated, and so refrigerated thereby, as never to arrive *ad mensuram suam legitimam*;——but that in case of the flaccidity and softness of the nurse or mother's breast,—by sinking into it, quoth *Parœus*, as into so much butter, the nose was comforted, nourish'd, plump'd up, refresh'd, refocillated, and set a growing for ever.

I have but two things to observe of *Paræus*; first, that he proves and explains all this with the utmost chastity and decorum of expression:—for which may his soul for ever rest in peace!

And, secondly, that besides the systems of *Prignitz* and *Scroderus*, which *Ambrose Paræus* his hypothesis effectually over-threw,—it overthrew at the same time the system of peace and harmony of our family; and for three days together, not only embroiled matters between my father and my mother, but turn'd likewise the whole house and every thing in it, except my uncle *Toby*, quite upside down.

Such a ridiculous tale of a dispute between a man and his wife, never surely in any age or country got vent through the key-hole of a street door!

My mother, you must know,——but I have fifty things more necessary to let you know first,—I have a hundred difficulties which I have promised to clear up, and a thousand distresses and domestic misadventures crouding in upon me thick and three-fold, one upon the neck of another,——a cow broke in (to-morrow morning) to my uncle *Toby*'s fortifications, and eat up two ratios and half of dried grass, tearing up the sods with it, which faced his horn-work and covered way.—*Trim* insists upon being tried by a court-martial,—the cow to be shot,—*Slop* to be *crucifix'd*,—myself to be *tristram'd*, and at my very baptism made a martyr of;——poor unhappy devils that we all are!—I want swaddling,——but there is no time to be lost in exclamations.——I have left my father lying across his bed, and my uncle *Toby* in his old fringed chair, sitting beside him, and promised I would go back to them in half an hour, and five and thirty minutes are laps'd already.

——Of all the perplexities a mortal author was ever seen in,—this certainly is the greatest,—for I have *Hafen Slawkenbergius*'s folio, Sir, to finish——a dialogue between my father and my uncle *Toby*, upon the solution of *Prignitz, Scoderus, Ambrose Paræus, Ponocrates* and *Grangousier* to relate,—a tale out of *Slawkenbergius* to translate, and all this in five minutes less than no time at all;—such a head!—would to heaven my enemies only saw the inside of it !

CHAPTER XXXIX

THERE was not any one scene more entertaining in our family,—and to do it justice in this point;——and I here put off my cap and lay it upon the table close beside my ink-horn, on purpose to make my declaration to the world concerning this one article, the more solemn,——that I believe in my soul, (unless my love and partiality to my understanding blinds me) the hand of the supreme Maker and first Designer of all things, never made or put a family together, (in that period at least of it, which I have sat down to write the story of)——where the characters of it were cast or contrasted with so dramatic a felicity as ours was, for this end; or in which the capacities of affording such exquisite scenes, and the powers of shifting them perpetually from morning to night, were lodged and intrusted with so unlimited a confidence, as in the SHANDY FAMILY.

Not any one of these was more diverting, I say, in this whimsical theatre of ours,—than what frequently arose out of this self-same chapter of long noses,——especially when my father's imagination was heated with the enquiry, and nothing would serve him but to heat my uncle *Toby*'s too.

My uncle *Toby* would give my father all possible fair play in this attempt; and with infinite patience would sit smoking his pipe for whole hours together, whilst my father was practising upon his head, and trying every accessible avenue to drive *Prignitz* and *Scroderus*'s solutions into it.

Whether they were above my uncle *Toby*'s reason,——or contrary to it,——or that his brain was like wet tinder, and no spark could possibly take hold,—or that it was so full of saps, mines, blinds, curtins, and such military disqualifications to his seeing clearly into *Prignitz* and *Scroderus*'s doctrines,—I say not,—let school-men—scullions, anatomists, and engineers, fight for it amongst themselves.——

'Twas some misfortune, I make no doubt, in this affair, that my father had every word of it to translate for the benefit of my uncle *Toby*, and render out of *Slawkenbergius*'s *Latin*, of which, as he was no great master, his translation was not always of the purest, —and generally least so where 'twas most wanted,—this naturally open'd a door to a second misfortune;—that in the warmer paroxisms of his zeal to open my uncle *Toby*'s eyes——my father's ideas run on, as much faster than the translation, as the translation out-

moved my uncle *Toby*'s;——neither the one or the other added
much to the perspicuity of my father's lecture.

CHAPTER XL

THE gift of ratiocination and making syllogisms,—I mean
in man,—for in superior classes of beings, such as angels
and spirits,—'tis all done, may it please your worships, as
they tell me, by INTUITION;—and beings inferior, as your worships
all know,——syllogize by their noses: though there is an island
swiming in the sea, though not altogether at its ease, whose inhabitants, if my intelligence deceives me not, are so wonderfully gifted,
as to syllogize after the same fashion, and oft-times to make very
well out too:——but that's neither here nor there——

The gift of doing it as it should be, amongst us,—or the great
and principal act of ratiocination in man, as logicians tell us, is the
finding out the agreement or disagreement of two ideas one with
another, by the intervention of a third; (called the *medius terminus*)
just as a man, as *Locke* well observes, by a yard, finds two men's
nine-pin-alleys to be of the same length, which could not be
brought together, to measure their equality, by *juxta-position*.

Had the same great reasoner looked on, as my father illustrated
his systems of noses, and observed my uncle *Toby*'s deportment,
—what great attention he gave to every word,—and as oft as he
took his pipe from his mouth, with what wonderful seriousness
he contemplated the length of it,——surveying it transversely as he
held it betwixt his finger and his thumb,——then foreright,—then
this way, and then that, in all its possible directions and fore-
shortenings,——he would have concluded my uncle *Toby* had got
hold of the *medius terminus*; and was syllogizing and measuring
with it the truth of each hypothesis of long noses, in order as my
father laid them before him. This, by the bye, was more than my
father wanted,—his aim in all the pains he was at in these philosophic lectures,—was to enable my uncle *Toby* not to *discuss*,——
but *comprehend*——to *hold* the grains and scruples of learning,—
not to *weigh* them.—My uncle *Toby*, as you will read in the next
chapter, did neither the one or the other.

CHAPTER XLI

'TIS A PITY, cried my father one winter's night, after a three hours painful translation of *Slawkenbergius*,—'tis a pity, cried my father, putting my mother's thread-paper into the book for a mark, as he spoke——that truth, brother *Toby*, should shut herself up in such impregnable fastnessess, and be so obstinate as not to surrender herself sometimes up upon the closest siege.——

Now it happened then, as indeed it had often done before, that my uncle *Toby*'s fancy, during the time of my father's explanation of *Prignitz* to him,——having nothing to stay it there, had taken a short flight to the bowling-green;——his body might as well have taken a turn there too,——so that with all the semblance of a deep school-man intent upon the *medius terminus*,——my uncle *Toby* was in fact as ignorant of the whole lecture, and all its pro's and con's, as if my father had been translating *Hafen Slawkenbergius* from the *Latin* tongue into the *Cherokeè*. But the word *siege*, like a talismanic power, in my father's metaphor, wafting back my uncle *Toby*'s fancy, quick as a note could follow the touch,—he open'd his ears,—and my father observing that he took his pipe out of his mouth, and shuffled his chair nearer the table, as with a desire to profit,—my father with great pleasure began his sentence again,——changing only the plan, and dropping the metaphor of the siege of it, to keep clear of some dangers my father apprehended from it.

'Tis a pity, said my father, that truth can only be on one side, brother *Toby*,—considering what ingenuity these learned men have all shewn in their solutions of noses.——Can noses be dissolved? replied my uncle *Toby*.——

——My father thrust back his chair,——rose up,——put on his hat,——took four long strides to the door,—jerked it open,—thrust his head half way out,—shut the door again,—took no notice of the bad hinge,—returned to the table,—pluck'd my mother's thread-paper out of *Slawkenbergius*'s book,—went hastily to his bureau,—walk'd slowly back, twisting my mother's thread-paper about his thumb,—unbutton'd his waistcoat,—— threw my mother's thread-paper into the fire,—bit her sattin pincushion in two, fill'd his mouth with bran,—confounded it;— but mark!—the oath of confusion was levell'd at my uncle *Toby*'s brain,——which was e'en confused enough already,——the curse came charged only with the bran,—the bran, may it please your honours,—was no more than powder to the ball.

'Twas well my father's passions lasted not long; for so long as they did last, they led him a busy life on't, and it is one of the most unaccountable problems that ever I met with in my observations of human nature, that nothing should prove my father's mettle so much, or make his passions go off so like gun-powder, as the unexpected strokes his science met with from the quaint simplicity of my uncle *Toby*'s questions.——Had ten dozen of hornets stung him behind in so many different places all at one time,—he could not have exerted more mechanical functions in fewer seconds,—or started half so much, as with one single *quære* of three words unseasonably popping in full upon him in his hobbyhorsical career.

'Twas all one to my uncle *Toby*,—he smoaked his pipe on, with unvaried composure,—his heart never intended offence to his brother,—and as his head could seldom find out where the sting of it lay,——he always gave my father the credit of cooling by himself.——He was five minutes and thirty-five seconds about it in the present case.

By all that's good! said my father, swearing, as he came to himself, and taking the oath out of *Ernulphus*'s digest of curses, (though to do my father justice it was a fault (as he told Dr. *Slop* in the affair of *Ernulphus*) which he as seldom committed as any man upon earth.)——By all that's good and great! brother *Toby*, said my father, if it was not for the aids of philosophy, which befriend one so much as they do,—you would put a man beside all temper.—Why, by the *solutions* of noses, of which I was telling you, I meant as you might have known, had you favoured me with one grain of attention, the various accounts which learned men of different kinds of knowledge have given the world, of the causes of short and long noses.—There is no cause but one, replied my uncle *Toby*,—why one man's nose is longer than another's, but because that God pleases to have it so.—That is *Grangousier*'s solution, said my father.—'Tis he, continued my uncle *Toby*, looking up, and not regarding my father's interruption, who makes us all, and frames and puts us together in such forms and proportions, and for such ends, as is agreeable to his infinite wisdom. ——'Tis a pious account, cried my father, but not philosophical,—there is more religion in it than sound science. 'Twas no inconsistent part of my uncle *Toby*'s character,——that he feared God, and reverenced religion.——So the moment my father finished his remark,—my uncle *Toby* fell a whistling *Lillabullero*, with more zeal (though more out of tune) than usual.——

What is become of my wife's thread-paper?

CHAPTER XLII

NO MATTER,——as an appendage to seamstressy, the thread-paper might be of some consequence to my mother,—of none to my father, as a mark in *Slawkenbergius*. *Slawkenbergius* in every page of him was a rich treasury of inexhaustible knowledge to my father,—he could not open him amiss; and he would often say in closing the book, that if all the arts and sciences in the world, with the books which treated of them, were lost,——should the wisdom and policies of governments, he would say, through disuse, ever happen to be forgot, and all that statesmen had wrote, or caused to be written, upon the strong or the weak sides of courts and kingdoms, should they be forgot also,—and *Slawkenbergius* only left,—there would be enough in him in all conscience, he would say, to set the word a-going again. A treasure therefore was he indeed! and institute of all that was necessary to be known of noses, and every thing else, ——at *matin*, noon, and vespers was *Hafen Slawkenbergius* his recreation and delight: 'twas for ever in his hands,—you would have sworn, Sir, it had been a canon's prayer-book,—so worn, so glazed, so contrited and attrited was it with fingers and with thumbs in all its parts, from one end even unto the other.

I am not such a bigot to *Slawkenbergius*, as my father;—there is a fund in him, no doubt; but in my opinion, the best, I don't say the most profitable, but the most amusing part of *Hafen Slawkenbergius*, is his tales,——and, considering he was a *German*, many of them told not without fancy:——these take up his second book, containing nearly one half of his folio, and are comprehended in ten decads, each decad containing ten tales.—— Philosophy is not built upon tales; and therefore 'twas certainly wrong in *Slawkenbergius* to send them into the world by that name;—there are a few of them in his eighth, ninth, and tenth decads, which I own seem rather playful and sportive, than speculative,—but in general they are to be looked upon by the learned as a detail of so many independent facts, all of them turning round somehow or other upon the main hinges of his subject, and collected by him with great fidelity, and added to his work as so many illustrations upon the doctrines of noses.

As we have leisure enough upon our hands,—if you give me leave, madam, I'll tell you the ninth tale of his tenth decad.

END of the THIRD VOLUME.

VOLUME IV

SLAWKENBERGII FABELLA*

V ESPERA *quâdam frigidulâ posteriori in parte mensis Augusti, peregrinus, mulo fusco colore insidens, manticâ a tergo, paucis indusijs, binis calceis, braccisque sericis coccinejs repletâ* Argentoratum *ingressus est.*

Militi eum percontanti, quum portus intraret dixit, se apud Nasorum promontorium fuisse, Francofurtum proficisci, et Argentoratum, transitu ad fines Sarmatiæ mensis intervallo, reversurum.

Miles peregrini in faciem suspexit—Di boni, nova forma nasi!

At multum mihi profuit, inquit peregrinus, carpum amento extrahens, e quo pependit acinaces: Loculo manum inseruit; & magnâ cum urbanitate, pilei parte anteriore tactâ manu sinistrâ ut extendit dextram, militi florinum dedit et processit.

Dolet mihi, ait miles, tympanistam nanum et valgum alloquens, virum adeo urbanum vaginam perdidisse; itinerari haud poterit nudâ acinaci, neque vaginam toto Argentorato, *habilem inveniet. —Nullam unquam habui, respondit peregrinus respiciens,—seque comiter inclinans—hoc more gesto, nudam acinacem elevans, mulo lentò progrediente, ut nasum tueri possim.*

Non immerito, benigne peregrine, respondit miles.

Nihili æstimo, ait ille tympanista, e pergamenâ factitius est.

Prout christianus sum, inquit miles, nasus ille, ni sexties major sit, meo esset conformis.

Crepitare audivi ait tympanista.

Mehercule! sanguinem emisit, respondit miles.

Miseret me, inquit tympanista, qui non ambo titigimus!

Eodem temporis puncto, quo hæc res argumentata fuit inter militem et tympanistam, disceptabatur ibidem tubicine & uxore suâ, qui tunc accesserunt, et peregrino prætereunte, restiterunt.

Quantus nasus! æque longus est, ait tubicina, ac tuba.

* As *Hafen-Slawkenbergius de Nasis* is extremely scarce, it may not be unacceptable to the learned reader to see the specimen of a few pages of his original; I will make no reflection upon it, but that his story-telling Latin is much more concise than his philosophic—and, I think, has more of Latinity in it.

SLAWKENBERGIUS'S TALE

I T WAS one cool refreshing evening, at the close of a very sultry day, in the latter end of the month of *August*, when a stranger, mounted upon a dark mule, with a small cloak-bag behind him, containing a few shirts, a pair of shoes, and a crimson-sattin pair of breeches, entered the town of *Strasburg*.

He told the centinel, who questioned him as he entered the gates, that he had been at the Promontory of NOSES—was going on to *Frankfort*—and should be back again at *Strasburg* that day month, in his way to the borders of *Crim Tartary*.

The centinel looked up into the stranger's face—never saw such a nose in his life.

—I have made a very good venture of it, quoth the stranger—so slipping his wrist out of the loop of a black ribban, to which a short scymetar was hung: He put his hand into his pocket, and with great courtesy touching the forepart of his cap with his left-hand, as he extended his right—he put a florin into the centinel's hand, and passed on.

It grieves me, said the centinel, speaking to a little dwarfish bandy-legg'd drummer, that so courteous a soul should have lost his scabbard—he cannot travel without one to his scymetar, and will not be able to get a scabbard to fit it in all *Strasburg*.——
I never had one, replied the stranger, looking back to the centinel, and putting his hand up to his cap as he spoke——I carry it, continued he thus—holding up his naked scymetar, his mule moving on slowly all the time, on purpose to defend my nose.

It is well worth it, gentle stranger, replied the centinel.

—'Tis not worth a single stiver, said the bandy-legg'd drummer —'tis a nose of parchment.

As I am a true catholic—except that it is six times as big—'tis a nose, said the centinel, like my own.

—I heard it crackle, said the drummer.

By dunder, said the centinel, I saw it bleed.

What a pity, cried the bandy-legg'd drummer, we did not both touch it!

At the very time that this dispute was maintaining by the centinel and the drummer—was the same point debating betwixt a trumpeter and a trumpeter's wife, who were just then coming up, and had stopped to see the stranger pass by.

Benedicity!——What a nose! 'tis as long, said the trumpeter's wife, as a trumpet.

Et ex eodem metallo, ait tubicen, velut sternutamento audias.

Tantum abest, respondit illa, quod fistulam dulcedine vincit.

Æneus est, ait tubicen.

Nequaquam, respondit uxor.

Rursum affirmo, ait tubicen, quod æneus est.

Rem penitus explorabo; prius, enim digito tangam, ait uxor, quam dormivero.

Mulus peregrini, gradu lento progressus est, ut unumquodque verbum controversiæ, non tantum inter militem et tympanistam, verum etiam inter tubicinem et uxorem ejus, audiret.

Nequaquam, ait ille, in muli collum fræna demittens, & manibus ambabus in pectus positis, (mulo lentè progrediente) nequoquam ait ille, respiciens, non necesse est ut res isthæc dilucidata foret. Minime gentium! meus nasus nunquam tangetur, dum spiritus hos reget artus—ad quid agendum? ait uxor burgomagistri.

Peregrinus illi non respondit. Votum faciebat tunc temporis sancto Nicolao, quo facto, sinu dextram inserens, e quâ negligenter pependit acinaces, lento gradu processit per plateam Argentorati latam quæ ad diversorium templo ex adversum ducit.

Peregrinus mulo descendens stabulo includi, & manticam inferri jussit: qua apertâ et coccineis sericis femoralibus extractis cum argenteo laciniato Περιζοματε, his sese induit, statimque, acinaci in manu, ad forum deambulavit.

Quod ubi peregrinus esset ingressus, uxorem tubicinis obviam euntem aspicit; illico cursum flectit, metuens ne nasus suus exploraretur, atque ad diversorium regressus est—exuit se vestibus; braccas coccineas sericas manticæ imposuit mulumque educi jussit.

And of the same mettle, said the trumpeter, as you hear by its sneezing.

—'Tis as soft as a flute, said she.

—'Tis brass, said the trumpeter.

—'Tis a pudding's end—said his wife.

I tell thee again, said the trumpeter, 'tis a brazen nose.

I'll know the bottom of it, said the trumpeter's wife, for I will touch it with my finger before I sleep.

The stranger's mule moved on at so slow a rate, that he heard every word of the dispute, not only betwixt the centinel and the drummer; but betwixt the trumpeter and the trumpeter's wife.

No! said he, dropping his reins upon his mule's neck, and laying both his hands upon his breast, the one over the other in a saint-like position (his mule going on easily all the time) No! said he, looking up—I am not such a debtor to the world—slandered and disappointed as I have been——as to give it that conviction—no! said he, my nose shall never be touched whilst heaven gives me strength—To do what? said a burgomaster's wife.

The stranger took no notice of the burgomaster's wife—he was making a vow to saint *Nicolas*; which done, having uncrossed his arms with the same solemnity with which he crossed them, he took up the reins of his bridle with his left-hand, and putting his right-hand into his bosom, with his scymetar hanging loosely to the wrist of it, he rode on as slowly as one foot of the mule could follow another thro' the principal streets of *Strasburg*, till chance brought him to the great inn in the market-place over-against the church.

The moment the stranger alighted, he ordered his mule to be led into the stable, and his cloak-bag to be brought in; then opening, and taking out of it, his crimson-sattin breeches, with a silver-fringed—(appendage to them, which I dare not translate) —he put his breeches, with his fringed cod-piece on, and forthwith with his short scymetar in his hand, walked out to the grand parade.

The stranger had just taken three turns upon the parade, when he perceived the trumpeter's wife at the opposite side of it—so turning short, in pain lest his nose should be attempted, he instantly went back to his inn——undressed himself, packed up his crimson-sattin breeches, &c. in his cloak-bag, and called for his mule.

Francofurtum proficiscor, ait ille, et Argentoratum quatuor abhinc hebdomadis revertar.

Bene curasti hoc jumentum (ait) muli faciem manu demulcens ——me, manticamque meam, plus sexcentis mille passibus portavit.

Longa via est! respondet hospes, nisi plurimum esset negoti.—— Enimvero ait peregrinus a nasorum promontorio redij, et nasum speciosissimum, egregiosissimumque quem unquam quisquam sortitus est, acquisivi?

Dum peregrinus hanc miram rationem, de seipso reddit, hospes et uxor ejus, oculis intentis, peregrini nasum contemplantur—Per sanctos, sanctasque omnes, ait hospitis uxor, nasis duodecim maximis, in toto Argentorato major est!—estne, ait illa mariti in aurem insusurrans, nonne est nasus prægrandis?

Dolus inest, anime mi, ait hospes—nasus est falsus.—

Verus est, respondit uxor.—

Ex abiete factus, est, ait ille, terebinthinum olet——

Carbunculus inest, ait uxor.

Mortuus est nasus, respondit hospes.

Vivus est, ait illa——& si ipsa vivam tangam.

Votum feci sancto Nicolao, ait peregrinus, nasum meum intactum fore usque ad—Quodnam tempus? illico respondit illa.

Minime tangetur, inquit ille (manibus in pectus compositis) usque ad illam horam—Quam horam? ait illa.—Nullam, respondit peregrinus, donec perveneo, ad—Quem locum,—obsecro? ait illa— Peregrinus nil respondens mulo conscenso discessit.

I am going forwards, said the stranger, for *Frankfort*——and shall be back at *Strasburg* this day month.

I hope, continued the stranger, stroking down the face of his mule with his left-hand as he was going to mount it, that you have been kind to this faithful slave of mine——it has carried me and my cloak-bag, continued he, tapping the mule's back, above six hundred leagues.

—'Tis a long journey, Sir, replied the master of the inn—— unless a man has great business.—Tut! tut! said the stranger, I have been at the Promontory of Noses; and have got me one of the goodliest and jolliest, thank heaven, that ever fell to a single man's lot.

Whilst the stranger was giving this odd account of himself, the master of the inn and his wife kept both their eyes fixed full upon the stranger's nose—By saint *Radagunda*, said the inn-keeper's wife to herself, there is more of it than in any dozen of the largest noses put together in all *Strasburg*! is it not, said she, whispering her husband in his ear, is it not a noble nose?

'Tis an imposture, my dear, said the master of the inn—'tis a false nose.—

'Tis a true nose, said his wife,—

'Tis made of fir-tree, said he,—I smell the turpentine.—

There's a pimple on it, said she.

'Tis a dead nose, replied the inn-keeper.

'Tis a live nose, and if I am alive myself, said the inn-keeper's wife, I will touch it.

I have made a vow to saint *Nicolas* this day, said the stranger, that my nose shall not be touched till—Here the stranger, suspending his voice, looked up—Till when? said she hastily.

It never shall be touched, said he, clasping his hands and, bringing them close to his breast, till that hour.——What hour? cried the inn-keeper's wife.——Never!—never! said the stranger, never till I am got—For heaven sake into what place? said she.— The stranger rode away without saying a word.

The stranger had not got half a league on his way towards *Frankfort*, before all the city of *Strasburg* was in an uproar about his nose. The *Compline* bells were just ringing to call the *Strasburgers* to their devotions, and shut up the duties of the day in prayer:——no soul in all *Strasburg* heard 'em—the city was like a swarm of bees——men, women, and children (the *Compline*-bells tinkling all the time) flying here and there—in at one door, out at another—this way and that way—long ways and cross ways—up one street, down another street—in at this ally, out at that——did you see it? did you see it? did you see it? O! did you see it?—who saw it? who did see it? for mercy's sake, who saw it?

Alack o'day! I was at vespers!——I was washing, I was starching, I was scouring, I was quilting—GOD help me! I never saw it—I never touch'd it!——would I had been a centinel, a bandy-legg'd drummer, a trumpeter, a trumpeter's wife, was the general cry and lamentation in every street and corner of *Strasburg*.

Whilst all this confusion and disorder triumphed throughout the great city of *Strasburg*, was the courteous stranger going on as gently upon his mule in his way to *Frankfort*, as if he had had no concern at all in the affair—talking all the way he rode in broken sentences, sometimes to his mule—sometimes to himself ——sometimes to his Julia.

O Julia, my lovely Julia!—nay I cannot stop to let thee bite that thistle—that ever the suspected tongue of a rival should have robbed me of enjoyment when I was upon the point of tasting it.—

—Pugh!—'tis nothing but a thistle—never mind it—thou shalt have a better supper at night.—

——Banish'd from my country—my friends—from thee.—

Poor devil, thou'rt sadly tired with thy journey!—come—get on a little faster—there's nothing in my cloak-bag but two shirts —a crimson-sattin pair of breeches, and a fringed—Dear Julia!

—But why to *Frankfort*?—is it that there is a hand unfelt, which secretly is conducting me through these meanders and unsuspected tracts!—

—Stumbling! by saint *Nicolas*! every step——why at this rate we shall be all night in getting in——

—To happiness—or am I to be the sport of fortune and slander —destined to be driven forth unconvicted—unheard—untouched ——if so, why did I not stay at *Strasburg*, where justice——but I had sworn!—Come, thou shalt drink—to *St. Nicolas*—O Julia! ——What dost thou prick up thy ears at?—'tis nothing but a man, &c.——

The stranger rode on communing in this manner with his mule and Julia—till he arrived at his inn, where, as soon as he arrived, he alighted—saw his mule, as he had promised it, taken good care of——took off his cloak-bag, with his crimson-sattin breeches, &c. in it——called for an omelet to his supper, went to his bed about twelve o'clock, and in five minutes fell fast asleep.

It was about the same hour when the tumult in *Strasburg* being abated for that night,——the *Strasburgers* had all got quietly into their beds—but not like the stranger, for the rest either of their minds or bodies; queen *Mab*, like an elf as she was, had taken the stranger's nose, and without reduction of its bulk, had that night been at the pains of slitting and dividing it into as many noses of different cuts and fashions, as there were heads in *Strasburg* to hold them. The abbess of *Quedlinberg*, who, with the four great dignitaries of her chapter, the prioress, the deaness, the sub-chantress, and senior canoness, had that week come to *Strasburg* to consult the university upon a case of conscience relating to their placket holes—was ill all the night.

The courteous stranger's nose had got perched upon the top of the pineal gland of her brain, and made such rousing work in the fancies of the four great dignitaries of her chapter, they could not get a wink of sleep the whole night thro' for it——there was no keeping a limb still amongst them—in short, they got up like so many ghosts.

The penitentiaries of the third order of saint *Francis*—— the nuns of mount *Calvary*—the *Præmonstratenses*——the *Clunienses**—the *Carthusians*, and all the severer orders of nuns who lay that night in blankets of hair-cloth, were still in a worse condition than the abbess of *Quedlinberg*—by tumbling and tossing, and tossing and tumbling from one side of their beds to the other the whole night long—the several sisterhoods had scratch'd and mawl'd themselves all to death—they got out of their beds almost flead alive—every body thought saint *Antony* had visited them for probation with his fire——they had never once, in short, shut their eyes the whole night long from vespers to matins.

The nuns of saint *Ursula* acted the wisest—they never attempted to go to bed at all.

The dean of *Strasburg*, the prebendaries, the capitulars and domiciliars (capitularly assembled in the morning to consider the case of butter'd buns) all wished they had followed the nuns of saint *Ursula*'s example.——In the hurry and confusion every thing had been in the night before, the bakers had all forgot to lay their leaven—there were no butter'd buns to be had for breakfast in all *Strasburg*—the whole close of the cathedral was in one eternal commotion—such a cause of restlessness and disquietude,

* *Hafen Slawkenbergius* means the Benedictine nuns of *Cluny*, founded in the year 940, by *Odo*, abbé de *Cluny*.

and such a zealous inquiry into the cause of that restlessness, had never happened in *Strasburg*, since *Martin Luther*, with his doctrines, had turned the city up-side down.

If the stranger's nose took this liberty of thrusting itself thus into the dishes* of religious orders, &c. what a carnival did his nose make of it, in those of the laity!—'tis more than my pen, worn to the stump as it is, has powers to describe; tho' I acknowledge, (*cries* Slawkenbergius, *with more gaiety of thought than I could have expected from him*) that there is many a good simile now subsisting in the world which might give my countrymen some idea of it; but at the close of such a folio as this, wrote for their sakes, and in which I have spent the greatest part of my life —tho' I own to them the simile is in being, yet would it not be unreasonable in them to expect I should have either time or inclination to search for it? Let it suffice to say, that the riot and disorder it occasioned in the *Straburgers* fantacies was so general —such an overpowering mastership had it got of all the faculties of the *Strasburgers* minds—so many strange things, with equal confidence on all sides, and with equal eloquence in all places, were spoken and sworn to concerning it, that turned the whole stream of all discourse and wonder towards it—every soul, good and bad—rich and poor—learned and unlearned—doctor and student—mistress and maid—gentle and simple—nun's flesh and woman's flesh in *Strasburg* spent their time in hearing tidings about it—every eye in *Strasburg* languished to see it——every finger—every thumb in *Strasburg* burned to touch it.

Now what might add, if any thing may be thought necessary to add to so vehement a desire—was this, that the centinel, the bandy-legg'd drummer, the trumpeter, the trumpeter's wife, the burgomaster's widow, the master of the inn, and the master of the inn's wife, how widely soever they all differed every one from another in their testimonies and descriptions of the stranger's nose—they all agreed together in two points—namely, that he was gone to *Frankfort*, and would not return to *Strasburg* till that day month; and secondly, whether his nose was true or false, that the stranger himself was one of the most perfect paragons of beauty—the finest made man!—the most genteel!—the most generous of his purse—the most courteous in his carriage that had ever entered the gates of *Strasburg*—that as he rode, with

* Mr. *Shandy*'s compliments to orators—is very sensible that *Slawkenbergius* has here changed his metaphor—which he is very guilty of;—that as a translator, Mr. *Shandy* has all along done what he could to make him stick to it—but that here 'twas impossible.

his scymetar slung loosely to his wrist, thro' the streets—and walked with his crimson-sattin breeches across the parade—'twas with so sweet an air of careless modesty, and so manly withal—as would have put the heart in jeopardy (had his nose not stood in his way) of every virgin who had cast her eyes upon him.

I call not upon that heart which is a stranger to the throbs and yearnings of curiosity, so excited to justify the abbess of *Quedlinberg*, the prioress, the deaness and subchantress for sending at noon-day for the trumpeter's wife: she went through the streets of *Strasburg* with her husband's trumpet in her hand;—the best apparatus the straitness of the time would allow her, for the illustration of her theory—she staid no longer than three days.

The centinel and the bandy-legg'd drummer!—nothing on this side of old *Athens* could equal them! they read their lectures under the city gates to comers and goers, with all the pomp of a *Chrysippus* and a *Crantor* in their porticos.

The master of the inn, with his ostler on his left-hand, read his also in the same stile,—under the portico or gateway of his stable-yard—his wife, hers more privately in a back room: all flocked to their lectures; not promiscuously—but to this or that, as is ever the way, as faith and credulity marshal'd them—in a word, each *Strasburger* came crouding for intelligence and every *Strasburger* had the intelligence he wanted.

'Tis worth remarking, for the benefit of all demonstrators in natural philosophy, &c. that as soon as the trumpeter's wife had finished the abbess of *Quedlinberg*'s private lecture, and had begun to read in public, which she did upon a stool in the middle of the great parade—she incommoded the other demonstrators mainly, by gaining incontinently the most fashionable part of the city of *Strasburg* for her auditory—But when a demonstrator in philosophy (cries *Slawkenbergius*) has a *trumpet* for an apparatus, pray what rival in science can pretend to be heard besides him?

Whilst the unlearned, thro' these conduits of intelligence, were all busied in getting down to the bottom of the well, where TRUTH keeps her little court—were the learned in their way as busy in pumping her up thro' the conduits of dialect induction—they concerned themselves not with facts—they reasoned—

Not one profession had thrown more light upon this subject than the faculty—had not all their disputes about it run into the affair of *Wens* and œdematous swellings, they could not keep clear of them for their bloods and souls—the stranger's nose had nothing to do either with wens or œdematous swellings.

It was demonstrated however very satisfactorily, that such a ponderous mass of heterogenious matter could not be congested and conglomerated to the nose, whilst the infant was *in Utero*, without destroying the statical balance of the fœtus, and throwing it plump upon its head nine months before the time.——

—The opponents granted the theory—they denied the consequences.

And if a suitable provision of veins, arteries, &c. said they, was not laid in, for the due nourishment of such a nose, in the very first stamina and rudiments of its formation before it came into the world (bating the case of Wens) it could not regularly grow and be sustained afterwards.

This was all answered by a dissertation upon nutriment, and the effect which nutriment had in extending the vessels, and in the increase and prolongation of the muscular parts to the greatest growth and expansion imaginable—In the triumph of which theory, they went so far as to affirm, that there was no cause in nature, why a nose might not grow to the size of the man himself.

The respondents satisfied the world this event could never happen to them so long as a man had but one stomach and one pair of lungs—For the stomach, said they, being the only organ destined for the reception of food, and turning it into chyle,—and the lungs the only engine of sanguification—it could possibly work off no more, than what the appetite brought it: or admitting the possibility of a man's overloading his stomach, nature had set bounds however to his lungs—the engine was of a determined size and strength, and could elaborate but a certain quantity in a given time—that is, it could produce just as much blood as was sufficient for one single man, and no more; so that, if there was as much nose as man—they proved a mortification must necessarily ensue; and forasmuch as there could not be a support for both, that the nose must either fall off from the man, or the man inevitably fall off from his nose.

Nature accommodates herself to these emergencies, cried the opponents—else what do you say to the case of a whole stomach —a whole pair of lungs, and but *half* a man, when both his legs have been unfortunately shot off?—

He dies of a plethora, said they—or must spit blood, and in a fortnight or three weeks go off in a consumption—

—It happens otherways—replied the opponents.——

It ought not, said they.

The more curious and intimate inquirers after nature and her doings, though they went hand in hand a good way together, yet they all divided about the nose at last, almost as much as the faculty itself.

They amicably laid it down, that there was a just and geometrical arrangement and proportion of the several parts of the human frame to its several destinations, offices, and functions, which could not be transgressed but within certain limits—that nature, though she sported—she sported within a certain circle;—and they could not agree about the diameter of it.

The logicians stuck much closer to the point before them than any of the classes of the literati;—they began and ended with the word nose; and had it not been for a *petitio principii*, which one of the ablest of them ran his head against in the beginning of the combat, the whole controversy had been settled at once.

A nose, argued the logician, cannot bleed without blood—and not only blood—but blood circulating in it to supply the phænomenon with a succession of drops—(a stream being but a quicker succession of drops, that is included, said he.)—Now death, continued the logician, being nothing but the stagnation of the blood—

I deny the definition—Death is the separation of the soul from the body, said his antagonist—Then we don't agree about our weapon, said the logician—Then there is an end of the dispute, replied the antagonist.

The civilians were still more concise; what they offered being more in the nature of a decree—than a dispute.

— Such a monstrous nose, said they, had it been a true nose, could not possibly have been suffered in civil society—and if false—to impose upon society with such false signs and tokens, was a still greater violation of its rights, and must have had still less mercy shewn it.

The only objection to this was, that if it proved any thing, it proved the stranger's nose was neither true nor false.

This left room for the controversy to go on. It was maintained by the advocates of the ecclesiastic court, that there was nothing to inhibit a decree, since the stranger *ex mero motu* had confessed he had been at the Promontory of Noses, and had got one of the goodliest, &c. &c.—To this it was answered, it was impossible there should be such a place as the Promontory of Noses, and the learned be ignorant where it lay. The commissary of the bishop of *Strasburg* undertook the advocates, explained this matter in a treatise upon proverbial phrases, shewing them, that the Promontory of Noses was a mere allegoric expression, importing no more than that nature had given him a long nose: in proof of which, with great learning, he cited the underwritten authorities*, which had decided the point incontestably, had it not appeared that a dispute about some franchises of dean and chapter-lands had been determined by it nineteen years before.

It happened—I must not say unluckily for Truth, because they were giving her a lift another way in so doing; that the two universities of *Strasburg*—the *Lutheran*, founded in the year 1538 by *Jacobus Sturmius*, counsellor of the senate,—and the *Popish*, founded by *Leopold*, arch-duke of *Austria*, were, during all this time, employing the whole depth of their knowledge (except just what the affair of the abbess of *Quedlinberg*'s placket-holes required)—in determining the point of *Martin Luther*'s damnation.

The *Popish* doctors had undertaken to demonstrate *a priori*; that from the necessary influence of the planets on the twenty-second day of *October* 1483——when the moon was in the twelfth house —*Jupiter*, *Mars*, and *Venus* in the third, the *Sun*, *Saturn*, and *Mercury* all got together in the fourth—that he must in course, and unavoidably, be a damn'd man—and that his doctrines, by a direct corollary, must be damn'd doctrines too.

By inspection into his horoscope, where five planets were in coition all at once with scorpio † (in reading this my father would always shake his head) in the ninth house which the *Arabians* allotted to religion—it appeared that *Martin Luther* did not care

* Nonnulli ex nostratibus eadem loquendi formulâ utun. Quinimo et Logistæ & Canonistæ — Vid. Parce Bar e Jas in d. L. Provicial. Constitut. de conjec. vid. Vol. Lib 4. Titul. 1. N. 7, quà etiam in re conspir. Om. de Promontorio Nas. Tichmak. ff. d. tit. 3. fol. 189. paffim. Vid. Glos. de contrahend, empt. &c. nec non J. Scrudr. in cap. §. refut. ff. per totum, cum his cons. Rever. J. Tubal, Sentent. & Prov. cap. 9. ff. 11, 12. obiter. V. et Librum, cui Tit. de Terris & Phras. Belg. ad finem, cum comment. N. Bardy Belg. Vid. Scrip. Argentotarens. de Antiq. Ecc. in Episc. Archiv, fid. coll. per Von Jacobum Koinshoven Folio Argent. 1583, præcip. ad finem. Quibus add. Rebuff in L. obvenire de Signif. Nom. ff. fol. & de Jure, Gent. & Civil, de protib. aliena feud, per federa, test. Joha. Luxius in prolegom. quem velim videas, de Analy. Cap. 1, 2, 3. Vid. Idea.

† Hæc mira, satisque horrenda. Planetarum coitio sub Scorpio Asterismo in nonâ cœli statione, quam Arabes religioni deputabant efficit *Martinum Lutherum* sacrilegum hereticum, christianæ religionis hostem acerrimum atque prophanum, ex horoscopi directione ad Martis coitum, religiosis-simus obiit, ejus Anima scelestissima ad infernos navigavit—ab Alecto, Tisiphone et Magera flagellis igneis cruciata pereniter.

—Lucas Gauricus in Tractatu astrologico de præteritis multorum hominum accidentibus per genituras examinatis.

one stiver about the matter—and that from the horoscope directed to the conjunction of *Mars*—they made it plain likewise he must die cursing and blaspheming—with the blast of which his soul (being steep'd in guilt) sailed before the wind, into the lake of hell fire.

The little objection of the *Lutheran* doctors to this, was, that it must certainly be the soul of another man, born *Oct.* 22, 1483, which was forced to sail down before the wind in that manner—inasmuch as it appeared from the register of *Islaben* in the county of *Mansfelt*, that *Luther* was not born in the year 1483, but in 84; and not on the 22d day of *October*, but on the 10th of *November*, the eve of *Martinmas*-day, from whence he had the name of *Martin*.

[—I must break off my translation for a moment; for if I did not, I know I should no more be able to shut my eyes in bed, than the abbess of *Quedlinberg*—It is to tell the reader, that my father never read this passage of *Slawkenbergius* to my uncle *Toby* but with triumph—not over my uncle *Toby*, for he never opposed him in it—but over the whole world.

—Now you see, brother *Toby*, he would say, looking up, "that christian names are not such indifferent things;"—had *Luther* here been called by any other name but *Martin*, he would have been damned to all eternity—Not that I look upon *Martin*, he would add, as a good name—far from it—'tis something better than a neutral, and but a little—yet little as it is, you see it was of some service to him.

My father knew the weakness of this prop to his hypothesis, as well as the best logician could shew him—yet so strange is the weakness of man at the same time, as it fell in his way, he could not for his life but make use of it; and it was certainly for this reason, that though there are many stories in *Hafen Slawkenbergius*'s Decads full as entertaining as this I am translating, yet there is not one amongst them which my father read over with half the delight—it flattered two of his strangest hypotheses together—his NAMES and his NOSES—I will be bold to say, he might have read all the books in the *Alexandrian* library, had not fate taken other care of them, and not have met with a book or a passage in one, which hit two such nails as these upon the head at one stroke.]

The two universities of *Strasburg* were hard tugging at this affair of *Luther*'s navigation. The Protestant doctors had demonstrated, that he had not sailed right before the wind, as the

Popish doctors had pretended; and as every one knew there was no sailing full in the teeth of it,—they were going to settle, in case he had sailed, how many points he was off; whether *Martin* had doubled the cape, or had fallen upon a lee-shore; and no doubt, as it was an enquiry of much edification, at least to those who understood this sort of NAVIGATION, they had gone on with it in spite of the size of the stranger's nose, had not the size of the stranger's nose drawn off the attention of the world from what they were about—it was their business to follow.——

The abbess of *Quedlinberg* and her four dignitaries was no stop; for the enormity of the stranger's nose running full as much in their fancies as their case of conscience—The affair of their placket-holes kept cold—In a word, the printers were ordered to distribute their types—all controversies dropp'd.

'Twas a square cap with a silk tassel upon the crown of it—to a nut shell—to have guessed on which side of the nose the two universities would split.

'Tis above reason, cried the doctors on one side.

'Tis below reason, cried the others.

'Tis faith, cried the one.

'Tis a fiddle-stick, said the other.

'Tis possible, cried the one.

'Tis impossible, said the other.

God's power is infinite, cried the Nosarians, he can do any thing.

He can do nothing, replied the Antinosarians, which implies contradictions.

He can make matter think, said the Nosarians.

As certainly as you can make a velvet cap out of a sow's ear, replied the Antinosarians.

He cannot make two and two five, replied the Popish doctors.—'Tis false, said their opponents.—

Infinite power is infinite power, said the doctors who maintained the *reality* of the nose.——It extends only to all possible things, replied the *Lutherans*.

By God in heaven, cried the Popish doctors, he can make a nose, if he thinks fit, as big as the steeple of *Strasburg*.

Now the steeple of *Strasburg* being the biggest and the tallest church-steeple to be seen in the whole world, the Anti-nosarians denied that a nose of 575 geometrical feet in length could be worn, at least by a middle-siz'd man—The Popish doctors swore it could—The *Lutheran* doctors said No;—it could not.

This at once started a new dispute, which they pursued a great way upon the extent and limitation of the moral and natural attributes of God—That controversy led them naturally into *Thomas Aquinas*, and *Thomas Aquinas* to the devil.

The stranger's nose was no more heard of in the dispute—it just served as a frigate to launch them into the gulph of school-divinity,—and then they all sailed before the wind.

Heat is in proportion to the want of true knowledge.

The controversy about the attributes, &c. instead of cooling, on the contrary had inflamed the *Strasburgers* imaginations to a most inordinate degree—The less they understood of the matter, the greater was their wonder about it—they were left in all the distresses of desire unsatisfied—saw their doctors, the *Parchmentarians*, the *Brassarians*, the *Turpentarians*, on one side—the Popish doctors on the other, like *Pantagruel* and his companions in quest of the oracle of the bottle, all embarked and out of sight.

——The poor *Strasburgers* left upon the beach!

—What was to be done?—No delay—the uproar increased— every one in disorder—the city gates set open.—

Unfortunate *Strasburgers*! was there in the store-house of nature—was there in the lumber-rooms of learning—was there in the great arsenal of chance, one single engine left undrawn forth to torture your curiosities, and stretch your desires, which was not pointed by the hand of fate to play upon your hearts?— I dip not my pen into my ink to excuse the surrender of yourselves—'tis to write your panegyrick. Shew me a city so macerated with expectation—who neither eat, or drank, or slept, or prayed, or hearkened to the calls either of religion or nature for seven and twenty days together, who could have held out one day longer.

On the twenty-eighth the courteous stranger had promised to return to *Strasburg*.

Seven thousand coaches (*Slawkenbergius* must certainly have made some mistake in his numerical characters) 7000 coaches— 15000 single horse chairs——20000 waggons, crouded as full as they could all hold with senators, counsellors, syndicks— beguines, widows, wives, virgins, canons, concubines, all in their coaches—The abbess of *Quedlinberg*, with the prioress, the deaness and sub-chantress leading the procession in one coach, and the dean of *Strasburg*, with the four great dignitaries of his chapter on her left-hand—the rest following higglety-pigglety as they could; some on horseback——some on foot—some led—some driven—some down the *Rhine*—some this way—some that—all set out at sun-rise to meet the courteous stranger on the road.

Haste we now towards the catastrophe of my tale—I say *Catastrophe* (cries *Slawkenbergius*) inasmuch as a tale, with parts rightly disposed, not only rejoiceth (*gaudet*) in the *Catastrophe* and *Peripeitia* of a DRAMA, but rejoiceth moreover in all the essential and integrant parts of it—it has its *Protasis, Epistasis, Catastasis*, its *Catastrophe* or *Peripeitia* growing one out of the other in it, in the order *Aristotle* first planted them—without which a tale had better never be told at all, says *Slawkenbergius*, but be kept to a man's self.

In all my ten tales, in all my ten decads, have I, *Slawkenbergius*, tied down every tale of them as tightly to this rule, as I have done this of the stranger and his nose.

—From his first parley with the centinel, to his leaving the city of *Strasburg*, after pulling off his crimson-sattin pair of breeches, is the *Protasis* or first entrance——where the characters of the *Personæ Dramatis* are just touched in, and the subject slightly begun.

The *Epistasis*, wherein the action is more fully entered upon and heightened, till it arrives at its state or height called the *Catastasis*, and which usually takes up the 2d and 3d act, is included within that busy period of my tale, betwixt the first night's uproar about the nose, to the conclusion of the trumpeter's wife's lectures upon it in the middle of the grand parade; and from the first embarking of the learned in the dispute—to the doctors finally sailing away, and leaving the *Strasburgers* upon the beach in distress, is the *Catastasis* or the ripening of the incidents and passions for their bursting forth in the fifth act.

This commences with the setting out of the *Strasburgers* in the *Frankfort* road, and terminates in unwinding the labyrinth and bringing the hero out of a state of agitation (as *Aristotle* calls it) to a state of rest and quietness.

This, says *Hafen Slawkenbergius*, constitutes the catastrophe or peripeitia of my tale—and that is the part of it I am going to relate.

We left the stranger behind the curtain asleep—he enters now upon the stage.

—What dost thou prick up thy ears at?—'tis nothing but a man upon a horse—was the last word the stranger uttered to his mule. It was not proper then to tell the reader, that the mule took his master's word for it; and without any more *ifs* or *ands*, let the traveller and his horse pass by.

The traveller was hastening with all diligence to get to *Strasburg* that night——What a fool am I, said the traveller to himself, when he had rode about a league farther, to think of getting into *Strasburg* this night—*Strasburg!*—the great *Strasburg!*—*Strasburg*, the capital of all *Alsatia! Strasburg*, an imperial city! *Strasburg*, a sovereign state! *Strasburg*, garrisoned with five thousand of the best troops in all the world!—Alas! If I was at the gates of *Strasburg* this moment, I could not gain admittance into it for a ducat,—nay a ducat and half—'tis too much—better go back to the last inn I have passed—than lie I know not where—or give I know not what. The traveller, as he made these reflections in his mind, turned his horse's head about, and three minutes after the stranger had been conducted into his chamber, he arrived at the same inn.

—We have bacon in the house, said the host, and bread—till eleven o'clock this night had three eggs in it—but a stranger, who arrived an hour ago, has had them dressed into an omlet, and we have nothing.———

—Alas! said the traveller, harrassed as I am, I want nothing but a bed—I have one as soft as is in *Alsatia*, said the host.

——The stranger, continued he, should have slept in it, for 'tis my best bed, but upon the score of his nose—He has got a defluxion, said the traveller—Not that I know, cried the host—But 'tis a camp-bed, and *Jacinta*, said he, looking towards the maid, imagined there was not room in it to turn his nose in—Why so? cried the traveller starting back—It is so long a nose, replied the host—The traveller fixed his eyes upon *Jacinta*, then upon the ground—kneeled upon his right knee—had just got his hand laid upon his breast—Trifle not with my anxiety, said he, rising up again—'Tis no trifle, said *Jacinta*, 'tis the most glorious nose!—The traveller fell upon his knee again—laid his hand upon his breast—then said he, looking up to heaven! thou hast conducted me to the end of my pilgrimage——'Tis *Diego!*

The traveller was the brother of the Julia, so often invoked that night by the stranger as he rode from *Strasburg* upon his mule; and was come, on her part, in quest of him. He had accompanied his sister from *Valadolid* across the *Pyrenean* mountains thro' *France*, and had many an entangled skein to wind off in pursuit of him thro' the many meanders and abrupt turnings of a lover's thorny tracks.

—Julia had sunk under it—and had not been able to go a step farther than to *Lyons*, where, with the many disquietudes of a tender heart, which all talk of—but few feel—she sicken'd, but had just strength to write a letter to *Diego*; and having conjured her brother never to see her face till he had found him out, and put the letter into his hands, Julia took to her bed.

Fernandez (for that was her brother's name)—tho' the camp-bed was as soft as any one in *Alsace*, yet he could not shut his eyes in it.—As soon as it was day he rose, and hearing *Diego* was risen too, he enter'd his chamber, and discharged his sister's commission.

The letter was as follows:

"Seig. DIEGO.

"Whether my suspicions of your nose were justly excited or not—'tis not now to inquire—it is enough I have not had firmness to put them to farther tryal.

"How could I know so little of myself, when I sent my *Duena* to forbid your coming more under my lattice? or how could I know so little of you, *Diego*, as to imagine you would not have staid one day in *Valadolid* to have given ease to my doubts?—Was I to be abandoned, *Diego*, because I was deceived? or was it kind to take me at my word, whether my suspicions were just or no, and leave me, as you did, a prey to much uncertainty and sorrow.

"In what manner Julia has resented this—my brother, when he puts this letter into your hands, will tell you: He will tell you in how few moments she repented of the rash message she had sent you—in what frantic haste she flew to her lattice, and how many days and nights together she leaned immoveably upon her elbow, looking thro' it towards the way which *Diego* was wont to come.

"He will tell you, when she heard of your departure—how her spirits deserted her—how her heart sicken'd—how piteously she mourn'd—how low she hung her head. O *Diego*! how many weary steps has my brother's pity led me by the hand languishing to trace out yours! how far has desire carried me beyond strength—and how oft have I fainted by the way, and sunk into his arms, with only power to cry out—O my *Diego*!

"If the gentleness of your carriage has not belied your heart, you will fly to me, almost as fast as you fled from me—haste as you will, you will arrive but to see me expire.—'Tis a bitter draught, *Diego*, but oh! 'tis embitter'd still more by dying *un*——."

[230]

She could proceed no farther.

Slawkenbergius supposes the word intended was *unconvinced*, but her strength would not enable her to finish her letter.

The heart of the courteous *Diego* overflowed as he read the letter—he ordered his mule forthwith and *Fernandez*'s horse to be saddled; and as no vent in prose is equal to that of poetry in such conflicts—chance, which as often directs us to remedies as to *diseases*, having thrown a piece of charcoal into the window—*Diego* availed himself of it, and whilst the ostler was getting ready his mule, he eased his mind against the wall as follows.

ODE

Harsh and untuneful are the notes of love,
Unless my Julia strikes the key,
Her hand alone can touch the part,
Whose dulcet movement charms the heart,
And governs all the man with sympathetic sway.

2d.

O Julia!

The lines were very natural—for they were nothing at all to the purpose, says *Slawkenbergius*, and 'tis a pity there were no more of them; but whether it was that Seig. *Diego* was slow in composing verses—or the ostler quick in saddling mules—is not averred; certain it was, that *Diego*'s mule and *Fernandez*'s horse were ready at the door of the inn, before *Diego* was ready for his second stanza; so without staying to finish his ode, they both mounted, sallied forth, passed the *Rhine*, traversed *Alsace*, shaped their course towards *Lyons*, and before the *Strusburgers* and the abbess of *Quedlinberg* had set out on their cavalcade, had *Fernandez, Diego*, and his *Julia*, crossed the *Pyrenean* mountains, and got safe to *Valadolid*.

'Tis needless to inform the geographical reader, that when *Diego* was in *Spain*, it was not possible to meet the courteous stranger in the *Frankfort* road; it is enough to say, that of all restless desires, curiosity being the strongest—the *Strasburgers* felt the full force of it; and that for three days and nights they were tossed to and fro in the *Frankfort* road, with the tempestuous fury of this passion, before they could submit to return home—When alas! an event was prepared for them, of all others the most grievous that could befal a free people.

As this revolution of the *Strasburgers* affairs is often spoken of,

[231]

and little understood, I will, in ten words, says *Slawkenbergius*, give the world an explanation of it, and with it put an end to my tale.

Every body knows of the grand system of Universal Monarchy, wrote by order of Mons. *Colbert*, and put in manuscript into the hands of *Lewis* the fourteenth, in the year 1664.

'Tis as well known, that one branch out of many of that system, was the getting possession of *Strasburg*, to favour an entrance at all times into *Suabia*, in order to disturb the quiet of *Germany*—and that in consequence of this plan, *Strasburg* unhappily fell at length into their hands.

It is the lot of few to trace out the true springs of this and such like revolutions—The vulgar look too high for them—Statesmen look too low—Truth (for once) lies in the middle.

What a fatal thing is the popular pride of a free city! cries one historian—The *Strasburgers* deemed it a diminution of their freedom to receive an imperial garrison—and so fell a prey to a *French* one.

The fate, says another, of the *Strasburgers*, may be a warning to all free people to save their money—They anticipated their revenues—brought themselves under taxes, exhausted their strength, and in the end became so weak a people, they had not strength to keep their gates shut, and so the *French* pushed them open.

Alas! alas! cries *Slawkenbergius*, 'twas not the *French*—'twas CURIOSITY pushed them open—The *French* indeed, who are ever upon the catch, when they saw the *Strasburgers*, men, women, and children, all marched out to follow the stranger's nose—each man followed his own, and marched in.

Trade and manufactures have decayed and gradually grown down ever since—but not from any cause which commercial heads have assigned; for it is owing to this only, that Noses have ever so run in their heads, that the *Strasburgers* could not follow their business.

Alas! alas! cries *Slawkenbergius*, making an exclamation—it is not the first—and I fear will not be the last fortress that has been either won——or lost by NOSES.

The END of *Slawkenbergius*'s TALE.

CHAPTER I

WITH all this learning upon Noses running perpetually in my father's fancy—with so many family prejudices—and ten decads of such tales running on for ever along with them—how was it possible with such exquisite—was it a true nose?—That a man with such exquisite feelings as my father had, could bear the shock at all below stairs—or indeed above stairs, in any other posture, but the very posture I have described.

—Throw yourself down upon the bed, a dozen times—taking care only to place a looking-glass first in a chair on one side of it, before you do it——But was the stranger's nose a true nose—or was it a false one?

To tell that before-hand, madam, would be to do injury to one of the best tales in the christian world; and that is the tenth of the tenth decad which immediately follows this.

This tale, crieth *Slawkenbergius* somewhat exultingly, has been reserved by me for the concluding tale of my whole work; knowing right well, that when I shall have told it, and my reader shall have read it thro'—'twould be even high time for both of us to shut up the book; inasmuch, continues *Slawkenbergius*, as I know of no tale which could possibly ever go down after it.

—'Tis a tale indeed!

This sets out with the first interview in the inn at *Lyons*, when *Fernandez* left the courteous stranger and his sister *Julia* alone in her chamber, and is overwritten,

The INTRICACIES

of

Diego and *Julia*.

Heavens! thou art a strange creature *Slawkenbergius*! what a whimsical view of the involutions of the heart of woman hast thou opened! how this can ever be translated, and yet if this specimen of *Slawkenbergius*'s tales, and the exquisitiveness of his moral should please the world—translated shall a couple of volumes be.—Else, how this can ever be translated into good *English*, I have no sort of conception.—There seems in some passages to want a sixth sense to do it rightly.——What can he mean by the lambent pupilability of slow, low, dry chat, five notes below the natural tone,—which you know, madam, is little more than a whisper? The moment I pronounced the words,

[233]

I could perceive an attempt towards a vibration in the strings, about the region of the heart.—The brain made no acknowledgment.—There's often no good understanding betwixt 'em.—I felt as if I understood it.——I had no ideas.—The movement could not be without cause.—I'm lost. I can make nothing of it, —unless, may it please your worships, the voice, in that case being little more than a whisper, unavoidably forces the eyes to approach not only within six inches of each other—but to look into the pupils—is not that dangerous?—But it can't be avoided—for to look up to the ceiling, in that case the two chins unavoidably meet—and to look down into each others laps, the foreheads come into immediate contact, which at once puts an end to the conference—I mean to the sentimental part of it.——What is left, madam, is not worth stooping for.

CHAPTER II

MY FATHER lay stretched across the bed as still as if the hand of death has pushed him down, for a full hour and a half, before he began to play upon the floor with the toe of that foot which hung over the bed-side; my uncle *Toby*'s heart was a pound lighter for it.—In a few moments, his left-hand, the knuckles of which had all the time reclined upon the handle of the chamber-pot, came to its feeling—he thrust it a little more within the valance—drew up his hand, when he had done, into his bosom—gave a hem!—My good uncle *Toby*, with infinite pleasure, answered it; and full gladly would have ingrafted a sentence of consolation upon the opening it afforded; but having no talents, as I said, that way, and fearing moreover that he might set out with something which might make a bad matter worse, he contented himself with resting his chin placidly upon the cross of his crutch.

Now whether the compression shortened my uncle *Toby*'s face into a more pleasurable oval,—or that the philanthropy of his heart, in seeing his brother beginning to emerge out of the sea of his afflictions, had braced up his muscles,—so that the compression upon his chin only doubled the benignity which was there before, is not hard to decide.—My father, in turning his eyes, was struck with such a gleam of sun-shine in his face, as melted down the sullenness of his grief in a moment.

He broke silence as follows.

CHAPTER III

D ID EVER man, brother *Toby*, cried my father, raising himself up upon his elbow, and turning himself round to the opposite side of the bed where my uncle *Toby* was sitting in his old fringed chair, with his chin resting upon his crutch—did ever a poor unfortunate man, brother *Toby*, cried my father, receive so many lashes?—The most I ever saw given, quoth my uncle *Toby*, (ringing the bell at the bed's head for *Trim*) was to a grenadier, I think in *Makay*'s regiment.

—Had my uncle *Toby* shot a bullet thro' my father's heart, he could not have fallen down with his nose upon the quilt more suddenly.

Bless me! said my uncle *Toby*.

CHAPTER IV

W AS IT *Makay*'s regiment, quoth my uncle *Toby*, where the poor grenadier was so unmercifully whipp'd at *Bruges* about the ducats.—O Christ! he was innocent! cried *Trim* with a deep sigh.——And he was whipp'd, may it please your honour, almost to death's door.—They had better have shot him outright as he begg'd, and he had gone directly to heaven, for he was as innocent as your honour.——I thank thee, *Trim*, quoth my uncle *Toby*. I never think of his, continued *Trim*, and my poor brother *Tom*'s misfortunes, for we were all three school-fellows, but I cry like a coward.—Tears are no proof of cowardice, *Trim*.—I drop them oft-times myself, cried my uncle *Toby*.—I know your honour does, replied *Trim*, and so am not ashamed of it myself.—But to think, may it please your honour, continued *Trim*, a tear stealing into the corner of his eye as he spoke—to think of two virtuous lads with hearts as warm in their bodies, and as honest as God could make them—the children of honest people, going forth with gallant spirits to seek their fortunes in the world—and fall into such evils!—poor *Tom*! to be tortured upon a rack for nothing—but marrying a *Jew*'s widow who sold sausages—honest *Dick Johnson*'s soul to be scourged out of his body, for the ducats another man put into his knapsack!—O!—these are misfortunes, cried *Trim*, pulling

[235]

out his handkerchief—these are misfortunes, may it please your honour, worth lying down and crying over.

—My father could not help blushing.

—'Twould be a pity, *Trim*, quoth my uncle *Toby*, thou shouldst ever feel sorrow of thy own—thou feelest it so tenderly for others.

—Alack-o-day, replied the corporal, brightening up his face—your honour knows I have neither wife or child——I can have no sorrows in this world.—My father could not help smiling.—

As few as any man, *Trim*, replied my uncle *Toby*; nor can I see how a fellow of thy light heart can suffer, but from the distress of poverty in thy old age—when thou art passed all services, *Trim*, —and hast out-lived thy friends—An' please your honour, never fear, replied *Trim* chearily—But I would have thee never fear, *Trim*, replied my uncle; and therefore, continued my uncle *Toby*, throwing down his crutch, and getting up upon his legs as he uttered the word *therefore*—in recompence, *Trim*, of thy long fidelity to me, and that goodness of thy heart I have had such proofs of—whilst thy master is worth a shilling—thou shalt never ask elsewhere, *Trim*, for a penny. *Trim* attempted to thank my uncle *Toby*,—but had not power—tears trickled down his cheeks faster than he could wipe them off—He laid his hands upon his breast—made a bow to the ground, and shut the door.

—I have left *Trim* my bowling-green, cried my uncle *Toby*—My father smiled—I have left him moreover a pension, continued my uncle *Toby*—My father looked grave.

CHAPTER V

IS THIS a fit time, said my father to himself, to talk of PENSIONS and GRENADIERS?

CHAPTER VI

WHEN my uncle *Toby* first mentioned the grenadier, my father, I said, fell down with his nose flat to the quilt, and as suddenly as if my uncle *Toby* had shot him; but it was not added, that every other limb and member of my father instantly relapsed with his nose into the same precise attitude in which he lay first described; so that when corporal *Trim* left the room, and my father found himself disposed to rise off the bed,—he had all the little preparatory movements to run over again, before he could do it.—Attitudes are nothing, madam,—'tis the transition from one attitude to another—like the preparation and resolution of the discord into harmony, which is all in all.

For which reason my father played the same jig over again with his toe upon the floor—pushed the chamber-pot still a little farther within the valance—gave a hem—raised himself up upon his elbow—and was just beginning to address himself to my uncle *Toby*—when recollecting the unsuccessfulness of his first effort in that attitude,—he got upon his legs, and in making the third turn across the room, he stopped short before my uncle *Toby*; and laying the three first fingers of his right-hand in the palm of his left, and stooping a little, he addressed himself to my uncle *Toby* as follows.

CHAPTER VII

WHEN I reflect, brother *Toby*, upon MAN; and take a view of that dark side of him which represents his life as open to so many causes of trouble—when I consider, brother *Toby*, how oft we eat the bread of affliction, and that we are born to it, as to the portion of our inheritance—I was born to nothing, quoth my uncle *Toby*, interrupting my father—but my commission. Zooks! said my father, did not my uncle leave you a hundred and twenty pounds a year?—What could I have done without it? replied my uncle *Toby*.—That's another concern, said my father testily—But I say, *Toby*, when one runs over the catalogue of all the cross reckonings and sorrowful *items* with which the heart of man is overcharged, 'tis wonderful by what hidden resources the mind is enabled to stand it out, and bear itself up, as it does against the impositions laid upon our nature.——'Tis by the assistance of Almighty God, cried my uncle *Toby*, looking up, and pressing the palms of his hands close together—'tis not from our own strength, brother *Shandy*—a sentinel in a wooden centry-box, might as well pretend to stand it out against a detachment of fifty men,—we are upheld by the grace and the assistance of the best of Beings.

—That is cutting the knot, said my father, instead of untying it.—But give me leave to lead you, brother *Toby*, a little deeper into this mystery.

With all my heart, replied my uncle *Toby*.

My father instantly exchanged the attitude he was in, for that in which *Socrates* is so finely painted by *Raffael* in his school of *Athens*; which your connoisseurship knows is so exquisitely imagined, that even the particular manner of the reasoning of *Socrates* is expressed by it—for he holds the fore-finger of his left-hand between the fore-finger and the thumb of his right, and seems as if he was saying to the libertine he is reclaiming—"*You grant me* this—and this: and this, and this, I don't ask of you— they follow of themselves in course."

So stood my father, holding fast his fore-finger betwixt his finger and his thumb, and reasoning with my uncle *Toby* as he sat in his old fringed chair, valanced around with party-coloured worsted bobs—O *Garrick*! what a rich scene of this would thy exquisite powers make! and how gladly would I write such another to avail myself of thy immortality, and secure my own behind it.

CHAPTER VIII

THOUGH man is of all others the most curious vehicle, said my father, yet at the same time 'tis of so slight a frame and so totteringly put together, that the sudden jerks and hard jostlings it unavoidably meets with in this rugged journey, would overset and tear it to pieces a dozen times a day—was it not, brother *Toby*, that there is a secret spring within us—Which spring, said my uncle *Toby*, I take to be Religion.—Will that set my child's nose on? cried my father, letting go his finger, and striking one hand against the other—It makes every thing straight for us, answered my uncle *Toby*—Figuratively speaking, dear *Toby*, it may, for aught I know, said my father; but the spring I am speaking of, is that great and elastic power within us of counterbalancing evil, which like a secret spring in a well-ordered machine, though it can't prevent the shock—at least it imposes upon our sense of it.

Now, my dear brother, said my father, replacing his fore-finger, as he was coming closer to the point,—had my child arrived safe into the world, unmartyr'd in that precious part of him—fanciful and extravagant as I may appear to the world in my opinion of christian names, and of that magic bias which good or bad names irresistably impress upon our characters and conducts— heaven is witness! that in the warmest transports of my wishes for the prosperity of my child, I never once wished to crown his head with more glory and honour, than what GEORGE or EDWARD would have spread around it.

But alas! continued my father, as the greatest evil has befallen him—I must counteract and undo it with the greatest good.

He shall be christened *Trismegistus*, brother.

I wish it may answer—replied my uncle *Toby*, rising up.

CHAPTER IX

WHAT a chapter of chances, said my father, turning himself about upon the first landing, as he and my uncle *Toby* were going down stairs——what a long chapter of chances do the events of this world lay open to us! Take pen and ink in hand, brother *Toby*, and calculate it fairly— I know no more of calculations than this balluster, said my uncle *Toby*, (striking short of it with his crutch, and hitting my father a desperate blow souse upon his shin-bone)—'Twas a hundred to one—cried my uncle *Toby*.——I thought, quoth my father, (rubbing his shin) you had known nothing of calculations, brother *Toby*.—'Twas a meer chance, said my uncle *Toby*—Then it adds one to the chapter—replied my father.

The double success of my father's repartees tickled off the pain of his shin at once—it was well it so fell out—(chance! again)— or the world to this day had never known the subject of my father's calculation—to guess it—there was no chance—What a lucky chapter of chances has this turned out! for it has saved me the trouble of writing one express, and in truth I have enow already upon my hands without it——Have not I promised the world a chapter of knots? two chapters upon the right and the wrong end of a woman? a chapter upon whiskers? a chapter upon wishes?—a chapter of noses?—No, I have done that— a chapter upon my uncle *Toby*'s modesty? to say nothing of a chapter upon chapters, which I will finish before I sleep—by my great grandfather's whiskers, I shall never get half of 'em through this year.

Take pen and ink in hand, and calculate it fairly, brother *Toby*, said my father, and it will turn out a million to one, that of all the parts of the body, the edge of the forceps should have the ill luck just to fall upon and break down that one part, which should break down the fortunes of our house with it.

It might have been worse, replied my uncle *Toby*—I don't comprehend, said my father—Suppose the hip had presented, replied my uncle *Toby*, as Dr. *Slop* foreboded.

My father reflected half a minute—looked down—touched the middle of his forehead slightly with his finger—

—True, said he.

CHAPTER X

IS IT not a shame to make two chapters of what passed in going down one pair of stairs? for we are got no farther yet than to the first landing, and there are fifteen more steps down to the bottom; and for aught I know, as my father and my uncle *Toby* are in a talking humour, there may be as many chapters as steps;—let that be as it will, Sir, I can no more help it than my destiny:—A sudden impulse comes across me——drop the curtain, *Shandy*—I drop it——Strike a line here across the paper, *Tristram*—I strike it—and hey for a new chapter?

The duce of any other rule have I to govern myself by in this affair—and if I had one—as I do all things out of all rule—I would twist it and tear it to pieces, and throw it into the fire when I had done—Am I warm? I am, and the cause demands it—a pretty story! is a man to follow rules—or rules to follow him?

Now this, you must know, being my chapter upon chapters, which I promised to write before I went to sleep, I thought it meet to ease my conscience entirely before I lay'd down, by telling the world all I knew about the matter at once: Is not this ten times better than to set out dogmatically with a sententious parade of wisdom, and telling the world a story of a roasted horse—that chapters relieve the mind—that they assist—or impose upon the imagination—and that in a work of this dramatic cast they are as necessary as the shifting of scenes—with fifty other cold conceits, enough to extinguish the fire which roasted him.—O! but to understand this, which is a puff at the fire of *Diana*'s temple—you must read *Longinus*—read away—if you are not a jot the wiser by reading him the first time over—never fear—read him again—*Avicenna* and *Licetus* read *Aristotle*'s metaphysicks forty times through a-piece, and never understood a single word.—But mark the consequence—*Avicenna* turned out a desperate writer at all kinds of writing—for he wrote books *de omni scribili*; and for *Licetus* (*Fortunio*) though all the world knows he was born a fœtus*, of no more than five inches and a half in length, yet he grew to that astonishing height in litera-ture, as to write a book with a title as long as himself——the learned know I mean his *Gonopsychanthropologia*, upon the origin of the human soul.

So much for my chapter upon chapters, which I hold to be the best chapter in my whole work; and take my word, whoever reads it, is full as well employed, as in picking straws.

CHAPTER XI

WE SHALL bring all things to rights, said my father, setting his foot upon the first step from the landing—— This *Trismegistus*, continued my father, drawing his leg back, and turning to my uncle *Toby* was the greatest (*Toby*) of all earthly beings—he was the greatest king—the greatest lawgiver—the greatest philosopher—and the greatest priest—— and engineer—said my uncle *Toby*.—

—In course, said my father.

* *Ce Fœtus* n'etoit pas plus grand que la paume de la main; mais son pere l'ayant éxaminè en qualitè de Médecin, & ayant trouvé que c'etoit quelque chose de plus qu'un Embryon, le fit transporter tout vivant à Rapallo, ou il le fit voir à Jerôme Bardi & à d'autres Medecins du lieu. On trouva qu'il ne lui manquoit rien d'essentiel à la vie; & son pere pour faire voir un essai de son expérience, entreprit d'achever l'ouvrage de la Nature, & de travailler à la formation de l'Enfant avec le même artifice que celui dont on se sert pour faire éclorre les Poulets en Egypte. Il instruisit une Nourisse de tout ce qu'elle avoit à faire, & ayant fait mettre son fil dans un four proprement accommodè, il reuissit à l'élever et a lui faire prendre ses accroissemens necessaires, par l'uniformité d'une chaleur étrangére mesurée exactement sur les dégrés d'un Thermométre, ou d'un autre instrument équivalent. (Vide Mich. Giustinian, ne gli Scritt. Liguri à Cart 223. 488.)

On auroit toujours été très-satisfait de l'industrie d'un Pere si experimenté dans l'Art de la Generation, quand il n'auroit pû prolonger la vie a son fils que pour quelques mois, ou pour peu d'années.

Mais quand on se represente que l'Enfant a vecu pres de quatre-vingts ans, & qu'il a composé quatre-vingts Ouvrages differents tous fruits d'une longue lecture—il faut convenir que tout ce qui est incroyable n'est pas toujours faux, & que la *Vraisemblance n'est pas toujours du coté de la Verité*.

Il n'avoit que dix-neuf ans lorsqu'il composa Gonopsychanthropologia de Origine Animæ humanæ.

(Les Enfans celebres, revûs & corriges par M. De la Monnoye de l'Academie Françoise.)

CHAPTER XII

— AND HOW does your mistress? cried my father, taking the same step over again from the landing, and calling to *Susannah*, whom he saw passing by the foot of the stairs with a huge pin-cushion in her hand—how does your mistress? As well, said *Susannah*, tripping by, but without looking up, as can be expected—What a fool am I! said my father, drawing his leg back again—let things be as they will, brother *Toby*, 'tis ever the precise answer—And how is the child, pray?—No answer. And where is doctor *Slop*? added my father, raising his voice aloud, and looking over the ballusters—*Susannah* was out of hearing.

Of all the riddles of a married life, said my father, crossing the landing in order to set his back against the wall, whilst he propounded it to my uncle *Toby*—of all the puzzling riddles, said he, in a marriage state,—of which you may trust me, brother *Toby*, there are more asses loads than all *Job*'s stock of asses could have carried—there is not one that has more intricacies in it than this—that from the very moment the mistress of the house is brought to bed, every female in it, from my lady's gentlewoman down to the cinder-wench, becomes an inch taller for it; and give themselves more airs upon that single inch, than all their other inches put together.

I think rather, replied my uncle *Toby*, that 'tis we who sink an inch lower.——If I meet but a woman with child—I do it—'Tis a heavy tax upon that half of our fellow-creatures, brother *Shandy*, said my uncle *Toby*—'Tis a piteous burden upon 'em, continued he, shaking his head.—Yes, yes, 'tis a painful thing—said my father, shaking his head too—but certainly since shaking of heads came into fashion, never did two heads shake together, in concert, from two such different springs.

God bless } 'em all—said my uncle *Toby* and my father, each
Duce take } to himself.

CHAPTER XIII

HOLLA!—you chairman!—here's sixpence—do step into that bookseller's shop, and call me a *day-tall* critick. I am very willing to give any one of 'em a crown to help me with his tackling, to get my father and my uncle *Toby* off the stairs, and to put them to bed.—

—'Tis even high time; for except a short nap, which they both got whilst *Trim* was boring the jack-boots—and which, by the bye, did my father no sort of good upon the score of the bad hinge—they have not else shut their eyes, since nine hours before the time that doctor *Slop* was led into the back parlour in that dirty pickle by *Obadiah*.

Was every day of my life to be as busy a day as this,—and to take up,—truce—

I will not finish that sentence till I have made an observation upon the strange state of affairs between the reader and myself, just as things stand at present—an observation never applicable before to any one biographical writer since the creation of the world, but to myself—and I believe will never hold good to any other, until its final destruction——and therefore, for the very novelty of it alone, it must be worth your worships attending to.

I am this month one whole year older than I was this time twelve-month; and having got, as you perceive, almost into the middle of my fourth volume—and no farther than to my first day's life—'tis demonstrative that I have three hundred and sixty-four days more life to write just now, than when I first set out; so that instead of advancing, as a common writer, in my work with what I have been doing at it—on the contrary, I am just thrown so many volumes back—was every day of my life to be as busy a day as this—And why not?—and the transactions and opinions of it to take up as much description—And for what reason should they be cut short? as at this rate I should just live 364 times faster than I should write—It must follow, an' please your worships, that the more I write, the more I shall have to write—and consequently, the more your worships read, the more your worships will have to read.

Will this be good for your worships eyes?

It will do well for mine; and, was it not that my OPINIONS will be the death of me, I perceive shall lead a fine life of it out of this self-same life of mine; or, in other words, shall lead a couple of fine lives together.

As for the proposal of twelve volumes a year, or a volume a month, it no way alters my prospect—write as I will, and rush as I may into the middle of things, as *Horace* advises,—I shall never overtake myself—whipp'd and driven to the last pinch, at the worst I shall have one day the start of my pen—and one day is enough for two volumes—and two volumes will be enough for one year.—

Heaven prosper the manufactures of paper under this propitious reign, which is now open'd to us,—as I trust its providence will prosper every thing else in it that is taken in hand.—

As for the propagation of Geese—I give myself no concern—Nature is all bountiful—I shall never want tools to work with.

—So then, friend! you have got my father and my uncle *Toby* off the stairs, and seen them to bed?—And how did you manage it?—You dropp'd a curtain at the stairs foot—I thought you had no other way for it—Here's a crown for your trouble.

CHAPTER XIV

—THEN reach me my breeches off the chair, said my father to *Susannah*—There is not a moment's time to dress you, Sir, cried *Susannah*—the child is as black in the face as my—As your, what? said my father, for like all orators, he was a dear searcher into comparisons—Bless me, Sir, said *Susannah*, the child's in a fit—And where's Mr. *Yorick*—Never where he should be, said *Susannah*, but his curate's in the dressing-room, with the child upon his arm, waiting for the name——and my mistress bid me run as fast as I could to know, as captain *Shandy* is the godfather, whether it should not be called after him.

Were one sure, said my father to himself, scratching his eyebrow, that the child was expiring, one might as well compliment my brother *Toby* as not—and 'twould be a pity, in such a case, to throw away so great a name as *Trismegistus* upon him—But he may recover.

No, no,—said my father to *Susannah*, I'll get up——There is no time, cried *Susannah*, the child's as black as my shoe. *Trismegistus*, said my father—But stay—thou art a leaky vessel

Susannah, added my father; canst thou carry *Trismegistus* in thy head, the length of the gallery without scattering—Can I? cried *Susannah*, shutting the door in a huff—If she can, I'll be shot, said my father, bouncing out of bed in the dark, and groping for his breeches.

Susannah ran with all speed along the gallery.

My father made all possible speed to find his breeches.

Susannah got the start, and kept it—'Tis *Tris*—something, cried *Susannah*—There is no christian name in the world, said the curate, beginning with *Tris*—but *Tristram*. Then 'tis *Tristram-gistus*, quoth *Susannah*.

—There is no *gistus* to it, noodle!—'tis my own name, replied the curate, dipping his hand as he spoke into the bason— *Tristram*! said he, *&c. &c. &c. &c.* so *Tristram* was I called, and *Tristram* shall I be to the day of my death.

My father followed *Susannah* with his night-gown across his arm, with nothing more than his breeches on, fastened through haste with but a single button, and that button through haste thrust only half into the button-hole.

—She has not forgot the name, cried my father, half opening the door No, no, said the curate, with a tone of intelligence— And the child is better, cried *Susannah*—And how does your mistress? As well, said *Susannah*, as can be expected—Pish! said my father, the button of his breeches slipping out of the button-hole—So that whether the interjection was levelled at *Susannah*, or the button-hole,—whether pish was an interjection of contempt or an interjection of modesty, is a doubt, and must be a doubt till I shall have time to write the three following favourite chapters, that is, my chapter of *chamber-maids*—my chapter of *pishes*, and my chapter of *button-holes*.

All the light I am able to give the reader at present is this, that the moment my father cried Pish! he whisk'd himself about—and with his breeches held up by one hand, and his night-gown thrown across the arm of the other, he returned along the gallery to bed, something slower than he came.

CHAPTER XV

I WISH I could write a chapter upon sleep.

A fitter occasion could never have presented itself, than what this moment offers, when all the curtains of the family are drawn—the candles put out—and no creature's eyes are open but a single one, for the other has been shut these twenty years, of my mother's nurse.

It is a fine subject!

And yet, as fine as it is, I would undertake to write a dozen chapters upon button-holes, both quicker and with more fame than a single chapter upon this.

Button-holes!——there is something lively in the very idea of 'em—and trust me, when I get amongst 'em—You gentry with great beards—look as grave as you will—I'll make merry work with my button-holes—I shall have 'em all to myself—'tis a maiden subject—I shall run foul of no man's wisdom or fine sayings in it.

But for sleep—I know I shall make nothing of it before I begin —I am no dab at your fine sayings in the first place—and in the next, I cannot for my soul set a grave face upon a bad matter, and tell the world—'tis the refuge of the unfortunate—the enfranchisement of the prisoner—the downy lap of the hopeless, the weary and the broken-hearted; nor could I set out with a lye in my mouth, by affirming, that of all the soft and delicious functions of our nature, by which the great Author of it, in his bounty, has been pleased to recompence the sufferings wherewith his justice and his good pleasure has wearied us,—that this is the chiefest (I know pleasures worth ten of it) or what a happiness it is to man, when the anxieties and passions of the day are over, and he lays down upon his back, that his soul shall be so seated within him, that which ever way she turns her eyes, the heavens shall look calm and sweet above her—no desire— or fear—or doubt that troubles the air, nor any difficulty past, present, or to come, that the imagination may not pass over without offence, in that sweet secession.

—"God's blessing, said *Sancho Panca*, be upon the man who first invented this self-same thing called sleep——it covers a man all over like a cloak." Now there is more to me in this, and it speaks warmer to my heart and affections, than all the dissertations squeez'd out of the heads of the learned together upon the subject.

—Not that I altogether disapprove of what *Montaigne* advances upon it—'tis admirable in its way.——(I quote by memory.)

The world enjoys other pleasures, says he, as they do that of sleep, without tasting or feeling it as it slips and passes by —We should study and ruminate upon it, in order to render proper thanks to him who grants it to us—for this end I cause myself to be disturbed in my sleep, that I may the better and more sensibly relish it—And yet I see few, says he again, who live with less sleep when need requires; my body is capable of a firm, but not of a violent and sudden agitation—I evade of late all violent exercises—I am never weary with walking—but from my youth, I never liked to ride upon pavements. I love to lie hard and alone, and even without my wife—This last word may stagger the faith of the world—but remember, "La Vraisemblance (as *Baylet* says in the affair of *Liceti*) n'est pas toujours du Cotè de la Verité." And so much for sleep.

CHAPTER XVI

IF MY wife will but venture him—brother *Toby*, *Trismegistus* shall be dress'd and brought down to us, whilst you and I are getting our breakfasts together.—

—Go, tell *Susannah*, *Obadiah*, to step here.

She is run up stairs, answered *Obadiah*, this very instant, sobbing and crying, and wringing her hands as if her heart would break.—

We shall have a rare month of it, said my father, turning his head from *Obadiah*, and looking wistfully in my uncle *Toby*'s face for some time—we shall have a devilish month of it, brother *Toby*, said my father, setting his arms a-kimbo, and shaking his head; fire, water, women, wind—brother *Toby*!—'Tis some misfortune, quoth my uncle *Toby*—That it is, cried my father,—to have so many jarring elements breaking loose, and riding triumph in every corner of a gentleman's house— Little boots it to the peace of a family, brother *Toby*, that you and I possess ourselves, and sit here silent and unmoved,— whilst such a storm is whistling over our heads.——

—And what's the matter, *Susannah*? They have called the child *Tristram*——and my mistress is just got out of an hysterick fit about it—No!—'tis not my fault, said *Susannah*—I told him it was *Tristram-gistus*.

——Make tea for yourself, brother *Toby*, said my father, taking down his hat—but how different from the sallies and agitations of voice and members which a common reader would imagine!

—For he spake in the sweetest modulation—and took down his hat with the gentlest movement of limbs, that ever affliction harmonized and attuned together.

—Go to the bowling-green for corporal *Trim*, said my uncle *Toby*, speaking to *Obadiah*, as soon as my father left the room.

CHAPTER XVII

WHEN the misfortune of my NOSE fell so heavily upon my father's head,—the reader remembers that he walked instantly up stairs, and cast himself down upon his bed; and from hence, unless he has a great insight into human nature, he will be apt to expect a rotation of the same ascending and descending movements from him, upon this misfortune of my NAME;——no.

The different weight, dear Sir,—nay even the different package of two vexations of the same weight,—makes a very wide difference in our manners of bearing and getting through with them.—It is not half an hour ago, when (in the great hurry and precipitation of a poor devil's writing for daily bread) I threw a fair sheet, which I had just finished, and carefully wrote out, slap into the fire, instead of the foul one.

Instantly I snatch'd off my wig, and threw it perpendicularly, with all imaginable violence, up to the top of the room—indeed I caught it as it fell—but there was an end of the matter; nor do I think any thing else in *Nature*, would have given such immediate ease; She, dear Goddess, by an instantaneous impulse, in all *provoking cases*, determines us to a sally of this or that member— or else she thrusts us into this or that place, or posture of body, we know not why—But mark, madam, we live amongst riddles and mysteries—the most obvious things, which come in our way, have dark sides, which the quickest sight cannot penetrate into; and even the clearest and most exalted understandings amongst us find ourselves puzzled and at a loss in almost every cranny of nature's works; so that this, like a thousand other things, falls out for us in a way, which tho' we cannot reason upon it,—yet we find the good of it, may it please your reverences and your worships—and that's enough for us.

Now, my father could not lie down with this affliction for his life—nor could he carry it up stairs like the other—He walked composedly out with it to the fish-pond.

Had my father leaned his head upon his hand, and reasoned an hour which way to have gone—reason, with all her force, could not have directed him to any thing like it: there is something, Sir, in fish-ponds—but what it is, I leave to system builders and fish-pond diggers betwixt 'em to find out—but there is something, under the first disorderly transport of the humours, so unaccountably becalming in an orderly and a sober walk towards one of them, that I have often wondered that neither *Pythagoras*, nor *Plato*, nor *Solon*, nor *Licurgus*, nor *Mahomet*, nor any of your noted law-givers, ever gave order about them.

CHAPTER XVIII

YOUR honour, said *Trim*, shutting the parlour door before he began to speak, has heard, I imagine, of this unlucky accident——O yes, *Trim*! said my uncle *Toby*, and it gives me great concern—I am heartily concerned too, but I hope your honour, replied *Trim*, will do me the justice to believe, that it was not in the least owing to me—To thee—*Trim*!—cried my uncle *Toby*, looking kindly in his face—'twas *Susannah*'s and the curate's folly betwixt them—What business could they have together, an'please your honour, in the garden?—In the gallery, thou meanest, replied my uncle *Toby*.

Trim found he was upon a wrong scent, and stopped short with a low bow—Two misfortunes, quoth the corporal to himself, are twice as many at least as are needful to be talked over at one time—the mischief the cow has done in breaking into the fortifications, may be told his honour hereafter—*Trim*'s casuistry and address, under the cover of his low bow, prevented all suspicion in my uncle *Toby*, so he went on with what he had to say to *Trim* as follows:

—For my own part, *Trim*, though I can see little or no difference betwixt my nephew's being called *Tristram* or *Trismegistus*—yet as the thing sits so near my brother's heart, *Trim*,—I would freely have given a hundred pounds rather than it should have happened.—A hundred pounds, an'please your honour, replied *Trim*,—I would not give a cherry-stone to boot—Nor would I, *Trim*, upon my own account, quoth my uncle *Toby*—but my brother, whom there is no arguing with in this case—maintains that a great deal more depends, *Trim*, upon christian names, than what ignorant people imagine;——for he says there never was a great or heroic action performed since the world began by one called *Tristram*—nay he will have it, *Trim*, that a man can neither be learned, or wise, or brave—'Tis all a fancy, an'please your honour—I fought just as well, replied the corporal, when the regiment called me *Trim*, as when they called me *James Butler*—And for my own part, said my uncle *Toby*, though I should blush to boast of myself, *Trim*,—yet had my name been *Alexander*, I could have done no more at *Namur* than my duty—Bless your honour! cried *Trim*, advancing three steps as he spoke, does a man think of his christian name when he goes upon the attack? —Or when he stands in the trench, *Trim*? cried my uncle *Toby*, looking firm—Or when he enters a breach? said *Trim*, pushing in between two chairs—Or forces the lines? cried my uncle, rising up, and pushing his crutch like a pike—Or facing a platoon, cried *Trim*, presenting his stick like a firelock—Or when he marches up the glacis, cried my uncle *Toby*, looking warm and setting his foot upon his stool.——

CHAPTER XIX

MY FATHER was returned from his walk to the fish-pond —and opened the parlour-door in the very height of the attack, just as my uncle *Toby* was marching up the glacis—*Trim* recovered his arms—never was my uncle *Toby* caught riding at such a desperate rate in his life! Alas! my uncle *Toby*! had not a weightier matter called forth all the ready eloquence of my father—how hadst thou then and thy poor HOBBY-HORSE too have been insulted!

My father hung up his hat with the same air he took it down;

and after giving a slight look at the disorder of the room, he took hold of one of the chairs which had formed the corporal's breach, and placing it over-against my uncle *Toby*, he sat down in it, and as soon as the tea-things were taken away and the door shut, he broke out in a lamentation as follows.

My Father's Lamentation

IT IS in vain longer, said my father, addressing himself as much to *Ernulphus*'s curse, which was laid upon the corner of the chimney-piece,—as to my uncle *Toby* who sat under it—it is in vain longer, said my father, in the most querulous monotone imaginable, to struggle as I have done against this most uncomfortable of human persuasions—I see it plainly, that either for my own sins, brother *Toby*, or the sins and follies of the *Shandy*-family, heaven has thought fit to draw forth the heaviest of its artillery against me; and that the prosperity of my child is the point upon which the whole force of it is directed to play——Such a thing would batter the whole universe about our ears, brother *Shandy*, said my uncle *Toby*,—if it was so—Unhappy *Tristram*! child of wrath! child of decrepitude! interruption! mistake! and discontent! What one misfortune or disaster in the book of embryotic evils, that could unmechanize thy frame, or entangle thy filaments! which has not fallen upon thy head, or ever thou camest into the world—what evils in thy passage into it!—What evils since!—produced into being, in the decline of thy father's days—when the powers of his imagination and of his body were waxing feeble—when radical heat and radical moisture, the elements which should have temper'd thine, were drying up; and nothing left to found thy stamina in, but negations——'tis pitiful—brother *Toby*, at the best, and called out for all the little helps that care and attention on both sides could give it. But how were we defeated! You know the event, brother *Toby*,—'tis too melancholy a one to be repeated now,—when the few animal spirits I was worth in the world, and with which memory, fancy, and quick parts should have been convey'd,—were all dispersed, confused, confounded, scattered, and sent to the devil.—

Here then was the time to have put a stop to this persecution against him;—and tried an experiment at least—whether calmness and serenity of mind in your sister, with a due attention, brother *Toby*, to her evacuations and repletions—and the rest of her non-naturals, might not, in a course of nine months gesta-

tion, have set all things to rights.—My child was bereft of these!
—What a teazing life did she lead herself, and consequently her
fœtus too, with that nonsensical anxiety of hers about lying-in
in town? I thought my sister submitted with the greatest patience,
replied my uncle *Toby*——I never heard her utter one fretful
word about it.—She fumed inwardly, cried my father; and that,
let me tell you, brother, was ten times worse for the child—and
then! what battles did she fight with me, and what perpetual
storms about the midwife—There she gave vent, said my uncle
Toby—Vent! cried my father, looking up—

But what was all this, my dear *Toby*, to the injuries done us by
my child's coming head foremost into the world, when all I
wished in this general wreck of his frame, was to have saved this
little casket unbroke, unrifled—

With all my precautions, how was my system turned topside
turvy in the womb with my child! his head exposed to the hand
of violence, and a pressure of 470 pounds averdupois weight
acting so perpendicularly upon its apex—that at this hour 'tis
ninety *per Cent.* insurance, that the fine network of the intellectual
web be not rent and torn to a thousand tatters.

—Still we could have done.——Fool, coxcomb, puppy—give
him but a NOSE—Cripple, Dwarf, Driviller, Goosecap—(shape
him as you will) the door of Fortune stands open—O *Licetus*!
Licetus! had I been blest with a fœtus five inches long and a half,
like thee—fate might have done her worst.

Still, brother *Toby*, there was one cast of the dye left for our
child after all—O *Tristram*! *Tristram*! *Tristram*!

We will send for Mr. *Yorick*, said my uncle *Toby*.

—You may send for whom you will, replied my father.

CHAPTER XX

WHAT a rate have I gone on at, curvetting and frisking
it away, two up and two down for four volumes
together, without looking once behind, or even on one
side of me, to see whom I trod upon!—I'll tread upon no one,—
quoth I to myself when I mounted—I'll take a good rattling
gallop; but I'll not hurt the poorest jack-ass upon the road—
So off I set—up one lane—down another, through this turn-pike

—over that, as if the arch-jockey of jockeys had got behind me.

Now ride at this rate with what good intention and resolution you may,—'tis a million to one you'll do some one a mischief, if not yourself—He's flung—he's off—he's lost his seat—he's down—he'll break his neck—see!—if he has not galloped full amongst the scaffolding of the undertaking criticks!—he'll knock his brains out against some of their posts—he's bounced out!—look—he's now riding like a madcap full tilt through a whole crowd of painters, fiddlers, poets, biographers, physicians, lawyers, logicians, players, schoolmen, churchmen, statesmen, soldiers, casuists, connoisseurs, prelates, popes, and engineers—Don't fear, said I—I'll not hurt the poorest jack-ass upon the king's high-way—But your horse throws dirt; see you've splash'd a bishop—I hope in God, 'twas only *Ernulphus*, said I—But you have squirted full in the faces of Mess. *Le Moyne*, *De Romigny*, and *De Marcilly*, doctors of the *Sorbonne*—That was last year, replied I—But you have trod this moment upon a king. ——Kings have bad times on't, said I, to be trod upon by such people as me.

—You have done it, replied my accuser.

I deny it, quoth I, and so have got off, and here am I standing with my bridle in one hand, and with my cap in the other, to tell my story—And what is it? You shall hear in the next chapter.

CHAPTER XXI

AS *FRANCIS* the First of *France* was one winterly night warming himself over the embers of a wood fire, and talking with his first minister of sundry things for the good of the state*—it would not be amiss, said the king, stirring up the embers with his cane, if this good understanding betwixt ourselves and *Switzerland* was a little strengthened—There is no end, Sire, replied the minister, in giving money to these people— they would swallow up the treasury of *France*—Poo! poo! answered the king——there are more ways, Mons. *le Premier*, of bribing states, besides that of giving money——I'll pay *Switzerland* the honour of standing godfather for my next child—Your

* Vide Menagiana, vol. 1.

majesty, said the minister, in so doing, would have all the grammarians in *Europe* upon your back;—*Switzerland*, as a republick, being a female, can in no construction be godfather—She may be godmother, replied *Francis*, hastily—so announce my intentions by a courier tomorrow morning.

I am astonished, said *Francis* the First, (that day fortnight) speaking to his minister as he entered the closet, that we have had no answer from *Switzerland*—Sire, I wait upon you this moment, said Mons. *le Premier*, to lay before you my dispatches upon that business.—They take it kindly? said the king—They do, Sire, replied the minister, and have the highest sense of the honour your majesty has done them—but the republick, as godmother, claims her right in this case, of naming the child.

In all reason, quoth the king—she will christen him *Francis*, or *Henry*, or *Lewis*, or some name that she knows will be agreeable to us. Your majesty is deceived, replied the minister—I have this hour received a dispatch from our resident, with the determination of the republick on that point also—And what name has the republick fixed upon for the Dauphin?—*Shadrach*, *Mesech*, and *Abed-nego*, replied the minister—By saint *Peter's* girdle, I will have nothing to do with the *Swiss*, cried *Francis* the First, pulling up his breeches and walking hastily across the floor.

Your majesty, replied the minister calmly, cannot bring yourself off.

We'll pay them in money—said the king.

Sire, there are not sixty thousand crowns in the treasury, answered the minister——I'll pawn the best jewel in my crown, quoth *Francis* the First.

Your honour stands pawn'd already in this matter, answered Monsieur *le Premier*.

Then, Mons. *le Premier*, said the king, by———we'll go to war with 'em.

CHAPTER XXII

ALBEIT, gentle reader, I have lusted earnestly, and endeavoured carefully (according to the measure of such slender skill as God has vouchsafed me, and as convenient leisure from other occasions of needful profit and healthful pastime have permitted) that these little books, which I here put into thy hands, might stand instead of many bigger books—yet have I carried myself towards thee in such fanciful guise of careless disport, that right sore am I ashamed now to entreat thy lenity seriously—in beseeching thee to believe it of me, that in the story of my father and his christian names,—I had no thoughts of treading upon *Francis* the First—nor in the affair of the nose— upon *Francis* the Ninth—nor in the character of my uncle *Toby*— of characterizing the militiating spirits of my country—the wound upon his groin, is a wound to every comparison of that kind,—nor by *Trim*,—that I meant the duke of *Ormond*—or that my book is wrote against predestination, or free will, or taxes— If 'tis wrote against any thing,——'tis wrote, an'please your worships, against the spleen; in order, by a more frequent and more convulsive elevation and depression of the diaphragm, and the succussations of the intercostal and abdominal muscles in laughter, to drive the *gall* and other *bitter juices* from the gall-bladder, liver, and sweet-bread of his majesty's subjects, with all the inimicitious passions which belong to them, down into their duodenums.

CHAPTER XXIII

—BUT can the thing be undone, *Yorick*? said my father—for in my opinion, continued he, it cannot. I am a vile canonist, replied *Yorick*—but of all evils, holding suspense to be the most tormenting, we shall at least know the worst of this matter. I hate these great dinners—said my father—The size of the dinner is not the point, answered *Yorick*—we want, Mr. *Shandy*, to dive into the bottom of this doubt, whether the name can be changed or not—and as the beards of so many commissaries, officials, advocates, proctors, registers, and of the most able of our school-divines, and others, are all to meet in the middle of one table, and *Didius* has so pressingly invited you,— who in your distress would miss such an occasion? All that is requisite, continued *Yorick*, is to apprize *Didius*, and let him manage a conversation after dinner so as to introduce the subject—Then my brother *Toby*, cried my father, clapping his two hands together, shall go with us.

—Let my old tye-wig, quoth my uncle *Toby*, and my laced regimentals, be hung to the fire all night, *Trim*.

CHAPTER XXV

—NO DOUBT, Sir—there is a whole chapter wanting here—
and a chasm of ten pages made in the book by it—but
the book-binder is neither a fool, or a knave, or a
puppy—nor is the book a jot more imperfect, (at least upon that
score)—but, on the contrary, the book is more perfect and complete by wanting the chapter, than having it, as I shall demon-
state to your reverences in this manner—I question first by-the-
bye, whether the same experiment might not be made as success-
fully upon sundry other chapters——but there is no end, an'
please your reverences, in trying experiments upon chapters—we
have had enough of it—So there's an end of that matter.

But before I begin my demonstration, let me only tell you,
that the chapter which I have torn out, and which otherwise
you would all have been reading just now, instead of this,—was
the description of my father's, my uncle *Toby*'s, *Trim*'s, and
Obadiah's setting out and journeying to the visitations at * * * *.

We'll go in the coach, said my father—Prithee, have the arms
been altered, *Obadiah*?—It would have made my story much
better, to have begun with telling you, that at the time my
mother's arms were added to the *Shandy*'s, when the coach was
repainted upon my father's marriage, it had so fallen out, that
the coach painter, whether by performing all his works with the
left-hand, like *Turpilius* the *Roman*, or *Hans Holbein* of *Basil*—or
whether 'twas more from the blunder of his head than hand—
or whether, lastly, it was from the sinister turn, which every thing
relating to our family was apt to take—It so fell out, however,
to our reproach, that instead of the *bend dexter*, which since
Harry the Eighth's reign was honestly our due——a *bend
sinister*, by some of these fatalities, had been drawn quite across
the field of the *Shandy*-arms. 'Tis scarce credible that the mind
of so wise a man as my father was, could be so much incommoded with so small a matter. The word coach—let it be whose
it would—or coach-man, or coach-horse, or coach-hire, could
never be named in the family, but he constantly complained of
carrying this vile mark of Illegitimacy upon the door of his own;
he never once was able to step into the coach, or out of it, without
turning round to take a view of the arms, and making a vow at
the same time, that it was the last time he would ever set his
foot in it again, till the *bend-sinister* was taken out—but like

the affair of the hinge, it was one of the many things which the *Destinies* had set down in their books—ever to be grumbled at (and in wiser families than ours)—but never to be mended.

—Has the *bend-sinister* been brush'd out, I say? said my father —There has been nothing brush'd out, Sir, answered *Obadiah*, but the lining. We'll go o'horse-back, said my father, turning to *Yorick*—Of all things in the world, except politicks, the clergy know the least of heraldry, said *Yorick*—No matter for that, cried my father—I should be sorry to appear with a blot in my escutcheon before them——Never mind the *bend-sinister*, said my uncle *Toby*, putting on his tye-wig—No, indeed, said my father,—you may go with my aunt *Dinah* to a visitation with a *bend-sinister*, if you think fit—My poor uncle *Toby* blush'd. My father was vexed at himself—No—my dear brother *Toby*, said my father, changing his tone—but the damp of the coach-lining about my loins, may give me the Sciatica again, as it did *December*, *January*, and *February* last winter—so if you please you shall ride my wife's pad—and as you are to preach, *Yorick*, you had better make the best of your way before,—and leave me to take care of my brother *Toby*, and to follow at our own rates.

Now the chapter I was obliged to tear out, was the description of this cavalcade, in which corporal *Trim* and *Obadiah*, upon two coach-horses a-breast, led the way as slow as a patrole—whilst my uncle *Toby*, in his laced regimentals and tye-wig, kept his rank with my father, in deep roads and dissertations alternately upon the advantage of learning and arms, as each could get the start.

—But the painting of this journey, upon reviewing it, appears to be so much above the stile and manner of any thing else I have been able to paint in this book, that it could not have remained in it, without depreciating every other scene; and destroying at the same time that necessary equipoise and balance, (whether of good or bad) betwixt chapter and chapter, from whence the just proportions and harmony of the whole work results. For my own part, I am but just set up in the business, so know little about it—but, in my opinion, to write a book is for all the world like humming a song—be but in tune with yourself, madam, 'tis no matter how high or how low you take it.—

—This is the reason, may it please your reverences, that some of the lowest and flattest compositions pass off very well—(as *Yorick* told my uncle *Toby* one night) by siege—My uncle *Toby* looked brisk at the sound of the word *siege*, but could make neither head or tail of it.

I'm to preach at court next Sunday, said *Homenas*—run over my notes—so I humm'd over doctor *Homenas*'s notes—the modulation's very well—'twill do, *Homenas*, if it holds on at this rate—so on I humm'd—and a tolerable tune I thought it was; and to this hour, may it please your reverences, had never found out how low, how flat, how spiritless and jejune it was, but that all of a sudden, up started an air in the middle of it, so fine, so rich, so heavenly—it carried my soul up with it into the other world; now had I, (as *Montaigne* complained in a parallel accident)—had I found the declivity easy, or the ascent accessible—certes I had been outwitted—Your notes, *Homenas*, I should have said, are good notes,—but it was so perpendicular a precipice—so wholly cut off from the rest of the work, that by the first note I humm'd, I found myself flying into the other world, and from thence discovered the vale from whence I came, so deep, so low, and dismal, that I shall never have the heart to descend into it again.

☞ A dwarf who brings a standard along with him to measure his own size—take my word, is a dwarf in more articles than one —And so much for tearing out of chapters.

CHAPTER XXVI

—SEE if he is not cutting it all into slips, and giving them about him to light their pipes!—'Tis abominable, answered *Didius*; it should not go unnoticed, said doctor *Kysarcius*— ☞ he was of the *Kysarcij* of the low countries.

Methinks, said *Didius*, half rising from his chair, in order to remove a bottle and a tall decanter, which stood in a direct line betwixt him and *Yorick*—you might have spared this sarcastick stroke, and have hit upon a more proper place, Mr. *Yorick*—or at least upon a more proper occasion to have shewn your contempt of what we have been about: If the Sermon is of no better worth than to light pipes with—'twas certainly, Sir, not good enough to be preached before so learned a body; and if 'twas good enough to be preached before so learned a body—'twas certainly, Sir, too good to light their pipes with afterwards.

—I have got him fast hung up, quoth *Didius* to himself, upon one of the two horns of my dilemma—let him get off as he can. I have undergone such unspeakable torments, in bringing forth this sermon, quoth *Yorick*, upon this occasion,—that I declare, *Didius*, I would suffer martyrdom—and if it was possible my horse with me, a thousand times over, before I would sit down and make such another: I was delivered of it at the wrong end of me—it came from my head instead of my heart—and it is for the pain it gave me, both in the writing and preaching of it, that I revenge myself of it, in this manner.—To preach, to shew the extent of our reading, or the subtleties of our wit—to parade it in the eyes of the vulgar with the beggarly accounts of a little learning, tinseled over with a few words which glitter, but convey little light and less warmth—is a dishonest use of the poor single half hour in a week which is put into our hands—'Tis not preaching the gospel—but ourselves—For my own part, continued *Yorick*, I had rather direct five words point blank to the heart—

As *Yorick* pronounced the word *point blank*, my uncle *Toby* rose up to say something upon projectiles——when a single word and no more, uttered from the opposite side of the table, drew every one's ears towards it—a word of all others in the dictionary the last in that place to be expected—a word I am ashamed to write—yet must be written—must be read;—illegal—uncanonical—guess ten thousand guesses, multiplied into themselves—rack—torture your invention for ever, you're where you was—In short, I'll tell it in the next chapter.

CHAPTER XXVII

Z OUNDS!——Z————ds! cried *Phutatorius*, partly to himself—and yet high enough to be heard—and what seemed odd, 'twas uttered in a construction of look, and in a tone of voice, somewhat between that of a man in amazement, and of one in bodily pain.

One or two who had very nice ears, and could distinguish the expression and mixture of the two tones as plainly as a *third* or a *fifth*, or any other chord in musick—were the most puzzled and perplexed with it—the *concord* was good in itself—but then 'twas quite out of the key, and no way applicable to the subject started;—so that with all their knowledge, they could not tell what in the world to make of it.

[270]

Others who knew nothing of musical expression, and merely lent their ears to the plain import of the *word*, imagined that *Phutatorius*, who was somewhat of a cholerick spirit, was just going to snatch the cudgels out of *Didius*'s hands, in order to bemawl *Yorick* to some purpose—and that the desperate monosyllable Z——ds was the exordium to an oration, which, as they judged from the sample, presaged but a rough kind of handling of him; so that my uncle *Toby*'s good nature felt a pang for what *Yorick* was about to undergo. But seeing *Phutatorius* stop short, without any attempt or desire to go on—a third party began to suppose, that it was no more than an involuntary respiration, casually forming itself into the shape of a twelve-penny oath— without the sin or substance of one.

Others, and especially one or two who sat next him, looked upon it on the contrary, as a real and substantial oath propensly formed against *Yorick*, to whom he was known to bear no good liking—which said oath, as my father philosophized upon it, actually lay fretting and fuming at that very time in the upper regions of *Phutatorius*'s purtenance; and so was naturally, and according to the due course of things, first squeezed out by the sudden influx of blood, which was driven into the right ventricle of *Phutatorius*'s heart, by the stroke of surprize which so strange a theory of preaching had excited.

How finely we argue upon mistaken facts!

There was not a soul busied in all these various reasonings upon the monosyllable which *Phutatorius* uttered,—who did not take this for granted, proceeding upon it as from an axiom, namely, that *Phutatorius*'s mind was intent upon the subject of debate which was arising between *Didius* and *Yorick*; and indeed as he looked first towards the one, and then towards the other, with the air of a man listening to what was going forwards,— who would not have thought the same? But the truth was, that *Phutatorius* knew not one word or one syllable of what was passing—but his whole thoughts and attention were taken up with a transaction which was going forwards at that very instant within the precincts of his own *Galligaskins*, and in a part of them, where of all others he stood most interested to watch accidents: So that notwithstanding he looked with all the attention in the world, and had gradually skrewed up every nerve and muscle in his face, to the utmost pitch the instrument would bear, in order, as it was thought, to give a sharp reply to *Yorick*, who sat over-against him—Yet I say, was *Yorick* never once in any one domicile of *Phutatorius*'s brain—but the true cause of his exclamation lay at least a yard below.

This I will endeavour to explain to you with all imaginable decency.

You must be informed then, that *Gastripheres*, who had taken a turn into the kitchen a little before dinner, to see how things went on—observing a wicker-basket of fine chesnuts standing upon the dresser, had ordered that a hundred or two or them might be roasted and sent in, as soon as dinner was over—*Gastripheres* inforcing his orders about them, that *Didius*, but *Phutatorius* especially, were particularly fond of 'em.

About two minutes before the time that my uncle *Toby* interrupted *Yorick*'s harangue—*Gastripheres*'s chesnuts were brought in—and as *Phutatorius*'s fondness for 'em, was uppermost in the waiter's head, he laid them directly before *Phutatorius*, wrapt up hot in a clean damask napkin.

Now whether it was physically impossible, with half a dozen hands all thrust into the napkin at a time—but that some one chesnut, of more life and rotundity than the rest, must be put in motion—it so fell out, however, that one was actually sent rolling off the table; and as *Phutatorius* sat straddling under—it fell perpendicularly into that particular aperture of *Phutatorius*'s breeches, for which, to the shame and indelicacy of our language be it spoke, there is no chaste word throughout all *Johnson*'s dictionary—let it suffice to say—it was that particular aperture, which in all good societies, the laws of decorum do strictly require, like the temple of *Janus* (in peace at least) to be universally shut up.

The neglect of this punctilio in *Phutatorius* (which by the bye should be a warning to all mankind) had opened a door to this accident.—

—Accident, I call it, in compliance to a received mode of speaking,—but in no opposition to the opinion either of *Acrites* or *Mythogeras* in this matter; I know they were both prepossessed and fully persuaded of it—and are so to this hour, That there was nothing of accident in the whole event—but that the chesnut's taking that particular course, and in a manner of its accord—and then falling with all its heat directly into that one particular place, and no other——was a real judgment upon *Phutatorius*, for that filthy and obscene treatise *de Concubinis retinendis*, which *Phutatorius* had published about twenty years ago—and was that identical week going to give the world a second edition of.

It is not my business to dip my pen in this controversy——
much undoubtedly may be wrote on both sides of the question—
all that concerns me as an historian, is to represent the matter of
fact, and render it credible to the reader, that the hiatus in
Phutatorius's breeches was sufficiently wide to receive the chesnut;—and that the chesnut, some how or other, did fall perpendicularly and piping hot into it, without *Phutatorius*'s perceiving
it, or any one else at that time.

The genial warmth which the chesnut imparted, was not
undelectable for the first twenty or five and twenty seconds,—
and did no more than gently solicit *Phutatorius*'s attention
towards the part:—But the heat gradually increasing, and in
a few seconds more getting beyond the point of all sober pleasure,
and then advancing with all speed into the regions of pain,—
the soul of *Phutatorius*, together with all his ideas, his thoughts,
his attention, his imagination, judgment, resolution, deliberation,
ratiocination, memory, fancy, with ten batallions of animal
spirits, all tumultuously crouded down, through different defiles
and circuits, to the place in danger, leaving all his upper regions,
as you may imagine, as empty as my purse.

With the best intelligence which all these messengers could
bring him back, *Phutatorius* was not able to dive into the secret
of what was going forwards below, nor could he make any kind
of conjecture, what the devil was the matter with it: However, as
he knew not what the true cause might turn out, he deemed it
most prudent, in the situation he was in at present, to bear it, if
possible, like a stoick; which, with the help of some wry faces
and compursions of the mouth, he had certainly accomplished,
had his imagination continued neuter—but the sallies of the
imagination are ungovernable in things of this kind—a thought
instantly darted into his mind, that tho' the anguish had the
sensation of glowing heat—it might, notwithstanding that, be
a bite as well as a burn; and if so, that possibly a *Newt* or an
Asker, or some such detested reptile, had crept up, and was
fastening his teeth—the horrid idea of which, with a fresh glow
of pain arising that instant from the chesnut, seized *Phutatorius*
with a sudden panick, and in the first terrifying disorder of the
passion it threw him, as it has done the best generals upon earth,
quite off his guard;—the effect of which was this, that he leapt
incontinently up, uttering as he rose that interjection of surprise
so much discanted upon, with the aposiopestick break after it,
marked thus, Z——ds—which, though not strictly canonical, was

still as little as any man cotld have said upon the occasion;——
and which, by the bye, whether canonical or not, *Phutatorius*
could no more help than he could the cause of it.

Though this has taken up some time in the narrative, it took
up little more time in the transaction, than just to allow time for
Phutatorius to draw forth the chesnut, and throw it down with
violence upon the floor—and for *Yorick*, to rise from his chair,
and pick the chesnut up.

It is curious to observe the triumph of slight incidents over the
mind:—What incredible weight they have in forming and
governing our opinions, both of men and things,—that trifles
light as air, shall waft a belief into the soul, and plant it so
immoveably within it,—that *Euclid*'s demonstrations, could they
be brought to batter it in breach, should not all have power to
overthrow it.

Yorick, I said, picked up the chesnut which *Phutatorius*'s
wrath had flung down—the action was trifling—I am ashamed to
account for it—he did it, for no reason, but that he thought the
chesnut not a jot worse for the adventure—and that he held
a good chesnut worth stooping for.—But this incident, trifling as
it was, wrought differently in *Phutatorius*'s head: He considered
this act of *Yorick*'s, in getting off his chair, and picking up the
chesnut, as a plain acknowledgment in him, that the chesnut was
originally his,—and in course, that it must have been the owner
of the chesnut, and no one else, who could have plaid him such
a prank with it: What greatly confirmed him in this opinion,
was this, that the table being parallelogramical and very narrow,
it afforded a fair opportunity for *Yorick*, who sat directly over-
against *Phutatorius*, of slipping the chesnut in—and consequently
that he did it. The look of something more than suspicion, which
Phutatorius cast full upon *Yorick* as these thoughts arose, too
evidently spoke his opinion—and as *Phutatorius* was naturally
supposed to know more of the matter than any person besides,
his opinion at once became the general one;—and for a reason
very different from any which have been yet given—in a little
time it was put out of all manner of dispute.

When great or unexpected events fall out upon the stage of this
sublunary world—the mind of man, which is an inquisitive kind
of a substance, naturally takes a flight, behind the scenes, to see
what is the cause and first spring of them—The search was not
long in this instance.

It was well known that *Yorick* had never a good opinior of the treatise which *Phutatorius* had wrote *de Concubinis retinendis*, as a thing which he feared had done hurt in the world—and 'twas easily found out, that there was a mystical meaning in *Yorick*'s prank—and that his chucking the chesnut hot into *Phutatorius*'s * * *__* * * * *, was a sarcastical fling at his book—the doctrines of which, they said, had inflamed many an honest man in the same place.

This conceit awaken'd *Somnolentus*—made *Agelastes* smile—and if you can recollect the precise look and air of a man's face intent in finding out a riddle—it threw *Gastripheres*'s into that form—and in short was thought by many to be a master-stroke of arch-wit.

This, as the reader has seen from one end to the other, was as groundless as the dreams of philosophy: *Yorick*, no doubt, as *Shakespear* said of his ancestor — "*was a man of jest*," but it was temper'd with something which withheld him from that, and many other ungracious pranks, of which he as undeservedly bore the blame;—but it was his misfortune all his life long to bear the imputation of saying and doing a thousand things of which (unless my esteem blinds me) his nature was incapable. All I blame him for—or rather, all I blame and alternately like him for, was that singularity of his temper, which would never suffer him to take pains to set a story right with the world, however in his power. In every ill usage of that sort, he acted precisely as in the affair of his lean horse—he could have explained it to his honour, but his spirit was above it; and besides, he ever looked upon the inventor, the propagator and believer of an illiberal report alike so injurious to him,—he could not stoop to tell his story to them—and so trusted to time and truth to do it for him.

This heroic cast produced him inconveniences in many respects —in the present, it was followed by the fixed resentment of *Phutatorius*, who, as *Yorick* had just made an end of his chesnut, rose up from his chair a second time, to let him know it—which indeed he did with a smile; saying only—that he would endeavour not to forget the obligation.

But you must mark and carefully separate and distinguish these two things in your mind.

—The smile was for the company.

—The threat was for *Yorick*.

CHAPTER XXVIII

—CAN you tell me, quoth *Phutatorius*, speaking to *Gastripheres* who sat next to him,—for one would not apply to a surgeon in so foolish an affair,—can you tell me, *Gastripheres*, what is best to take out the fire?—Ask *Eugenius*, said *Gastripheres*—That greatly depends, said *Eugenius*, pretending ignorance of the adventure, upon the nature of the part— If it is a tender part, and a part which can conveniently be wrapt up—It is both the one and the other, replied *Phutatorius*, laying his hand as he spoke, with an emphatical nod of his head upon the part in question, and lifting up his right leg at the same time to ease and ventilate it—If that is the case, said *Eugenius*, I would advise you, *Phutatorius*, not to tamper with it by any means; but if you will send to the next printer, and trust your cure to such a simple thing as a soft sheet of paper just come off the press— you need do nothing more than twist it round—The damp paper, quoth *Yorick* (who sat next to his friend *Eugenius*) though I know it has a refreshing coolness in it—yet I presume is no more than the vehicle—and that the oil and lamp-black with which the paper is so strongly impregnated, does the business—Right, said *Eugenius*, and is of any outward application I would venture to recommend the most anodyne and safe.

Was it my case, said *Gastripheres*, as the main thing is the oil and lamp-black, I should spread them thick upon a rag, and clap it on directly. That would make a very devil of it, replied *Yorick* —And besides, added *Eugenius*, it would not answer the intention, which is the extream neatness and elegance of the prescription, which the faculty hold to be half in half—for consider, if the type is a very small one, (which it should be) the sanative particles, which come into contact in this form, have the advantage of being spread so infinitely thin and with such a mathematical equality (fresh paragraphs and large capitals excepted) as no art or management of the spatula can come up to. It falls out very luckily, replied *Phutatorius*, that the second edition of my treatise *de Concubinis retinendis*, is at this instant in the press —You may take any leaf of it, said *Eugenius*—No matter which —provided, quoth *Yorick*, there is no bawdry in it—

They are just now, replied *Phutatorius*, printing off the ninth chapter—which is the last chapter but one in the book—Pray what is the title to that chapter, said *Yorick*, making a respectful bow to *Phutatorius* as he spoke—I think, answered *Phutatorius*, 'tis that, *de re concubinariâ*.

For heaven's sake keep out of that chapter, quoth *Yorick*. —By all means—added *Eugenius*.

CHAPTER XXIX

—NOW, quoth *Didius*, rising up, and laying his right-hand with his fingers spread upon his breast—had such a blunder about a christian-name happened before the reformation—(It happened the day before yesterday, quoth my uncle *Toby* to himself) and when baptism was administer'd in *Latin*——('Twas all in *English*, said my uncle)—Many things might have coincided with it, and upon the authority of sundry decreed cases, to have pronounced the baptism null, with a power of giving the child a new name—Had a priest, for instance, which was no uncommon thing, through ignorance of the *Latin* tongue, baptized a child of Tom-o'Stiles, *in nomino patriæ & filia & spiritum sanctos,*—the baptism was held null—I beg your pardon, replied *Kysarcius,*—in that case, as the mistake was only in the *terminations,* the baptism was valid—and to have rendered it null, the blunder of the priest should have fallen upon the first syllable of each noun—and not, as in your case, upon the last.—

My father delighted in subtleties of this kind, and listen'd with infinite attention.

Gastripheres, for example, continued *Kysarcius,* baptizes a child of *John Stradling*'s, *in Gomine* gatris, &c. &c. instead of *in Nomine* patris, &c.—Is this a baptism? No,—say the ablest canonists; inasmuch as the radix of each word is hereby torn up, and the sense and meaning of them removed and changed quite to another object; for *Gomine* does not signify a name, nor *gatris* a father—What do they signify? said my uncle *Toby*—Nothing at all—quoth *Yorick*—Ergo, such a baptism is null, said *Kysarcius* —In course, answered *Yorick*, in a tone two parts jest and one part earnest—

But in the case cited, continued *Kysarcius,* where *patrim* is put for *patris, filia* for *filij,* and so on—as it is a fault only in the declension, and the roots of the words continue untouch'd, the inflexions of their branches, either this way or that, does not in any sort hinder the baptism, inasmuch as the same sense continues in the words as before—But then, said *Didius*, the intention of the priest's pronouncing them grammatically, must have been proved to have gone along with it—Right, answered *Kysarcius*; and of this, brother *Didius*, we have an instance in a decree of the decretals of Pope *Leo* the IIId.—But my brother's child, cried my uncle *Toby*, has nothing to do with the Pope—'tis the plain child of a Protestant gentleman, christen'd *Tristram* against the wills and wishes both of its father and mother, and all who are a-kin to it—

If the wills and wishes, said *Kysarcius*, interrupting my uncle *Toby*, of those only who stand related to Mr. *Shandy*'s child, were to have weight in this matter, Mrs. *Shandy*, of all people, has the least to do in it—My uncle *Toby* lay'd down his pipe, and my father drew his chair still closer to the table to hear the conclusion of so strange an introduction.

It has not only been a question, captain *Shandy*, amongst the * best lawyers and civilians in this land, continued *Kysarcius*, "*Whether the mother be of kin to her child*,"—but after much dispassionate enquiry and jactitation of the arguments on all sides,—it has been adjudged for the negative,—namely, "*That the mother is not of kin to her child*†." My father instantly clapp'd his hand upon my uncle *Toby*'s mouth, under colour of whispering in his ear—the truth was, he was alarmed for *Lillabullero*—and having a great desire to hear more of so curious an argument—he begg'd my uncle *Toby*, for heaven's sake, not to disappoint him in it—My uncle *Toby* gave a nod—resumed his pipe, and contenting himself with whistling *Lillabullero* inwardly—*Kysarcius*, *Didius*, and *Triptolemus* went on with the discourse as follows.

This determination, continued *Kysarcius*, how contrary soever it may seem to run to the stream of vulgar ideas, yet had reason strongly on its side; and has been put out of all manner of dispute from the famous case, known commonly by the name of the Duke of *Suffolk*'s case:—It is cited in *Brook*, said *Triptolemus*—And taken notice of by Lord *Coke*, added *Didius*—And you may find it in *Swinburn* on Testaments, said *Kysarcius*.

The case, Mr. *Shandy*, was this.

In the reign of *Edward* the Sixth, *Charles* Duke of *Suffolk* having issue a son by one venter, and a daughter by another venter, made his last will, wherein he devised goods to his son,

* Vid. Swinburn on Testaments, Part 7. § 8.
† Vid. Brook Abridg. Tit. Administr. N. 47.

and died; after whose death the son died also—but without will, without wife, and without child—his mother and his sister by the father's side (for she was born of the former venter) then living. The mother took the administration of her son's goods, according to the statute of the 21st of *Harry* the Eighth, whereby it is enacted, That in case any person die intestate, the administration of his goods shall be committed to the next of kin.

The administration being thus (surreptitiously) granted to the mother, the sister by the father's side commenced a suit before the Ecclesiastical Judge, alledging, 1st, That she herself was next of kin; and 2dly, That the mother was not of kin at all to the party deceased; and therefore pray'd the court, that the administration granted to the mother might be revoked, and be committed unto her, as next of kin to the deceased, by force of the said statute.

Hereupon, as it was a great cause, and much depending upon its issue—and many causes of great property likely to be decided in times to come, by the precedent to be then made—the most learned, as well in the laws of this realm, as in the civil law, were consulted together, whether the mother was of kin to her son, or no.—Whereunto not only the temporal lawyers—but the church-lawyers—the juris-consulti—the juris-prudentes—the civilians—the advocates—the commissaries—the judges of the consistory and prerogative courts of *Canterbury* and *York*, with the master of the faculties, were all unanimously of opinion, That the mother was not of * kin to her child—

And what said the Duchess of *Suffolk* to it? said my uncle *Toby*.

The unexpectedness of my uncle *Toby*'s question, confounded *Kysarcius* more than the ablest advocate——He stopp'd a full minute, looking in my uncle *Toby*'s face without replying—and in that single minute *Triptolemus* put by him, and took the lead as follows.

'Tis a ground and principle in the law, said *Triptolemus*, that things do not ascend, but descend in it; and I make no doubt 'tis for this cause, that however true it is, that the child may be of the blood or seed of its parents—that the parents, nevertheless, are not of the blood and seed of it; inasmuch as the parents are not begot by the child, but the child by the parents—For so they write, *Liberi sunt de sanguine patris & matris, sed pater et mater non sunt de sanguine liberorum.*

* Mater non numeratur inter consanguineos. Bald. in ult. C. de Verb. signific.

—But this, *Triptolemus*, cried *Didius*, proves too much—for from this authority cited it would follow, not only what indeed is granted on all sides, that the mother is not of kin to her child—but the father likewise——It is held, said *Triptolemus*, the better opinion; because the father, the mother, and the child, though they be three persons, yet are they but (*una caro* *) one flesh; and consequently no degree of kindred—or any method of acquiring one *in nature*—There you push the argument again too far, cried *Didius*—for there is no prohibition *in nature*, though there is in the levitical law,—but that a man may beget a child upon his grandmother—in which case, supposing the issue a daughter, she would stand in relation both of——But who ever thought, cried *Kysarcius*, of laying with his grandmother?——The young gentleman, replied *Yorick*, whom *Selden* speaks of—who not only thought of it, but justified his intention to his father by the argument drawn from the law of retaliation——"You lay'd, Sir, with my mother, said the lad—why may not I lay with yours?"——'Tis the *Argumentum commune*, added *Yorick*.—'Tis as good, replied *Eugenius*, taking down his hat, as they deserve.

The company broke up——

CHAPTER XXX

—AND pray, said my uncle *Toby*, leaning upon *Yorick*, as he and my father were helping him leisurely down the stairs—don't be terrified, madam, this stair-case conversation is not so long as the last—And pray, *Yorick*, said my uncle *Toby*, which way is this said affair of *Tristram* at length settled by these learned men? Very satisfactorily, replied *Yorick*; no mortal, Sir, has any concern with it—for Mrs. *Shandy* the mother is nothing at all akin to him—and as the mother's is the surest side—Mr. *Shandy*, in course, is still less than nothing—In short, he is not as much akin to him, Sir, as I am—

—That may well be, said my father, shaking his head.

—Let the learned say what they will, there must certainly, quoth my uncle *Toby*, have been some sort of consanguinity betwixt the duchess of *Suffolk* and her son—

The vulgar are of the same opinion, quoth *Yorick*, to this hour.

*Vide Brook Abridg. tit. Administr. N. 47.

CHAPTER XXXI

THOUGH my father was hugely tickled with the subtleties of these learned discourses—'twas still but like the anointing of a broken bone—The moment he got home, the weight of his afflictions returned upon him but so much the heavier, as is ever the case when the staff we lean on slips from under us— He became pensive—walked frequently forth to the fish-pond— let down one loop of his hat—sigh'd often—forbore to snap— and, as the hasty sparks of temper, which occasion snapping, so much assist perspiration and digestion, as *Hippocrates* tells us— he had certainly fallen ill with the extinction of them, had not his· thoughts been critically drawn off, and his health rescued by a fresh train of disquietudes left him, with a legacy of a thousand pounds by my aunt *Dinah*—

My father had scarce read the letter, when taking the thing by the right end, he instantly begun to plague and puzzle his head how to lay it out mostly to the honour of his family—A hundred and fifty odd projects took possession of his brains by turns—he would do this, and that, and t'other—He would got to *Rome*— he would go to law—he would buy stock—he would buy *John Hobson*'s farm—he would new fore-front his house, and add a new wing to make it even—There was a fine water-mill on this side, and he would build a wind-mill on the other side of the river in full view to answer it—But above all things in the world, he would inclose the great *Ox-moor*, and send out my brother *Bobby* immediately upon his travels.

But as the sum was *finite*, and consequently could not do every thing—and in truth very few of these to any purpose,—of all the projects which offered themselves upon this occasion, the two last seemed to make the deepest impression; and he would infallibly have determined upon both at once, but for the small inconvenience hinted at above, which absolutely put him under a necessity of deciding in favour either of the one or the other.

This was not altogether so easy to be done; for though 'tis certain my father had long before set his heart upon this necessary part of my brother's education, and like a prudent man had actually determined to carry it into execution, with the first money that returned from the second creation of actions in the *Missisippi*-scheme, in which he was an adventurer—yet the *Ox-moor*, which was a fine, large, whinny, undrained, unimproved common, belonging to the *Shandy*-estate, had almost as old a claim upon him: He had long and affectionately set his heart upon turning it likewise to some account.

But having never hitherto been pressed with such a conjuncture of things, as made it necessary to settle either the priority or justice of their claims,—like a wise man he had refrained entering into any nice or critical examination about them: So that upon the dismission of every other project at this crisis,—— the two old projects, the Ox-moor and my BROTHER, divided him again; and so equal a match were they for each other, as to become the occasion of no small contest in the old gentleman's mind,—which of the two should be set o'going first.

—People may laugh as they will——but the case was this.

It had ever been the custom of the family, and by length of time was almost become a matter of common right, that the eldest son of it should have free ingress, egress, and regress into foreign parts before marriage,—not only for the sake of bettering his own private parts, by the benefit of exercise and change of so much air—but simply for the mere delectation of his fancy, by the feather put into his cap, of having been abroad—*tantum valet*, my father would say, *quantum sonat*.

Now as this was a reasonable, and in course a most christian indulgence—to deprive him of it, without why or wherefore,— and thereby make an example of him, as the first *Shandy* unwhirl'd about *Europe* in a post-chaise, and only because he was a heavy lad—would be using him ten times worse than a *Turk*.

On the other hand, the case of the *Ox-moor* was full as hard.

Exclusive of the original purchase-money, which was eight hundred pounds—it had cost the family eight hundred pounds more in a law-suit about fifteen years before—besides the Lord knows what trouble and vexation.

It had been moreover in possession of the *Shandy*-family ever since the middle of the last century; and though it lay full in view before the house, bounded on one extremity by the water-mill, and on the other by the projected wind-mill spoken of above,—and for all these reasons seemed to have the fairest title of any part of the estate to the care and protection of the family —yet by an unaccountable fatality, common to men, as well as the ground they tread on,—it had all along most shamefully been overlook'd; and to speak the truth of it, had suffered so much by it, that it would have made any man's heart have bled

(*Obadiah* said) who understood the value of land, to have rode over it, and only seen the condition it was in.

However, as neither the purchasing this tract of ground—nor indeed the placing of it where it lay, were either of them, properly speaking, of my father's doing—he had never thought himself any way concerned in the affair—till the fifteen years before, when the breaking out of that cursed law-suit mentioned above (and which had arose about its boundaries)—which being altogether my father's own act and deed, it naturally awakened every other argument in its favour; and upon summing them all up together, he saw, not merely in interest, but in honour, he was bound to do something for it—and that now or never was the time.

I think there must certainly have been a mixture of ill-luck in it, that the reasons on both sides should happen to be so equally balanced by each other; for though my father weigh'd them in all humours and conditions—spent many an anxious hour in the most profound and abstracted meditation upon what was best to be done——reading books of farming one day— books of travels another—laying aside all passion whatever— viewing the arguments on both sides in all their lights and circumstances——communing every day with my uncle *Toby*— arguing with *Yorick*, and talking over the whole affair of the *Ox-moor* with *Obadiah*—yet nothing in all that time appeared so strongly in behalf of the one, which was not either strictly applicable to the other, or at least so far counterbalanced by some consideration of equal weight, as to keep the scales even.

For to be sure, with proper helps, and in the hands of some people, tho' the *Ox-moor* would undoubtedly have made a different appearance in the world from what it did, or ever would do in the condition it lay—yet every tittle of this was true, with regard to my brother *Bobby*—let *Obadiah* say what he would.——

In point of interest—the contest, I own, at first sight, did not appear so undecisive betwixt them; for whenever my father took pen and ink in hand, and set about calculating the simple expence of paring and burning, and fencing in the *Ox-moor*, &c. &c.— with the certain profit it would bring him in return—the latter turned out so prodigiously in his way of working the account, that you would have sworn the *Ox-moor* would have carried all before it. For it was plain he should reap a hundred lasts of rape, at twenty pounds a last, the very first year—besides an excellent crop of wheat the year following—and the year after that, to speak within bounds, a hundred——but, in all likelihood, a hundred and fifty—if not two hundred quarters of pease and beans—besides potatoes without end—But then, to think he was all this while breeding up my brother like a hog to eat them—knocked all on the head again, and generally left the old gentleman in such a state of suspence—that, as he often declared to my uncle *Toby*—he knew no more than his heels what to do.

No body, but he who has felt it, can conceive what a plaguing thing it is to have a man's mind torn asunder by two projects of equal strength, both obstinately pulling in a contrary direction at the same time: For to say nothing of the havock, which by a certain consequence is unavoidably made by it all over the finer system of the nerves, which you know convey the animal spirits and more subtle juices from the heart to the head, and so on—— It is not to be told in what a degree such a wayward kind of friction works upon the more gross and solid parts, wasting the fat and impairing the strength of a man every time as it goes backwards and forwards.

My father had certainly sunk under this evil, as certainly as he had done under that of my CHRISTIAN NAME—had he not been rescued out of it as he was out of that, by a fresh evil—the misfortune of my brother *Bobby*'s death.

What is the life of man! Is it not to shift from side to side?—from sorrow to sorrow?——to button up one cause of vexation! —and unbutton another!

CHAPTER XXXII

FROM this moment I am to be considered as heir-apparent to the *Shandy* family—and it is from this point properly, that the story of my LIFE and my OPINIONS sets out; with all my hurry and precipitation I have but been clearing the ground to raise the building——and such a building do I foresee it will turn out, as never was planned, and as never was executed since *Adam*. In less than five minutes I shall have thrown my pen into the fire, and the little drop of thick ink which is left remaining at the bottom of my inkhorn, after it—I have but half a score things to do in the time——I have a thing to name—a thing to lament—a thing to hope—a thing to promise, and a thing to threaten—I have a thing to suppose—a thing to declare—a thing to conceal—a thing to chuse, and a thing to pray for.—This chapter, therefore, I *name* the chapter of THINGS—and my next chapter to it, that is, the first chapter of my next volume, if I live, shall be my chapter upon WHISKERS, in order to keep up some sort of connection in my works.

The thing I lament is, that things have crowded in so thick upon me, that I have not been able to get into that part of my work, towards which, I have all the way, looked forwards, with so much earnest desire; and that is the campaigns, but especially the amours of my uncle *Toby*, the events of which are of so singular a nature, and so Cervantick a cast, that if I can so manage it, as to convey but the same impressions to every other brain, which the occurrences themselves excite in my own——I will answer for it the book shall make its way in the world, much better than its master has done before it——Oh *Tristram*! *Tristram*! can this but be once brought about——the credit, which will attend thee as an author, shall counterbalance the many evils which have befallen thee as a man—thou wilt feast upon the one —when thou hast lost all sense and remembrance of the other!

No wonder I itch so much as I do, to get at these amours— They are the choicest morsel of my whole story! and when I do get at 'em—assure yourselves, good folks,—(nor do I value whose squeamish stomach takes offence at it) I shall not be at all nice in the choice of my words;——and that's the thing I have to *declare*.—I shall never get all through in five minutes, that I fear—and the thing I *hope* is, that your worships and reverences are not offended—if you are, depend upon't I'll give you something, my good gentry, next year, to be offended at—— that's my dear *Jenny*'s way—but who my *Jenny* is—and which is the right and which the wrong end of a woman, is the thing to be *concealed*—it shall be told you the next chapter but one, to my chapter of button-holes,—and not one chapter before.

And now that you have just got to the end of these four volumes——the thing I have to *ask* is, how you feel your heads? my own akes dismally—as for your healths, I know, they are much better——True *Shandeism*, think what you will against it, opens the heart and lungs, and like all those affections which partake of its nature, it forces the blood and other vital fluids of the body to run freely thro' its channels, and makes the wheel of life run long and chearfully round.

Was I left like *Sancho Pança*, to chuse my kingdom, it should

not be maritime—or a kingdom of blacks to make a penny of——
no, it should be a kingdom of hearty laughing subjects: And as
the bilious and more saturnine passions, by creating disorders in
the blood and humours, have as bad an influence, I see, upon the
body politick as body natural—and as nothing but a habit of
virtue can fully govern those passions, and subject them to
reason—I should add to my prayer—that God would give my
subjects grace to be as WISE as they were MERRY; and then
should I be the happiest monarch, and they the happiest people
under heaven—

And so, with this moral for the present, may it please your
worships and your reverences, I take my leave of you till this
time twelve-month, when (unless this vile cough kills me in the
mean time) I'll have another pluck at your beards, and lay open
a story to the world you little dream of.

END of the FOURTH VOLUME.

VOLUME V

Dixero si quid fortè jocosius, hoc mihi juris
Cum venia dabis.——   HOR.

——Si quis calumnietur levius esse quam decet theologum, aut
mordacius quam deceat Christianum——non Ego, sed Democritus
dixit.——   ERASMUS.

TO THE RIGHT HONOURABLE
JOHN
LORD VISCOUNT SPENCER

My Lord,

I HUMBLY beg leave to offer you these two Volumes; they are the best my talents, with such bad health as I have, could produce:—had providence granted me a larger stock of either, they had been a much more proper present to your Lordship.

I beg your Lordship will forgive me, if, at the same time I dedicate this work to you, I join Lady SPENCER, in the liberty I take of inscribing the story of *Le Fever* in the sixth volume to her name; for which I have no other motive, which my heart has informed me of, but that the story is a humane one.

I am,
My Lord,
Your Lordship's
Most devoted,
And most humble Servant,
LAUR. STERNE.

CHAPTER I

IF IT HAD not been for those two mettlesome tits, and that madcap of a postilion, who drove them from Stilton to Stamford, the thought had never entered my head. He flew like lightning——there was a slope of three miles and a half—— we scarce touched the ground——the motion was most rapid— most impetuous—'twas communicated to my brain—my heart partook of it——"By the great God of day," said I, looking towards the sun, and thrusting my arm out of the fore-window of the chaise, as I made my vow, "I will lock up my study door the moment I get home, and throw the key of it ninety feet below the surface of the earth, into the draw-well at the back of my house."

The London waggon confirmed me in my resolution: it hung tottering upon the hill, scarce progressive, drag'd—drag'd up by eight *heavy beasts*——"by main strength!—quoth I, nodding— but your betters draw the same way—and something of every bodies!——O rare!"

Tell me, ye learned, shall we for ever be adding so much to the *bulk*—so little to the *stock*?

Shall we for ever make new books, as apothecaries make new mixtures, by pouring only out of one vessel into another?

Are we for ever to be twisting, and untwisting the same rope? for ever in the same track—for ever at the same pace?

Shall we be destined to the days of eternity, on holy-days, as well as working-days, to be shewing the *relicks of learning*, as monks do the relicks of their saints—without working one—one single miracle with them?

Who made MAN, with powers which dart him from earth to heaven in a moment—that great, that most excellent, and most noble creature of the world—the *miracle* of nature, as Zoroaster in his book περὶ φύσεως called him—the SHEKINAH of the divine presence, as Chrysostom—the *image* of God, as Moses— the *ray* of divinity, as Plato—the *marvel* of *marvels*, as Aristotle— to go sneaking on at this pitiful—pimping—pettifogging rate?

I scorn to be as abusive as Horace upon the occasion——but if there is no catachresis in the wish, and no sin in it, I wish from my soul, that every imitator in *Great Britain*, *France*, and *Ireland*, had the farcy for his pains; and that there was a good farcical house, large enough to hold—aye—and sublimate them, *shag-rag*

[289]

and *bob-tail*, male and female, all together: and this leads me to the affair of *Whiskers*——but, by what chain of ideas—I leave as a legacy in *mort main* to Prudes and Tartufs, to enjoy and make the most of.

Upon Whiskers

I'm sorry I made it——'twas as inconsiderate a promise as ever entered a man's head——A chapter upon whiskers! alas! the world will not bear it——'tis a delicate world—but I knew not of what mettle it was made—nor had I ever seen the underwritten fragment; otherwise, as surely as noses are noses, and whiskers are whiskers still; (let the world say what it will to the contrary) so surely would I have steered clear of this dangerous chapter.

The Fragment

* * * * * * * * * * * * * * * * * * *
* * * * * * *——You are half asleep, my good lady, said the old gentleman, taking hold of the old lady's hand and giving it a gentle squeeze, as he pronounced the word *Whiskers*——shall we change the subject? By no means, replied the old lady—I like your account of these matters: so throwing a thin gauze handkerchief over her head, and leaning it back upon the chair with her face turned towards him, and advancing her two feet as she reclined herself—I desire, continued she, you will go on.

The old gentleman went on as follows.——Whiskers! cried the queen of *Navarre*, dropping her knotting-ball, as *La Fosseuse* uttered the word——Whiskers; madam, said *La Fosseuse*, pinning the ball to the queen's apron, and making a courtesy as she repeated it.

La Fosseuse's voice was naturally soft and low, yet 'twas an articulate voice: and every letter of the word *whiskers* fell distinctly upon the queen of *Navarre*'s ear—Whiskers! cried the queen, laying a greater stress upon the word, and as if she had still distrusted her ears—Whiskers; replied *La Fosseuse*, repeating the word a third time—There is not a cavalier, madam, of his age in *Navarre*, continued the maid of honour, pressing the page's interest upon the queen, that has so gallant a pair—Of what? cried *Margaret*, smiling——Of whiskers, said *La Fosseuse*, with infinite modesty.

The word whiskers still stood its ground, and continued to be made use of in most of the best companies throughout the little kingdom of *Navarre*, notwithstanding the indiscreet use which *La Fosseuse* had made of it: the truth was, *La Fosseuse* had pronounced the word, not only before the queen, but upon sundry other occasions at court, with an accent which always implied something of a mystery——And as the court of *Margaret*, as all the world knows, was at that time a mixture of gallantry and devotion——and whiskers being as applicable to the one, as the other, the word naturally stood its ground—it gain'd full as much as it lost; that is, the clergy were for it—the laity were against it—and for the women,——*they* were divided.——

The excellency of the figure and mien of the young Sieur *de Croix*, was at that time beginning to draw the attention of the maids of honour towards the terrase before the palace gate, where the guard was mounted. The Lady *de Baussiere* fell deeply in love with him,—*La Battarelle* did the same—it was the finest weather for it, that ever was remembered in *Navarre*—*La Guyol*, *La Maronette*, *La Sabatiere*, fell in love with the Sieur *de Croix* also—*La Rebours* and *La Fosseuse* knew better—*De Croix* had failed in an attempt to recommend himself to *La Rebours*; and *La Rebours* and *La Fosseuse* were inseparable.

The queen of *Navarre* was sitting with her ladies in the painted bow-window, facing the gate of the second court, as *De Croix* passed through it—He is handsome, said the Lady *Baussiere*.—He has a good mien, said *La Battarelle*.—He is finely shaped, said *La Guyol*.—I never saw an officer of the horse-guards in my life, said *La Maronette*, with two such legs—Or who stood so well upon them, said *La Sabatiere*——But he has no whiskers, cried *La Fosseuse*—Not a pile, said *La Rebours*.

The queen went directly to her oratory, musing all the way, as she walked through the gallery, upon the subject; turning it this way and that way in her fancy——*Ave Maria* + ——what can *La Fosseuse* mean? said she, kneeling down upon the cushion.

La Guyol, *La Battarelle*, *La Maronette*, *La Sabatiere*, retired instantly to their chambers—Whiskers! said all four of them to themselves, as they bolted their doors on the inside.

The Lady *Carnavallette* was counting her beads with both hands, unsuspected under her farthingal—from St. *Antony* down to St. *Ursula* inclusive, not a saint passed through her fingers without whiskers; St. *Francis*, St. *Dominick*, St. *Bennet*, St. *Basil*, St. *Bridget*, had all whiskers.

The Lady *Baussiere* had got into a wilderness of conceits, with moralizing too intricately upon *La Fosseuse*'s text—She mounted her palfry, her page followed her—the host passed by—the lady *Baussiere* rode on.

One denier, cried the order of mercy—one single denier, in behalf of a thousand patient captives, whose eyes look towards heaven and you for their redemption.

—The Lady *Baussiere* rode on.

Pity the unhappy, said a devout, venerable, hoary-headed man, meekly holding up a box, begirt with iron, in his withered hands ——I beg for the unfortunate—good, my lady, 'tis for a prison— for an hospital—'tis for an old man—a poor man undone by shipwreck, by suretyship, by fire——I call God and all his angels to witness—'tis to cloath the naked—to feed the hungry—'tis to comfort the sick and the broken hearted.

—The Lady *Baussiere* rode on.

A decayed kinsman bowed himself to the ground.

—The Lady *Baussiere* rode on.

He ran begging bare-headed on one side of her palfry, con-juring her by the former bonds of friendship, alliance, con-sanguinity, &c.—Cousin, aunt, sister, mother—for virtue's sake, for your own, for mine, for Christ's sake remember me—pity me.

—The Lady *Baussiere* rode on.

Take hold of my whiskers, said the Lady *Baussiere*——The page took hold of her palfry. She dismounted at the end of the terrace.

There are some trains of certain ideas which leave prints of themselves about our eyes and eye-brows; and there is a con-sciousness of it, somewhere about the heart, which serves but to make these etchings the stronger—we see, spell, and put them together without a dictionary.

Ha, ha! hee, hee! cried *La Guyol* and *La Sabatiere*, looking close at each others prints——Ho, ho! cried *La Battarelle* and *Maronette*, doing the same:—Whist! cried one—st, st,—said a second,—hush, quoth a third——poo, poo, replied a fourth— gramercy! cried the Lady *Carnavallette*;—'twas she who be-whisker'd St. *Bridget*.

La Fosseuse drew her bodkin from the knot of her hair, and having traced the outline of a small whisker, with the blunt end of it, upon one side of her upper lip, put it into *La Rebours*'s hand. *La Rebours* shook her head.

The Lady *Baussiere* cough'd thrice into the inside of her muff— *La Guyol* smiled—Fy, said the Lady *Baussiere*. The queen of

Navarre touched her eye with the tip of her fore finger—as much as to say, I understand you all.

'Twas plain to the whole court the word was ruined: *La Fosseuse* had given it a wound, and it was not the better for passing through all these defiles——It made a faint stand, however, for a few months; by the expiration of which, the Sieur *de Croix*, finding it high time to leave *Navarre* for want of whiskers—the word in course became indecent, and (after a few efforts) absolutely unfit for use.

The best word, in the best language of the best world, must have suffered under such combinations.—The curate of *d'Estella* wrote a book against them, setting forth the dangers of accessory ideas, and warning the *Navarois* against them.

Does not all the world know, said the curate *d'Estella* at the conclusion of his work, that Noses ran the same fate some centuries ago in most parts of *Europe*, which Whiskers have now done in the kingdom of *Navarre*—The evil indeed spread no further then—, but have not beds and bolsters, and night-caps and chamber-pots stood upon the brink of destruction ever since? Are not trouse, and placket-holes, and pump-handles—and spigots and faucets, in danger still, from the same association?—Chastity, by nature the gentlest of all affections—give it but its head—'tis like a ramping and a roaring lion.

The drift of the curate *d'Estella*'s argument was not understood.—They ran the scent the wrong way.—The world bridled his ass at the tail.—And when the *extreams* of DELICACY, and the *beginnings* of CONCUPISCENCE, hold their next provincial chapter together, they may decree that bawdy also.

CHAPTER II

WHEN my father received the letter which brought him the melancholy account of my brother *Bobby*'s death, he was busy calculating the expence of his riding post from *Calais* to *Paris*, and so on to *Lyons*.

'Twas a most inauspicious journey; my father having had every foot of it to travel over again, and his calculation to begin afresh, when he had almost got to the end of it, by *Obadiah*'s opening the door to acquaint him the family was out of yeast—and to ask whether he might not take the great coach-horse early in the morning, and ride in search of some.—With all my heart, *Obadiah*, said my father, (pursuing his journey)—take the coach-horse, and welcome.—But he wants a shoe, poor creature! said *Obadiah*.—Poor creature! said my uncle *Toby*, vibrating the note back again, like a string in unison. Then ride the *Scotch* horse, quoth my father hastily.—He cannot bear a saddle upon his back, quoth *Obadiah*, for the whole world.——The devil's in that horse; then take PATRIOT, cried my father, and shut the door.—— PATRIOT is sold, said *Obadiah*.—Here's for you! cried my father, making a pause, and looking in my uncle *Toby*'s face, as if the thing had not been a matter of fact.—Your worship ordered me to sell him last *April*, said *Obadiah*.—Then go on foot for your pains, cried my father.—I had much rather walk than ride, said *Obadiah*, shutting the door.

What plagues! cried my father, going on with his calculation.—But the waters are out, said *Obadiah*,—opening the door again.

Till that moment my father, who had a map of *Sanson*'s, and a book of the post roads before him, had kept his hand upon the head of his compasses, with one foot of them fixed upon *Nevers*, the last stage he had paid for—purposing to go on from that point with his journey and calculation, as soon as *Obadiah* quitted the room; but this second attack of *Obadiah*'s, in opening the door and laying the whole country under water, was too much.—He let go his compasses—or rather with a mixed motion betwixt accident and anger, he threw them upon the table; and then there was nothing for him to do, but to return back to *Calais* (like many others) as wise as he had set out.

When the letter was brought into the parlour, which contained the news of my brother's death, my father had got forwards again upon his journey to within a stride of the compasses of the very same stage of *Nevers*.—By your leave, Mons. *Sanson*, cried my father, striking the point of his compasses through *Nevers* into the table,—and nodding to my uncle *Toby*, to see what was in the letter,—twice of one night is too much for an *English* gentleman and his son, Mons. *Sanson*, to be turned back from so lousy a town as *Nevers*,—what think'st thou, *Toby*, added my father in a sprightly tone.—Unless it be a garrison town, said my uncle *Toby*,—for then—I shall be a fool, said my father, smiling to himself, as long as I live.—So giving a second nod— and keeping his compasses still upon *Nevers* with one hand, and holding his book of the post-roads in the other—half calculating and half listening, he leaned forwards upon the table with both elbows, as my uncle *Toby* hummed over the letter.

— — — — — — — — — — —

— — — — — — — — — — —

— — — he's gone! said my uncle *Toby*.—Where—Who? cried my father.—My nephew, said my uncle *Toby*.——What—without leave—without money——without governor? cried my father in amazement. No:—he is dead, my dear brother, quoth my uncle *Toby*.—Without being ill? cried my father again.—I dare say not, said my uncle *Toby*, in a low voice, and fetching a deep sigh from the bottom of his heart, he has been ill enough, poor lad! I'll answer for him—for he is dead.

When *Agrippina* was told of her son's death, *Tacitus* informs us, that not being able to moderate the violence of her passions, she abruptly broke off her work—My father stuck his compasses into *Nevers*, but so much the faster.—What contrarieties! his, indeed, was a matter of calculation—*Agrippina*'s must have been quite a different affair; who else could pretend to reason from history?

How my father went on, in my opinion, deserves a chapter to itself.——

CHAPTER III

—AND A CHAPTER it shall have, and a devil of a one too—so look to yourselves.

'Tis either *Plato*, or *Plutarch*, or *Seneca*, or *Xenophon*, or *Epictetus*, or *Theophrastus*, or *Lucian*—or some one perhaps of later date—either *Cardan*, or *Budæus*, or *Petrarch*, or *Stella*—or possibly it may be some divine or father of the church, St. *Austin*, or St. *Cyprian*, or *Barnard*, who affirms that it is an irresistable and natural passion to weep for the loss of our friends or children —and *Seneca* (I'm positive) tells us somewhere, that such griefs evacuate themselves best by that particular channel.—And accordingly we find, that *David* wept for his son *Absolom*—*Adrian* for his *Antinous*—*Niobe* for her children, and that *Apollodorus* and *Crito* both shed tears for *Socrates* before his death.

My father managed his affliction otherwise; and indeed differently from most men either ancient or modern; for he neither wept it away, as the *Hebrews* and the *Romans*—or slept it off, as the *Laplanders*—or hang'd it, as the *English*, or drowned it, as the *Germans*—nor did he curse it, or damn it, or excommunicate it, or rhyme it, or lillabullero it.——

——He got rid of it, however.

Will your worships give me leave to squeeze in a story between these two pages?

When *Tully* was bereft of his dear daughter *Tullia*, at first he laid it to his heart,—he listened to the voice of nature, and modulated his own unto it.—O my *Tullia*! my daughter! my child!—still, still, still,—'twas O my *Tullia*!——my *Tullia*! Methinks I see my *Tullia*, I hear my *Tullia*, I talk with my *Tullia*.—But as soon as he began to look into the stores of philosophy, and consider how many excellent things might be said upon the occasion—no body upon earth can conceive, says the great orator, how happy, how joyful it made me.

My father was as proud of his eloquence as MARCUS TULLIUS CICERO could be for his life, and for aught I am convinced of to the contrary at present, with as much reason: it was indeed his strength—and his weakness too.——His strength—for he was by nature eloquent,—and his weakness—for he was hourly a dupe to it; and provided an occasion in life would but permit him to shew his talents, or say either a wise thing, a witty, or a shrewd one—(bating the case of a systematick misfortune)—he had all he wanted.—A blessing which tied up my father's tongue, and a misfortune which set it loose with a good grace, were pretty equal: sometimes, indeed, the misfortune was the better of the two; for instance, where the pleasure of the harangue was as *ten*, and the pain of the misfortune but as *five*—my father gained half in half, and consequently was as well again off, as it never had befallen him.

This clue will unravel what otherwise would seem very inconsistent in my father's domestick character; and it is this, that in the provocations arising from the neglects and blunders of servants, or other mishaps unavoidable in a family, his anger, or rather the duration of it, eternally ran counter to all conjecture.

My father had a favourite little mare, which he had consigned over to a most beautiful Arabian horse, in order to have a pad out of her for his own riding: he was sanguine in all his projects; so talked about his pad every day with as absolute a security, as if it had been reared, broke,—and bridled and saddled at his door ready for mounting. By some neglect or other in *Obadiah*, it so fell out, that my father's expectations were answered with nothing better than a mule, and as ugly a beast of the kind as ever was produced.

My mother and my uncle *Toby* expected my father would be the death of *Obadiah*—and that there never would be an end of the disaster.——See here! you rascal, cried my father, pointing to the mule, what you have done!—It was not me, said *Obadiah*. —How do I know that? replied my father.

Triumph swam in my father's eyes, at the repartee—the *Attic* salt brought water into them—and so *Obadiah* heard no more about it.

Now let us go back to my brother's death.

Philosophy has a fine saying for every thing.—For *Death* it has an entire set; the misery was, they all at once rushed into my father's head, that 'twas difficult to string them together, so as to make any thing of a consistent show out of them.—He took them as they came.

"'Tis an inevitable chance—the first statute in *Magnâ Chartâ*— it is an everlasting act of parliament, my dear brother,— —*All must die.*

"If my son could not have died, it had been matter of wonder, —not that he is dead.

"Monarchs and princes dance in the same ring with us.

"—*To die*, is the great debt and tribute due unto nature: tombs and monuments, which should perpetuate our memories, pay it themselves; and the proudest pyramid of them all, which wealth and science have erected, has lost its apex, and stands obtruncated in the traveller's horizon." (My father found he got great ease, and went on)—"Kingdoms and provinces, and towns and cities, have they not their periods? and when those principles and powers, which at first cemented and put them together, have performed their several evolutions, they fall back."—Brother *Shandy*, said my uncle *Toby*, laying down his pipe at the word *evolutions*— Revolutions, I meant, quoth my father,—by heaven! I meant revolutions, brother *Toby*—evolutions is nonsense.—'Tis not nonsense—said my uncle *Toby*.——But is it not nonsense to break the thread of such a discourse, upon such an occasion? cried my father—do not—dear *Toby*, continued he, taking him by the hand, do not—do not, I beseech thee, interrupt me at this crisis.—My uncle *Toby* put his pipe into his mouth.

"Where is *Troy* and *Mycenæ*, and *Thebes* and *Delos*, and *Persepolis*, and *Agrigentum*"—continued my father, taking up his book of post-roads, which he had laid down.—"What is become, brother *Toby*, of *Nineveh* and *Babylon*, of *Cizicum* and *Mitylenæ?* The fairest towns that ever the sun rose upon, are now no more: the names only are left, and those (for many of them are wrong spelt) are falling themselves by piecemeals to decay and in length of time will be forgotten, and involved with every thing in a perpetual night: the world itself, brother *Toby*, must—must come to an end.

"Returning out of *Asia*, when I sailed from *Ægina* towards *Megara*," (*when can this have been? thought my uncle Toby*) "I began to view the country round about. *Ægina* was behind me, *Megara* was before, *Pyræus* on the right hand, *Corinth* on the left.—What flourishing towns now prostrate upon the earth! Alas! alas! said I to myself, that man should disturb his soul for the loss of a child, when so much as this lies awfully buried in his presence——Remember, said I to myself again—remember thou art a man."—

Now my uncle *Toby* knew not that this last paragraph was an extract of *Servius Sulpicius*'s consolatory letter to *Tully*.—He had as little skill, honest man, in the fragments, as he had in the whole pieces of antiquity.—And as my father, whilst he was concerned in the *Turky* trade, had been three or four different times in the *Levant*, in one of which he had staid a whole year and a half at *Zant*, my uncle *Toby* naturally concluded, that in some one of these periods he had taken a trip across the *Archipelago* into *Asia*; and that all this sailing affair with *Ægina* behind, and *Megara* before, and *Pyræus* on the right hand, &c. &c. was nothing more than the true course of my father's voyage and reflections.—'Twas certainly in his *manner*, and many an undertaking critick would have built two stories higher upon worse foundations.—And pray, brother, quoth my uncle *Toby*, laying the end of his pipe upon my father's hand in a kindly way of interruption—but waiting till he finished the account—what year of our Lord was this?—'Twas no year of our Lord, replied my father.—That's impossible, cried my uncle *Toby*.—Simpleton! said my father,—'twas forty years before Christ was born.

My uncle *Toby* had but two things for it; either to suppose his brother to be the wandering *Jew*, or that his misfortunes had disordered his brain.—"May the Lord God of heaven and earth protect him and restore him," said my uncle *Toby*, praying silently for my father, and with tears in his eyes.

—My father placed the tears to a proper account, and went on with his harangue with great spirit.

"There is not such great odds, brother *Toby*, betwixt good and evil, as the world imagines"——(this way of setting off, by the bye, was not likely to cure my uncle *Toby*'s suspicions.)—"Labour, sorrow, grief, sickness, want, and woe, are the sauces of life."— Much good may it do them—said my uncle *Toby* to himself.——

"My son is dead!—so much the better;—'tis a shame in such a tempest to have but one anchor.

"But he is gone for ever from us!—be it so. He is got from under the hands of his barber before he was bald.—He is but risen from a feast before he was surfeited—from a banquet before he had got drunken.

"The *Thracians* wept when a child was born"—(and we were very near it, quoth my uncle *Toby*)—"and feasted and made merry when a man went out of the world; and with reason.— Death opens the gate of fame, and shuts the gate of envy after it, —it unlooses the chain of the captive, and puts the bondsman's talk into another man's hands.

"Shew me the man, who knows what life is, who dreads it, and I'll shew thee a prisoner who dreads his liberty.

"Is it not better, my dear brother *Toby*, (for mark—our appetites are but diseases)—is it not better not to hunger at all, than to eat? —not to thirst, than to take physick to cure it?

"Is it not better to be freed from cares and agues, from love and melancholy, and the other hot and cold fits of life, than like a galled traveller, who comes weary to his inn, to be bound to begin his journey afresh?

"There is no terror, brother *Toby*, in its looks, but what it borrows from groans and convulsions—and the blowing of noses, and the wiping away of tears with the bottoms of curtains in a dying man's room.—Strip it of these, what is it—'Tis better in battle than in bed, said my uncle *Toby*.—Take away its herses, its mutes, and its mourning,—its plumes, scutcheons, and other mechanic aids—What is it?—*Better in battle!* continued my father, smiling, for he had absolutely forgot my brother *Bobby*— 'tis terrible no way—for consider, brother *Toby*,—when we *are*— death is *not*;—and when death *is*—we are *not*. My uncle *Toby* laid down his pipe to consider the proposition; my father's eloquence was too rapid to stay for any man—away it went,—and hurried my uncle *Toby*'s ideas along with it.——

"For this reason, continued my father, 'tis worthy to recollect, how little alteration in great men, the approaches of death have made.—*Vespasian* died in a jest upon his close stool—*Galba* with a sentence—*Septimius Severus* in a dispatch—*Tiberius* in dissimulation, and *Cæsar Augustus* in a compliment.—I hope, 'twas a sincere one—quoth my uncle *Toby*.

—'Twas to his wife,—said my father.

CHAPTER IV

—AND lastly—for all the choice anecdotes which history can produce of this matter, continued my father,—this, like the gilded dome which covers in the fabrick—crowns all.—

'Tis of *Cornelius Gallus*, the prætor—which I dare say, brother *Toby*, you have read.—I dare say I have not, replied my uncle.—He died said my father, as * * * * * * * * * * * * * * *—And if it was with his wife, said my uncle *Toby*—there could be no hurt in it.—That's more than I know—replied my father.

CHAPTER V

MY MOTHER was going very gingerly in the dark along the passage which led to the parlour, as my uncle *Toby* pronounced the word *wife*.—'Tis a shrill, penetrating sound of itself, and *Obadiah* had helped it by leaving the door a little a-jar, so that my mother heard enough of it, to imagine herself the subject of the conversation: so laying the edge of her finger across her two lips—holding in her breath, and bending her head a little downwards, with a twist of her neck—(not towards the door, but from it, by which means her ear was brought to the chink)—she listened with all her powers:——the listening slave, with the Goddess of Silence at his back, could not have given a finer thought for an intaglio.

In this attitude I am determined to let her stand for five minutes: till I bring up the affairs of the kitchen (as *Rapin* does those of the church) to the same period.

CHAPTER VI

THOUGH in one sense, our family was certainly a simple machine, as it consisted of a few wheels; yet there was thus much to be said for it, that these wheels were set in motion by so many different springs, and acted one upon the other from such a variety of strange principles and impulses,——that though it was a simple machine, it had all the honour and advantages of a complex one,——and a number of as odd movements within it, as ever were beheld in the inside of a *Dutch* silk-mill.

Amongst these there was one, I am going to speak of, in which, perhaps, it was not altogether so singular, as in many others; and it was this, that whatever motion, debate, harangue, dialogue, project, or dissertation, was going forwards in the parlour, there was generally another at the same time, and upon the same subject, running parallel along with it in the kitchen.

Now to bring this about, whenever an extraordinary message, or letter, was delivered in the parlour,—or a discourse suspended till a servant went out—or the lines of discontent were observed to hang upon the brows of my father or mother—or, in short, when any thing was supposed to be upon the tapis worth knowing or listening to, 'twas the rule to leave the door, not absolutely shut, but somewhat a-jar—as it stands just now,—which, under covert of the bad hinge, (and that possibly might be one of the many reasons why it was never mended) it was not difficult to manage; by which means, in all these cases, a passage was generally left, not indeed as wide as the *Dardanells*, but wide enough, for all that, to carry on as much of this windward trade, as was sufficient to save my father the trouble of governing his house;— my mother at this moment stands profiting by it.—*Obadiah* did the same thing, as soon as he had left the letter upon the table which brought the news of my brother's death; so that before my father had well got over his surprize, and entered upon his harangue,— had *Trim* got upon his legs, to speak his sentiments upon the subject.

A curious observer of nature, had he been worth the inventory of all *Job*'s stock—though, by the bye, *your curious observers are seldom worth a groat*—would have given the half of it, to have heard Corporal *Trim* and my father, two orators so contrasted by nature and education, haranguing over the same bier.

My father a man of deep reading—prompt memory—with *Cato*, and *Seneca*, and *Epictetus*, at his fingers ends.—

[301]

The corporal—with nothing—to remember—of no deeper reading than his muster-roll—or greater names at his finger's end, than the contents of it.

The one proceeding from period to period, by metaphor and allusion, and striking the fancy as he went along, (as men of wit and fancy do) with the entertainment and pleasantry of his pictures and images.

The other, without wit or antithesis, or point, or turn, this way or that; but leaving the images on one side, and the pictures on the other, going strait forwards as nature could lead him, to the heart. O *Trim*! would to heaven thou had'st a better historian! —would!—thy historian had a better pair of breeches!——O ye criticks! will nothing melt you?

CHAPTER VII

—MY YOUNG master in *London* is dead! said *Obadiah*.— —A green sattin night-gown of my mother's, which had been twice scoured, was the first idea which *Obadiah*'s exclamation brought into *Susannah*'s head.—Well might *Locke* write a chapter upon the imperfections of words.— Then, quoth *Susannah*, we must all go into mourning.—But note a second time: the word *mourning*, notwithstanding *Susannah* made use of it herself—failed also of doing its office; it excited not one single idea, tinged either with grey or black,—all was green.——The green sattin night-gown hung there still.

—O! 'twill be the death of my poor mistress, cried *Susannah*.— My mother's whole wardrobe followed.—What a procession! her red damask,—her orange-tawny,—her white and yellow lutestrings,—her brown taffata,—her bone-laced caps, her bedgowns, and comfortable under-petticoats.—Not a rag was left behind.—"*No,—she will never look up again*," said *Susannah*.

We had a fat foolish scullion—my father, I think, kept her for her simplicity;—she had been all autumn struggling with a dropsy. —He is dead! said *Obadiah*,—he is certainly dead!—So am not I, said the foolish scullion.

——Here is sad news, *Trim*! cried *Susannah*, wiping her eyes as *Trim* step'd into the kitchen,—master *Bobby* is dead and *buried*,— the funeral was an interpolation of *Susannah*'s,—we shall have all to go into mourning, said *Susannah*.

[302]

I hope not, said *Trim*.—You hope not! cried *Susannah*
earnestly.—The mourning ran not in *Trim*'s head, whatever it did
in *Susannah*'s,—I hope—said *Trim*, explaining himself, I hope in
God the news is not true. I heard the letter read with my own ears,
answered *Obadiah*; and we shall have a terrible piece of work of
it in stubbing the ox-moor.—Oh! he's dead, said *Susannah*.—As
sure, said the scullion, as I am alive.

I lament for him from my heart and my soul, said *Trim*, fetching a sigh.—Poor creature!—poor boy! poor gentleman!

—He was alive last *Whitsontide*, said the coachman.—*Whitsontide!* alas! cried *Trim*, extending his right arm, and falling instantly into the same attitude in which he read the sermon,—
what is *Whitsontide, Jonathan*, (for that was the coachman's
name) or *Shrovetide*, or any tide or time past, to this? Are we not
here now, continued the corporal, (striking the end of his stick
perpendicularly upon the floor, so as to give an idea of health and
stability)—and are we not—(dropping his hat upon the ground)
gone! in a moment!—'Twas infinitely striking! *Susannah* burst
into a flood of tears.—We are not stocks and stones.—*Jonathan,
Obadiah*, the cook-maid, all melted.—The foolish fat scullion
herself, who was scouring a fish-kettle upon her knees, was rous'd
with it.—The whole kitchen crouded about the corporal.

Now as I perceive plainly, that the preservation of our constitution in church and state,—and possibly the preservation of the
whole world—or what is the same thing, the distribution and
balance of its property and power, may in time to come depend
greatly upon the right understanding of this stroke of the corporal's
eloquence—I do demand your attention,—your worships and
reverences, for any ten pages together, take them where you will
in any other part of the work, shall sleep for it at your ease.

I said, "we were not stocks and stones"—'tis very well. I should
have added, nor are we angels, I wish we were,—but men
cloathed with bodies, and governed by our imaginations;—and
what a junketting piece of work of it there is, betwixt these and
our seven senses, especially some of them, for my own part, I own
it, I am ashamed to confess. Let it suffice to affirm, that of all the
senses, the eye, (for I absolutely deny the touch, though most of
your *Barbati*, I know, are for it) has the quickest commerce with
the soul,—gives a smarter stroke, and leaves something more
inexpressible upon the fancy, than words can either convey—or
sometimes get rid of.

—I've gone a little about—no matter, 'tis for health—let us

only carry it back in our mind to the mortality of *Trim*'s hat.—
"Are we not here now,—and gone in a moment?"—There was
nothing in the sentence—'twas one of your self-evident truths we
have the advantage of hearing every day; and if *Trim* had not
trusted more to his hat than his head—he had made nothing
at all of it.

————"Are we not here now;"—continued the corporal, "and
are we not"—(dropping his hat plumb upon the ground—and
pausing, before he pronounced the word)—"gone! in a moment?"
The descent of the hat was as if a heavy lump of clay had been
kneaded into the crown of it.——Nothing could have expressed
the sentiment of mortality, of which it was the type and fore-
runner, like it,—his hand seemed to vanish from under it,—it fell
dead,—the corporal's eye fix'd upon it, as upon a corps,—and
Susannah burst into a flood of tears.

Now—Ten thousand, and ten thousand times ten thousand
(for matter and motion are infinite) are the ways by which a hat
may be dropped upon the ground, without any effect.——Had he
flung it, or thrown it, or cast it, or skimmed it, or squirted, or let
it slip or fall in any possible direction under heaven,—or in the
best direction that could be given to it,—had he dropped it like
a goose—like a puppy—like an ass—or in doing it, or even after
he had done, had he looked like a fool,—like a ninny—like a
nicompoop—it had fail'd, and the effect upon the heart had been
lost.

Ye who govern this mighty world and its mighty concerns with
the *engines* of eloquence,—who heat it, and cool it, and melt it,
and mollify it,——and then harden it again to *your purpose*——

Ye who wind and turn the passions with this great windlass,—
and, having done it, lead the owners of them, whither ye think
meet—

Ye, lastly, who drive——and why not, Ye also who are driven,
like turkeys to market, with a stick and a red clout—meditate
—meditate, I beseech you, upon *Trim*'s hat.

CHAPTER VIII

STAY——I have a small account to settle with the reader, before *Trim* can go on with his harangue.—It shall be done in two minutes.

Amongst many other book-debts, all of which I shall discharge in due time,—I own myself a debtor to the world for two items,—a chapter upon *chamber-maids and button-holes*, which, in the former part of my work, I promised and fully intended to pay off this year: but some of your worships and reverences telling me, that the two subjects, especially so connected together, might endanger the morals of the world,—I pray the chapter upon chamber-maids and button-holes may be forgiven me,—and that they will accept of the last chapter in lieu of it; which is nothing, an't please your reverences, but a chapter of *chamber-maids, green-gowns, and old hats.*

Trim took his off the ground,—put it upon his head,—and then went on with his oration upon death, in manner and form following.

CHAPTER IX

——TO US, *Jonathan*, who know not what want or care is— who live here in the service of two of the best of masters— (bating in my own case his majesty King *William* the Third, whom I had the honour to serve both in *Ireland* and *Flanders*)—I own it, that from *Whitsontide* to within three weeks of *Christmas*,—'tis not long—'tis like nothing;—but to those, *Jonathan*, who know what death is, and what havock and destruction he can make, before a man can well wheel about—'tis like a whole age.—O *Jonathan*! 'twould make a good-natured man's heart bleed, to consider, continued the corporal, (standing perpendicularly) how low many a brave and upright fellow has been laid since that time!—And trust me, *Susy*, added the corporal, turning to *Susannah*, whose eyes were swiming in water,—before that time comes round again,—many a bright eye will be dim.—*Susannah* placed it to the right side of the page— she wept—but she court'sied too.—Are we not, continued *Trim*, looking still at *Susannah*—are we not like a flower of the field— a tear of pride stole in betwixt every two tears of humiliation—

[305]

else no tongue could have described *Susannah*'s affliction—is not all flesh grass? —'Tis clay,—'tis dirt.—They all looked directly at the scullion,—the scullion had just been scouring a fish-kettle. —It was not fair.——

—What is the finest face that ever man looked at!—I could hear *Trim* talk so for ever, cried *Susannah*,—what is it! (*Susannah* laid her hand upon *Trim*'s shoulder)—but corruption?—— *Susannah* took it off.

—Now I love you for this—and 'tis this delicious mixture within you which makes you dear creatures what you are—and he who hates you for it——all I can say of the matter, is—That he has either a pumkin for his head—or a pippin for his heart,— and whenever he is dissected 'twill be found so.

CHAPTER X

WHETHER *Susannah*, by taking her hand too suddenly from off the corporal's shoulder, (by the whisking about of her passions)——broke a little the chain of his reflections——

Or whether the corporal began to be suspicious, he had got into the doctor's quarters, and was talking more like the chaplain than himself——

Or whether————Or whether——for in all such cases a man of invention and parts may with pleasure fill a couple of pages with suppositions——which of all these was the cause, let the curious physiologist, or the curious any body determine ——'tis certain, at least, the corporal went on thus with his harangue.

For my own part, I declare it, that out of doors, I value not death at all:—not this .. added the corporal, snapping his fingers, —but with an air which no one but the corporal could have given to the sentiment.—In battle, I value death not this ... and let him not take me cowardly, like poor *Joe Gibbins*, in scouring his gun. —What is he? A pull of a trigger—a push of a bayonet an inch this way or that—makes the difference.—Look along the line—to the right—see! *Jack*'s down! well,—'tis worth a regiment of horse to him.—No—'tis *Dick*. Then *Jack*'s no worse.—Never mind which,—we pass on,—in hot pursuit the wound itself which brings him is not felt,—the best way is to stand up to him,—the man who flies, is in ten times more danger than the man who marches up into his jaws.—I've look'd him, added the corporal, an hundred times in the face,—and know what he is.—He's nothing, *Obadiah*, at all in the field.—But he's very frightful in a house, quoth *Obadiah*.——I never mind it myself, said *Jonathan*, upon a coach-box.—It must, in my opinion, be most natural in bed, replied *Susannah*.—And could I escape him by creeping into the worst calf's skin that ever was made into a knapsack, I would do it there—said *Trim*—but that is nature.

——Nature is nature, said *Jonathan*.—And that is the reason, cried *Susannah*, I so much pity my mistress.—She will never get the better of it.—Now I pity the captain the most of any one in the family, answered *Trim*.——Madam will get ease of heart in weeping,—and the Squire in talking about it,—but my poor master will keep it all in silence to himself.—I shall hear him sigh in his bed for a whole month together, as he did for lieutenant *Le Fever*. An' please your honour, do not sigh so piteously, I would say to him as I laid besides him. I cannot help it, *Trim*, my master would say,——'tis so melancholy an accident—I cannot get it off my heart—Your honour fears not death yourself.—I hope, *Trim*, I fear nothing, he would say, but the doing a wrong thing.——Well, he would add, whatever betides, I will take care of *Le Fever*'s boy.—And with that, like a quieting draught, his honour would fall asleep.

I like to hear *Trim*'s stories about the captain, said *Susannah*.— He is a kindly-hearted gentleman, said *Obadiah*, as ever lived.— Aye,—and as brave a one too, said the corporal, as ever stept before a platoon.—There never was a better officer in the king's army,—or a better man in God's world; for he would march up to the mouth of a cannon, though he saw the lighted match at the very touch-hole,—and yet, for all that, he has a heart as soft as a child for other people.——He would not hurt a chicken.——I would sooner, quoth *Jonathan*, drive such a gentleman for seven pounds a year—than some for eight.—Thank thee, *Jonathan*! for thy twenty shillings,—as much, *Jonathan*, said the corporal, shaking him by the hand, as if thou hadst put the money into my own pocket.——I would serve him to the day of my death out of love. He is a friend and a brother to me,—and could I be sure my poor brother *Tom* was dead,—continued the corporal, taking out his handkerchief,—was I worth ten thousand pounds, I would leave every shilling of it to the captain.——*Trim* could not refrain from tears at this testamentary proof he gave of his

affection to his master.——The whole kitchen was affected.——
Do tell us this story of the poor lieutenant, said *Susannah*.——
With all my heart, answered the corporal.

Susannah, the cook, *Jonathan*, *Obadiah*, and corporal *Trim*,
formed a circle about the fire; and as soon as the scullion had
shut the kitchen door,—the corporal begun.

CHAPTER XI

I AM A *Turk* if I had not as much forgot my mother, as if
Nature had plaistered me up, and set me down naked upon
the banks of the river *Nile*, without one.——Your most
obedient servant, Madam—I've cost you a great deal of trouble,
—I wish it may answer;—but you have left a crack in my back,
—and here's a great piece fallen off here before,—and what must
I do with this foot?——I shall never reach *England* with it.

For my own part I never wonder at any thing;—and so often
has my judgment deceived me in my life, that I always suspect it,
right or wrong,—at least I am seldom hot upon cold subjects.
For all this, I reverence truth as much as any body; and when it
has slipped us, if a man will but take me by the hand, and go
quietly and search for it, as for a thing we have both lost, and can
neither of us do well without,—I'll go to the world's end with him:
——But I hate disputes,—and therefore (bating religious points,
or such as touch society) I would almost subscribe to any thing
which does not choak me in the first passage, rather than be
drawn into one——But I cannot bear suffocation,——and bad
smells worst of all.——For which reasons, I resolved from the
beginning, That if ever the army of martyrs was to be augmented,
—or a new one raised,—I would have no hand in it, one way or
t'other.

CHAPTER XII

—B UT TO return to my mother.
My uncle *Toby*'s opinion, Madam, "that there could
be no harm in *Cornelius Gallus*, the *Roman* prætor's lying
with his wife;"——or rather the last word of that opinion,—(for
it was all my mother heard of it) caught hold of her by the weak

part of the whole sex:——You shall not mistake me,—I mean her curiosity,—she instantly concluded herself the subject of the conversation, and with that prepossession upon her fancy, you will readily conceive every word my father said, was accommodated either to herself, or her family concerns.

——Pray, Madam, in what street does the lady live, who would not have done the same?

From the strange mode of *Cornelius*'s death, my father had made a transition to that of *Socrates*, and was giving my uncle *Toby* an abstract of his pleading before his judges;——'twas irresistable:——not the oration of *Socrates*,—but my father's temptation to it.——He had wrote the * Life of *Socrates* himself the year before he left off trade, which, I fear, was the means of hastening him out of it;——so that no one was able to set out with so full a sail, and in so swelling a tide of heroic loftiness upon the occasion, as my father was. Not a period in *Socrates*'s oration, which closed with a shorter word than *transmigration*, or *annihilation*,—or a worse thought in the middle of it than *to be—or not to be*,—the entering upon a new and untried state of things,—or, upon a long, a profound and peaceful sleep, without dreams, without disturbance;——*That we and our children were born to die,—but neither of us born to be slaves.*——No—there I mistake; that was part of *Eleazer*'s oration, as recorded by *Josephus* (*de Bell. Judaic.*)——*Eleazer* owns he had it from the philosophers of *India*; in all likelihood *Alexander* the Great, in his irruption into *India*, after he had over-run *Persia*, amongst the many things he stole,—stole that sentiment also; by which means it was carried, if not all the way by himself, (for we all know he died at *Babylon*) at least by some of his maroders, into *Greece*,—from *Greece* it got to *Rome*,—from *Rome* to *France*,—and from *France* to *England*:——So things come round.——

By land carriage I can conceive no other way.——

By water the sentiment might easily have come down the *Ganges* into the *Sinus Gangeticus*, or *Bay of Bengal*, and so into the *Indian Sea*; and following the course of trade, (the way from *India* by the *Cape of Good Hope* being then unknown) might be carried with other drugs and spices up the *Red Sea* to *Joddah*, the port of *Mekka*, or else to *Tor* or *Sues*, towns at the bottom of the gulf; and from thence by karrawans to *Coptos*, but three days

* This book my father would never consent to publish; 'tis in manuscript, with some other tracts of his, in the family, all, or most of which will be printed in due time.

journey distant, so down the *Nile* directly to *Alexandria*, where the SENTIMENT would be landed at the very foot of the great staircase of the *Alexandrian* library,——and from that store-house it would be fetched.——Bless me! what a trade was driven by the learned in those days!

CHAPTER XIII

—NOW MY father had a way, a little like that of *Job*'s (in case there ever was such a man——if not, there's an end of the matter.——

Though, by the bye, because your learned men find some difficulty in fixing the precise æra in which so great a man lived; —whether, for instance, before or after the patriarchs, &c.—— to vote, therefore, that he never lived *at all*, is a little cruel,—'tis not doing as they would be done by—happen that as it may)—— My father, I say, had a way, when things went extremely wrong with him, especially upon the first sally of his impatience,—of wondering why he was begot,—wishing himself dead;—sometimes worse:——And when the provocation ran high, and grief touched his lips with more than ordinary powers,—Sir, you scarce could have distinguished him from *Socrates* himself.——Every word would breathe the sentiments of a soul disdaining life, and careless about all its issues; for which reason, though my mother was a woman of no deep reading, yet the abstract of *Socrates*'s oration, which my father was giving my uncle *Toby*, was not altogether new to her.—She listened to it with composed intelligence, and would have done so to the end of the chapter, had not my father plunged (which he had no occasion to have done) into that part of the pleading where the great philosopher reckons up his connections, his alliances, and children; but renounces a security to be so won by working upon the passions of his judges. —"I have friends—I have relations,—I have three desolate children,"—says *Socrates*.—

——Then, cried my mother, opening the door,——you have one more, Mr. *Shandy*, than I know of.

By heaven! I have one less,—said my father, getting up and walking out of the room.

[310]

CHAPTER XIV

—THEY ARE *Socrates*'s children, said my uncle *Toby*. He has been dead a hundred years ago, replied my mother.

My uncle *Toby* was no chronologer—so not caring to advance a step but upon safe ground, he laid down his pipe deliberately upon the table, and rising up, and taking my mother most kindly by the hand, without saying another word, either good or bad, to her, he led her out after my father, that he might finish the ecclaircissment himself.

CHAPTER XV

HAD THIS volume been a farce, which, unless every one's life and opinions are to be looked upon as a farce as well as mine, I see no reason to suppose—the last chapter, Sir, had finished the first act of it, and then this chapter must have set off thus.

Ptr..r..r..ing—twing—twang—prut—trut——'tis a cursed bad fiddle.—Do you know whether my fiddle's in tune or no?—trut.. prut..—They should be *fifths*.——'Tis wickedly strung—tr... a.e.i.o.u.-twang.—The bridge is a mile too high, and the sound-post absolutely down,—else—trut . . prut—hark! 'tis not so bad a tone.—Diddle diddle, diddle diddle, diddle diddle, dum. There is nothing in playing before good judges,—but there's a man there—no—not him with the bundle under his arm—the grave man in black.—S'death! not the gentleman with the sword on.— Sir, I had rather play a *Caprichio* to *Calliope* herself, than draw my bow across my fiddle before that very man; and yet, I'll stake my *Cremona* to a *Jew*'s trump, which is the greatest musical odds that ever were laid, that I will this moment stop three hundred and fifty leagues out of tune upon my fiddle, without punishing one single nerve that belongs to him.—Twaddle diddle, tweddle diddle,—twiddle diddle,——twoddle diddle,—twuddle diddle, ——prut-trut—krish—krash—krush.—I've undone you, Sir,— but you see he is no worse,—and was *Apollo* to take his fiddle after me, he can make him no better.

Diddle diddle, diddle diddle, diddle diddle—hum—dum—drum.

—Your worships and your reverences love musick—and God

has made you all with good ears—and some of you play delightfully yourselves——trut-prut,—prut-trut.

O! there is—whom I could sit and hear whole days,—whose talents lie in making what he fiddles to be felt,—who inspires me with his joys and hopes, and puts the most hidden springs of my heart into motion.——If you would borrow five guineas of me, Sir,—which is generally ten guineas more than I have to spare— or you, Messrs. Apothecary and Taylor, want your bills paying, —that's your time.

CHAPTER XVI

THE FIRST thing which entered my father's head, after affairs were a little settled in the family, and *Susannah* had got possession of my mother's green sattin night-gown,— was to sit down coolly, after the example of *Xenophon*, and write a TRISTRA-*pædia*, or system of education for me; collecting first for that purpose his own scattered thoughts, counsels, and notions; and binding them together, so as to form an INSTITUTE for the government of my childhood and adolescence. I was my father's last stake—he had lost my brother *Bobby* entirely,—he had lost, by his own computation, full three fourths of me—that is, he had been unfortunate in his three first great casts for me—my geniture, nose, and name,—there was but this one left; and accordingly my father gave himself up to it with as much devotion as ever my uncle *Toby* had done to his doctrine of projectils.—The difference between them was, that my uncle *Toby* drew his whole knowledge of projectils from *Nicholas Tartaglia*—My father spun his, every thread of it, out of his own brain,—or reeled and crosstwisted what all other spinners and spinsters had spun before him, that 'twas pretty near the same torture to him.

In about three years, or something more, my father had got advanced almost into the middle of his work.—Like all other writers, he met with disappointments.—He imagined he should be able to bring whatever he had to say, into so small a compass, that when it was finished and bound, it might be rolled up in my mother's hussive.—Matter grows under our hands.—Let no man say,—"Come—I'll write a *duodecimo*."

My father gave himself up to it, however, with the most painful diligence, proceeding step by step in every line, with the same kind of caution and circumspection (though I cannot say upon quite so religious a principle) as was used by *John de la Casse*, the lord archbishop of *Benevento*, in compassing his *Galatea*; in which his Grace of *Benevento* spent near forty years of his life; and when the thing came out, it was not of above half the size or the thickness of a *Rider's* Almanack.—How the holy man managed the affair, unless he spent the greatest part of his time in combing his whiskers, or playing at *primero* with his chaplain,—would pose any mortal not let into the true secret;—and therefore 'tis worth explaining to the world, was it only for the encouragement of those few in it, who write not so much to be fed—as to be famous.

I own had *John de la Casse*, the archbishop of *Benevento*, for whose memory (notwithstanding his *Galatea*) I retain the highest veneration,—had he been, Sir, a slender clerk—of dull wit—slow parts—costive head, and so forth,—he and his *Galatea* might have jogged on together to the age of *Methusalah* for me,—the phænomenon had not been worth a parenthesis.—

But the reverse of this was the truth: *John de la Casse* was a genius of fine parts and fertile fancy; and yet with all these great advantages of nature, which should have pricked him forwards with his *Galatea*, he lay under an impuissance at the same time of advancing above a line and an half in the compass of a whole summer's day: this disability in his Grace arose from an opinion he was afflicted with,—which opinion was this,—*viz.* that whenever a Christian was writing a book (not for his private amusement, but) where his intent and purpose was *bonâ fide*, to print and publish it to the world, his first thoughts were always the temptations of the evil one.—This was the state of ordinary writers: but when a personage of venerable character and high station, either in church or state, once turned author,—he maintained, that from the very moment he took pen in hand—all the devils in hell broke out of their holes to cajole him.—'Twas Term-time with them,—every thought, first and last, was captious; —how specious and good soever,—'twas all one;—in whatever form or colour it presented itself to the imagination,—'twas still a stroke of one or other of 'em levelled at him, and was to be fenced off.—So that the life of a writer, whatever he might fancy to the contrary, was not so much a state of *composition*, as a state of *warfare*; and his probation in it, precisely that of any other man militant upon earth,—both depending alike, not half so much upon the degrees of his WIT—as his RESISTANCE.

My father was hugely pleased with this theory of *John de la*

Casse, archbishop of *Benevento*; and (had it not cramped him a little in his creed) I believe would have given ten of the best acres in the *Shandy* estate, to have been the broacher of it.—How far my father actually believed in the devil, will be seen, when I come to speak of my father's religious notions, in the progress of this work: 'tis enough to say here, as he could not have the honour of it, in the literal sense of the doctrine—he took up with the allegory of it;—and would often say, especially when his pen was a little retrograde, there was as much good meaning, truth, and knowledge, couched under the veil of *John de la Casse*'s parabolical representation,—as was to be found in any one poetic fiction, or mystick record of antiquity.—Prejudice of education, he would say, *is the devil*,—and the multitudes of them which we suck in with our mother's milk—*are the devil and all.*——We are haunted with them, brother *Toby*, in all our lucubrations and researches; and was a man fool enough to submit tamely to what they obtruded upon him,—what would his book be? Nothing,— he would add, throwing his pen away with a vengeance,—nothing but a farrago of the clack of nurses, and of the nonsense of the old women (of both sexes) throughout the kingdom.

This is the best account I am determined to give of the slow progress my father made in his *Tristra-pædia*; at which (as I said) he was three years and something more, indefatigably at work, and at last, had scarce compleated, by his own reckoning, one half of his undertaking: the misfortune was, that I was all that time totally neglected and abandoned to my mother; and what was almost as bad, by the very delay, the first part of the work, upon which my father had spent the most of his pains, was rendered entirely useless,——every day a page or two became of no consequence.——

——Certainly it was ordained as a scourge upon the pride of human wisdom, That the wisest of us all, should thus outwit ourselves, and eternally forego our purposes in the intemperate act of pursuing them.

In short, my father was so long in all his acts of resistance,—or in other words,—he advanced so very slow with his work, and I began to live and get forwards at such a rate, that if an event had not happened,——which, when we get to it, if it can be told with decency, shall not be concealed a moment from the reader ——I verily believe, I had put by my father, and left him drawing a sun-dial, for no better purpose than to be buried under ground.

CHAPTER XVII

—'TWAS nothing,—I did not lose two drops of blood by it ——'twas not worth calling in a surgeon, had he lived next door to us——thousands suffer by choice, what I did by accident.——Doctor *Slop* made ten times more of it, than there was occasion:——some men rise, by the art of hanging great weights upon small wires,—and I am this day (*August* the 10th, 1761) paying part of the price of this man's reputation.—— O 'twould provoke a stone, to see how things are carried on in this world!——The chamber-maid had left no ******* *** under the bed:——Cannot you contrive, master, quoth *Susannah*, lifting up the sash with one hand, as she spoke, and helping me up into the window seat with the other,—cannot you manage, my dear, for a single time to **** *** ** *** ******?

I was five years old.——*Susannah* did not consider that nothing was well hung in our family,—so slap came the sash down like lightening upon us;—Nothing is left,—cried *Susannah*,—nothing is left—for me, but to run my country.——

My uncle *Toby*'s house was a much kinder sanctuary; and so *Susannah* fled to it.

CHAPTER XVIII

WHEN *Susannah* told the corporal the misadventure of the sash, with all the circumstances which attended the *murder* of me,—(as she called it)—the blood forsook his cheeks;—all accessaries in murder, being principals,—*Trim*'s conscience told him he was as much to blame as *Susannah*,—and if the doctrine had been true, my uncle *Toby* had as much of the blood-shed to answer for to heaven, as either of 'em;—so that neither reason or instinct, separate or together, could possibly have guided *Susannah*'s steps to so proper an asylum. It is in vain to leave this to the Reader's imagination:——to form any kind of hypothesis that will render these propositions feasible, he must cudgel his brains sore,—and to do it without,—he must have such brains as no reader ever had before him.——Why should I put them either to tryal or to torture? 'Tis my own affair: I'll explain it myself.

[315]

CHAPTER XIX

T IS A PITY, *Trim*, said my uncle *Toby*, resting with his hand upon the corporal's shoulder, as they both stood surveying their works,—that we have not a couple of field pieces to mount in the gorge of that new redoubt;——'twould secure the lines all along there, and make the attack on that side quite complete:——get me a couple cast, *Trim*.

Your honour shall have them, replied *Trim*, before to-morrow morning.

It was the joy of *Trim*'s heart,—nor was his fertile head ever at a loss for expedients in doing it, to supply my uncle *Toby* in his campaigns, with whatever his fancy called for; had it been his last crown, he would have sate down and hammered it into a paderero to have prevented a single wish in his Master. The corporal had already,—what with cutting off the ends of my uncle *Toby*'s spouts—hacking and chiseling up the sides of his leaden gutters,—melting down his pewter shaving bason,—and going at last, like *Lewis* the fourteenth, on to the top of the church, for spare ends, &c.——he had that very campaign brought no less than eight new battering cannons, besides three demi-culverins into the field; my uncle *Toby*'s demand for two more pieces for the redoubt, had set the corporal at work again; and no better resource offering, he had taken the two leaden weights from the nursery window: and as the sash pullies, when the lead was gone, were of no kind of use, he had taken them away also, to make a couple of wheels for one of their carriages.

He had dismantled every sash window in my uncle *Toby*'s house long before, in the very same way,—though not always in the same order; for sometimes the pullies had been wanted, and not the lead,—so then he began with the pullies,—and the pullies being picked out, then the lead became useless,—and so the lead went to pot too.

——A great MORAL might be picked handsomly out of this, but I have not time—'tis enough to say, wherever the demolition began, 'twas equally fatal to the sash window.

CHAPTER XX

THE corporal had not taken his measures so badly in this stroke of artilleryship, but that he might have kept the matter entirely to himself, and left *Susannah* to have sustained the whole weight of the attack, as she could;—true courage is not content with coming off so.——The corporal, whether as general or comptroller of the train,—'twas no matter,——had done that, without which, as he imagined, the misfortune could never have happened,—*at least in* Susannah's *hands*;——How would your honours have behaved?——He determined at once, not to take shelter behind *Susannah*,—but to give it; and with this resolution upon his mind, he marched upright into the parlour, to lay the whole *manœuvre* before my uncle *Toby*.

My uncle *Toby* had just then been giving *Yorick* an account of the Battle of *Steenkirk*, and of the strange conduct of count *Solmes* in ordering the foot to halt, and the horse to march where it could not act; which was directly contrary to the king's commands, and proved the loss of the day.

There are incidents in some families so pat to the purpose of what is going to follow,—they are scarce exceeded by the invention of a dramatic writer;—I mean of ancient days.——

Trim, by the help of his forefinger, laid flat upon the table, and the edge of his hand striking a-cross it at right angles, made a shift to tell his story so, that priests and virgins might have listened to it;—and the story being told,—the dialogue went on as follows:

CHAPTER XXI

—I WOULD be picquetted to death, cried the corporal, as he concluded *Susannah*'s story, before I would suffer the woman to come to any harm,—'twas my fault, an' please your honour,—not her's.

Corporal *Trim*, replied my uncle *Toby*, putting on his hat which lay upon the table,——if any thing can be said to be a fault, when the service absolutely requires it should be done,—'tis I certainly who deserve the blame,——you obeyed your orders.

Had count *Solmes*, *Trim*, done the same at the battle of *Steenkirk*, said *Yorick*, drolling a little upon the corporal, who had

been run over by a dragoon in the retreat,——he had saved thee;
——Saved! cried *Trim*, interrupting *Yorick*, and finishing the
sentence for him after his own fashion,——he had saved five
battalions, an' please your reverence, every soul of them:——
there was *Cutt*'s—continued the corporal, clapping the forefinger
of his right hand upon the thumb of his left, and counting round
his hand,——there was *Cutt*'s,——*Mackay*'s——*Angus*'s,——
Graham's——and *Leven*'s, all cut to pieces;——and so had the
English life-guards too, had it not been for some regiments upon
the right, who marched up boldly to their relief, and received the
enemy's fire in their faces, before any one of their own platoons
discharged a musket,——they'll go to heaven for it,—added
Trim.—*Trim* is right, said my uncle *Toby*, nodding to *Yorick*,
——he's perfectly right. What signified his marching the horse,
continued the corporal, where the ground was so strait, and the
French had such a nation of hedges, and copses, and ditches, and
fell'd trees laid this way and that to cover them; (as they always
have.)——Count *Solmes* should have sent us,——we would have
fired muzzle to muzzle with them for their lives.——There was
nothing to be done for the horse:——he had his foot shot off
however for his pains, continued the corporal, the very next campaign at *Landen*.—Poor *Trim* got his wound there, quoth my
uncle *Toby*.——'Twas owing, an' please your honour, entirely to
count *Solmes*,——had we drub'd them soundly at *Steenkirk*,
they would not have fought us at *Landen*.——Possibly not,——
Trim, said my uncle *Toby*;——though if they have the advantage
of a wood, or you give them a moment's time to intrench themselves, they are a nation which will pop and pop for ever at you.
——There is no way but to march cooly up to them,——receive
their fire, and fall in upon them, pell-mell—— Ding dong, added
Trim.——Horse and foot, said my uncle *Toby*.——Helter skelter,
said *Trim*.——Right and left, cried my uncle *Toby*.——Blood an'
ounds, shouted the corporal;——the battle raged,——*Yorick*
drew his chair a little to one side for safety, and after a moment's
pause, my uncle *Toby* sinking his voice a note,—resumed the
discourse as follows:

CHAPTER XXII

KING *WILLIAM*, said my uncle *Toby*, addressing himself to *Yorick*, was so terribly provoked at count *Solmes* for disobeying his orders, that he would not suffer him to come into his presence for many months after.——I fear, answered *Yorick*, the squire will be as much provoked at the corporal, as the King at the count.——But 'twould be singularly hard in this case, continued he, if corporal *Trim*, who has behaved so diametrically opposite to count *Solmes*, should have the fate to be rewarded with the same disgrace;——too oft in this world, do things take that train.——I would spring a mine, cried my uncle *Toby*, rising up,——and blow up my fortifications, and my house with them, and we would perish under their ruins, ere I would stand by and see it.——*Trim* directed a slight,——but a grateful bow towards his master,——and so the chapter ends.

CHAPTER XXIII

—THEN, *Yorick*, replied my uncle *Toby*, you and I will lead the way abreast,——and do you, corporal, follow a few paces behind us.——And *Susannah*, an' please your honour, said *Trim*, shall be put in the rear.——'Twas an excellent disposition,—and in this order, without either drums beating, or colours flying, they marched slowly from my uncle *Toby*'s house to *Shandy hall*.

——I wish, said *Trim*, as they entered the door,—instead of the sash-weights, I had cut off the church-spout, as I once thought to have done.—You have cut off spouts enow, replied *Yorick*.——

CHAPTER XXIV

AS MANY pictures as have been given of my father, how like him soever in different airs and attitudes,—not one, or all of them, can ever help the reader to any kind of preconception of how my father would think, speak, or act, upon any untried occasion or occurrence of life.—There was that infinitude

[319]

of oddities in him, and of chances along with it, by which handle he would take a thing,—it baffled, Sir, all calculations.——The truth was, his road lay so very far on one side, from that wherein most men travelled,—that every object before him presented a face and section of itself to his eye, altogether different from the plan and elevation of it seen by the rest of mankind.—In other words, 'twas a different object,—and in course was differently considered:

This is the true reason, that my dear *Jenny* and I, as well as all the world besides us, have such eternal squabbles about nothing. —She looks at her outside,—I, at her in—. How is it possible we should agree about her value?

CHAPTER XXV

'TIS A POINT settled,—and I mention it for the comfort of *Confucius*,* who is apt to get entangled in telling a plain story—that provided he keeps along the line of his story,— he may go backwards and forwards as he will,—'tis still held to be no digression.

This being premised, I take the benefit of the *act of going backwards* myself.

CHAPTER XXVI

FIFTY THOUSAND pannier loads of devils—(not of the Archbishop of *Benevento*'s,—I mean of *Rabelais*'s devils) with their tails chopped off by their rumps, could not have made so diabolical a scream of it, as I did—when the accident befell me: it summoned up my mother instantly into the nursery, —so that *Susannah* had but just time to make her escape down the back stairs, as my mother came up the fore.

Now, though I was old enough to have told the story myself,— and young enough, I hope, to have done it without malignity; yet *Susannah*, in passing by the kitchen, for fear of accidents, had left it in short-hand with the cook—the cook had told it with a commentary to *Jonathan*, and *Jonathan* to *Obadiah*; so that by the time my father had rung the bell half a dozen times, to know what

* Mr. *Shandy* is supposed to mean ***** *** ***, Esq; member for ******,——and not the *Chinese* Legislator.

was the matter above,—was *Obadiah* enabled to give him a particular account of it, just as it had happened.—I thought as much, said my father, tucking up his night-gown;—and so walked up stairs.

One would imagine from this——(though for my own part I somewhat question it)—that my father before that time, had actually wrote that remarkable chapter in the *Tristrapædia*, which to me is the most original and entertaining one in the whole book;—and that is the *chapter upon sash-windows*, with a bitter *Philippick* at the end of it, upon the forgetfulness of chambermaids.—I have but two reasons for thinking otherwise.

First, Had the matter been taken into consideration, before the event happened, my father certainly would have nailed up the sash-window for good an' all;—which, considering with what difficulty he composed books.—he might have done with ten times less trouble, than he could have wrote the chapter: this argument I foresee holds good against his writing the chapter, even after the event; but 'tis obviated under the second reason, which I have the honour to offer to the world in support of my opinion, that my father did not write the chapter upon sash-windows and chamber-pots, at the time supposed,—and it is this.

——That, in order to render the *Tristrapædia* complete,—I wrote the chapter myself.

CHAPTER XXVII

MY FATHER put on his spectacles—looked,—took them off,—put them into the case—all in less than a statutable minute; and without opening his lips, turned about, and walked precipitately down stairs: my mother imagined he had stepped down for lint and basilicon; but seeing him return with a couple of folios under his arm, and *Obadiah* following him with a large reading desk, she took it for granted 'twas an herbal, and so drew him a chair to the bedside, that he might consult upon the case at his ease.

——If it be but right done,—said my father, turning to the Section—*de sede vel subjecto circumcisionis*,——for he had brought up *Spencer de Legibus Hebræorum Ritualibus*—and *Maimonides*, in order to confront and examine us altogether.—

——If it be but right done, quoth he:—Only tell us, cried my

mother, interrupting him, what herbs.——For that, replied my father, you must send for Dr. *Slop*.

My mother went down, and my father went on, reading the section as follows.

* *

* * * * * * * * * *——Very well,—said my father,

* * * * * * * * * * * * * * * * * * * *

* * * * * * * *—nay, if it has that convenience——and so without stopping a moment to settle it first in his mind, whether the *Jews* had it from the *Egyptians*, or the *Egyptians* from the *Jews*,—he rose up, and rubbing his forehead two or three times across with the palm of his hand, in the manner we rub out the footsteps of care, when evil has trod lighter upon us than we foreboded,—he shut the book, and walked down stairs.—Nay, said he, mentioning the name of a different great nation upon every step as he set his foot upon it—if the EGYPTIANS,—the SYRIANS,—the PHOENICIANS,—the ARABIANS,—the CAPADOCIANS,——if the COLCHI, and TROGLODYTES did it——if SOLON and PYTHAGORAS submitted,—what is TRISTRAM?——Who am I, that I should fret or fume one moment about the matter?

CHAPTER XXVIII

DEAR *Yorick*, said my father smiling, (for *Yorick* had broke his rank with my uncle *Toby* in coming through the narrow entry, and so had stept first into the parlour)—this *Tristram* of ours, I find, comes very hardly by all his religious rites.—Never was the son of *Jew, Christian, Turk*, or *Infidel* initiated into them in so oblique and slovenly a manner.—But he is no worse, I trust, said *Yorick*.—There has been certainly, continued my father, the duce and all to do in some part or other of the ecliptic, when this offspring of mine was formed.—That, you are a better judge of than I, replied *Yorick*.—Astrologers, quoth my father, know better than us both:—the trine and sextil aspects have jumped awry,—or the opposite of the ascendents have not hit it, as they should,—or the lords of the genitures (as they call them) have been at *bo-peep*,—or something has been wrong above, or below with us.

'Tis possible, answered *Yorick*.——But is the child, cried my uncle *Toby*, the worse?—The *Troglodytes* say not, replied my father.—And your theologists, *Yorick*, tell us—Theologically?

said *Yorick*,—or speaking after the manner of * apothecaries?
—† statesmen?—or ‡ washer-women?

——I'm not sure, replied my father,—but they tell us, brother
Toby, he's the better for it.——Provided, said *Yorick*, you travel
him into *Egypt*.——Of that, answered my father, he will have the
advantage, when he sees the *Pyramids*.——

Now every word of this, quoth my uncle *Toby*, is *Arabick* to
me.——I wish, said *Yorick*, 'twas so, to half the world.

—§ ILUS, continued my father, circumcised his whole army one
morning.—Not without a court martial? cried my uncle *Toby*.
——Though the learned, continued he, taking no notice of my
uncle *Toby*'s remark, but turning to *Yorick*,—are greatly divided
still who *Ilus* was;—some say *Saturn*;—some the supream Being;
—others, no more than a brigadier general under *Pharoah-neco*.
——Let him be who he will, said my uncle *Toby*, I know not by
what article of war he could justify it.

The controvertists, answered my father, assign two and twenty
different reasons for it:—others indeed, who have drawn their
pens on the opposite side of the question, have shewn the world
the futility of the greatest part of them.—But then again, our best
polemic divines—I wish there was not a polemic divine, said
Yorick, in the kingdom;—one ounce of practical divinity—is worth
a painted ship load of all their reverences have imported these
fifty years.—Pray, Mr. *Yorick*, quoth my uncle *Toby*,—do tell me
what a polemic divine is.——The best description, captain
Shandy, I have ever read, is of a couple of 'em, replied *Yorick*, in
the account of the battle fought single hands betwixt *Gymnast*
and captain *Tripet*; which I have in my pocket.——I beg I may
hear it, quoth my uncle *Toby* earnestly.—You shall, said *Yorick*.
And as the corporal is waiting for me at the door,—and I know
the description of a battle, will do the poor fellow more good
than his supper,—I beg, brother, you'll give him leave to come in.
—With all my soul, said my father.——*Trim* came in, erect and
happy as an emperour; and having shut the door, *Yorick* took
a book from his right-hand coat pocket, and read, or pretended
to read, as follows:

* Χαλεπῆς νόσου, καὶ δυσιάτου ἀπαλλαγὴ, ἣν ἄνθρακα
καλοῦσιν.   PHILO.
† Τα τεμνόμιενα τῶν ἐθνῶν πολυγονώτατα, καὶ πολυανθρωπό-
τατα εἶναι.
‡ Καθαριότητος εἵνεκεν.   BOCHART.
§ Ὁ Ἴλος τὰ αἰδοῖα περιτέμνεται, ταὐτὸ ποιῆσαι καὶ τοὺς
ἅμ᾽ αὐτῷ συμμάχους καταναγκάσας.   SANCHUNIATHO.

CHAPTER XXIX

—"**W**HICH words being heard by all the soldiers which were there, divers of them being inwardly terrified, did shrink back and make room for the assailant: all this did *Gymnast* very well remark and consider; and therefore, making as if he would have alighted from off his horse, as he was poising himself on the mounting-side, he most nimbly (with his short sword by his thigh) shifting his feet in the stirrup and performing the stirrup-leather feat, whereby, after the inclining of his body downwards, he forthwith launched himself aloft into the air, and placed both his feet together upon the saddle, standing upright, with his back turned towards his horse's head,—Now (said he) my case goes forward. Then suddenly in the same posture wherein he was, he fetched a gambol upon one foot, and turning to the left-hand, failed not to carry his body perfectly round, just into his former position, without missing one jot.— Ha! said *Tripet*, I will not do that at this time,—and not without cause. Well, said *Gymnast*, I have failed,—I will undo this leap; then with a marvellous strength and agility, turning towards the right-hand, he fetched another frisking gambol as before; which done, he set his right-hand thumb upon the bow of the saddle, raised himself up, and sprung into the air, poising and upholding his whole weight upon the muscle and nerve of the said thumb, and so turned and whirled himself about three times: at the fourth, reversing his body and overturning it upside-down, and fore-side back, without *touching any thing*, he brought himself betwixt the horse's two ears, and then giving himself a jerking swing, he seated himself upon the crupper——"

(This can't be fighting, said my uncle *Toby*.——The corporal shook his head at it.——Have patience, said *Yorick*.)

"Then (*Tripet*) pass'd his right leg over his saddle, and placed himself *en croup*.—But, said he, 'twere better for me to get into the saddle; then putting the thumbs of both hands upon the crupper before him, and thereupon leaning himself, as upon the only supporters of his body, he incontinently turned heels over head in the air, and straight found himself betwixt the bow of the saddle in a tolerable seat; then springing into the air with a summerset, he turned him about like a wind-mill, and made above a hundred frisks, turns and demi-pommadas."—(Good God! cried *Trim*,

losing all patience,—one home thrust of a bayonet is worth it all.
——I think so too, replied *Yorick*.——

—I am of a contrary opinion, quoth my father.

CHAPTER XXX

—NO,—I think I have advanced nothing, replied my father
making answer to a question which *Yorick* had taken
the liberty to put to him,—I have advanced nothing in
the *Tristrapædia*, but what is as clear as any one proposition in
Euclid.—Reach me, *Trim*, that book from off the scrutoir:——it
has oft times been in my mind, continued my father, to have read
it over both to you, *Yorick*, and to my brother *Toby*, and I think
it a little unfriendly in myself, in not having done it long ago:——
shall we have a short chapter or two now,—and a chapter or two
hereafter, as occasions serve; and so on, till we get through the
whole? My uncle *Toby* and *Yorick* made the obeisance which was
proper; and the corporal, though he was not included in the compliment, laid his hand upon his breast, and made his bow at the
same time.——The company smiled. *Trim*, quoth my father, has
paid the full price for staying out the *entertainment.*——He did
not seem to relish the play, replied *Yorick*.——'Twas a Tom-fool-
battle, an' please your reverence, of captain *Tripet*'s and that
other officer, making so many summersets, as they advanced;——
the *French* come on capering now and then in that way,—but not
quite so much.

My uncle *Toby* never felt the consciousness of his existence
with more complacency than what the corporal's, and his own
reflections, made him do at that moment;——he lighted his pipe,
——*Yorick* drew his chair closer to the table,—*Trim* snuff'd the
candle,—my father stir'd up the fire,—took up the book,—
cough'd twice, and begun.

CHAPTER XXXI

THE FIRST thirty pages, said my father, turning over the
leaves,—are a little dry; and as they are not closely connected with the subject,——for the present we'll pass them
by: 'tis a prefatory introduction, continued my father, or an
introductory preface (for I am not determined which name to

give it) upon political or civil government; the foundation of which being laid in the first conjunction betwixt male and female, for procreation of the species——I was insensibly led into it.—— 'Twas natural, said *Yorick*.

The original of society, continued my father, I'm satisfied is, what *Politian* tells us, *i.e.* merely conjugal; and nothing more than the getting together of one man and one woman;—to which, (according to *Hesiod*) the philosopher adds a servant:——but supposing in the first beginning there were no men servants born ——he lays the foundation of it, in a man,—a woman—and a bull.——I believe 'tis an ox, quoth *Yorick*, quoting the passage (οἶκον μὲν πρῶτιϑτα, γυναῖκα τε, Βουν τ' ἀροτηρα)——A bull must have given more trouble than his head was worth.——But there is a better reason still, said my father, (dipping his pen into his ink) for, the ox being the most patient of animals, and the most useful withal in tilling the ground for their nourishment,—was the properest instrument, and emblem too, for the new joined couple, that the creation could have associated with them.—And there is a stronger reason, added my uncle *Toby*, than them all for the ox.—My father had not power to take his pen out of his ink-horn, till he had heard my uncle *Toby*'s reason.—For when the ground was tilled, said my uncle *Toby*, and made worth inclosing, then they began to secure it by walls and ditches, which was the origin of fortification.——True, true; dear *Toby*, cried my father, striking out the bull, and putting the ox in his place.

My father gave *Trim* a nod, to snuff the candle, and resumed his discourse.

——I enter upon this speculation, said my father carelessly, and half shutting the book, as he went on,—merely to shew the foundation of the natural relation between a father and his child; the right and jurisdiction over whom he acquires these several ways—

1st, by marriage.

2d, by adoption.

3d, by legitimation.

And 4th, by procreation; all which I consider in their order.

I lay a slight stress upon one of them; replied *Yorick*——the act, especially where it ends there, in my opinion lays as little obligation upon the child, as it conveys power to the father.—You are wrong,—said my father argutely, and for this plain reason

* * * * * * * * * * * * * * * * * * * *

* * * * * * * * * * * * * * * *. — I own,

added my father, that the offspring, upon this account, is not so under the power and jurisdiction of the *mother*.—But the reason, replied *Yorick*, equally holds good for her.——She is under authority herself, said my father:—and besides, continued my father, nodding his head and laying his finger upon the side of his nose, as he assigned his reason,—*she is not the principal agent*, Yorick.—In what? quoth my uncle *Toby*, stopping his pipe.— Though by all means, added my father (not attending to my uncle *Toby*) "*The son ought to pay her respect*," as you may read, *Yorick*, at large in the first book of the Institutes of *Justinian*, at the eleventh title and the tenth section.—I can read it as well, replied *Yorick*, in the Catechism.

CHAPTER XXXII

TRIM can repeat every word of it by heart, quoth my uncle *Toby*.—Pugh! said my father, not caring to be interrupted with *Trim*'s saying his Catechism. He can upon my honour, replied my uncle *Toby*.—Ask him, Mr. *Yorick*, any question you please.——

—The fifth Commandment, *Trim*—said *Yorick*, speaking mildly, and with a gentle nod, as to a modest Catechumen. The corporal stood silent.—You don't ask him right, said my uncle *Toby*, raising his voice, and giving it rapidly like the word of command;——The fifth——— cried my uncle *Toby*.—I must begin with the first, an' please your honour, said the corporal.——

—*Yorick* could not forbear smiling.—Your reverence does not consider, said the corporal, shouldering his stick like a musket, and marching into the middle of the room, to illustrate his position,—that 'tis exactly the same thing, as doing one's exercise in the field.—

"*Join your right hand to your firelock*, " cried the corporal, giving the word of command, and performing the motion.—

"*Poise your firelock*" cried the corporal, doing the duty still of both adjutant and private man.—

"*Rest your firelock;*"—one motion, an' please your reverence, you see leads into another.—If his honour will begin but with the *first*—

THE FIRST—cried my uncle *Toby*, setting his hand upon his side

—* * * * * * * * * * * * * * * * * * *

THE SECOND—cried my uncle *Toby*, waving his tobacco-pipe, as he would have done his sword at the head of a regiment.—The corporal went through his *manual* with exactness; and having *honoured his father and mother*, made a low bow, and fell back to the side of the room.

Every thing in this world, said my father, is big with jest,—and has wit in it, and instruction too,—if we can but find it out.

—Here is the *scaffold work* of INSTRUCTION, its true point of folly, without the BUILDING behind it.—

—Here is the glass for pedagogues, preceptors, tutors, governours, gerund-grinders and bear-leaders to view themselves in, in their true dimensions.—

Oh! there is a husk and shell, *Yorick*, which grows up with learning, which their unskilfulness knows not how to fling away!

—SCIENCES MAY BE LEARNED BY ROTE, BUT WISDOM NOT.

Yorick thought my father inspired.—I will enter into obligations this moment, said my father, to lay out all my aunt *Dinah*'s legacy, in charitable uses (of which, by the bye, my father had no high opinion) if the corporal has any one determinate idea annexed to any one word he has repeated.—Prythee, *Trim*, quoth my father, turning round to him,—What do'st thou mean, by "*honouring thy father and mother?*"

Allowing them, an' please your honour, three-halfpence a day out of my pay, when they grew old.—And didst thou do that, *Trim*? said *Yorick*.—He did indeed, replied my uncle *Toby*.—Then, *Trim*, said *Yorick*, springing out of his chair, and taking the corporal by the hand, thou art the best commentator upon that part of the *Decalogue*; and I honour thee more for it, corporal *Trim*, than if thou hadst had a hand in the *Talmud* itself..

CHAPTER XXXIII

O BLESSED health! cried my father, making an exclamation, as he turned over the leaves to the next chapter,—thou art above all gold and treasure; 'tis thou who enlargest the soul,—and openest all.it's powers to receive instruction and to relish virtue.—He that has thee, has little more to wish for;—and he that is so wretched as to want thee,—wants every thing with thee.

I have concentrated all that can be said upon this important head, said my father, into a very little room, therefore we'll read the chapter quite thro'.

My father read as follows:

"The whole secret of health depending upon the due contention for mastery betwixt the radical heat and the radical moisture"—You have proved that matter of fact, I suppose, above, said *Yorick*. Sufficiently, replied my father.

In saying this, my father shut the book,—not as if he resolved to read no more of it, for he kept his forefinger in the chapter:——nor pettishly,—for he shut the book slowly; his thumb resting, when he had done it, upon the upper-side of the cover, as his three fingers supported the lower-side of it, without the least compressive violence.——

I have demonstrated the truth of that point, quoth my father, nodding to *Yorick*, most sufficiently in the preceding chapter.

Now could the man in the moon be told, that a man in the earth had wrote a chapter, sufficiently demonstrating, That the secret of all health depended upon the due contention for mastery betwixt the *radical heat* and the *radical moisture*,—and that he had managed the point so well, that there was not one single word wet or dry upon radical heat or radical moisture, throughout the whole chapter,—or a single syllable in it, *pro* or *con*, directly or indirectly, upon the contention betwixt these two powers in any part of the animal œconomy——

"O thou eternal maker of all beings!"—he would cry, striking his breast with his right hand, (in case he had one)—"Thou whose power and goodness can enlarge the faculties of thy creatures to this infinite degree of excellence and perfection,—What have we MOONITES done?"

CHAPTER XXXIV

WITH TWO strokes, the one at *Hippocrates*, the other at Lord *Verulam*, did my father atchieve it.

The stroke at the prince of physicians, with which he began, was no more than a short insult upon his sorrowful complaint of the *Ars longa*,—and *Vita brevis.*——Life short, cried my father,—and the art of healing tedious! And who are we to thank for both the one and the other, but the ignorance of quacks themselves,—and the stage-loads of chymical nostrums, and peripatetic lumber, with which in all ages, they have first flatter'd the world, and at last deceived it.

——O my lord *Verulam*! cried my father, turning from *Hippocrates*, and making his second stroke at him, as the principal of nostrum-mongers, and the fittest to be made an example of to the rest,——What shall I say to thee, my great lord *Verulam*? What shall I say to thy internal spirit,—thy opium,—thy salt-petre, ——thy greasy unctions,—thy daily purges,—thy nightly glisters, and succedaneums?

——My father was never at a loss what to say to any man, upon any subject; and had the least occasion for the exordium of any man breathing: how he dealt with his lordship's opinion,——you shall see;——but when—I know not:——we must first see what his lordship's opinion was.

CHAPTER XXXV

"THE TWO great causes, which conspire with each other to shorten life, says lord *Verulam*, are first——

"The internal spirit, which like a gentle flame, wastes the body down to death:—And secondly, the external air, that parches the body up to ashes:—which two enemies attacking us on both sides of our bodies together, at length destroy our organs, and render them unfit to carry on the functions of life."

This being the state of the case; the road to Longevity was plain; nothing more being required, says his lordship, but to repair the waste committed by the internal spirit, by making the substance of it more thick and dense, by a regular course of opiates on one side, and by refrigerating the heat of it on the other, by three grains and a half of salt-petre every morning before you got up.——

Still this frame of ours was left exposed to the inimical assaults of the air without;—but this was fenced off again by a course of greasy unctions, which so fully saturated the pores of the skin, that no spicula could enter;——nor could any one get out.—— This put a stop to all perspiration, sensible and insensible, which being the cause of so many scurvy distempers—a course of glisters was requisite to carry off redundant humours,—and render the system compleat.

What my father had to say to my lord of *Verulam*'s opiates, his salt-petre, and greasy unctions and glisters, you shall read,—but not to-day—or to-morrow: time presses upon me,—my reader is impatient—I must get forwards.——You shall read the chapter at your leisure, (if you chuse it) as soon as ever the *Tristrapædia* is published.——

Sufficeth it at present, to say, my father levelled the hypothesis with the ground, and in doing that, the learned know, he built up and established his own.——

CHAPTER XXXVI

THE whole secret of health, said my father, beginning the sentence again, depending evidently upon the due contention betwixt the radical heat and radical moisture within us; —the least imaginable skill had been sufficient to have maintained it, had not the school-men confounded the task, merely (as *Van Helmont*, the famous chymist, has proved) by all along mistaking the radical moisture for the tallow and fat of animal bodies.

Now the radical moisture is not the tallow or fat of animals, but an oily and balsamous substance; for the fat and tallow, as also the phlegm or watery parts are cold; whereas the oily and balsamous parts are of a lively heat and spirit, which accounts for the observation of *Aristotle*, "*Quod omne animal post coitum est triste.*"

Now it is certain, that the radical heat lives in the radical moisture, but whether *vice versâ*, is a doubt: however, when the one decays, the other decays also; and then is produced, either an unnatural heat, which causes an unnatural dryness——or an unnatural moisture, which causes dropsies.——So that if a child, as he grows up, can but be taught to avoid running into fire or water, as either of 'em threaten his destruction,——'twill be all that is needful to be done upon that head.——

CHAPTER XXXVII

THE description of the siege of *Jerico* itself, could not have engaged the attention of my uncle *Toby* more powerfully than the last chapter;—his eyes were fixed upon my father, throughout it;—he never mentioned radical heat and radical moisture, but my uncle *Toby* took his pipe out of his mouth, and shook his head; and as soon as the chapter was finished, he beckoned to the corporal to come close to his chair, to ask him the following question,—*aside*.—— *. It was at the siege of *Limerick*, an' please your honour, replied the corporal, making a bow.

The poor fellow and I, quoth my uncle *Toby*, addressing himself to my father, were scarce able to crawl out of our tents, at the time the siege of *Limerick* was raised, upon the very account you mention.——Now what can have got into that precious noddle of thine, my dear brother *Toby*? cried my father, mentally.—— By Heaven! continued he, communing still with himself, it would puzzle an *Œdipus* to bring it in point.——

I believe, an' please your honour, quoth the corporal, that if it had not been for the quantity of brandy we set fire to every night, and the claret and cinnamon with which I plyed your honour off; —And the geneva, *Trim*, added my uncle *Toby*, which did us more good than all—I verily believe, continued the corporal, we had both, an' please your honour, left our lives in the trenches, and been buried in them too.——The noblest grave, corporal! cried my uncle *Toby*, his eyes sparkling as he spoke, that a soldier could wish to lie down in.——But a pitiful death for him! an' please your honour, replied the corporal.

All this was as much *Arabick* to my father, as the rites of the *Colchi* and *Troglodites* had been before to my uncle *Toby*; my father could not determine whether he was to frown or smile.——

My uncle *Toby*, turning to *Yorick*, resumed the case at *Limerick*, more intelligibly than he had begun it,—and so settled the point for my father at once.

CHAPTER XXXVIII

I T WAS undoubtedly, said my uncle *Toby*, a great happiness for myself and the corporal, that we had all along a burning fever, attended with a most raging thirst, during the whole five and twenty days the flux was upon us in the camp; otherwise what my brother calls the radical moisture, must, as I conceive it, inevitably have got the better.——My father drew in his lungs top-full of air, and looking up, blew it forth again, as slowly as he possibly could.——

——It was heaven's mercy to us, continued my uncle *Toby*, which put it into the corporal's head to maintain that due contention betwixt the radical heat and the radical moisture, by reinforcing the fever, as he did all along, with hot wine and spices; whereby the corporal kept up (as it were) a continual firing, so that the radical heat stood its ground from the beginning to the end, and was a fair match for the moisture, terrible as it was.—— Upon my honour, added my uncle *Toby*, you might have heard the contention within our bodies, brother *Shandy*, twenty toises. —If there was no firing, said *Yorick*.

Well—said my father, with a full aspiration, and pausing a while after the word——Was I a judge, and the laws of the country which made me one permitted it, I would condemn some of the worst malefactors, provided they had had their clergy————

———————— *Yorick* foreseeing the sentence was likely to end with no sort of mercy, laid his hand upon my father's breast, and begged he would respite it for a few minutes, till he asked the corporal a question.——Prithee, *Trim*, said *Yorick*, without staying for my father's leave,—tell us honestly—what is thy opinion concerning this self-same radical heat and radical moisture?

With humble submission to his honour's better judgment, quoth the corporal, making a bow to my uncle *Toby*—Speak thy opinion freely, corporal, said my uncle *Toby*.—The poor fellow is my servant,—not my slave,—added my uncle *Toby*, turning to my father.——

The corporal put his hat under his left arm, and with his stick hanging upon the wrist of it, by a black thong split into a tassel about the knot, he marched up to the ground where he had performed his catechism; then touching his under jaw with the thumb and fingers of his right hand before he opened his mouth,——he delivered his notion thus.

CHAPTER XXXIX

JUST AS the corporal was humming, to begin—in waddled Dr. *Slop*.—'Tis not two-pence matter—the corporal shall go on in the next chapter, let who will come in.——

Well, my good doctor, cried my father sportively, for the transitions of his passions were unaccountably sudden,—and what has this whelp of mine to say to the matter?——

Had my father been asking after the amputation of the tail of a puppy-dog—he could not have done it in a more careless air: the system which Dr. *Slop* had laid down, to treat the accident by, no way allowed of such a mode of enquiry.—He sat down.

Pray, Sir, quoth my uncle *Toby*, in a manner which could not go unanswered,—in what condition is the boy?—'Twill end in a *phimosis*, replied Dr. *Slop*.

I am no wiser than I was, quoth my uncle *Toby*,—returning his pipe into his mouth.——Then let the corporal go on, said my father, with his medical lecture.—The corporal made a bow to his old friend, Dr. *Slop*, and then delivered his opinion concerning radical heat and radical moisture, in the following words.

CHAPTER XL

THE CITY of *Limerick*, the siege of which was begun under his majesty king *William* himself, the year after I went into the army—lies, an' please your honours, in the middle of a devilish wet, swampy country.—'Tis quite surrounded, said my uncle *Toby*, with the *Shannon*, and is, by its situation, one of the strongest fortified places in *Ireland*.——

I think this is a new fashion, quoth Dr. *Slop*, of beginning a medical lecture.—'Tis all true, answered *Trim*.—Then I wish the faculty would follow the cut of it, said *Yorick*.—'Tis all cut through, an' please your reverence, said the corporal, with drains and bogs; and besides, there was such a quantity of rain fell during the siege, the whole country was like a puddle,—'twas that, and nothing else, which brought on the flux, and which had like to have killed both his honour and myself; now there was no such thing, after the first ten days, continued the corporal, for a soldier to lie dry in his tent, without cutting a ditch round it, to draw off the water;—nor was that enough, for those who could afford it, as his honour could, without setting fire every night to a pewter dish full of brandy, which took off the damp of the air, and made the inside of the tent as warm as a stove.————

And what conclusion dost thou draw, Corporal *Trim*, cried my father, from all these premises?

I infer, an' please your worship, replied *Trim*, that the radical moisture is nothing in the world but ditch-water—and that the radical heat, of those who can go to the expence of it, is burnt brandy—the radical heat and moisture of a private man, an' please your honours, is nothing but ditch-water—and a dram of geneva——and give us but enough of it, with a pipe of tobacco, to give us spirits, and drive away the vapours—we know not what it is to fear death.

I am at a loss, Captain *Shandy*, quoth Doctor *Slop*, to determine in which branch of learning your servant shines most, whether in physiology, or divinity.—*Slop* had not forgot *Trim*'s comment upon the sermon.—

It is but an hour ago, replied *Yorick*, since the corporal was examined in the latter, and pass'd muster with great honour.——

The radical heat and moisture, quoth Doctor *Slop*, turning to my father, you must know, is the basis and foundation of our being, as the root of a tree is the source and principle of its vegetation.—It is inherent in the seeds of all animals, and may be preserved sundry ways, but principally in my opinion by *consubstantials, impriments,* and *occludents.*——Now this poor fellow, continued Dr. *Slop*, pointing to the corporal, has had the misfortune to have heard some superficial emperic discourse upon this nice point.——That he has,—said my father.——Very likely, said my uncle.—I'm sure of it—quoth *Yorick*.—

CHAPTER XLI

DOCTOR *SLOP* being called out to look at a cataplasm he had ordered, it gave my father an opportunity of going on with another chapter in the *Tristrapædia*.——Come! chear up, my lads; I'll shew you land——for when we have tugged through that chapter, the book shall not be opened again this twelvemonth.—Huzza!—

CHAPTER XLII

—FIVE years with a bib under his chin;
   Four years in travelling from Christ-cross-row to
   Malachi;
A year and a half in learning to write his own name;
Seven long years and more τεπτω-ing it, at Greek and Latin;
Four years at his *probations* and his *negations*—the fine statue still lying in the middle of the marble block,—and nothing done, but his tools sharpened to hew it out!—'Tis a piteous delay!— Was not the great *Julius Scaliger* within an ace of never getting his tools sharpened at all?———Forty-four years old was he before he could manage his Greek;—and *Peter Damianus*, lord bishop of *Ostia*, as all the world knows, could not so much as read, when he was of man's estate.—And *Baldus* himself, as eminent as he turned out after, entered upon the law so late in life, that every body imagined he intended to be an adovcate in the other world: no wonder, when *Eudamidas*, the son of *Archidamas*, heard *Xenocrates* at seventy-five disputing about *wisdom*, that he asked gravely,—*If the old man be yet disputing and enquiring concerning wisdom,—what time will he have to make use of it?*

Yorick listened to my father with great attention; there was a seasoning of wisdom unaccountably mixed up with his strangest whims, and he had sometimes such illuminations in the darkest of his eclipses, as almost attoned for them:—be wary, Sir, when you imitate him.

I am convinced, *Yorick*, continued my father, half reading and half discoursing, that there is a North west passage to the intellectual world; and that the soul of man has shorter ways of going to work, in furnishing itself with knowledge and instruction, than we generally take with it.——But alack! all fields have not a river or a spring running besides them;—every child, *Yorick*! has not a parent to point it out.

——The whole entirely depends, added my father, in a low voice, upon the *auxiliary verbs*, Mr. *Yorick*.

Had *Yorick* trod upon *Virgil*'s snake, he could not have looked more surprised.—I am surprised too, cried my father, observing it,—and I reckon it as one of the greatest calamities which ever befell the republick of letters, That those who have been entrusted with the education of our children, and whose business it was to open their minds, and stock them early with ideas, in order to set

[336]

the imagination loose upon them, have made so little use of the auxiliary verbs in doing it, as they have done——So that, except *Raymond Lullius*, and the elder *Pelegrini*, the last of which arrived to such perfection in the use of 'em, with his topics, that in a few lessons, he could teach a young gentleman to discourse with plausibility upon any subject, *pro* and *con*, and to say and write all that could be spoken or written concerning it, without blotting a word, to the admiration of all who beheld him.—I should be glad, said *Yorick*, interrupting my father, to be made to comprehend this matter. You shall, said my father.

The highest stretch of improvement a single word is capable of, is a high metaphor,——for which, in my opinion, the idea is generally the worse, and not the better;——but be that as it may, —when the mind has done that with it—there is an end,—the mind and the idea are at rest,—until a second idea enters;—— and so on.

Now the use of the *Auxiliaries* is, at once to set the soul a going by herself upon the materials as they are brought her; and by the versability of this great engine, round which they are twisted, to open new tracks of enquiry, and make every idea engender millions.

You excite my curiosity greatly, said *Yorick*.

For my own part, quoth my uncle *Toby*, I have given it up.—— The *Danes*, an' please your honour, quoth the corporal, who were on the left at the siege of *Limerick*, were all auxiliaries.—— And very good ones, said my uncle *Toby*.—But the auxiliaries, *Trim*, my brother is talking about,—I conceive to be different things.——

——You do? said my father, rising up.

CHAPTER XLIII

MY FATHER took a single turn across the room, then sat down and finished the chapter.

The verbs auxiliary we are concerned in here, continued my father, are, *am*; *was*; *have*; *had*; *do*; *did*; *make*; *made*; *suffer*; *shall*; *should*; *will*; *would*; *can*; *could*; *owe*; *ought*; *used*; or *is wont*.—And these varied with tenses, *present*, *past*, *future*, and conjugated with the verb *see*,—or with these questions added to them;—*Is it? Was it? Will it be? Would it be? May it be?*

Might it be? And these again put negatively,`Is it not? Was it not?* *Ought it not?*—Or affirmatively,—*It is*; *It was*; *It ought to be.* Or chronologically,—*Has it been always? Lately? How long ago?* Or hypothetically,—*If it was*; *If it was not?* What would follow? ———If the *French* should beat the *English*? If the *Sun* go out of the *Zodiac*?

Now, by the right use and application of these, continued my father, in which a child's memory should be exercised, there is no one idea can enter his brain how barren soever, but a magazine of conceptions and conclusions may be drawn forth from it.——— Did'st thou ever see a white bear? cried my father, turning his head round to *Trim*, who stood at the back of his chair:—No, an' please your honour, replied the corporal.———But thou could'st discourse about one, *Trim*, said my father, in case of need?——— How is it possible, brother, quoth my uncle *Toby*, if the corporal never saw one?———'Tis the fact I want; replied my father,—and the possibility of it, is as follows:

A WHITE BEAR! Very well. Have I ever seen one? Might I ever have seen one? Am I ever to see one? Ought I ever to have seen one? Or can I ever see one?

Would I had seen a white bear? (for how can I imagine it?)

If I should see a white bear, what should I say? If I should never see a white bear, what then?

If I never have, can, must or shall see a white bear alive; have I ever seen the skin of one? Did I ever see one painted?— described? Have I never dreamed of one?

Did my father, mother, uncle, aunt, brothers or sisters, ever see a white bear? What would they give? How would they behave? How would the white bear have behaved? Is he wild? Tame? Terrible? Rough? Smooth?

—Is the white bear worth seeing?—

—Is there no sin in it?—

Is it better than a BLACK ONE?

END of the FIFTH VOLUME.

VOLUME VI

CHAPTER I

—WE'LL not stop two moments, my dear Sir,—only, as
we have got thro' these five volumes, (do, Sir, sit down
upon a set——they are better than nothing) let us just
look back upon the country we have pass'd through.——

——What a wilderness has it been! and what a mercy that we
have not both of us been lost, or devoured by wild beasts in it.

Did you think the world itself, Sir, had contained such a number
of Jack Asses?——How they view'd and review'd us as we passed
over the rivulet at the bottom of that little valley!——and when
we climbed over that hill, and were just getting out of sight—
good God! what a braying did they all set up together!

——Prithee, shepherd! who keeps all those Jack Asses? * * *

——Heaven be their comforter——What! are they never
curried?——Are they never taken in in winter?——Bray bray—
bray. Bray on,—the world is deeply your debtor;——louder
still—that's nothing;—in good sooth, you are ill-used:——Was
I a Jack Asse, I solemnly declare, I would bray in G-sol-re-ut
from morning, even unto night.

CHAPTER II

WHEN my father had danced his white bear backwards
and forwards through half a dozen pages, he closed the
book for good an' all,—and in a kind of triumph
redelivered it into *Trim*'s hand, with a nod to lay it upon the
'scrutoire where he found it.——*Tristram*, said he, shall be made
to conjugate every word in the dictionary, backwards and forwards the same way;——every word, *Yorick*, by this means, you
see, is converted into a thesis or an hypothesis;—every thesis and
hypothesis have an off-spring of propositions;—and each proposition has it own consequences and conclusions; every one of
which leads the mind on again, into fresh tracks of enquiries
and doubtings.——The force of this engine, added my father,
is incredible, in opening a child's head.——'Tis enough, brother
Shandy, cried my uncle *Toby*, to burst it into a thousand
splinters.——

I presume, said *Yorick*, smiling,—it must be owing to this,——

(for let logicians say what they will, it is not to be accounted for sufficiently from the bare use of the ten predicaments)——That the famous *Vincent Quirino*, amongst the many other astonishing feats of his childhood, of which the Cardinal *Bembo* has given the world so exact a story,—should be able to paste up in the publick schools at *Rome*, so early as in the eighth year of his age, no less than four thousand, five hundred, and sixty different theses, upon the most abstruse points of the most abstruse theology;—and to defend and maintain them in such sort, as to cramp and dumbfound his opponents.——What is that, cried my father, to what is told us of *Alphonsus Tostatus*, who, almost in his nurse's arms, learned all the sciences and liberal arts without being taught any one of them?——What shall we say of the great *Piereskius*?—That's the very man, cried my uncle *Toby*, I once told you of, brother *Shandy*, who walked a matter of five hundred miles, reckoning from *Paris* to *Schevling*, and from *Schevling* back again, merely to see *Stevinus*'s flying chariot.—— He was a very great man! added my uncle *Toby*; (meaning *Stevinus*)—He was so; brother *Toby*, said my father, (meaning *Piereskius*)——and had multiplied his ideas so fast, and increased his knowledge to such a prodigious stock, that, if we may give credit to an anecdote concerning him, which we cannot withhold here, without shaking the authority of all anecdotes whatever—at seven years of age, his father committed entirely to his care the education of his younger brother, a boy of five years old, —with the sole management of all his concerns.—Was the father as wise as the son? quoth my uncle *Toby*:—I should think not, said *Yorick*:—But what are these, continued my father—(breaking out in a kind of enthusiasm)—what are these, to those prodigies of childhood in *Grotius*, *Scioppius*, *Heinsius*, *Politian*, *Pascal*, *Joseph Scaliger*, *Ferdinand de Cordouè*, and others—some of which left off their *substantial forms* at nine years old, or sooner, and went on reasoning without them;—others went through their classics at seven;—wrote tragedies at eight;— *Ferdinand de Cordouè* was so wise at nine,—'twas thought the Devil was in him;——and at *Venice* gave such proofs of his knowledge and goodness, that the monks imagined he was *Antichrist*, or nothing.——Others were masters of fourteen languages at ten,—finished the course of their rhetoric, poetry, logic, and ethics at eleven,—put forth their commentaries upon *Servius* and *Martianus Capella* at twelve,—and at thirteen received their degrees in philosophy, laws, and divinity:——But

[342]

you forget the great *Lipsius*, quoth *Yorick*, who composed a work*
the day he was born;——They should have wiped it up, said my
uncle *Toby*, and said no more about it.

CHAPTER III

WHEN the cataplasm was ready, a scruple of *decorum* had
unseasonably rose up in *Susannah*'s conscience, about
holding the candle, whilst *Slop* tied it on; *Slop* had not
treated *Susannah*'s distemper with anodines,—and so a quarrel
had ensued betwixt them.

——Oh! oh!——said *Slop*, casting a glance of undue freedom
in *Susannah*'s face, as she declined the office;——then, I think
I know you, madam——You know me, Sir! cried *Susannah*
fastidiously, and with a toss of her head, levelled evidently, not
at his profession, but at the doctor himself,——you know me!
cried *Susannah* again.——Doctor *Slop* clapped his finger and his
thumb instantly upon his nostrils;——*Susannah*'s spleen was
ready to burst at it;——'Tis false, said *Susannah*.—Come, come,
Mrs. Modesty, said *Slop*, not a little elated with the success of his
last thrust,——if you won't hold the candle, and look—you may
hold it and shut your eyes:—That's one of your popish shifts,
cried *Susannah*:—'Tis better, said *Slop*, with a nod, than no shift
at all, young woman;——I defy you, Sir, cried *Susannah*, pulling
her shift sleeve below her elbow.

It was almost impossible for two persons to assist each other
in a surgical case with a more splenetic cordiality.

Slop snatched up the cataplasm,——*Susannah* snatched up the
candle;——A little this way, said *Slop*; *Susannah* looking one
way, and rowing another, instantly set fire to *Slop*'s wig, which
being somewhat bushy and unctuous withal, was burnt out before
it was well kindled.——You impudent whore! cried *Slop*,—(for
what is passion, but a wild beast)—you impudent whore, cried
Slop, getting upright, with the cataplasm in his hand;——I never

---

* Nous aurions quelque interêt, says *Baillet*, de montrer qu'il n' a rien
de ridicule s'il étoit véritable, au moins dans le sens énigmatique que *Nicius
Erythræus* a tâché de lui donner. Cet auteur dit que pour comprendre
comme *Lipse*, a pû composer un ouvrage le premier jour de sa vie, il faut,
s'imaginer, que ce premier jour n'est pas celui de sa naissance charnelle,
mais celui au quel il a commencé d'user de la raison; il veut que ç'ait été
a l'age de *neuf* ans; et il nous veut persuader que ce fut en cet âge, que *Lipse*
fit un poem.——Le tour est ingenieux, &c. &c.

was the destruction of any body's nose, said *Susannah*,—which is more than you can say:——Is it? cried *Slop*, throwing the cataplasm in her face;——Yes, it is, cried *Susannah*, returning the compliment with what was left in the pan.——

CHAPTER IV

DOCTOR *SLOP* and *Susannah* filed cross-bills against each other in the parlour; which done, as the cataplasm had failed, they retired into the kitchen to prepare a fomentation for me;—and whilst that was going, my father determined the point as you will read.

CHAPTER V

YOU SEE 'tis high time, said my father, addressing himself equally to my uncle *Toby* and *Yorick*, to take this young creature out of these women's hands, and put him into those of a private governor. *Marcus Antoninus* provided fourteen governors all at once to superintend his son *Commodus*'s education,—and in six weeks he cashiered five of them;—I know very well, continued my father, that *Commodus*'s mother was in love with a gladiator at the time of her conception, which accounts for a great many of *Commodus*'s cruelties when he became emperor; —but still I am of opinion, that those five whom *Antoninus* dismissed, did *Commodus*'s temper, in that short time, more hurt than the other nine were able to rectify all their lives long.

Now as I consider the person who is to be about my son, as the mirror in which he is to view himself from morning to night, and by which he is to adjust his looks, his carriage, and perhaps the inmost sentiments of his heart;—I would have one, *Yorick*, if possible, polished at all points, fit for my child to look into.—— This is very good sense, quoth my uncle *Toby* to himself.

——There is, continued my father, a certain mien and motion of the body and all its parts, both in acting and speaking, which argues a man *well within*; and I am not at all surprized that *Gregory* of *Nazianzum*, upon observing the hasty and untoward gestures of *Julian*, should foretel he would one day become an apostate;——or that St. *Ambrose* should turn his *Amanuensis* out

of doors, because of an indecent motion of his head, which went backwards and forwards like a flail;——or that *Democritus* should conceive *Protagoras* to be a scholar, from seeing him bind up a faggot, and thrusting, as he did it, the small twigs inwards.
——There are a thousand unnoticed openings, continued my father, which let a penetrating eye at once into a man's soul; and I maintain it, added he, that a man of sense does not lay down his hat in coming into a room,—or take it up in going out of it, but something escapes, which discovers him.

It is for these reasons, continued my father, that the governor I make choice of shall neither * lisp, or squint, or wink, or talk loud, or look fierce, or foolish;——or bite his lips, or grind his teeth, or speak through his nose, or pick it, or blow it with his fingers.——

He shall neither walk fast,—or slow, or fold his arms,—for that is laziness;—or hang them down,—for that is folly; or hide them in his pocket, for that is nonsense.——

He shall neither strike, or pinch, or tickle,—or bite, or cut his nails, or hawk, or spit, or snift, or drum with his feet or fingers in company;——nor (according to *Erasmus*) shall he speak to any one in making water,—nor shall he point to carrion or excrement.——Now this is all nonsense again, quoth my uncle *Toby* to himself.——

I will have him, continued my father, cheerful, faceté, jovial; at the same time, prudent, attentive to business, vigilant, acute, argute, inventive, quick in resolving doubts and speculative questions;——he shall be wise and judicious, and learned:——And why not humble, and moderate, and gentle tempered, and good? said *Yorick*:——And why not, cried my uncle *Toby*, free, and generous, and bountiful, and brave?——He shall, my dear *Toby*, replied my father, getting up and shaking him by his hand.
—Then, brother *Shandy*, answered my uncle *Toby*, raising himself off the chair, and laying down his pipe to take hold of my father's other hand,—I humbly beg I may recommend poor *Le Fever*'s son to you;——a tear of joy of the first water sparkled in my uncle *Toby*'s eye,—and another, the fellow to it, in the corporal's, as the proposition was made;——you will see why when you read *Le Fever*'s story:——fool that I was! nor can I recollect, (nor perhaps you) without turning back to the place, what it was that hindered me from letting the corporal tell it in his own words; —but the occasion is lost,—I must tell it now in my own.

* Vid. *Pellegrina*.

[345]

CHAPTER VI

The Story of LE FEVER.

IT WAS some time in the summer of that year in which *Dendermond* was taken by the allies,—which was about seven years before my father came into the country,—and about as many, after the time, that my uncle *Toby* and *Trim* had privately decamped from my father's house in town, in order to lay some of the finest sieges to some of the finest fortified cities in *Europe*—when my uncle *Toby* was one evening getting his supper, with *Trim* sitting behind him at a small sideboard,—I say, sitting —for in consideration of the corporal's lame knee (which sometimes gave him exquisite pain)—when my uncle *Toby* dined or supped alone, he would never suffer the corporal to stand; and the poor fellow's veneration for his master was such, that, with a proper artillery, my uncle *Toby* could have taken *Dendermond* itself, with less trouble than he was able to gain this point over him; for many a time when my uncle *Toby* supposed the corporal's leg was at rest, he would look back, and detect him standing behind him with the most dutiful respect: this bred more little squabbles betwixt them, than all other causes for five and twenty years together—But this is neither here nor there—why do I mention it?——Ask my pen,—it governs me,—I govern not it.

He was one evening sitting thus at his supper, when the landlord of a little inn in the village came into the parlour with an empty phial in his hand, to beg a glass or two of sack; 'Tis for a poor gentleman,—I think, of the army, said the landlord, who has been taken ill at my house four days ago, and has never held up his head since, or had a desire to taste any thing, till just now, that he has a fancy for a glass of sack and a thin toast,——*I think*, says he, taking his hand from his forehead, *it would comfort me.*——

——If I could neither beg, borrow, or buy such a thing,— added the landlord,—I would almost steal it for the poor gentleman, he is so ill.——I hope in God he will still mend, continued he,—we are all of us concerned for him.

Thou art a good natured soul, I will answer for thee, cried my uncle *Toby*; and thou shalt drink the poor gentleman's health in a glass of sack thyself,—and take a couple of bottles with my service, and tell him he is heartily welcome to them, and to a dozen more if they will do him good.

Though I am persuaded, said my uncle *Toby*, as the landlord shut the door, he is a very compassionate fellow—*Trim*,—yet I cannot help entertaining a high opinion of his guest too; there must be something more than common in him, that in so short a time should win so much upon the affections of his host;—— And of his whole family, added the corporal, for they are all concerned for him.——Step after him, said my uncle *Toby*,—do *Trim*,—and ask if he knows his name.

——I have quite forgot it, truly, said the landlord, coming back into the parlour with the corporal,—but I can ask his son again:——Has he a son with him then? said my uncle *Toby*.— A boy, replied the landlord, of about eleven or twelve years of age;—but the poor creature has tasted almost as little as his father; he does nothing but mourn and lament for him night and day:——He has not stirred from the bedside these two days.

My uncle *Toby* laid down his knife and fork, and thrust his plate from before him, as the landlord gave him the account; and *Trim*, without being ordered, took away without saying one word, and in a few minutes after brought him his pipe and tobacco.

——Stay in the room a little, said my uncle *Toby*.——

Trim!——said my uncle *Toby*, after he lighted his pipe, and smoak'd about a dozen whiffs.——*Trim* came in front of his master and made his bow;—my uncle *Toby* smoak'd on, and said no more.——Corporal! said my uncle *Toby*——the corporal made his bow.——My uncle *Toby* proceeded no farther, but finished his pipe.

Trim! said my uncle *Toby*, I have a project in my head, as it is a bad night, of wrapping myself up warm in my roquelaure, and paying a visit to this poor gentleman.——Your honour's roquelaure, replied the corporal, has not once been had on, since the night before your honour received your wound, when we mounted guard in the trenches before the gate of St. *Nicholas*;——and besides it is so cold and rainy a night, that what with the roquelaure, and what with the weather, 'twill be enough to give your honour your death, and bring on your honour's torment in your groin. I fear so; replied my uncle *Toby*, but I am not at rest in my mind, *Trim*, since the account the landlord has given me.—— I wish I had not known so much of this affair,—added my uncle *Toby*,—or that I had known more of it:——How shall we manage it? Leave it, an't please your honour, to me, quoth the corporal;

——I'll take my hat and stick and go to the house and recon-
noitre, and act accordingly; and I will bring your honour a full
account in an hour.——Thou shalt go, *Trim*, said my uncle *Toby*,
and here's a shilling for thee to drink with his servant.——I shall
get it all out of him, said the corporal, shutting the door.

My uncle *Toby* filled his second pipe; and had it not been, that
he now and then wandered from the point, with considering
whether it was not full as well to have the curtain of the tennaile
a straight line, as a crooked one,—he might be said to have
thought of nothing else but poor *Le Fever* and his boy the whole
time he smoaked it.

CHAPTER VII

The Story of LE FEVER *continued.*

I T WAS not till my uncle *Toby* had knocked the ashes out of
his third pipe, that corporal *Trim* returned from the inn,
and gave him the following account.

I despaired at first, said the corporal, of being able to bring
back your honour any kind of intelligence concerning the poor
sick lieutenant—Is he in the army then? said my uncle *Toby*——
He is: said the corporal——And in what regiment? said my
uncle *Toby*——I'll tell your honour, replied the corporal, every
thing straight forwards, as I learnt it.—Then, *Trim*, I'll fill another
pipe, said my uncle *Toby*, and not interrupt thee till thou hast done;
so sit down at thy ease, *Trim*, in the window seat, and begin thy
story again. The corporal made his old bow, which generally
spoke as plain as a bow could speak it— *Your honour is good*:——
And having done that, he sat down, as he was ordered,—and
begun the story to my uncle *Toby* over again in pretty near the
same words.

I despaired at first, said the corporal, of being able to bring
back any intelligence to your honour about the lieutenant and his
son; for when I asked where his servant was, from whom I made
myself sure of knowing every thing which was proper to be
asked,—That's a right distinction, *Trim*, said my uncle *Toby*—
I was answered, an' please your honour, that he had no servant
with him;——that he had come to the inn with hired horses,
which, upon finding himself unable to proceed, (to join, I suppose,
the regiment) he had dismissed the morning after he came.—If

I get better, my dear, said he, as he gave his purse to his son to pay the man,—we can hire horses from hence.——But alas! the poor gentleman will never get from hence, said the landlady to me,—for I heard the death-watch all night long;——and when he dies, the youth, his son, will certainly die with him; for he is broken hearted already.

I was hearing this account, continued the corporal, when the youth came into the kitchen, to order the thin toast the landlord spoke of;——but I will do it for my father myself, said the youth. ——Pray let me save you the trouble, young gentleman, said I, taking up a fork for the purpose, and offering him my chair to sit down upon by the fire, whilst I did it.——I believe, Sir, said he, very modestly, I can please him best myself.——I am sure, said I, his honour will not like the toast the worse for being toasted by an old soldier.——The youth took hold of my hand, and instantly burst into tears.——Poor youth! said my uncle *Toby*,—he has been bred up from an infant in the army, and the name of a soldier, *Trim*, sounded in his ears like the name of a friend;—I wish I had him here.

——I never in the longest march, said the corporal, had so great a mind to my dinner, as I had to cry with him for company: —What could be the matter with me, an' please your honour? Nothing in the world, *Trim*, said my uncle *Toby*, blowing his nose,—but that thou art a good natured fellow.

When I gave him the toast, continued the corporal, I thought it was proper to tell him I was Captain *Shandy*'s servant, and that your honour (though a stranger) was extremely concerned for his father;—and that if there was any thing in your house or cellar——(And thou might'st have added my purse too, said my uncle *Toby*)——he was heartily welcome to it:——He made a very low bow, (which was meant to your honour) but no answer, —for his heart was full—so he went up stairs with the toast;— I warrant you, my dear, said I, as I opened the kitchen door, your father will be well again.——Mr. *Yorick*'s curate was smoking a pipe by the kitchen fire,—but said not a word good or bad to comfort the youth.——I thought it wrong; added the corporal ——I think so too, said my uncle *Toby*.

When the lieutenant had taken his glass of sack and toast, he felt himself a little revived, and sent down into the kitchen, to let me know, that in about ten minutes he should be glad if I would step up stairs.——I believe, said the landlord, he is going to say his prayers,——for there was a book laid upon the chair by his bedside, and as I shut the door, I saw his son take up a cushion.—

I thought, said the curate, that you gentlemen of the army, Mr. *Trim*, never said your prayers at all.——I heard the poor gentleman say his prayers last night, said the landlady, very devoutly, and with my own ears, or I could not have believed it. ——Are you sure of it? replied the curate.——A soldier, an' please your reverence, said I, prays as often (of his own accord) as a parson;——and when he is fighting for his king, and for his own life, and for his honour too, he has the most reason to pray to God of any one in the whole world—— 'Twas well said of thee, *Trim*, said my uncle *Toby*.——But when a soldier, said I, an' please your reverence, has been standing for twelve hours together in the trenches, up to his knees in cold water,—or engaged, said I, for months together in long and dangerous marches;—harrassed, perhaps, in his rear to-day;— harrassing others to-morrow;—detached here;—countermanded there;—resting this night out upon his arms;—beat up in his shirt the next;—benumbed in his joints;—perhaps without straw in his tent to kneel on;—must say his prayers *how* and *when* he can.—I believe, said I,—for I was piqued, quoth the corporal, for the reputation of the army,—I believe, an' please your reverence, said I, that when a soldier gets time to pray,—he prays as heartily as a parson,—though not with all his fuss and hypocrisy.—— Thou shouldst not have said that, *Trim*, said my uncle *Toby*,—for God only knows who is a hypocrite, and who is not:——At the great and general review of us all, corporal, at the day of judgment, (and not till then)—it will be seen who has done their duties in this world,—and who has not; and we shall be advanced, *Trim*, accordingly.——I hope we shall, said *Trim*.——It is in the Scripture, said my uncle *Toby*; and I will shew it thee to-morrow: ——In the mean time we may depend upon it, *Trim*, for our comfort, said my uncle *Toby*, that God Almighty is so good and just a governor of the world, that if we have but done our duties in it,— it will never be enquired into, whether we have done them in a red coat or a black one:——I hope not; said the corporal—— But go on, *Trim*, said my uncle *Toby*, with thy story.

When I went up, continued the corporal, into the lieutenant's room, which I did not do till the expiration of the ten minutes,— he was lying in his bed with his head raised upon his hand, with his elbow upon the pillow, and a clean white cambrick handkerchief beside it:——The youth was just stooping down to take up

[350]

the cushion, upon which I supposed he had been kneeling,—the book was laid upon the bed,—and as he rose, in taking up the cushion with one hand, he reached out his other to take it away at the same time.——Let it remain there, my dear, said the lieutenant.

He did not offer to speak to me, till I had walked up close to his bed-side:—If you are Captain *Shandy*'s servant, said he, you must present my thanks to your master, with my little boy's thanks along with them, for his courtesy to me;—if he was of *Levens*'s—said the lieutenant.—I told him your honour was— Then, said he, I served three campaigns with him in *Flanders*, and remember him,—but 'tis most likely, as I had not the honour of any acquaintance with him, that he knows nothing of me.—— You will tell him, however, that the person his good nature has laid under obligations to him, is one *Le Fever*, a lieutenant in *Angus*'s——but he knows me not,—said he, a second time, musing;——possibly he may my story—added he—pray tell the captain, I was the ensign at *Breda*, whose wife was most unfortunately killed with a musket shot, as she lay in my arms in my tent.——I remember the story, an't please your honour, said I, very well.——Do you so? said he, wiping his eyes with his handkerchief,—then well may I.—In saying this, he drew a little ring out of his bosom, which seemed tied with a black ribband about his neck, and kiss'd it twice——Here, *Billy*, said he,—— the boy flew across the room to the bed-side,—and falling down upon his knee, took the ring in his hand, and kissed it too,—then kissed his father, and sat down upon the bed and wept.

I wish, said my uncle *Toby*, with a deep sigh,—I wish, *Trim*, I was asleep.

Your honour, replied the corporal, is too much concerned; —shall I pour your honour out a glass of sack to your pipe?—— Do, *Trim*, said my uncle *Toby*.

I remember, said my uncle *Toby*, sighing again, the story of the ensign and his wife, with a circumstance his modesty omitted; —and particularly well that he, as well as she, upon some account or other, (I forget what) was universally pitied by the whole regiment;—but finish the story thou art upon:—'Tis finished already, said the corporal,—for I could stay no longer,—so wished his honour a good night; young *Le Fever* rose from off the bed, and saw me to the bottom of the stairs; and as we went down together, told me, they had come from *Ireland*, and were on their route to join the regiment in *Flanders*.——But alas! said the corporal,—the lieutenant's last day's march is over.—Then what is to become of his poor boy? cried my uncle *Toby*.

CHAPTER VIII

The Story of LE FEVER *continued.*

IT WAS to my uncle *Toby*'s eternal honour,——though I tell it only for the sake of those, who, when coop'd in betwixt a natural and a positive law, know not for their souls, which way in the world to turn themselves——That notwithstanding my uncle *Toby* was warmly engaged at that time in carrying on the siege of *Dendermond*, parallel with the allies, who pressed theirs on so vigorously, that they scarce allowed him time to get his dinner——that nevertheless he gave up *Dendermond*, though he had already made a lodgment upon the counterscarp;—and bent his whole thoughts towards the private distresses at the inn; and, except that he ordered the garden gate to be bolted up, by which he might be said to have turned the siege of *Dendermond* into a blockade,—he left *Dendermond* to itself,—to be relieved or not by the *French* king, as the *French* king thought good; and only considered how he himself should relieve the poor lieutenant and his son.

——That kind BEING, who is a friend to the friendless, shall recompence thee for this.

Thou hast left this matter short, said my uncle *Toby* to the corporal, as he was putting him to bed,——and I will tell thee in what, *Trim*.——In the first place, when thou madest an offer of my services to *Le Fever*,—as sickness and travelling are both expensive, and thou knowest he was but a poor lieutenant, with a son to subsist as well as himself, out of his pay,—that thou didst not make an offer to him of my purse; because, had he stood in need, thou knowest, *Trim*, he had been as welcome to it as myself.——Your honour knows, said the corporal, I had no orders;——True, quoth my uncle *Toby*,—thou didst very right, *Trim*, as a soldier,—but certainly very wrong as a man.

In the second place, for which, indeed, thou hast the same excuse, continued my uncle *Toby*,——when thou offeredst him whatever was in my house,—thou shouldst have offered him my house too:——A sick brother officer should have the best

[352]

quarters, *Trim*, and if we had him with us,—we could tend and look to him:——Thou art an excellent nurse thyself, *Trim*,—and what with thy care of him, and the old woman's, and his boy's, and mine together, we might recruit him again at once, and set him upon his legs.——

——In a fortnight or three weeks, added my uncle *Toby*, smiling,—he might march.——He will never march, an' please your honour, in this world, said the corporal:——He will march; said my uncle *Toby*, rising up from the side of the bed, with one shoe off:——An' please your honour, said the corporal, he will never march, but to his grave:——He shall march, cried my uncle *Toby*, marching the foot which had a shoe on, though without advancing an inch,—he shall march to his regiment.——He cannot stand it, said the corporal;——He shall be supported, said my uncle *Toby*;——He'll drop at last, said the corporal, and what will become of his boy?——He shall not drop, said my uncle *Toby*, firmly.——A-well-o'day,—do what we can for him, said *Trim*, maintaining his point,—the poor soul will die:—— He shall not die, by G—, cried my uncle *Toby*.

—The ACCUSING SPIRIT which flew up to heaven's chancery with the oath, blush'd as he gave it in;—and the RECORDING ANGEL as he wrote it down, dropp'd a tear upon the word, and blotted it out for ever.

CHAPTER IX

MY UNCLE *TOBY* went to his bureau,—put his purse into his breeches pocket, and having ordered the corporal to go early in the morning for a physician,—he went to bed, and fell asleep.

CHAPTER X

The Story of LE FEVER *concluded.*

THE SUN looked bright the morning after, to every eye in the village but *Le Fever*'s and his afflicted son's; the hand of death press'd heavy upon his eye-lids,——and hardly could the wheel at the cistern turn round its circle,—when my uncle *Toby*, who had rose up an hour before his wonted time, entered the lieutenant's room, and without preface or apology, sat himself down upon the chair by the bed-side, and independently of all modes and customs, opened the curtain in the manner an old friend and brother officer would have done it, and asked him how he did,—how he had rested in the night,—what was his complaint,—where was his pain,—and what he could do to help him:——and without giving him time to answer any one of the enquiries, went on and told him of the little plan which he had been concerting with the corporal the night before for him.——

——You shall go home directly, *Le Fever*, said my uncle *Toby*, to my house,—and we'll send for a doctor to see what's the matter,—and we'll have an apothecary,—and the corporal shall be your nurse;——and I'll be your servant, *Le Fever*.

There was a frankness in my uncle *Toby*,—not the *effect* of familiarity,—but the *cause* of it,—which let you at once into his soul, and shewed you the goodness of his nature; to this, there was something in his looks, and voice, and manner, superadded, which eternally beckoned to the unfortunate to come and take shelter under him; so that before my uncle *Toby* had half finished the kind offers he was making to the father, had the son insensibly pressed up close to his knees, and had taken hold of the breast of his coat, and was pulling it towards him.——The blood and spirits of *Le Fever*, which were waxing cold and slow within him, and were retreating to their last citadel, the heart,—rallied back,—the film forsook his eyes for a moment,—he looked up wishfully in my uncle *Toby*'s face,—then cast a look upon his boy,——and that *ligament*, fine as it was,—was never broken.——

Nature instantly ebb'd again,——the film returned to its place, ——the pulse fluttered——stopp'd——went on——throb'd—— stopp'd again——moved——stopp'd——shall I go on?——No.

CHAPTER XI

I AM SO impatient to return to my own story, that what remains of young *Le Fever*'s, that is, from this turn of his fortune, to the time my uncle *Toby* recommended him for my preceptor, shall be told in a very few words, in the next chapter.— All that is necessary to be added to this chapter is as follows.—

That my uncle *Toby*, with young *Le Fever* in his hand, attended the poor lieutenant, as chief mourners, to his grave.

[354]

That the governor of *Dendermond* paid his obsequies all military honours,—and that *Yorick*, not to be behind hand—paid him all ecclesiastic—for he buried him in his chancel:—And it appears likewise, he preached a funeral sermon over him—— I say it *appears*,—for it was *Yorick*'s custom, which I suppose a general one with those of his profession, on the first leaf of every sermon which he composed, to chronicle down the time, the place, and the occasion of its being preached: to this, he was ever wont to add some short comment or stricture upon the sermon itself, seldom, indeed, much to its credit:—For instance, *This sermon upon the jewish dispensation—I don't like it at all;— Though I own there is a world of* WATER-LANDISH *knowledge in it, —but 'tis all tritical, and most tritically put together.——This is but a flimsy kind of a composition; what was in my head when I made it?*

——N.B. *The excellency of this text is, that it will suit any sermon,—and of this sermon,——that it will suit any text.——*

——*For this sermon I shall be hanged,—for I have stolen the greatest part of it. Doctor* Paidagunes *found me out.* ☞ *Set a thief to catch a thief.——*

On the back of half a dozen I find written, *So, so*, and no more ——and upon a couple *Moderato*; by which, as far as one may gather from *Altieri*'s *Italian* dictionary,—but mostly from the authority of a piece of green whipcord, which seemed to have been the unravelling of *Yorick*'s whip-lash, with which he has left us the two sermons marked *Moderato*, and the half dozen of *So, so*, tied fast together in one bundle by themselves,—one may safely suppose he meant pretty near the same thing.

There is but one difficulty in the way of this conjecture, which is this, that the *moderato*'s are five times better than the *so, so*'s; —shew ten times more knowledge of the human heart;—have seventy times more wit and spirit in them;—(and, to rise properly in my climax)—discover a thousand times more genius;—and to crown all, are infinitely more entertaining than those tied up with them;—for which reason, whene'er *Yorick*'s *dramatic* sermons are offered to the world, though I shall admit but one out of the whole number of the *so, so*'s, I shall, nevertheless, adventure to print the two *moderato*'s without any sort of scruple.

What *Yorick* could mean by the words *lentamente,—tenutè,— grave,*—and sometimes *adagio*,—as applied to theological compositions, and with which he has characterized some of these sermons, I dare not venture to guess.——I am more puzzled still

[355]

upon finding a *l' octava alta*! upon one;——*Con strepito* upon the back of another;——*Scicilliana* upon a third;——*Alla capella* upon a fourth;——*Con l'arco* upon this;——*Senza l'arco* upon that.——All I know is, that they are musical terms, and have a meaning;——and as he was a musical man, I will make no doubt, but that by some quaint application of such metaphors to the compositions in hand, they impressed very distinct ideas of their several characters upon his fancy,—whatever they may do upon that of others.

Amongst these, there is that particular sermon which has unaccountably led me into this digression——The funeral sermon upon poor *Le Fever*, wrote out very fairly, as if from a hasty copy.—I take notice of it the more, because it seems to have been his favourite composition——It is upon mortality; and is tied length-ways and cross-ways with a yarn thrum, and then rolled up and twisted round with a half sheet of dirty blue paper, which seems to have been once the cast cover of a general review, which to this day smells horribly of horse-drugs.——Whether these marks of humiliation were designed,—I something doubt;—— because at the end of the sermon, (and not at the beginning of it)— very different from his way of treating the rest, he had wrote——

Bravo!

——Though not very offensively,——for it is at two inches, at least, and a half's distance from, and below the concluding line of the sermon, at the very extremity of the page, and in that right hand corner of it, which, you know, is generally covered with your thumb; and, to do it justice, it is wrote besides with a crow's quill so faintly in a small *Italian* hand, as scarce to sollicit the eye towards the place, whether your thumb is there or not,—so that from the *manner of it*, it stands half excused; and being wrote moreover with very pale ink, diluted almost to nothing,— 'tis more like a *ritratto* of the shadow of vanity, than of VANITY herself—of the two; resembling rather a faint thought of transient applause, secretly stirring up in the heart of the composer, than a gross mark of it, coarsely obtruded upon the world.

With all these extenuations, I am aware, that in publishing this, I do no service to *Yorick*'s character as a modest man;—but all men have their failings! and what lessens this still farther, and almost wipes it away, is this, that the word was struck through sometime afterwards (as appears from a different tint of the ink) with a line quite across it in this manner, ~~BRAVO~~——as if he

[356]

had retracted, or was ashamed of the opinion he had once entertained of it.

These short characters of his sermons were always written, excepting in this one instance, upon the first leaf of his sermon, which served as a cover to it; and usually upon the inside of it, which was turned towards the text;—but at the end of his discourse, where, perhaps, he had five or six pages, and sometimes, perhaps, a whole score to turn himself in,—he took a larger circuit, and, indeed, a much more mettlesome one;—as if he had snatched the occasion of unlacing himself with a few more frolicksome strokes at vice, than the straitness of the pulpit allowed.— These, though hussar-like, they skirmish lightly and out of all order, are still auxiliaries on the side of virtue—; tell me then, Mynheer Vander Blonederdondergewdenstronke, why they should not be printed together?

CHAPTER XII

WHEN my uncle *Toby* had turned every thing into money, and settled all accounts betwixt the agent of the regiment and *Le Fever*, and betwixt *Le Fever* and all mankind,—— there remained nothing more in my uncle *Toby*'s hands, than an old regimental coat and a sword; so that my uncle *Toby* found little or no opposition from the world in taking administration. The coat my uncle gave *Toby* the corporal;——Wear it, *Trim*, said my uncle *Toby*, as long as it will hold together, for the sake of the poor lieutenant——And this,——said my uncle *Toby*, taking up the sword in his hand, and drawing it out of the scabbard as he spoke——and this, *Le Fever*, I'll save for thee,— 'tis all the fortune, continued my uncle *Toby*, hanging it up upon a crook, and pointing to it,—'tis all the fortune, my dear *Le Fever*, which God has left thee; but if he has given thee a heart to fight thy way with it in the world,—and thou doest it like a man of honour,—'tis enough for us.

As soon as my uncle *Toby* had laid a foundation, and taught him to inscribe a regular polygon in a circle, he sent him to a public school, where, excepting *Whitsontide* and *Christmas*, at which times the corporal was punctually dispatched for him,— he remained to the spring of the year seventeen; when the stories of the emperor's sending his army into *Hungary* against the

Turks, kindling a spark of fire in his bosom, he left his *Greek* and *Latin* without leave, and throwing himself upon his knees before my uncle *Toby*, begged his father's sword, and my uncle *Toby*'s leave along with it, to go and try his fortune under *Eugene*.—— Twice did my uncle *Toby* forget his wound, and cry out, *Le Fever*! I will go with thee, and thou shalt fight beside me——And twice he laid his hand upon his groin, and hung down his head in sorrow and disconsolation.——

My uncle *Toby* took down the sword from the crook, where it had hung untouched ever since the lieutenant's death, and delivered it to the corporal to brighten up;——and having detained *Le Fever* a single fortnight to equip him, and contract for his passage to *Leghorn*,—he put the sword into his hand,—— If thou art brave, *Le Fever*, said my uncle *Toby*, this will not fail thee,——but Fortune, said he (musing a little)——Fortune may ——And if she does,—added my uncle *Toby*, embracing him, come back again to me, *Le Fever*, and we will shape thee another course.

The greatest injury could not have oppressed the heart of *Le Fever* more than my uncle *Toby*'s paternal kindness;——he parted from my uncle *Toby*, as the best of sons from the best of fathers——both dropped tears——and as my uncle *Toby* gave him his last kiss, he slipped sixty guineas, tied up in an old purse of his father's, in which was his mother's ring, into his hand,— and bid God bless him.

CHAPTER XIII

L*E FEVER* got up to the Imperial army just time enough to try what metal his sword was made of, at the defeat of the *Turks* before *Belgrade*; but a series of unmerited mischances had pursued him from that moment, and trod close upon his heels for four years together after: he had withstood these buffetings to the last, till sickness overtook him at *Marseilles*, from whence he wrote my uncle *Toby* word, he had lost his time, his services, his health, and, in short, every thing but his sword; ——and was waiting for the first ship to return back to him.

As this letter came to hand about six weeks before *Susannah*'s accident, *Le Fever* was hourly expected; and was uppermost in my uncle *Toby*'s mind all the time my father was giving him and

Yorick a description of what kind of a person he would chuse for a preceptor to me: but as my uncle *Toby* thought my father at first somewhat fanciful in the accomplishments he required, he forbore mentioning *Le Fever*'s name,——till the character, by *Yorick*'s interposition, ending unexpectedly, in one, who should be gentle tempered, and generous, and good, it impressed the image of *Le Fever*, and his interest upon my uncle *Toby* so forceably, he rose instantly off his chair; and laying down his pipe, in order to take hold of both my father's hands——I beg, brother *Shandy*, said my uncle *Toby*, I may recommend poor *Le Fever*'s son to you——I beseech you, do, added *Yorick*——He has a good heart, said my uncle *Toby*——And a brave one too, an' please your honour, said the corporal.

——The best hearts, *Trim*, are ever the bravest, replied my uncle *Toby*.——And the greatest cowards, an' please your honour, in our regiment, were the greatest rascals in it.——There was serjeant *Kumbur*, and ensign——

——We'll talk of them, said my father, another time.

CHAPTER XIV

WHAT a jovial and a merry world would this be, may it please your worships, but for that inextricable labyrinth of debts, cares, woes, want, grief, discontent, melancholy, large jointures, impositions, and lies!

Doctor *Slop*, like a son of a w——, as my father called him for it,—to exalt himself,—debased me to death,—and made ten thousand times more of *Susannah*'s accident, than there was any grounds for; so that in a week's time, or less, it was in every body's mouth, *That poor Master Shandy* * * * * * * * * * * * entirely.—And FAME, who loves to double every thing,—in three days more, had sworn positively she saw it, —and all the world, as usual, gave credit to her evidence—— "That the nursery window had not only * ;—— but that * 's also."

Could the world have been sued like a BODY-CORPORATE,— my father had brought an action upon the case, and trounced it sufficiently; but to fall foul of individuals about it——as every soul who had mentioned the affair, did it with the greatest pity imaginable;——'twas like flying in the very face of his best friends:——And yet to acquiesce under the report, in silence— was to acknowledge it openly,—at least in the opinion of one half of the world; and to make a bustle again, in contradicting it,— was to confirm it as strongly in the opinion of the other half.——

——Was ever poor devil of a country gentleman so hampered? said my father.

I would shew him publickly, said my uncle *Toby*, at the market cross.

——'Twill have no effect, said my father.

CHAPTER XV

I 'LL PUT him, however, into breeches said my father,—let the world say what it will.

CHAPTER XVI

THERE are a thousand resolutions, Sir, both in church and state, as well as in matters, Madam, of a more private concern;—which, though they have carried all the appearance in the world of being taken, and entered upon in a hasty, hare-brained, and unadvised manner, were, notwithstanding this, (and could you or I have got into the cabinet, or stood behind the curtain, we should have found it was so) been weighed, poized, and perpended——argued upon——canvassed through ——entered into, and examined on all sides with so much coolness, that the GODDESS of COOLNESS herself (I do not take upon me to prove her existence) could neither have wished it, or done it better.

Of the number of these was my father's resolution of putting me into breeches; which, though determined at once,—in a kind of huff, and a defiance of all mankind, had, nevertheless, been *pro'd* and *conn'd*, and judicially talked over betwixt him and my mother about a month before, in two several *beds of justice*, which my father had held for that purpose. I shall explain the nature of these beds of justice in my next chapter; and in the chapter following that, you shall step with me, Madam, behind the curtain, only to hear in what kind of manner my father and my mother debated between themselves, this affair of the breeches,—from which you may form an idea, how they debated all lesser matters.

CHAPTER XVII

THE ancient *Goths* of *Germany*, who (the learned *Cluverius* is positive) were first seated in the country between the *Vistula* and the *Oder*, and who afterwards incorporated the *Herculi*, the *Bugians*, and some other *Vandallick* clans to 'em,—had all of them a wise custom of debating every thing of importance to their state, twice; that is,—once drunk, and once sober:——Drunk—that their counsels might not want vigour;——and sober—that they might not want discretion.

Now my father being entirely a water-drinker,—was a long time gravelled almost to death, in turning this as much to his advantage, as he did every other thing, which the ancients did or said; and it was not till the seventh year of his marriage, after a thousand fruitless experiments and devices, that he hit upon an expedient which answered the purpose;——and that was when any difficult and momentous point was to be settled in the family, which required great sobriety, and great spirit too, in its determination,——he fixed and set apart the first *Sunday* night in the month, and the *Saturday* night which immediately preceded it, to argue it over, in bed with my mother: By which contrivance, if you consider, Sir, with yourself, * * * * * * * * *
* * * * * * * * * * * * * * * * * *
* * * * * * * * * * * * *.

These my father, humourously enough, called his *beds of justice*;——for from the two different counsels taken in these two different humours, a middle one was generally found out, which touched the point of wisdom as well, as if he had got drunk and sober a hundred times.

It must not be made a secret of to the world, that this answers full as well in literary discussions, as either in military or conjugal; but it is not every author that can try the experiment as the *Goths* and *Vandals* did it——or if he can, may it be always for his body's health; and to do it, as my father did it,—am I sure it would be always for his soul's.——

My way is this:——

In all nice and ticklish discussions,—(of which, heaven knows, there are but too many in my book)—where I find I cannot take a step without the danger of having either their worships or their reverences upon my back——I write one half *full*,—and t'other *fasting*;——or write it all full,—and correct it fasting; ——or write it fasting,—and correct it full, for they all come to the same thing:——So that with a less variation from my father's plan, than my father's from the *Gothick*——I feel myself upon a par with him in his first bed of justice,—and no way inferior to him in his second.——These different and almost irreconcileable effects, flow uniformly from the wise and wonderful mechanism of nature,—of which,—be her's the honour.——All that we can do, is to turn and work the machine to the improvement and better manufactury of the arts and sciences.——

Now, when I write full,—I write as if I was never to write fasting again as long as I live;——that is, I write free from the cares, as well as the terrors of the world.——I count not the number of my scars,—nor does my fancy go forth into dark entries and bye corners to ante-date my stabs.——In a word, my pen takes its course; and I write on as much from the fullness of my heart, as my stomach.——

But when, an' please your honours, I indite fasting, 'tis a different history.——I pay the world all possible attention and respect,—and have as great a share (whilst it lasts) of that understrapping virtue of discretion, as the best of you.——So that betwixt both, I write a careless kind of a civil, nonsensical, good humoured *Shandean* book, which will do all your hearts good——

——And all your heads too,—provided you understand it.

CHAPTER XVIII

WE SHOULD begin, said my father, turning himself half round in bed, and shifting his pillow a little towards my mother's, as he opened the debate——We should begin to think, Mrs. *Shandy*, of putting this boy into breeches.——

We should so,—said my mother.——We defer it, my dear, quoth my father, shamefully.——

I think we do, Mr. *Shandy*,—said my mother.

——Not but the child looks extremely well, said my father, in his vests and tunicks.——

[362]

——He does look very well in them,—replied my mother.——

——And for that reason it would be almost a sin, added my father, to take him out of 'em.——

——It would so,—said my mother:——But indeed he is growing a very tall lad,—rejoin'd my father.

——He is very tall for his age, indeed,—said my mother.——

——I can not (making two syllables of it) imagine, quoth my father, who the duce he takes after.——

I cannot conceive, for my life,—said my mother.——

Humph!——said my father.

(The dialogue ceased for a moment.)

——I am very short myself,—continued my father, gravely.

You are very short, Mr. *Shandy*,—said my mother.

Humph! quoth my father to himself, a second time: in muttering which, he plucked his pillow a little further from my mother's, —and turning about again, there was an end of the debate for three minutes and a half.

——When he gets these breeches made, cried my father in a higher tone, he'll look like a beast in 'em.

He will be very aukward in them at first, replied my mother.—

——And 'twill be lucky, if that's the worst on't, added my father.

It will be very lucky, answered my mother. ⸴

I suppose, replied my father,—making some pause first,— he'll be exactly like other people's children.——

Exactly, said my mother.——

——Though I should be sorry for that, added my father: and so the debate stopped again.

——They should be of leather, said my father, turning him about again.—They will last him, said my mother, the longest.

But he can have no linings to 'em, replied my father.——

He cannot, said my mother.

'Twere better to have them of fustian, quoth my father.

Nothing can be better, quoth my mother.——

——Except dimity,—replied my father:——'Tis best of all, —replied my mother.

——One must not give him his death, however,—interrupted my father.

By no means, said my mother:——and so the dialogue stood still again.

I am resolved, however, quoth my father, breaking silence the fourth time, he shall have no pockets in them.——

——There is no occasion for any, said my mother.——

[363]

I mean in his coat and waistcoat,—cried my father.

——I mean so too,—replied mother.

——Though if he gets a gig or a top——Pour souls! it is a crown and a scepter to them,—they should have where to secure it. ——

Order it as you please, Mr. *Shandy*, replied my mother.——

——But don't you think it right? added my father, pressing the point home to her.

Perfectly, said my mother, if it pleases you, Mr. *Shandy*.——

——There's for you! cried my father, losing temper——Pleases me!——You never will distinguish, Mrs. *Shandy*, nor shall I ever teach you to do it, betwixt a point of pleasure and a point of convenience.——This was on the *Sunday* night;——and further this chapter sayeth not.

CHAPTER XIX

AFTER my father had debated the affair of the breeches with my mother,—he consulted *Albertus Rubenius* upon it; and *Albertus Rubenius* used my father ten times worse in the consultation (if possible) than even my father had used my mother: For as *Rubenius* had wrote a quarto *express, De re Vestiaria Veterum,*—it was *Rubenius*'s business to have given my father some lights.—On the contrary, my father might as well have thought of extracting the seven cardinal virtues out of a long beard,—as of extracting a single word out of *Rubenius* upon the subject.

Upon every other article of ancient dress, *Rubenius* was very communicative to my father;—gave him a full and satisfactory account of

The Toga, or loose gown.

The Chlamys.

The Ephod.

The Tunica, or Jacket.

The Synthesis.

The Pænula.

The Lacema, with its Cucullus.

The Paludamentum.

The Prætexta.

The Sagum, or soldier's jerkin.

The Trabea: of which, according to *Suetonius,* there were three kinds.—

————But what are all these to the breeches? said my father.
Rubenius threw him down upon the counter all kinds of shoes
which had been in fashion with the *Romans*.————There was,

> The open shoe.
> The close shoe.
> The slip shoe.
> The wooden shoe.
> The soc.
> The buskin.

And The military shoe with hob-nails in it, which *Juvenal*
takes notice of.

There were, The clogs.

> The patins.
> The pantoufles.
> The brogues.
> The sandals, with latchets to them.

There was, The felt shoe.

> The linen shoe.
> The laced shoe.
> The braided shoe.
> The calceus incisus.

And The calceus rostratus.

Rubenius shewed my father how well they all fitted,—in what
manner they laced on,—with what points, straps, thongs, lachets,
ribands, jaggs, and ends.————

————But I want to be informed about the breeches, said my
father.

Albertus Rubenius informed my father that the *Romans* manu-
factured stuffs of various fabricks,————some plain,—some striped,
—others diapered throughout the whole contexture of the
wool, with silk and gold————That linen did not begin to be
in common use, till towards the declension of the empire, when
the *Egyptians* coming to settle amongst them, brought it into
vogue.

————That persons of quality and fortune distinguished themselves by the fineness and whiteness of their cloaths; which colour
(next to purple, which was appropriated to the great offices) they
most affected and wore on their birth-days and public rejoicings.

————That it appeared from the best historians of those times, that
they frequently sent their cloaths to the fuller, to be cleaned and
whitened;————but that the inferior people, to avoid that expence,
generally wore brown cloaths, and of a something coarser tex-

ture,—till towards the beginning of *Augustus*'s reign, when the slave dressed like his master, and almost every distinction of habiliment was lost, but the *Latus Clavus*.

And what was the *Latus Clavus*? said my father.

Rubenius told him, that the point was still litigating amongst the learned:——That *Egnatius, Sigonius, Bossius Ticinensis, Bayfius, Budæus, Salmasius, Lipsius, Lazius, Isaac Causobon*, and *Joseph Scaliger*, all differed from each other,—and he from them: That some took it to be the button,—some the coat itself,—others only the colour of it:—That the great *Bayfius*, in his Wardrobe of the Ancients, chap. 12.—honestly said, he knew not what it was,—whether a tibula,—a stud,—a button,—a loop,—a buckle, —or clasps and keepers.——

——My father lost the horse, but not the saddle——They are *hooks and eyes*, said my father——and with hooks and eyes he ordered my breeches to be made.

CHAPTER XX

WE ARE now going to enter upon a new scene of events.——

——Leave we then the breeches in the taylor's hands. with my father standing over him with his cane, reading him as he sat at work a lecture upon the *latus clavus*, and pointing to the precise part of the waistband, where he was determined to have it sewed on.——

Leave we my mother—(truest of all the *Poco-curante*'s of her sex!)—careless about it, as about every thing else in the world which concerned her;—that is,—indifferent whether it was done this way or that,—provided it was but done at all.——

Leave we *Slop* likewise to the full profits of all my dishonours.——

Leave we poor *Le Fever* to recover, and get home from *Marseilles* as he can.——And last of all,—because the hardest of all——

Let us leave, if possible, *myself*:——But 'tis impossible,— I must go along with you to the end of the work.

CHAPTER XXI

IF THE reader has not a clear conception of the rood and the half of ground which lay at the bottom of my uncle *Toby*'s kitchen garden, and which was the scene of so many of his delicious hours,—the fault is not in me,—but in his imagination;—for I am sure I gave him so minute a description, I was almost ashamed of it.

When FATE was looking forwards one afternoon, into the great transactions of future times,—and recollected for what purposes this little plot, by a decree fast bound down in iron, had been destined,—she gave a nod to NATURE—'twas enough— Nature threw half a spade full of her kindliest compost upon it, with just so *much* clay in it, as to retain the forms of angles and indentings,—and so *little* of it too, as not to cling to the spade, and render works of so much glory, nasty in foul weather.

My uncle *Toby* came down, as the reader has been informed, with plans along with him, of almost every fortified town in *Italy* and *Flanders*; so let the Duke of *Marlborough*, or the allies, have set down before what town they pleased, my uncle *Toby* was prepared for them.

His way, which was the simplest one in the world, was this; as soon as ever a town was invested—(but sooner when the design was known) to take the plan of it, (let it be what town it would) and enlarge it upon a scale to the exact size of his bowling-green; upon the surface of which, by means of a large role of pack-thread, and a number of small piquets driven into the ground, at the several angles and redans, he transferred the lines from his paper; then taking the profile of the place, with its works, to determine the depths and slopes of the ditches,—the talus of the glacis, and the precise height of the several banquets, parapets, &c.—he set the corporal to work——and sweetly went it on:——The nature of the soil,—the nature of the work itself,— and above all, the good nature of my uncle *Toby* sitting by from morning to night, and chatting kindly with the corporal upon past-done deeds,—left LABOUR little else but the ceremony of the name.

When the place was finished in this manner, and put into a proper posture of defence,—it was invested,—and my uncle *Toby* and the corporal began to run their first parallel.——I beg I may not be interrupted in my story, by being told, *That the first* *parallel should be at least three hundred toises distant from the main body of the place,—and that I have not left a single inch for it :——*for my uncle *Toby* took the liberty of incroaching upon his kitchen garden, for the sake of enlarging his works on the bowling green, and for that reason generally ran his first and second parallels betwixt two rows of his cabbages and his collyflowers; the conveniences and inconveniences of which will be considered at large in the history of my uncle *Toby*'s and the corporal's campaigns, of which, this I'm now writing is but a sketch, and will be finished, if I conjecture right, in three pages (but there is no guessing)——The campaigns themselves will take up as many books; and therefore I apprehend it would be hanging too great a weight of one kind of matter in so flimsy a performance as this, to rhapsodize them, as I once intended, into the body of the work——surely they had better be printed apart,——we'll consider the affair——so take the following sketch of them in the mean time.

CHAPTER XXII

WHEN the town, with its works, was finished, my uncle *Toby* and the corporal began to run their first parallel ——not at random, or any how——but from the same points and distances the allies had begun to run theirs; and regulating their approaches and attacks, by the accounts my uncle *Toby* received from the daily papers,—they went on, during the whole siege, step by step with the allies.

When the duke of *Marlborough* made a lodgment,——my uncle *Toby* made a lodgment too.——And when the face of a bastion was battered down, or a defence ruined,—the corporal took his mattock and did as much,—and so on;——gaining ground, and making themselves masters of the works one after another, till the town fell into their hands.

To one who took pleasure in the happy state of others,—there could not have been a greater sight in the world, than, on a post-morning, in which a practicable breach had been made by the duke of *Marlborough*, in the main body of the place,—to have stood behind the horn-beam hedge, and observed the spirit with which my uncle *Toby*, with *Trim* behind him, sallied forth;—— the one with the *Gazette* in his hand,—the other with a spade on his shoulder to execute the contents.——What an honest

triumph in my uncle *Toby*'s looks as he marched up to the ramparts! What intense pleasure swimming in his eye as he stood over the corporal, reading the paragraph ten times over to him, as he was at work, lest, peradventure, he should make the breach an inch too wide,—or leave it an inch too narrow——But when the *chamade* was beat, and the corporal helped my uncle up it, and followed with the colours in his hand, to fix them upon the ramparts—Heaven! Earth! Sea!——but what avails apostrophes?
——with all your elements, wet or dry, ye never compounded so intoxicating a draught.

In this track of happiness for many years, without one interruption to it, except now and then when the wind continued to blow due west for a week or ten days together, which detained the *Flanders* mail, and kept them so long in torture,—but still 'twas the torture of the happy——In this track, I say, did my uncle *Toby* and *Trim* move for many years, every year of which, and sometimes every month, from the invention of either the one or the other of them, adding some new conceit or quirk of improvement to their operations, which always opened fresh springs of delight in carrying them on.

The first year's campaign was carried on from beginning to end, in the plain and simple method I've related.

In the second year, in which my uncle *Toby* took *Liege* and *Ruremond*, he thought he might afford the expence of four handsome draw-bridges, two of which I have given an exact description, in the former part of my work.

At the latter end of the same year he added a couple of gates with portcullises:——These last were converted afterwards in orgues, as the better thing; and during the winter of the same year, my uncle *Toby*, instead of a new suit of cloaths, which he always had at *Christmas*, treated himself with a handsome sentry-box, to stand at the corner of the bowling-green, betwixt which point and the foot of the glacis, there was left a little kind of an esplanade for him and the corporal to confer and hold councils of war upon.

——The sentry-box was in case of rain.

All these were painted white three times over the ensuing spring, which enabled my uncle *Toby* to take the field with great splendour.

My father would often say to *Yorick*, that if any mortal in the whole universe had done such a thing, except his brother *Toby*, it would have been looked upon by the world as one of the most refined satyrs upon the parade and prancing manner, in which *Lewis* XIV. from the beginning of the war, but particularly that very year, had taken the field——But 'tis not my brother *Toby*'s nature, kind soul! my father would add, to insult any one.

——But let us go on.

CHAPTER XXIII

I MUST observe, that although in the first year's campaign, the word *town* is often mentioned,—yet there was no town at that time within the polygon; that addition was not made till the summer following the spring in which the bridges and sentry-box were painted, which was the third year of my uncle *Toby*'s campaigns,—when upon his taking *Amberg, Bonn,* and *Rhinberg,* and *Huy* and *Limbourg,* one after another, a thought came into the corporal's head, that to talk of taking so many towns, *without one* TOWN *to show for it,*—was a very nonsensical way of going to work, and so proposed to my uncle *Toby,* that they should have a little model of a town built for them,—to be run up together of slit deals, and then painted, and clapped within the interior polygon to serve for all.

My uncle *Toby* felt the good of the project instantly, and instantly agreed to it, but with the addition of two singular improvements, of which he was almost as proud, as if he had been the original inventor of the project itself.

The one was to have the town built exactly in the stile of those, of which it was most likely to be the representative:——with grated windows, and the gable ends of the houses, facing the streets, &c. &c.—as those in *Ghent* and *Bruges,* and the rest of the towns in *Brabant* and *Flanders.*

The other was, not to have the houses run up together, as the corporal proposed, but to have every house independant, to hook on, or off, so as form into the plan of whatever town they pleased. This was put directly into hand, and many and many a look of mutual congratulation was exchanged between my uncle *Toby* and the corporal, as the carpenter did the work.

——It answered prodigiously the next summer——the town was a perfect *Proteus*——It was *Landen,* and *Trerebach,* and *Santvliet,* and *Drusen,* and *Hagenau,*—and then it was *Ostend* and *Menin,* and *Aeth* and *Dendermond.*——

[370]

———Surely never did any TOWN act so many parts, since *Sodom* and *Gomorrah*, as my uncle *Toby*'s town did.

In the fourth year, my uncle *Toby* thinking a town looked foolishly without a church, added a very fine one with a steeple.
———*Trim* was for having bells in it;———my uncle *Toby* said, the mettle had better be cast into cannon.

This led the way the next campaign for half a dozen brass field pieces,—to be planted three and three on each side of my uncle *Toby*'s sentry-box; and in a short time, these led the way for a train of somewhat larger,—and so on—(as must always be the case in hobby-horsical affairs) from pieces of half an inch bore, till it came at last to my father's jack boots.

The next year, which was that in which *Lisle* was besieged, and at the close of which both *Ghent* and *Bruges* fell into our hands,— my uncle *Toby* was sadly put to it for *proper* ammunition;—— I say proper ammunition——because his great artillery would not bear powder; and 'twas well for the *Shandy* family they would not——For so full were the papers, from the beginning to the end of the siege, of the incessant firings kept up by the besiegers, ——and so heated was my uncle *Toby*'s imagination with the accounts of them, that he had infallibly shot away all his estate.

SOMETHING therefore was wanting, as a *succedaneum*, especially in one or two of the more violent paroxysms of the siege, to keep up something like a continual firing in the imagination,——and this *something*, the corporal, whose principal strength lay in invention, supplied by an entire new system of battering of his own,—without which, this had been objected to by military critics, to the end of the world, as one of the great *desiderata* of my uncle *Toby*'s apparatus.

This will not be explained the worse, for setting off, as I generally do, at a little distance from the subject.

CHAPTER XXIV

WITH TWO or three other trinkets, small in themselves, but of great regard, which poor *Tom*, the corporal's unfortunate brother, had sent him over, with the account of his marriage with the *Jew*'s widow——there was A *Montero*-cap and two *Turkish* tobacco pipes.

The *Montero*-cap I shall describe by and bye.——The *Turkish* tobacco pipes had nothing particular in them; they were fitted up and ornamented as usual, with flexible tubes of *Morocco* leather and gold wire, and mounted at their ends, the one of them with ivory,—the other with black ebony, tipp'd with silver.

My father, who saw all things in lights different from the rest of the world, would say to the corporal, that he ought to look upon these two presents more as tokens of his brother's nicety, than his affection.——*Tom* did not care, *Trim*, he would say, to put on the cap, or to smoak in the tobacco-pipe of a *Jew*.—— God bless your honour, the corporal would say, (giving a strong reason to the contrary)—how can that be.——

The Montero-cap was scarlet, of a superfine *Spanish* cloth, died in grain, and mounted all round with furr, except about four inches in the front, which was faced with a light blue, slightly embroidered,—and seemed to have been the property of a *Portuguese* quarter-master, not of foot, but of horse, as the word denotes.

The corporal was not a little proud of it, as well for its own sake, as the sake of the giver, so seldom or never put it on but upon GALA-days; and yet never was a Montero-cap put to so many uses; for in all controverted points, whether military or culinary, provided the corporal was sure he was in the right,—it was either his *oath*,—his *wager*,—or his *gift*.

——'Twas his gift in the present case.

I'll be bound, said the corporal, speaking to himself, to *give* away my Montero-cap to the first beggar who comes to the door, if I do not manage this matter to his honour's satisfaction.

The completion was no further off, than the very next morning; which was that of the storm of the counterscarp betwixt the *Lower Deule*, to the right, and the gate St. *Andrew*,—and on the left, between St. *Magdalen*'s and the river.

As this was the most memorable attack in the whole war,— the most gallant and obstinate on both sides,—and I must add the most bloody too, for it cost the allies themselves that morning above eleven hundred men,—my uncle *Toby* prepared himself for it with a more than ordinary solemnity.

The eve which preceded, as my uncle *Toby* went to bed, he ordered his ramallie wig, which had laid inside out for many years in the corner of an old campaigning trunk, which stood by his bedside, to be taken out and laid upon the lid of it, ready for the morning;—and the very first thing he did in his shirt, when he had stepped out of bed, my uncle *Toby*, after he had turned the rough side outwards,—put it on:——This done, he proceeded next to his breeches, and having buttoned the waistband, he forthwith buckled on his sword belt, and had got his sword half way in,—when he considered he should want shaving, and that it would be very inconvenient doing it with his sword on,— so took it off:——In assaying to put on his regimental coat and waistcoat, my uncle *Toby* found the same objection in his wig,— so that went off too:—So that what with one thing, and what with another, as always falls out when a man is in the most haste,— 'twas ten o'clock, which was half an hour later than his usual time, before my uncle *Toby* sallied out.

CHAPTER XXV

MY UNCLE *TOBY* had scarce turned the corner of his yew hedge, which separated his kitchen garden from his bowling green, when he perceived the corporal had began the attack without him.——

Let me stop and give you a picture of the corporal's apparatus; and of the corporal himself in the height of this attack just as it struck my uncle *Toby*, as he turned towards the sentry-box, where the corporal was at work,——for in nature there is not such another,——nor can any combination of all that is grotesque and whimsical in her works produce its equal.

The corporal——

——Tread lightly on his ashes, ye men of genius,——for he was your kinsman:

Weed his grave clean, ye men of goodness,—for he was your brother.—Oh corporal! had I thee, but now,—now, that I am able to give thee a dinner and protection,—how would I cherish thee! thou should'st wear thy Montero-cap ever hour of the day, and every day of the week,—and when it was worn out, I would purchase thee a couple like it:——But alas! alas! alas! now that I can do this, in spight of their reverences—the occasion is lost— for thou art gone;—thy genius fled up to the stars from whence it came;—and that warm heart of thine, with all its generous and open vessels, compressed into a *clod of the valley*!

——But what——what is this, to that future and dreaded page, where I look towards the velvet pall, decorated with the military ensigns of thy master—the first—the foremost of created beings;

[373]

——where, I shall see thee, faithful servant! laying his sword and scabbard with a trembling hand across his coffin, and then returning pale as ashes to the door, to take his mourning horse by the bridle, to follow his hearse, as he directed thee;——where —all my father's systems shall be baffled by his sorrows; and, in spight of his philosophy, I shall behold him, as he inspects the lackered plate, twice taking his spectacles from off his nose, to wipe away the dew which nature has shed upon them——When I see him cast in the rosemary with an air of disconsolation, which cries through my ears,——O *Toby*! in what corner of the world shall I seek thy fellow?

——Gracious powers! which erst have opened the lips of the dumb in his distress, and made the tongue of the stammerer speak plain——when I shall arrive at this dreaded page, deal not with me, then, with a stinted hand.

CHAPTER XXVI

THE corporal, who the night before had resolved in his mind, to supply the grand *desideratum*, of keeping up something like an incessant firing upon the enemy during the heat of the attack,—had no further idea in his fancy at that time, than a contrivance of smoaking tobacco against the town, out of one of my uncle *Toby*'s six field pieces, which were planted on each side of his sentry-box; the means of effecting which occuring to his fancy at the same time, though he had pledged his cap, he thought it in no danger from the miscarriage of his projects.

Upon turning it this way, and that, a little in his mind, he soon began to find out, that by means of his two *Turkish* tobacco-pipes, with the supplement of three smaller tubes of wash-leather at each of their lower ends, to be tagg'd by the same number of tin pipes fitted to the touch holes, and sealed with clay next the cannon, and then tied hermetically with waxed silk at their several insertions into the *Morocco* tube,—he should be able to fire the six field pieces all together, and with the same ease as to fire one.——

——Let no man say from what taggs and jaggs hints may not be cut out for the advancement of human knowledge. Let no man who has read my father's first and second *beds of justice*, ever rise up and say again, from collision of what kinds of bodies, light may, or may not be struck out, to carry the arts and sciences up to perfection.——Heaven! thou knowest how I love them;—— thou knowest the secrets of my heart, and that I would this moment give my shirt——Thou art a fool, *Shandy*, says *Eugenius*, —for thou hast but a dozen in the world,—and 'twill break thy set.——

No matter for that, *Eugenius*; I would give the shirt off my back to be burnt into tinder, were it only to satisfy one feverish enquirer, how many sparks at one good stroke, a good flint and steel could strike into the tail of it.——Think ye not that in striking these *in*,—he might, peradventure, strike something *out*? as sure as a gun.——

——But this project, by the bye.

The corporal sat up the best part of the night in bringing *his* to perfection; and having made a sufficient proof of his cannon, with charging them to the top with tobacco,—he went with contentment to bed.

CHAPTER XXVII

THE corporal had slipped out about ten minutes before my uncle *Toby*, in order to fix his apparatus, and just give the enemy a shot or two before my uncle *Toby* came.

He had drawn the six field-pieces for this end, all close up together in front of my uncle *Toby*'s sentry-box, leaving only an interval of about a yard and a half betwixt the three, on the right and left, for the convenience of charging, *&c.*—and the sake possibly of two batteries, which he might think double the honour of one.

In the rear, and facing this opening, with his back to the door of the sentry-box, for fear of being flanked, had the corporal wisely taken his post:——He held the ivory pipe, appertaining to the battery on the right, betwixt the finger and thumb of his right hand,—and the ebony pipe tipp'd with silver, which appertained to the battery on the left, betwixt the finger and thumb of the other——and with his right knee fixed firm upon the ground, as if in the front rank of his platoon, was the corporal, with his Montero-cap upon his head, furiously playing off his two cross batteries at the same time against the counterguard, which faced the counterscarp, where the attack was to be made that morning.

His first intention, as I said, was no more than giving the enemy a single puff or two;—but the pleasure of the *puffs*, as well as the *puffing*, had insensibly got hold of the corporal, and drawn him on from puff to puff, into the very height of the attack, by the time my uncle *Toby* joined him.

'Twas well for my father, that my uncle *Toby* had not his will to make that day.

CHAPTER XXVIII

MY UNCLE *TOBY* took the ivory pipe out of the corporal's hand,—looked at it for half a minute, and returned it.

In less than two minutes my uncle *Toby* took the pipe from the corporal again, and raised it half way to his mouth——then hastily gave it back a second time.

The corporal redoubled the attack,——my uncle *Toby* smiled,——then looked grave,——then smiled for a moment,——then looked serious for a long time;——Give me hold of the ivory pipe, *Trim*, said my uncle *Toby*——my uncle *Toby* put it to his lips,——drew it back directly,——gave a peep over the horn-beam hedge;——never did my uncle *Toby*'s mouth water so much for a pipe in his life.——My uncle *Toby* retired into the sentry-box with the pipe in his hand.——

——Dear uncle *Toby*! don't go into the sentry-box with the pipe,—there's no trusting a man's self with such a thing in such a corner.

CHAPTER XXIX

I BEG the reader will assist me here, to wheel off my uncle *Toby*'s ordnance behind the scenes,——to remove his sentry-box, and clear the theatre, *if possible*, of horn-works and half moons, and get the rest of his military apparatus out of the way;——that done, my dear friend *Garrick*, we'll snuff the candles bright,—sweep the stage with a new broom,—draw up the curtain, and exhibit my uncle *Toby* dressed in a new character, throughout which the world can have no idea how he will act: and yet, if pity be akin to love,—and bravery no alien to it, you have seen enough of my uncle *Toby* in these, to trace these family likenesses, betwixt the two passions (in case there is one) to your heart's content.

Vain science! thou assists us in no case of this kind—and thou puzzlest us in every one.

There was, Madam, in my uncle *Toby*, a singleness of heart which misled him so far out of the little serpentine tracks in which things of this nature usually go on; you can—you can have no conception of it: with this, there was a plainness and simplicity of thinking, with such an unmistrusting ignorance of the plies and foldings of the heart of woman;——and so naked and defenceless did he stand before you, (when a siege was out of his head) that you might have stood behind any one of your serpentine walks, and shot my uncle *Toby* ten times in a day, through his liver, if nine times in a day, Madam, had not served your purpose.

With all this, Madam,—and what confounded every thing as much on the other hand, my uncle *Toby* had that unparalleled modesty of nature I once told you of, and which, by the bye, stood eternal sentry upon his feelings, that you might as soon—— But where am I going? these reflections croud in upon me ten pages at least too soon, and take up that time, which I ought to bestow upon facts.

CHAPTER XXX

OF THE few legitimate sons of *Adam*, whose breasts never felt what the sting of love was,—(maintaining first, all mysogynists to be bastards)—the greatest heroes of ancient and modern story have carried off amongst them, nine parts in ten of the honour; and I wish for their sakes I had the key of my study out of my draw-well, only for five minutes, to tell you their names—recollect them I cannot—so be content to accept of these, for the present, in their stead.——

There was the great king *Aldrovandus*, and *Bosphorus*, and *Capadocius*, and *Dardanus*, and *Pontus*, and *Asius*,——to say nothing of the iron-hearted *Charles* the XIIth, whom the Countess of K * * * * * herself could make nothing of.——There was *Babylonicus*, and *Mediterraneus*, and *Polixenes*, and *Persicus*, and *Prusicus*, not one of whom (except *Capadocius* and *Pontus*, who were both a little suspected) ever once bowed down his breast to the goddess——The truth is, they had all of them something else to do—and so had my uncle *Toby*—till Fate—till Fate I say, envying his name the glory of being handed down to posterity with *Aldrovandus*'s and the rest,—she basely patched up the peace of *Utrecht*.

——Believe me, Sirs, 'twas the worst deed she did that year.

CHAPTER XXXI

AMONGST the many ill consequences of the treaty of *Utrecht*, it was within a point of giving my uncle *Toby* a surfeit of sieges; and though he recovered his appetite afterwards, yet *Calais* itself left not a deeper scar in *Mary*'s heart, than *Utrecht* upon my uncle *Toby*'s. To the end of his life he never could hear *Utrecht* mentioned upon any account whatever, —or so much as read an article of news extracted out of the *Utrecht Gazette*, without fetching a sigh, as if his heart would break in twain.

My father, who was a great MOTIVE-MONGER, and consequently a very dangerous person for a man to sit by, either laughing or crying,—for he generally knew your motive for doing both, much better than you knew it yourself—would always console my uncle *Toby* upon these occasions, in a way which shewed plainly, he imagined my uncle *Toby* grieved for nothing in the whole affair, so much as the loss of his *hobby-horse*.——Never mind, brother *Toby*, he would say,—by God's blessing we shall have another war break out again some of these days; and when it does,—the belligerent powers, if they would hang themselves, cannot keep us out of play.——I defy 'em, my dear *Toby*, he would add, to take countries without taking towns,——or towns without sieges.

My uncle *Toby* never took this back-stroke of my father's at his hobby-horse kindly.——He thought the stroke ungenerous; and the more so, because in striking the horse, he hit the rider too, and in the most dishonourable part a blow could fall; so that upon these occasions, he always laid down his pipe upon the table with more fire to defend himself than common.

I told the reader, this time two years, that my uncle *Toby* was not eloquent; and in the very same page gave an instance to the contrary:——I repeat the observation, and a fact which con-

tradicts it again.—He was not eloquent,—it was not easy to my
uncle *Toby* to make long harangues,—and he hated florid ones;
but there were occasions where the stream overflowed the man,
and ran so counter to its usual course, that in some parts my
uncle *Toby*, for a time, was at least equal to *Tertullus*——but in
others, in my own opinion, infinitely above him.

My father was so highly pleased with one of these apologetical
orations of my uncle *Toby*'s, which he had delivered one evening
before him and *Yorick*, that he wrote it down before he went to
bed.

I have had the good fortune to meet with it amongst my
father's papers, with here and there an insertion of his own,
betwixt two crooks, thus [   ], and is endorsed,

My brother TOBY'*s justification of his own principles and conduct*
in wishing to continue the war.

I may safely say, I have read over this apologetical oration of my
uncle *Toby*'s a hundred times, and think it so fine a model of
defence,—and shews so sweet a temperament of gallantry and
good principles in him, that I give it the world, word for word,
(interlineations and all) as I find it.

CHAPTER XXXII

My uncle TOBY'*s apologetical oration.*

I AM NOT insensible, brother *Shandy*, that when a man, whose
profession is arms, wishes, as I have done, for war,—it has
an ill aspect to the world;——and that, how just and right
soever his motives and intentions may be,—he stands in an
uneasy posture in vindicating himself from private views in
doing it.

For this cause, if a soldier is a prudent man, which he may be,
without being a jot the less brave, he will be sure not to utter his
wish in the hearing of an enemy; for say what he will, an enemy
will not believe him.——He will be cautious of doing it even to
a friend,—lest he may suffer in his esteem:——But if his heart is
overcharged, and a secret sigh for arms must have its vent, he will
reserve if for the ear of a brother, who knows his character to
the bottom, and what his true notions, dispositions, and principles
of honour are: What, I *hope*, I have been in all these, brother
Shandy, would be unbecoming in me to say:——much worse,

I know, have I been than I ought,—and something worse, perhaps, than I think: But such as I am, you, my dear brother
Shandy, who have sucked the same breasts with me,—and with
whom I have been brought up from my cradle,—and from whose
knowledge, from the first hours of our boyish pastimes, down to
this, I have concealed no one action of my life, and scarce
a thought in it——Such as I am, brother, you must by this time
know me, with all my vices, and with all my weaknesses too,
whether of my age, my temper, my passions, or my understanding.

Tell me then, my dear brother *Shandy*, upon which of them it
is, that when I condemned the peace of *Utrecht*, and grieved the
war was not carried on with vigour a little longer, you should
think your brother did it upon unworthy views; or that in wishing for war, he should be bad enough to wish more of his fellow
creatures slain,—more slaves made, and more families driven
from their peaceful habitations, merely for his own pleasure:
——Tell me, brother *Shandy*, upon what one deed of mine do you
ground it? [*The devil a deed do I know of, dear* Toby, *but one for
a hundred pounds, which I lent thee to carry on these cursed sieges.*]

If, when I was a school-boy, I could not hear a drum beat, but
my heart beat with it—was it my fault?——Did I plant the
propensity there?——did I sound the alarm within, or Nature?

When *Guy*, Earl of *Warwick*, and *Parismus* and *Parismenus*,
and *Valentine* and *Orson*, and the *Seven Champions of England*
were handed around the school,—were they not all purchased
with my own pocket money? Was that selfish, brother *Shandy*?
When we read over the siege of *Troy*, which lasted ten years and
eight months,——though with such a train of artillery as we had
at *Namur*, the town might have been carried in a week—was
I not as much concerned for the destruction of the *Greeks* and
Trojans as any boy of the whole school? Had I not three strokes
of a ferula given me, two on my right hand and one on my left,
for calling *Helena* a bitch for it? Did any one of you shed more
tears for *Hector*? And when king *Priam* came to the camp to beg
his body, and returned weeping back to *Troy* without it,—you
know, brother, I could not eat my dinner.——

——Did that bespeak me cruel? Or because, brother *Shandy*,
my blood flew out into the camp, and my heart panted for war,
—was it a proof it could not ache for the distresses of war too?

O brother! 'tis one thing for a soldier to gather laurels,—and
'tis another to scatter cypress.——[*Who told thee, my dear* Toby,
that cypress was used by the ancients on mournful occasions?]

[380]

————'Tis one thing, brother *Shandy*, for a soldier to hazard his own life—to leap first down into the trench, where he is sure to be cut in pieces:————'Tis one thing, from public spirit and a thirst of glory, to enter the breach the first man,—to stand in the foremost rank, and march bravely on with drums and trumpets, and colours flying about his ears:————'Tis one thing, I say, brother *Shandy*, to do this—and 'tis another thing to reflect on the miseries of war;—to view the desolations of whole countries, and consider the intolerable fatigues and hardships which the soldier himself, the instrument who works them, is forced (for six pence a day, if he can get it) to undergo.

Need I be told, dear *Yorick*, as I was by you, in *Le Fever*'s funeral sermon, *That so soft and gentle a creature, born to love, to mercy, and kindness, as man is, was not shaped for this?*———— But why did you not add, *Yorick*,—if not by NATURE—that he is so by NECESSITY?————For what is war? what is it, *Yorick*, when fought as ours has been, upon principles of *liberty*, and upon principles of *honour*————what is it, but the getting together of quiet and harmless people, with their swords in their hands, to keep the ambitious and the turbulent within bounds? And heaven is my witness, brother *Shandy*, that the pleasure I have taken in these things,—and that infinite delight, in particular, which has attended my sieges in my bowling green, has arose within me, and I hope in the corporal too, from the consciousness we both had, that in carrying them on, we were answering the great ends of our creation.

CHAPTER XXXIII

I TOLD the Christian reader————I say *Christian*————hoping he is one————and if he is not, I am sorry for it————and only beg he will consider the matter with himself, and not lay the blame entirely upon this book,————

I told him, Sir————for in good truth, when a man is telling a story in the strange way I do mine, he is obliged continually to be going backwards and forwards to keep all tight together in the reader's fancy————which, for my own part, if I did not take heed to do more than at first, there is so much unfixed and equivocal matter starting up, with so many breaks and gaps in it,—and so little service do the stars afford, which, nevertheless, I hang up in some of the darkest passages, knowing that the world is apt to lose its way, with all the lights the sun itself at noon day can give it——and now, you see, I am lost myself!——

——But 'tis my father's fault; and whenever my brains come to be dissected, you will perceive, without spectacles, that he has left a large uneven thread, as you sometimes see in an unsaleable piece of cambrick, running along the whole length of the web, and so untowardly, you cannot so much as cut out a * *, (here I hang up a couple of lights again)——or a fillet, or a thumb-stall, but it is seen or felt.——

Quanto id diligentius in liberis procreandis cavendum, sayeth *Cardan*. All which being considered, and that you see 'tis morally impracticable for me to wind this round to where I set out——

I begin the chapter over again.

CHAPTER XXXIV

I TOLD the Christian reader in the beginning of the chapter which preceded my uncle *Toby*'s apologetical oration,—though in a different trope from what I shall make use of now, That the peace of *Utrecht* was within an ace of creating the same shyness betwixt my uncle *Toby* and his hobby-horse, as it did betwixt the queen and the rest of the confederating powers.

There is an indignant way in which a man sometimes dismounts his horse, which as good as says to him, "I'll go afoot, Sir, all the days of my life, before I would ride a single mile upon your back again." Now my uncle *Toby* could not be said to dismount his horse in this manner; for in strictness of language, he could not be said to dismount his horse at all——his horse rather flung him——and somewhat *viciously*, which made my uncle *Toby* take it ten times more unkindly. Let this matter be settled by state jockies as they like.——It created, I say, a sort of shyness betwixt my uncle *Toby* and his hobby-horse.——He had no occasion for him from the month of *March* to *November*, which was the summer after the articles were signed, except it was now and then to take a short ride out, just to see that the fortifications and harbour of *Dunkirk* were demolished, according to stipulation.

The *French* were so backwards all that summer in setting about that affair, and Monsieur *Tugghe*, the deputy from the magistrates of *Dunkirk*, presented so many affecting petitions to the queen,—

[382]

beseeching her majesty to cause only her thunderbolts to fall
upon the martial works, which might have incurred her dis-
pleasure,—but to spare—to spare the mole, for the mole's sake;
which, in its naked situation, could be no more than an object
of pity——and the queen (who was but a woman) being of
a pitiful disposition,—and her ministers also, they not wishing
in their hearts to have the town dismantled, for these private
reasons, * * * * * * * * * * * * * * * *
* * *____

* * * * * * * * * * * * * * * * * *

* * * * *; so that the whole went heavily on with my uncle
Toby; insomuch, that it was not within three full months, after
he and the corporal had constructed the town, and put it in
a condition to be destroyed, that the several commandants,
commissaries, deputies, negotiators, and intendants, would permit him to set about it.——Fatal interval of inactivity!

The corporal was for beginning the demolition, by making
a breach in the ramparts, or main fortifications of the town——
No,—that will never do, corporal, said my uncle *Toby*, for in
going that way to work with the town, the *English* garrison will
not be safe in it an hour; because if the *French* are treacherous
——They are as treacherous as devils, an' please your honour,
said the corporal——It gives me concern always when I hear it,
Trim, said my uncle *Toby*,—for they don't want personal
bravery; and if a breach is made in the ramparts, they may enter
it, and make themselves masters of the place when they please:
——Let them enter it, said the corporal, lifting up his pioneer's
spade in both his hands, as if he was going to lay about him with
it, let them enter, an' please your honour, if they dare.——In
cases like this, corporal, said my uncle *Toby*, slipping his right
hand down to the middle of his cane, and holding it afterwards
truncheon-wise, with his forefinger extended,——'tis no part of
the consideration of a commandant, what the enemy dare,—or
what they dare not do; he must act with prudence. We will begin
with the outworks both towards the sea and the land, and particularly with fort *Louis*, the most distant of them all, and demolish it first,—and the rest, one by one, both on our right and left,
as we retreat towards the town;——then we'll demolish the mole,
—next fill up the harbour,—then retire into the citadel, and blow
it up into the air; and having done that, corporal, we'll embark
for *England*.——We are there, quoth the corporal, recollecting
himself——Very true, said my uncle *Toby*—looking at the church.

CHAPTER XXXV

A DELUSIVE, delicious consultation or two of this kind, betwixt my uncle *Toby* and *Trim*, upon the demolition of *Dunkirk*,—for a moment rallied back the ideas of those pleasures, which were slipping from under him:——still—still all went on heavily——the magic left the mind the weaker—STILLNESS, with SILENCE at her back, entered the solitary parlour, and drew their gauzy mantle over my uncle *Toby*'s head;——and LISTLESSNESS, with her lax fibre and undirected eye, sat quietly down beside him in his arm chair.——No longer *Amberg*, and *Rhinberg*, and *Limbourg*, and *Huy*, and *Bonn*, in one year,—and the prospect of *Landen*, and *Trerebach*, and *Drusen*, and *Dendermond*, the next,—hurried on the blood:—No longer did saps, and mines, and blinds, and gabions, and palisadoes, keep out this fair enemy of man's repose:——No more could my uncle *Toby*, after passing the *French* lines, as he eat his egg at supper, from thence break into the heart of *France*,—cross over the *Oyes*, and with all *Picardie* open behind him, march up to the gates of *Paris*, and fall asleep with nothing but ideas of glory:——No more was he to dream, he had fixed the royal standard upon the tower of the *Bastile*, and awake with it streaming in his head.

——Softer visions,—gentler vibrations stole sweetly in upon his slumbers;—the trumpet of war fell out of his hands,—he took up the lute, sweet instrument! of all others the most delicate! the most difficult!——how wilt thou touch it, my dear uncle *Toby*?

CHAPTER XXXVI

N OW, because I have once or twice said, in my inconsiderate way of talking, That I was confident the following memoirs of my uncle *Toby*'s courtship of widow *Wadman*, whenever I got time to write them, would turn out one of the most compleat systems, both of the elementary and practical part of love and love-making, that ever was addressed to the world——are you to imagine from thence, that I shall set out with a description of *what love is*? whether part God and part Devil, as *Plotinus* will have it——

[384]

———Or by a more critical equation, and supposing the whole of love to be as ten——to determine, with *Ficinus*, "*How many parts of it—the one,—and how many the other;*"—or whether it is *all of it one great Devil*, from head to tail, as *Plato* has taken upon him to pronounce; concerning which conceit of his, I shall not offer my opinion:—but my opinion of *Plato* is this; that he appears, from this instance, to have been a man of much the same temper and way of reasoning with doctor *Baynyard*, who being a great enemy to blisters, as imagining that half a dozen of 'em on at once, would draw a man as surely to his grave, as a herse and six—rashly concluded, that the Devil himself was nothing in the world, but one great bouncing *Cantharidis.*———

I have nothing to say to people who allow themselves this monstrous liberty in arguing, but what *Nazianzen* cried out (*that is polemically*) to *Philagrius*——

"ʽΕυγε!" *O rare! 'tis fine reasoning, Sir, indeed!*—"ὅτι φιλοσοφεῖς ἐν Πάθευι"—*and most nobly do you aim at truth, when you philosophize about it in your moods and passions.*

Nor is it to be imagined, for the same reason, I should stop to enquire, whether love is a disease,——or embroil myself with *Rhasis* and *Dioscorides*, whether the seat of it is in the brain or liver;—because this would lead me on, to an examination of the two very opposite manners, in which patients have been treated ——the one, of *Aætius*, who always begun with a cooling glyster of hempseed and bruised cucumbers;—and followed on with thin potations of water lillies and purslane—to which he added a pinch of snuff, of the herb *Hanea;*—and where *Aætius* durst venture it,—his topaz-ring.

——The other, that of *Gordonius*, who (in his cap. 15. *de Amore*) directs they should be thrashed, "*ad putorem usque,*"—— till they stink again.

These are disquisitions, which my father, who had laid in a great stock of knowledge of this kind, will be very busy with, in the progress of my uncle *Toby*'s affairs: I must anticipate thus much, That from his theories of love, (with which, by the way, he contrived to crucify my uncle *Toby*'s mind, almost as much as his amours themselves)—he took a single step into practice;— and by means of a camphorated cerecloth, which he found means to impose upon the taylor for buckram, whilst he was making my uncle *Toby* a new pair of breeches, he produced *Gordonius*'s effect upon my uncle *Toby* without the disgrace,

[385]

What changes this produced, will be read in its proper place: all that is needful to be added to the anecdote, is this,——That whatever effect it had upon my uncle *Toby*,——it had a vile effect upon the house;——and if my uncle *Toby* had not smoaked it down as he did, it might have had a vile effect upon my father too.

CHAPTER XXXVII

—'TWILL COME out of itself by and bye.——All I contend for is, that I am not *obliged* to set out with a definition of what love is; and so long as I can go on with my story intelligibly, with the help of the word itself, without any other idea to it, than what I have in common with the rest of the world, why should I differ from it a moment before the time?——When I can get on no further,—and find myself entangled on all sides of this mystick labyrinth,—my Opinion will then come in, in course,—and lead me out.

At present, I hope I shall be sufficiently understood, in telling the reader, my uncle *Toby fell in love:*

—Not that the phrase is at all to my liking: for to say a man is *fallen* in love,—or that he is *deeply* in love,—or up to the ears in love,—and sometimes even *over head and ears in it,*—carries an idiomatical kind of implication, that love is a thing *below* a man:—this is recurring again to *Plato*'s opinion, which, with all his divinityship,—I hold to be damnable and heretical;—and so much for that.

Let love therefore be what it will,—my uncle *Toby* fell into it.

——And possibly, gentle reader, with such a temptation—so wouldst thou: For never did thy eyes behold, or thy concupiscence covet any thing in this world, more concupiscible than widow *Wadman*.

CHAPTER XXXVIII

TO CONCEIVE this right,—call for pen and ink—here's paper ready to your hand.——Sit down, Sir, paint her to your own mind——as like your mistress as you can——as unlike your wife as your conscience will let you—'tis all one to me——please but your own fancy in it.

[386]

VOLUME SIX

————Was ever any thing in Nature so sweet!—so exquisite!
————Then, dear Sir, how could my uncle *Toby* resist it?
Thrice happy book! thou wilt have one page, at least, within
thy covers, which MALICE will not blacken, and which IGNORANCE
cannot misrepresent.

CHAPTER XXXIX

As *SUSANNAH* was informed by an express from Mrs.
Bridget, of my uncle *Toby*'s falling in love with her mistress, fifteen days before it happened,—the contents of
which express, *Susannah* communicated to my mother the next
day,—it has just given me an opportunity of entering upon my
uncle *Toby*'s amours a fortnight before their existence.

I have an article of news to tell you, Mr. *Shandy*, quoth my
mother, which will surprise you greatly.————

Now my father was then holding one of his second beds of
justice, and was musing within himself about the hardships of
matrimony, as my mother broke silence.————

————My brother *Toby*, quoth she, is going to be married to
Mrs. *Wadman*.

————Then he will never, quoth my father, be able to lie
diagonally in his bed again as long as he lives.

It was a consuming vexation to my father, that my mother
never asked the meaning of a thing she did not understand.

————That she is not a woman of science, my father would say
—is her misfortune—but she might ask a question.—

My mother never did.————In short, she went out of the world
at last without knowing whether it turned *round*, or stood *still*.
————My father had officiously told her above a thousand times
which way it was,—but she always forgot.

For these reasons a discourse seldom went on much further
betwixt them, than a proposition,—a reply, and a rejoinder; at
the end of which, it generally took breath for a few minutes, (as
in the affair of the breeches) and then went on again.

If he marries, 'twill be the worse for us,—quoth my mother.

Not a cherry-stone, said my father,—he may as well batter
away his means upon that, as any thing else.

————To be sure, said my mother: so here ended the proposition,
—the reply,—and the rejoinder, I told you of.

It will be some amusement to him, too,————said my father.

A very great one, answered my mother, if he should have children.——

——Lord have mercy upon me,—said my father to himself ___ * .

CHAPTER XL

I AM NOW beginning to get fairly into my work; and by the help of a vegetable diet, with a few of the cold seeds, I make no doubt but I shall be able to go on with my uncle *Toby*'s story, and my own, in a tolerable straight line. Now,

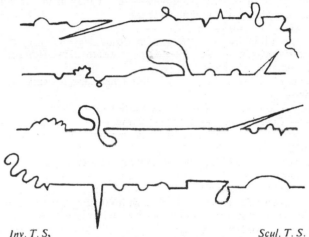

Inv. T. S.   *Scul. T. S.*

These were the four lines I moved in through my first, second, third, and fourth volumes.——In the fifth volume I have been very good,——the precise line I have described in it being this:

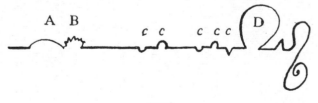

By which it appears, that except at the curve, marked A. where I took a trip to *Navarre*,—and the indented curve B. which is the short airing when I was there with the lady *Baussiere* and her page,—I have not taken the least frisk of a digression, till *John de la Casse*'s devils led me the round you see marked D.—for as for *c c c c c* they are nothing but parentheses, and the common *ins* and *outs* incident to the lives of the greatest ministers of state; and when compared with what men have done,—or with my own transgressions at the letters A B D—they vanish into nothing.

In this last volume I have done better still—for from the end of *Le Fever*'s episode, to the beginning of my uncle *Toby*'s campaigns,—I have scarce stepped a yard out of my way.

If I mend at this rate, it is not impossible——by the good leave of his grace of *Benevento*'s devils——but I may arrive hereafter at the excellency of going on even thus;

———

which is a line drawn as straight as I could draw it, by a writing-master's ruler, (borrowed for that purpose) turning neither to the right hand or to the left.

This *right line*,—the path-way for Christians to walk in! say divines——

——The emblem of moral rectitude! says *Cicero*——

——The *best line*! say cabbage-planters——is the shortest line, says *Archimedes*, which can be drawn from one given point to another.——

I wish your ladyships would lay this matter to heart in your next birthday suits!

——What a journey!

Pray can you tell me,—that is, without anger, before I write my chapter upon straight lines——by what mistake——who told them so——or how it has come to pass, that your men of wit and genius have all along confounded this line, with the line of GRAVITATION.

END of the SIXTH VOLUME.

VOLUME VII

Non enim excursus hic ejus, sed opus ipsum est.
PLIN. Lib. quintus Epistola sexta.

CHAPTER I

NO——I THINK, I said, I would write two volumes every year, provided the vile cough which then tormented me, and which to this hour I dread worse than the devil, would but give me leave——and in another place——(but where, I can't recollect now) speaking of my book as a *machine*, and laying my pen and ruler down cross-wise upon the table, in order to gain the greater credit to it—I swore it should be kept a-going at that rate these forty years if it pleased but the fountain of life to bless me so long with health and good spirits.

Now as for my spirits, little have I to lay to their charge—nay so very little (unless the mounting me upon a long stick, and playing the fool with me nineteen hours out of the twenty-four, be accusations) that on the contrary, I have much—much to thank 'em for: cheerily have ye made me tread the path of life with all the burdens of it (except its cares) upon my back; in no one moment of my existence, that I remember, have ye once deserted me, or tinged the objects which came in my way, either with sable, or with a sickly green; in dangers ye gilded my horizon with hope, and when DEATH himself knocked at my door—ye bad him come again; and in so gay a tone of careless indifference, did ye do it, that he doubted of his commission——

"There must certainly be some mistake in this matter," quoth he.

Now there is nothing in this world I abominate worse, than to be interrupted in a story——and I was that moment telling *Eugenius* a most tawdry one in my way, of a nun who fancied herself a shell-fish, and of a monk damn'd for eating a muscle, and was shewing him the grounds and justice of the procedure——

"—Did ever so grave a personage get into so vile a scrape?" quoth *Death*. Thou hast had a narrow escape, *Tristram*, said *Eugenius*, taking hold of my hand as I finish'd my story——

But there is no *living*, *Eugenius*, replied I, at this rate; for as this *son of a whore* has found out my lodgings——

—You call him rightly, said *Eugenius*,—for by sin, we are told, he enter'd the world——I care not which way he enter'd, quoth I, provided he be not in such a hurry to take me out with him—for I have forty volumes to write, and forty thousand things to say and do, which no body in the world will say and do for me, except thyself; and as thou seest he has got me by the throat (for *Eugenius* could scarce hear me speak across the table) and that

I am no match for him in the open field, had I not better, whilst these few scatter'd spirits remain, and these two spider legs of mine (holding one of them up to him) are able to support me—had I not better, *Eugenius*, fly for my life? 'Tis my advice, my dear *Tristram*, said *Eugenius*——Then by heaven! I will lead him a dance he little thinks of—for I will gallop, quoth I, without looking once behind me, to the banks of the *Garonne*; and if I hear him clattering at my heels——I'll scamper away to mount *Vesuvius*——from thence to *Joppa*, and from *Joppa* to the world's end, where, if he follows me, I pray God he may break his neck——

—He runs more risk *there*, said *Eugenius*, than thou.

Eugenius's wit and affection brought blood into the cheek from whence it had been some months banish'd—'twas a vile moment to bid adieu in; he led me to my chaise——*Allons!* said I; the post boy gave a crack with his whip——off I went like a cannon, and in half a dozen bounds got into *Dover*.

CHAPTER II

NOW HANG IT! quoth I, as I look'd towards the *French* coast—a man should know something of his own country too, before he goes abroad——and I never gave a peep into *Rochester* church, or took notice of the dock of *Chatham*, or visited St. *Thomas* at *Canterbury*, though they all three laid in my way——

—But mine, indeed, is a particular case——

So without arguing the matter further with *Thomas o'Becket*, or any one else—I skip'd into the boat, and in five minutes we got under sail and scudded away like the wind.

Pray captain, quoth I, as I was going down into the cabin, is a man never overtaken by *Death* in this passage?

Why, there is not time for a man to be sick in it, replied he——What a cursed lyar! for I am sick as a horse, quoth I, already——what a brain!——upside down!——hey dey! the cells are broke loose one into another, and the blood, and the lymph, and the nervous juices, with the fix'd and volatile salts, are all jumbled into one mass——good g—! every thing turns round in it like a thousand whirlpools—I'd give a shilling to know if I shan't write the clearer for it——

Sick! sick! sick! sick!——

——When shall we get to land? captain—they have hearts like stones——O I am deadly sick!——reach me that thing, boy—— 'tis the most discomfiting sickness——I wish I was at the bottom —Madam! how is it with you? Undone! undone! un—— O! undone! Sir— What the first time?——No, 'tis the second, third, sixth, tenth time, Sir,—hey-dey——what a trampling over head! —hollo! cabin boy! what's the matter—

The wind chopp'd about! s'Death!—then I shall meet him full in the face.

What luck!—'tis chopp'd about again, master—O the devil chop it——

Captain, quoth she, for heaven's sake, let us get ashore.

CHAPTER III

I T IS a great inconvenience to a man in a haste, that there are three distinct roads between *Calais* and *Paris*, in behalf of which there is so much to be said by the several deputies from the towns which lie along them, that half a day is easily lost in settling which you'll take.

First, the road by *Lisle* and *Arras*, which is the most about—— but most interesting, and instructing.

The second that by *Amiens*, which you may go, if you would see *Chantilly*——

And that by *Beauvais*, which you may go, if you will.

For this reason a great many chuse to go by *Beauvais*.

CHAPTER IV

"N OW BEFORE I quit *Calais*," a travel-writer would say, "it would not be amiss to give some account of it."— Now I think it very much amiss—that a man cannot go quietly through a town, and let it alone, when it does not meddle with him, but that he must be turning about and drawing his pen at every kennel he crosses over, merely o' my conscience, for the sake of drawing it; because, if we may judge from what has been wrote of these things, by all who have *wrote and gallop'd*—or who

[395]

have *gallop'd and wrote*, which is a different way still; or who, for more expedition than the rest, have *wrote-galloping*, which is the way I do at present——from the great *Addison* who did it with his satchel of school-books hanging at his a— and galling his beast's crupper at every stroke—there is not a galloper of us all who might not have gone on ambling quietly in his own ground (in case he had any) and have wrote all he had to write, dry shod, as well as not.

For my own part, as heaven is my judge, and to which I shall ever make my last appeal—I know no more of *Calais*, (except the little my barber told me of it, as he was whetting his razor) than I do this moment of *Grand Cairo*; for it was dusky in the evening when I landed, and dark as pitch in the morning when I set out, and yet by merely knowing what is what, and by drawing this from that in one part of the town, and by spelling and putting this and that together in another—I would lay any travelling odds, that I this moment write a chapter upon *Calais* as long as my arm; and with so distinct and satisfactory a detail of every item, which is worth a stranger's curiosity in the town—that you would take me for the town clerk of *Calais* itself—and where, Sir, would be the wonder? was not *Democritus*, who laughed ten times more than I—town-clerk of *Abdera*? and was not (I forget his name) who had more discretion than us both, town-clerk of *Ephesus*?

——it should be penn'd moreover, Sir, with so much knowledge and good sense, and truth, and precision——

—Nay—if you don't believe me, you may read the chapter for your pains.

CHAPTER V

CALAIS, *Calatium, Calusium, Calesium.*
         This town, if we may trust it's archives, the authority of which I see no reason to call in question in this place— was *once* no more than a small village belonging to one of the first Counts *de Guines*; and as it boasts at present of no less than fourteen thousand inhabitants, exclusive of four hundred and twenty distinct families in the *basse ville*, or suburbs——it must have grown up by little and little, I suppose, to it's present size.

Though there are four convents, there is but one parochial

church in the whole town; I had not an opportunity of taking its exact dimensions, but it is pretty easy to make a tolerable conjecture of 'em—for as there are fourteen thousand inhabitants in the town, if the church holds them all, it must be considerably large—and if it will not—'tis a very great pity they have not another—it is built in form of a cross, and dedicated to the *Virgin Mary*; the steeple which has a spire to it, is placed in the middle of the church, and stands upon four pillars elegant and light enough, but sufficiently strong at the same time—it is decorated with eleven altars, most of which are rather fine than beautiful. The great altar is a masterpiece in its kind; 'tis of white marble, and as I was told near sixty feet high—had it been much higher, it had been as high as mount Calvary itself—therefore, I suppose it must be high enough in all conscience.

There was nothing struck me more than the great *Square*; tho' I cannot say 'tis either well paved or well built; but 'tis in the heart of the town, and most of the streets, especially those in that quarter, all terminate in it; could there have been a fountain in all *Calais*, which it seems there cannot, as such an object would have been a great ornament, it is not to be doubted, but that the inhabitants would have had it in the very centre of this square,—not that it is properly a square,—because 'tis forty feet longer from east to west, than from north to south; so that the *French* in general have more reason on their side in calling them *Places* than *Squares*, which strictly speaking, to be sure they are not.

The town-house seems to be but a sorry building, and not to be kept in the best repair; otherwise it had been a second great ornament to this place; it answers however its destination, and serves very well for the reception of the magistrates, who assemble in it from time to time; so that 'tis presumable, justice is regularly distributed.

I had heard much of it, but there is nothing at all curious in the *Courgain*; 'tis a distinct quarter of the town inhabited solely by sailors and fishermen; it consists of a number of small streets, neatly built and mostly of brick; 'tis extremely populous, but as that may be accounted for from the principles of their diet,—there is nothing curious in that neither.——A traveller may see it to satisfy himself—he must not omit however taking notice of *La Tour de Guet*, upon any account; 'tis so called from its particular destination, because in war it serves to discover and give notice of the enemies which approach the place, either by sea or land;——but 'tis monstrous high, and catches the eye

[397]

so continually, you cannot avoid taking notice of it, if you would.

It was a singular disappointment to me, that I could not have permission to take an exact survey of the fortifications, which are the strongest in the world, and which, from first to last, that is, from the time they were set about by *Philip of France* Count of *Bologne*, to the present war, wherein many reparations were made, have cost (as I learned afterwards from an engineer in *Gascony*)—above a hundred millions of livres. It is very remarkable that at the *Tête de Gravelenes*, and where the town is naturally the weakest, they have expended the most money; so that the out-works stretch a great way into the campaign, and consequently occupy a large tract of ground.—However, after all that is *said* and *done*, it must be acknowledged that *Calais* was never upon any account so considerable from itself, as from its situation, and that easy enterance which it gave our ancestors upon all occasions into *France*: it was not without its inconveniences also; being no less troublesome to the *English* in those times, than *Dunkirk* has been to us, in ours; so that it was deservedly looked upon as the key to both kingdoms, which no doubt is the reason that there have arisen so many contentions who should keep it: of these, the siege of *Calais*, or rather the blockade (for it was shut up both by land and sea) was the most memorable, as it withstood the efforts of *Edward* the third a whole year, and was not terminated at last but by famine and extream misery; the gallantry of *Eustace de St. Pierre*, who first offered himself a victim for his fellow citizens, has rank'd his name with heroes. As it will not take up above fifty pages, it would be injustice to the reader, not to give him a minute account of that romantic transaction, as well as of the siege itself, in *Rapin*'s own words:

CHAPTER VI

—BUT COURAGE! gentle reader!——I scorn it——'tis enough to have thee in my power——but to make use of the advantage which the fortune of the pen has now gained over thee, would be too much——No——! by that all powerful fire which warms the visionary brain, and lights the spirits through unworldly tracts! ere I would force a helpless creature upon this hard service, and make thee pay, poor soul! for fifty pages which I have no right to sell thee,—naked as I am,

I would browse upon the mountains, and smile that the north wind brought me neither my tent or my supper.

—So put on, my brave boy! and make the best of thy way to *Boulogne*.

CHAPTER VII

—BOULOGNE!——hah!—so we are all got together—— debtors and sinners before heaven; a jolly set of us—but I can't stay and quaff it off with you—I'm pursued myself like a hundred devils, and shall be overtaken before I can well change horses:——for heaven's sake, make haste——'Tis for high treason, quoth a very little man, whispering as low as he could to a very tall man that stood next him——Or else for murder; quoth the tall man——Well thrown, *Size-Ace*! quoth I. No; quoth a third, the gentleman has been committing —— ——.

Ah! *ma chere fille*! said I, as she tripp'd by, from her matins —you look as rosy as the morning (for the sun was rising, and it made the compliment the more gracious)——No; it can't be that, quoth a fourth——(she made a curt'sy to me—I kiss'd my hand) 'tis debt; continued he: 'Tis certainly for debt; quoth a fifth; I would not pay that gentleman's debts, quoth *Ace*, for a thousand pounds; Nor would I, quoth *Size*, for six times the sum— Well thrown, *Size-Ace*, again! quoth I;—but I have no debt but the debt of NATURE, and I want but patience of her, and I will pay her every farthing I owe her——How can you be so hardhearted, MADAM, to arrest a poor traveller going along without molestation to any one, upon his lawful occasions? do stop that death-looking, long-striding scoundrel of a scare-sinner, who is posting after me——he never would have followed me but for you——if it be but for a stage, or two, just to give me start of him, I beseech you, madam —————— do, dear lady ——.

——Now, in troth, 'tis a great pity, quoth mine *Irish* host, that all this good courtship should be lost; for the young gentlewoman has been after going out of hearing of it all along——.

——Simpleton! quoth I.

——So you have nothing *else* in *Boulogne* worth seeing?

—By Jasus! there is the finest SEMINARY for the HUMANITIES——.

—There cannot be a finer; quoth I.

CHAPTER VIII

WHEN the precipitancy of a man's wishes hurries on his ideas ninety times faster than the vehicle he rides in—woe be to truth! and woe be to the vehicle and its tackling (let 'em be made of what stuff you will) upon which he breathes forth the disappointment of his soul!

As I never give general characters either of men or things in choler, "*the most haste, the worst speed,*" was all the reflection I made upon the affair, the first time it happen'd;—the second, third, fourth, and fifth time, I confined it respectively to those times, and accordingly blamed only the second, third, fourth, and fifth post-boy for it, without carrying my reflections further; but the event continuing to befall me from the fifth, to the sixth, seventh, eighth, ninth, and tenth time, and without one exception, I then could not avoid making a national reflection of it, which I do in these words:

That something is always wrong in a French post-chaise upon first setting out.

Or the proposition may stand thus:

A French postilion has always to alight before he has got three hundred yards out of town.

What's wrong now?——Diable!——a rope's broke!——a knot has slipt!——a staple's drawn!——a bolt's to whittle!——a tag, a rag, a jag, a strap, a buckle, or a buckle's tongue, want altering.——

Now true as all this is, I never think myself impower'd to excommunicate thereupon either the post-chaise, or its driver—— nor do I take it into my head to swear by the living G—, I would rather go a foot ten thousand times——or that I will be damn'd if ever I get into another——but I take the matter coolly before me, and consider, that some tag, or rag, or jag, or bolt, or buckle, or buckle's tongue, will ever be a wanting, or want altering, travel where I will——so I never chaff, but take the good and the bad as they fall in my road, and get on:——Do so, my lad! said I; he had lost five minutes already, in alighting in order to get at a luncheon of black bread which he had cramm'd into the chaise-pocket, and was remounted and going leisurely on, to relish it the better——Get on, my lad, said I, briskly—but in the most per-suasive tone imaginable, for I jingled a four and twenty sous piece against the glass, taking care to hold the flat side towards him, as he look'd back: the dog grinn'd intelligence from his right ear to his left, and behind his sooty muzzle discover'd such a pearly row of teeth, that *Sovereignty* would have pawn'd her jewels for them.——

Just heaven! { What masticators!——
{ What bread!——

and so, as he finish'd the last mouthful of it, we enter'd the town of *Montreuil*.

CHAPTER IX

THERE is not a town in all *France*, which in my opinion, looks better in the map, than MONTREUIL;——I own, it does not look so well in the book of post roads; but when you come to see it—to be sure it looks most pitifully.

There is one thing however in it at present very handsome; and that is the inn-keeper's daughter: She has been eighteen months at *Amiens*, and six at *Paris*, in going through her classes; so knits, and sews, and dances, and does the little coquetries very well.——

—A slut! in running them over within these five minutes that I have stood looking at her, she has let fall at least a dozen loops in a white thread stocking——Yes, yes—I see, you cunning gipsy!——'tis long, and taper—you need not pin it to your knee—and that 'tis your own—and fits you exactly.——

——That Nature should have told this creature a word about a *statue's thumb*!——

—But as this sample is worth all their thumbs——besides I have her thumbs and fingers in at the bargain if they can be any guide to me,—and as *Janatone* withal (for that is her name) stands so well for a drawing——may I never draw more, or rather may I draw like a draught-horse, by main strength all the days of my life,—if I do not draw her in all her proportions, and with as determin'd a pencil, as if I had her in the wettest drapery.——

—But your worships chuse rather that I give you the length, breadth, and perpendicular height of the great parish church, or a drawing of the fascade of the abbey of Saint *Austreberte* which has been transported from *Artois* hither—every thing is just I suppose as the masons and carpenters left them,—and if the belief in *Christ* continues so long, will be so these fifty years to come—so your worships and reverences, may all measure them at your leisures——but he who measures thee, *Janatone*, must do

[401]

it now—thou carriest the principles of change within thy frame; and considering the chances of a transitory life, I would not answer for thee a moment; e'er twice twelve months are pass'd and gone, thou mayest grow out like a pumkin, and lose thy shapes——or, thou mayest go off like a flower, and lose thy beauty——nay, thou mayest go off like a hussy—and lose thyself.——I would not answer for my aunt *Dinah*, was she alive—— 'faith, scarce for her picture——were it but painted by *Reynolds*—

—But if I go on with my drawing, after naming that son of *Apollo*, I'll be shot——

So you must e'en be content with the original; which if the evening is fine in passing thro' *Montreuil*, you will see at your chaise door, as you change horses; but unless you have as bad a reason for haste as I have—you had better stop:——She has a little of the *devote*: but that, Sir, is a terce to a nine in your favour——

—L— help me! I could not count a single point: so had been piqued, and repiqued, and capotted to the devil.

CHAPTER X

ALL WHICH being considered, and that *Death* moreover might be much nearer me than I imagined——I wish I was at *Abbeville*, quoth I, were it only to see how they card and spin——so off we set.

   * *de Montreuil a Nampont* - poste et demi
     de Nampont a *Bernay* - - - poste
     de *Bernay* a *Nouvion* - - - poste
     de *Nouvion* a ABBEVILLE poste

——but the carders and spinners were all gone to bed.

CHAPTER XI

WHAT a vast advantage is travelling! only it heats one; but there is a remedy for that, which you may pick out of the next chapter.

   * Vid. Book of French post-roads, page 36, edition of 1762.

CHAPTER XII

WAS I in a condition to stipulate with death, as I am this moment with my apothecary, how and where I will take his glister——I should certainly declare against submitting to it before my friends; and therefore, I never seriously think upon the mode and manner of this great catastrophe, which generally takes up and torments my thoughts as much as the catastrophe itself, but I constantly draw the curtain across it with this wish, that the *Disposer* of all things may so order it, that it happen not to me in my own house——but rather in some decent inn——at home, I know it,——the concern of my friends, and the last services of wiping my brows and smoothing my pillow, which the quivering hand of pale affection shall pay me, will so crucify my soul, that I shall die of a distemper which my physician is not aware of: but in an inn, the few cold offices I wanted, would be purchased with a few guineas, and paid me with an undisturbed, but punctual attention——but mark. This inn, should not be the inn at *Abbeville*——if there was not another inn in the universe, I would strike that inn out of the capitulation: so

Let the horses be in the chaise exactly by four in the morning ——Yes, by four, Sir,——or by *Genevieve*! I'll raise a clatter in the house, shall wake the dead.

CHAPTER XIII

"MAKE them like unto a wheel," is a bitter sarcasm, as all the learned know, against the *grand tour*, and that restless spirit for making it, which *David* prophetically foresaw would haunt the children of men in the latter days; and therefore, as thinketh the great bishop *Hall*, 'tis one of the severest imprecations which *David* ever utter'd against the enemies of the Lord—and, as if he had said, "I wish them no worse luck than always to be rolling about"—So much motion, continues he, (for he was very corpulent)—is so much unquietness; and so much of rest, by the same analogy, is so much of heaven.

Now, I (being very thin) think differently; and that so much of motion, is so much of life, and so much of joy——and that to stand still, or get on but slowly, is death and the devil——

[403]

Hollo! Ho!——the whole world's asleep!——bring out the horses——grease the wheels——tie on the mail——and drive a nail into that moulding——I'll not lose a moment——

Now the wheel we are talking of, and *whereinto* (but not *whereonto*, for that would make an *Ixion*'s wheel of it) he curseth his enemies, according to the bishop's habit of body, should certainly be a post-chaise wheel, whether they were set up in *Palestine* at that time or not——and my wheel, for the contrary reasons, must as certainly be a cart-wheel groaning round its revolution once in an age; and of which sort, were I to turn commentator, I should make no scruple to affirm, they had great store in that hilly country.

I love the *Pythagoreans* (much more than ever I dare tell my dear *Jenny*) for their "χωρισμὸν ἀπὸ του Σώματος, εἰς τὸ Καλῶς Φιλοσοφεῖν"——[their] "*getting out of the body, in order to think well.*" No man thinks right whilst he is in it; blinded, as he must be, with his congenial humours, and drawn differently aside, as the bishop and myself have been, with too lax or too tense a fibre ——REASON is, half of it, SENSE; and the measure of heaven itself is but the measure of our present appetites and concoctions——

——But which of the two, in the present case, do you think to be mostly in the wrong?

You, certainly: quoth she, to disturb a whole family so early.

CHAPTER XIV

BUT SHE did not know I was under a vow not to shave my beard till I got to *Paris*;——yet I hate to make mysteries of nothing;——'tis the cold cautiousness of one of those little souls from which *Lessius* (*lib.* 13. *de moribus divinis, cap.* 24.) hath made his estimate, wherein he setteth forth, That one *Dutch* mile, cubically multiplied, will allow room enough, and to spare, for eight hundred thousand millions, which he supposes to be as great a number of souls (counting from the fall of *Adam*) as can possibly be damn'd to the end of the world.

From what he has made this second estimate——unless from the parental goodness of God—I don't know——I am much more at a loss what could be in *Franciscus Ribbera*'s head, who pretends that no less a space than one of two hundred *Italian* miles multiplied into itself, will be sufficient to hold the like number——he certainly must have gone upon some of the old *Roman* souls, of which he had read, without reflecting how much, by a gradual and most tabid decline, in a course of eighteen hundred years, they must unavoidably have shrunk, so as to have come, when he wrote, almost to nothing.

In *Lessius*'s time, who seems the cooler man, they were as little as can be imagined——

——We find them less *now*——

And next winter we shall find them less again; so that if we go on from little to less, and from less to nothing, I hesitate not one moment to affirm, that in half a century, at this rate, we shall have no souls at all; which being the period beyond which I doubt likewise of the existence of the Christian faith, 'twill be one advantage that both of 'em will be exactly worn out together——

Blessed *Jupiter*! and blessed every other heathen god and goddess! for now ye will all come into play again, and with *Priapus* at your tails——what jovial times!——but where am I? and into what a delicious riot of things am I rushing? I——I who must be cut short in the midst of my days, and taste no more of 'em than what I borrow from my imagination——peace to thee, generous fool! and let me go on.

CHAPTER XV

—" **S** O HATING, I say, to make mysteries of *nothing*"—— I intrusted it with the post-boy, as soon as ever I got off the stones; he gave a crack with his whip to balance the compliment; and with the thill-horse trotting, and a sort of an up and a down of the other, we danced it along to *Ailly au clochers*, famed in days of yore for the finest chimes in the world; but we danced through it without music——the chimes being greatly out of order—(as in truth they were through all *France*).

And so making all possible speed, from
    Ailly au clochers, I got to *Hixcourt*, from *Hixcourt*, I got to
    Pequignay, and from *Pequignay*, I got to AMIENS,
concerning which town I have nothing to inform you, but what I have informed you once before——and that was——that *Janatone* went there to school.

CHAPTER XVI

IN THE whole catalogue of those whiffling vexations which come puffing across a man's canvas, there is not one of a more teasing and tormenting nature, than this particular one which I am going to describe——and for which, (unless you travel with an *avance-courier*, which numbers do in order to prevent it)——there is no help: and it is this.

That be you in never so kindly a propensity to sleep——tho' you are passing perhaps through the finest country—upon the best roads,—and in the easiest carriage for doing it in the world ——nay was you sure you could sleep fifty miles straight forwards, without once opening your eyes——nay what is more, was you as demonstratively satisfied as you can be of any truth in *Euclid*, that you should upon all accounts be full as well asleep as awake——nay perhaps better——Yet the incessant returns of paying for the horses at every stage,——with the necessity thereupon of putting your hand into your pocket, and counting out from thence, three livres fifteen sous (sous by sous) puts an end to so much of the project, that you cannot execute above six miles of it (or supposing it is a post and half, that is but nine) ——were it to save your soul from destruction.

——I'll be even with 'em, quoth I, for I'll put the precise sum into a piece of paper, and hold it ready in my hand all the way: "Now I shall have nothing to do" said I (composing myself to rest) "but to drop this gently into the post-boy's hat, and not say a word." ——Then there wants two sous more to drink——or there is a twelve sous piece of *Louis* XIV. which will not pass—or a livre and some odd liards to be brought over from the last stage, which Monsieur had forgot; which altercations (as a man cannot dispute very well asleep) rouse him: still is sweet sleep retrievable; and still might the flesh weigh down the spirit, and recover itself of these blows—but then, by heaven! you have paid but for a single post—whereas 'tis a post and a half; and this obliges you to pull out your book of post-roads, the print of which is so very small, it forces you to open your eyes, whether you will or no: then Monsieur *le Curè* offers you a pinch of snuff——or a poor soldier shews you his leg——or a shaveling his box——or the priestesse of the cistern will water your wheels——they do not want it——but she swears by her *priesthood* (throwing it back) that they do:——then you have all these points to argue, or consider over in your mind; in doing of which, the rational powers get so thoroughly awakened——you may get 'em to sleep again as you can.

It was entirely owing to one of these misfortunes, or I had pass'd clean by the stables of *Chantilly*——

——But the postilion first affirming, and then persisting in it to my face, that there was no mark upon the two sous piece, I open'd my eyes to be convinced—and seeing the mark upon it, as plain as my nose—I leap'd out of the chaise in a passion, and so saw everything at *Chantilly* in spite.—I tried it but for three posts and a half, but believe 'tis the best principle in the world to travel speedily upon; for as few objects look very inviting in that mood—you have little or nothing to stop you; by which means it was that I pass'd through St. *Dennis*, without turning my head so much as on side towards the Abby——

——Richness of their treasury! stuff and nonsense!—bating their jewels, which are all false, I would not give three sous for any one thing in it, but *Jaidas*'s *lantern*——nor for that either, only as it grows dark, it might be of use.

CHAPTER XVII

CRACK, crack——crack, crack——crack, crack——so this is *Paris*! quoth I (continuing in the same mood)—— and this is *Paris*!——humph!——*Paris*! cried I, repeating the name the third time——

The first, the finest, the most brilliant——

—The streets however are nasty;

But it looks, I suppose, better than it smells——crack, crack ——crack, crack——What a fuss thou makest!—as if it concern'd the good people to be inform'd, That a man with pale face, and clad in black, had the honour to be driven into *Paris* at nine o'clock at night, by a postilion in a tawny yellow jerkin turned up with red calamanco——crack, crack——crack, crack——crack, crack——I wish thy whip——

——But 'tis the spirit of thy nation; so crack—crack on.

Ha!——and no one gives the wall!——but in the School of Urbanity herself, if the walls are besh—t —how can you do otherwise?

And prithee when do they light the lamps? What?—never in

[407]

the summer months!——Ho! 'tis the time of sallads.——O rare!
sallad and soup—soup and sallad—sallad and soup, *encore*——
——'Tis *too much* for sinners.

Now I cannot bear the barbarity of it; how can that unconscionable coachman talk so much bawdy to that lean horse? don't
you see, friend, the streets are so villainously narrow, that there
is not room in all *Paris* to turn a wheel-barrow? In the grandest
city of the whole world, it would not have been amiss, if they
had been left a thought wider; nay were it only so much in every
single street, as that a man might know (was it only for satisfaction) on which side of it he was walking.

One—two—three—four—five—six—seven—eight—nine—ten.
—Ten cook's shops! and twice the number of barber's! and all
within three minutes driving! one would think that all the cooks
in the world on some great merry-meeting with the barbers, by
joint consent had said—Come, let us all go live at *Paris*: the
French love good eating——they are all *gourmands*——we shall
rank high; if their god is their belly——their cooks must be
gentlemen: and forasmuch as *the periwig maketh the man*, and the
periwig-maker maketh the periwig——*ergo*, would the barbers
say, we shall rank higher still—we shall be above you all—we
shall be * *Capitouls* at least—*pardi!* we shall all wear swords——
—And so, one would swear, (that is by candle-light,—but there
is no depending upon it) they continue to do, to this day.

CHAPTER XVIII

THE *FRENCH* are certainly misunderstood:——but
whether the fault is theirs, in not sufficienuy explaining
themselves; or speaking with that exact limitation and precision which one would expect on a point of such importance, and
which, moreover, is so likely to be contested by us——or whether
the fault may not be altogether on our side, in not understanding
their language always so critically as to know "what they would
be at"——I shall not decide; but 'tis evident to me, when they
affirm, "*That they who have seen Paris, have seen every thing,*"
they must mean to speak of those who have seen it by day-light.

As for candle-light—I give it up——I have said before, there
was no depending upon it—and I repeat it again; but not

* Chief Magistrate in *Toulouse, &c. &c. &c.*

because the lights and shades are too sharp—or the tints confounded—or that there is neither beauty or keeping, &c. . . . for
that's not truth—but it is an uncertain light in this respect, That
in all the five hundred grand Hôtels, which they number up to you
in *Paris*—and the five hundred good things, at a modest computation (for 'tis only allowing one good thing to a Hôtel) which by
candle-light are best to be *seen, felt, heard and understood* (which,
by the bye is a quotation from *Lilly*)——the devil a one of us out
of fifty, can get our heads fairly thrust in amongst them.

This is no part of the *French* computation: 'tis simply this.

That by the last survey taken in the year one thousand seven
hundred and sixteen, since which time there have been considerable augmentations, *Paris* doth contain nine hundred streets;
(*viz.*)

In the quarter called the *City*—there are fifty three streets.

In St. *James* of the Shambles, fifty five streets.

In St. *Oportune*, thirty four streets.

In the quarter of the *Louvre*, twenty five streets.

In the *Palace Royal*, or St. *Honorius*, forty nine streets.

In *Mont. Martyr*, forty one streets.

In St. *Eustace*, twenty nine streets.

In the *Halles*, twenty seven streets.

In St. *Dennis*, fifty five streets.

In St. *Martin*, fifty four streets.

In St. *Paul*, or the *Mortellerie*, twenty seven streets.

The *Greve*, thirty eight streets.

In St. *Avoy*, or the *Verrerie*, nineteen streets.

In the *Marais*, or the *Temple*, fifty two streets.

In St. *Antony*'s, sixty eight streets.

In the *Place Maubert*, eighty one streets.

In St. *Bennet*, sixty streets.

In St. *Andrews de Arcs*, fifty one streets.

In the quarter of the *Luxembourg*, sixty two streets.

And in that of St. *Germain*, fifty five streets, into any of which you
may walk; and that when you have seen them with all that belongs
to them, fairly by day-light—their gates, their bridges, their
squares, their statues——and have crusaded it moreover
through all their parish churches, by no means omitting St. *Roche*
and *Sulplice*——and to crown all, have taken a walk to the four
palaces, which you may see either with or without the statues and
pictures, just as you chuse—

——Then you will have seen——

————but, 'tis what no one needeth to tell you, for you will read it yourself upon the portico of the *Louvre*, in these words,

   * EARTH NO SUCH FOLKS!—NO FOLKS E'ER SUCH A TOWN
AS PARIS IS!—SING, DERRY, DERRY, DOWN.

The *French* have a *gay* way of treating every thing that is Great; and that is all can be said upon it.

CHAPTER XIX

IN MENTIONING the word *gay* (as in the close of the last chapter) it puts one (*i.e.* an author) in mind of the word *spleen* ————especially if he has any thing to say upon it: not that by any analysis—or that from any table of interest or genealogy, there appears much more ground of alliance betwixt them, than betwixt light and darkness, or any two of the most unfriendly opposites in nature————only 'tis an undercraft of authors to keep up a good understanding amongst words, as politicians do amongst men—not knowing how near they may be under a necessity of placing them to each other—which point being now gain'd, and that I may place mine exactly to my mind, I write it down here—

SPLEEN

This, upon leaving *Chantilly*, I declared to be the best principle in the world to travel speedily upon; but I gave it only as matter of opinion, I still continue in the same sentiments—only I had not then experience enough of its working to add this, that though you do get on at a tearing rate, yet you get on but uneasily to yourself at the same time; for which reason I here quit it entirely, and for ever, and 'tis heartily at one's service—it has spoiled me the digestion of a good supper, and brought on a bilious diarrhæa, which has brought me back again to my first principle on which I set out————and with which I shall now scamper it away to the banks of the *Garonne*.

————No;————I cannot stop a moment to give you the character of the people—their genius—their manners—their customs—their laws—their religion—their government—their manufactures—their commerce—their finances, with all the resources and hidden springs which sustain them: qualified as I may be, by

* Non Orbis gentem, non urbem gens habet ullam
————————ulla parem.

spending three days and two nights amongst them, and during all that time, making these things the entire subject of my enquiries and reflections——

Still—still I must away——the roads are paved—the posts are short—the days are long—'tis no more than noon—I shall be at *Fontainbleau* before the king——

—Was he going there? not that I know——

CHAPTER XX

NOW I hate to hear a person, especially if he be a traveller, complain that we do not get on so fast in *France* as we do in *England*; whereas we get on much faster, *consideratis, considerandis*; thereby always meaning, that if you weigh their vehicles with the mountains of baggage which you lay both before and behind upon them—and then consider their puny horses, with the very little they give them—'tis a wonder they get on at all: their suffering is most unchristian, and 'tis evident thereupon to me, that a *French* post-horse would not know what in the world to do, was it not for the two words * * * * * * and * * * * * * in which there is as much sustenance, as if you gave him a peck of corn: now as these words cost nothing, I long from my soul to tell the reader what they are; but here is the question—they must be told him plainly, and with most distinct articulation, or it will answer no end—and yet to do it in that plain way—though their reverences may laugh at it in the bed-chamber—full well I wot, they will abuse it in the parlour: for which cause, I have been volving and revolving in my fancy some time, but to no purpose, by what clean device or facete contrivance I might so modulate them, that whilst I satisfy *that ear* which the reader chuses to *lend* me—I might not dissatisfy the other which he keeps to himself.

——My ink burns my finger to try——and when I have—— 'twill have a worse consequence——it will burn (I fear) my paper.

——No;——I dare not——

But if you wish to know how the *abbess* of *Andoüillets*, and a novice of her convent got over the difficulty (only first wishing myself all imaginable success)—I'll tell you without the least scruple.

CHAPTER XXI

THE ABBESS of *Andoüillets*, which if you look into the large set of provincial maps now publishing at *Paris*, you will find situated amongst the hills which divide *Burgundy* from *Savoy*, being in danger of an *Anchylosis* or stiff joint (the *sinovia* of her knee becoming hard by long matins) and having tried every remedy——first, prayers and thanksgiving; then invocations to all the saints in heaven promiscuously——then particularly to every saint who had ever had a stiff leg before her—— then touching it with all the reliques of the convent, principally with the thigh-bone of the man of *Lystra*, who had been impotent from his youth——then wrapping it up in her veil when she went to bed——then cross-wise her rosary——then bringing in to her aid the secular arm, and anointing it with oils and hot fat of animals——then treating it with emollient and resolving fomentations——then with poultices of marsh-mallows, mallows, bonus Henricus, white lillies and fenugreek——then taking the woods, I mean the smoak of 'em, holding her scapulary across her lap ——then decoctions of wild chicory, water cresses, chervil, sweet cecily and cochlearia——and nothing all this while answering, was prevailed on at last to try the hot baths of *Bourbon*——so having first obtain'd leave of the visitor-general to take care of her existence—she ordered all to be got ready for her journey: a novice of the convent of about seventeen, who had been troubled with a whitloe in her middle finger, by sticking it constantly into the abbess's cast poultices, &c.—had gained such an interest, that overlooking a sciatical old nun, who might have been set up for ever by the hot baths of *Bourbon, Margarita*, the little novice, was elected as the companion of the journey.

An old calesh, belonging to the abbess, lined with green frize, was ordered to be drawn out into the sun—the gardener of the convent being chosen muleteer, led out the two old mules to clip the hair from the rump-ends of their tails, whilst a couple of lay-sisters were busied, the one in darning the lining, and the other in sewing on the shreds of yellow binding, which the teeth of time had unravelled——the under-gardener dress'd the muleteer's hat in hot wine-lees——and a taylor sat musically at it, in a shed over against the convent, in assorting four dozen of bells for the harness, whistling to each bell as he tied it on with a thong——

——The carpenter and the smith of *Andoüillets* held a council of wheels; and by seven, the morning after, all look'd spruce, and was ready at the gate of the convent for the hot-baths of *Bourbon* —two rows of the unfortunate stood ready there an hour before.

The abbess of *Andoüillets*, supported by *Margarita* the novice, advanced slowly to the calesh, both clad in white, with their black rosaries hanging at their breasts——

——There was a simple solemnity in the contrast: they entered the calesh; the nuns in the same uniform, sweet emblem of innocence, each occupied a window, and as the abbess and *Margarita* look'd up—each (the sciatical poor nun excepted)—each stream'd out the end of her veil in the air—then kiss'd the lily hand which let it go: the good abbess and *Margarita* laid their hands saint-wise upon their breasts—look'd up to heaven—then to them— and look'd "God bless you, dear sisters."

I declare I am interested in this story, and wish I had been there.

The gardener, who I shall now call the muleteer, was a little, hearty, broadset, good-natured, chattering, toping kind of a fellow, who troubled his head very little with the *hows* and *whens* of life; so had mortgaged a month of his conventical wages in a borrachio, or leathern cask of wine, which he had disposed behind the calesh, with a large russet coloured riding coat over it, to guard it from the sun; and as the weather was hot, and he, not a niggard of his labours, walking ten times more than he rode— he found more occasions than those of nature, to fall back to the rear of his carriage; till by frequent coming and going, it had so happen'd, that all his wine had leak'd out at the *legal* vent of the borrachio, before one half of the journey was finish'd.

Man is a creature born to habitudes. The day had been sultry —the evening was delicious—the wine was generous—the *Burgundian* hill on which it grew was steep—a little tempting bush over the door of a cool cottage at the foot of it, hung vibrating in full harmony with the passions—a gentle air rustled distinctly through the leaves—"Come—come, thirsty muleteer—come in."

——The muleteer was a son of *Adam*. I need not say one word more. He gave the mules, each of 'em, a sound lash, and looking in the abbess's and *Margarita*'s faces (as he did it)—as much as to say, "here I am"—he gave a second good crack—as much as to say to his mules, "get on"——so slinking behind, he enter'd the little inn at the foot of the hill.

The muleteer, as I told you, was a little, joyous, chirping fellow, who thought not of to-morrow, nor of what had gone before, or what was to follow it, provided he got but his scantling of *Bur-*

[413]

gundy, and a little chit-chat along with it; so entering into a long conversation, as how he was chief gardener to the convent of *Andoüillets*, *&c. &c.* and out of friendship for the abbess and Mademoiselle *Margarita*, who was only in her noviciate, he had come along with them from the confines of *Savoy*, *&c.—&c.—* and as how she had got a white swelling by her devotions——and what a nation of herbs he had procured to mollify her humours, *&c. &c.* and that if the waters of *Bourbon* did not mend that leg— she might as well be lame of both—*&c. &c. &c.*—He so contrived his story as absolutely to forget the heroine of it—and with her, the little novice, and what was a more ticklish point to be forgot than both—the two mules; who being creatures that take advantage of the world, inasmuch as their parents took it of them—and they not being in a condition to return the obligation *downwards* (as men and women and beasts are)—they do it side-ways, and long-ways, and back-ways—and up hill, and down hill, and which way they can.——Philosophers, with all their ethics, have never considered this rightly—how should the poor muleteer then, in his cups, consider it at all? he did not in the least—'tis time we do; let us leave him then in the vortex of his element, the happiest and most thoughtless of mortal men——and for a moment let us look after the mules, the abbess, and *Margarita*.

By virtue of the muleteer's two last strokes, the mules had gone quietly on, following their own consciences up the hill, till they had conquer'd about one half of it; when the elder of them, a shrewd crafty old devil, at the turn of an angle, giving a side glance, and no muleteer behind them——

By my fig! said she, swearing, I'll go no further——And if I do, replied the other—they shall make a drum of my hide.——

And so with one consent they stopp'd thus——

CHAPTER XXII

—GET ON with you, said the abbess.
——Wh——ysh——ysh——cried *Margarita*.
Sh——a——shu - u——shu——u—sh——aw—— shaw'd the abbess.

——Whu—v—w——whew—w—w—whuv'd *Margarita*, pursing up her sweet lips betwixt a hoot and a whistle.

Thump—thump—thump—obstreperated the abbess of *An-*

doüillets with the end of her gold-headed cane against the bottom
of the calesh——
——The old mule let a f—

CHAPTER XXIII

WE ARE ruin'd and undone, my child, said the abbess to
Margarita——we shall be here all night——we shall be
plunder'd——we shall be ravish'd——
——We shall be ravish'd, said *Margarita*, as sure as a gun.
Sancta Maria! cried the abbess (forgetting the O!)—why was
I govern'd by this wicked stiff joint? why did I leave the convent
of *Andoüillets*? and why didst thou not suffer thy servant to go
unpolluted to her tomb?
O my finger! my finger! cried the novice, catching fire at the
word *servant*—why was I not content to put it here, or there, any
where rather than be in this strait?
——Strait! said the abbess.
Strait——said the novice; for terrour had struck their understandings——the one knew not what she said——the other what
she answer'd.
O my virginity! virginity! cried the abbess.
——inity!——inity! said the novice, sobbing.

CHAPTER XXIV

MY DEAR mother, quoth the novice, coming a little to
herself,——there are two certain words, which I have
been told will force any horse, or ass, or mule, to go up
a hill whether he will or no; be he never so obstinate or ill-
will'd, the moment he hears them utter'd, he obeys. They are
words magic! cried the abbess, in the utmost horrour—No; replied
Margarita calmly—but they are words sinful—What are they?
quoth the abbess, interrupting her: They are sinful in the first
degree, answered *Margarita*,—they are mortal—and if we are
ravish'd and die unabsolved of them, we shall both——but you
may pronounce them to me, quoth the abbess of *Andoüillets*——
They cannot, my dear mother, said the novice, be pronounced at
all; they will make all the blood in one's body fly up into one's
face——But you may whisper them in my ear, quoth the abbess.

[415]

Heaven! hadst thou no guardian angel to delegate to the inn at the bottom of the hill? was there no generous and friendly spirit unemploy'd——no agent in nature, by some monitory shivering, creeping along the artery which led to his heart, to rouze the muleteer from his banquet?——no sweet minstrelsy to bring back the fair idea of the abbess and *Margarita*, with their black rosaries!

Rouse! rouse!——but 'tis too late—the horrid words are pronounced this moment——

——and how to tell them——Ye, who can speak of every thing existing, with unpolluted lips——instruct me——guide me——

CHAPTER XXV

ALL SINS whatever, quoth the abbess, turning casuist in the distress they were under, are held by the confessor of our convent to be either mortal or venial: there is no further division. Now a venial sin being the slightest and least of all sins,—being halved—by taking, either only the half of it, and leaving the rest—or, by taking it all, and amicably halving it betwixt yourself and another person—in course becomes diluted into no sin at all.

Now I see no sin in saying, *bou, bou, bou, bou, bou,* a hundred times together; nor is there any turpitude in pronouncing the syllable *ger, ger, ger, ger, ger,* were it from our matins to our vespers: Therefore, my dear daughter, continued the abbess of *Andoüillets*—I will say *bou*, and thou shalt say *ger* ; and then alternately, as there is no more sin in *fou* then in *bou*—Thou shalt say *fou*—and I will come in (like fa, sol, la, re, mi, ut, at our complines) with *ter*. And accordingly the abbess, giving the pitch note, set off thus:

> Abbess, ⎱ Bou—bou—bou—
> *Margarita,* ⎰ ——ger,—ger,—ger
> *Margarita,* ⎱ Fou—fou—fou—
> Abbess, ⎰ ——ter,—ter,—ter.

The two mules acknowledged the notes by a mutual lash of their tails; but it went no further.——'Twill answer by an' by, said the novice.

> Abbess, ⎱ Bou- bou- bou- bou- bou- bou-
> *Margarita,* ⎰ —ger, ger, ger, ger, ger, ger,

Quicker still, cried *Margarita*.

Fou, fou, fou, fou, fou fou, fou, fou, fou.

Quicker still, cried *Margarita*.

Bou, bou, bou, bou, bou, bou, bou, bou, bou.

Quicker still—God preserve me! said the abbess—They do not understand us, cried *Margarita*—But the Devil does, said the abbess of *Andoüillets*.

CHAPTER XXVI

WHAT a tract of country have I run!—how many degrees nearer to the warm sun am I advanced, and how many fair and goodly cities have I seen, during the time you have been reading, and reflecting, Madam, upon this story! There's FONTAINBLEAU, and SENS, and JOIGNY, and AUXERRE, and DIJON the capital of *Burgundy*, and CHALLON, and MÂCON the capital of the *Mâconese*, and a score more upon the road to LYONS——and now I have run them over——I might as well talk to you of so many market-towns in the moon, as tell you one word about them: it will be this chapter at the least, if not both this and the next entirely lost, do what I will——

—Why, 'tis a strange story! *Tristram*.

——Alas! Madam, had it been upon some melancholy lecture of the cross—the peace of meekness, or the contentment of resignation——I had not been incommoded: or had I thought of writing it upon the purer abstractions of the soul, and that food of wisdom, and holiness, and contemplation, upon which the spirit of man (when separated from the body) is to subsist for ever——You would have come with a better appetite from it——

——I wish I never had wrote it: but as I never blot any thing out——let us use some honest means to get it out of our heads directly.

——Pray reach me my fool's cap——I fear you sit upon it, Madam——'tis under the cushion——I'll put it on——

Bless me! you have had it upon your head this half hour.—— There then let it stay, with a

> Fa-ra diddle di
> and a fa-ri diddle d
> and a high-dum—dye-dum
> fiddle——dumb - c.

And now, Madam, we may venture, I hope, a little to go on.

CHAPTER XXVII

——ALL YOU need say of *Fontainbleau* (in case you are ask'd) is, that it stands about forty miles (south *something*) from *Paris*, in the middle of a large forest——That there is something great in it——That the king goes there once, every two or three years, with his whole court, for the pleasure of the chase—and that during that carnival of sporting, any *English* gentleman of fashion (you need not forget yourself) may be accommodated with a nag or two, to partake of the sport, taking care only not to out-gallop the king——

Though there are two reasons why you need not talk loud of this to every one.

First, Because 'twill make the said nags the harder to be got; and

Secondly, 'Tis not a word of it true.——*Allons!*

As for SENS——you may dispatch it in a word————"'*Tis an archiepiscopal see.*"

——For JOIGNY—the less, I think, one says of it, the better.

But for AUXERRE—I could go on for ever: for in my *grand tour* through *Europe*, in which, after all, my father (not caring to trust me with any one) attended me himself, with my uncle *Toby*, and *Trim*, and *Obadiah*, and indeed most of the family, except my mother, who being taken up with a project of knitting my father a pair of large worsted breeches—(the thing is common sense)— and she not caring to be put out of her way, she staid at home at SHANDY-HALL, to keep things right during the expedition; in which, I say, my father stopping us two days at *Auxerre*, and his researches being ever of such a nature, that they would have found fruit even in a desert——he has left me enough to say upon AUXERRE: in short, wherever my father went——but 'twas more remarkably so, in this journey through *France* and *Italy*, than in any other stages of his life——his road seemed to lie so much on one side of that, wherein all other travellers had gone before him —he saw kings and courts and silks of all colours, in such strange lights——and his remarks and reasonings upon the characters, the manners and customs of the countries we pass'd over, were so opposite to those of all other mortal men, particularly those of my uncle *Toby* and *Trim*—(to say nothing of myself)—and to crown all—the occurrences and scrapes which we were perpetually meeting and getting into, in consequence of his systems and opiniatry—they were of so odd, so mixed and tragicomical a con-

[418]

texture—That the whole put together, it appears of so different a shade and tint from any tour of *Europe*, which was ever executed—That I will venture to pronounce—the fault must be mine and mine only—if it be not read by all travellers and travel-readers, till travelling is no more,—or which comes to the same point—till the world, finally, takes it into it's head to stand still.—

——But this rich bale is not to be open'd now; except a small thread or two of it, merely to unravel the mystery of my father's stay at AUXERRE.

——As I have mentioned it—'tis too slight to be kept suspended; and when 'tis wove in, there's an end of it.

We'll go, brother *Toby*, said my father, whilst dinner is coddling—to the abby of Saint *Germain*, if it be only to see these bodies, of which Monsieur *Sequier* has given such a recommendation.——I'll go see any body; quoth my uncle *Toby*; for he was all compliance thro' every step of the journey——Defend me! said my father—they are all mummies——Then one need not shave; quoth my uncle *Toby*——Shave! no—cried my father—'twill be more like relations to go with our beards on—So out we sallied, the corporal lending his master his arm, and bringing up the rear, to the abby of Saint *Germain*.

Every thing is very fine, and very rich, and very superb, and very magnificent, said my father, addressing himself to the sacristan, who was a young brother of the order of *Benedictines*—but our curiosity has led us to see the bodies, of which Monsieur *Sequier* has given the world so exact a description.—The sacristan made a bow, and lighting a torch first, which he had always in the vestry ready for the purpose, he led us into the tomb of St. *Heribald*——This, said the sacristan, laying his hand upon the tomb, was a renowned prince of the house of *Bavaria*, who under the successive reigns of *Charlemagne*, *Louis le Debonair*, and *Charles the Bald*, bore a great sway in the government, and had a principal hand in bringing every thing into order and discipline——

Then he has been as great, said my uncle, in the field, as in the cabinet——I dare say he has been a gallant soldier—He was a monk—said the sacristan.

My uncle *Toby* and *Trim* sought comfort in each others faces—but found it not: my father clapp'd both his hands upon his codpiece, which was a way he had when any thing hugely tickled him; for though he hated a monk and the very smell of a monk worse

[419]

than all the devils in hell——Yet the shot hitting my uncle *Toby* and *Trim* so much harder than him, 'twas a relative triumph; and put him into the gayest humour in the world.

——And pray what do you call this gentleman? quoth my father, rather sportingly: This tomb, said the young *Benedictine*, looking downwards, contains the bones of Saint MAXIMA, who came from *Ravenna* on purpose to touch the body——

——Of Saint MAXIMUS, said my father, popping in with his saint before him—they were two of the greatest saints in the whole martyrology, added my father——Excuse me, said the sacristan——'twas to touch the bones of Saint *Germain* the builder of the abby —— And what did she get by it? said my uncle *Toby* ——What does any woman get by it? said my father—— MARTYRDOME; replied the young *Benedictine*, making a bow down to the ground, and uttering the word with so humble, but decisive a cadence, it disarmed my father for a moment. 'Tis supposed, continued the *Benedictine*, that St. *Maxima* has lain in this tomb four hundred years, and two hundred before her canonization——'Tis but a slow rise, brother *Toby*, quoth my father, in this self same army of martyrs.——A desperate slow one, an' please your honour, said *Trim*, unless one could purchase ——I should rather sell out entirely, quoth my uncle *Toby*—— I am pretty much of your opinion, brother *Toby*, said my father.

——Poor St. *Maxima*! said my uncle *Toby* low to himself, as we turn'd from her tomb: She was one of the fairest and most beautiful ladies either of *Italy* or *France*, continued the sacrist ——But who the duce has got lain down here, besides her, quoth my father, pointing with his cane to a large tomb as we walked on ——It is Saint *Optat*, Sir, answered the sacristan——And properly is Saint *Optat* plac'd! said my father: And what is Saint *Optat*'s story? continued he, Saint *Optat*, replied the sacristan, was a bishop——

——I thought so, by heaven! cried my father, interrupting him ——Saint *Optat*!——how should Saint *Optat* fail? so snatching out his pocket-book, and the young *Benedictine* holding him the torch as he wrote, he set it down as a new prop to his system of christian names, and I will be bold to say, so disinterested was he in the search of truth, that had he found a treasure in St. *Optat*'s tomb, it would not have made him half so rich: 'Twas as successful a short visit as ever was paid to the dead; and so highly was his fancy pleas'd with all that had passed in it,—that he determined at once to stay another day in *Auxerre*.

[420]

—I'll see the rest of these good gentry to-morrow, said my father, as we cross'd over the square—And while you are paying that visit, brother *Shandy*, quoth my uncle *Toby*—the corporal and I will mount the ramparts.

CHAPTER XXVIII

—NOW THIS is the most puzzled skein of all—for in this last chapter, as far at least as it has help'd me through *Auxerre*, I have been getting forwards in two different journies together, and with the same dash of the pen—for I have got entirely out of *Auxerre* in this journey which I am writing now, and I am got half way out of *Auxerre* in that which I shall write hereafter——There is but a certain degree of perfection in every thing; and by pushing at something beyond that, I have brought myself into such a situation, as no traveller ever stood before me; for I am this moment walking across the market-place of *Auxerre* with my father and my uncle *Toby*, in our way back to dinner—and I am this moment also entering *Lyons* with my postchaise broke into a thousand pieces—and I am moreover this moment in a handsome pavillion built by *Pringello**, upon the banks of the *Garonne*, which Mons. *Sligniac* has lent me, and where I now sit rhapsodizing all these affairs.

——Let me collect myself, and pursue my journey.

CHAPTER XXIX

I AM GLAD of it, said I, settling the account with myself as I walk'd into *Lyons*——my chaise being all laid higgledy-piggledy with my baggage in a cart, which was moving slowly before me——I am heartily glad, said I, that 'tis all broke to pieces; for now I can go directly by water to *Avignon*, which will carry me on a hundred and twenty miles of my journey, and not cost me seven livres——and from thence, continued I, bringing forwards the account, I can hire a couple of mules—or asses, if

---

* The same Don *Pringello*, the celebrated *Spanish* architect, of whom my cousin *Antony* has made such honourable mention in a scholium to the Tale inscribed to his name.   Vide. p. 129, small edit.

I like, (for no body knows me) and cross the plains of *Languedoc*, for almost nothing——I shall gain four hundred livres by the misfortune, clear into my purse; and pleasure! worth—worth double the money by it. With what velocity, continued I, clapping my two hands together, shall I fly down the rapid *Rhône*, with the VIVARES on my right-hand, and DAUPHINY on my left, scarce seeing the ancient cities of *Vienne, Valence,* and *Vivieres.* What a flame will it rekindle in the lamp, to snatch a blushing grape from the *Hermitage* and *Cotê roti,* as I shoot by the foot of them? and what a fresh spring in the blood! to behold upon the banks advancing and retiring, the castles of romance, whence courteous knights have whilome rescued the distress'd——and see vertiginous, the rocks, the mountains, the cataracts, and all the hurry which Nature is in with all her great works about her——

As I went on thus, methought my chaise, the wreck of which look'd stately enough at the first, insensibly grew less and less in its size; the freshness of the painting was no more—the gilding lost its lustre—and the whole affair appeared so poor in my eyes —so sorry!—so contemptible! and, in a word, so much worse than the abbess of *Andoüillets* itself—that I was just opening my mouth to give it to the devil—when a pert vamping chaise-undertaker, stepping nimbly across the street, demanded if Monsieur would have his chaise refitted——No, no, said I, shaking my head sideways—Would Monsieur choose to sell it? rejoin'd the undertaker—With all my soul, said I—the iron work is worth forty livres—and the glasses worth forty more—and the leather you may take to live on.

—What a mine of wealth, quoth I, as he counted me the money, has this post chaise brought me in? And this is my usual method of book-keeping, at least with the disasters of life—making a penny of every one of 'em as they happen to me——

——Do, my dear *Jenny,* tell the world for me, how I behaved under one, the most oppressive of its kind which could befall me as a man, proud, as he ought to be, of his manhood——

'Tis enough, said'st thou, coming close up to me, as I stood with my garters in my hand, reflecting upon what had *not* pass'd ——'Tis enough, *Tristram,* and I am satisfied, said'st thou, whispering these words in my ear, **** ** **** *** ******;— **** ** ****——any other man would have sunk down to the center——

—Every thing is good for something, quoth I.

——I'll go into *Wales* for six weeks, and drink goat's-whey—
and I'll gain seven years longer life for the accident. For which
reason I think myself inexcusable, for blaming Fortune so often
as I have done, for pelting me all my life long, like an ungracious
dutchess, as I call'd her, with so many small evils: surely if I have
any cause to be angry with her, 'tis that she has not sent me great
ones—a score of good cursed, bouncing losses, would have been
as good as a pension to me.

——One of a hundred a year, or so, is all I wish—I would not
be at the plague of paying land tax for a larger.

CHAPTER XXX

TO THOSE who call vexations, VEXATIONS, as knowing what
they are, there could not be a greater, than to be the best
part of a day in *Lyons*, the most opulent and flourishing city
in *France*, enriched with the most fragments of antiquity—and
not be able to see it. To be withheld upon *any* account, must be
a vexation; but to be withheld *by* a vexation——must certainly
be, what philosophy justly calls

VEXATION
upon
VEXATION.

I had got my two dishes of milk coffee (which by the bye is
excellently good for a consumption, but you must boil the milk
and coffee together—otherwise 'tis only coffee and milk)—and
as it was no more than eight in the morning, and the boat did not
go off till noon, I had time to see enough of *Lyons* to tire the patience of all the friends I had in the world with it. I will take a walk
to the cathedral, said I, looking at my list, and see the wonderful
mechanism of this great clock of *Lippius* of *Basil*, in the first
place——
Now, of all things in the world, I understand the least of
mechanism——I have neither genius, or taste, or fancy—and
have a brain so entirely unapt for every thing of that kind, that
I solemnly declare I was never yet able to comprehend the principles of motion of a squirrel cage, or a common knife-grinder's
wheel—tho' I have many an hour of my life look'd up with great
devotion at the one—and stood by with as much patience as any
christian ever could do, at the other——

I'll go see the surprising movements of this great clock, said I, the very first thing I do: and then I will pay a visit to the great library of the *Jesuits*, and procure, if possible, a sight of the thirty volumes of the general history of *China*, wrote (not in the *Tartarian*) but in the *Chinese* language, and in the *Chinese* character too.

Now I almost know as little of the *Chinese* language, as I do of the mechanism of *Lippius*'s clock-work; so, why these should have jostled themselves into the two first articles of my list—— I leave to the curious as a problem of Nature. I own it looks like one of her ladyship's obliquities; and they who court her, are interested in finding out her humour as much as I.

When these curiosities are seen, quoth I, half addressing myself to my *valet de place*, who stood behind me——'twill be no hurt if WE go to the church of St. *Ireneus*, and see the pillar to which *Christ* was tied——and after that, the house where *Pontius Pilate* lived——'Twas at the next town, said the *valet de place*—at *Vienne*; I am glad of it, said I, rising briskly from my chair, and walking across the room with strides twice as long as my usual pace—— "for so much the sooner shall I be at the *Tomb of the two lovers*."

What was the cause of this movement, and why I took such long strides in uttering this——I might leave to the curious too; but as no principle of clock-work is concern'd in it——'twill be as well for the reader if I explain it myself.

CHAPTER XXXI

O! THERE is a sweet æra in the life of man, when, (the brain being tender and fibrillous, and more like pap than any thing else)——a story read of two fond lovers, separated from each other by cruel parents, and by still more cruel destiny——

Amandus——He

Amanda——She——

each ignorant of the other's course,

He——east

She——west

Amandus taken captive by the *Turks*, and carried to the emperor of *Morocco*'s court, where the princess of *Morocco* falling in love with him, keeps him twenty years in prison, for the love of his *Amanda*——

She—(*Amanda*) all the time wandering barefoot, and with dis-

hevell'd hair, o'er rocks and mountains enquiring for *Amandus*——
——*Amandus! Amandus!*— making every hill and valley to echo
back his name——

Amandus! Amandus!

at every town and city sitting down forlorn at the gate—Has
Amandus!—has my *Amandus* enter'd?——till,——going round,
and round, and round the world——chance unexpected bringing
them at the same moment of the night, though by different ways,
to the gate of *Lyons* their native city, and each in well known
accents calling out aloud,

Is *Amandus* } still alive?
Is my *Amanda* }

they fly into each others arms, and both drop down dead for joy.

There is a soft æra in every gentle mortal's life, where such
a story affords more *pabulum* to the brain, than all the *Frusts*, and
Crusts, and *Rusts* of antiquity, which travellers can cook up for it.

——'Twas all that stuck on the right side of the cullender in my
own, of what *Spon* and others, in their accounts of *Lyons*, had
strained into it; and finding, moreover, in some Itinerary, but in
what God knows——That sacred to the fidelity of *Amandus* and
Amanda, a tomb was built without the gates, where to this hour,
lovers call'd upon them to attest their truths,——I never could
get into a scrape of that kind in my life, but this *tomb of the lovers*
would, some how or other, come in at the close——nay such
a kind of empire had it establish'd over me, that I could seldom
think or speak of *Lyons*—and sometimes not so much as see even
a *Lyons-waistcoat*, but this remnant of antiquity would present
itself to my fancy; and I have often said in my wild way of running on——tho' I fear with some irreverence——"I thought this
shrine (neglected as it was) as valuable as that of *Mecca*, and so
little short, except in wealth, of the *Santa Casa* itself, that some
time or other, I would go a pilgrimage (though I had no other
business at *Lyons*) on purpose to pay it a visit.

In my list, therefore, of *Videnda* at *Lyons*, this, tho' *last*—was
not, you see, *least*; so taking a dozen or two of longer strides than
usual across my room, just whilst it passed my brain, I walked
down calmly into the *Basse Cour*, in order to sally forth; and having called for my bill—as it was uncertain whether I should return
to my inn, I had paid it——had moreover given the maid ten sous,
and was just receiving the dernier compliments of Monsieur *Le
Blanc*, for a pleasant voyage down the *Rhône*——when I was
stopped at the gate——

[425]

CHAPTER XXXII

—'TWAS BY a poor ass who had just turned in with a couple of large panniers upon his back, to collect eleemosunary turnip tops and cabbage leaves; and stood dubious, with his two forefeet on the inside of the threshold, and with his two hinder feet towards the street, as not knowing very well whether he was to go in, or no.

Now, 'tis an animal (be in what hurry I may) I cannot bear to strike——there is a patient endurance of sufferings, wrote so unaffectedly in his looks and carriage, which pleads so mightily for him, that it always disarms me; and to that degree, that I do not like to speak unkindly to him: on the contrary, meet him where I will—whether in town or country—in cart or under panniers—whether in liberty or bondage——I have ever something civil to say to him on my part; and as one word begets another (if he has as little to do as I)——I generally fall into conversation with him; and surely never is my imagination so busy as in framing his responses from the etchings of his countenance—and where those carry me not deep enough——in flying from my own heart into his, and seeing what is natural for an ass to think—as well as a man, upon the occasion. In truth, it is the only creature of all the classes of beings below me, with whom I can do this: for parrots, jackdaws, &c.——I never exchange a word with them ——nor with the apes, &c. for pretty near the same reason; they act by rote, as the others speak by it, and equally make me silent: nay my dog and my cat, though I value them both——(and for my dog he would speak if he could)—yet some how or other, they neither of them possess the talents for conversation——I can make nothing of a discourse with them, beyond the *proposition*, the *reply*, and *rejoinder*, which terminated my father's and my mother's conversations, in his beds of justice——and those utter'd—there's an end of the dialogue——

—But with an ass, I can commune for ever.

Come *Honesty*! said I,—seeing it was impracticable to pass betwixt him and the gate——art thou for coming in, or going out?

The ass twisted his head round to look up the street——

Well—replied I—we'll wait a minute for thy driver:

——He turned his head thoughtful about, and looked wistfully the opposite way——

I understand thee perfectly; answered I——if thou takest a

wrong step in this affair, he will cudgel thee to death——Well! a minute is but a minute, and if it saves a fellow creature a drubbing, it shall not be set down as ill-spent.

He was eating the stem of an artichoke as this discourse went on, and in the little peevish contentions of nature betwixt hunger and unsavouriness, had dropt it out of his mouth half a dozen times, and pick'd it up again——God help thee, Jack! said I, thou hast a bitter breakfast on't—and many a bitter day's labour—and many a bitter blow, I fear, for its wages——'tis all—all bitterness to thee, whatever life is to others.——And now thy mouth, if one knew the truth of it, is as bitter, I dare say, as soot—(for he had cast aside the stem) and thou hast not a friend perhaps in all this world, that will give thee a macaroon.——In saying this, I pull'd out a paper of 'em, which I had just purchased, and gave him one—and at this moment that I am telling it, my heart smites me, that there was more of pleasantry in the conceit, of seeing *how* an ass would eat a macaroon——than of benevolence in giving him one, which presided in the act.

When the ass had eaten his macaroon, I press'd him to come in ——the poor beast was heavy loaded——his legs seem'd to tremble under him——he hung rather backwards, and as I pull'd at his halter, it broke short in my hand——he look'd up pensive in my face—"Don't thrash me with it—but if you will, you may" ——If I do, said I, I'll be d——d.

The word was but one half of it pronounced, like the abbess of *Andoüillets*—(so there was no sin in it)—when a person coming in, let fall a thundering bastinado upon the poor devil's crupper, which put an end to the ceremony.

Out upon it!

cried I——but the interjection was equivocal——and, I think wrong placed too—for the end of an osier which had started out from the contexture of the ass's pannier, had caught hold of my breeches pocket as he rush'd by me, and rent it in the most disasterous direction you can imagine——so that the

Out upon it! in my opinion, should have come in here——but this I leave to be settled by

The
REVIEWERS
of
MY BREECHES.

which I have brought over along with me for that purpose.

[427]

CHAPTER XXXIII

W HEN all was set to rights, I came down stairs again into the *basse cour* with my *valet de place*, in order to sally out towards the tomb of the two lovers, &c.—and was a second time stopp'd at the gate——not by the ass—but by the person who struck him; and who, by that time, had taken possession (as is not uncommon after a defeat) of the very spot of ground where the ass stood.

It was a commissary sent to me from the post-office, with a rescript in his hand for the payment of some six livres odd sous.

Upon what account? said I.——'Tis upon the part of the king, replied the commissary, heaving up both his shoulders——

——My good friend, quoth I——as sure as I am I—and you are you——

——And who are you? said he.———Don't puzzle me; said I.

CHAPTER XXXIV

—B UT IT is an indubitable verity, continued I, addressing myself to the commissary, changing only the form of my asseveration——that I owe the king of *France* nothing but my good-will; for he is a very honest man, and I wish him all health and pastime in the world——

Pardonnez moi—replied the commissary, you are indebted to him six livres four sous, for the next post from hence to St. *Fons*, in your rout to *Avignon*—which being a post royal, you pay double for the horses and postilion—otherwise 'twould have amounted to no more than three livres, two sous——

——But I don't go by land; said I.

——You may if you please; replied the commissary——

Your most obedient servant——said I, making him a low bow——

The commissary, with all the sincerity of grave good breeding—made me one, as low again.——I never was more disconcerted with a bow in my life.

——The devil take the serious character of these people! quoth I—(aside) they understand no more of IRONY than this——

The comparison was standing close by with his panniers—

but something seal'd up my lips—I could not pronounce the name—

Sir, said I, collecting myself—it is not my intention to take post——

—But you may—said he, persisting in his first reply—you may take post if you chuse——

—And I may take salt to my pickled herring, said I, if I chuse——

—But I do not chuse—

—But you must pay for it, whether you do or no——

Aye! for the salt; said I (I know)——

—And for the post too; added he. Defend me; cried I——

I travel by water—I am going down the *Rhône* this very afternoon—my baggage is in the boat—and I have actually paid nine livres for my passage——

C'est tout egal—'tis all one; said he.

Bon Dieu! what, pay for the way I go! and for the way I do *not* go!

——*C'est tout egal*; replied the commissary——

——The devil it is! said I—but I will go to ten thousand *Bastiles* first——

O *England! England!* thou land of liberty, and climate of good sense, thou tenderest of mothers—and gentlest of nurses, cried I, kneeling upon one knee, as I was beginning my apostrophe——

When the director of Madam *Le Blanc*'s conscience coming in at that instant, and seeing a person in black, with a face as pale as ashes, at his devotions—looking still paler by the contrast and distress of his drapery—ask'd, if I stood in want of the aids of the church——

I go by WATER—said I—and here's another will be for making me pay for going by OYL.

CHAPTER XXXV

AS I perceived the commissary of the post-office would have his six livres four sous, I had nothing else for it, but to say some smart thing upon the occasion, worth the money: And so I set off thus——

——And pray Mr. Commissary, by what law of courtesy is a defenceless stranger to be used just the reverse from what you use a *Frenchman* in this matter?

By no means; said he.

Excuse me; said I—for you have begun, Sir, with first tearing off my breeches—and now you want my pocket——

Whereas—had you first taken my pocket, as you do with your own people—and then left me bare a—'d after—I had been a beast to have complain'd——

As it is——

——'Tis contrary to the *law of nature.*

——'Tis contrary to *reason.*

——'Tis contrary to the GOSPEL.

But not to this—said he—putting a printed paper into my hand.

PAR LE ROY.

—— ——'Tis a pithy prolegomenon, quoth I—and so read on —
— —
— — — — — — — — — — — — — — — — — —

——By all which it appears, quoth I, having read it over, a little too rapidly, that if a man sets out in a post-chaise from *Paris*—he must go on travelling in one, all the days of his life—or pay for it.——Excuse me, said the commissary, the spirit of the ordinance is this—That if you set out with an intention of running post from *Paris* to *Avignon, &c.* you shall not change that intention or mode of travelling, without first satisfying the fermiers for two posts further than the place you repent at—and 'tis founded, continued he, upon this, that the REVENUES are not to fall short through your *fickleness*——

——O by heavens! cried I—if fickleness is taxable in *France*—we have nothing to do but make the best peace with you we can—

AND SO THE PEACE WAS MADE;

——And if it is a bad one—as *Tristram Shandy* laid the corner stone of it—nobody but *Tristram Shandy* ought to be hanged.

CHAPTER XXXVI

THOUGH I was sensible I had said as many clever things to the commissary as came to six livres four sous, yet I was determined to note down the imposition amongst my remarks before I retir'd from the place; so putting my hand into my coat pocket for my remarks—(which by the bye, may be a caution to travellers to take a little more care of *their* remarks for the future) "my remarks were *stolen*"—Never did sorry traveller make such a pother and racket about his remarks as I did about mine, upon the occasion.

Heaven! earth! sea! fire! cried I, calling in every thing to my aid but what I should——My remarks are stolen!—what shall I do?—Mr. Commissary! pray did I drop any remarks as I stood besides you?——

You dropp'd a good many very singular ones; replied he—— Pugh! said I, those were but a few, not worth above six livres two sous—but these are a large parcel——He shook his head—— Monsieur *Le Blanc*! Madam *Le Blanc*! did you see any papers of mine?—you maid of the house! run up stairs—*François*! run up after her——

——I must have my remarks——they were the best remarks, cried I, that ever were made—the wisest—the wittiest——What shall I do?—which way shall I turn myself?

Sancho Pança, when he lost his ass's FURNITURE, did not exclaim more bitterly.

CHAPTER XXXVII

WHEN the first transport was over, and the registers of the brain were beginning to get a little out of the confusion into which this jumble of cross accidents had cast them— it then presently occurr'd to me, that I had left my remarks in the pocket of the chaise—and that in selling my chaise, I had sold my remarks along with, to the chaise-vamper.   I leave this void space that the reader may swear into it, any oath that he is most accustomed to——For my own part, if ever I swore a *whole* oath into a vacancy in my life, I think it was into that—— *** **** **, said I—and so my remarks through *France*, which were as full of wit, as an egg is full of meat, and as well worth four hundred guineas, as the said egg is worth a penny— Have I been selling here to a chaise-vamper—for four *Louis d'Ors*—and giving him a post-chaise (by heaven) worth six into the bargain; had it been to *Dodsley*, or *Becket*, or any creditable bookseller, who was either leaving off business, and wanted a post-chaise—or who was beginning it—and wanted my remarks, and two or three guineas along with them—I could have borne it—— but to a chaise-vamper!—shew me to him this moment *François* —said I—the *valet de place* put on his hat, and led the way—and I pull'd off mine, as I pass'd the commissary, and followed him.

CHAPTER XXXVIII

WHEN we arrived at the chaise-vamper's house, both the house and the shop were shut up; it was the eighth of September, the nativity of the blessed Virgin *Mary*, mother of God—

——Tantarra - ra - tan - tivi——the whole world was going out a May-poling—frisking here—capering there—no body cared a button for me or my remarks; so I sat me down upon a bench by the door, philosophating upon my condition: by a better fate than usually attends me, I had not waited half an hour, when the mistress came in, to take the papilliotes from off her hair, before she went to the May-poles——

The *French* women, by the bye, love May-poles, *a la folie*— that is, as much as their matins——give 'em but a May-pole, whether in May, June, July, or September—they never count the times——down it goes——'tis meat, drink, washing, and lodging to 'em——and had we but the policy, an' please your worships (as wood is a little scarce in *France*) to send them but plenty of May-poles——

The women would set them up; and when they had done, they would dance round them (and the men for company) till they were all blind.

The wife of the chaise-vamper step'd in, I told you, to take the papilliotes from off her hair——the toilet stands still for no man ——so she jerk'd off her cap, to begin with them as she open'd the door, in doing which, one of them fell upon the ground—— I instantly saw it was my own writing——

—O Seignieur! cried I—you have got all my remarks upon your head, Madam!——*J'en suis bien mortifiée*, said she——'tis well, thinks I, they have stuck there—for could they have gone deeper, they would have made such confusion in a *French* woman's noddle—She had better have gone with it unfrizled, to the day of eternity.

Tenez—said she—so without any idea of the nature of my suffering, she took them from her curls, and put them gravely one by one into my hat——one was twisted this way——another twisted that——ay! by my faith; and when they are published, quoth I,——

They will be worse twisted still.

CHAPTER XXXIX

AND NOW for *Lippius*'s clock! said I, with the air of a man, who had got thro' all his difficulties——nothing can prevent us seeing that, and the *Chinese* history, &c. except the time, said *François*——for 'tis almost eleven—then we must speed the faster, said I, striding it away to the cathedral.

I cannot say, in my heart, that it gave me any concern in being told by one of the minor canons, as I was entering the west door, —That *Lippius*'s great clock was all out of joints, and had not gone for some years——It will give me the more time, thought I, to peruse the *Chinese* history; and besides I shall be able to give the world a better account of the clock in it's decay, than I could have done in its flourishing condition——

——And so away I posted to the college of the Jesuits.

Now it is with the project of getting a peep at the history of *China* in *Chinese* characters—as with many others I could.mention, which strike the fancy only at a distance; for as I came nearer and nearer to the point—my blood cool'd—the freak gradually went off, till, at length I would not have given a cherry-stone to have it gratified——The truth was, my time was short, and my heart was at the Tomb of the Lovers——I wish to God, said I, as I got the rapper in my hand, that the key of the library may be but lost; it fell out as well——

For all the JESUITS *had got the cholic*—and to that degree, as never was known in the memory of the oldest practitioner.

CHAPTER XL

AS I KNEW the geography of the Tomb of the Lovers, as well as if I had lived twenty years in *Lyons*, namely, that it was upon the turning of my right hand, just without the gate, leading to the *Fauxbourg de Vaise*——I dispatch'd *François* to the boat, that I might pay the homage I so long ow'd it, without a witness of my weakness.—I walk'd with all imaginable joy towards the place——when I saw the gate which intercepted the tomb, my heart glowed within me——

—Tender and faithful spirits! cried I, addressing myself to *Amandus* and *Amanda*—long—long have I tarried to drop this tear upon your tomb——I come——I come——

When I came—there was no tomb to drop it upon.

What would I have given for my uncle *Toby* to have whistled, Lillabullero!

CHAPTER XLI

NO MATTER how, or in what mood—but I flew from the tomb of the lovers—or rather I did not fly *from* it—(for there was no such thing existing) and just got time enough to the boat to save my passage;—and e'er I had sailed a hundred yards, the *Rhône* and the *Saôn* met together, and carried me down merrily betwixt them.

But I have described this voyage down the *Rhône*, before I made it——

—— So now I am at *Avignon*—and as there is nothing to see but the old house, in which the duke of *Ormond* resided, and nothing to stop me but a short remark upon the place, in three minutes you will see me crossing the bridge upon a mule, with *François* upon a horse with my portmanteau behind him, and the owner of both, striding the way before us with a long gun upon his shoulder, and a sword under his arm, least peradventure we should run away with his cattle. Had you seen my breeches in entering *Avignon*,——Though you'd have seen them better, I think, as I mounted—you would not have thought the precaution amiss, or found in your heart to have taken it, in dudgeon: for my own part, I took it most kindly; and determined to make him a present of them, when we got to the end of our journey, for the trouble they had put him to, of arming himself at all points against them.

Before I go further, let me get rid of my remark upon *Avignon*, which is this; That I think it wrong, merely because a man's hat has been blown off his head by chance the first night he comes to *Avignon*,——that he should therefore say, "*Avignon* is more subject to high winds than any town in all *France*:" for which reason I laid no stress upon the accident till I had inquired of the master of the inn about it, who telling me seriously it was so——and hearing moreover, the windyness of *Avignon* spoke of in the country about as a proverb—I set it down, merely to ask the learned what can be the cause——the consequence I saw—for they are all Dukes, Marquisses, and Counts, there——the duce a Baron, in all *Avignon*——so that there is scarce any talking to them, on a windy day.

[434]

Prithee friend, said I, take hold of my mule for a moment——
for I wanted to pull off one of my jack-boots, which hurt my heel
—the man was standing quite idle at the door of the inn, and as
I had taken it into my head, he was someway concerned about the
house or stable, I put the bridle into his hand—so begun with my
boot:—when I had finished the affair, I turned about to take the
mule from the man, and thank him——

——*But Monsieur le Marquis* had walked in——

CHAPTER XLII

I HAD now the whole south of *France*, from the banks of the
Rhône to those of the *Garonne* to traverse upon my mule at
my own leisure—*at my own leisure*——for I had left Death,
the lord knows——and He only—how far behind me——"I have
followed many a man thro' *France*, quoth he—but never at this
mettlesome rate"——Still he followed,——and still I fled him
——but I fled him chearfully——still he pursued—but like one
who pursued his prey without hope——as he lag'd, every step he
lost, softened his looks——why should I fly him at this rate?

So notwithstanding all the commissary of the post-office had
said, I changed the *mode* of my travelling once more; and after so
percipitate and rattling a course as I had run, I flattered my fancy
with thinking of my mule, and that I should traverse the rich
plains of *Languedoc* upon his back, as slowly as foot could fall.

There is nothing more pleasing to a traveller——or more
terrible to travel-writers, than a large rich plain; especially if it is
without great rivers or bridges; and presents nothing to the eye,
but one unvaried picture of plenty: for after they have once told
you that 'tis delicious! or delightful! (as the case happens)—that
the soil was grateful, and that nature pours out all her abundance, &c. . . . they have then a large plain upon their hands,
which they know not what to do with—and which is of little or
no use to them but to carry them to some town; and that town,
perhaps of little more, but a new place to start from to the next
plain—and so on.

—This is most terrible work; judge if I don't manage my plains
better.

CHAPTER XLIII

I HAD NOT gone above two leagues and a half, before the man with his gun, began to look at his priming.

I had three several times loiter'd *terribly* behind; half a mile at least every time: once, in deep conference with a drum-maker, who was making drums for the fairs of *Baucaira* and *Tarascone*—I did not understand the principles——

The second time, I cannot so properly say, I stopp'd——for meeting a couple of *Franciscans* straiten'd more for time than myself, and not being able to get to the bottom of what I was about——I had turn'd back with them——

The third, was an affair of trade with a gossip, for a hand basket of *Provence* figs for four sous; this would have been transacted at once; but for a case of conscience at the close of it; for when the figs were paid for, it turn'd out, that there were two dozen of eggs cover'd over with vine-leaves at the bottom of the basket—as I had no intention of buying eggs—I made no sort of claim of them—as for the space they had occupied—what signified it? I had figs enow for my money——

—But it was my intention to have the basket—it was the gossip's intention to keep it, without which, she could do nothing with her eggs——and unless I had the basket, I could do as little with my figs, which were too ripe already, and most of 'em burst at the side: this brought on a short contention, which terminated in sundry proposals, what we should both do——

—How we disposed of our eggs and figs, I defy you, or the Devil himself, had he not been there (which I am persuaded he was) to form the least probable conjecture: You will read the whole of it——not this year, for I am hastening to the story of my uncle *Toby*'s amours—but you will read it in the collection of those which have arose out of the journey across this plain—— and which, therefore, I call my

PLAIN STORIES.

How far my pen has been fatigued like those of other travellers, in this journey of it, over so barren a track—the world must judge—but the traces of it, which are now all set o' vibrating together this moment, tell me 'tis the most fruitful and busy period of my life; for as I had made no convention with my man with the gun as to time—by stopping and talking to every soul

[436]

I met who was not in a full trot—joining all parties before me—
waiting for every soul behind—hailing all those who were coming
through cross roads—arresting all kinds of beggars, pilgrims,
fiddlers, fryars—not passing by a woman in a mulberry-tree with
out commending her legs, and tempting her into conversation
with a pinch of snuff——In short, by seizing every handle, of
what size or shape soever, which chance held out to me in this
journey—I turned my *plain* into a *city*—I was always in company,
and with great variety too; and as my mule loved society as much
as myself, and had some proposals always on his part to offer to
every beast he met—I am confident we could have passed through
Pall Mall or St. *James's Street* for a month together, with fewer
adventures—and seen less of human nature.

O! there is that sprightly frankness which at once unpins every
plait of a *Languedocian's* dress—that whatever is beneath it, it
looks so like the simplicity which poets sing of in better days—
I will delude my fancy, and believe it is so.

'Twas in the road betwixt *Nismes* and *Lunel*, where there is the
best *Muscatto* wine in all *France*, and which by the bye belongs
to the honest canons of MONTPELLIER—and foul befall the man
who has drank it at their table, who grudges them a drop of it.

——The sun was set—they had done their work; the nymphs
had tied up their hair afresh—and the swains were preparing for
a carousal——My mule made a dead point——'Tis the fife and
tabourin, said I——I'm frighten'd to death, quoth he——They
are running at the ring of pleasure, said I, giving him a prick——
By Saint *Boogar*, and all the saints at the backside of the door of
purgatory, said he—(making the same resolution with the abbess
of *Andoüillets*) I'll not go a step further——'Tis very well, Sir, said
I—I never will argue a point with one of your family, as long as
I live; so leaping off his back, and kicking off one boot into this
ditch, and t'other into that—I'll take a dance, said I——so
stay you here.

A sun-burnt daughter of Labour rose up from the groupe to
meet me as I advanced towards them; her hair, which was a dark
chesnut, approaching rather to a black, was tied up in a knot, all
but a single tress.

We want a cavalier, said she, holding out both her hands, as if
to offer them——And a cavalier ye shall have; said I, taking hold
of both of them.

Hadst thou, *Nannette*, been array'd like a dutchesse!

——But that cursed slit in thy petticoat!

Nannette cared not for it.

We could not have done without you, said she, letting go one hand, with self-taught politeness, leading me up with the other.

A lame youth, whom *Apollo* had recompenced with a pipe, and to which he had added a tabourin of his own accord, ran sweetly over the prelude, as he sat upon the bank——Tie me up this tress instantly, said *Nannette*, putting a piece of string into my hand ——It taught me to forget I was a stranger——The whole knot fell down——We had been seven years acquainted.

The youth struck the note upon the tabourin—his pipe followed, and off we bounded——"the duce take that slit!"

The sister of the youth who had stolen her voice from heaven, sung alternately with her brother——'twas a *Gascoigne* roundelay.

VIVA LA JOIA!
FIDON LA TRISTESSA!

The nymphs join'd in unison, and their swains an octave below them——

I would have given a crown to have it sew'd up—*Nannette* would not have given a sous—*Viva la joia!* was in her lips— *Viva la joia!* was in her eyes. A transient spark of amity shot across the space betwixt us——She look'd amiable!——Why could I not live and end my days thus? Just disposer of our joys and sorrows, cried I, why could not a man sit down in the lap of content here—and dance, and sing, and say his prayers, and go to heaven with this nut brown maid? capriciously did she bend her head on one side, and dance up insiduous——Then 'tis time to dance off, quoth I; so changing only partners and tunes, I danced it away from *Lunel* to *Montpellier*——from thence to *Pesçnas*, *Beziers*——I danced it along through *Narbonne, Carcasson*, and *Castle Naudairy*, till at last I danced myself into *Perdrillo*'s pavillion, where pulling a paper of black lines, that I might go on straight forwards, without digression or parenthesis, in my uncle *Toby*'s amours——

I begun thus——

END of the SEVENTH VOLUME.

VOLUME VIII

CHAPTER I

BUT SOFTLY——for in these sportive plains, and under this genial sun, where at this instant all flesh is running out piping, fiddling, and dancing to the vintage, and every step that's taken, the judgment is surprised by the imagination, I defy, notwithstanding all that has been said upon *straight lines** in sundry pages of my book—I defy the best cabbage planter that ever existed, whether he plants backwards or forwards, it makes little difference in the account (except that he will have more to answer for in the one case than in the other)—I defy him to go on cooly, critically, and canonically, planting his cabbages one by one, in straight lines, and stoical distances, especially if slits in petticoats are unsew'd up—without ever and anon straddling out, or sidling into some bastardly digression——In *Freeze-land, Fog-land* and some other lands I wot of—it may be done——

But in this clear climate of fantasy and perspiration, where every idea, sensible and insensible, gets vent—in this land, my dear *Eugenius*—in this fertile land of chivalry and romance, where I now sit, unskrewing my ink-horn to write my uncle *Toby*'s amours, and with all the meanders of JULIA's track in quest of her DIEGO, in full view of my study window—if thou comest not and takest me by the hand——

What a work is it likely to turn out!

Let us begin it.

CHAPTER II

IT IS with LOVE as with CUCKOLDOM——

——But now I am talking of beginning a book, and have long had a thing upon my mind to be imparted to the reader, which if not imparted now, can never be imparted to him as long as I live (whereas the COMPARISON may be imparted to him any hour in the day)——I'll just mention it, and begin in good earnest.

The thing is this.

That of all the several ways of beginning a book which are now in practice throughout the known world, I am confident my own way of doing it is the best——I'm sure it is the most religious

* Vid. Vol. VI. p. 389.

——for I begin with writing the first sentence——and trusting to Almighty God for the second.

'Twould cure an author for ever of the fuss and folly of opening his street-door, and calling in his neighbours and friends, and kinsfolk, with the devil and all his imps, with their hammers and engines, &c. only to observe how one sentence of mine follows another, and how the plan follows the whole.

I wish you saw me half starting out of my chair, with what confidence, as I grasp the elbow of it, I look up——catching the idea, even sometimes before it half way reaches me——

I believe in my conscience I intercept many a thought which heaven intended for another man.

Pope and his Portrait* are fools to me——no martyr is ever so full of faith or fire——I wish I could say of good works too—— but I have no

Zeal or Anger——or
Anger or Zeal——

And till gods and men agree together to call it by the same name ——the errantest TARTUFFE, in science—in politics—or in religion, shall never kindle a spark within me, or have a worse word, or a more unkind greeting, than what he will read in the next chapter.

CHAPTER III

—BON JOUR!——good-morrow?—so you have got your cloak on betimes!——but 'tis a cold morning, and you judge the matter rightly——'tis better to be well mounted, than go o'foot——and obstructions in the glands are dangerous ——And how goes it with thy concubine—thy wife—and thy little ones o'both sides? and when did you hear from the old gentleman and lady—your sister, aunt, uncle and cousins—— I hope they have got better of their colds, coughs, claps, tooth-aches, fevers, stranguries, sciaticas, swellings, and sore-eyes.—— What a devil of an apothecary! to take so much blood—give such a vile purge—puke—poultice—plaister—night-draught— glister—blister?——And why so many grains of calomel? *santa Maria!* and such a dose of opium! periclitating, pardi! the whole family of ye, from head to tail——By my great aunt *Dinah*'s old black velvet mask! I think there was no occasion for it.

* Vid. *Pope*'s Portrait.

Now this being a little bald about the chin, by frequently putting off and on, *before* she was got with child by the coachman—not one of our family would wear it after. To cover the MASK afresh, was more than the mask was worth——and to wear a mask which was bald, or which could be half seen through, was as bad as having no mask at all——

This is the reason, may it please your reverences, that in all our numerous family, for these four generations, we count no more than one archbishop, a *Welch* judge, some three or four aldermen, and a single mountebank——

In the sixteenth century, we boast of no less than a dozen alchymists.

CHAPTER IV

" I T IS with Love as with Cuckoldom"——the suffering party is at least the *third*, but generally the last in the house who knows any thing about the matter: this comes, as all the world knows, from having half a dozen words for one thing; and so long, as what in this vessel of the human frame, is *Love*—may be *Hatred,* in that——*Sentiment* half a yard higher——and *Nonsense*————no Madam,—not there——I mean at the part I am now pointing to with my forefinger——how can we help ourselves?

Of all mortal, and immortal men too, if you please, who ever soliloquized upon this mystic subject, my uncle *Toby* was the worst fitted, to have push'd his researches thro' such a contention of feelings; and he had infallibly let them all run on, as we do worse matters, to see what they would turn out——had not *Bridget*'s pre-notification of them to *Susannah*, and *Susannah*'s repeated manifesto's thereupon to all the world, made it necessary for my uncle *Toby* to look into the affair.

CHAPTER V

W HY weavers, gardeners, and gladiators—or a man with a pined leg (proceeding from some ailment in the *foot*)— should ever have had some tender nymph breaking her heart in secret for them, are points well and duely settled and accounted for, by ancient and modern physiologists.

[443]

A water-drinker, provided he is a profess'd one, and does it without fraud or covin, is precisely in the same predicament: not that, at first sight, there is any consequence, or shew of logic in it, "That a rill of cold water dribbling through my inward parts, should light up a torch in my *Jenny*'s—"

——The proposition does not strike one; on the contrary, it seems to run opposite to the natural workings of causes and effects——

But it shews the weakness and imbecility of human reason.

——"And in perfect good health with it?"

—The most perfect—Madam, that friendship herself could wish me——

—"And drink nothing!—nothing but water?"

—Impetuous fluid! the moment thou presses against the flood-gates of the brain——see how they give way!——

In swims CURIOSITY, beckoning to her damsels to follow—they dive into the centre of the current——

FANCY sits musing upon the bank, and with her eyes following the stream, turns straws and bulrushes into masts and bowsprits—And DESIRE, with vest held up to the knee in one hand, snatches at them, as they swim by her, with the other——

O ye water-drinkers! is it then by this delusive fountain, that ye have so often governed and turn'd this world about like a mill-wheel—grinding the faces of the impotent—be-powdering their ribs—be-peppering their noses, and changing sometimes even the very frame and face of nature——

—If I was you, quoth *Yorick*, I would drink more water, *Eugenius.*—And, if I was you, *Yorick*, replied *Eugenius*, so would I.

Which shews they had both read *Longinus*——

For my own part, I am resolved never to read any book but my own, as long as I live.

CHAPTER VI

I WISH my uncle *Toby* had been a water-drinker; for then the thing had been accounted for, That the first moment Widow *Wadman* saw him, she felt something stirring within her in his favour—Something!—something.

—Something perhaps more than friendship—less than love—something—no matter what—no matter where—I would not give a single hair off my mule's tail, and be obliged to pluck it off myself (indeed the villain has not many to spare, and is not a little vicious into the bargain) to be let by your worships into the secret——

But the truth is, my uncle *Toby* was not a water-drinker; he drank it neither pure nor mix'd, or any how, or any where, except fortuitously upon some advanced posts, where better liquor was not to be had——or during the time he was under cure; when the surgeon telling him it would extend the fibres, and bring them sooner into contact——my uncle *Toby* drank it for quietness sake.

Now as all the world knows, that no effect in nature can be produced without a cause and as it is as well known, that my uncle *Toby*, was neither a weaver—a gardener, or a gladiator—— unless as a captain, you will needs have him one—but then he was only a captain of foot—and besides the whole is an equivocation—There is nothing left for us to suppose, but that my uncle *Toby*'s leg——but that will avail us little in the present hypothesis, unless it had proceeded from some ailment *in the foot*— whereas his leg was not emaciated from any disorder in his foot— for my uncle *Toby*'s leg was not emaciated at all. It was a little stiff and awkward, from a total disuse of it, for the three years he lay confined at my father's house in town; but it was plump and muscular, and in all other respects as good and promising a leg as the other.

I declare, I do not recollect any one opinion or passage of my life, where my understanding was more at a loss to make ends meet, and torture the chapter I had been writing, to the service of the chapter following it, than in the present case: one would think I took a pleasure in running into difficulties of this kind, merely to make fresh experiments of getting out of 'em——Inconsiderate soul that thou art! What! are not the unavoidable distresses with which, as an author and a man, thou art hemm'd in on every side of thee——are they, *Tristram*, not sufficient, but thou must entangle thyself still more?

Is it not enough that thou art in debt, and that thou hast ten cart-loads of thy fifth and sixth volumes still—still unsold, and art almost at thy wit's ends, how to get them off thy hands.

To this hour art thou not tormented with the vile asthma thou gattest in skating against the wind in *Flanders*? and is it but two months ago, that in a fit of laughter, on seeing a cardinal make water like a quirister (with both hands) thou brakest a vessel in

[445]

thy lungs, whereby, in two hours, thou lost as many quarts of blood; and hadst thou lost as much more, did not the faculty tell thee———it would have amounted to a gallon?———

CHAPTER VII

—BUT FOR heaven's sake, let us not talk of quarts or gallons ——let us take the story straight before us; it is so nice and intricate a one, it will scarce bear the transposition of a single tittle; and some how or other, you have got me thrust almost into the middle of it—

—I beg we may take more care.

CHAPTER VIII

MY UNCLE *TOBY* and the corporal had posted down with so much heat and precipitation, to take possession of the spot of ground we have so often spoke of, in order to open their campaign as early as the rest of the allies; that they had forgot one of the most necessary articles of the whole affair; it was neither a pioneer's spade, a pick-ax, or a shovel—

—It was a bed to lie on: so that as *Shandy Hall* was at that time unfurnished; and the little inn where poor *Le Fever* died, not yet built; my uncle *Toby* was constrained to accept of a bed at Mrs. *Wadman*'s, for a night or two, till corporal *Trim* (who to the character of an excellent valet, groom, cook, sempster, surgeon and engineer, super-added that of an excellent upholsterer too) with the help of a carpenter and a couple of taylors, constructed one in my uncle *Toby*'s house.

A daughter of *Eve*, for such was Widow *Wadman*, and 'tis all the character I intend to give of her—

—"*That she was a perfect woman;*" had better be fifty leagues off—or in her warm bed—or playing with a case-knife—or any thing you please—than make a man the object of her attention, when the house and all the furniture is her own.

There is nothing in it out of doors and in broad day-light, where a woman has a power, physically speaking, of viewing a man in more lights than one—but here, for her soul, she can see him in no light without mixing something of her own goods and chattels along with him——till by reiterated acts of such combinations, he gets foisted into her inventory——

—And then good night.

But this is not matter of SYSTEM; for I have delivered that above ——nor is it matter of BREVIARY——for I make no man's creed but my own——nor matter of FACT——at least that I know of; but 'tis matter copulative and introductory to what follows.

CHAPTER IX

I DO NOT speak it with regard to the coarseness or cleanness of them—or the strength of their gussets——but pray do not night-shifts differ from day-shifts as much in this particular, as in any thing else in the world; That they so far exceed the others in length, that when you are laid down in them, they fall almost as much below the feet, as the day-shifts fall short of them?

Widow *Wadman*'s night-shifts (as was the mode I suppose in King *William*'s and Queen *Anne*'s reigns) were cut however after this fashion; and if the fashion is changed, (for in *Italy* they are come to nothing)——so much the worse for the public; they were two *Flemish* ells and a half in length; so that allowing a moderate woman two ells, she had half an ell to spare, to do what she would with.

Now from one little indulgence gain'd after another, in the many bleak and decemberly nights of a seven years' widowhood, things had insensibly come to this pass, and for the two last years had got establish'd into one of the ordinances of the bed-chamber —That as soon as Mrs. *Wadman* was put to bed, and had got her legs stretched down to the bottom of it, of which she always gave *Bridget* notice—*Bridget* with all suitable decorum, having first open'd the bed-cloaths at the feet, took hold of the half ell of cloath we are speaking of, and having gently, and with both her hands, drawn it downwards to its furthest extension, and then contracted it again side long by four or five even plaits, she took a large corking pin out of her sleeve, and with the point directed towards her, pin'd the plaits all fast together a little above the hem; which done she tuck'd all in tight at the feet, and wish'd her mistress a good night.

This was constant, and without any other variation than this; that on shivering and tempestuous nights, when *Bridget* untuck'd

the feet of the bed, &c. to do this——she consulted no thermo-
meter but that of her own passions; and so performed it standing
—kneeling—or squatting, according to the different degrees of
faith, hope, and charity, she was in, and bore towards her mistress
that night. In every other respect the *etiquette* was sacred, and
might have vied with the most mechanical one of the most
inflexible bed-chamber in *Christendom*.

The first night, as soon as the corporal had conducted my uncle
Toby up stairs, which was about ten——Mrs. *Wadman* threw
herself into her arm chair, and crossing her left knee with her
right, which formed a resting-place for her elbow, she reclin'd her
cheek upon the palm of her hand, and leaning forwards, ruminated
till midnight upon both sides of the question.

The second night she went to her bureau, and having ordered
Bridget to bring her up a couple of fresh candles and leave them
upon the table, she took out her marriage-settlement, and read it
over with great devotion: and the third night (which was the last
of my uncle *Toby*'s stay) when *Bridget* had pull'd down the night-
shift, and was assaying to stick in the corking pin——

——With a kick of both heels at once, but at the same time the
most natural kick that could be kick'd in her situation——for
supposing ****** *** to be the sun in its meridian, it was a north-
east kick——she kick'd the pin out of her fingers——the *etiquette*
which hung upon it, down—down it fell to the ground, and was
shivered into a thousand atoms.

From all which it was plain that widow *Wadman* was in love
with my uncle *Toby*.

CHAPTER X

M
Y UNCLE *TOBY*'S head at that time was full of other
matters, so that it was not till the demolition of *Dunkirk*,
when all the other civilities of *Europe* were settled, that
he found leisure to return this.

This made an armistice (that is speaking with regard to my
uncle *Toby*—but with respect to Mrs. *Wadman*, a vacancy)—of
almost eleven years. But in all cases of this nature, as it is the
second blow, happen at what distance of time it will, which makes
the fray——I chuse for that reason to call these the amours of my
uncle *Toby* with Mrs. *Wadman*, rather than the amours of Mrs.
Wadman with my uncle *Toby*.

This is not a distinction without a difference.

It is not like the affair of *an old hat cock'd*——and *a cock'd old hat*, about which your reverences have so often been at odds with one another——but there is a difference here in the nature of things——

And let me tell you, gentry, a wide one too.

CHAPTER XI

NOW AS widow *Wadman* did love my uncle *Toby*——and my uncle *Toby* did not love widow *Wadman*, there was nothing for widow *Wadman* to do but to go on and love my uncle *Toby*——or let it alone.

Widow *Wadman* would do neither the one or the other——

——Gracious heaven!——but I forget I am a little of her temper myself; for whenever it so falls out, which it sometimes does about the equinoxes, that an earthly goddess is so much this, and that, and t'other, that I cannot eat my breakfast for her——and that she careth not three halfpence whether I eat my breakfast or no——

——Curse on her! and so I send her to *Tartary*, and from *Tartary* to *Terra del Fuogo*, and so on to the devil: in short there is not an infernal nitch where I do not take her divinityship and stick it.

But as the heart is tender, and the passions in these tides ebb and flow ten times in a minute, I instantly bring her back again; and as I do all things in extremes, I place her in the very centre of the milky-way——

Brightest of stars! thou wilt shed thy influence upon some one——

——The duce take her and her influence too——for at that word I lose all patience——much good may it do him!——By all that is hirsute and gashly! I cry, taking off my furr'd cap, and twisting it round my finger——I would not give sixpence for a dozen such!

——But 'tis an excellent cap too (putting it upon my head, and pressing it close to my ears)—and warm—and soft; especially if you stroke it the right way—but alas! that will never be my luck ——(so here my philosophy is shipwreck'd again)

——No; I shall never have a finger in the pye (so here I break my metaphor)——

[449]

Crust and crumb
Inside and out
Top and bottom——I detest it, I hate it, I repudiate it——I'm
sick at the sight of it——
　'Tis all pepper,
　　　　garlick,
　　　　staragen,
　　　　salt, and
　　　　devil's dung——by the great arch cook of cooks, who
does nothing, I think, from morning to night, but sit down by the
fire-side and invent inflammatory dishes for us, I would not touch
it for the world——

——O *Tristram*! *Tristram*! cried *Jenny*.

O *Jenny*! *Jenny*! replied I, and so went on with the twelfth
chapter.

CHAPTER XII

—"**N**OT TOUCH it for the world" did I say——
Lord, how I have heated my imagination with
this metaphor!

CHAPTER XIII

WHICH shews, let your reverences and worships say what
you will of it (for as for *thinking*——all who *do* think—
think pretty much alike, both upon it and other matters)
——LOVE is certainly, at least alphabetically speaking, one of
the most

A gitating
B ewitching
C onfounded
D evilish affairs of life——the most
E xtravagant
F utilitous
G alligaskinish
H andy-dandyish
I racundulous (there is no K to it) and
L yrical of all human passions: at the same time, the most

M isgiving

N innyhammering

O bstipating

P ragmatical

S tridulous

R idiculous—though by the bye the R should have gone first—But in short 'tis of such a nature, as my father once told my uncle *Toby* upon the close of a long dissertation upon the subject——"You can scarce," said he, "combine two ideas together upon it, brother *Toby*, without an hypallage"——What's that? cried my uncle *Toby*.

The cart before the horse, replied my father——

——And what has he to do there? cried my uncle *Toby*——

Nothing, quoth my father, but to get in——or let it alone.

Now widow *Wadman*, as I told you before, would do neither the one or the other.

She stood however ready harnessed and caparisoned at all points to watch accidents.

CHAPTER XIV

THE FATES, who certainly all fore-knew of these amours of widow *Wadman* and my uncle *Toby*, had, from the first creation of matter and motion (and with more courtesy than they usually do things of this kind) established such a chain of causes and effects hanging so fast to one another, that it was scarce possible for my uncle *Toby* to have dwelt in any other house in the world, or to have occupied any other garden in *Christendom*, but the very house and garden which join'd and laid parallel to Mrs. *Wadman*'s; this, with the advantage of a thickset arbour in Mrs. *Wadman*'s garden, but planted in the hedge-row of my uncle *Toby*'s, put all the occasions into her hands which Love-militancy wanted; she could observe my uncle *Toby*'s motions, and was mistress likewise of his councils of war; and as his unsuspecting heart had given leave to the corporal, through the mediation of *Bridget*, to make her a wicker-gate of communication to enlarge her walks, it enabled her to carry on her approaches to the very door of the sentry-box; and sometimes out of gratitude, to make the attack, and endeavour to blow my uncle *Toby* up in the very sentry-box itself.

CHAPTER XV

I T IS A great pity——but 'tis certain from every day's observation of man, that he may be set on fire like a candle, at either end—provided there is a sufficient wick standing out; if there is not—there's an end of the affair; and if there is—by lighting it at the bottom, as the flame in that case has the misfortune generally to put out itself—there's an end of the affair again.

For my part, could I always have the ordering of it which way I would be burnt myself—for I cannot bear the thoughts of being burnt like a beast—I would oblige a housewife constantly to light me at the top; for then I should burn down decently to the socket; that is, from my head to my heart, from my heart to my liver, from my liver to my bowels, and so on by the meseraick veins and arteries, through all the turns and lateral insertions of the intestines and their tunicles, to the blind gut——

——I beseech you, doctor *Slop*, quoth my uncle *Toby*, interrupting him as he mentioned the *blind gut*, in a discourse with my father the night my mother was brought to bed of me——I beseech you, quoth my uncle *Toby*, to tell me which is the blind gut; for, old as I am, I vow I do not know to this day where it lies.

The *blind gut*, answered doctor *Slop*, lies betwixt the *Illion* and *Colon*——

——In a man? said my father.

——'Tis precisely the same, cried doctor *Slop*, in a woman——
That's more than I know; quoth my father.

CHAPTER XVI

—A ND SO to make sure of both systems, Mrs. *Wadman* predetermined to light my uncle *Toby* neither at this end or that; but like a prodigal's candle, to light him, if possible, at both ends at once.

Now, through all the lumber rooms of military furniture, including both of horse and foot, from the great arsenal of *Venice* to the *Tower* of *London* (exclusive) if Mrs. *Wadman* had been rummaging for seven years together, and with *Bridget* to help her, she could not have found any one *blind* or *mantelet* so fit for her purpose, as that which the expediency of my uncle *Toby*'s affairs had fix'd up ready to her hands.

I believe I have not told you——but I don't know—possibly I have——be it as it will, 'tis one of the number of those many things, which a man had better do over again, than dispute about it—That whatever town or fortress the corporal was at work upon, during the course of their campaign, my uncle *Toby* always took care on the inside of his sentry-box, which was towards his left hand, to have a plan of the place, fasten'd up with two or three pins at the top, but loose at the bottom, for the conveniency of holding it up to the eye, &c. . . . as occasions required; so that when an attack was resolved upon, Mrs. *Wadman* had nothing more to do, when she had got advanced to the door of the sentry-box, but to extend her right hand; and edging in her left foot at the same movement, to take hold of the map or plan, or upright, or whatever it was, and with outstretched neck meeting it half way,—to advance it towards her; on which my uncle *Toby*'s passions were sure to catch fire——for he would instantly take hold of the other corner of the map in his left hand, and with the end of his pipe, in the other, begin an explanation.

When the attack was advanced to this point;——the world will naturally enter into the reasons of Mrs. *Wadman*'s next stroke of generalship——which was, to take my uncle *Toby*'s tobacco-pipe out of his hand as soon as she possibly could; which, under one pretence or other, but generally that of pointing more distinctly at some redoubt or breast-work in the map, she would effect before my uncle *Toby* (poor soul!) had well march'd above half a dozen toises with it.

—It obliged my uncle *Toby* to make use of his forefinger.

The difference it made in the attack was this; That in going upon it, as in the first case, with the end of her forefinger against the end of my uncle *Toby*'s tobacco-pipe, she might have travelled with it, along the lines, from *Dan* to *Beersheba*, had my uncle *Toby*'s lines reach'd so far, without any effect: For as there was no arterial or vital heat in the end of the tobacco-pipe, it could excite no sentiment——it could neither give fire by pulsation—— or receive it by sympathy——'twas nothing but smoak.

Whereas, in following my uncle *Toby*'s forefinger with hers, close thro' all the little turns and indentings of his works—— pressing sometimes against the side of it——then treading upon it's nail——then tripping it up——then touching it here——then there, and so on——it set something at least in motion.

[453]

This, tho' slight skirmishing, and at a distance from the main body, yet drew on the rest; for here, the map usually falling with the back of it, close to the side of the sentry-box, my uncle *Toby*, in the simplicity of his soul, would lay his hand flat upon it, in order to go on with his explanation; and Mrs. *Wadman*, by a manœuvre as quick as thought, would as certainly place her's close besides it; this at once opened a communication, large enough for any sentiment to pass or repass, which a person skill'd in the elementary and practical part of love-making, has occasion for———

By bringing up her forefinger parallel (as before) to my uncle *Toby*'s———it unavoidably brought the thumb into action———and the forefinger and thumb being once engaged, as naturally brought in the whole hand. Thine, dear uncle *Toby*! was never now in its right place———Mrs. *Wadman* had it ever to take up, or, with the gentlest pushings, protrusions, and equivocal compressions, that a hand to be removed is capable of receiving———to get it press'd a hair breadth of one side out of her way.

Whilst this was doing, how could she forget to make him sensible, that it was her leg (and no one's else) at the bottom of the sentry-box, which slightly press'd against the calf of his———So that my uncle *Toby* being thus attacked and sore push'd on both his wings—was it a wonder, if now and then, it put his centre into disorder?———

———The duce take it! said my uncle *Toby*.

CHAPTER XVII

THESE attacks of Mrs. *Wadman*, you will readily conceive to be of different kinds; varying from each other, like the attacks which history is full of, and from the same reasons. A general looker on, would scarce allow them to be attacks at all ———or if he did, would confound them all together———but I write not to them: it will be time enough to be a little more exact in my descriptions of them, as I come up to them, which will not be for some chapters; having nothing more to add in this, but that in a bundle of original papers and drawings which my father took care to roll up by themselves, there is a plan of *Bouchain* in perfect preservation (and shall be kept so, whilst I have power to preserve any thing) upon the lower corner of which, on the right hand side, there is still remaining the marks of a snuffy finger and thumb, which there is all the reason in the world to imagine, were Mrs. *Wadman*'s; for the opposite side of the margin, which I suppose to have been my uncle *Toby*'s, is absolutely clean: This seems an authenticated record of one of these attacks; for there are vestigia of the two punctures partly grown up, but still visible on the opposite corner of the map, which are unquestionably the very holes, through which it has been pricked up in the sentry-box——

By all that is priestly! I value this precious relick, with it's *stigmata* and *pricks*, more than all the relicks of the *Romish* church——always excepting, when I am writing upon these matters, the pricks which enter'd the flesh of St. *Radagunda* in the desert, which in your road from FESSE to CLUNY, the nuns of that name will shew you for love.

CHAPTER XVIII

I THINK, an' please your honour, quoth *Trim*, the fortifications are quite destroyed——and the bason is upon a level with the mole——I think so too; replied my uncle *Toby* with a sigh half suppress'd——but step into the parlour, *Trim*, for the stipulation——it lies upon the table.

It has lain there these six weeks, replied the corporal, till this very morning that the old woman kindled the fire with it—

——Then, said my uncle *Toby*, there is no further occasion for our services. The more, an' please your honour, the pity, said the corporal; in uttering which he cast his spade into the wheelbarrow, which was beside him, with an air the most expressive of disconsolation that can be imagined, and was heavily turning about to look for his pick-ax, his pioneer's shovel, his picquets and other little military stores, in order to carry them off the field——when a heigh ho! from the sentry-box, which, being made of thin slit deal, reverberated the sound more sorrowfully to his ear, forbad him.

——No; said the corporal to himself, I'll do it before his honour rises to-morrow morning; so taking his spade out of the wheel-barrow again, with a little earth in it, as if to level something at the foot of the glacis——but with a real intent to approach nearer to his master, in order to divert him——he loosen'd a sod or two——pared their edges with his spade, and having given them a gentle blow or two with the back of it, he sat himself down close by my uncle *Toby*'s feet, and began as follows.

CHAPTER XIX

I T WAS a thousand pities——though I believe, an' please your honour, I am going to say but a foolish kind of a thing for a soldier——

A soldier, cried my uncle *Toby*, interrupting the corporal, is no more exempt from saying a foolish thing, *Trim*, than a man of letters——But not so often; an' please your honour, replied the corporal——My uncle *Toby* gave a nod.

It was a thousand pities then, said the corporal, casting his eye upon *Dunkirk*, and the mole, as *Servius Sulpicius*, in returning out of *Asia* (when he sailed from *Ægina* towards *Megara*) did upon *Corinth* and *Pyreus*——

——"It was a thousand pities, an' please your honour, to destroy these works——and a thousand pities to have let them stood."——

——Thou art right, *Trim*, in both cases: said my uncle *Toby* ——This, continued the corporal, is the reason, that from the beginning of their demolition to the end——I have never once whistled, or sung, or laugh'd, or cry'd, or talk'd of pass'd done deeds, or told your honour one story good or bad——

——Thou hast many excellencies, *Trim*, said my uncle *Toby*, and I hold it not the least of them, as thou happenest to be a story-teller, that of the number thou hast told me, either to amuse me in my painful hours, or divert me in my grave ones—thou hast seldom told me a bad one——

——Because, an' please your honour, except one of a *King of Bohemia and his seven castles*,—they are all true; for they are about myself——

I do not like the subject the worse, *Trim*, said my uncle *Toby*, on that score: But prithee what is this story? thou hast excited my curiosity.

I'll tell it your honour, quoth the corporal, directly—Provided, said my uncle *Toby*, looking earnestly towards *Dunkirk* and the mole again——provided it is not a merry one; to such, *Trim*, a man should ever bring one half of the entertainment along with

[456]

him; and the disposition I am in at present would wrong both thee, *Trim*, and thy story——It is not a merry one by any means, replied the corporal—Nor would I have it altogether a grave one, added my uncle *Toby*——It is neither the one nor the other, replied the corporal, but will suit your honour exactly——Then I'll thank thee for it with all my heart, cried my uncle *Toby*, so prithee begin it, *Trim*.

The corporal made his reverence; and though it is not so easy a matter as the world imagines, to pull off a lank Montero-cap with grace——or a whit less difficult, in my conceptions, when a man is sitting squat upon the ground, to make a bow so teeming with respect as the corporal was wont, yet by suffering the palm of his right hand, which was towards his master, to slip backward upon the grass, a little beyond his body, in order to allow it the greater sweep——and by an unforced compression, at the same time, of his cap with the thumb and the two forefingers of his left, by which the diameter of the cap became reduced, so that it might be said, rather to be insensibly squeez'd—than pull'd off with a flatus——the corporal acquitted himself of both, in a better manner than the posture of his affairs promised; and having hemmed twice, to find in what key his story would best go, and best suit his master's humour—he exchanged a single look of kinness with him, and set off thus.

The Story of the King of Bohemia and his
seven castles.

THERE was a certain King of *Bo*——*he*——

As the corporal was entering the confines of *Bohemia*, my uncle *Toby* obliged him to halt for a single moment; he had set out bare-headed, having since he pull'd off his Montero-cap in the latter end of the last chapter, left it lying beside him on the ground.

——The eye of Goodness espieth all things——so that before the corporal had well got through the first five words of his story, had my uncle *Toby* twice touch'd his Montero-cap with the end of his cane, interrogatively——as much as to say, Why don't you put it on, *Trim*? *Trim* took it up with most respectful slowness, and casting a glance of humiliation as he did it, upon the embroidery of the fore-part, which being dismally tarnish'd and fray'd moreover in some of the principal leaves and boldest parts of the pattern, he lay'd it down again betwixt his two feet, in order to moralize upon the subject.

――'Tis every word of it but too true, cried my uncle *Toby*, that thou art about to observe――

"*Nothing in this world*, Trim, *is made to last for ever.*"

――But when tokens, dear *Tom*, of thy love and remembrance wear out, said *Trim*, what shall we say?

There is no occasion, *Trim*, quoth my uncle *Toby*, to say any thing else; and was a man to puzzle his brains till Doom's day, I believe, *Trim*, it would be impossible.

The corporal perceiving my uncle *Toby* was in the right, and that it would be in vain for the wit of man to think of extracting a purer moral from his cap, without further attempting it, he put it on; and passing his hand across his forehead to rub out a pensive wrinkle, which the text and the doctrine between them had engender'd, he return'd, with the same look and tone of voice, to his story of the King of *Bohemia* and his seven castles.

The Story of the King of *Bohemia* and his
seven castles, continued.

THERE was a certain King of *Bohemia*, but in whose reign, except his own, I am not able to inform your honour――

I do not desire it of thee, *Trim*, by any means, cried my uncle *Toby*.

――It was a little before the time, an' please your honour, when giants were beginning to leave off breeding;—but in what year of our Lord that was――

――I would not give a half-penny to know, said my uncle *Toby*.

――Only, an' please your honour, it makes a story look the better in the face――

――'Tis thy own, *Trim*, so ornament it after thy own fashion; and take any date, continued my uncle *Toby*, looking pleasantly upon him—take any date in the whole world thou choosest, and put it to—thou art heartily welcome――

The corporal bowed; for of every century, and of every year of that century, from the first creation of the world down to *Noah's* flood; and from *Noah's* flood to the birth of *Abraham*; through all the pilgrimages of the patriarchs, to the departure of the *Israelites* out of *Egypt*――and throughout all the Dynasties, Olympiads, Urbecondita's, and other memorable epochas of the different nations of the world, down to the coming of *Christ*, and from thence to the very moment in which the corporal was telling his story――had my uncle *Toby* subjected this vast empire of time

[458]

and all its abysses at his feet; but as MODESTY scarce touches with a finger what LIBERALITY offers her with both hands open——the corporal contented himself with the very *worst year* of the whole bunch; which, to prevent your honours of the Majority and Minority from tearing the very flesh off your bones in contestation, 'Whether that year is not always the last cast-year of the last cast-almanack'——I tell you plainly it was; but from a different reason than you wot of——

——It was the year next him——which being the year of our Lord seventeen hundred and twelve, when the duke of *Ormond* was playing the devil in *Flanders*——the corporal took it, and set out with it afresh on his expedition to *Bohemia*.

The Story of the King of *Bohemia* and his
seven castles, continued.

IN THE year of our Lord one thousand seven hundred and twelve, there was, an' please your honour——

——To tell thee truly, *Trim*, quoth my uncle *Toby*, any other date would have pleased me much better, not only on account of the sad stain upon our history that year, in marching off our troops, and refusing to cover the siege of *Quesnoi*, though *Fagel* was carrying on the works with such incredible vigour—— but likewise on the score, *Trim*, of thy own story; because if there are—and which, from what thou hast dropt, I partly suspect to be the fact—if there are giants in it——

There is but one, an' please your honour——

——'Tis as bad as twenty, replied my uncle *Toby*——thou should'st have carried him back some seven or eight hundred years out of harm's way, both of criticks and other people; and therefore I would advise thee, if ever thou tellest it again——

——If I live, an' please your honour, but once to get through it, I will never tell it again, quoth *Trim*, either to man, woman, or child——Poo—poo! said my uncle *Toby*—but with accents of such sweet encouragement did he utter it, that the corporal went on with his story with more alacrity than ever.

The Story of the King of *Bohemia* and his
seven castles, continued.

THERE was, an' please your honour, said the corporal, raising his voice and rubbing the palms of his two hands cheerily together as he begun, a certain King of *Bohemia*——

——Leave out the date entirely, *Trim*, quoth my uncle *Toby*, leaning forwards, and laying his hand gently upon the corporal's shoulder to temper the interruption—leave it out entirely, *Trim*; a story passes very well without these niceties, unless one is pretty sure of 'em——Sure of 'em! said the corporal, shaking his head—

Right; answered my uncle *Toby*, it is not easy, *Trim*, for one, bred up as thou and I have been to arms, who seldom looks further forward than to the end of his musket, or backwards beyond his knapsack, to know much about this matter——God bless your honour! said the corporal, won by the *manner* of my uncle *Toby*'s reasoning, as much as by the reasoning itself, he has something else to do; if not on action, or a march, or upon duty in his garrison—he has his firelock, an' please your honour, to furbish—his accoutrements to take care of—his regimentals to mend—himself to shave and keep clean, so as to appear always like what he is upon the parade; what business, added the corporal triumphantly, has a soldier, an' please your honour, to know any thing at all of *geography*?

——Thou would'st have said *chronology*, *Trim*, said my uncle *Toby*; for as for geography, 'tis of absolute use to him; he must be acquainted intimately with every country and its boundaries where his profession carries him; he should know every town and city, and village and hamlet, with the canals, the roads, and hollow ways which lead up to them; there is not a river or a rivulet he passes, *Trim*, but he should be able at first sight to tell thee what is its name—in what mountains it takes its rise—what is its course—how far it is navigable—where fordable—where not; he should know the fertility of every valley, as well as the hind who ploughs it; and be able to describe, or, if it is required, to give thee an exact map of all the plains and defiles, the forts, the acclivities, the woods and morasses, thro' and by which his army is to march; he should know their produce, their plants, their minerals, their waters, their animals, their seasons, their climates, their heats and cold, their inhabitants, their customs, their language, their policy, and even their religion.

Is it else to be conceived, corporal, continued my uncle *Toby*, rising up in his sentry-box, as he began to warm in this part of his discourse—how *Marlborough* could have marched his army from the banks of the *Maes* to *Belburg*; from *Belburg* to *Kerpenord*—(here the corporal could sit no longer) from *Kerpenord*, *Trim*, to *Kalsaken*; from *Kalsaken* to *Newdorf*; from *Newdorf* to *Landenbourg*; from *Landenbourg* to *Mildenheim*; from *Mildenheim* to *Elchingen*; from *Elchingen* to *Gingen*; from *Gingen* to *Bal-*

merchoffen; from *Balmerchoffen* to *Skellenburg*, where he broke
in upon the enemy's works; forced his passage over the *Danube*;
cross'd the *Lech*—pushed on his troops into the heart of the
empire, marching at the head of them through *Friburg*, *Hoken-
wert*, and *Schonevelt*, to the plains of *Blenheim* and *Hochstet*?——
Great as he was, corporal, he could not have advanced a step, or
made one single day's march without the aids of *Geography*——
As for *Chronology*, I own, *Trim*, continued my uncle *Toby*, sitting
down again coolly in his sentry-box, that of all others, it seems a
science which the soldier might best spare, was it not for the
lights which that science must one day give him, in determining
the invention of powder; the furious execution of which, renvers-
ing every thing like thunder before it, has become a new æra to us
of military improvements, changing so totally the nature of
attacks and defences both by sea and land, and awakening so
much art and skill in doing it, that the world cannot be too exact
in ascertaining the precise time of its discovery, or too inquisitive
in knowing what great man was the discoverer, and what occasions gave birth to it.

   I am far from controverting, continued my uncle *Toby*, what
historians agree in, that in the year of our Lord 1380, under the
reign of *Wencelaus*, son of *Charles* the fourth——a certain priest,
whose name was *Schwartz*, shew'd the use of powder to the
Venetians, in their wars against the *Genoese*; but 'tis certain he
was not the first; because if we are to believe *Don Pedro* the
bishop of *Leon*—How came priests and bishops, an' please your
honour, to trouble their heads so much about gun-powder? God
knows, said my uncle *Toby*——his providence brings good out of
every thing—and he avers, in his chronicle of King *Alphonsus*,
who reduced *Toledo*, That in the year 1343, which was full thirty
seven years before that time, the secret of powder was well known,
and employed with success, both by *Moors* and *Christians*, not
only in their sea-combats, at that period, but in many of their
most memorable sieges in *Spain* and *Barbary*—And all the world
knows, that Friar *Bacon* had wrote expressly about it, and had
generously given the world a receipt to make it by, above a hundred and fifty years before even *Schwartz* was born—And that the
Chinese, added my uncle *Toby*, embarass us, and all accounts of it
still more, by boasting of the invention some hundreds of years
even before him——

   —They are a pack of liars, I believe, cried *Trim*——

   ——They are some how or other deceived, said my uncle *Toby*,

in this matter, as is plain to me from the present miserable state of military architecture amongst them; which consists of nothing more than a fossè with a brick wall without flanks—and for what they give us as a bastion at each angle of it, 'tis so barbarously constructed, that it looks for all the world————
Like one of my seven castles, an' please your honour, quoth *Trim.*

My uncle *Toby*, tho' in the utmost distress for a comparison, most courteously refused *Trim*'s offer—till *Trim* telling him, he had half a dozen more in *Bohemia*, which he knew not how to get off his hands——my uncle *Toby* was so touch'd with the pleasantry of heart of the corporal——that he discontinued his dissertation upon gunpowder——and begged the corporal forthwith to go on with his story of the King of *Bohemia* and his seven castles.

The Story of the King of *Bohemia* and his seven castles, continued.

THIS *unfortunate* King of *Bohemia*, said *Trim*——Was he unfortunate then? cried my uncle *Toby*, for he had been so wrapt up in his dissertation upon gun-powder and other military affairs, that tho' he had desired the corporal to go on, yet the many interruptions he had given, dwelt not so strong upon his fancy, as to account for the epithet——Was he *unfortunate* then, *Trim*? said my uncle *Toby*, pathetically——The corporal, wishing first the *word* and all its synonimas at the devil, forthwith began to run back in his mind, the principal events in the King of *Bohemia*'s story; from every one of which, it appearing that he was the most fortunate man that ever existed in the world——it put the corporal to a stand: for not caring to retract his epithet——and less, to explain it——and least of all, to twist his tale (like men of lore) to serve a system——he looked up in my uncle *Toby*'s face for assistance——but seeing it was the very thing, my uncle *Toby* sat in expectation of himself——after a hum and a haw, he went on——

The King of *Bohemia*, an' please your honour, replied the corporal, was *unfortunate*, as thus——That taking great pleasure and delight in navigation and all sort of sea-affairs——and there *happening* throughout the whole kingdom of *Bohemia*, to be no sea-port town whatever——

How the duce should there—*Trim*? cried my uncle *Toby*; for *Bohemia* being totally inland, it could have happen'd no otherwise ——It might; said *Trim*, if it had pleased God——

[462]

My uncle *Toby* never spoke of the being and natural attributes of God, but with diffidence and hesitation——

——I believe not, replied my uncle *Toby*, after some pause—— for being inland, as I said, and having *Silesia* and *Moravia* to the east; *Lusatia* and *Upper Saxony* to the north; *Franconia* to the west; and *Bavaria* to the south: *Bohemia* could not have been propell'd to the sea, without ceasing to be *Bohemia*——nor could the sea, on the other hand, have come up to *Bohemia*, without overflowing a great part of *Germany*, and destroying millions of unfortunate inhabitants who could make no defence against it ——Scandalous! cried *Trim*—Which would bespeak, added my uncle *Toby*, mildly, such a want of compassion in Him who is the Father of it——that, I think, *Trim*——the thing could have happen'd no way.

The corporal made the bow of unfeigned conviction; and went on.

Now the King of *Bohemia* with his queen and courtiers *happening* one fine summer's evening to walk out——Aye! there the word *happening* is right, *Trim*, cried my uncle *Toby*; for the King of *Bohemia* and his queen might have walk'd out, or let it alone; ——'twas a matter of contingency, which might happen, or not, just as chance ordered it.

King *William* was of an opinion, an' please your honour, quoth *Trim*, that every thing was predestined for us in this world; insomuch, that he would often say to his soldiers, that "every ball had it's billet." He was a great man, said my uncle *Toby*——And I believe, continued *Trim*, to this day, that the shot which disabled me at the battle of *Landen*, was pointed at my knee for no other purpose, but to take me out of his service, and place me in your honour's, where I should be taken so much better care of in my old age——It shall never, *Trim*, be construed otherwise, said my uncle *Toby*.

The heart, both of the master and the man, were alike subject to sudden overflowings;——a short silence ensued.

Besides, said the corporal, resuming the discourse—but in a gayer accent——if it had not been for that single shot, I had never, an' please your honour, been in love——

So, thou wast once in love, *Trim*! said my uncle *Toby*, smiling—

Souse! replied the corporal—over head and ears! an' please your honour. Prithee when? where?—and how came it to pass? ——I never heard one word of it before; quoth my uncle *Toby*: ——I dare say, answered *Trim*, that every drummer and serjeant's

[463]

son in the regiment knew of it——Its high time I should——
said my uncle *Toby*.

Your honour remembers with concern, said the corporal, the
total rout and confusion of our camp and army at the affair of
Landen; every one was left to shift for himself; and if it had not
been for the regiments of *Wyndham*, *Lumley*, and *Galway*, which
covered the retreat over the bridge of *Neerspeeken*, the king
himself could scarce have gain'd it——he was press'd hard, as
your honour knows, on every side of him——

Gallant mortal! cried my uncle *Toby*, caught up with enthusiasm—this moment, now that all is lost, I see him galloping across
me, corporal, to the left, to bring up the remains of the *English*
horse along with him to support the right, and tear the laurel from
Luxembourg's brows, if yet 'tis possible——I see him with the
knot of his scarfe just shot off, infusing fresh spirits into poor
Galway's regiment—riding along the line—then wheeling about,
and charging *Conti* at the head of it——Brave! brave by heaven!
cried my uncle *Toby*—he deserves a crown——As richly, as
a thief a halter; shouted *Trim*.

My uncle *Toby* knew the corporal's loyalty;—otherwise the
comparison was not at all to his mind——it did not altogether
strike the corporal's fancy when he had made it——but it could
not be recall'd——so he had nothing to do, but proceed.

As the number of wounded was prodigious, and no one had
time to think of any thing, but his own safety—Though *Talmash*,
said my uncle *Toby*, brought off the foot with great prudence——
But I was left upon the field, said the corporal. Thou wast so;
poor fellow! replied my uncle *Toby*——So that it was noon the
next day, continued the corporal, before I was exchanged, and put
into a cart with thirteen or fourteen more, in order to be convey'd to our hospital.

There is no part of the body, an' please your honour, where
a wound occasions more intolerable anguish than upon the
knee——

Except the groin; said my uncle *Toby*. An' please your honour,
replied the corporal, the knee, in my opinion, must certainly be
the most acute, there being so many tendons and what-d'ye-
call-'ems all about it.

It is for that reason, quoth my uncle *Toby*, that the groin is
infinitely more sensible——there being not only as many tendons
and what-d'ye-call-'ems (for I know their names as little as thou
do'st)——about it——but moreover ***——

[464]

Mrs. *Wadman*, who had been all the time in her arbour—instantly stopp'd her breath—unpinn'd her mob at the chin, and stood up upon one leg——

The dispute was maintained with amicable and equal force betwixt my uncle *Toby* and *Trim* for some time; till *Trim* at length recollecting that he had often cried at his master's sufferings, but never shed a tear at his own—was for giving up the point, which my uncle *Toby* would not allow——'Tis a proof of nothing, *Trim*, said he, but the generosity of thy temper——

So that whether the pain of a wound in the groin (*cæteris paribus*) is greater than the pain of a wound in the knee——or

Whether the pain of a wound in the knee is not greater than the pain of a wound in the groin——are points which to this day remain unsettled.

CHAPTER XX

THE anguish of my knee, continued the corporal, was excessive in itself; and the uneasiness of the cart, with the roughness of the roads which were terribly cut up—making bad still worse—every step was death to me: so that with the loss of blood, and the want of care-taking of me, and a fever I felt coming on besides——(Poor soul! said my uncle *Toby*) all together, an' please your honour, was more than I could sustain.

I was telling my sufferings to a young woman at a peasant's house, where our cart, which was the last of the line, had halted; they had help'd me in, and the young woman had taken a cordial out of her pocket and dropp'd it upon some sugar, and seeing it had cheer'd me, she had given it me a second and a third time—— So I was telling her, an' please your honour, the anguish I was in, and was saying it was so intolerable to me, that I had much rather lie down upon the bed, turning my face towards one which was in the corner of the room—and die, than go on——when, upon her attempting to lead me to it, I fainted away in her arms. She was a good soul! as your honour, said the corporal, wiping his eyes, will hear.

I thought *love* had been a joyous thing, quoth my uncle *Toby*.

'Tis the most serious thing, an' please your honour (sometimes) that is in the world.

By the persuasion of the young woman, continued the corporal, the cart with the wounded men set off without me: she had assured them I should expire immediately if I was put into the cart. So when I came to myself——I found myself in a still quiet cottage, with no one but the young woman, and the peasant and his wife. I was laid across the bed in the corner of the room, with my wounded leg upon a chair, and the young woman beside me, hold-ing the corner of her handkerchief dipp'd in vinegar to my nose with one hand, and rubbing my temples with the other.

I took her at first for the daughter of the peasant (for it was no inn)—so had offer'd her a little purse with eighteen florins, which my poor brother *Tom* (here *Trim* wip'd his eyes) had sent me as a token, by a recruit, just before he set out for *Lisbon*——

——I never told your honour that piteous story yet——here *Trim* wiped his eyes a third time.

The young woman call'd the old man and his wife into the room, to shew them the money, in order to gain me credit for a bed and what little necessaries I should want, till I should be in a condition to be got to the hospital——Come then! said she, tying up the little purse—I'll be your banker—but as that office alone will not keep me employ'd, I'll be your nurse too.

I thought by her manner of speaking this, as well as by her dress, which I then began to consider more attentively—that the young woman could not be the daughter of the peasant.

She was in black down to her toes, with her hair conceal'd under a cambrick border, laid close to her forehead: she was one of those kind of nuns, an' please your honour, of which, your honour knows, there are a good many in *Flanders* which they let go loose——By thy description, *Trim*, said my uncle *Toby*, I dare say she was a young *Beguine*, of which there are none to be found any where but in the *Spanish Netherlands*—except at *Amsterdam* ——they differ from nuns in this, that they can quit their cloister if they choose to marry; they visit and take care of the sick by pro-fession——I had rather, for my own part, they did it out of good-nature.

——She often told me, quoth *Trim*, she did it for the love of *Christ*—I did not like it.——I believe, *Trim*, we are both wrong, said my uncle *Toby*—we'll ask Mr. *Yorick* about it to-night at my brother *Shandy*'s——so put me in mind; added my uncle *Toby*.

The young *Beguine*, continued the corporal, had scarce given herself time to tell me "she would be my nurse," when she hastily turned about to begin the office of one, and prepare something

[466]

for me——and in a short time—though I thought it a long one—
she came back with flannels, &c. &c. and having fomented my
knee soundly for a couple of hours, &c. and made me a thin basin
of gruel for my supper—she wish'd me rest, and promised to be
with me early in the morning.——She wish'd me, an' please your
honour, what was not to be had. My fever ran very high that
night—her figure made sad disturbance within me—I was every
moment cutting the world in two—to give her half of it—and
every moment was I crying, That I had nothing but a knapsack
and eighteen florins to share with her——The whole night long
was the fair *Beguine*, like an angel, close by my bedside, holding
back my curtain and offering me cordials—and I was only
awakened from my dream by her coming there at the hour
promised, and giving them in reality. In truth, she was scarce
ever from me, and so accustomed was I to receive life from her
hands, that my heart sickened, and I lost colour when she left the
room: and yet, continued the corporal, (making one of the
strangest reflections upon it in the world)——

——"*It was not love*"——for during the three weeks she was
almost constantly with me, fomenting my knee with her hand,
night and day—I can honestly say, an' please your
honour—that * * * * * * * * * * * * * * * once.

That was very odd, *Trim*, quoth my uncle *Toby*——
I think so too—said Mrs. *Wadman*.
It never did, said the corporal.

CHAPTER XXI

——**B**UT 'TIS no marvel, continued the corporal—seeing my
uncle *Toby* musing upon it—for Love, an' please your
honour, is exactly like war, in this; that a soldier, though
he has escaped three weeks compleat o'*Saturday*-night,—may
nevertheless be shot through his heart on *Sunday* morning——*It
happened so here*, an' please your honour, with this difference
only—that it was on *Sunday* in the afternoon, when I fell in love
all at once with a sisserara——it burst upon me, an' please your
honour, like a bomb——scarce giving me time to say, "God
bless me."

I thought, *Trim*, said my uncle *Toby*, a man never fell in love so
very suddenly.

Yes, an' please your honour, if he is in the way of it——
replied *Trim*.

I prithee, quoth my uncle *Toby*, inform me how this matter
happened.

——With all pleasure, said the corporal, making a bow.

CHAPTER XXII

I HAD escaped, continued the corporal, all that time from
falling in love, and had gone on to the end of the chapter, had
it not been predestined otherwise——there is no resisting
our fate.

It was on a *Sunday*, in the afternoon, as I told your
honour——

The old man and his wife had walked out——

Every thing was still and hush as midnight about the house——

There was not so much as a duck or a duckling about the
yard——

——When the fair *Beguine* came in to see me.

My wound was then in a fair way of doing well—the inflamma-
tion had been gone off for some time, but it was succeeded with
an itching both above and below my knee, so insufferable, that
I had not shut my eyes the whole night for it.

Let me see it, said she, kneeling down upon the ground parallel
to my knee, and laying her hand upon the part below it——It
only wants rubbing a little, said the *Beguine*; so covering it with
the bed cloaths, she began with the forefinger of her right-hand
to rub under my knee, guiding her fore-finger backwards and forwards by the edge of the flannel which kept on the dressing.

In five or six minutes I felt slightly the end of her second finger
——and presently it was laid flat with the other, and she continued rubbing in that way round and round for a good while; it
then came into my head, that I should fall in love—I blush'd when
I saw how white a hand she had—I shall never, an' please your
honour, behold another hand so white whilst I live——

——Not in that place: said my uncle *Toby*——

Though it was the most serious affair in nature to the corporal
—he could not forbear smiling.

The young *Beguine*, continued the corporal, perceiving it was
of great service to me—from rubbing, for some time, with two

fingers—proceeded to rub at length, with three—till by little and little she brought down the fourth, and then rubb'd with her whole hand: I will never say another word, an' please your honour, upon hands again—but it was softer than satin——

——Prithee, *Trim*, commend it as much as thou wilt, said my uncle *Toby*; I shall hear thy story with the more delight——The corporal thank'd his master most unfeignedly; but having nothing to say upon the *Beguine*'s hand, but the same over again——he proceeded to the effects of it.

The fair *Beguine*, said the corporal, continued rubbing with her whole hand under my knee—till I fear'd her zeal would weary her——"I would do a thousand times more," said she, "for the love of *Christ*"——In saying which she pass'd her hand across the flannel, to the part above my knee, which I had equally complained of, and rubb'd it also.

I perceived, then, I was beginning to be in love——

As she continued rub-rub-rubbing—I felt it spread from under her hand, an' please your honour, to every part of my frame——

The more she rubb'd, and the longer strokes she took——the more the fire kindled in my veins——till at length, by two or three strokes longer than the rest——my passion rose to the highest pitch——I seiz'd her hand——

——And then, thou clapped'st it to thy lips, *Trim*, said my uncle *Toby*——and madest a speech.

Whether the corporal's amour terminated precisely in the way my uncle *Toby* described it, is not material; it is enough that it contain'd in it the essence of all the love-romances which ever have been wrote since the beginning of the world.

CHAPTER XXIII

AS SOON as the corporal had finished the story of his amour—or rather my uncle *Toby* for him—Mrs. *Wadman* silently salled forth from her arbour, replaced the pin in her mob, pass'd the wicker-gate, and advanced slowly towards my uncle *Toby*'s sentry-box: the disposition which *Trim* had made in my uncle *Toby*'s mind, was too favourable a crisis to be let slipp'd——

——The attack was determin'd upon: it was facilitated still more by my uncle *Toby*'s having ordered the corporal to wheel off the pioneer's shovel, the spade, the pick-axe, the picquets, and other military stores which lay scatter'd upon the ground where *Dunkirk* stood—The corporal had march'd—the field was clear.

Now consider, Sir, what nonsense it is, either in fighting, or writing, or any thing else (whether in rhyme to it, or not) which a man has occasion to do—to act by plan: for if ever Plan, independent of all circumstances, deserved registering in letters of gold (I mean in the archives of *Gotham*)—it was certainly the PLAN of Mrs. *Wadman*'s attack of my uncle *Toby* in his sentry-box, BY PLAN——Now the Plan hanging up in it at this juncture, being the Plan of *Dunkirk*—and the tale of *Dunkirk* a tale of relaxation, it opposed every impression she could make: and besides, could she have gone upon it—the manœuvre of fingers and hands in the attack of the sentry-box, was so outdone by that of the fair *Beguine*'s in *Trim*'s story—that just then, that particular attack, however successful before—became the most heartless attack that could be made——

O! let woman alone for this. Mrs. *Wadman* had scarce open'd the wicker-gate, when her genius sported with the change of circumstances.

——She formed a new attack in a moment.

CHAPTER XXIV

—I AM HALF distracted, captain *Shandy*, said Mrs. *Wadman*, holding up her cambrick handkerchief to her left eye, as she approach'd the door of my uncle *Toby*'s sentry-box——a mote——or sand——or something——I know not what, has got into this eye of mine——do look into it—it is not in the white——

In saying which, Mrs. *Wadman* edged herself close in beside my uncle *Toby*, and squeezing herself down upon the corner of his bench, she gave him an opportunity of doing it without rising up ——Do look into it—said she.

Honest soul! thou didst look into it with as much innocency of heart, as ever child look'd into a raree-shew-box; and 'twere as much a sin to have hurt thee.

——If a man will be peeping of his own accord into things of that nature——I've nothing to say to it——

My uncle *Toby* never did: and I will answer for him, that he would have sat quietly upon a sopha from June to January, (which you know, takes in both the hot and cold months) with an eye as fine as the *Thracian** *Rodope*'s besides him, without being able to tell, whether it was a black or a blue one.

The difficulty was to get my uncle *Toby*, to look at one at all. 'Tis surmounted. And

I see him yonder with his pipe pendulous in his hand, and the ashes falling out of it—looking—and looking—then rubbing his eyes——and looking again, with twice the good nature that ever *Gallileo* look'd for a spot in the sun.

——In vain! for by all the powers which animate the organ—— Widow *Wadman*'s left eye shines this moment as lucid as her right ——there is neither mote, or sand, or dust, or chaff, or speck, or particle of opake matter floating in it——There is nothing, my dear paternal uncle! but one lambent delicious fire, furtively shooting out from every part of it, in all directions, into thine——

——If thou lookest, uncle *Toby*, in search of this mote one moment longer——thou art undone.

CHAPTER XXV

AN EYE is for all the world exactly like a cannon, in this respect; That it is not so much the eye or the cannon, in themselves, as it is the carriage of the eye——and the carriage of the cannon, by which both the one and the other are enabled to do so much execution. I don't think the comparison a bad one: However, as 'tis made and placed at the head of the chapter, as much for use as ornament, all I desire in return, is, that whenever I speak of Mrs. *Wadman*'s eyes (except once in the next period) that you keep it in your fancy.

I protest, Madam, said my uncle *Toby*, I can see nothing whatever in your eye.

It is not in the white; said Mrs. *Wadman*: my uncle *Toby* look'd with might and main into the pupil——

Now of all the eyes, which ever were created——from your own, Madam, up to those of *Venus* herself, which certainly were as venereal a pair of eyes as every stood in a head——there never was an eye of them all, so fitted to rob my uncle *Toby* of his repose, as the very eye, at which he was looking—it was not,

* Rodope Thracia tam inevitabili fascino instructa, tam exacte oculis intuens attraxit, ut si in illam quis incidisset, fieri non posset, quin caperetur ——I know not who.

Madam, a rolling eye—a romping or a wanton one—nor was it an eye sparkling—petulant or imperious—of high claims and terrifying exactions, which would have curdled at once that milk of human nature, of which my uncle *Toby* was made up——but 'twas an eye full of gentle salutations——and soft responses—— speaking——not like the trumpet stop of some ill-made organ, in which many an eye I talk to, holds coarse converse——but whispering soft——like the last low accents of an expiring saint ——"How can you live comfortless, captain *Shandy,* and alone, without a bosom to lean your head on——or trust your cares to?"

It was an eye——

But I shall be in love with it myself, if I say another word about it.

——It did my uncle *Toby*'s business.

CHAPTER XXVI

THERE is nothing shews the characters of my father and my uncle *Toby*, in a more entertaining light, than their different manner of deportment, under the same accident——for I call not love a misfortune, from a persuasion, that a man's heart is ever the better for it——Great God! what must my uncle *Toby*'s have been, when 'twas all benignity without it.

My father, as appears from many of his papers, was very subject to this passion, before he married——but from a little sub-acid kind of drollish impatience in his nature, whenever it befell him, he would never submit to it like a christian; but would pish, and huff, and bounce, and kick, and play the Devil, and write the bitterest Philippicks against the eye that ever man wrote——there is one in verse upon some body's eye or other, that for two or three nights together, had put him by his rest; which in his first transport of resentment against it, he begins thus:

"A Devil 'tis——and mischief such doth work
As never yet did *Pagan, Jew,* or *Turk*." *

In short during the whole paroxism, my father was all abuse and foul language, approaching rather towards malediction—— only he did not do it with as much method as *Ernulphus*——he was too impetuous; nor with *Ernulphus*'s policy——for tho' my

* This will be printed with my father's life of *Socrates, &c. &c.*

father, with the most intolerant spirit, would curse both this and that, and every thing under heaven, which was either aiding or abetting to his love——yet never concluded his chapter of curses upon it, without cursing himself in at the bargain, as one of the most egregious fools and coxcombs, he would say, that ever was let loose in the world.

My uncle *Toby*, on the contrary, took it like a lamb——sat still and let the poison work in his veins without resistance——in the sharpest exacerbations of his wound (like that on his groin) he never dropt one fretful or discontented word——he blamed neither heaven nor earth——or thought or spoke an injurious thing of any body, or any part of it; he sat solitary and pensive with his pipe——looking at his lame leg——then whiffing out a sentimental heigh ho! which mixing with the smoak, incommoded no one mortal.

He took it like a lamb——I say.

In truth he had mistook it at first; for having taken a ride with my father, that very morning, to save if possible a beautiful wood, which the dean and chapter were hewing down to give to the poor*; which said wood being in full view of my uncle *Toby*'s house, and of singular service to him in his description of the battle of *Wynnendale*—by trotting on too hastily to save it—— upon an uneasy saddle—worse horse, &c. &c. . . it had so happened, that the serous part of the blood had got betwixt the two skins, in the nethermost part of my uncle *Toby*——the first shootings of which (as my uncle *Toby* had no experience of love) he had taken for a part of the passion—till the blister breaking in the one case—and the other remaining—my uncle *Toby* was presently convinced, that his wound was not a skin-deep-wound ——but that it had gone to his heart.

CHAPTER XXVII

THE world is ashamed of being virtuous——My uncle *Toby* knew little of the world; and therefore when he felt he was in love with Widow *Wadman*, he had no conception that the thing was any more to be made a mystery of, than if Mrs. *Wadman*, had given him a cut with a gap'd knife across his finger: Had

---

* Mr. *Shandy* must mean the poor *in spirit*; inasmuch as they divided the money amongst themselves.

it been otherwise——yet as he ever look'd upon *Trim* as a humble friend; and saw fresh reasons every day of his life, to treat him as such——it would have made no variation in the manner in which he informed him of the affair.

"I am in love, corporal!" quoth my uncle *Toby*.

CHAPTER XXVIII

IN LOVE!——said the corporal—your honour was very well the day before yesterday, when I was telling your honour the story of the King of *Bohemia—Bohemia!* said my uncle *Toby*———musing a long time——What became of that story, *Trim*?

—We lost it, an' please your honour, somehow betwixt us—but your honour was as free from love then, as I am——'twas, just whilst thou went'st off with the wheel-barrow—with Mrs. *Wadman*, quoth my uncle *Toby*——She has left a ball here—added my uncle *Toby*—pointing to his breast——

——She can no more, an' please your honour, stand a siege, than she can fly—cried the corporal——

——But as we are neighbours, *Trim*,—the best way I think is to let her know it civilly first—quoth my uncle *Toby*.

Now if I might presume, said the corporal, to differ from your honour——

—Why else, do I talk to thee *Trim*: said my uncle *Toby*, mildly——

—Then I would begin, an' please your honour, with making a good thundering attack upon her, in return—and telling her civilly afterwards—for if she knows any thing of your honour's being in love, before hand——L—d help her!—she knows no more at present of it, *Trim*, said my uncle *Toby*—than the child unborn——

Precious souls!———

Mrs. *Wadman* had told it with all its circumstances, to Mrs. *Bridget* twenty-four hours before; and was at that very moment sitting in council with her, touching some slight misgivings with regard to the issue of the affair, which the Devil, who never lies dead in a ditch, had put into her head—before he would allow half time, to get quietly through her *te Deum*———

I am terribly afraid, said widow *Wadman*, in case I should

marry him, *Bridget*—that the poor captain will not enjoy his health, with the monstrous wound upon his groin——

It may not, Madam, be so very large, replied *Bridget*, as you think——and I believe besides, added she—that 'tis dried up——

——I could like to know—merely for his sake, said Mrs. *Wadman*——

—We'll know the long and the broad of it, in ten days—answered Mrs. *Bridget*, for whilst the captain is paying his addresses to you—I'm confident Mr. *Trim* will be for making love to me—and I'll let him as much as he will—added *Bridget*—to get it all out of him——

The measures were taken at once——and my uncle *Toby* and the corporal went on with theirs.

Now, quoth the corporal, setting his left hand a kimbo, and giving such a flourish with his right, as just promised success—and no more——if your honour will give me leave to lay down the plan of this attack——

——Thou wilt please me by it, *Trim*, said my uncle *Toby*, exceedingly—and as I foresee thou must act in it as my *aid de camp*, here's a crown, corporal, to begin with, to steep thy commission.

Then, an' please your honour, said the corporal (making a bow first for his commission)—we will begin with getting your honour's laced cloaths out of the great campaign trunk, to be well-air'd, and have the blue and gold taken up at the sleeves—and I'll put your white ramallie-wig fresh into pipes—and send for a taylor, to have your honour's thin scarlet breeches turn'd——

—I had better take the red plush ones, quoth my uncle *Toby*
——They will be too clumsy—said the corporal.

CHAPTER XXIX

—THOU wilt get a brush and a little chalk to my sword——
'Twill be only in your honour's way, replied *Trim*.

CHAPTER XXX

—BUT YOUR honour's two razors shall be new set—and I will get my Montero-cap furbish'd up, and put on poor lieutenant *Le Fever*'s regimental coat, which your honour gave me to wear for his sake—and as soon as your honour is clean shaved—and has got your clean shirt on, with your blue and gold, or your fine scarlet——sometimes one and sometimes t'other—and every thing is ready for the attack—we'll march up boldly, as if 'twas to the face of a bastion; and whilst your honour engages Mrs. *Wadman* in the parlour, to the right——I'll attack Mrs. *Bridget* in the kitchen, to the left; and having seiz'd that pass, I'll answer for it, said the corporal, snapping his fingers over his head —that the day is our own.

I wish I may but manage it right; said my uncle *Toby*—but I declare, corporal I had rather march up to the very edge of a trench——

—A woman is quite a different thing—said the corporal.

—I suppose so, quoth my uncle *Toby*.

CHAPTER XXXI

IF ANY thing in this world, which my father said, could have provoked my uncle *Toby*, during the time he was in love, it was the perverse use my father was always making of an expression of *Hilarion* the hermit; who, in speaking of his abstinence, his watchings, flagellations, and other instrumental parts of his religion—would say—tho' with more facetiousness than became an hermit—"That they were the means he used, to make his *ass* (meaning his body) leave off kicking."

It pleased my father well; it was not only a laconick way of expressing——but of libelling, at the same time, the desires and appetites of the lower part of us; so that for many years of my father's life, 'twas his constant mode of expression—he never used the word *passions* once—but *ass* always instead of them——So that he might be said truly, to have been upon the bones, or the back of his own ass, or else of some other man's, during all that time.

[476]

I must here observe to you, the difference betwixt
    My father's ass
    and my hobby-horse—in order to keep characters as
separate as may be, in our fancies as we go along.

For my hobby-horse, if you recollect a little, is no way a
vicious beast; he has scarce one hair or lineament of the ass about
him——'Tis the sporting little filly-folly which carries you out for
the present hour—a maggot, a butterfly, a picture, a fiddle-stick—
an uncle *Toby*'s siege—or an *any thing*, which a man makes a shift
to get a stride on, to canter it away from the cares and solici-
tudes of life—'Tis as useful a beast as is in the whole creation—
nor do I really see how the world could do without it——

——But for my father's ass——oh! mount him—mount him
—mount him—(that's three times, is it not?)—mount him not:—
'tis a beast concupiscent—and foul befall the man, who does not
hinder him from kicking.

CHAPTER XXXII

WELL! dear brother *Toby*, said my father, upon his first
seeing him after he fell in love—and how goes it with
your Ass?
Now my uncle *Toby* thinking more of the *part* where he had had
the blister, than of *Hilarion*'s metaphor—and our preconceptions
having (you know) as great a power over the sounds of words as
the shapes of things, he had imagined, that my father, who was
not very ceremonious in his choice of words, had enquired after
the part by its proper name; so notwithstanding my mother,
doctor *Slop*, and Mr. *Yorick*, were sitting in the parlour, he
thought it rather civil to conform to the term my father had made
use of than not. When a man is hemm'd in by two indecorums,
and must commit one of 'em—I always observe—let him choose
which he will, the world will blame him—so I should not be
astonished if it blames my uncle *Toby*.

My A—e, quoth my uncle *Toby*, is much better—brother
Shandy——My father had formed great expectations from his
Ass in this onset; and would have brought him on again; but
doctor *Slop* setting up an intemperate laugh—and my mother
crying out L— bless us!—it drove my father's Ass off the field—
and the laugh then becoming general—there was no bringing him
back to the charge, for some time——

And so the discourse went on without him.

Every body, said my mother, says you are in love, brother *Toby* —and we hope it is true.

I am as much in love, sister, I believe, replied my uncle *Toby*, as any man usually is——Humph! said my father——and when did you know it? quoth my mother——

——When the blister broke; replied my uncle *Toby*.

My uncle *Toby*'s reply put my father into good temper—so he charged o'foot.

CHAPTER XXXIII

AS THE antients agree, brother *Toby*, said my father, that there are two different and distinct kinds of *love*, according to the different parts which are affected by it—the Brain or Liver——I think when a man is in love, it behoves him a little to consider which of the two he is fallen into.

What signifies it, brother *Shandy*, replied my uncle *Toby*, which of the two it is, provided it will but make a man marry, and love his wife, and get a few children.

——A few children! cried my father, rising out of his chair, and looking full in my mother's face, as he forced his way betwixt her's and doctor *Slop*'s—a few children! cried my father, repeating my uncle *Toby*'s words as he walk'd to and fro'——

——Not, my dear brother *Toby*, cried my father, recovering himself all at once, and coming close up to the back of my uncle *Toby*'s chair—not that I should be sorry had'st thou a score—on the contrary I should rejoice—and be as kind, *Toby*, to every one of them as a father—

My uncle *Toby* stole his hand unperceived behind his chair, to give my father's a squeeze——

——Nay, moreover, continued he, keeping hold of my uncle *Toby*'s hand—so much do'st thou possess, my dear *Toby*, of the milk of human nature, and so little of its asperities—'tis piteous the world is not peopled by creatures which resemble thee; and was I an *Asiatick* monarch, added my father, heating himself with his new project—I would oblige thee, provided it would not impair thy strength—or dry up thy radical moisture too fast—or weaken thy memory or fancy, brother *Toby*, which these gymnicks inordinately taken, are apt to do—else, dear *Toby*, I would procure thee

[478]

the most beautiful woman in my empire, and I would oblige thee, *nolens*, *volens*, to beget for me one subject every *month*——

As my father pronounced the last word of the sentence—my mother took a pinch of snuff.

Now I would not, quoth my uncle *Toby*, get a child, *nolens*, *volens*, that is, whether I would or no, to please the greatest prince upon earth——

——And 'twould be cruel in me, brother *Toby*, to compell thee; said my father—but 'tis a case put to shew thee, that it is not thy begetting a child—in case thou should'st be able—but the system of Love and marriage thou goest upon, which I would set thee right in——

There is at least, said *Yorick*, a great deal of reason and plain sense in captain *Shandy*'s opinion of love; and 'tis amongst the ill spent hours of my life which I have to answer for, that I have read so many flourishing poets and rhetoricians in my time, from whom I never could extract so much——

I wish, *Yorick*, said my father, you had read *Plato*; for there you would have learnt that there are two LOVES—I know there were two RELIGIONS, replied *Yorick*, amongst the ancients—— one—for the vulgar, and another for the learned; but I think ONE LOVE might have served both of them very well——

It could not; replied my father—and for the same reasons: for of these Loves, according to *Ficinus*'s comment upon *Velastus*, the one is *rational*——

——the other is *natural*——

the first ancient——without mother——where *Venus* had nothing to do: the second, begotten of *Jupiter* and *Dione*—

——Pray brother, quoth my uncle *Toby*, what has a man who believes in God to do with this? My father could not stop to answer, for fear of breaking the thread of his discourse——

This latter, continued he, partakes wholly of the nature of *Venus*.

The first, which is the golden chain let down from heaven, excites to love heroic, which comprehends in it, and excites to the desire of philosophy and truth——the second, excites to *desire*, simply——

——I think the procreation of children as beneficial to the world, said *Yorick*, as the finding out the longitude——

——To be sure, said my mother, *love* keeps peace in the world—

——In the *house*—my dear, I own——It replenishes the earth; said my mother——

[479]

But it keeps heaven empty—my dear; replied my father.

——'Tis Virginity, cried *Slop*, triumphantly, which fills paradise.

Well push'd nun! quoth my father.

CHAPTER XXXIV

MY FATHER had such a skirmishing, cutting kind of a slashing way with him in his disputations, thrusting and ripping, and giving every one a stroke to remember him by in his turn—that if there were twenty people in company—in less than half an hour he was sure to have every one of 'em against him.

What did not a little contribute to leave him thus without an ally, was, that if there was any one post more untenable than the rest, he would be sure to throw himself into it; and to do him justice, when he was once there, he would defend it so gallantly, that 'twould have been a concern, either to a brave man, or a good-natured one, to have seen him driven out.

Yorick, for this reason, though he would often attack him— yet could never bear to do it with all his force.

Doctor *Slop*'s VIRGINITY, in the close of the last chapter, had got him for once on the right side of the rampart; and he was beginning to blow up all the convents in *Christendom* about *Slop*'s ears, when corporal *Trim* came into the parlour to inform my uncle *Toby*, that his thin scarlet breeches, in which the attack was to be made upon Mrs. *Wadman*, would not do; for, that the taylor, in ripping them up, in order to turn them, had found they had been turn'd before——Then turn them again, brother, said my father rapidly, for there will be many a turning of 'em yet before all's done in the affair——They are as rotten as dirt, said the corporal——Then by all means, said my father, bespeak a new pair, brother——for though I know, continued my father, turning himself to the company, that Widow *Wadman* has been deeply in love with my brother *Toby* for many years, and has used every art and circumvention of woman to outwit him into the same passion, yet now that she has caught him——her fever will be pass'd it's height——

——She has gain'd her point.

In this case, continued my father, which *Plato*, I am persuaded, never thought of——Love, you see, is not so much a SENTIMENT as a SITUATION, into which a man enters, as my brother *Toby* would do, into a *corps*——no matter whether he loves the service or no——being once in it—he acts as if he did; and takes every step to shew himself a man of prowesse.

The hypothesis, like the rest of my father's, was plausible enough, and my uncle *Toby* had but a single word to object to it —in which *Trim* stood ready to second him——but my father had not drawn his conclusion——

For this reason, continued my father (stating the case over again) notwithstanding all the world knows, that Mrs. *Wadman affects* my brother *Toby*—and my brother *Toby* contrariwise *affects* Mrs. *Wadman*, and no obstacle in nature to forbid the music striking up this very night, yet will I answer for it, that this self-same tune will not be play'd this twelvemonth.

We have taken our measures badly, quoth my uncle *Toby*, looking up interrogatively in *Trim*'s face.

I would lay my Montero-cap, said *Trim*——Now *Trim*'s Montero-cap, as I once told you, was his constant wager; and having furbish'd it up that very night, in order to go upon the attack—it made the odds look more considerable——I would lay, an' please your honour, my Montero-cap to a shilling—was it proper, continued *Trim* (making a bow) to offer a wager before your honours——

——There is nothing improper in it, said my father—'tis a mode of expression; for in saying thou would'st lay thy Montero-cap to a shilling—all thou meanest is this—that thou believest——

——Now, What do'st thou believe?

That widow *Wadman*, an' please your worship, cannot hold it out ten days——

And whence, cried *Slop*, jeeringly, hast thou all this knowledge of woman, friend?

By falling in love with a popish clergy-woman; said *Trim*.

'Twas a *Beguine*, said my uncle *Toby*.

Doctor *Slop* was too much in wrath to listen to the distinction; and my father taking that very crisis to fall in helter-skelter upon the whole order of Nuns and *Beguines*, a set of silly, fusty baggages——*Slop* could not stand it——and my uncle *Toby* having some measures to take about his breeches—and *Yorick* about his fourth general division—in order for their several attacks next day—the company broke up: and my father being left alone, and having half an hour upon his hands betwixt that and bed-time;

[481]

he called for pen, ink, and paper, and wrote my uncle *Toby* the following letter of instructions.

My dear brother *Toby*,

WHAT I am going to say to thee, is upon the nature of women, and of love-making to them; and perhaps it is as well for thee—tho' not so well for me—that thou hast occasion for a letter of instructions upon that head, and that I am able to write it to thee.

Had it been the good pleasure of him who disposes of our lots —and thou no sufferer by the knowledge, I had been well content that thou should'st have dipp'd the pen this moment into the ink, instead of myself; but that not being the case————Mrs. *Shandy* being now close besides me, preparing for bed——I have thrown together without order, and just as they have come into my mind, such hints and documents as I deem may be of use to thee; intending, in this, to give thee a token of my love; not doubting, my dear *Toby*, of the manner in which it will be accepted.

In the first place, with regard to all which concerns religion in the affair——though I perceive from a glow in my cheek, that I blush as I begin to speak to thee upon the subject, as well knowing, notwithstanding thy unaffected secrecy, how few of its offices thou neglectest—yet I would remind thee of one (during the continuance of thy courtship) in a particular manner, which I would not have omitted; and that is, never to go forth upon the enterprize, whether it be in the morning or the afternoon, without first recommending thyself to the protection of Almighty God, that he may defend thee from the evil one.

Shave the whole top of thy crown clean, once at least every four or five days, but oftner if convenient; lest in taking off thy wig before her, thro' absence of mind, she should be able to discover how much has been cut away by Time——how much by *Trim.*

—'Twere better to keep ideas of baldness out of her fancy.

Always carry it in thy mind, and act upon it, as a sure maxim, *Toby*——

"*That women are timid:*" And 'tis well they are——else there would be no dealing with them.

Let not thy breeches be too tight, or hang too loose about thy thighs, like the trunk-hose of our ancestors.

——A just medium prevents all conclusions.

Whatever thou hast to say, be it more or less, forget not to utter it in a low soft tone of voice. Silence, and whatever approaches it, weaves dreams of midnight secrecy into the brain: For this cause, if thou canst help it, never throw down the tongs and poker.

Avoid all kinds of pleasantry and facetiousness in thy discourse with her, and do whatever lies in thy power at the same time, to keep from her all books and writings which tend thereto: there are some devotional tracts, which if thou canst entice her to read over—it will be well: but suffer her not to look into *Rabelais*, or *Scarron*, or *Don Quixote*——

——They are all books which excite laughter; and thou knowest, dear *Toby*, that there is no passion so serious as lust.

Stick a pin in the bosom of thy shirt, before thou enterest her parlour.

And if thou art permitted to sit upon the same sopha with her, and she gives thee occasion to lay thy hand upon hers—beware of taking it——thou can'st not lay thy hand on hers, but she will feel the temper of thine. Leave that and as many other things as thou canst, quite undetermined; by so doing, thou will have her curiosity on thy side; and if she is not conquer'd by that, and thy Ass continues still kicking, which there is great reason to suppose——Thou must begin, with first losing a few ounces of blood below the ears, according to the practice of the ancient *Scythians*, who cured the most intemperate fits of the appetite by that means.

Avicenna, after this, is for having the part anointed with the syrrup of hellebore, using proper evacuations and purges——and I believe rightly. But thou must eat little or no goat's flesh, nor red deer——nor even foal's flesh by any means; and carefully abstain——that is, as much as thou canst, from peacocks, cranes, coots, didappers, and water-hens——

As for thy drink—I need not tell thee, it must be the infusion of VERVAIN, and the herb HANEA, of which *Ælian* relates such effects ——but if thy stomach palls with it—discontinue it from time to time, taking cucumbers, melons, purslane, water-lillies, woodbine, and lettice, in the stead of them.

There is nothing further for thee, which occurs to me at present——

—Unless the breaking out of a fresh war——So wishing every thing, dear *Toby*, for the best,

I rest thy affectionate brother,

WALTER SHANDY.

[483]

CHAPTER XXXV

WHILST my father was writing his letter of instructions, my uncle *Toby* and the corporal were busy in preparing every thing for the attack. As the turning of the thin scarlet breeches was laid aside (at least for the present) there was nothing which should put it off beyond the next morning; so accordingly it was resolv'd upon, for eleven o'clock.

Come, my dear, said my father to my mother—'twill be but like a brother and sister, if you and I take a walk down to my brother *Toby*'s to——countenance him in this attack of his.

My uncle *Toby* and the corporal had been accoutred both some time, when my father and mother enter'd, and the clock striking eleven, were that moment in motion to sally forth—but the account of this is worth more, than to be wove into the fag end of the eighth volume of such a work as this.——My father had no time but to put the letter of instructions into my uncle *Toby*'s coat-pocket——and join with my mother in wishing his attack prosperous.

I could like, said my mother, to look through the key-hole out of *curiosity*——Call it by it's right name, my dear, quoth my father—

And look through the key-hole as long as you will.

END of the EIGHTH VOLUME.

VOLUME IX

Si quid urbaniusculè lusum a nobis, per Musas et Charitas et omnium poetarum Numina, Oro te, ne me malè capias.

A

DEDICATION

TO A GREAT MAN

HAVING, *a priori*, intended to dedicate *The Amours of my uncle Toby* to Mr. *** —— I see more reasons, *a posteriori*, for doing it to Lord *******.

I should lament from my soul, if this exposed me to the jealousy of their Reverences; because, *a posteriori*, in Court-latin, signifies the kissing hands for preferment—or any thing else—in order to get it.

My opinion of Lord ******* is neither better nor worse, than it was of Mr. ***. Honours, like impressions upon coin, may give an ideal and local value to a bit of base metal; but Gold and Silver will pass all the world over without any other recommendation than their own weight.

The same good will that made me think of offering up half an hour's amusement to Mr. *** when out of place—operates more forcibly at present, as half an hour's amusement will be more serviceable and refreshing after labour and sorrow, than after a philosophical repast.

Nothing is so perfectly *amusement* as a total change of ideas; no ideas are so totally different as those of Ministers, and innocent Lovers: for which reason, when I come to talk of Statesmen and Patriots, and set such marks upon them as will prevent confusion and mistakes concerning them for the future—I propose to dedicate that Volume to some gentle Shepherd,

> Whose Thoughts proud Science never taught to stray,
> Far as the Stateman's walk or Patriot-way;
> Yet *simple Nature* to his hopes had given
> Out of a cloud-capp'd head a humbler heaven;
> Some *untam'd* World in depth of woods embraced—
> Some happier Island in the watry-waste—
> And where admitted to that equal sky,
> His *faithful Dogs* should bear him company.

In a word, by thus introducing an entire new set of objects to his Imagination, I shall unavoidably give a *Diversion* to his passionate and love-sick Contemplations. In the mean time,

I am

THE AUTHOR.

CHAPTER I

I CALL all the powers of time and chance, which severally check us in our careers in this world, to bear me witness, that I could never yet get fairly to my uncle *Toby*'s amours, till this very moment, that my mother's *curiosity*, as she stated the affair,——or a different impulse in her, as my father would have it——wished her to take a peep at them through the key-hole.

"Call it, my dear, by its right name, quoth my father, and look through the key-hole as long as you will."

Nothing but the fermentation of that little subacid humour, which I have often spoken of, in my father's habit, could have vented such an insinuation——he was however frank and generous in his nature, and at all times open to conviction; so that he had scarce got to the last word of this ungracious retort, when his conscience smote him.

My mother was then conjugally swinging with her left arm twisted under his right, in such wise, that the inside of her hand rested upon the back of his—she raised her fingers, and let them fall—it could scarce be call'd a tap; or if it was a tap——'twould have puzzled a casuist to say, whether 'twas a tap of remonstrance, or a tap of confession: my father, who was all sensibilities from head to foot, class'd it right—Conscience redoubled her blow— he turn'd his face suddenly the other way, and my mother suppos- ing his body was about to turn with it in order to move home- wards, by a cross movement of her right leg, keeping her left as its centre, brought herself so far in front, that as he turned his head, he met her eye———Confusion again! he saw a thousand reasons to wipe out the reproach, and as many to reproach him- self——a thin, blue, chill, pellucid chrystal with all its humours so at rest, the least mote or speck of desire might have been seen at the bottom of it, had it existed——it did not——and how I happen to be so lewd myself, particularly a little before the vernal and autumnal equinoxes——Heaven above knows—— My mother——madam——was so at no time, either by nature, by institution, or example.

A temperate current of blood ran orderly through her veins in all months of the year, and in all critical moments both of the day and night alike; nor did she superinduce the least heat into her humours from the manual effervescencies of devotional tracts, which having little or no meaning in them, nature is oft times obliged to find one——And as for my father's example! 'twas so far from being either aiding or abetting thereunto, that 'twas the whole business of his life to keep all fancies of that kind out of her head——Nature had done her part, to have spared him this trouble; and what was not a little inconsistent, my father knew it ——And here am I sitting, this 12th day of August, 1766, in a purple jerkin and yellow pair of slippers, without either wig or cap on, a most tragicomical completion of his prediction, "That I should neither think, nor act like any other man's child, upon that very account."

The mistake of my father, was in attacking my mother's motive, instead of the act itself: for certainly key-holes were made for other purposes; and considering the act, as an act which interfered with a true proposition, and denied a key-hole to be what it was——it became a violation of nature; and was so far, you see, criminal.

It is for this reason, an' please your Reverences, That key-holes are the occasions of more sin and wickedness, than all other holes in this world put together.

——which leads me to my uncle *Toby*'s amours.

CHAPTER II

THOUGH the Corporal had been as good as his word in putting my uncle *Toby*'s great ramallie-wig into pipes, yet the time was too short to produce any great effects from it: it had lain many years squeezed up in the corner of his old campaign trunk; and as bad forms are not so easy to be got the better of, and the use of candle-ends not so well understood, it was not so pliable a business as one would have wished. The corporal with cheary eye and both arms extended, had fallen back perpendicular from it a score times, to inspire it, if possible, with a better air——had SPLEEN given a look at it, 'twould have cost her ladyship a smile——it curl'd every where but where the corporal would have it; and where a buckle or two, in his opinion, would have done it honour, he could as soon have raised the dead.

Such it was——or rather such would it have seem'd upon any other brow; but the sweet look of goodness which sat upon my uncle *Toby*'s, assimilated every thing around it so sovereignly to itself, and Nature had moreover wrote GENTLEMAN with so fair a hand in every line of his countenance, that even his tarnish'd gold-laced hat and huge cockade of flimsy taffeta became him; and though not worth a button in themselves, yet the moment my uncle *Toby* put them on, they became serious objects, and altogether seem'd to have been picked up by the hand of Science to set him off to advantage.

Nothing in this world could have co-operated more powerfully towards this, than my uncle *Toby*'s blue and gold——*had not Quantity in some measure been necessary to Grace:* in a period of fifteen or sixteen years since they had been made, by a total inactivity in my uncle *Toby*'s life, for he seldom went further than the bowling-green—his blue and gold had become so miserably too strait for him, that it was the utmost difficulty the Corporal was able to get him into them: the taking them up at the sleeves, was of no advantage.——They were laced however down the back, and at the seams of the sides, &c. in the mode of King *William*'s reign; and to shorten all description, they shone so bright against the sun that morning, and had so metallick, and doughty an air with them, that had my uncle *Toby* thought of attacking in armour, nothing could have so well imposed upon his imagination.

As for the thin scarlet breeches, they had been unripp'd by the taylor between the legs, and left at *sixes and sevens*——

——Yes, Madam,——but let us govern our fancies. It is enough they were held impracticable the night before, and as there was no alternative in my uncle *Toby*'s wardrobe, he sallied forth in the red plush.

The Corporal had array'd himself in poor *Le Fever*'s regimental coat; and with his hair tuck'd up under his Montero-cap, which he had furbish'd up for the occasion, march'd three paces distant from his master: a whiff of military pride had puff'd out his shirt at the wrist; and upon that in a black leather thong clipp'd into a tassel beyond the knot, hung the Corporal's stick——My uncle *Toby* carried his cane like a pike.

——It looks well at least; quoth my father to himself.

CHAPTER III

MY UNCLE *TOBY* turn'd his head more than once behind him, to see how he was supported by the Corporal; and the Corporal as oft as he did it, gave a slight flourish with his stick—but not vapouringly; and with the sweetest accent of most respectful encouragement, bid his honour "never fear."

Now my uncle *Toby* did fear; and grievously too: he knew not (as my father had reproach'd him) so much as the right end of a Woman from the wrong, and therefore was never altogether at his ease near any one of them——unless in sorrow or distress; then infinite was his pity; nor would the most courteous knight of romance have gone further, at least upon one leg, to have wiped away a tear from a woman's eye; and yet excepting once that he was beguiled into it by Mrs. *Wadman*, he had never looked stedfastly into one; and would often tell my father in the simplicity of his heart, that it was almost (if not about) as bad as talking bawdy.——

——And suppose it is? my father would say.

CHAPTER IV

SHE CANNOT, quoth my uncle *Toby*, halting, when they had march'd up to within twenty paces of Mrs. *Wadman*'s door —she cannot, Corporal, take it amiss.——

——She will take it, an' please your honour, said the Corporal, just as the *Jew*'s widow at *Lisbon* took it of my brother *Tom*.——

——And how was that? quoth my uncle *Toby*, facing quite about to the Corporal.

Your honour, replied the Corporal, knows of *Tom*'s misfortunes; but this affair has nothing to do with them any further than this, That if *Tom* had not married the widow——or had it pleased God after their marriage, that they had but put pork into their sausages, the honest soul had never been taken out of his warm bed, and dragg'd to the inquisition——'Tis a cursed place —added the Corporal, shaking his head,—when once a poor creature is in, he is in, an' please your honour, for ever.

'Tis very true; said my uncle *Toby* looking gravely at Mrs. *Wadman*'s house, as he spoke.

[490]

Nothing, continued the Corporal, can be so sad as confinement for life—or so sweet, an' please your honour, as liberty.

Nothing, *Trim*——said my uncle *Toby*, musing——

Whilst a man is free—cried the corporal, giving a flourish with his stick thus——

A thousand of my father's most subtle syllogisms could not have said more for celibacy.

My uncle *Toby* look'd earnestly towards his cottage and his bowling green.

The Corporal had unwarily conjured up the Spirit of calculation with his wand; and he had nothing to do, but to conjure him down again with his story, and in this form of Exorcism, most un-ecclesiastically did the Corporal do it.

CHAPTER V

AS *TOM'S* place, an' please your honour, was easy—and the weather warm—it put him upon thinking seriously of settling himself in the world; and as it fell out about that time, that a *Jew* who kept a sausage shop in the same street, had the ill luck to die of a strangury, and leave his widow in possession of a rousing trade——*Tom* thought (as every body in *Lisbon* was doing the best he could devise for himself) there could be no harm in offering her his service to carry it on: so without any introduction to the widow, except that of buying a pound of sausages at her shop—*Tom* set out—counting the matter thus within himself, as he walk'd along; that let the worst come of it that could, he should at least get a pound of sausages for their worth—but, if things went well, he should be set up; inasmuch as he should get not only a pound of sausages—but a wife—and a sausage-shop, an' please your honour, into the bargain.

Every servant in the family, from high to low, wish'd *Tom* success; and I can fancy, an' please your honour, I see him this moment with his white dimity waistcoat and breeches, and hat a little o' one side, passing jollily along the street, swinging his stick, with a smile and a chearful word for every body he met: ——But alas! *Tom*! thou smilest no more, cried the Corporal, looking on one side of him upon the ground, as if he apostrophized him in his dungeon.

Poor fellow! said my uncle *Toby*, feelingly.

He was an honest, light-hearted lad, an' please your honour, as ever blood warm'd——

——Then he resembled thee, *Trim*, said my uncle *Toby*, rapidly.

The Corporal blush'd down to his fingers ends—a tear of sentimental bashfulness—another of gratitude to my uncle *Toby*—and a tear of sorrow for his brother's misfortunes, started into his eye and ran sweetly down his cheek together; my uncle *Toby*'s kindled as one lamp does at another; and taking hold of the breast of *Trim*'s coat (which had been that of *Le Fever*'s) as if to ease his lame leg, but in reality to gratify a finer feeling—he stood silent for a minute and a half; at the end of which he took his hand away, and the corporal making a bow, went on with his story of his brother and the *Jew*'s widow.

CHAPTER VI

WHEN *Tom*, an' please your honour, got to the shop, there was nobody in it, but a poor negro girl, with a bunch of white feathers slightly tied to the end of a long cane, flapping away flies—not killing them——'Tis a pretty picture! said my uncle *Toby*—she had suffered persecution, *Trim*, and had learnt mercy——

[492]

——She was good, an' please your honour, from nature as well as from hardships; and there are circumstances in the story of that poor friendless slut that would melt a heart of stone, said *Trim*; and some dismal winter's evening, when your honour is in the humour, they shall be told you with the rest of *Tom*'s story, for it makes a part of it——

Then do not forget, *Trim*, said my uncle *Toby*.

A Negro has a soul? an' please your honour, said the Corporal (doubtingly).

I am not much versed, Corporal, quoth my uncle *Toby*, in things of that kind; but I suppose, God would not leave him without one, any more than thee or me——

——It would be putting one sadly over the head of another, quoth the Corporal.

It would so; said my uncle *Toby*. Why then, an' please your honour, is a black wench to be used worse than a white one?

I can give no reason, said my uncle *Toby*——

——Only, cried the Corporal, shaking his head, because she has no one to stand up for her——

——'Tis that very thing, *Trim*, quoth my uncle *Toby*,——which recommends her to protection——and her brethren with her; 'tis the fortune of war which has put the whip into our hands *now*—— where it may be hereafter, heaven knows!——but be it where it will, the brave, *Trim*! will not use it unkindly.

——God forbid, said the Corporal.

Amen, responded my uncle *Toby*, laying his hand upon his heart.

The Corporal returned to his story, and went on——but with an embarrassment in doing it, which here and there a reader in this world will not be able to comprehend; for by the many sudden transitions all along, from one kind and cordial passion to another, in getting thus far on his way, he had lost the sportable key of his voice which gave sense and spirit to his tale: he attempted twice to resume it, but could not please himself; so giving a stout hem! to rally back the retreating spirits, and aiding Nature at the same time with his left arm a-kimbo on one side, and with his right a little extended, supporting her on the other— the Corporal got as near the note as he could; and in that attitude, continued his story.

CHAPTER VII

A S *TOM*, an' please your honour, had no business at that
time with the *Moorish* girl, he passed on into the room
beyond to talk to the *Jew*'s widow about love——and his
pound of sausages; and being, as I have told your honour, an
open, cheary-hearted lad, with his character wrote in his looks
and carriage, he took a chair, and without much apology, but
with great civility at the same time, placed it close to her at the
table, and sat down.

There is nothing so awkward, as courting a woman, an' please
your honour, whilst she is making sausages——So *Tom* began
a discourse upon them; first gravely,——"as how they were made
——with what meats, herbs and spices"—Then a little gayly—as,
"With what skins——and if they never burst——Whether the
largest were not the best"——and so on—taking care only as he
went along, to season what he had to say upon sausages, rather
under, than over;——that he might have room to act in——

It was owing to the neglect of that very precaution, said my
uncle *Toby*, laying his hand upon *Trim*'s shoulder, That Count
de la Motte lost the battle of *Wynnendale*: he pressed too speedily
into the wood; which if he had not done, *Lisle* had not fallen into
our hands, nor *Ghent* and *Bruges*, which both followed her
example; it was so late in the year, continued my uncle *Toby*, and
so terrible a season came on, that if things had not fallen out as
they did, our troops must have perished in the open field.——

——Why therefore, may not battles, an' please your honour,
as well as marriages, be made in heaven?—My uncle *Toby*
· mused.——

Religion inclined him to say one thing, and his high idea of
military skill tempted him to say another; so not being able to
frame a reply exactly to his mind——my uncle *Toby* said nothing
at all; and the Corporal finished his story.

As *Tom* perceived, an' please your honour, that he gained
ground, and that all he had said upon the subject of sausages was
kindly taken, he went on to help her a little in making them.——
First, by taking hold of the ring of the sausage whilst she stroked
the forced meat down with her hand—then by cutting the strings
into proper lengths, and holding them in his hand, whilst she took
them out one by one—then, by putting them across her mouth,
that she might take them out as she wanted them—and so on

from little to more, till at last he adventured to tie the sausage himself, whilst she held the snout.——

——Now a widow, an' please your honour, always chuses a second husband as unlike the first as she can: so the affair was more than half settled in her mind before *Tom* mentioned it.

She made a feint however of defending herself, by snatching up a sausage:——*Tom* instantly laid hold of another——

But seeing *Tom*'s had more gristle in it——

She signed the capitulation——and *Tom* sealed it; and there was an end of the matter.

CHAPTER VIII

ALL womankind, continued *Trim*, (commenting upon his story) from the highest to the lowest, an' please your honour, love jokes; the difficulty is to know how they chuse to have them cut; and there is no knowing that, but by trying as we do with our artillery in the field, by raising or letting down their breeches, till we hit the mark.——

——I like the comparison, said my uncle *Toby*, better than the thing itself——

——Because your honour, quoth the Corporal, loves glory, more than pleasure.

I hope, *Trim*, answered my uncle *Toby*, I love mankind more than either; and as the knowledge of arms tends so apparently to the good and quiet of the world——and particularly that branch of it which we have practised together in our bowling-green, has no object but to shorten the strides of AMBITION, and intrench the lives and fortunes of the *few*, from the plunderings of the *many* ——whenever that drum beats in our ears, I trust, Corporal, we shall neither of us want so much humanity and fellow-feeling as to face about and march.

In pronouncing this, my uncle *Toby* faced about, and march'd firmly as at the head of his company——and the faithful Corporal, shouldering his stick, and striking his hand upon his coat-skirt as he took his first step——march'd close behind him down the avenue.

——Now what can their two noddles be about? cried my father to my mother——by all that's strange, they are besieging Mrs. *Wadman* in form, and are marching round her house to mark out the lines of circumvallation.

I dare say, quoth my mother——But stop, dear Sir——
for what my mother dared to say upon the occasion——and what
my father did say upon it——with her replies and his rejoinders,
shall be read, perused, paraphrased, commented and discanted
upon—or to say it all in a word, shall be thumb'd over by
Posterity in a chapter apart——I say, by Posterity—and care not,
if I repeat the word again—for what has this book done more than
the *Legation of Moses*, or the *Tale of a Tub*, that it may not swim
down the gutter of Time along with them?

I will not argue the matter: Time wastes too fast: every letter
I trace tells me with what rapidity Life follows my pen; the days
and hours of it, more precious, my dear *Jenny*! than the rubies
about thy neck, are flying over our heads like light clouds of
a windy day, never to return more——every thing presses on——
whilst thou art twisting that lock,——see! it grows grey; and
every time I kiss thy hand to bid adieu, and every absence which
follows it, are preludes to that eternal separation which we are
shortly to make.——

——Heaven have mercy upon us both!

CHAPTER IX

NOW, for what the world thinks of that ejaculation——
I would not give a groat.

CHAPTER X

MY MOTHER had gone with her left arm twisted in my
father's right, till they had got to the fatal angle of the
old garden wall, where Doctor *Slop* was overthrown by
Obadiah on the coach-horse: as this was directly opposite to the
front of Mrs. *Wadman*'s house, when my father came to it, he
gave a look across; and seeing my uncle *Toby* and the corporal
within ten paces of the door, he turn'd about——"Let us just stop
a moment, quoth my father, and see with what ceremonies my
brother *Toby* and his man *Trim* make their first entry——it will
not detain us, added my father, a single minute."——No matter,
if it be ten minutes, quoth my mother.

[496]

——It will not detain us half a one; said my father.

The Corporal was just then setting in with the story of his brother *Tom* and the *Jew*'s widow: the story went on—and on—— it had episodes in it——it came back, and went on——and on again; there was no end of it——the reader found it very long——

——G— help my father! he pish'd fifty times at every new attitude, and gave the corporal's stick, with all its flourishings and danglings, to as many devils as chose to accept of them.

When issues of events like these my father is waiting for, are hanging in the scales of fate, the mind has the advantage of changing the principle of expectation three times, without which it would not have power to see it out.

Curiosity governs the *first moment*; and the second moment is all œconomy to justify the expence of the first——and for the third, fourth, fifth, and sixth moments, and so on to the day of judgment—'tis a point of HONOUR.

I need not be told, that the ethic writers have assigned this all to Patience; but that VIRTUE methinks, has extent of dominion sufficient of her own, and enough to do in it, without invading the few dismantled castles which HONOUR has left him upon the earth.

My father stood it out as well as he could with these three auxiliaries to the end of *Trim*'s story; and from thence to the end of my uncle *Toby*'s panegyrick upon arms, in the chapter following it; when seeing, that instead of marching up to Mrs. *Wadman*'s door, they both faced about and march'd down the avenue diametrically opposite to his expectation—he broke out at once with that little subacid soreness of humour which, in certain situations, distinguished his character from that of all other men.

CHAPTER XI

—"NOW WHAT can their two noddles be about?" cried my father——*&c*,——

I dare say, said my mother, they are making fortifications——

——Not on Mrs. *Wadman*'s premises! cried my father, stepping back——

I suppose not: quoth my mother.

I wish, said my father, raising his voice, the whole science of fortification at the devil, with all its trumpery of saps, mines, blinds, gabions, fausse-brays and cuvetts——

——They are foolish things——said my mother.

Now she had a way, which by the bye, I would this moment give away my purple jerkin, and my yellow slippers into the bargain, if some of your reverences would imitate—and that was never to refuse her assent and consent to any proposition my father laid before her, merely because she did not understand it, or had no ideas to the principal word or term of art, upon which the tenet or proposition rolled. She contented herself with doing all that her godfathers and godmothers promised for her—but no more; and so would go on using a hard word twenty years together—and replying to it too, if it was a verb, in all its moods and tenses, without giving herself any trouble to enquire about it.

This was an eternal source of misery to my father, and broke the neck, at the first setting out, of more good dialogues between them, than could have done the most petulant contradiction—— the few which survived were the better for the *cuvetts*——

—"They are foolish things;" said my mother.

——Particularly the *cuvetts*; replied my father.

'Twas enough—he tasted the sweet of triumph—and went on.

—Not that they are, properly speaking, Mrs. *Wadman*'s premises, said my father, partly correcting himself—because she is but tenant for life——

——That makes a great difference—said my mother——

—In a fool's head, replied my father——

Unless she should happen to have a child—said my mother——

——But she must persuade my brother *Toby* first to get her one—

——To be sure, Mr. *Shandy*, quoth my mother.

——Though if it comes to persuasion—said my father—Lord have mercy upon them.

Amen: said my mother, *piano*.

Amen: cried my father, *fortissimè*.

Amen: said my mother again—but with such a sighing cadence of personal pity at the end of it, as discomfited every fibre about my father—he instantly took out his almanack; but before he could untie it, *Yorick*'s congregation coming out of church, became a full answer to one half of his business with it—and my mother telling him it was a sacrament day—left him as little in doubt, as to the other part—He put his almanack into his pocket.

The first Lord of the Treasury thinking of *ways and means*, could not have returned home, with a more embarrassed look.

CHAPTER XII

UPON looking back from the end of the last chapter and surveying the texture of what has been wrote, it is necessary, that upon this page and the five following, a good quantity of heterogeneous matter be inserted, to keep up that just balance betwixt wisdom and folly, without which a book would not hold together a single year: nor is it a poor creeping digression (which but for the name of, a man might continue as well going on in the king's highway) which will do the business ——no; if it is to be a digression, it must be a good frisky one, and upon a frisky subject too, where neither the horse or his rider are to be caught, but by rebound.

The only difficulty, is raising powers suitable to the nature of the service: FANCY is capricious—WIT must not be searched for—and PLEASANTRY (good-natured slut as she is) will not come in at a call, was an empire to be laid at her feet.

——The best way for a man, is to say his prayers——

Only if it puts him in mind of his infirmities and defects as well ghostly as bodily—for that purpose, he will find himself rather worse after he has said them than before—for other purposes, better.

For my own part there is not a way either moral or mechanical under heaven that I could think of, which I have not taken with myself in this case: sometimes by addressing myself directly to the soul herself, and arguing the point over and over again with her upon the extent of her own faculties——

——I never could make them an inch the wider——

Then by changing my system, and trying what could be made of it upon the body, by temperance, soberness and chastity: These are good, quoth I, in themselves—they are good, absolutely;—they are good, relatively;—they are good for health—they are good for happiness in this world—they are good for happiness in the next——

In short, they were good for every thing but the thing wanted; and there they were good for nothing, but to leave the soul just as heaven made it: as for the theological virtues of faith and hope, they give it courage; but then that sniveling virtue of Meekness (as my father would always call it) takes it quite away again, so you are exactly where you started.

Now in all common and ordinary cases, there is nothing which I have found to answer so well as this——

——Certainly, if there is any dependence upon Logic, and that I am not blinded by self-love, there must be something of true genius about me, merely upon this symptom of it, that I do not know what envy is: for never do I hit upon any invention or device which tendeth to the furtherance of good writing, but I instantly make it public; willing that all mankind should write as well as myself.

——Which they certainly will, when they think as little.

CHAPTER XIII

NOW IN ordinary cases, that is, when I am only stupid, and the thoughts rise heavily and pass gummous through my pen——
Or that I am got, I know not how, into a cold unmetaphorical vein of infamous writing, and cannot take a plumb-lift out of it *for my soul*; so must be obliged to go on writing like a *Dutch* commentator to the end of the chapter, unless something be done——
——I never stand confering with pen and ink one moment; for if a pinch of snuff or a stride or two across the room will not do the business for me—I take a razor at once; and having tried the edge of it upon the palm of my hand, without further ceremony, except that of first lathering my beard, I shave it off; taking care only if I do leave a hair, that it be not a grey one; this done, I change my shirt—put on a better coat—send for my last wig—put my topaz ring upon my finger; and in a word, dress myself from one end to the other of me, after my best fashion.

Now the devil in hell must be in it, if this does not do: for consider, Sir, as every man chuses to be present at the shaving of his own beard (though there is no rule without an exception) and unavoidably sits overagainst himself the whole time it is doing, in case he has a hand in it—the Situation, like all others, has notions of her own to put into the brain.——

——I maintain it, the conceits of a rough-bearded man, are seven years more terse and juvenile for one single operation; and if they did not run a risk of being quite shaved away, might be carried up by continual shavings, to the highest pitch of sublimity —How Homer could write with so long a beard, I don't know—— and as it makes against my hypothesis, I as little care——But let us return to the Toilet.

[500]

Ludovicus Sorbonensis makes this entirely an affair of the body (ἐξωτερικὴ πρᾶξις) as he calls it——but he is deceived: the soul and body are joint-sharers in every thing they get: A man cannot dress but his ideas get cloath'd at the same time; and if he dresses like a gentleman, every one of them stands presented to his imagination, genteelized along with him—so that he has nothing to do, but take his pen, and write like himself.

For this cause, when your honours and reverences would know whether I writ clean and fit to be read, you will be able to judge full as well by looking into my Laundress's bill, as my book: there was one single month in which I can make it appear, that I dirtied one and thirty shirts with clean writing; and after all, was more abus'd, curs'd, criticis'd and confounded, and had more mystic heads shaken at me, for what I had wrote in that one month, than in all the other months of that year put together.

——But their honours and reverences had not seen my *bills*.

CHAPTER XIV

AS I NEVER had any intention of beginning the Digression, I am making all this preparation for, till I come to the 15th chapter——I have this chapter to put to whatever use I think proper——I have twenty this moment ready for it—— I could write my chapter of Button-holes in it——

Or my chapter of *Pishes*, which should follow them——

Or my chapter of *Knots*, in case their reverences have done with them——they might lead me into mischief: the safest way is to follow the tract of the learned, and raise objections against what I have been writing, tho' I declare beforehand, I know no more than my heels how to answer them.

And first, it may be said, there is a pelting kind of *thersitical* satire, as black as the very ink 'tis wrote with——(and by the bye, whoever says so, is indebted to the muster-master general of the *Grecian* army, for suffering the name of so ugly and foul-mouth'd a man as *Thersites* to continue upon his roll——for it has furnished him with an epithet)——in these productions he will urge, all the personal washings and scrubbings upon earth do a sinking genius no sort of good——but just the contrary, inasmuch as the dirtier the fellow is, the better generally he succeeds in it.

To this, I have no other answer——at least ready——but that

the Archbishop of *Benevento* wrote his *nasty* Romance of the *Galatea*, as all the world knows, in a purple coat, waistcoat, and purple pair of breeches; and that the penance set him of writing a commentary upon the book of the *Revelations*, as severe as it was look'd upon by one part of the world, was far from being deem'd so, by the other, upon the single account of that *Investment*.

Another objection, to all this remedy, is its want of universality; forasmuch as the shaving part of it, upon which so much stress is laid, by an unalterable law of nature excludes one half of the species entirely from its use: all I can say is, that female writers, whether of *England*, or of *France*, must e'en go without it——

As for the *Spanish* ladies——I am in no sort of distress——

CHAPTER XV

THE fifteenth chapter is come at last; and brings nothing with it but a sad signature of "How our pleasures slip from under us in this world;"

For in talking of my digression——I declare before heaven I have made it! What a strange creature is mortal man! said she.

'Tis very true, said I——but 'twere better to get all these things out of our heads, and return to my uncle *Toby*.

CHAPTER XVI

WHEN my uncle *Toby* and the Corporal had marched down to the bottom of the avenue, they recollected their business lay the other way; so they faced about and marched up streight to Mrs. *Wadman*'s door.

I warrant your honour; said the Corporal, touching his Montero-cap with his hand, as he passed him in order to give a knock at the door——My uncle *Toby*, contrary to his invariable way of treating his faithful servant, said nothing good or bad: the truth was, he had not altogether marshal'd his ideas; he wish'd for another conference, and as the Corporal was mounting up the three steps before the door—he hem'd twice—a portion of my uncle *Toby*'s most modest spirits fled, at each expulsion, towards the Corporal; he stood with the rapper of the door suspended for a full minute in his hand, he scarce knew why. *Bridget* stood perdue within, with her finger and her thumb upon the latch, benumb'd with expectation; and Mrs. *Wadman*, with an eye ready to be deflowered again, sat breathless behind the window-curtain of her bed-chamber, watching their approach.

Trim! said my uncle *Toby*——but as he articulated the word, the minute expired, and *Trim* let fall the rapper.

My uncle *Toby* perceiving that all hopes of a conference were knock'd on the head by it————whistled Lillabullero.

CHAPTER XVII

AS MRS. *BRIDGET*'S finger and thumb were upon the latch, the Corporal did not knock as oft as perchance your honour's taylor——I might have taken my example something nearer home; for I owe mine, some five and twenty pounds at least, and wonder at the man's patience——

——But this is nothing at all to the world: only 'tis a cursed thing to be in debt; and there seems to be a fatality in the exchequers of some poor princes, particularly those of our house, which no Economy can bind down in irons: for my own part, I'm persuaded there is not any one prince, prelate, pope, or potentate, great or small upon earth, more desirous in his heart of keeping streight with the world than I am——or who takes more likely means for it. I never give above half a guinea——or walk with boots—or cheapen tooth-picks——or lay out a shilling upon a band-box the year round; and for the six months I'm in the country, I'm upon so small a scale, that with all the good temper in the world, I out-do *Rousseau*, a bar length——for I keep neither man or boy, or horse, or cow, or dog, or cat, or any thing that can eat or drink, except a thin poor piece of a Vestal (to keep my fire in) and who has generally as bad an appetite as myself——but if you think this makes a philosopher of me—— I would not, my good people! give a rush for your judgments.

True philosophy——but there is no treating the subject whilst my uncle is whistling Lillabullero.

——Let us go into the house.

CHAPTER XVIII

CHAPTER XIX

CHAPTER XX

——— *
* * * * * * * *.
* * * * * * * * * * * * * * * * * * * *
* * * * * * * * * * * * * * * ———

—YOU SHALL see the very place, Madam; said my uncle
Toby.

Mrs. *Wadman* blush'd——look'd towards the door
——turn'd pale——blush'd slightly again——recovered her
natural colour——blush'd worse than ever; which for the sake of
the unlearned reader, I translate thus——

"L—d! I cannot look at it——
What would the world say if I look'd at it?
I should drop down, if I look'd at it—
I wish I could look at it——
There can be no sin in looking at it.
——I will look at it."

Whilst all this was running through Mrs. *Wadman*'s imagination, my uncle *Toby* had risen from the sopha, and got to the
other side of the parlour-door, to give *Trim* an order about it in
the passage——

* * * * * * * * * * * * * * —— I believe it is
in the garret, said my uncle *Toby*——I saw it there, an' please
your honour, this morning, answered *Trim*——Then prithee,
step directly for it, *Trim*, said my uncle *Toby*, and bring it into the
parlour.

The Corporal did not approve of the orders, but most chearfully
obey'd them. The first was not an act of his will—the second was;
so he put on his Montero-cap, and went as fast as his lame knee
would let him. My uncle *Toby* returned into the parlour, and sat
himself down again upon the sopha.

——You shall lay your finger upon the place—said my uncle
Toby.——I will not touch it, however, quoth Mrs. *Wadman* to
herself.

This requires a second translation:—it shews what little
knowledge is got by mere words—we must go up to the first
springs.

Now in order to clear up the mist which hangs upon these
three pages, I must endeavour to be as clear as possible
myself.

[506]

Rub your hands thrice across your foreheads—blow your noses —cleanse your emunctories—sneeze, my good people!—God bless you——

Now give me all the help you can.

CHAPTER XXI

AS THERE are fifty different ends (counting all ends in—— as well civil as religious) for which a woman takes a hus- band, she first sets about and carefully weighs, then separates and distinguishes in her mind, which of all that number of ends, is hers: then by discourse, enquiry, argumentation and inference, she investigates and finds out whether she has got hold of the right one——and if she has——then, by pulling it gently this way and that way, she further forms a judgment, whether it will not break in the drawing.

The imagery under which *Slawkenbergius* impresses this upon his reader's fancy, in the beginning of his third Decad, is so ludicrous, that the honour I bear the sex, will not suffer me to quote it——otherwise 'tis not destitute of humour.

"She first, saith *Slawkenbergius*, stops the ass, and holding his halter in her left hand (lest he should get away) she thrusts her right hand into the very bottom of his pannier to search for it— For what?—you'll not know the sooner, quoth *Slawkenbergius*, for interrupting me——

"I have nothing, good Lady, but empty bottles;" says the ass.

"I'm loaded with tripes;" says the second.

——And thou art little better, quoth she to the third; for nothing is there in thy panniers but trunk-hose and pantofles— and so to the fourth and fifth, going on one by one through the whole string, till coming to the ass which carries it, she turns the pannier upside down, looks at it—considers it—samples it— measures it—stretches it—wets it—dries it—then takes her teeth both to the warp and weft of it——

——Of what? for the love of Christ!

I am determined, answered *Slawkenbergius*, that all the powers upon earth shall never wring that secret from my breast.

CHAPTER XXII

WE LIVE in a world beset on all sides with mysteries and riddles—and so 'tis no matter—else it seems strange, that Nature, who makes every thing so well to answer its destination, and seldom or never errs, unless for pastime, in giving such forms and aptitudes to whatever passes through her hands, that whether she designs for the plough, the caravan, the cart—or whatever other creature she models, be it but an ass's foal, you are sure to have the thing you wanted; and yet at the same time should so eternally bungle it as she does, in making so simple a thing as a married man.

Whether it is in the choice of the clay——or that it is frequently spoiled in the baking; by an excess of which a husband may turn out too crusty (you know) on one hand——or not enough so, through defect of heat, on the other——or whether this great Artificer is not so attentive to the little Platonic exigences *of that part* of the species, for whose use she is fabricating *this*——or that her Ladyship sometimes scarce knows what sort of a husband will do——I know not: we will discourse about it after supper.

It is enough, that neither the observation itself, or the reasoning upon it, are at all to the purpose——but rather against it; since with regard to my uncle *Toby*'s fitness for the marriage state, nothing was ever better: she had formed him of the best and kindliest clay——had temper'd it with her own milk, and breathed into it the sweetest spirit——she had made him all gentle, generous and humane——she had fill'd his heart with trust and confidence, and disposed every passage which led to it, for the communication of the tenderest offices——she had moreover considered the other causes for which matrimony was ordained—

And accordingly * * * * * * * * * * * * * *
* * * * * * * * * * * * * * * * * * *.

The DONATION was not defeated by my uncle *Toby*'s wound.

Now this last article was somewhat apocryphal; and the Devil, who is the great disturber of our faiths in this world, had raised scruples in Mrs. *Wadman*'s brain about it; and like a true devil as he was, had done his own work at the same time, by turning my uncle *Toby*'s Virtue thereupon into nothing but *empty bottles*, *tripes*, *trunk-hose*, and *pantofles*.

CHAPTER XXIII

MRS. *BRIDGET* had pawn'd all the little stock of honour a poor chambermaid was worth in the world, that she would get to the bottom of the affair in ten days; and it was built upon one of the most concessible *postulatum* in nature: namely, that whilst my uncle *Toby* was making love to her mistress, the Corporal could find nothing better to do, than make love to her——"*And I'll let him as much as he will,*" said *Bridget*, "*to get it out of him.*"

Friendship has two garments; an outer, and an under one. *Bridget* was serving her mistress's interests in the one—and doing the thing which most pleased herself in the other; so had as many stakes depending upon my uncle *Toby*'s wound, as the Devil himself——Mrs. *Wadman* had but one—and as it possibly might be her last (without discouraging Mrs. *Bridget*, or discrediting her talents) was determined to play her cards herself.

She wanted not encouragement: a child might have look'd into his hand——there was such a plainness and simplicity in his playing out what trumps he had—— with such an unmistrusting ignorance of the *ten-ace*——and so naked and defenceless did he sit upon the same sopha with widow *Wadman*, that a generous heart would have wept to have won the game of him.

Let us drop the metaphor.

CHAPTER XXIV

— **A**ND THE story too—if you please: for though I have all along been hastening towards this part of it, with so much earnest desire, as well knowing it to be the choicest morsel of what I had to offer to the world, yet now that I am got to it, any one is welcome to take my pen, and go on with the story for me that will—I see the difficulties of the descriptions I'm going to give—and feel my want of powers.

It is one comfort at least to me, that I lost some fourscore ounces of blood this week in a most uncritical fever which attacked me at the beginning of this chapter; so that I have still some hopes remaining, it may be more in the serous or globular parts of the blood, than in the subtile *aura* of the brain——be it which it will—an Invocation can do no hurt——and I leave the affair entirely to the *invoked*, to inspire or to inject me according as he sees good.

THE INVOCATION

GENTLE Spirit of sweetest humour, who erst didst sit upon the easy pen of my beloved CERVANTES; Thou who glided'st daily through his lattice, and turned'st the twilight of his prison into noon-day brightness by thy presence——tinged'st his little urn of water with heaven-sent Nectar, and all the time he wrote of *Sancho* and his master, didst cast thy mystic mantle o'er his wither'd * stump, and wide extended it to all the evils of his life———

——Turn in hither, I beseech thee!——behold these breeches! ——they are all I have in the world——that piteous rent was given them at *Lyons*———

My shirts! see what a deadly schism has happen'd amongst 'em —for the laps are in *Lombardy*, and the rest of 'em here—I never had but six, and a cunning gypsey of a laundress at *Milan* cut me off the *fore*-laps of five—To do her justice, she did it with some consideration—for I was returning *out* of *Italy*.

And yet, notwithstanding all this, and a pistol tinder-box which was moreover filch'd from me at *Sienna*, and twice that I pay'd five *Pauls* for two hard eggs, once at *Raddicoffini*, and a second time at *Capua*—I do not think a journey through *France* and *Italy*, provided a man keeps his temper all the way, so bad a thing as some people would make you believe: there must be *ups* and *downs*, or how the duce should we get into vallies where Nature spreads so many tables of entertainment.—'Tis nonsense to imagine they will lend you their voitures to be shaken to pieces for nothing; and unless you pay twelve sous for greasing your wheels, how should the poor peasant get butter to his bread?—We really expect too much—and for the livre or two above par for your suppers and bed—at the most they are but one shilling and nine-pence halfpenny——who would embroil their philosophy for it? for heaven's and for your own sake, pay it——pay it with both hands open, rather than leave *Disappointment* sitting drooping upon the eye of your fair Hostess and her Damsels in the gate-way, at your departure——and besides, my dear Sir, you get a sisterly kiss of each of 'em worth a pound——at least I did——

* He lost his hand at the battle of *Lepanto*.

——For my uncle *Toby*'s amours running all the way in my head, they had the same effect upon me as if they had been my own ——I was in the most perfect state of bounty and good will; and felt the kindliest harmony vibrating within me, with every oscillation of the chaise alike; so that whether the roads were rough or smooth, it made no difference; every thing I saw, or had to do with, touch'd upon some secret spring either of sentiment or rapture.

——They were the sweetest notes I ever heard; and I instantly let down the fore-glass to hear them more distinctly——'Tis *Maria*; said the postillion, observing I was listening——Poor *Maria*, continued he, (leaning his body on one side to let me see her, for he was in a line betwixt us) is sitting upon a bank playing her vespers upon her pipe, with her little goat beside her.

The young fellow utter'd this with an accent and a look so perfectly in tune to a feeling heart, that I instantly made a vow, I would give him a four and twenty sous piece, when I got to *Moulins*——

——And who is *poor Maria?* said I.

The love and pity of all the villages around us; said the postillion——it is but three years ago, that the sun did not shine upon so fair, so quick-witted and amiable a maid; and better fate did *Maria* deserve, than to have her Banns forbid, by the intrigues of the curate of the parish who published them——

He was going on, when *Maria*, who had made a short pause, put the pipe to her mouth and began the air again——they were the same notes;——yet were ten times sweeter: It is the evening service to the Virgin, said the young man——but who has taught her to play it—or how she came by her pipe, no one knows; we think that Heaven has assisted her in both; for ever since she has been unsettled in her mind, it seems her only consolation——she has never once had the pipe out of her hand, but plays that *service* upon it almost night and day.

The postillion delivered this with so much discretion and natural eloquence, that I could not help decyphering something in his face above his condition, and should have sifted out his history, had not poor *Maria*'s taken such full possession of me.

We had got up by this time almost to the bank where *Maria* was sitting: she was in a thin white jacket with her hair, all but two tresses, drawn up into a silk net, with a few olive-leaves twisted a little fantastically on one side——she was beautiful; and if ever I felt the full force of an honest heart-ache, it was the moment I saw her——

[511]

——God help her! poor damsel! above a hundred masses, said the postillion, have been said in the several parish churches and convents around, for her,——but without effect; we have still hopes, as she is sensible for short intervals, that the Virgin at last will restore her to herself; but her parents, who know her best, are hopeless upon that score, and think her senses are lost for ever.

As the postillion spoke this, MARIA made a cadence so melancholy, so tender and querulous, that I sprung out of the chaise to help her, and found myself sitting betwixt her and her goat before I relapsed from my enthusiasm.

MARIA look'd wistfully for some time at me, and then at her goat——and then at me——and then at her goat again, and so on, alternately——

——Well, *Maria*, said I softly——What resemblance do you find?

I do intreat the candid reader to believe me, that it was from the humblest conviction of what a *Beast* man is,——that I ask'd the question; and that I would not have let fallen an unseasonable pleasantry in the venerable presence of Misery, to be entitled to all the wit that ever *Rabelais* scatter'd——and yet I own my heart smote me, and that I so smarted at the very idea of it, that I swore I would set up for Wisdom and utter grave sentences the rest of my days——and never——never attempt again to commit mirth with man, woman, or child, the longest day I had to live.

As for writing nonsense to them——I believe, there was a reserve—but that I leave to the world.

Adieu, *Maria*!—adieu, poor hapless damsel!——some time, but not *now*, I may hear thy sorrows from thy own lips——but I was deceived; for that moment she took her pipe and told me such a tale of woe with it, that I rose up, and with broken and irregular steps walk'd softly to my chaise.

——What an excellent inn at *Moulins*!

CHAPTER XXV

WHEN we have got to the end of this chapter (but not before) we must all turn back to the two blank chapters, on the account of which my honour has lain bleeding this half hour——I stop it, by pulling off one of my yellow slippers and throwing it with all my violence to the opposite side of my room, with a declaration at the heel of it——

[512]

——That whatever resemblance it may bear to half the chapters which are written in the world, or, for aught I know, may be now writing in it—that it was as casual as the foam of *Zeuxis* his horse: besides, I look upon a chapter which has, *only nothing in it*, with respect; and considering what worse things there are in the world——That it is no way a proper subject for satire——

——Why then was it left so? And here, without staying for my reply, shall I be call'd as many blockheads, numsculs, doddypoles, dunderheads, ninny-hammers, goosecaps, joltheads, nicompoops, and sh—t-a-beds——and other unsavory appellations, as ever the cake-bakers of *Lernè*, cast in the teeth of King *Garagantua*'s shepherds——And I'll let them do it, as *Bridget* said, as much as they please; for how was it possible they should foresee the necessity I was under of writing the 25th chapter of my book, before the 18th, &c.

——So I don't take it amiss——All I wish is, that it may be a lesson to the world, "*to let people tell their stories their own way.*"

The Eighteenth Chapter

AS MRS. *BRIDGET* open'd the door before the corporal had well given the rap, the interval betwixt that and my uncle *Toby*'s introduction into the parlour, was so short, that Mrs. *Wadman* had but just time to get from behind the curtain ——lay a Bible upon the table, and advance a step or two towards the door to receive him.

My uncle *Toby* saluted Mrs. *Wadman*, after the manner in which women were saluted by men in the year of our Lord God one thousand seven hundred and thirteen——then facing about, he march'd up abreast with her to the sopha, and in three plain words——though not before he was sat down——nor after he was sat down——but as he was sitting down, told her, "*he was in love*"——so that my uncle *Toby* strained himself more in the declaration than he needed.

Mrs. *Wadman* naturally looked down, upon a slit she had been darning up in her apron, in expectation every moment, that my uncle *Toby* would go on; but having no talents for amplification, and LOVE moreover of all others being a subject of which he was the least a master——When he had told Mrs. *Wadman* once that he loved her, he let it alone, and left the matter to work after its own way.

[513]

My father was always in raptures with this system of my uncle *Toby*'s, as he falsely called it, and would often say, that could his brother *Toby* to his processe have added but a pipe of tobacco——he had wherewithal to have found his way, if there was faith in a *Spanish* proverb, towards the hearts of half the women upon the globe.

My uncle *Toby* never understood what my father meant; nor will I presume to extract more from it, than a condemnation of an error which the bulk of the world lie under——but the *French*, every one of em' to a man, who believe in it, almost as much as the REAL PRESENCE, "*That talking of love, is making it.*"

——I would as soon set about making a black-pudding by the same receipt.

Let us go on: Mrs. *Wadman* sat in expectation my uncle *Toby* would do so, to almost the first pulsation of that minute, wherein silence on one side or the other, generally becomes indecent: so edging herself a little more towards him, and raising up her eyes, sub-blushing, as she did it——she took up the gauntlet——or the discourse (if you like it better) and communed with my uncle *Toby*, thus.

The cares and disquietudes of the marriage state, quoth Mrs. *Wadman*, are very great. I suppose so—said my uncle *Toby*: and therefore when a person, continued Mrs. *Wadman*, is so much at his ease as you are—so happy, captain *Shandy*, in yourself, your friends and your amusements—I wonder, what reasons can incline you to the state——

——They are written, quoth my uncle *Toby*, in the Common-Prayer Book.

Thus far my uncle *Toby* went on warily, and kept within his depth, leaving Mrs. *Wadman* to sail upon the gulph as she pleased.

——As for children—said Mrs. *Wadman*—though a principal end perhaps of the institution, and the natural wish, I suppose, of every parent—yet do not we all find, they are certain sorrows, and very uncertain comforts? and what is there, dear Sir, to pay one for the heart-achs—what compensation for the many tender and disquieting apprehensions of a suffering and defenceless mother who brings them into life? I declare, said my uncle *Toby*, smit with pity, I know of none; unless it be the pleasure which it has pleased God——

——A fiddlestick! quoth she.

Chapter the Nineteenth

NOW THERE are such an infinitude of notes, tunes, cants, chants, airs, looks, and accents with which the word *fiddlestick* may be pronounced in all such causes as this, every one of 'em impressing a sense and meaning as different from the other, as *dirt* from *cleanliness*—That Casuists (for it is an affair of conscience on that score) reckon up no less than fourteen thousand in which you may do either right or wrong.

Mrs. *Wadman* hit upon the *fiddlestick*, which summoned up all my uncle *Toby*'s modest blood into his cheeks—so feeling within himself that he had somehow or other got beyond his depth, he stopt short; and without entering further either into the pains or pleasures of matrimony, he laid his hand upon his heart, and made an offer to take them as they were, and share them along with her.

When my uncle *Toby* had said this, he did not care to say it again; so casting his eye upon the Bible which Mrs. *Wadman* had laid upon the table, he took it up; and popping, dear soul! upon a passage in it, of all others the most interesting to him—which was the siege of *Jericho*—he set himself to read it over—leaving his proposal of marriage, as he had done his declaration of love, to work with her after its own way. Now it wrought neither as an astringent or a loosener; nor like opium, or bark, or mercury, or buckthorn, or any one drug which nature had bestowed upon the world—in short, it work'd not at all in her; and the cause of that was, that there was something working there before——Babbler that I am! I have anticipated what it was a dozen times; but there is fire still in the subject——allons.

CHAPTER XXVI

IT IS natural for a perfect stranger who is going from *London* to *Edinburgh*, to enquire before he sets out, how many miles to *York*; which is about the half way——nor does any body wonder, if he goes on and asks about the Corporation, &c.—

It was just as natural for Mrs. *Wadman*, whose first husband was all his time afflicted with a Sciatica, to wish to know how far from the hip to the groin; and how far she was likely to suffer more or less in her feelings, in the one case than in the other.

She had accordingly read *Drake*'s anatomy from one end to the other. She had peeped into *Wharton* upon the brain, and borrowed * *Graaf* upon the bones and muscles; but could make nothing of it.

She had reason'd likewise from her own powers——laid down theorems——drawn consequences, and come to no conclusion.

To clear up all, she had twice asked Doctor *Slop*, "if poor captain *Shandy* was ever likely to recover of his wound——?"

——He is recovered, Doctor *Slop* would say——

What! quite?

——Quite: madam——

But what do you mean by a recovery? Mrs. *Wadman* would say.

Doctor *Slop* was the worst man alive at definitions; and so Mrs. *Wadman* could get no knowledge: in short, there was no way to extract it, but from my uncle *Toby* himself.

There is an accent of humanity in an enquiry of this kind which lulls SUSPICION to rest——and I am half persuaded the serpent got pretty near it, in his discourse with *Eve*; for the propensity in the sex to be deceived could not be so great, that she should have boldness to hold chat with the devil, without it——But there is an accent of humanity——how shall I describe it?—'tis an accent which covers the part with a garment, and gives the enquirer a right to be as particular with it, as your body-surgeon.

"——Was it without remission?—

"——Was it more tolerable in bed?

"——Could he lie on both sides alike with it?

"—Was he able to mount a horse?

"—Was motion bad for it?" *et cætera*. were so tenderly spoke to, and so directed towards my uncle *Toby*'s heart, that every item of them sunk ten times deeper into it than the evils themselves ——but when Mrs. *Wadman* went round about by *Namur* to get at my uncle *Toby*'s groin; and engaged him to attack the point of the advanced counterscarp, and *pêle mêle* with the *Dutch* to take the counterguard of *St. Roch* sword in hand—and then with tender notes playing upon his ear, led him all bleeding by the hand out of the trench, wiping her eye, as he was carried to his tent——Heaven! Earth! Sea!—all was lifted up—the springs of nature rose above their levels—an angel of mercy sat besides him on the sopha—his heart glow'd with fire—and had he been worth a thousand, he had lost every heart of them to Mrs. *Wadman*.

* This must be a mistake in Mr. *Shandy*; for *Graaf* wrote upon the pancreatick juice, and the parts of generation.

—And whereabouts, dear Sir, quoth Mrs. *Wadman*, a little categorically, did you receive this sad blow?——In asking this question, Mrs. *Wadman* gave a slight glance towards the waistband of my uncle *Toby*'s red plush breeches, expecting naturally, as the shortest reply to it, that my uncle *Toby* would lay his forefinger upon the place——It fell out otherwise——for my uncle *Toby* having got his wound before the gate of *St. Nicolas*, in one of the traverses of the trench, opposite to the salient angle of the demi-bastion of *St. Roch*; he could at any time stick a pin upon the identical spot of ground where he was standing when the stone struck him: this struck instantly upon my uncle *Toby*'s sensorium——and with it, struck his large map of the town and citadel of *Namur* and its environs, which he had purchased and pasted down upon a board by the Corporal's aid, during his long illness—it had lain with other military lumber in the garret ever since, and accordingly the corporal was detached into the garret to fetch it.

My uncle *Toby* measured off thirty toises, with Mrs. *Wadman*'s scissars, from the returning angle before the gate of *St. Nicolas*; and with such a virgin modesty laid her finger upon the place, that the goddess of Decency, if then in being—if not, 'twas her shade—shook her head, and with a finger wavering across her eyes—forbid her to explain the mistake.

Unhappy Mrs. *Wadman*!——

——For nothing can make this chapter go off with spirit but an apostrophe to thee——but my heart tells me, that in such a crisis an apostrophe is but an insult in disguise, and ere I would offer one to a woman in distress—let the chapter go to the devil; provided any damn'd critick *in keeping* will be but at the trouble to take it with him.

CHAPTER XXVII

MY UNCLE *TOBY*'S Map is carried down into the kitchen.

CHAPTER XXVIII

— AND HERE is the *Maes*—and this is the *Sambre*; said the Corporal, pointing with his right hand extended a little towards the map, and his left upon Mrs. *Bridget*'s shoulder——but not the shoulder next him—and this, said he, is the town of *Namur*—and this the citadel—and there lay the *French* —and here lay his honour and myself——and in this cursed trench, Mrs. *Bridget*, quoth the Corporal, taking her by the hand, did he receive the wound which crush'd him so miserably *here* ——In pronouncing which he slightly press'd the back of her hand towards the part he felt for——and let it fall.

We thought, Mr. *Trim*, it had been more in the middle——said Mrs. *Bridget*——

That would have undone us for ever—said the Corporal.

——And left my poor mistress undone too—said *Bridget*.

The Corporal made no reply to the repartee, but by giving Mrs. *Bridget* a kiss.

Come—come—said *Bridget*—holding the palm of her left-hand parallel to the plane of the horizon, and sliding the fingers of the other over it, in a way which could not have been done, had there been the least wart or protuberance——'Tis every syllable of it false, cried the Corporal, before she had half finished the sentence——

—I know it to be fact, said *Bridget*, from credible witnesses.

——Upon my honour, said the Corporal, laying his hand upon his heart, and blushing as he spoke with honest resentment —'tis a story, Mrs. *Bridget*, as false as hell—Not, said *Bridget*, interrupting him, that either I or my mistress care a halfpenny about it, whether 'tis so or no——only that when one is married, one would chuse to have such a thing by one at least——

It was somewhat unfortunate for Mrs. *Bridget*, that she had begun the attack with her manual exercise; for the Corporal instantly * .

CHAPTER XXIX

I T WAS like the momentary contest in the moist eye-lids of an *April* morning, "Whether *Bridget* should laugh or cry."

She snatch'd up a rolling-pin——'twas ten to one, she had laugh'd——

She laid it down——she cried; and had one single tear of 'em but tasted of bitterness, full sorrowful would the Corporal's heart have been that he had used the argument; but the Corporal understood the sex, a *quart major to a terce* at least, better than my uncle *Toby*, and accordingly he assailed Mrs. *Bridget* after this manner.

I know, Mrs. *Bridget*, said the Corporal, giving her a most respectful kiss, that thou art good and modest by nature, and art withal so generous a girl in thyself, that if I know thee rightly, thou wouldst not wound an insect, much less the honour of so gallant and worthy a soul as my master, wast thou sure to be made a countess of —— but thou hast been set on, and deluded, dear *Bridget*, as is often a woman's case, "to please others more than themselves——"

Bridget's eyes poured down at the sensations the Corpora excited.

——Tell me——tell me then, my dear *Bridget*, continued the Corporal, taking hold of her hand, which hung down dead by her side,——and giving a second kiss—whose suspicion has misled thee?

Bridget sobb'd a sob or two——then open'd her eyes——the Corporal wiped 'em with the bottom of her apron——she then open'd her heart and told him all.

CHAPTER XXX

M Y UNCLE *TOBY* and the Corporal had gone on separately with their operations the greatest part of the campaign, and as effectually cut off from all communication of what either the one or the other had been doing, as if they had been separated from each other by the *Maes* or the *Sambre*.

My uncle *Toby*, on his side, had presented himself every afternoon in his red and silver, and blue and gold alternately, and sustained an infinity of attacks in them, without knowing them to be attacks—and so had nothing to communicate——

The Corporal, on his side, in taking *Bridget*, by it had gain'd considerable advantages——and consequently had much to communicate——but what were the advantages——as well, as what was the manner by which he had seiz'd them, required so nice an historian that the Corporal durst not venture upon it; and as sensible as he was of glory, would rather have been contented to have gone barehead and without laurels for ever, than torture his master's modesty for a single moment——

——Best of honest and gallant servants!——But I have apostrophiz'd thee, *Trim*! once before——and could I apotheosize thee also (that is to say) with good company——I would do it *without ceremony* in the very next page.

CHAPTER XXXI

NOW my uncle *Toby* had one evening laid down his pipe upon the table, and was counting over to himself upon his finger ends, (beginning at his thumb) all Mrs. *Wadman*'s perfections one by one; and happening two or three times together, either by omitting some, or counting others twice over, to puzzle himself sadly before he could get beyond his middle finger—Prithee, *Trim*! said he, taking up his pipe again,—— bring me a pen and ink: *Trim* brought paper also.

Take a full sheet——*Trim*! said my uncle *Toby*, making a sign with his pipe at the same time to take a chair and sit down close by him at the table. The Corporal obeyed——placed the paper directly before him——took a pen and dip'd it in the ink.

—She has a thousand virtues, *Trim*! said my uncle *Toby*——

Am I to set them down, an' please your honour? quoth the Corporal.

——But they must be taken in their ranks, replied my uncle *Toby*; for of them all, *Trim*, that which wins me most, and which is a security for all the rest, is the compassionate turn and singular humanity of her character—I protest, added my uncle *Toby*, looking up, as he protested it, towards the top of the ceiling——That was I her brother, *Trim*, a thousand fold, she could not make more constant or more tender enquiries after my sufferings—— though now no more.

The Corporal made no reply to my uncle *Toby*'s protestation, but by a short cough—he dip'd the pen a second time into the inkhorn; and my uncle *Toby* pointing with the end of his pipe as close to the top of the sheet at the left hand corner of it, as he could get it——the Corporal wrote down the word
HUMANITY - - - - thus.

Prithee, Corporal, said my uncle *Toby*, as soon as *Trim* had done it——how often does Mrs. *Bridget* enquire after the wound on the cap of thy knee, which thou received'st at the battle of *Landen*?

She never, an' please your honour, enquires after it at all.

That, Corporal, said my uncle *Toby*, with all the triumph the goodness of his nature would permit——That shews the difference in the character of the mistress and maid——had the fortune of war allotted the same mischance to me, Mrs. *Wadman* would have enquired into every circumstance relating to it a hundred times——She would have enquired, an' please your honour, ten times as often about your honour's groin——The pain, *Trim*, is equally excruciating,——and Compassion has as much to do with the one as the other——

——God bless your honour! cried the Corporal——what has a woman's compassion to do with a wound upon the cap of a man's knee? had your honour's been shot into ten thousand splinters at the affair of *Landen*, Mrs. *Wadman* would have troubled her head as little about it as *Bridget*; because, added the Corporal, lowering his voice and speaking very distinctly, as he assigned his reason——

"The knee is such a distance from the main body—whereas the groin, your honour knows, is upon the very *curtin* of the *place*."

My uncle *Toby* gave a long whistle——but in a note which could scarce be heard across the table.

The Corporal had advanced too far to retire——in three words he told the rest——

My uncle *Toby* laid down his pipe as gently upon the fender, as if it had been spun from the unravellings of a spider's web——

——Let us go to my brother *Shandy*'s, said he.

CHAPTER XXXII

THERE will be just time, whilst my uncle *Toby* and *Trim* are walking to my father's, to inform you, that Mrs. *Wadman* had, some moons before this, made a confident of my mother; and that Mrs. *Bridget*, who had the burden of her own, as well as her mistress's secret to carry, had got happily delivered of both to *Susannah* behind the garden-wall.

As for my mother, she saw nothing at all in it, to make the least bustle about——but *Susannah* was sufficient by herself for all the ends and purposes you could possibly have, in exporting a family secret; for she instantly imparted it by signs to *Jonathan* ——·—and *Jonathan* by tokens to the cook, as she was basting a loin of mutton; the cook sold it with some kitchen-fat to the postillion for a groat, who truck'd it with the dairy maid for something of about the same value——and though whisper'd in the hay-loft, FAME caught the notes with her brazen trumpet and sounded them upon the house-top—In a word, not an old woman in the village or five miles round, who did not understand the difficulties of my uncle *Toby*'s siege, and what were the secret articles which had delay'd the surrender.——

My father, whose way was to force every event in nature into an hypothesis, by which means never man crucified TRUTH at the rate he did——had but just heard of the report as my uncle *Toby* set out; and catching fire suddenly at the trespass done his brother by it, was demonstrating to *Yorick*, notwithstanding my mother was sitting by——not only, "That the devil was in women, and that the whole of the affair was lust;" but that every evil and disorder in the world of what kind or nature soever, from the first fall of *Adam*, down to my uncle *Toby*'s (inclusive) was owing one way or other to the same unruly appetite.

Yorick was just bringing my father's hypothesis to some temper, when my uncle *Toby* entering the room with marks of infinite benevolence and forgiveness in his looks, my father's eloquence rekindled against the passion——and as he was not very nice in the choice of his words when he was wroth——as soon as my uncle *Toby* was seated by the fire, and had filled his pipe, my father broke out in this manner.

CHAPTER XXXIII

—THAT provision should be made for continuing the race of so great, so exalted and godlike a Being as man—I am far from denying—but philosophy speaks freely of every thing; and therefore I still think and do maintain it to be a pity, that it should be done by means of a passion which bends down the faculties, and turns all the wisdom, contemplations, and operations of the soul backwards——a passion, my dear, continued my father, addressing himself to my mother, which couples and equals wise men with fools, and makes us come out of our caverns and hiding-places more like satyrs and four-footed beasts than men.

I know it will be said, continued my father (availing himself of the *Prolepsis*) that in itself, and simply taken——like hunger, or thirst, or sleep——'tis an affair neither good or bad—or shameful or otherwise.——Why then did the delicacy of *Diogenes* and *Plato* so recalcitrate against it? and wherefore, when we go about to make and plant a man, do we put out the candle? and for what reason is it, that all the parts thereof—the congredients—the preparations—the instruments, and whatever serves thereto, are so held as to be conveyed to a cleanly mind by no language, translation, or periphrasis whatever?

——The act of killing and destroying a man, continued my father raising his voice—and turning to my uncle *Toby*—you see, is glorious—and the weapons by which we do it are honourable ——We march with them upon our shoulders——We strut with them by our sides——We gild them——We carve them——We in-lay them——We enrich them——Nay, if it be but a *scoundril* cannon, we cast an ornament upon the breech of it.—

——My uncle *Toby* laid down his pipe to intercede for a better epithet——and *Yorick* was rising up to batter the whole hypothesis to pieces——

——When *Obadiah* broke into the middle of the room with a complaint, which cried out for an immediate hearing.

The case was this:

My father, whether by ancient custom of the manor, or as improprietor of the great tythes, was obliged to keep a Bull for the service of the Parish, and *Obadiah* had led his cow upon a *pop-visit* to him one day or other the preceeding summer—I say, one day or other—because as chance would have it, it was the day on which he was married to my father's house-maid——so one was a reckoning to the other. Therefore when *Obadiah*'s wife was brought to bed—*Obadiah* thanked God——

——Now, said *Obadiah*, I shall have a calf: so *Obadiah* went daily to visit his cow.

She'll calve on *Monday*—on *Tuesday*—or *Wednesday* at the farthest——

The cow did not calve——no—she'll not calve till next week ——the cow put it off terribly——till at the end of the sixth week *Obadiah*'s suspicions (like a good man's) fell upon the Bull.

Now the parish being very large, my father's Bull, to speak the truth of him, was no way equal to the department; he had, however, got himself, somehow or other, thrust into employment— and as he went through the business with a grave face, my father had a high opinion of him.

——Most of the townsmen, an' please your worship, quoth *Obadiah*, believe that 'tis all the Bull's fault——

——But may not a cow be barren? replied my father, turning to Doctor *Slop*.

It never happens: said Dr. *Slop*, but the man's wife may have come before her time naturally enough——Prithee has the child hair upon his head?—added Dr. *Slop*——

——It is as hairy as I am; said *Obadiah*.——*Obadiah* had not been shaved for three weeks——Wheu—u——u——— cried my father; beginning the sentence with an exclamatory whistle——and so, brother *Toby*, this poor Bull of mine, who is as good a Bull as ever p—ss'd, and might have done for *Europa* herself in purer times—had he but two legs less, might have been driven into Doctors Commons and lost his character——which to a Town Bull, brother *Toby*, is the very same thing as his life——

L—d! said my mother, what is all this story about?——

A COCK and a BULL, said *Yorick*——And one of the best of its kind, I ever heard.

END of the NINTH VOLUME.

A

Sentimental Journey

THROUGH

FRANCE AND ITALY

By Mr. Yorick

The present text of *A Sentimental Journey*, except for some minor corrections, follows the text of the first edition. (For details of its composition and publication see Chronological Table.)

VOLUME I

SENTIMENTAL JOURNEY

THROUGH FRANCE AND ITALY

—THEY order, said I, this matter better in France—
—You have been in France? said my gentleman, turning quick upon me with the most civil triumph in the world.—Strange! quoth I, debating the matter with myself, That one and twenty miles sailing, for 'tis absolutely no further from Dover to Calais, should give a man these rights—I'll look into them: so giving up the argument—I went straight to my lodgings, put up half dozen a shirts and a black pair of silk breeches—"the coat I have on, said I, looking at the sleeve, will do"—took a place in the Dover stage; and the packet sailing at nine the next morning —by three I had got sat down to my dinner upon a fricassee'd chicken so incontestably in France, that had I died that night of an indigestion, the whole world could not have suspended the effects of the * *Droits d'aubaine*—my shirts, and black pair of silk breeches—portmanteau and all must have gone to the King of France—even the little picture which I have so long worn, and so often have told thee, Eliza, I would carry with me into my grave, would have been torn from my neck.—Ungenerous!—to seize upon the wreck of an unwary passenger, whom your subjects had beckon'd to their coast—by heaven! SIRE, it is not well done; and much does it grieve me, 'tis the monarch of a people so civilized and courteous, and so renown'd for sentiment and fine feelings, that I have to reason with——

But I have scarce set foot in your dominions——

CALAIS

WHEN I had finish'd my dinner, and drank the King of France's health, to satisfy my mind that I bore him no spleen, but, on the contrary, high honour for the humanity of his temper—I rose up an inch taller for the accommodation.

* All the effects of strangers (Swiss and Scotch excepted) dying in France, are seized by virtue of this law, tho' the heir be upon the spot——the profit of these contingencies being farm'd, there is no redress.

—No—said I—the Bourbon is by no means a cruel race: they may be misled like other people; but there is a mildness in their blood. As I acknowledged this, I felt a suffusion of a finer kind upon my cheek—more warm and friendly to man, than what Burgundy (at least of two livres a bottle, which was such as I had been drinking) could have produced.

—Just God! said I, kicking my portmanteau aside, what is there in this world's goods which should sharpen our spirits, and make so many kind-hearted brethren of us, fall out so cruelly as we do by the way?

When man is at peace with man, how much lighter than a feather is the heaviest of metals in his hand! he pulls out his purse, and holding it airily and uncompress'd, looks round him, as if he sought for an object to share it with—In doing this, I felt every vessel in my frame dilate—the arteries beat all chearily together, and every power which sustained life, perform'd it with so little friction, that 'twould have confounded the most *physical precieuse* in France: with all her materialism, she could scarce have called me a machine—

I'm confident, said I to myself, I should have overset her creed.

The accession of that idea, carried nature, at that time, as high as she could go—I was at peace with the world before, and this finish'd the treaty with myself—

—Now, was I a King of France, cried I—what a moment for an orphan to have begg'd his father's portmanteau of me!

THE MONK

CALAIS

I HAD scarce utter'd the words, when a poor monk of the order of St. Francis came into the room to beg something for his convent. No man cares to have his virtues the sport of contingencies—or one man may be generous, as another man is puissant—*sed non, quo ad hanc*—or be it as it may—for there is no regular reasoning upon the ebbs and flows of our humours; they may depend upon the same causes, for ought I know, which influence the tides themselves—'twould oft be no discredit to us, to suppose it was so: I'm sure at least for myself, that in many a case I should be more highly satisfied, to have it said by the world, "I had had an affair with the moon, in which there was neither sin nor shame," than have it pass altogether as my own act and deed, wherein there was so much of both.

—But be this as it may. The moment I cast my eyes upon him, I was predetermined not to give him a single sous; and accordingly I put my purse into my pocket—button'd it up—set myself a little more upon my centre, and advanced up gravely to him: there was something, I fear, forbidding in my look: I have his figure this moment before my eyes, and think there was that in it which deserved better.

The monk, as I judged from the break in his tonsure, a few scatter'd white hairs upon his temples, being all that remained of it, might be about seventy—but from his eyes, and that sort of fire which was in them, which seemed more temper'd by courtesy than years, could be no more than sixty—Truth might lie between—He was certainly sixty-five; and the general air of his countenance, notwithstanding something seem'd to have been planting wrinkles in it before their time, agreed to the account.

It was one of those heads, which Guido has often painted—mild, pale—penetrating, free from all common-place ideas of fat contented ignorance looking downwards upon the earth—it look'd forwards; but look'd, as if it look'd at something beyond this world. How one of his order came by it, heaven above, who let it fall upon a monk's shoulders, best knows: but it would have suited a Bramin, and had I met it upon the plains of Indostan, I had reverenced it.

The rest of his outline may be given in a few strokes; one might put it into the hands of any one to design, for 'twas neither elegant or otherwise, but as character and expression made it so: it was a thin, spare form, something above the common size, if it lost not the distinction by a bend forwards in the figure—but it was the attitude of Intreaty; and as it now stands presented to my imagination, it gain'd more than it lost by it.

When he had enter'd the room three paces, he stood still; and laying his left hand upon his breast, (a slender white staff with which he journey'd being in his right)—when I had got close up to him, he introduced himself with the little story of the wants of his convent, and the poverty of his order—and did it with so simple a grace—and such an air of deprecation was there in the whole cast of his look and figure—I was bewitch'd not to have been struck with it—

—A better reason was, I had predetermined not to give him a single sous.

THE MONK

CALAIS

—'TIS very true, said I, replying to a cast upwards with his eyes, with which he had concluded his address—'tis very true—and heaven be their resource who have no other but the charity of the world, the stock of which, I fear, is no way sufficient for the many *great claims* which are hourly made upon it.

As I pronounced the words *great claims*, he gave a slight glance with his eye downwards upon the sleeve of his tunick—I felt the full force of the appeal—I acknowledge it, said I—a coarse habit, and that but once in three years, with meagre diet—are no great matters; and the true point of pity is, as they can be earn'd in the world with so little industry, that your order should wish to procure them by pressing upon a fund which is the property of the lame, the blind, the aged, and the infirm—the captive who lies down counting over and over again the days of his afflictions, languishes also for his share of it; and had you been of the *order of mercy*, instead of the order of St. Francis, poor as I am, continued I, pointing at my portmanteau, full chearfully should it have been open'd to you, for the ransom of the unfortunate—The monk made me a bow—but of all others, resumed I, the unfortunate of our own country, surely, have the first rights; and I have left thousands in distress upon our own shore—The monk gave a cordial wave with his head—as much as to say, No doubt, there is misery enough in every corner of the world, as well as within our convent—But we distinguish, said I, laying my hand upon the sleeve of his tunick, in return for his appeal—we distinguish, my good Father! betwixt those who wish only to eat the bread of their own labour—and those who eat the bread of other people's, and have no other plan in life, but to get through it in sloth and ignorance, *for the love of God.*

The poor Franciscan made no reply: a hectic of a moment pass'd across his cheek, but could not tarry—Nature seemed to have had done with her resentments in him; he shewed none—but letting his staff fall within his arm, he press'd both his hands with resignation upon his breast, and retired.

THE MONK

CALAIS

MY HEART smote me the moment he shut the door—Psha! said I with an air of carelessness, three several times—but it would not do: every ungracious syllable I had utter'd, crouded back into my imagination: I reflected, I had no right over the poor Franciscan, but to deny him; and that the punishment of that was enough to the disappointed without the addition of unkind language—I consider'd his grey hairs—his courteous figure seem'd to re-enter and gently ask me what injury he had done me?—and why I could use him thus—I would have given twenty livres for an advocate—I have behaved very ill; said I within myself; but I have only just set out upon my travels; and shall learn better manners as I get along.

THE DESOBLIGEANT

CALAIS

WHEN a man is discontented with himself, it has one advantage however, that it puts him into an excellent frame of mind for making a bargain. Now there being no travelling through France and Italy without a chaise—and nature generally prompting us to the thing we are fittest for, I walk'd out into the coach yard to buy or hire something of that kind to my purpose: an old *Desobligeant in the furthest corner of the court, hit my fancy at first sight, so I instantly got into it, and finding it in tolerable harmony with my feelings, I ordered the waiter to call Monsieur Dessein the master of the hotel—but Monsieur Dessein being gone to vespers, and not caring to face the Franciscan whom I saw on the opposite side of the court, in conference with a lady just arrived, at the inn—I drew the taffeta curtain betwixt us, and being determined to write my journey, I took out my pen and ink, and wrote the preface to it in the *Desobligeant*.

* A chaise, so called in France, from its holding but one person.

[533]

PREFACE

IN THE DESOBLIGEANT

I T MUST have been observed by many a peripatetic philosopher, That nature has set up by her own unquestionable authority certain boundaries and fences to circumscribe the discontent of man: she has effected her purpose in the quietest and easiest manner by laying him under almost insuperable obligations to work out his ease, and to sustain his sufferings at home. It is there only that she has provided him with the most suitable objects to partake of his happiness, and bear a part of that burden which in all countries and ages, has ever been too heavy for one pair of shoulders. 'Tis true we are endued with an imperfect power of spreading our happiness sometimes beyond *her* limits, but 'tis so ordered, that from the want of languages, connections, and dependencies, and from the difference in education, customs and habits, we lie under so many impediments in communicating our sensations out of our own sphere, as often amount to a total impossibility.

It will always follow from hence, that the balance of sentimental commerce is always against the expatriated adventurer: he must buy what he has little occasion for at their own price— his conversation will seldom be taken in exchange for theirs without a large discount—and this, by the by, eternally driving him into the hands of more equitable brokers for such conversation as he can find, it requires no great spirit of divination to guess at his party—

This brings me to my point; and naturally leads me (if the seesaw of this *Desobligeant* will but let me get on) into the efficient as well as the final causes of travelling—

Your idle people that leave their native country and go abroad for some reason or reasons which may be derived from one of these general causes—

Infirmity of body,
Imbecility of mind, or
Inevitable necessity.

The first two include all those who travel by land or by water, labouring with pride, curiosity, vanity or spleen, subdivided and combined *in infinitum*.

The third class includes the whole army of peregrine martyrs; more especially those travellers who set out upon their travels with the benefit of the clergy, either as delinquents travelling under the direction of governors recommended by the magistrate—or young gentlemen transported by the cruelty of parents and guardians, and travelling under the direction of governors recommended by Oxford, Aberdeen and Glasgow.

There is a fourth class, but their number is so small that they would not deserve a distinction, was it not necessary in a work of this nature to observe the greatest precision and nicety, to avoid a confusion of character. And these men I speak of, are such as cross the seas and sojourn in a land of strangers with a view of saving money for various reasons and upon various pretences: but as they might also save themselves and others a great deal of unnecessary trouble by saving their money at home—and as their reasons for travelling are the least complex of any other species of emigrants, I shall distinguish these gentlemen by the name of

Simple Travellers.

Thus the whole circle of travellers may be reduced to the following *Heads*.

Idle Travellers,
Inquisitive Travellers,
Lying Travellers,
Proud Travellers,
Vain Travellers,
Splenetic Travellers.

Then follow the Travellers of Necessity.

The delinquent and felonious Traveller,
The unfortunate and innocent Traveller,
The simple Traveller,

And last of all (if you please) The Sentimental Traveller (meaning thereby myself) who have travell'd, and of which I am now sitting down to give an account—as much out of *Necessity*, and the *besoin de* Voyager, as any one in the class.

I am well aware, at the same time, as both my travels and observations will be altogether of a different cast from any of my fore-runners; that I might have insisted upon a whole nitch entirely to myself—but I should break in upon the confines of the *Vain* Traveller, in wishing to draw attention towards me, till I have some better grounds for it, than the mere *Novelty of my Vehicle*.

It is sufficient for my reader, if he has been a traveller himself, that with study and reflection hereupon he may be able to determine his own place and rank in the catalogue—it will be one step towards knowing himself; as it is great odds, but he retains some tincture and resemblance, of what he imbibed or carried out, to the present hour.

The man who first transplanted the grape of Burgundy to the Cape of Good Hope (observe he was a Dutch man) never dreamt of drinking the same wine at the Cape, that the same grape produced upon the French mountains—he was too phlegmatic for that—but undoubtedly he expected to drink some sort of vinous liquor; but whether good, bad, or indifferent—he knew enough of this world to know, that it did not depend upon his choice, but that what is generally called *chance* was to decide his success: however, he hoped for the best; and in these hopes, by an intemperate confidence in the fortitude of his head, and the depth of his discretion, *Mynheer* might possibly overset both in his new vineyard; and by discovering his nakedness, become a laughing-stock to his people.

Even so it fares with the poor Traveller, sailing and posting through the politer kingdoms of the globe in pursuit of knowledge and improvements.

Knowledge and improvements are to be got by sailing and posting for that purpose; but whether useful knowledge and real improvements, is all a lottery—and even where the adventurer is successful, the acquired stock must be used with caution and sobriety to turn to any profit—but as the chances run prodigiously the other way both as to the acquisition and application, I am of opinion, That a man would act as wisely, if he could prevail upon himself, to live contented without foreign knowledge or foreign improvements, especially if he lives in a country that has no absolute want of either—and indeed, much grief of heart has it oft and many a time cost me, when I have observed how many a foul step the inquisitive Traveller has measured to see sights and look into discoveries; all which, as Sancho Pança said to Don Quixote, they might have seen dry-shod at home. It is an age so full of light, that there is scarce a country or corner of Europe whose beams are not crossed and interchanged with others—Knowledge in most of its branches, and in most affairs, is like music in an Italian street, whereof those may partake, who pay nothing—But there is no nation under heaven—and God is my record, (before whose tribunal I must one day come and give an account of this work)—that I do not speak it vauntingly— But there is no nation under heaven abounding with more variety

[536]

of learning—where the sciences may be more fitly woo'd, or more surely won than here—where art is encouraged, and will so soon rise high—where Nature (take her all together) has so little to answer for—and, to close all, where there is more wit and variety of character to feed the mind with—Where then, my dear countrymen, are you going—

—We are only looking at this chaise, said they—Your most obedient servant, said I, skipping out of it, and pulling off my hat—We were wondering, said one of them, who, I found, was an *inquisitive traveller*—what could occasion its motion.——'Twas the agitation, said I coolly, of writing a preface—I never heard, said the other, who was a *simple traveller*, of a preface wrote in a *Desobligeant*.—It would have been better, said I, in a *Vis a Vis*.

—*As an English man does not travel to see English men*, I retired to my room.

CALAIS

I PERCEIVED that something darken'd the passage more than myself, as I stepp'd along it to my room; it was effectually Mons. Dessein, the master of the hotel, who had just return'd from vespers, and, with his hat under his arm, was most complaisantly following me, to put me in mind of my wants. I had wrote myself pretty well out of conceit with the *Desobligeant*; and Mons. Dessein speaking of it, with a shrug, as if it would no way suit me, it immediately struck my fancy that it belong'd to some *innocent traveller*, who, on his return home, had left it to Mons. Dessein's honour to make the most of. Four months had elapsed since it had finish'd its career of Europe in the corner of Mons. Dessein's coachyard; and having sallied out from thence but a vampt-up business at the first, though it had been twice taken to pieces on Mount Sennis, it had not profited much by its adventures—but by none so little as the standing so many months unpitied in the corner of Mons. Dessein's coach-yard. Much indeed was not to be said for it—but something might—and when a few words will rescue misery out of her distress, I hate the man who can be a churl of them.

—Now was I the master of this hotel, said I, laying the point of my fore-finger on Mons. Dessein's breast, I would inevitably make a point of getting rid of this unfortunate *Desobligeant*—it stands swinging reproaches at you every time you pass by it—

Mon Dieu! said Mons. Dessein—I have no interest—Except the interest, said I, which men of a certain turn of mind take, Mons. Dessein, in their own sensations—I'm persuaded, to a man who feels for others as well as for himself, every rainy night, disguise it as you will, must cast a damp upon your spirits —You suffer, Mons. Dessein, as much as the machine—

I have always observed, when there is as much *sour* as *sweet* in a compliment, that an Englishman is eternally at a loss within himself, whether to take it, or let it alone: a Frenchman never is: Mon. Dessein made me a bow.

C'est bien vrai, said he—But in this case I should only exchange one disquietude for another, and with loss: figure to yourself, my dear Sir, that in giving you a chaise which would fall to pieces before you had got half way to Paris—figure to yourself how much I should suffer, in giving an ill impression of myself to a man of honour, and lying at the mercy, as I must do, *d'un homme d'esprit.*

The dose was made up exactly after my own prescription; so I could not help taking it—and returning Mons. Dessein his bow, without more casuistry we walk'd together towards his Remise, to take a view of his magazine of chaises.

IN THE STREET

CALAIS

IT MUST needs be a hostile kind of a world, when the buyer (if it be but of a sorry post-chaise) cannot go forth with the seller thereof into the street to terminate the difference betwixt them, but he instantly falls into the same frame of mind and views his conventionist with the same sort of eye, as if he was going along with him to Hyde-park corner to fight a duel. For my own part, being but a poor sword's-man, and no way a match for Monsieur *Dessein*, I felt the rotation of all the movements within me, to which the situation is incident—I looked at Monsieur *Dessein* through and through—ey'd him as he walked along in profile—then, *en face*—thought he look'd like a Jew—then a Turk—disliked his wig—cursed him by my gods—wished him at the devil—

[538]

—And is all this to be lighted up in the heart for a beggarly account of three or four louisd'ors, which is the most I can be over-reach'd in?—Base passion! said I, turning myself about, as a man naturally does upon a sudden reverse of sentiment—base, ungentle passion! thy hand is against every man, and every man's hand against thee—heaven forbid! said she, raising her hand up to her forehead, for I had turned full in front upon the lady whom I had seen in conference with the monk—she had followed us unperceived—Heaven forbid indeed! said I, offering her my own—she had a black pair of silk gloves open only at the thumb and two fore-fingers, so accepted it without reserve—and I led her up to the door of the Remise.

Monsieur *Dessein* had *diabled* the key above fifty times before he found out he had come with a wrong one in his hand: we were as impatient as himself to have it open'd; and so attentive to the obstacle, that I continued holding her hand almost without knowing it; so that Monsieur *Dessein* left us together with her hand in mine, and with our faces turned towards the door of the Remise, and said he would be back in five minutes.

Now a colloquy of five minutes, in such a situation, is worth one of as many ages, with your faces turned towards the street: in the latter case, 'tis drawn from the objects and occurrences without—when your eyes are fixed upon a dead blank—you draw purely from yourselves. A silence of a single moment upon Monsieur *Dessein*'s leaving us, had been fatal to the situation—she had infallibly turned about—so I begun the conversation instantly.—

—But what were the temptations, (as I write not to apologize for the weaknesses of my heart in this tour,—but to give an account of them)—shall be described with the same simplicity, with which I felt them.

THE REMISE DOOR

CALAIS

WHEN I told the reader that I did not care to get out of the *Desobligeant*, because I saw the monk in close conference with a lady just arrived at the inn—I told him the truth; but I did not tell him the whole truth; for I was full as much restrained by the appearance and figure of the lady he was talking to. Suspicion crossed my brain, and said, he was telling her what had passed: something jarred upon it within me —I wished him at his convent.

When the heart flies out before the understanding, it saves the judgment a world of pains—I was certain she was of a better order of beings—however, I thought no more of her, but went on and wrote my preface.

The impression returned, upon my encounter with her in the street; a guarded frankness with which she gave me her hand, shewed, I thought, her good education and her good sense; and as I led her on, I felt a pleasurable ductility about her, which spread a calmness over all my spirits—

—Good God! how a man might lead such a creature as this round the world with him!—

I had not yet seen her face—'twas not material; for the drawing was instantly set about, and long before we had got to the door of the Remise, *Fancy* had finished the whole head, and pleased herself as much with its fitting her goddess, as if she had dived into the TIBER for it—but thou art a seduced, and a seducing slut; and albeit thou cheatest us seven times a day with thy pictures and images, yet with so many charms dost thou do it, and thou deckest out thy pictures in the shapes of so many angels of light, 'tis a shame to break with thee.

When we had got to the door of the Remise, she withdrew her hand from across her forehead, and let me see the original— it was a face of about six and twenty—of a clear transparent brown, simply set off without rouge or powder—it was not critically handsome, but there was that in it, which in the frame of mind I was in, which attached me much more to it—it was interesting; I fancied it wore the characters of a widow'd look, and in that state of its declension, which had passed the two first paroxysms of sorrow, and was quietly beginning to reconcile itself to its loss—but a thousand other distresses might have traced the same lines; I wish'd to know what they had been— and was ready to enquire, (had the same *bon ton* of conversation permitted, as in the days of Esdras)—" *What aileth thee? and why art thou disquieted? and why is thy understanding troubled?*"— In a word, I felt benevolence for her; and resolved some way or other to throw in my mite of courtesy—if not of service.

Such were my temptations—and in this disposition to give way to them, was I left alone with the lady with her hand in mine, and with our faces both turned closer to the door of the Remise than what was absolutely necessary.

THE REMISE DOOR

CALAIS

THIS certainly, fair lady! said I, raising her hand up a little lightly as I begun, must be one of Fortune's whimsical doings: to take two utter strangers by their hands—of different sexes, and perhaps from different corners of the globe, and in one moment place them together in such a cordial situation, as Friendship herself could scarce have atchieved for them, had she projected it for a month—

—And your reflection upon it, shews how much, Monsieur, she has embarassed you by the adventure.—

When the situation is, what we would wish, nothing is so ill-timed as to hint at the circumstances which make it so: you thank Fortune, continued she—you had reason—the heart knew it, and was satisfied; and who but an English philosopher would have sent notices of it to the brain to reverse the judgment?

In saying this, she disengaged her hand with a look which I thought a sufficient commentary upon the text.

It is a miserable picture which I am going to give of the weakness of my heart, by owning, that it suffered a pain, which worthier occasions could not have inflicted.—I was mortified with the loss of her hand, and the manner in which I had lost it carried neither oil nor wine to the wound: I never felt the pain of a sheepish inferiority so miserably in my life.

The triumphs of a true feminine heart are short upon these discomfitures. In a very few seconds she laid her hand upon the cuff of my coat, in order to finish her reply; so some way or other, God knows how, I regained my situation.

—She had nothing to add.

I forthwith began to model a different conversation for the lady, thinking from the spirit as well as moral of this, that I had been mistaken in her character; but upon turning her face towards me, the spirit which had animated the reply was fled—the muscles relaxed, and I beheld the same unprotected look of distress which first won me to her interest—melancholy! to see such sprightliness the prey of sorrow.—I pitied her from my soul; and though it may seem ridiculous enough to a torpid heart,—I could have taken her into my arms, and cherished her, though it was in the open street, without blushing.

The pulsations of the arteries along my fingers pressing across

[541]

hers, told her what was passing within me: she looked down—
a silence of some moments followed.

I fear, in this interval, I must have made some slight efforts
towards a closer compression of her hand, from a subtle sensation I felt in the palm of my own—not as if she was going to
withdraw hers—but, as if she thought about it—and I had
infallibly lost it a second time, had not instinct more than reason
directed me to the last resource in these dangers—to hold it
loosely, and in a manner as if I was every moment going to release
it, of myself; so she let it continue, till Monsieur *Dessein* returned
with the key; and in the mean time I set myself to consider how
I should undo the ill impressions which the poor monk's story,
in case he had told it her, must have planted in her breast against
me.

THE SNUFF-BOX

CALAIS

THE good old monk was within six paces of us, as the idea of
him cross'd my mind; and was advancing towards us a little
out of the line, as if uncertain whether he should break in
upon us or no.—He stopp'd, however, as soon as he came up to
us, with a world of frankness; and having a horn snuff-box in his
hand, he presented it open to me—You shall taste mine—said
I, pulling out my box (which was a small tortoise one) and putting
it into his hand—'Tis most excellent, said the monk; Then do me
the favour, I replied, to accept of the box and all, and when you
take a pinch out of it, sometimes recollect it was the peace-
offering of a man who once used you unkindly, but not from his
heart.

The poor monk blush'd as red as scarlet. *Mon Dieu!* said he,
pressing his hands together—you never used me unkindly.—
I should think, said the lady, he is not likely. I blush'd in my turn;
but from what movements, I leave to the few who feel to analyse
—Excuse me, Madame, replied I—I treated him most unkindly;
and from no provocations—'Tis impossible, said the lady.—My
God! cried the monk, with a warmth of asseveration which seemed
not to belong to him—the fault was in me, and in the indiscretion
of my zeal—the lady opposed it, and I joined with her in maintaining it was impossible, that a spirit so regulated as his, could
give offence to any.

[542]

I knew not that contention could be rendered so sweet and pleasurable a thing to the nerves as I then felt it.—We remained silent, without any sensation of that foolish pain which takes place, when in such a circle you look for ten minutes in one another's faces without saying a word. Whilst this lasted, the monk rubb'd his horn box upon the sleeve of his tunick; and as soon as it had acquired a little air of brightness by the friction—he made a low bow, and said, 'twas too late to say whether it was the weakness or goodness of our tempers which had involved us in this contest—but be it as it would—he begg'd we might exchange boxes—in saying this, he presented his to me with one hand, as he took mine from me in the other; and having kiss'd it—with a stream of good nature in his eyes he put it into his bosom—and took his leave.

I guard this box, as I would the instrumental parts of my religion, to help my mind on to something better: in truth, I seldom go abroad without it; and oft and many a time have I called up by it the courteous spirit of its owner to regulate my own, in the justlings of the world; they had found full employment for his, as I learnt from his story, till about the forty-fifth year of his age, when upon some military services ill requited, and meeting at the same time with a disappointment in the tenderest of passions, he abandon'd the sword and the sex together, and took sanctuary, not so much in his convent as in himself.

I feel a damp upon my spirits, as I am going to add, that in my last return through Calais, upon inquiring after Father Lorenzo, I heard he had been dead near three months, and was buried, not in his convent, but, according to his desire, in a little cimetiery belonging to it, about two leagues off: I had a strong desire to see where they had laid him—when, upon pulling out his little horn box, as I sat by his grave, and plucking up a nettle or two at the head of it, which had no business to grow there, they all struck together so forcibly upon my affections, that I burst into a flood of tears—but I am as weak as a woman; and I beg the world not to smile, but pity me.

THE REMISE DOOR

CALAIS

I HAD never quitted the lady's hand all this time; and had held it so long, that it would have been indecent to have let it go, without first pressing it to my lips: the blood and spirits, which had suffer'd a revulsion from her, crouded back to her, as I did it.

Now the two travellers who had spoke to me in the coach-yard, happening at that crisis to be passing by, and observing our communications, naturally took it into their heads that we must be *man and wife* at least; so stopping as soon as they came up to the door of the Remise, the one of them, who was the inquisitive traveller, ask'd us, if we set out for Paris the next morning?— I could only answer for myself, I said; and the lady added, she was for Amiens.—We dined there yesterday, said the simple traveller —You go directly through the town, added the other, in your road to Paris. I was going to return a thousand thanks for the intelligence, *that Amiens was in the road to Paris*; but, upon pulling out my poor monk's little horn box to take a pinch of snuff—I made them a quiet bow, and wishing them a good passage to Dover—they left us alone—

—Now where would be the harm, said I to myself, if I was to beg of this distressed lady to accept of half of my chaise?—and what mighty mischief could ensue?

Every dirty passion, and bad propensity in my nature, took the alarm, as I stated the proposition—It will oblige you to have a third horse, said AVARICE, which will put twenty livres out of your pocket.—You know not who she is, said CAUTION—or what scrapes the affair may draw you into, whisper'd COWARDICE—

Depend upon it, Yorick! said DISCRETION, 'twill be said you went off with a mistress, and came by assignation to Calais for that purpose—

—You can never after, cried HYPOCRISY aloud, shew your face in the world—or rise, quoth MEANNESS, in the church—or be any thing in it, said PRIDE, but a lousy prebendary.

—But 'tis a civil thing, said I—and as I generally act from the first impulse, and therefore seldom listen to these cabals, which serve no purpose, that I know of, but to encompass the heart with adamant—I turn'd instantly about to the lady—

[544]

—But she had glided off unperceived, as the cause was pleading, and had made ten or a dozen paces down the street, by the time I had made the determination; so I set off after her with a long stride, to make her the proposal with the best address I was master of; but observing she walk'd with her cheek half resting upon the palm of her hand—with the slow, short-measur'd step of thoughtfulness, and with her eyes, as she went step by step, fix'd upon the ground, it struck me, she was trying the same cause herself.—God help her! said I, she has some mother-in-law, or tartufish aunt, or nonsensical old woman, to consult upon the occasion, as well as myself: so not caring to interrupt the processe, and deeming it more gallant to take her at discretion than by surprize, I faced about, and took a short turn or two before the door of the Remise, whilst she walk'd musing on one side.

IN THE STREET

CALAIS

HAVING, on first sight of the lady, settled the affair in my fancy, "that she was of the better order of beings"—and then laid it down as a second axiom, as indisputable as the first, That she was a widow, and wore a character of distress —I went no further; I got ground enough for the situation which pleased me—and had she remained close beside my elbow till midnight, I should have held true to my system, and considered her only under that general idea.

She had scarce got twenty paces distant from me, ere something within me called out for a more particular inquiry—it brought on the idea of a further separation—I might possibly never see her more—the heart is for saving what it can; and I wanted the traces thro' which my wishes might find their way to her, in case I should never rejoin her myself: in a word, I wish'd to know her name—her family's—her condition; and as I knew the place to which she was going, I wanted to know from whence she came: but there was no coming at all this intelligence: a hundred little delicacies stood in the way. I form'd a score different plans—There was no such thing as a man's asking her directly—the thing was impossible.

A little French *debonaire* captain, who came dancing down the street, shewed me, it was the easiest thing in the world; for popping in betwixt us, just as the lady was returning back to the door of the Remise, he introduced himself to my acquaintance, and before he had well got announced, begg'd I would do him the honour to present him to the lady—I had not been presented myself—so turning about to her, he did it just as well by asking her, if she had come from Paris?—No: she was going that rout, she said.—*Vous n'etez pas de Londre?*—She was not, she replied. —Then Madame must have come thro' Flanders.—*Apparamment vous etez Flammande?* said the French captain.—The lady answered, she was.—*Peutetre, de Lisle?* added he—She said, she was not of Lisle.—Nor Arras?—nor Cambray?—nor Ghent?— nor Brussels? She answered, she was of Brussels.

He had had the honour, he said, to be at the bombardment of it last war—that it was finely situated, *pour cela*—and full of noblesse when the Imperialists were driven out by the French (the lady made a slight curtsy)—so giving her an account of the affair, and of the share he had had in it—he begg'd the honour to know her name—so made his bow.

—*Et Madame a son Mari?*—said he, looking back when he had made two steps—and without staying for an answer—danced down the street.

Had I served seven years apprenticeship to good breeding, I could not have done as much.

THE REMISE

CALAIS

AS THE little French captain left us, Mons. Dessein came up with the key of the Remise in his hand, and forthwith let us into his magazine of chaises.

The first object which caught my eye, as Mons. Dessein open'd the door of the Remise, was another old tatter'd *Desobligeant*: and notwithstanding it was the exact picture of that which had hit my fancy so much in the coach-yard but an hour before—the very sight of it stirr'd up a disagreeable sensation within me now; and I thought 'twas a churlish beast into whose heart the idea could first enter, to construct such a machine; nor had I much more charity for the man who could think of using it.

I observed the lady was as little taken with it as myself: so Mons. Dessein led us on to a couple of chaises which stood abreast, telling us as he recommended them, that they had been purchased by my Lord A. and B. to go the *grand tour*, but had gone no further than Paris, so were in all respects as good as new— They were too good—so I pass'd on to a third, which stood behind, and forthwith began to chaffer for the price—But 'twill scarce hold two, said I, opening the door and getting in—Have the goodness, Madam, said Mons. Dessein, offering his arm, to step in—The lady hesitated half a second, and stepp'd in; and the waiter that moment beckoning to speak to Mons. Dessein, he shut the door of the chaise upon us, and left us.

THE REMISE

CALAIS

C'EST *bien comique*, 'tis very droll, said the lady smiling, from the reflection that this was the second time we had been left together by a parcel of nonsensical contingencies —*c'est bien comique*, said she—

—There wants nothing, said I, to make it so, but the comick use which the gallantry of a Frenchman would put it to—to make love the first moment, and an offer of his person the second.

'Tis their *fort*: replied the lady.

It is supposed so at least—and how it has come to pass, continued I, I know not; but they have certainly got the credit of understanding more of love, and making it better than any other nation upon earth: but for my own part I think them errant bunglers, and in truth the worst set of marksmen that ever tried Cupid's patience.

—To think of making love by *sentiments*!

I should as soon think of making a genteel suit of cloaths out of remnants:—and to do it—pop—at first sight by declaration— is submitting the offer and themselves with it, to be sifted, with all their *pours* and *contres*, by an unheated mind.

The lady attended as if she expected I should go on.

Consider then, madam, continued I, laying my hand upon hers—

That grave people hate Love for the name's sake—

That selfish people hate it for their own—

Hypocrites for heaven's—

And that all of us both old and young, being ten times worse

[547]

frighten'd than hurt by the very *report*—What a want of knowledge in this branch of commerce a man betrays, whoever lets the word come out of his lips, till an hour or two at least after the time, that his silence upon it becomes tormenting. A course of small, quiet attentions, not so pointed as to alarm—nor so vague as to be misunderstood,—with now and then a look of kindness, and little or nothing said upon it—leaves Nature for your mistress, and she fashions it to her mind.—

Then I solemnly declare, said the lady, blushing—you have been making love to me all this while.

THE REMISE

CALAIS

MONSIEUR *DESSEIN* came back to let us out of the chaise, and acquaint the lady, the Count de L——— her brother was just arrived at the hotel. Though I had infinite good will for the lady, I cannot say, that I rejoiced in my heart at the event—and could not help telling her so—for it is fatal to a proposal, Madam, said I, that I was going to make you—

—You need not tell me what the proposal was, said she, laying her hand upon both mine, as she interrupted me.—A man, my good Sir, has seldom an offer of kindness to make to a woman, but she has a presentiment of it some moments before—

Nature arms her with it, said I, for immediate preservation—But I think, said she, looking in my face, I had no evil to apprehend—and to deal frankly with you, had determined to accept it. —If I had—(she stopped a moment)—I believe your good will would have drawn a story from me, which would have made pity the only dangerous thing in the journey.

In saying this, she suffered me to kiss her hand twice, and with a look of sensibility mixed with a concern she got out of the chaise—and bid adieu.

IN THE STREET

CALAIS

I NEVER finished a twelve-guinea bargain so expeditiously in my life: my time seemed heavy upon the loss of the lady, and knowing every moment of it would be as two, till I put myself into motion—I ordered post horses directly, and walked towards the hotel.

Lord! said I, hearing the town clock strike four, and recollecting that I had been little more than a single hour in Calais—

—What a large volume of adventures may be grasped within this little span of life by him who interests his heart in every thing and who, having eyes to see, what time and chance are perpetually holding out to him as he journeyeth on his way, misses nothing he can *fairly* lay his hands on.—

—If this won't turn out something—another will—no matter— 'tis an assay upon human nature—I get my labour for my pains —'tis enough—the pleasure of the experiment has kept my senses, and the best part of my blood awake, and laid the gross to sleep.

I pity the man who can travel from *Dan* to *Beersheba*, and cry, 'Tis all barren—and so it is; and so is all the world to him who will not cultivate the fruits it offers. I declare, said I, clapping my hands chearily together, that was I in a desart, I would find out wherewith in it to call forth my affections—If I could not do better, I would fasten them upon some sweet myrtle, or seek some melancholy cypress to connect myself to—I would court their shade, and greet them kindly for their protection—I would cut my name upon them, and swear they were the loveliest trees throughout the desert: if their leaves wither'd, I would teach myself to mourn, and when they rejoiced, I would rejoice along with them.

The learned SMELFUNGUS travelled from Boulogne to Paris— from Paris to Rome—and so on—but he set out with the spleen and jaundice, and every object he pass'd by was discoloured or distorted—He wrote an account of them, but 'twas nothing but the account of his miserable feelings.

I met Smelfungus in the grand portico of the Pantheon—he. was just coming out of it—*'Tis nothing but a huge cock-pit**, said he—I wish you had said nothing worse of the Venus of Medicis, replied I—for in passing through Florence, I had heard he had

* Vide S———'s Travels.

fallen foul upon the goddess, and used her worse than a common strumpet, without the least provocation in nature.

I popp'd upon Smelfungus again at Turin, in his return home; and a sad tale of sorrowful adventures had he to tell, "wherein he spoke of moving accidents by flood and field, and of the cannibals which each other eat: the Anthropophagi"—he had been flea'd alive, and bedevil'd, and used worse than St. Bartholomew, at every stage he had come at—

—I'll tell it, cried Smelfungus, to the world. You had better tell it, said I, to your physician.

Mundungus, with an immense fortune, made the whole tour; going on from Rome to Naples—from Naples to Venice—from Venice to Vienna—to Dresden, to Berlin, without one generous connection or pleasurable anecdote to tell of; but he had travell'd straight on looking neither to his right hand or his left, lest Love or Pity should seduce him out of his road.

Peace be to them! if it is to be found; but heaven itself, was it possible to get there with such tempers, would want objects to give it—every gentle spirit would come flying upon the wings of Love to hail their arrival—Nothing would the souls of Smelfungus and Mundungus hear of, but fresh anthems of joy, fresh raptures of love, and fresh congratulations of their common felicity—I heartily pity them: they have brought up no faculties for this work; and was the happiest mansion in heaven to be allotted to Smelfungus and Mundungus, they would be so far from being happy, that the souls of Smelfungus and Mundungus would do penance there to all eternity.

MONTRIUL

I HAD ONCE lost my portmanteau from behind my chaise, and twice got out in the rain, and one of the times up to the knees in dirt, to help the postillion to tie it on, without being able to find out what was wanting—Nor was it till I got to Montriul, upon the landlord's asking me if I wanted not a servant, that it occurred to me, that that was the very thing.

A servant! That I do most sadly, quoth I—Because, Monsieur, said the landlord, there is a clever young fellow, who would be very proud of the honour to serve an Englishman—But why an English one, more than any other?—They are so generous, said the landlord—I'll be shot if this is not a livre out of my pocket, quoth I to myself, this very night—But they have wherewithal to be so, Monsieur, added he—Set down one livre more for that, quoth I—It was but last night, said the landlord, *qu'un my Lord Anglois presentoit un ecu a la fille de chambre*—*Tant pis, pour Mad*^{lle} *Janatone*, said I.

Now Janatone being the landlord's daughter, and the landlord supposing I was young in French, took the liberty to inform me, I should not have said *tant pis*—but, *tant mieux*. *Tant mieux, toujours, Monsieur*, said he, when there is anything to be got—*tant pis*, when there is nothing. It comes to the same thing, said I. *Pardonnez moi*, said the landlord.

I cannot take a fitter opportunity to observe once for all, that *tant pis* and *tant mieux* being two of the great hinges in French conversation, a stranger would do well to set himself right in the use of them, before he gets to Paris.

A prompt French Marquis at our ambassador's table demanded of Mr. H——, if he was H—— the poet? No, said H—— mildly—*Tant pis* replied the Marquis.

It is H—— the historian, said another—*Tant mieux*, said the Marquis. And Mr. H——, who is a man of an excellent heart, return'd thanks for both.

When the landlord had set me right in this matter, he called in La Fleur, which was the name of the young man he had spoke of —saying only first, That as for his talents, he would presume to say nothing—Monsieur was the best judge what would suit him; but for the fidelity of La Fleur, he would stand responsible in all he was worth.

The landlord deliver'd this in a manner which instantly set my mind to the business I was upon—and La Fleur, who stood waiting without, in that breathless expectation which every son of nature of us have felt in our turns, came in.

MONTRIUL

I AM APT to be taken with all kinds of people at first sight; but never more so, than when a poor devil comes to offer his service to so poor a devil as myself; and as I know this weakness, I always suffer my judgment to draw back something on that very account—and this more or less, according to the mood I am in, and the case—and I may add the gender too, of the person I am to govern.

When La Fleur enter'd the room, after every discount I could make for my soul, the genuine look and air of the fellow determined the matter at once in his favour; so I hired him first—and then began to inquire what he could do: But I shall find out his talents, quoth I, as I want them—besides, a Frenchman can do every thing.

Now poor La Fleur could do nothing in the world but beat a drum, and play a march or two upon the fife. I was determined to make his talents do; and can't say my weakness was ever so insulted by my wisdom, as in the attempt.

La Fleur had set out early in life, as gallantly as most Frenchmen do, with *serving* for a few years; at the end of which, having satisfied the sentiment, and found moreover, That the honour of beating a drum was likely to be its own reward, as it open'd no further track of glory to him—he retired *a ses terres*, and lived *comme il plaisoit a Dieu*—that is to say, upon nothing.

—And so, quoth *Wisdome*, you have hired a drummer to attend you in this tour of your's thro' France and Italy! Psha! said I, and do not one half of our gentry go with a hum-drum *compagnon du voiage* the same round, and have the piper and the devil and all to pay besides? When man can extricate himself with an *equivoque* in such an unequal match—he is not ill of—But you can do something else, La Fleur? said I——*O qu'oui!*—he could make spatterdashes, and play a little upon the fiddle—Bravo! said Wisdome—Why, I play a bass myself, said I—we shall do very well.—You can shave, and dress a wig a little, La Fleur?—He had all the dispositions in the world—It is enough for heaven! said I, interrupting him—and ought to be enough for me—So supper coming in, and having a frisky English spaniel on one side of my chair, and a French valet, with as much hilarity in his countenance as ever nature painted in one, on the other—I was satisfied to my heart's content with my empire; and if monarchs knew what they would be at, they might be as satisfied as I was.

MONTRIUL

A S LA FLEUR went the whole tour of France and Italy with me, and will be often upon the stage, I must interest the reader a little further in his behalf, by saying, that I had never less reason to repent of the impulses which generally do determine me, than in regard to this fellow—he was a faithful, affectionate, simple soul as ever trudged after the heels of a philosopher; and notwithstanding his talents of drum-beating and spatterdash-making, which, tho' very good in themselves, happen'd to be of no great service to me, yet was I hourly recompenced by the festivity of his temper—it supplied all defects—I had a constant resource in his looks in all difficulties and distresses of my own—I was going to have added, of his too; but La Fleur was out of the reach of every thing; for whether 'twas hunger or thirst, or cold or nakedness, or watchings, or whatever stripes of ill luck La Fleur met with in our journeyings, there was no index in his physiognomy to point them out by— he was eternally the same; so that if I am a piece of a philosopher, which Satan now and then puts it into my head I am— it always mortifies the pride of the conceit, by reflecting how much I owe to the complexional philosophy of this poor fellow, for shaming me into one of a better kind. With all this, La Fleur had a small cast of the coxcomb—but he seemed at first sight to be more a coxcomb of nature than of art; and before I had been three days in Paris with him—he seemed to be no coxcomb at all.

MONTRIUL

T HE NEXT morning La Fleur entering upon his employment, I delivered to him the key of my portmanteau with an inventory of my half a dozen shirts and silk pair of breeches; and bid him fasten all upon the chaise—get the horses put to— and desire the landlord to come in with his bill.

C'est un garçon de bonne fortune, said the landlord, pointing through the window to half a dozen wenches who had got round about La Fleur, and were most kindly taking their leave of him, as the postillion was leading out the horses. La Fleur kissed all their hands round and round again, and thrice he wiped his eyes, and thrice he promised he would bring them all pardons from Rome.

The young fellow, said the landlord, is beloved by all the town, and there is scarce a corner in Montriul where the want of him will not be felt: he has but one misfortune in the world, continued he, "He is always in love."—I am heartily glad of it, said I,—'twill save me the trouble every night of putting my breeches under my head. In saying this, I was making not so much La Fleur's eloge, as my own, having been in love with one princess or another almost all my life, and I hope I shall go on so, till I die, being firmly persuaded, that if ever I do a mean action, it must be in some interval betwixt one passion and another: whilst this interregnum lasts, I always perceive my heart locked up—I can scarce find in it, to give Misery a sixpence; and therefore I always get out of it as fast as I can, and the moment I am rekindled, I am all generosity and good will again; and would do any thing in the world either for, or with any one, if they will but satisfy me there is no sin in it.

—But in saying this—surely I am commending the passion—not myself.

A FRAGMENT

—THE town of Abdera, notwithstanding Democritus lived there trying all the powers of irony and laughter to reclaim it, was the vilest and most profligate town in all Thrace. What for poisons, conspiracies and assassinations—libels, pasquinades and tumults, there was no going there by day—'twas worse by night.

Now, when things were at the worst, it came to pass, that the Andromeda of Euripides being represented at Abdera, the whole orchestra was delighted with it: but of all the passages which delighted them, nothing operated more upon their imaginations, than the tender strokes of nature which the poet had wrought up in that pathetic speech of Perseus,

O Cupid, prince of God and men, &c.

Every man almost spoke pure iambics the next day, and talk'd of nothing but Perseus his pathetic address—"O Cupid! prince of God and men"—in every street of Abdera, in every house—"O Cupid! Cupid!"—in every mouth, like the natural notes of some sweet melody which drops from it whether it will or no—

nothing but "Cupid! Cupid! prince of God and men"—The fire caught—and the whole city, like the heart of one man, open'd itself to Love.

No pharmacopolist could sell one grain of helebore—not a single armourer had a heart to forge one instrument of death —Friendship and Virtue met together, and kiss'd each other in the street—the golden age return'd, and hung o'er the town of Abdera—every Abderite took his oaten pipe, and every Abderitish woman left her purple web, and chastly sat her down and listen'd to the song—

'Twas only in the power, says the Fragment, of the God whose empire extendeth from heaven to earth, and even to the depths of the sea, to have done this.

MONTRIUL

WHEN all is ready, and every article is disputed and paid for in the inn, unless you are a little sour'd by the adventure, there is always a matter to compound at the door, before you can get into your chaise; and that is with the sons and daughters of poverty, who surround you. Let no man say, "let them go to the devil"—'tis a cruel journey to send a few miserables, and they have had sufferings enow without it: I always think it better to take a few sous out in my hand; and I would counsel every gentle traveller to do so likewise; he need not be so exact in setting down his motives for giving them—they will be register'd elsewhere.

For my own part, there is no man gives so little as I do; for few that I know have so little to give: but as this was the first publick act of my charity in France, I took the more notice of it.

A well-a-way! said I. I have but eight sous in the world, shewing them in my hand, and there are eight poor men and eight poor women for 'em.

A poor tatter'd soul without a shirt on instantly withdrew his claim, by retiring two steps out of the circle, and making a disqualifying bow on his part. Had the whole parterre cried out, *Place aux dames*, with one voice, it would not have conveyed the sentiment of a deference for the sex with half the effect.

Just heaven! for what wise reasons hast thou order'd it, that beggary and urbanity, which are at such variance in other countries, should find a way to be at unity in this?

[555]

—I insisted upon presenting him with a single sous, merely for his *politesse.*

A poor little dwarfish brisk fellow, who stood over-against me in the circle, putting something first under his arm, which had once been a hat, took his snuff-box out of his pocket, and generously offer'd a pinch on both sides of him: it was a gift of consequence, and modestly declined—The poor little fellow press'd it upon them with a nod of welcomeness—*Prenez en—prenez*, said he, looking another way; so they each took a pinch —Pity thy box should ever want one ! said I to myself; so I put a couple of sous into it—taking a small pinch out of his box, to enhance their value, as I did it—He felt the weight of the second obligation more than that of the first—'twas doing him an honour—the other was only doing him a charity—and he made me a bow down to the ground for it.

—Here! said I to an old soldier with one hand, who had been campaign'd and worn out to death in the service—here's a couple of sous for thee—*Vive le Roi !* said the old soldier.

I had then but three sous left: so I gave one, simply *pour l'amour de Dieu*, which was the footing on which it was begg'd— The poor woman had a dislocated hip; so it could not be well, upon any other motive.

Mon cher et tres charitable Monsieur—There's no opposing this, said I.

My Lord Anglois—the very sound was worth the money—so I gave *my last sous for it*. But in the eagerness of giving, I had overlook'd a *pauvre honteux*, who had no one to ask a sous for him, and who, I believed, would have perish'd, ere he could have ask'd one for himself: he stood by the chaise a little without the circle, and wiped a tear from a face which I thought had seen better days—Good God! said I—and I have not one single sous left to give him—But you have a thousand! cried all the powers of nature, stirring within me—so I gave him—no matter what—I am ashamed to say *how much*, now—and was ashamed to think, how little, then: so if the reader can form any conjecture of my disposition, as these two fixed points are given him, he may judge within a livre or two what was the precise sum.

I could afford nothing for the rest, but, *Dieu vous benisse—Et le bon Dieu vous benisse encore*—said the old soldier, the dwarf, &c. The *pauvre honteux* could say nothing—he pull'd out a little handkerchief, and wiped his face as he turned away—and I thought he thank'd me more than them all.

THE BIDET

HAVING settled all these little matters, I got into my post-chaise with more ease than ever I got into a post-chaise in my life; and La Fleur having got one large jack-boot on the far side of a little *bidet**, and another on this (for I count nothing of his legs)—he canter'd away before me as happy and as perpendicular as a prince.—

—But what is happiness! what is grandeur in this painted scene of life! A dead ass, before we had got a league, put a sudden stop to La Fleur's career—his bidet would not pass by it—a contention arose betwixt them, and the poor fellow was kick'd out of his jack-boots the very first kick.

La Fleur bore his fall like a French christian, saying neither more or less upon it, than, Diable! so presently got up and came to the charge again astride his bidet, beating him up to it as he would have beat his drum.

The bidet flew from one side of the road to the other, then back again—then this way—then that way, and in short every way but by the dead ass.—La Fleur insisted upon the thing—and the bidet threw him.

What's the matter, La Fleur, said I, with this bidet of thine?—. *Monsieur*, said he, *c'est un cheval le plus opiniatré du monde*— Nay, if he is a conceited beast, he must go his own way, replied I—so La Fleur got off him, and giving him a good sound lash, the bidet took me at my word, and away he scampered back to Montriul.—*Peste!* said La Fleur.

It is not *mal a propos* to take notice here, that tho' La Fleur availed himself but of two different terms of exclamation in this encounter—namely, *Diable!* and *Peste!* that there are nevertheless three, in the French language; like the positive, comparative, and superlative, one or the other of which serve for every unexpected throw of the dice in life.

Le Diable! which is the first, and positive degree, is generally used upon ordinary emotions of the mind, where small things only fall out contrary to your expectations—such as—the throwing once doublets—La Fleur's being kick'd off his horse, and so forth—cuckoldom, for the same reason, is always—*Le Diable!*

But in cases where the cast has something provoking in it, as in

* Post horse.

that of the bidet's running away after, and leaving La Fleur aground in jack-boots—'tis the second degree.

'Tis then *Peste!*

And for the third—

—But here my heart is wrung with pity and fellow-feeling, when I reflect what miseries must have been their lot, and how bitterly so refined a people must have smarted, to have forced them upon the use of it.—

Grant me, O ye powers which touch the tongue with eloquence in distress!—whatever is my *cast*, Grant me but decent words to exclaim in, and I will give my nature way.

—But as these were not to be had in France, I resolved to take every evil just as it befell me without any exclamation at all.

La Fleur, who had made no such covenant with himself, followed the bidet with his eyes till it was got out of sight—and then, you may imagine, if you please, with what word he closed the whole affair.

As there was no hunting down a frighten'd horse in jack-boots, there remained no alternative but taking La Fleur either behind the chaise, or into it.—

I preferred the latter, and in half an hour we got to the posthouse at Nampont.

NAMPONT

THE DEAD ASS

—AND this, said he, putting the remains of a crust into his wallet—and this, should have been thy portion, said he, hadst thou been alive to have shared it with me. I thought by the accent, it had been an apostrophe to his child; but 'twas to his ass, and to the very ass we had seen dead in the road, which had occasioned La Fleur's misadventure. The man seemed to lament it much; and it instantly brought into my mind Sancho's lamentation for his; but he did it with more true touches of nature.

The mourner was sitting upon a stone bench at the door, with the ass's pannel and its bridle on one side, which he took up from time to time—then laid them down—look'd at them and shook his head. He then took his crust of bread out of his wallet again, as if to eat it; held it some time in his hand—then laid it upon the bit of his ass's bridle—looked wistfully at the little arrangement he had made—and then gave a sigh.

The simplicity of his grief drew numbers about him, and La Fleur amongst the rest, whilst the horses were getting ready; as I continued sitting in the post-chaise, I could see and hear over their heads.

—He said he had come last from Spain, where he had been from the furthest borders of Franconia; and had got so far on his return home, when his ass died. Every one seem'd desirous to know what business could have taken so old and poor a man so far a journey from his own home.

It had pleased heaven, he said, to bless him with three sons, the finest lads in all Germany; but having in one week lost two of the eldest of them by the small-pox, and the youngest falling ill of the same distemper, he was afraid of being bereft óf them all; and made a vow, if Heaven would not take him from him also, he would go in gratitude to St. Iago in Spain.

When the mourner got thus far on his story, he stopp'd to pay nature her tribute—and wept bitterly.

He said, Heaven had accepted the conditions; and that he had set out from his cottage with this poor creature, who had been a patient partner of his journey—that it had eat the same bread with him all the way, and was unto him as a friend.

Every body who stood about, heard the poor fellow with concern——La Fleur offered him money.—The mourner said he did not want it—it was not the value of the ass—but the loss of him.—The ass, he said, he was assured loved him—and upon this told them a long story of a mischance upon their passage over the Pyrenean mountains which had separated them from each other three days; during which time the ass had sought him as much as he had sought the ass, and that they had neither scarce eat or drank till they met.

Thou hast one comfort, friend, said I, at least in the loss of thy poor beast; I'm sure thou hast been a merciful master to him. —Alas! said the mourner, I thought so, when he was alive— but now that he is dead I think otherwise.—I fear the weight of myself and my afflictions together have been too much for him— they have shortened the poor creature's days, and I fear I have them to answer for.—Shame on the world! said I to myself— Did we love each other, as this poor soul but loved his ass— 'twould be something.—

[559]

NAMPONT

THE POSTILLION

THE concern which the poor fellow's story threw me into, required some attention: the postillion paid not the least to it, but set off upon the *pavè* in a full gallop.

The thirstiest soul in the most sandy desert of Arabia could not have wished more for a cup of cold water, than mine did for grave and quiet movements; and I should have had an high opinion of the postillion had he but stolen off with me in something like a pensive pace.—On the contrary, as the mourner finished his lamentation, the fellow gave an unfeeling lash to each of his beasts, and set off clattering like a thousand devils.

I called to him as loud as I could, for heaven's sake to go slower—and the louder I called the more unmercifully he galloped.—the deuce take him and his galloping too—said I—he'll go on tearing my nerves to pieces till he has worked me into a foolish passion, and then he'll go slow, that I may enjoy the sweets of it.

The postillion managed the point to a miracle: by the time he had got to the foot of a steep hill about half a league from Nampont,—he had put me out of temper with him—and then with myself, for being so!

My case then required a different treatment; and a good rattling gallop would have been of real service to me.—

—Then, prithee get on—get on, my good lad, said I.

The postillion pointed to the hill—I then tried to return back to the story of the poor German and his ass—but I had broke the clue—and could no more get into it again, than the postillion could into a trot.—

—The deuce go, said I, with it all! Here am I sitting as candidly disposed to make the best of the worst, as ever wight was, and all runs counter.

There is one sweet lenitive at least for evils, which nature holds out to us; so I took it kindly at her hands, and fell asleep; and the first word which roused me was *Amiens.*

—Bless me! said I, rubbing my eyes—this is the very town where my poor lady is to come.

AMIENS

THE words were scarce out of my mouth, when the Count de L * * *'s post-chaise, with his sister in it, drove hastily by: she had just time to make me a bow of recognition—and of that particular kind of it, which told me she had not yet done with me. She was as good as her look; for, before I had quite finished my supper, her brother's servant came into the room with a billet, in which she said, she had taken the liberty to charge me with a letter, which I was to present myself to Madame R * * * the first morning I had nothing to do at Paris. There was only added, she was sorry, but from what *penchant* she had not considered, that she had been prevented telling me her story—that she still owed it me; and if my rout should ever lay through Brussels, and I had not by then forgot the name of Madame de L * * *—that Madame de L * * * would be glad to discharge her obligation.

Then I will meet thee, said I, fair spirit! at Brussels—'tis only returning from Italy through Germany to Holland, by the rout of Flanders, home—'twill scarce be ten posts out of my way; but were it ten thousand! with what a moral delight will it crown my journey, in sharing in the sickening incidents of a tale of misery told to me by such a sufferer? to see her weep! and though I cannot dry up the fountain of her tears, what an exquisite sensation is there still left, in wiping them away from off the cheeks of the first and fairest of women, as I'm sitting with my handkerchief in my hand in silence the whole night besides her.

There was nothing wrong in the sentiment; and yet I instantly reproached my heart with it in the bitterest and most reprobate of expressions.

It had ever, as I told the reader, been one of the singular blessings of my life, to be almost every hour of it miserably in love with some one; and my last flame happening to be blown out by a whiff of jealousy on the sudden turn of a corner, I had lighted it up afresh at the pure taper of Eliza but about three months before—swearing as I did it, that it should last me through the whole journey—Why should I dissemble the matter? I had sworn to her eternal fidelity—she had a right to my whole heart—to divide my affections was to lessen them—to expose them, was to risk them: where there is risk, there may be loss:—and what wilt thou have, Yorick! to answer to a heart so full of trust and confidence—so good, so gentle and un-reproaching?

—I will not go to Brussels, replied I, interrupting myself—but my imagination went on—I recall'd her looks at that crisis of our separation when neither of us had power to say Adieu! I look'd at the picture she had tied in a black ribband about my neck—and blush'd as I look'd at it—I would have given the world to have kiss'd it,—but was ashamed—And shall this tender flower, said I, pressing it between my hands—shall it be smitten to its very root—and smitten, Yorick! by thee, who hast promised to shelter it in thy breast?

Eternal fountain of happiness! said I, kneeling down upon the ground—be thou my witness—and every pure spirit which tastes it, be my witness also, That I would not travel to Brussels, unless Eliza went along with me, did the road lead me towards heaven.

In transports of this kind, the heart, in spite of the under-standing, will always say too much.

THE LETTER

AMIENS

FORTUNE had not smiled upon La Fleur; for he had been unsuccessful in his feats of chivalry—and not one thing had offer'd to signalize his zeal for my service from the time he had enter'd into it, which was almost four and twenty hours. The poor soul burn'd with impatience; and the Count de L * * *'s servant's coming with the letter, being the first practicable occasion which offered, La Fleur had laid hold of it; and in order to do honour to his master, had taken him into a back parlour in the Auberge, and treated him with a cup or two of the best wine in Picardy; and the Count de L * * *'s servant in return, and not to be behind hand in politeness with La Fleur, had taken him back with him to the Count's hôtel. La Fleur's *prevenancy* (for there was a passport in his very looks) soon set every servant in the kitchen at ease with him; and as a Frenchman, whatever be his talents, has no sort of prudery in shewing them, La Fleur, in less than five minutes, had pull'd out his fife, and leading off the dance himself with the first note, set the *fille de chambre*, the *maitre d'hotel*, the cook, the scullion, and all the houshold, dogs and cats, besides an old monkey, a dancing: I suppose there never was a merrier kitchen since the flood.

Madame de L * * *, in passing from her brother's apartments to her own, hearing so much jollity below stairs, rung up her *fille de chambre* to ask about it; and hearing it was the English gentleman's servant who had set the whole house merry with his pipe, she order'd him up.

As the poor fellow could not present himself empty, he had loaden'd himself in going up stairs with a thousand compliments to Madame de L * * *, on the part of his master—added a long apocrypha of inquiries after Madame de L * * *'s health—told her, that Monsieur his master was *au desespoire* for her re-establishment from the fatigues of her journey—and, to close all, that Monsieur had received the letter which Madame had done him the honour——And he has done me the honour, said Madame de L * * *, interrupting La Fleur, to send a billet in return.

Madame de L * * * had said this with such a tone of reliance upon the fact, that La Fleur had not power to disappoint her expectations—he trembled for my honour—and possibly might not altogether be unconcerned for his own, as a man capable of being attached to a master who could be a wanting *en egards vis a vis d'une femme*; so that when Madame de L * * * asked La Fleur if he had brought a letter—*O qu'oui*, said La Fleur: so laying down his hat upon the ground, and taking hold of the flap of his right side pocket with his left hand, he began to search for the letter with his right—then contrary-wise—*Diable!*—then sought every pocket—pocket by pocket, round, not forgetting his fob—*Peste!*—then La Fleur emptied them upon the floor—pulled out a dirty cravat—a handkerchief—a comb—a whip lash—a night-cap—then gave a peep into his hat—*Quelle etourderie!* He had left the letter upon the table in the Auberge—he would run for it, and be back with it in three minutes.

I had just finished my supper when La Fleur came in to give me an account of his adventure: he told the whole story simply as it was; and only added, that if Monsieur had forgot (*par hazard*) to answer Madame's letter, the arrangment gave him an opportunity to recover the *faux pas*—and if not, that things were only as they were.

Now I was not altogether sure of my *etiquette*, whether I ought to have wrote or no; but if I had—a devil himself could not have been angry: 'twas but the officious zeal of a well-meaning creature for my honour; and however he might have mistook the

[563]

road—or embarrassed me in so doing—his heart was in no
fault—I was under no necessity to write—and what weighed
more than all—he did not look as if he had done amiss.

—'Tis all very well, La Fleur, said I.—'Twas sufficient. La
Fleur flew out of the room like lightening, and return'd with pen,
ink, and paper, in his hand; and coming up to the table, laid them
close before me, with such a delight in his countenance, that
I could not help taking up the pen.

I begun and begun again; and though I had nothing to say,
and that nothing might have been express'd in half a dozen lines,
I made half a dozen different beginnings, and could no way
please myself.

In short, I was in no mood to write.

La Fleur stepp'd out and brought a little water in a glass to
dilute my ink—then fetch'd sand and seal-wax—It was all one:
I wrote, and blotted, and tore off, and burnt, and wrote again—
Le Diable l'emporte! said I half to myself—I cannot write this
self-same letter; throwing the pen down despairingly as I said it.

As soon as I had cast down the pen, La Fleur advanced with the
most respectful carriage up to the table, and making a thousand
apologies for the liberty he was going to take, told me he had
a letter in his pocket wrote by a drummer in his regiment to
a·corporal's wife, which, he durst say, would suit the occasion.

I had a mind to let the poor fellow have his humour—Then
prithee, said I, let me see it.

La Fleur instantly pull'd out a little dirty pocket-book cramm'd
full of small letters and billet-doux in a sad condition, and laying
it upon the table, and then untying the string which held them all
together, run them over one by one, till he came to the letter in
question—*La voila!* said he, clapping his hands: so unfolding it
first, he laid it before me, and retired three steps from the table
whilst I read it.

THE LETTER

Madame,

JE SUIS penetré de la douleur la plus vive, et reduit en même
temps au desespoir par ce retour imprevû du Corporal qui
rend notre entrevue de ce soir la chose du monde la plus
impossible.

Mais vive la joie! et toute la mienne sera de penser a vous.

L'amour n'est *rien* sans sentiment.

Et le sentiment est encore *moins* sans amour.

On dit qu'on ne doit jamais se desesperer.

On dit aussi que Monsieur le Corporal monte la garde Mecredi: alors ce sera mon tour.

 Chacun a son tour.

En attendant—Vive l'amour! et vive la bagatelle!

  Je suis, MADAME,

  Avec toutes les sentiments les plus respecteux et les plus tendres tout a vous,

    JAQUES ROQUE.

It was but changing the Corporal into the Count—and saying nothing about mounting guard on Wednesday—and the letter was neither right or wrong—so to gratify the poor fellow, who stood trembling for my honour, his own, and the honour of his letter,—I took the cream gently off it, and whipping it up in my own way—I seal'd it up and sent him with it to Madame de L * * *—and the next morning we pursued our journey to Paris.

PARIS

WHEN a man can contest the point by dint of equipage, and carry on all floundering before him with half a dozen lackies and a couple of cooks—'tis very well in such a place as Paris—he may drive in at which end of a street he will.

A poor prince who is weak in cavalry, and whose whole infantry does not exceed a single man, had best quit the field; and signalize himself in the cabinet, if he can get up into it—I say *up into it*—for there is no descending perpendicular amongst 'em with a "*Me voici! mes enfans*"—here I am—whatever many may think.

I own my first sensations, as soon as I was left solitary and alone in my own chamber in the hotel, were far from being so flattering as I had prefigured them. I walked up gravely to the window in my dusty black coat, and looking through the glass saw all the world in yellow, blue, and green, running at the ring of pleasure. —The old with broken lances, and in helmets which had lost their vizards—the young in armour bright which shone like gold, beplumed with each gay feather of the east—all—all tilting at it like fascinated knights in tournaments of yore for fame and love.—

Alas, poor Yorick! cried I, what art thou doing here? On the very first onset of all this glittering clatter, thou art reduced to an atom—seek—seek some winding alley, with a tourniquet at the end of it, where chariot never rolled or flambeau shot its rays—there thou mayest solace thy soul in converse sweet with some kind *grisset* of a barber's wife, and get into such coteries!—

—May I perish! if I do, said I, pulling out the letter which I had to present to Madame de R * * *.—I'll wait upon this lady, the very first thing I do. So I called La Fleur to go seek me a barber directly—and come back and brush my coat.

THE WIG

PARIS

WHEN the barber came, he absolutely refused to have any thing to do with my wig: 'twas either above or below his art: I had nothing to do, but to take one ready made of his own recommendation.

—But I fear, friend! said I, this buckle won't stand.—You may immerge it, replied he, into the ocean, and it will stand—

What a great scale is every thing upon in this city! thought I—The utmost stretch of an English periwig-maker's ideas could have gone no further than to have "dipped it into a pail of water"—What difference! 'tis like time to eternity.

I confess I do hate all cold conceptions, as I do the puny ideas which engender them; and am generally so struck with the great works of nature, that for my own part, if I could help it, I never would make a comparison less than a mountain at least. All that can be said against the French sublime in this instance of it, is this—that the grandeur is *more* in the *word*; and *less* in the *thing*. No doubt the ocean fills the mind with vast ideas; but Paris being so far inland, it was not likely I should run post a hundred miles out of it, to try the experiment——the Parisian barber meant nothing.—

The pail of water standing besides the great deep, make certainly but a sorry figure in speech—but 'twill be said—it has one advantage—'tis in the next room, and the truth of the buckle may be tried in it without more ado, in a single moment

In honest truth, and upon a more candid revision of the matter, *The French expression professes more than it performs.*

I think I can see the precise and distinguishing marks of national characters more in these nonsensical *minutiæ*, than in the most important matters of state; where great men of all nations talk and stalk so much alike, that I would not give ninepence to chuse amongst them.

I was so long in getting from under my barber's hands, that it was too late of thinking of going with my letter to Madame R * * * that night: but when a man is once dressed at all points for going out, his reflections turn to little account, so taking down the name of the Hotel de Modene where I lodged, I walked forth without any determination where to go—I shall consider of that, said I, as I walk along.

THE PULSE

PARIS

HAIL ye small sweet courtesies of life, for smooth do ye make the road of it! like grace and beauty which beget inclinations to love at first sight; 'tis ye who open this door and let the stranger in.

—Pray, Madame, said I, have the goodness to tell me which way I must turn to go to the Opera comique:—Most willingly, Monsieur, said she, laying aside her work—

I had given a cast with my eye into half a dozen shops as I came along in search of a face not likely to be disordered by such an interruption; till at last, this hitting my fancy, I had walked in.

She was working a pair of ruffles as she sat in a low chair on the far side of the shop facing the door—

—*Tres volontiers*; most willingly, said she, laying her work down upon a chair next her, and rising up from the low chair she was sitting in, with so chearful a movement and so chearful a look, that had I been laying out fifty louis d'ors with her, I should have said—"This woman is grateful."

You must turn, Monsieur, said she, going with me to the door of the shop, and pointing the way down the street I was to take —you must turn first to your left hand—*mais prenez garde*— there are two turns; and be so good as to take the second—

then go down a little way and you'll see a church, and when you are past it, give yourself the trouble to turn directly to the right, and that will lead you to the foot of the *pont neuf*, which you must cross—and there, any one will do himself the pleasure to shew you—

She repeated her instructions three times over to me with the same good natur'd patience the third time as the first;—and if *tones and manners* have a meaning, which certainly they have, unless to hearts which shut them out—she seem'd really interested, that I should not lose myself.

I will not suppose it was the woman's beauty, notwithstanding she was the handsomest grisset, I think, I ever saw, which had much to do with the sense I had of her courtesy; only I remember, when I told her how much I was obliged to her, that I looked very full in her eyes,—and that I repeated my thanks as often as she had done her instructions. .

I had not got ten paces from the door; before I found I had forgot every tittle of what she had said—so looking back, and seeing her still standing in the door of the shop as if to look whether I went right or not—I returned back, to ask her whether the first turn was to my right or left—for that I had absolutely forgot.—Is it possible! said she, half laughing.—'Tis very possible, replied I, when a man is thinking more of a woman, than of her good advice.

As this was the real truth—she took it, as every woman takes a matter of right, with a slight courtesy.

—*Attendez!* said she, laying her hand upon my arm to detain me, whilst she called a lad out of the back-shop to get ready a parcel of gloves. I am just going to send him, said she, with a packet into that quarter, and if you will have the complaisance to step in, it will be ready in a moment, and he shall attend you to the place.—So I walk'd in with her to the far side of the shop, and taking up the ruffle in my hand which she laid upon the chair, as if I had a mind to sit, she sat down herself in her low chair, and I instantly sat myself down besides her.

—He will be ready, Monsieur, said she, in a moment—And in that moment, replied I, most willingly would I say something very civil to you for all these courtesies. Any one may do a casual act of good nature, but a continuation of them shews it is a part of the temperature; and certainly, added I, if it is the same blood which comes from the heart, which descends to the extremes (touching her wrist) I am sure you must have one of the best pulses of any woman in the world—Feel it, said she, holding out her arm. So laying down my hat, I took hold of her fingers in one hand, and applied the two fore-fingers of my other to the artery.—

—Would to heaven! my dear Eugenius, thou hadst passed by, and beheld me sitting in my black coat, and in my lack-a-day-sical manner, counting the throbs of it, one by one, with as much true devotion as if I had been watching the critical ebb or flow of her fever—How wouldst thou have laugh'd and moralized upon my new profession?—and thou shouldst have laugh'd and moralized on—Trust me, my dear Eugenius, I should have said, "there are worse occupation in this world *than feeling a woman's pulse.*"—But a Grisset's! thou wouldst have said—and in an open shop! Yorick—

—So much the better: for when my views are direct, Eugenius, I care not if all the world saw me feel it.

THE HUSBAND

PARIS

I HAD counted twenty pulsations, and was going on fast towards the fortieth, when her husband coming unexpected from a back parlour into the shop, put me a little out in my reckoning.—'Twas no body but her husband, she said—so I began a fresh score—Monsieur is so good, quoth she, as he pass'd us by, as to give himself the trouble of feeling my pulse—The husband took off his hat, and making me a bow, said, I did him too much honour—and having said that, he put on his hat and walk'd out.

Good God! said I to myself, as he went out—and can this man be the husband of this woman?

Let it not torment the few who know what must have been the grounds of this exclamation, if I explain it to those who do not.

In London a shopkeeper and a shopkeeper's wife seem to be one bone and one flesh: in the several endowments of mind and body, sometimes the one, sometimes the other has it, so as in general to be upon a par, and to tally with each other as nearly as man and wife need to do.

In Paris, there are scarce two orders of beings more different: for the legislative and executive powers of the shop not resting

[569]

in the husband, he seldom comes there—in some dark and dismal room behind, he sits commerceless in his thrum night-cap, the same rough son of Nature that Nature left him.

The genius of a people where nothing but the monarchy is *salique*, having ceded this department, with sundry others, totally to the women—by a continual higgling with customers of all ranks and sizes from morning to night, like so many rough pebbles shook long together in a bag, by amicable collisions, they have worn down their asperities and sharp angles, and not only become round and smooth, but will receive, some of them, a polish like a brilliant—Monsieur *le Mari* is little better than the stone under your feet—

—Surely—surely man! it is not good for thee to sit alone—thou wast made for social intercourse and gentle greetings, and this improvement of our natures from it, I appeal to, as my evidence.

—And how does it beat, Monsieur? said she.—With all the benignity, said I, looking quietly in her eyes, that I expected—She was going to say something civil in return—but the lad came into the shop with the gloves—*A propos*, said I; I want a couple of pair myself.

THE GLOVES

PARIS

THE beautiful Grisset rose up when I said this, and going behind the counter, reach'd down a parcel and untied it: I advanced to the side over-against her: they were all too large. The beautiful Grisset measured them one by one across my hand—It would not alter the dimensions—She begg'd I would try a single pair, which seemed to be the least—She held it open—my hand slipp'd into it at once—It will not do, said I, shaking my head a little—No, said she, doing the same thing.

There are certain combined looks of simple subtlety—where whim, and sense, and seriousness, and nonsense, are so blended, that all the languages of Babel set loose together could not express them—they are communicated and caught so instantaneously, that you can scarce say which party is the infecter. I leave it to your men of words to swell pages about it—it is enough in the present to say again, the gloves would not do; so folding our hands within our arms, we both loll'd upon the counter—it was narrow, and there was just room for the parcel to lay between us.

The beautiful Grisset look'd sometimes at the gloves, then side-ways to the window, then at the gloves—and then at me. I was not disposed to break silence—I follow'd her example: so I look'd at the gloves, then to the window, then at the gloves, and then at her—and so on alternately.

I found I lost considerably in every attack—she had a quick black eye, and shot through two such long and silken eye-lashes with such penetration, that she look'd into my very heart and reins—It may seem strange, but I could actually feel she did—

It is no matter, said I, taking up a couple of the pairs next me, and putting them into my pocket.

I was sensible the beautiful Grisset had not ask'd above a single livre above the price—I wish'd she had ask'd a livre more, and was puzzling my brains how to bring the matter about—Do you think, my dear Sir, said she, mistaking my embarrassment, that I could ask a *sous* too much of a stranger—and of a stranger whose politeness, more than his want of gloves, has done me the honour to lay himself at my mercy?—*M'en croyez capable?*—Faith! not I, said I; and if you were, you are welcome—So counting the money into her hand, and with a lower bow than one generally makes to a shopkeeper's wife, I went out, and her lad with his parcel followed me.

THE TRANSLATION

PARIS

THERE was no body in the box I was let into but a kindly old French officer. I love the character, not only because I honour the man whose manners are softened by a profession which makes bad men worse; but that I once knew one—for he is no more—and why should I not rescue one page from violation by writing his name in it, and telling the world it was Captain Tobias Shandy, the dearest of my flock and friends, whose philanthropy I never think of at this long distance from his death—but my eyes gush out with tears. For his sake, I have a predilection for the whole corps of veterans; and so I strode over the two back rows of benches, and placed myself beside him.

The old officer was reading attentively a small pamphlet, it might be the book of the opera, with a large pair of spectacles. As soon as I sat down, he took his spectacles off, and putting them into a shagreen case, return'd them and the book into his pocket together. I half rose up, and made him a bow.

Translate this into any civilized language in the world—the sense is this:

"Here's a poor stranger come in to the box—he seems as if he knew no body; and is never likely, was he to be seven years in Paris, if every man he comes near keeps his spectacles upon his nose—'tis shutting the door of conversation absolutely in his face—and using him worse than a German."

The French officer might as well have said it all aloud; and if he had, I should in course have put the bow I made him into French too, and told him, "I was sensible of his attention, and return'd him a thousand thanks for it."

There is not a secret so aiding to the progress of sociality, as to get master of this *short hand*, and be quick in rendering the several turns of looks and limbs, with all their inflections and delineations, into plain words. For my own part, by long habitude, I do it so mechanically, that when I walk the streets of London, I go translating all the way; and have more than once stood behind in the circle, where not three words have been said, and have brought off twenty different dialogues with me, which I could have fairly wrote down and sworn to.

I was going one evening to Martini's concert at Milan, and was just entering the door of the hall, when the Marquesina di F * * * was coming out in a sort of a hurry—she was almost upon me before I saw her; so I gave a spring to one side to let her pass—She had done the same, and on the same side too; so we ran our heads together: she instantly got to the other side to get out: I was just as unfortunate as she had been; for I had sprung to that side, and opposed her passage again—We both flew together to the other side, and then back—and so on—it was ridiculous; we both blush'd intolerably; so I did at last the thing I should have done at first—I stood stock still, and the Marquesina had no more difficulty. I had no power to go into the room, till I had made her so much reparation as to wait and follow her with my eye to the end of the passage—She look'd back twice, and walk'd along it rather side-ways, as if she would make room for any one coming up stairs to pass her—No, said I—that's a vile translation: the Marquesina has a right to the best apology I can make her; and that opening is left for me to do it in—so I ran and begg'd pardon for the embarrassment I had given her, saying it was my intention to have made her way. She answered, she was guided by the same intention towards me —so we reciprocally thank'd each other. She was at the top of the stairs; and seeing no *chichesbee* near her, I begg'd to hand her to her coach—so we went down the stairs, stopping at every third step to talk of the concert and the adventure—Upon my word, Madame, said I when I had handed her in, I made six different efforts to let you go out—And I made six efforts, replied she, to let you enter—I wish to heaven you would make a seventh, said I—With all my heart, said she, making room— Life is too short to be long about the forms of it—so I instantly stepp'd in, and she carried me home with her—And what became of the concert, St. Cecilia, who, I suppose, was at it, knows more than I.

I will only add, that the connection which arose out of that translation, gave me more pleasure than any one I had the honour to make in Italy.

THE DWARF

PARIS

I HAD never heard the remark made by any one in my life, except by one; and who that was, will probably come out in this chapter; so that being pretty much unprepossessed, there must have been grounds for what struck me the moment I cast my eyes over the *parterre*—and that was, the unaccountable sport of nature in forming such numbers of dwarfs—No doubt, she sports at certain times in almost every corner of the world; but in Paris, there is no end to her amusements—The goddess seems almost as merry as she is wise.

As I carried my idea out of the *opera comique* with me, I measured every body I saw walking in the streets by it—Melancholy application! especially where the size was extremely little— the face extremely dark—the eyes quick—the nose long—the teeth white—the jaw prominent—to see so many miserables, by force of accidents driven out of their own proper class into the very verge of another, which it gives me pain to write down— every third man a pigmy!—some by ricketty heads and hump backs—others by bandy legs—a third set arrested by the hand of Nature in the sixth and seventh years of their growth—a fourth,

[573]

in their perfect and natural state, like dwarf apple-trees; from the first rudiments and stamina of their existence, never meant to grow higher.

A medical traveller might say, 'tis owing to undue bandages—a splenetic one, to want of air—and an inquisitive traveller, to fortify the system, may measure the height of their houses—the narrowness of their streets, and in how few feet square in the sixth and seventh stories such numbers of the *Bourgoisie* eat and sleep together; but I remember, Mr. Shandy the elder, who accounted for nothing like any body else, in speaking one evening of these matters, averred, that children, like other animals, might be increased almost to any size, provided they came right into the world; but the misery was, the citizens of Paris were so coop'd up, that they had not actually room enough to get them—I do not call it getting any thing, said he—'tis getting nothing—Nay, continued he, rising in his argument, 'tis getting worse than nothing, when all you have got, after twenty or five and twenty years of the tenderest care and most nutritious aliment bestowed upon it, shall not at last be as high as my leg. Now, Mr. Shandy being very short, there could be nothing more said upon it.

As this is not a work of reasoning, I leave the solution as I found it, and content myself with the truth only of the remark, which is verified in every lane and by-lane of Paris. I was walking down that which leads from the Carousal to the Palais Royal, and observing a little boy in some distress at the side of the gutter, which ran down the middle of it, I took hold of his hand, and help'd him over. Upon turning up his face to look at him after, I perceived he was about forty——Never mind, said I; some good body will do as much for me when I am ninety.

I feel some little principles within me, which incline me to be merciful towards this poor blighted part of my species, who have neither size or strength to get on in the world—I cannot bear to see one of them trod upon; and had scarce got seated beside my old French officer, ere the disgust was exercised, by seeing the very thing happen under the box we sat in.

At the end of the orchestra, and betwixt that and the first side-box, there is a small esplanade left, where, when the house is full, numbers of all ranks take sanctuary. Though you stand, as in the parterre, you pay the same price as in the orchestra. A poor defenceless being of this order had got thrust some how or other into this luckless place—the night was hot, and he was surrounded by beings two feet and a half higher than himself.

[574]

The dwarf suffered inexpressibly on all sides; but the thing which incommoded him most, was a tall corpulent German, near seven feet high, who stood directly betwixt him and all possibility of his seeing either the stage or the actors. The poor dwarf did all he could to get a peep at what was going forwards, by seeking for some little opening betwixt the German's arm and his body, trying first one side, then the other; but the German stood square in the most unaccommodating posture that can be imagined—the dwarf might as well have been placed at the bottom of the deepest draw-well in Paris; so he civilly reach'd up his hand to the German's sleeve, and told him his distress—The German turn'd his head back, look'd down upon him as Goliah did upon David—and unfeelingly resumed his posture.

I was just then taking a pinch of snuff out of my monk's little horn box—And how would thy meek and courteous spirit, my dear monk! so temper'd to *bear and forbear*!—how sweetly would it have lent an ear to this poor soul's complaint!

The old French officer seeing me lift up my eyes with an emotion, as I made the apostrophe, took the liberty to ask me what was the matter—I told him the story in three words; and added, how inhuman it was.

By this time the dwarf was driven to extremes, and in his first transports, which are generally unreasonable, had told the German he would cut off his long queue with his knife—The German look'd back coolly, and told him he was welcome if he could reach it.

An injury sharpened by an insult, be it to who it will, makes every man of sentiment a party: I could have leaped out of the box to have redressed it.—The old French officer did it with much less confusion; for leaning over a little, and nodding to a centinel, and pointing at the same time with his finger at the distress—the centinel made his way up to it.—There was no occasion to tell the grievance—the thing told itself; so thrusting back the German instantly with his musket—he took the poor dwarf by the hand, and placed him before him.—This is noble! said I, clapping my hands together—And yet you would not permit this, said the old officer, in England.

—In England, dear Sir, said I, *we sit all at our ease.*

The old French officer would have set me at unity with myself, in case I had been at variance,—by saying it was a *bon mot*—and as a *bon mot* is always worth something at Paris, he offered me a pinch of snuff.

THE ROSE

PARIS

I T WAS now my turn to ask the old French officer "What was the matter?" for a cry of "*Haussez les mains, Monsieur l'Abbe*," re-echoed from a dozen different parts of the parterre, was as unintelligible to me, as my apostrophe to the monk had been to him.

He told me, it was some poor Abbe in one of the upper loges, who he supposed had got planted perdu behind a couple of grissets in order to see the opera, and that the parterre espying him, were insisting upon his holding up both his hands during the representation.—And can it be supposed, said I, that an ecclesiastick would pick the Grisset's pockets? The old French officer smiled, and whispering in my ear, open'd a door of knowledge which I had no idea of—

Good God! said I, turning pale with astonishment—it is possible, that a people so smit with sentiment should at the same time be so unclean, and so unlike themselves—*Quelle grossierte!* added I.

The French officer told me, it was an illiberal sarcasm at the church, which had begun in the theatre about the time the Tartuffe was given in it, by Moliere—but, like other remains of Gothic manners, was declining—Every nation, continued he, have their refinements and *grossiertes*, in which they take the lead, and lose it of one another by turns—that he had been in most countries, but never in one where he found not some delicacies, which others seemed to want. *Le* POUR, *et le* CONTRE *se trouvent en chaque nation*; there is a balance, said he, of good and bad every where; and nothing but the knowing it is so can emancipate one half of the world from the prepossessions which it holds against the other—that the advantage of travel, as it regarded the *sçavoir vivre*, was by seeing a great deal both of men and manners; it taught us mutual toleration; and mutual toleration, concluded he, making me a bow, taught us mutual love.

The old French officer delivered this with an air of such candour and good sense, as coincided with my first favourable impressions of his character—I thought I loved the man; but I fear I mistook the object—'twas my own way of thinking—the difference was, I could not have expressed it half so well.

It is alike troublesome to both the rider and his beast—if the latter goes pricking up his ears, and starting all the way at every object which he never saw before—I have as little torment of this kind as any creature alive; and yet I honestly confess, that many a thing gave me pain, and that I blush'd at many a word the first month—which I found inconsequent and perfectly innocent the second.

Madame de Rambouliet, after an acquaintance of about six weeks with her, had done me the honour to take me in her coach about two leagues out of town—Of all women, Madame de Rambouliet is the most correct; and I never wish to see one of more virtues and purity of heart—In our return back, Madame de Rambouliet desired me to pull the cord—I asked her if she wanted anything—*Rien que pisser*, said Madame de Rambouliet—

Grieve not, gentle traveller, to let Madame de Rambouliet p—ss on—And, ye fair mystic nymphs! go each one *pluck your rose*, and scatter them in your path—for Madame de Rambouliet did no more—I handed Madame de Rambouliet out of the coach; and had I been the priest of the chaste CASTALIA, I could not have served at her fountain with a more respectful decorum.

END OF VOL I.

VOLUME II

THE FILLE DE CHAMBRE

PARIS

WHAT the old French officer had deliver'd upon travelling, bringing Polonius's advice to his son upon the same subject into my head—and that bringing in Hamlet; and Hamlet the rest of Shakespear's works, I stopp'd at the Quai de Conti in my return home, to purchase the whole set.

The bookseller said he had not a set in the world—*Comment!* said I; taking one up out of a set which lay upon the counter betwixt us.——He said they were sent him only to be got bound, and were to be sent back to Versailles in the morning to the Count de B****.

—And does the Count de B****, said I, read Shakespear? *C'est un Esprit fort,* replied the bookseller.—He loves English books; and what is more to his honour, Monsieur, he love the English too.—You speak this so civilly, said I, that 'tis enough to oblige an Englishman to lay out a Louis d'or or two at your shop —the bookseller made a bow, and was going to say something, when a young decent girl of about twenty, who by her air and dress seemed to be *fille de chambre* to some devout woman of fashion, came into the shop and asked for *Les Egarments du Cœur & de l'Esprit:* the bookseller gave her the book directly; she pulled out a little green sattin purse run round with a ribband of the same colour, and putting her finger and thumb into it, she took out the money, and paid for it. As I had nothing more to stay me in the shop, we both walked out at the door together.

——And what have you to do, my dear, said I, with *The Wanderings of the Heart,* who scarce know yet you have one? nor till love has first told you it, or some faithless shepherd has made it ache, can'st thou ever be sure it is so.—*Le Dieu m'en guard!* said the girl.—With reason, said I; for if it is a good one, 'tis pity it should be stolen: 'tis a little treasure to thee, and gives a better air to your face, than if it was dress'd out with pearls.

The young girl listened with a submissive attention, holding her sattin purse by its ribband in her hand all the time—'Tis a very small one, said I, taking hold of the bottom of it—she held it towards me—and there is very little in it, my dear, said I; but be but as good as thou art handsome, and heaven will fill it: I had a parcel of crowns in my hand to pay for Shakespear; and as she had let go the purse intirely, I put a single one in; and tying up the ribband in a bow-knot, returned it to her.

The young girl made me more a humble court'sy than a low one—'twas one of those quiet, thankful sinkings where the spirit bows itself down—the body does no more than tell it.— I never gave a girl a crown in my life which gave me half the pleasure.

My advice, my dear, would not have been worth a pin to you, said I, if I had not given this along with it: but now, when you see the crown, you'll remember it—so don't, my dear, lay it out in ribbands.

Upon my word, Sir, said the girl, earnestly, I am incapable—in saying which, as is usual in little bargains of honour, she gave me her hand—*En verite, Monsieur, je mettrai cet argent apart*, said she.

When a virtuous convention is made betwixt man and woman, it sanctifies their most private walks: so notwithstanding it was dusky, yet as both our roads lay the same way, we made no scruple of walking along the Quai de Conti together.

She made me a second court'sy in setting off, and before we got twenty yards from the door, as if she had not done enough before, she made a sort of a little stop to tell me again—she. thank'd me.

It was a small tribute, I told her, which I could not avoid paying to virtue, and would not be mistaken in the person I had been rendering it to for the world—but I see innocence, my dear, in your face—and foul befal the man who ever lays a snare in its way!

The girl seem'd affected some way or other with what I said— she gave a low sigh—I found I was not impowered to enquire at all after it—so said nothing more till I got to the corner of the Rue de Nevers, where we were to part.

But is this the way, my dear, said I, to the hotel de Modene? she told me it was—or, that I might go by the Rue de Guineygaude, which was the next turn.—Then I'll go, my dear, by the Rue de Guineygaude, said I, for two reasons; first I shall please myself, and next I shall give you the protection of my company as far on your way as I can. The girl was sensible I was civil— and said, she wish'd the hotel de Modene was in the Rue de St. Pierre——You live there? said I.—She told me she was *fille de chambre* to Madame R****—Good God! said I, 'tis the very lady for whom I have brought a letter from Amiens—The girl told me that Madame R****, she believed expected a stranger with a letter, and was impatient to see him—so I desired the girl to present my compliments to Madame R****, and say I would certainly wait upon her in the morning.

We stood still at the corner of the Rue de Nevers whilst this pass'd—We then we stopp'd a moment whilst she disposed of her *Egarments de Cœur*, &c. more commodiously than carrying them in her hand—they were two volumes; so I held the second for her whilst she put the first into her pocket; and then she held her pocket, and I put in the other after it.

'Tis sweet to feel by what fine-spun threads our affections are drawn together.

We set off a-fresh, and as she took her third step, the girl put her hand within my arm—I was just bidding her—but she did it of herself with that undeliberating simplicity, which shew'd it was out of her head that she had never seen me before. For my own part, I felt the conviction of consanguinity so strongly, that I could not help turning half round to look in her face, and see if I could trace out any thing in it of a family likeness—Tut! said I, are we not all relations?

When we arrived at the turning up of the Rue de Guineygaude, I stopp'd to bid her adieu for good an all: the girl would thank me again for my company and kindness—She bid me adieu twice—I repeated it as often; and so cordial was the parting between us, that had it happen'd any where else, I'm not sure but I should have signed it with a kiss of charity, as warm and holy as an apostle.

But in Paris, as none kiss each other but the men, I did what amounted to the same thing——

——I bid God bless her.

THE PASSPORT

PARIS

WHEN I got home to my hotel, La Fleur told me I had been enquired after by the Lieutenant de Police—The duce take it! said I, I know the reason. It is time the reader should know it, for in the order of things in which it happened, it was omitted; not that it was out of my head, but that had I told it then, it might have been forgot now—and now is the time I want it.

I had left London with so much precipitation, that it never enter'd my mind that we were at war with France; and had reach'd Dover, and look'd through my glass at the hills beyond Boulogne, before the idea presented itself; and with this in its train, that there was no getting there without a passport. Go but to the end of a street, I have a mortal aversion for returning back no wiser than I set out; and as this was one of the greatest efforts I had ever made for knowledge, I could less bear the thoughts of it: so hearing the Count de **** had hired the packet, I begg'd he would take me in his *suite*. The Count had some little knowledge of me, so made little or no difficulty—only said, his inclination to serve me could reach no further than Calais, as he was to return by way of Brussels to Paris: however, when I had once pass'd there, I might get to Paris without interruption; but that in Paris I must make friends and shift for myself.—Let me get to Paris, Monsieur le Count, said I, and I shall do very well. So I embark'd, and never thought more of the matter.

When La Fleur told me the Lieutenant de Police had been enquiring after me, the thing instantly recurred—and by the time La Fleur had well told me, the master of the hotel came into my room to tell me the same thing, with this addition to it, that my passport had been particularly ask'd after: the master of the hotel concluded with saying, He hoped I had one.—Not I, faith! said I.

The master of the hotel retired three steps from me, as from an infected person, as I declared this—and poor La Fleur advanced three steps towards me, and with that sort of movement which a good soul makes to succour a distress'd one—The fellow won my heart by it; and from that single *trait*, I knew his character as perfectly, and could rely upon it as firmly, as if he had served me with fidelity for seven years.

Mon seigneur! cried the master of the hotel—but recollecting himself as he made the exclamation, he instantly changed the tone of it—If Monsieur, said he, has not a passport (*apparament*) in all likelihood he has friends in Paris who can procure him one. —Not that I know of, quoth I, with an air of indifference.—Then *certes*, replied he, you'll be sent to the Bastile or the Chatelet, *aumoins*.—Poo! said I, the king of France is a good natured soul —he'll hurt no body.—*Cela n'empeche pas*, said he—you will certainly be sent to the Bastile to-morrow morning.—But I've taken your lodgings for a month, answer'd I, and I'll not quit them a day before the time for all the kings of France in the world.

La Fleur whispered in my ear, That no body could oppose the king of France.

Pardi! said my host, *ces Messieurs Anglois sont des gens tres extraordinaires*—and having both said and sworn it, he went out.

THE PASSPORT

THE HOTEL AT PARIS

I COULD not find in my heart to torture La Fleur's with a serious look upon the subject of my embarrassment, which was the reason I had treated it so cavalierly: and to shew him how light it lay upon my mind, I dropt the subject entirely; and whilst he waited upon me at supper, talk'd to him with more than usual gaiety about Paris, and of the opera comique.—La Fleur had been there himself, and had followed me through the streets as far as the bookseller's shop; but seeing me come out with the young *fille de chambre*, and that we walk'd down the Quai de Conti together, La Fleur deem'd it unnecessary to follow me a step further—so making his own reflections upon it, he took a shorter cut, and got to the hotel in time to be inform'd of the affair of the Police against my arrival.

As soon as the honest creature had taken away, and gone down to sup himself, I then began to think a little seriously about my situation.—

—And here, I know, Eugenius, thou wilt smile at the remembrance of a short dialogue which pass'd betwixt us the moment I was going to set out—I must tell it here.

Eugenius, knowing that I was as little subject to be overburthen'd with money as thought, had drawn me aside to interrogate me how much I had taken care for; upon telling him the exact sum, Eugenius shook his head, and said it would not do; so pull'd out his purse in order to empty it into mine.—I've enough in conscience, Eugenius, said I. Indeed, Yorick, you have not, replied Eugenius; I know France and Italy better than you.——But you don't consider, Eugenius, said I, refusing his offer, that before I have been three days in Paris, I shall take care to say or do something or other for which I shall get clapp'd up into the Bastile, and that I shall live there a couple of months entirely at the king of France's expence.—I beg pardon, said Eugenius, drily; really, I had forgot that resource.

[585]

Now the event I treated gaily came seriously to my door.

Is it folly, or nonchalance, or philosophy, or pertinacity—or what is it in me, that, after all, when La Fleur had gone down stairs, and I was quite alone, that I could not bring down my mind to think of it otherwise than I had then spoken of it to Eugenius?

—And as for the Bastile! the terror is in the word—Make the most of it you can, said I to myself, the Bastile is but another word for a tower—and a tower is but another word for a house you can't get out of—Mercy on the gouty! for they are in it twice a year—but with nine livres a day, and pen and ink and paper, and patience, albeit a man can't get out, he may do very well within—at least for a month or six weeks; at the end of which, if he is a harmless fellow his innocence appears, and he comes out a better and wiser man than he went in.

I had some occasion (I forget what) to step into the court-yard, as I settled this account; and remember I walk'd down stairs in no small triumph with the conceit of my reasoning—Beshrew the *sombre* pencil! said I, vauntingly; for I envy not its powers, which paints the evils of life with so hard and deadly a colouring: the mind sits terrified at the objects she has magnified herself and blackened; reduce them to their proper size and hue she overlooks them—'Tis true, said I, correcting the proposition, the Bastile is not an evil to be despised—but strip it of its towers—fill up the fossè—unbarricade the doors—call it simply a confinement, and suppose 'tis some tyrant of a distemper—and not of a man which holds you in it—the evil vanishes, and you bear the other half without complaint.

I was interrupted in the hey-day of this soliloquy, with a voice which I took to be of a child, which complained "it could not get out."—I look'd up and down the passage, and seeing neither man, woman, or child, I went out without further attention.

In my return back through the passage, I heard the same words repeated twice over; and looking up, I saw it was a starling hung in a little cage.—"I can't get out—I can't get out," said the starling.

I stood looking at the bird: and to every person who came through the passage it ran fluttering to the side towards which they approach'd it, with the same lamentation of its captivity.—"I can't get out," said the starling—God help thee! said I, but I'll let thee out, cost what it will; so I turn'd about the cage to get to the door; it was twisted and double twisted so fast with wire, there was no getting it open without pulling the cage to pieces—I took both hands to it.

The bird flew to the place where I was attempting his deliverance, and thrusting his head through the trellis, press'd his breast against it, as if impatient—I fear, poor creature! said I, I cannot set thee at liberty—"No," said the starling—"I can't get out— I can't get out," said the starling.

I vow, I never had my affections more tenderly awakened; or do I remember an incident in my life, where the dissipated spirits, to which my reason had been a bubble, were so suddenly call'd home. Mechanical as the notes were, yet so true in tune to nature were they chanted, that in one moment they overthrew all my systematic reasonings upon the Bastile; and I heavily walk'd up stairs, unsaying every word I had said in going down them.

Disguise thyself as thou wilt, still slavery! said I, still thou art a bitter draught; and though thousands in all ages have been made to drink of thee, thou art no less bitter on that account.— 'Tis thou, thrice sweet and gracious goddess! addressing myself to LIBERTY, whom all in public or in private worship, whose taste is grateful, and ever wilt be so, till NATURE herself shall change—no *tint* of words can spot thy snowy mantle, or chymic power turn thy sceptre into iron—with thee to smile upon him as he eats his crust, the swain is happier than his monarch, from whose court thou art exiled—Gracious heaven! cried I, kneeling down upon the last step but one in my ascent—grant me but health, thou great Bestower of it, and give me but this fair goddess as my companion, and shower down thy mitres, if it seems good unto thy divine providence, upon those heads which are aching for them!

THE CAPTIVE

PARIS

THE bird in his cage pursued me into my room; I sat down close to my table, and leaning my head upon my hand, I begun to figure to myself the miseries of confinement. I was in a right frame for it, and so I gave full scope to my imagination.

I was going to begin with the millions of my fellow creatures born to no inheritance but slavery; but finding, however affecting

the picture was, that I could not bring it near me, and that the
multitude of sad groups in it did but distract me—

—I took a single captive, and having first shut him up in his
dungeon, I then look'd through the twilight of his grated door to
take his picture.

I beheld his body half wasted away with long expectation and
confinement, and felt what kind of sickness of the heart it was
which arises from hope deferr'd. Upon looking nearer I saw him
pale and feverish: in thirty years the western breeze had not once
fann'd his blood—he had seen no sun, no moon in all that time—
nor had the voice of friend or kinsman breathed through his
lattice—his children—

But here my heart began to bleed—and I was forced to go on
with another part of the portrait.

He was sitting upon the ground upon a little straw, in the
furthest corner of his dungeon, which was alternately his chair
and bed: a little calendar of small sticks were laid at the head
notch'd all over with the dismal days and nights he had pass'd
there—he had one of these little sticks in his hand, and with
a rusty nail he was etching another day of misery to add to the
heap. As I darkened the little light he had, he lifted up a hopeless
eye towards the door, then cast it down, shook his head, and
went on with his work of affliction. I heard his chains upon his
legs, as he turn'd his body to lay his little stick upon the bundle—
He gave a deep sigh—I saw the iron enter into his soul—I burst
into tears—I could not sustain the picture of confinement which
my fancy had drawn—I started up from my chair, and calling La
Fleur, I bid him bespeak me a *remise*, and have it ready at the
door of the hotel by nine in the morning.

I'll go directly, said I, myself to Monsieur le Duke de Choiseul.

La Fleur would have put me to bed; but not willing he should
see any thing upon my cheek, which would cost the honest fellow
a heartache, I told him I would go to bed by myself—and bid him
go do the same.

THE STARLING

ROAD TO VERSAILLES

I GOT into my *remise* the hour I proposed: La Fleur got up behind, and I bid the coachman make the best of his way to Versailles.

As there was nothing in this road, or rather nothing which I look for in travelling, I cannot fill up the blank better than with a short history of this self-same bird, which became the subject of the last chapter.

Whilst the honourable Mr. **** was waiting for a wind at Dover it had been caught upon the cliffs, before it could well fly, by an English lad who was his groom; who not caring to destroy it, had taken it in his breast into the packet—and by course of feeding it, and taking it once under his protection, in a day or two grew fond of it, and got it safe along with him to Paris.

At Paris the lad had laid out a livre in a little cage for the starling, and as he had little to do better the five months his master stay'd there, he taught it in his mother's tongue the four simple words—(and no more)—to which I own'd myself so much its debtor.

Upon his master's going on for Italy, the lad had given it to the master of the hotel—But his little song for liberty, being in an *unknown* language at Paris, the bird had little or no store set by him—so La Fleur bought both him and his cage for me for a bottle of Burgundy.

In my return from Italy I brought him with me to the country in whose language he had learn'd his notes—and telling the story of him to Lord A—Lord A begg'd the bird of me: in a week Lord A gave him to Lord B—Lord B made a present of him to Lord C —and Lord C's gentleman sold him to Lord D's for a shilling— Lord D gave him to Lord E—and so on—half round the alphabet —From that rank he pass'd into the lower house, and pass'd the hands of as many commoners——But as all these wanted to *get in* —and my bird wanted to get out—he had almost as little store set by him in London as in Paris.

It is impossible but many of my readers must have heard of him; and if any by mere chance have ever seen him—I beg leave to inform them, that that bird was my bird—or some vile copy set up to represent him.

I have nothing further to add upon him, but that from that time to this, I have borne this poor starling as the crest to my arms.—Thus:

And let the heralds officers twist his neck about if they dare.

THE ·ADDRESS

VERSAILLES

I SHOULD not like to have my enemy take a view of my mind, when I am going to ask protection of any man: for which reason I generally endeavour to protect myself; but this going to Monsieur le Duc de C***** was an act of compulsion—had it been an act of choice, I should have done it, I suppose, like other people.

How many mean plans of dirty address, as I went along, did my servile heart form!—I deserved the Bastile for every one of them.

Then nothing would serve me, when I got within sight of Versailles, but putting words and sentences together, and conceiving attitudes and tones to wreath myself into Monsieur le Duc de C*****'s good graces—This will do, said I—Just as well, retorted I again, as a coat carried up to him by an adventurous taylor, without taking his measure—Fool! continued I—see Monsieur le Duc's face first—observe what character is written in it—take notice in what posture he stands to hear you—mark the turns and expressions of his body and limbs—And for the tone—the first sound which comes from his lips will give it you— and from all these together you'll compound an address at once upon the spot, which cannot disgust the Duke—the ingredients are his own, and most likely to go down.

Well! said I, I wish it well over—Coward again! as if man to man was not equal throughout the whole surface of the globe: and if in the field—why not face to face in the cabinet too? And trust me, Yorick, whenever it is not so, man is false to himself, and betrays his own succours ten times where nature does it once. Go to the Duc de C***** with the Bastile in thy looks—my life for it, thou wilt be sent back to Paris in half an hour with an escort.

I believe so, said I—Then I'll go to the Duke, by heaven! with all the gaity and debonairness in the world.—

—And there you are wrong again, replied I—A heart at ease, Yorick, flies into no extremes—'tis ever on its center.—Well! well! cried I, as the coachman turn'd in at the gates, I find I shall do very well: and by the time he had wheel'd round the court, and brought me up to the door, I found myself so much the better for my own lecture, that I neither ascended the steps like a victim to justice, who was to part with life upon the topmost—nor did I mount them with a skip and a couple of strides, as I do when I fly up, Eliza! to thee to meet it.

As I enter'd the door of the saloon, I was met by a person who possibly might be the maitre d'hotel, but had more the air of one of the under secretaries, who told me the Duc de C***** was busy— I am utterly ignorant, said I, of the forms of obtaining an audience, being an absolute stranger, and what is worse in the present con- jecture of affairs, being an Englishman too.——He replied, that did not increase the difficulty.—I made him a slight bow, and told him, I had something of importance to say to Monsieur le Duc. The secretary look'd towards the stairs, as if he was about to leave me to carry up this account to some one—But I must not mislead you, said I; for what I have to say is of no manner of importance to Monsieur le Duc de C*****, but of great impor- tance to myself.—*C'est une autre affaire*, replied he——Not at all,

[591]

said I, to a man of gallantry.—But pray, good Sir, continued I, when can a stranger hope to have *accesse*?—In not less than two hours, said he, looking at his watch. The number of equipages in the court-yard seem'd to justify the calculation, that I could have no nearer a prospect—and as walking backwards and forwards in the saloon, without a soul to commune with, was for the time as bad as being in the Bastile itself, I instantly went back to my *remise*, and bid the coachman drive me to the Cordon Bleu, which was the nearest hotel.

I think there is a fatality in it—I seldom go to the place I set out for.

LE PATISSER

VERSAILLES

BEFORE I had got half-way down the street, I changed my mind: as I am at Versailles, thought I, I might as well take a view of the town; so I pull'd the cord, and ordered the coachman to drive round some of the principal streets—I suppose the town is not very large, said I.—The coachman begg'd pardon for setting me right, and told me it was very superb, and that numbers of the first dukes and marquises and counts had hotels —The Count de B****, of whom the bookseller at the Quai de Conti had spoke so handsomely the night before, came instantly into my mind.—And why should I not go, thought I, to the Count de B****, who has so high an idea of English books and Englishmen, and tell him my story? so I changed my mind a second time—In truth it was the third; for I had intended that day for Madame de R**** in the Rue St. Pierre, and had devoutly sent her word by her *fille de chambre* that I would assuredly wait upon her—but I am govern'd by circumstances—I cannot govern them: so seeing a man standing with a basket on the other side of the street, as if he had something to sell, I bid La Fleur go up to him and enquire for the Count's hotel.

La Fleur return'd a little pale; and told me it was a Chevalier de St. Louis selling *patés*—It is impossible, La Fleur! said I.—La Fleur could no more account for the phenomenon than myself; but persisted in his story: he had seen the croix set in gold, with its red ribband, he said, tied to his button-hole—and had look'd into the basket, and seen the *patés* which the Chevalier was selling; so could not be mistaken in that.

[592]

Such a reverse in man's life awakens a better principle than curiosity: I could not help looking for some time at him as I sat in the *remise*—the more I look'd at him, his croix, and his basket, the stronger they wove themselves into my brain—I got out of the *remise* and went towards him.

He was begirt with a clean linen apron which fell below his knees, and with a sort of a bib went half way up his breast; upon the top of this, but a little below the hem, hung his croix. His basket of little *patés* was cover'd over with a white damask napkin; another of the same kind was spread at the bottom; and there was a look of *propreté* and neatness throughout, that one might have bought his *patés* of him, as much from appetite as sentiment.

He made an offer of them to neither; but stood still with them at the corner of a hotel, for those to buy who chose it without solicitation.

He was about forty-eight—of a sedate look, something approaching to gravity.—I did not wonder.—I went up rather to the basket than him, and having lifted up the napkin, and taking one of his *patés* into my hand, I begg'd he would explain the appearance which affected me.

He told me in a few words, that the best part of his life had pass'd in the service, in which, after spending a small patrimony, he had obtain'd a company and the croix with it; but that at the conclusion of the last peace, his regiment being reformed, and the whole corps, with those of some other regiments, left without any provision, he found himself in a wide world without friends, without a livre—and indeed, said he, without any thing but this— (pointing, as he said it, to his croix)—The poor chevalier won my pity, and he finish'd the scene with winning my esteem too.

The king, he said, was the most generous of princes, but his generosity could neither relieve or reward every one, and it was only his misfortune to be amongst the number. He had a little wife, he said, whom he loved, who did the *patisserie*; and added, he felt no dishonour in defending her and himself from want in this way—unless Providence had offer'd him a better.

It would be wicked to with-hold a pleasure from the good in passing over what happen'd to this poor Chevalier of St. Louis about nine months after.

It seems he usually took his stand near the iron gates which lead up to the palace, and as his croix had caught the eye of numbers, numbers had made the same enquiry which I had done —He had told them the same story, and always with so much modesty and good sense, that it had reach'd at last the king's ears —who hearing the Chevalier had been a gallant officer, and respected by the whole regiment as a man of honour and integrity, he broke up his little trade by a pension of fifteen hundred livres a year.

As I have told this to please the reader, I beg he will allow me to relate another, out of its order, to please myself—the two stories reflect light upon each other, and 'tis a pity they should be parted.

THE SWORD

RENNES

WHEN states and empires have their periods of declension, and feel in their turns what distress and poverty is —I stop not to tell the causes which gradually brought the house d'E**** in Britany into decay. The Marquis d'E**** had fought up against his condition with great firmness; wishing to preserve, and still shew to the world, some little fragments of what his ancestors had been—their indiscretions had put it out of his power. There was enough left for the little exigencies of *obscurity*—But he had two boys who look'd up to him for *light*— he thought they deserved it.—He had tried his sword—it could not open the way—the *mounting* was too expensive—and simple œconomy was not a match for it—there was no resource but commerce.

In any other province in France, save Britany, this was smiting the root for ever of the little tree his pride and affection wish'd to see re-blossom—But in Britany, there being a provision for this, he avail'd himself of it; and taking an occasion when the states were assembled at Rennes, the Marquis, attended with his two boys, enter'd the court; and having pleaded the right of an ancient law of the duchy, which, though seldom claim'd, he said, was no less in force; he took his sword from his side—Here, said he, take it; and be trusty guardians of it, till better times put me in condition to reclaim it.

The president accepted the Marquis's sword—he stay'd a few minutes to see it deposited in the archives of his house, and departed.

The Marquis and his whole family embarked the next day for Martinico, and in about nineteen or twenty years of successful application to business, with some unlook'd-for bequests from distant branches of his house—return'd home to reclaim his nobility and to support it.

It was an incident of good fortune which will never happen to any traveller but a sentimental one, that I should be at Rennes at the very time of this solemn requisition: I call it solemn—it was so to me.

The Marquis enter'd the court with his whole family: he supported his lady—his eldest son supported his sister, and his youngest was at the other extreme of the line next his mother—he put his handkerchief to his face twice—

—There was a dead silence. When the Marquis had approach'd within six paces of the tribunal, he gave the Marchioness to his youngest son, and advancing three steps before his family—he reclaim'd his sword. His sword was given him, and the moment he got it into his hand he drew it almost out of the scabbard—'twas the shining face of a friend he had once given up—he look'd attentively along it, beginning at the hilt, as if to see whether it was the same—when observing a little rust which it had contracted near the point, he brought it near his eye, and bending his head down over it, I think I saw a tear fall upon the place: I could not be deceived by what followed.

"I shall find," said he, "some *other way*, to get it off."

When the Marquis had said this, he return'd his sword into its scabbard, made a bow to the guardians of it—and, with his wife and daughter and his two sons following him, walk'd out.

O how I envied him his feelings!

THE PASSPORT

VERSAILLES

I FOUND no difficulty in getting admittance to Monsieur le Count de B****. The set of Shakespears was laid upon the table, and he was tumbling them over. I walk'd up close to the table, and giving first such a look at the books as to make him conceive I knew what they were, I told him I had come without any one to present me, knowing I should meet with a friend in his apartment who, I trusted, would do it for me—It is my countryman the great Shakespear, said I, pointing to his works—*et ayez* *la bonté, mon cher ami*, apostrophizing his spirit, added I, *de me faire cet honneur là.*——

The Count smil'd at the singularity of the introduction; and seeing I look'd a little pale and sickly, insisted upon my taking an arm-chair: so I sat down; and to save him conjectures upon a visit so out of all rule, I told him simply of the incident in the book-seller's shop, and how that had impell'd me rather to go to him with the story of a little embarrassment I was under, than to any other man in France—And what is your embarrassment? Let me hear it, said the Count. So I told him the story just as I have told it the reader—

—And the master of my hotel, said I, as I concluded it, will needs have it, Monsieur le Count, that I shall be sent to the Bastile—but I have no apprehensions, continued I—for in falling into the hands of the most polish'd people in the world, and being conscious I was a true man, and not come to spy the nakedness of the land, I scarce thought I laid at their mercy.—It does not suit the gallantry of the French, Monsieur le Count, said I, to shew it against invalids.

An animated blush came into the Count de B****'s cheeks, as I spoke this—*Ne craignez rien*—Don't fear, said he—Indeed I don't, replied I again—Besides, continued I a little sportingly, I have come laughing all the way from London to Paris, and I do not think Monsieur le Duc de Choiseul is such an enemy to mirth, as to send me back crying for my pains.

My application tő you, Monsieur le Compte de B**** (making him a low bow) is to desire he will not.

The Count heard me with great good nature, or I had not said half as much—and once or twice said—*C'est bien dit*. So I rested my cause there—and determined to say no more about it.

The Count led the discourse: we talk'd of indifferent things—of books and politicks, and men—and then of women—God bless them all! said I, after much discourse about them, there is not a man upon earth who loves them so much as I do: after all the foibles I have seen, and all the satires I have read against them, still I love them; being firmly persuaded that a man who has not a sort of an affection for the whole sex, is incapable of ever loving a single one as he ought.

Heh bien! Monsieur l'Anglois, said the Count, gaily—You are not come to spy the nakedness of the land—I believe you—*ni encore*, I dare say, *that* of our women—But permit me to conjecture—if, *par hazard*, they fell in your way, that the prospect would not affect you.

I have something within me which cannot bear the shock of the least indecent insinuation; in the sportability of chit-chat I have often endeavoured to conquer it, and with infinite pain have hazarded a thousand things to a dozen of the sex together—the least of which I could not venture to a single one, to gain heaven.

Excuse me, Monsieur le Count, said I—as for the nakedness of your land, if I saw it, I should cast my eyes over it with tears in them—and for that of your women (blushing at the idea he had excited in me) I am so evangelical in this, and have such a fellow-feeling for what ever is *weak* about them, that I would cover it with a garment, if I knew how to throw it on—But I could wish, continued I, to spy the *nakedness* of their hearts, and through the different disguises of customs, climates, and religion, find out what is good in them to fashion my own by—and therefore am I come.

It is for this reason, Monsieur le Count, continued I, that I have not seen the Palais royal—nor the Luxembourg—nor the Façade of the Louvre—nor have attempted to swell the catalogues we have of pictures, statues, and churches—I conceive every fair being as a temple, and would rather enter in, and see the original drawings and loose sketches hung up in it, than the transfiguration of Raphael itself.

The thirst of this, continued I, as impatient as that which inflames the breast of the connoisseur, has led me from my own home into France—and from France will lead me through Italy—'tis a quiet journey of the heart in pursuit of NATURE, and those affections which rise out of her, which make us love each other—and the world, better than we do.

The Count said a great many civil things to me upon the occasion; and added very politely how much he stood obliged to Shakespear for making me known to him—But, *a-propos*, said he, Shakespear is full of great things—he forgot a small punctilio of announcing your name—it puts you under a necessity of doing it yourself.

THE PASSPORT

VERSAILLES

THERE is not a more perplexing affair in life to me, than to set about telling any one who I am—for there is scarce any body I cannot give a better account of than of myself; and I have often wish'd I could do it in a single word—and have an end of it. It was the only time and occasion in my life, I could accomplish this to any purpose—for Shakespear lying upon the table, and recollecting I was in his books, I took up Hamlet, and turning immediately to the grave-diggers scene in the fifth act, I lay'd my finger upon YORICK, and advancing the book to the Count, with my finger all the way over the name—Me, *Voici!* said I.

Now whether the idea of poor Yorick's skull was put out of the Count's mind, by the reality of my own, or by what magic he could drop a period of seven or eight hundred years, makes nothing in this account—'tis certain the French conceive better than they combine—I wonder at nothing in this world, and the less at this; inasmuch as one of the first of our own church, for whose candour and paternal sentiments I have the highest veneration, fell into the same mistake in the very same case.—"He could not bear," he said, "to look into sermons wrote by the king of Denmark's jester."——Good, my lord! said I—but there are two Yoricks. The Yorick your lordship thinks of, has been dead and buried eight hundred years ago; he flourish'd in Horwendillus's court—the other Yorick is myself, who have flourish'd, my lord, in no court—He shook his head—Good God! said I, you might as well confound Alexander the Great, with Alexander the Coppersmith, my lord——'Twas all one, he replied—

—If Alexander king of Macedon could have translated your lordship, said I, I'm sure your Lordship would not have said so.

The poor Count de B**** fell but into the same *error*—

——*Et, Monsieur, est il Yorick?* cried the Count.—*Je le suis,* said I.—*Vous?—Moi—moi qui ai l'honneur de vous parler, Monsieur le Compte—Mon Dieu!* said he, embracing me—*Vous etes Yorick.*

The Count instantly put the Shakespear into his pocket, and left me alone in his room.

THE PASSPORT

VERSAILLES

I COULD not conceive why the Count de B**** had gone so abruptly out of the room, any more than I could conceive why he had put the Shakespear into his pocket—*Mysteries which must explain themselves are not worth the loss of time which a conjecture about them takes up:* 'twas better to read Shakespear; so taking up, "*Much Ado about Nothing*," I transported myself instantly from the chair I sat in to Messina in Sicily, and got so busy with Don Pedro and Benedick and Beatrice, that I thought not of Versailles, the Count, or the Passport.

Sweet pliability of man's spirit, that can at once surrender itself to illusions, which cheat expectation and sorrow of their weary moments!—long—long since had ye number'd out my days, had I not trod so great a part of them upon this enchanted ground. When my way is too rough for my feet, or too steep for my strength, I get off it, to some smooth velvet path which fancy has scattered over with rose-buds of delights; and having taken a few turns in it, come back strengthen'd and refresh'd—When evils press sore upon me, and there is no retreat from them in this world, then I take a new course—I leave it—and as I have a clearer idea of the elysian fields than I have of heaven, I force myself, like Eneas, into them—I see him meet the pensive shade of his forsaken Dido—and wish to recognize it—I see the injured spirit wave her head, and turn off silent from the author of her miseries and dishonours—I lose the feelings for myself in hers—and in those affections which were wont to make me mourn for her when I was at school.

Surely this is not walking in a vain shadow—nor does man disquiet himself in vain *by it*—he oftener does so in trusting the issue of his commotions to reason only.—I can safely say for myself, I was never able to conquer any one single bad sensation in my heart so decisively, as by beating up as fast as I could for some kindly and gentle sensation, to fight it upon its own ground.

When I had got to the end of the third act, the Count de B**** entered with my Passport in his hand. Mons. le Duc de C****, said the Count, is as good a prophet, I dare say, as he is a statesman—*Un homme qui rit*, said the Duke, *ne sera jamais dangereuz,* —Had it been for any one but the king's jester, added the Count,

[599]

I could not have got it these two hours.—*Pardonnez moi, Monsieur le Compte*, said I—I am not the king's jester.—But you are Yorick?—Yes.—*Et vous plaisantez?*—I answered, Indeed I did jest—but was not paid for it—'twas entirely at my own expence.

We have no jester at court, Mons. le Count, said I, the last we had was in the licentious reign of Charles the IId—since which time our manners have been so gradually refining, that our court at present is so full of patriots, who wish for *nothing* but the honours and wealth of their country—and our ladies are all so chaste, so spotless, so good, so devout—there is nothing for a jester to make a jest of—

Voila un persiflage! cried the Count.

THE PASSPORT

VERSAILLES

AS THE Passport was directed to all lieutenant governors, governors, and commandants of cities, generals of armies, justiciaries, and all officers of justice, to let Mr. Yorick, the king's jester, and his baggage, travel quietly along—I own the triumph of obtaining the Passport was not a little tarnish'd by the figure I cut in it—But there is nothing unmixt in this world; and some of the gravest of our divines have carried it so far as to affirm, that enjoyment itself was attended even with a sigh—and that the greatest *they knew of* terminated *in a general way*, in little better than a convulsion.

I remember the grave and learned Bevoriskius, in his commentary upon the generations from Adam, very naturally breaks off in the middle of a note to give an account to the world of a couple of sparrows upon the out-edge of his window, which had incommoded him all the time he wrote, and at last had entirely taken him off from his genealogy.

—'Tis strange! writes Bevoriskius; but the facts are certain, for I have had the curiosity to mark them down one by one with my pen—but the cock-sparrow during the little time that I could have finished the other half this note, has actually interrupted me with the reiteration of his caresses three and twenty times and a half.

How merciful, adds Bevoriskius, is heaven to his creatures!

Ill fated Yorick! that the gravest of thy brethren should be able to write that to the world, which stains thy face with crimson, to copy in even thy study.

But this is nothing to my travels—So I twice—twice beg pardon for it.

CHARACTER

VERSAILLES

AND HOW do you find the French? said the Count de B****, after he had given me the Passport.

The reader may suppose, that after so obliging a proof of courtesy, I could not be at a loss to say something handsome to the enquiry.

—*Mais passe, pour cela*—Speak frankly, said he; do you find all the urbanity in the French which the world give us the honour of? —I had found every thing, I said, which confirmed it—*Vraiment*, said the Count.—*Les François sont polis.*—To an excess, replied I.

The Count took notice of the word *excesse;* and would have it I meant more than I said. I defended myself a long time as well as I could against it—he insisted I had a reserve, and that I would speak my opinion frankly.

I believe, Mons. le Count, said I, that man has a certain compass, as well as an instrument; and that the social and other calls have occasion by turns for every key in him; so that if you begin a note too high or too low, there must be a want either in the upper or under part, to fill up the system of harmony.—The Count de B**** did not understand music, so desired me to explain it some other way. A polish'd nation, my dear Count, said I, makes every one its debtor; and besides, urbanity itself, like the fair sex, has so many charms, it goes against the heart to say it can do ill; and yet, I believe, there is but a certain line of perfection that man, take him altogether, is empower'd to arrive at—if he gets beyond, he rather exchanges qualities, than gets them. I must not presume to say how far this has affected the French in the subject we are speaking of—but should it ever be the case of the English, in the progress of their refinements, to arrive at the same polish which distinguishes the French, if we did not lose the *politesse de cœur*, which inclines men more to humane actions, than courteous ones, we should at least lose that distinct variety and originality of character, which distinguishes them, not only from each other, but from all the world besides.

I had a few king William's shillings as smooth as glass in my pocket; and foreseeing they would be of use in the illustration of my hypothesis, I had got them into my hand, when I had proceeded so far—

See, Monsieur le Count, said I, rising up, and laying them before him upon the table—by jingling and rubbing one against another for seventy years together in one body's pocket or another's, they are become so much alike you can scarce distinguish one shilling from another.

The English, like antient medals, kept more apart, and passing but few peoples hands, preserve the first sharpnesses which the fine hand of nature has given them—they are not so pleasant to feel—but in return, the legend is so visible, that at the first look you see whose image and superscription they bear.—But the French, Mons. le Count, added I, wishing to soften what I had said, have so many excellencies, they can the better spare this— they are a loyal, a gallant, a generous, an ingenious, and good-temper'd people as is under heaven—if they have a fault—they are too *serious*.

Mon Dieu! cried the Count, rising out of his chair.

Mais vous plaisantez, said he, correcting his exclamation.— I laid my hand upon my breast, and with earnest gravity assured him it was my most settled opinion.

The Count said he was mortified, he could not stay to hear my reasons, being engaged to go that moment to dine with the Duc de C*****.

But if it is not too far to come to Versailles to eat your soup with me, I beg, before you leave France, I may have the pleasure of knowing you retract your opinion—or, in what manner you support it.—But if you do support it, Mons. Anglois, said he, you must do it with all your powers, because you have the whole world against you.—I promised the Count I would do myself the honour of dining with him before I set out for Italy—so took my leave.

THE TEMPTATION

PARIS

WHEN I alighted at the hotel, the porter told me a young women with a band-box had been that moment enquiring for me.—I do not know, said the porter, whether she is gone away or no. I took the key of my chamber of him, and went up stairs; and when I had got within ten steps of the top of the landing before my door, I met her coming easily down.

It was the fair *fille de chambre* I had walked along the Quai de Conti with: Madame de R**** had sent her upon some commissions to a *merchande de modes* within a step or two of the hotel de Modene; and as I had fail'd in waiting upon her, had bid her enquire if I had left Paris; and if so, whether I had not left a letter address'd to her.

As the fair *fille de chambre* was so near my door she turned back, and went into the room with me for a moment or two whilst I wrote a card.

It was a fine still evening in the latter end of the month of May— the crimson window curtains (which were of the same colour of those of the bed) were drawn close—the sun was setting, and reflected through them so warm a tint into the fair *fille de chambre*'s face, I thought she blush'd—the idea of it made me blush myself —we were quite alone; and that super-induced a second blush before the first could get off.

There is a sort of a pleasing half guilty blush, where the blood is more in fault than the man—'tis sent impetuous from the heart, and virtue flies after it—not to call it back, but to make the sensation of it more delicious to the nerves—'tis associated.—

But I'll not describe it.—I felt something at first within me which was not in strict unison with the lesson of virtue I had given her the night before—I sought five minutes for a card—I knew I had not one—I took up a pen—I laid it down again—my hand trembled—the devil was in me.

I know as well as any one he is an adversary whom if we resist he will fly from us—but I seldom resist him at all; from a terror, that though I may conquer, I may still get a hurt in the combat— so I give up the triumph, for security; and instead of thinking to make him fly, I generally fly myself.

The fair *fille de chambre* came close up to the bureau where I was looking for a card—took up first the pen I cast down, then offered to hold me the ink: she offer'd it so sweetly, I was going to accept it—but I durst not—I have nothing, my dear, said I, to write upon.—Write it, said she, simply, upon any thing.—

I was just going to cry out, Then I will write it, fair girl! upon thy lips.

—If I do, said I, I shall perish—so I took her by the hand, and led her to the door, and begg'd she would not forget the lesson I had given her—She said, Indeed she would not—and as she utter'd it with some earnestness, she turned about, and gave me both her hands, closed together, into mine—it was impossible not to compress them in that situation—I wish'd to let them go; and all the time I held them, I kept arguing within myself against it—and still I held them on.—In two minutes I found I had all the battle to fight over again—and I felt my legs and every limb about me tremble at the idea.

The foot of the bed was within a yard and a half of the place where we were standing—I had still hold of her hands—and how it happened I can give no account, but I neither ask'd her—nor drew her—nor did I think of the bed—but so it did happen, we both sat down.

I'll just shew you, said the fair *fille de chambre*, the little purse I have been making to-day to hold your crown. So she put her hand into her right pocket, which was next me, and felt for it for some time—then into the left—"She had lost it."—I never bore expectation more quietly—it was in her right pocket at last—she pulled it out; it was of green taffeta, lined with a little bit of white quilted sattin, and just big enough to hold the crown—she put it into my hand—it was pretty; and I held it ten minutes with the back of my hand resting upon her lap—looking sometimes at the purse, sometimes on one side of it.

A stitch or two had broke out in the gathers of my stock—the fair *fille de chambre*, without saying a word, took out her little hussive, threaded a small needle, and sew'd it up—I foresaw it would hazard the glory of the day; and as she passed her hand in silence across and across my neck in the manœuvre, I felt the laurels shake which fancy had wreath'd about my head.

A strap had given way in her walk, and the buckle of her shoe was just falling off—See, said the *fille de chambre*, holding up her foot—I could not for my soul but fasten the buckle in return, and putting in the strap—and lifting up the other foot with it, when I had done, to see both were right—in doing it too suddenly—it unavoidably threw the fair *fille de chambre* off her center—and then—

THE CONQUEST

YES——and then—Ye whose clay-cold heads and luke-warm hearts can argue down or mask your passions, tell me, what trespass is it that man should have them? or how his spirit stands answerable to the father of spirits, but for his conduct under them?

If nature has so wove her web of kindness, that some threads of love and desire are entangled with the piece, must the whole web be rent in drawing them out?—Whip me such stoics, great governor of nature! said I to myself—Wherever thy providence shall place me for the trials of my virtue—whatever is my danger—whatever is my situation—let me feel the movements which rise out of it, and which belong to me as a man, and if I govern them as a good one, I will trust the issues to thy justice—for thou hast made us, and not we ourselves.

As I finish'd my address, I raised the fair *fille de chambre* up by the hand, and led her out of the room—she stood by me till I lock'd the door and put the key in my pocket—*and then*—the victory being quite decisive—and not till then, I press'd my lips to her cheek, and, taking her by the hand again, led her safe to the gate of the hotel.

THE MYSTERY

PARIS

IF A MAN knows the heart, he will know it was impossible to go back instantly to my chamber—it was touching a cold key with a flat third to it, upon the close of a piece of musick, which had call'd forth my affections—therefore, when I let go the hand of the *fille de chambre*, I remain'd at the gate of the hotel for some time, looking at every one who pass'd by, and forming conjectures upon them, till my attention got fix'd upon a single object, which confounded all kind of reasoning upon him.

It was a tall figure of a philosophic serious, adust look, which pass'd and repass'd sedately along the street, making a turn of about sixty paces on each side of the gate of the hotel—the man was about fifty-two—had a small cane under his arm—was dress'd in a dark drab-colour'd coat, waistcoat, and breeches, which seem'd to have seen some years service—they were still clean, and there was a little air of frugal *propreté* throughout him. By his pulling off his hat, and his attitude of accosting a good many in his way, I saw he was asking charity; so I got a sous or two out of my pocket ready to give him, as he took me in his turn—he pass'd by me without asking any thing—and yet did not go five steps further before he ask'd charity of a little woman— I was much more likely to have given of the two.—He had scarce done with the woman, when he pull'd off his hat to another who was coming the same way.—An ancient gentleman came slowly— and, after him, a young smart one—he let them both pass, and ask'd nothing: I stood observing him half an hour, in which time he had made a dozen turns backwards and forwards, and found that he invariably pursued the same plan.

There were two things very singular in this, which set my brain to work, and to no purpose—the first was, why the man should *only* tell his story to the sex—and secondly, what kind of story it was, and what species of eloquence it could be, which soften'd the hearts of the women, which he knew 'twas to no purpose to practise upon the men.

There were two other circumstances which entangled this mystery—the one was, he told every woman what he had to say in her ear, and in a way which had much more the air of a secret than a petition—the other was, it was always successful—he never stopp'd a woman, but she pull'd out her purse, and immediately gave him something.

I could form no system to explain the phenomenon.

I had got a riddle to amuse me for the rest of the evening, so I walk'd up stairs to my chamber.

THE CASE OF CONSCIENCE

PARIS

I WAS immediately followed up by the master of the hotel, who came into my room to tell me I must provide lodgings elsewhere.—How so, friend? said I.—He answered, I had had a young woman lock'd up with me two hours that evening in my bed-chamber, and 'twas against the rules of his house.—Very well, said I, we'll all part friends then—for the girl is no worse—and I am no worse—and you will be just as I found you.——It was

[606]

enough, he said, to overthrow the credit of his hotel.—*Voyez vous,
Monsieur*, said he, pointing to the foot of the bed we had been
sitting upon.—I own it had something of the appearance of an
evidence; but my pride not suffering me to enter into any detail of
the case, I exhorted him to let his soul sleep in peace, as I resolved
to let mine do that night, and that I would discharge what I owed
him at breakfast.

I should not have minded, *Monsieur*, said he, if you had had
twenty girls—'Tis a score more, replied I, interrupting him, than
I ever reckon'd upon—Provided, added he, it had been but in
a morning.—And does the difference of the time of the day at
Paris make a difference in the sin?—It made a difference, he said,
in the scandal.—I like a good distinction in my heart, and cannot
say I was intolerably out of temper with the man.—I own it is
necessary, re-assumed the master of the hotel, that a stranger at
Paris should have the opportunities presented to him of buying
lace and silk stockings and ruffles, *et tout cela*—and 'tis nothing
if a woman comes with a band box.——O' my conscience, said I,
she had one; but I never look'd into it.—Then, *Monsieur*, said he,
has bought nothing.—Not one earthly thing, replied I.—Because,
said he, I could recommend one to you who would use you *en
conscience*.—But I must see her this night, said I.—He made me
a low bow and walk'd down.

Now shall I triumph over this maitre d'hotel, cried I—and
what then?—Then I shall let him see I know he is a dirty fellow.—
And what then?—What then!—I was too near myself to say it
was for the sake of others.—I had no good answer left—there was
more of spleen than principle in my project, and I was sick of it
before the execution.

In a few minutes the Grisset came in with her box of lace—I'll
buy nothing however, said I, within myself.

The Grisset would shew me every thing—I was hard to please:
she would not seem to see it; she open'd her little magazine, laid
all her laces one after another before me—unfolded and folded
them up again one by one with the most patient sweetness—
I might buy—or not—she would let me have every thing at my
own price—the poor creature seem'd anxious to get a penny; and
laid herself out to win me, and not so much in a manner which
seem'd artful, as in one I felt simple and caressing.

If there is not a fund of honest cullibility in man, so much the
worse—my heart relented, and I give up my second resolution as
quietly as the first—Why should I chastise one for the trespass of

[607]

another?—If thou art tributary to this tyrant of an host, thought I, looking up in her face, so much harder is thy bread.

If I had not had more than four Louis d'ors in my purse, there was no such thing as rising up and shewing her the door, till I had first laid three of them out in a pair of ruffles.

—The master of the hotel will share the profit with her—no matter—then I have only paid as many a poor soul has *paid* before me for an act he *could* not do, or think of.

THE RIDDLE

PARIS

WHEN La Fleur came up to wait upon me at supper, he told me how sorry the master of the hotel was for his affront to me in bidding me change my lodgings.

A man who values a good night's rest will not lay down with enmity in his heart if he can help it—So I bid La Fleur tell the master of the hotel, that I was sorry on my side for the occasion I had given him—and you may tell him, if you will, La Fleur, added I, that if the young woman should call again, I shall not see her.

This was a sacrifice not to him, but myself, having resolved, after so narrow an escape, to run no more risks, but to leave Paris, if it was possible, with all the virtue I enter'd in.

C'est deroger à noblesse, Monsieur, said La Fleur, making me a bow down to the ground as he said it—*Et encore Monsieur,* said he, may change his sentiments—and if (*par hazard*) he should like to amuse himself—I find no amusement in it, said I, interrupting him—

Mon Dieu! said La Fleur—and took away.

In an hour's time he came to put me to bed, and was more than commonly officious—something hung upon his lips to say to me, or ask me, which he could not get off: I could not conceive what it was; and indeed gave myself little trouble to find it out, as I had another riddle so much more interesting upon my mind, which was that of the man's asking charity before the door of the hotel —I would have given any thing to have got to the bottom of it; and that, not out of curiosity—'tis so low a principle of enquiry, in general, I would not purchase the gratification of it with a two-sous piece—but a secret, I thought, which so soon and so certainly soften'd the heart of every woman you came near, was

[608]

a secret at least equal to the philosopher's stone: had I had both the Indies, I would have given up one to have been master of it.

I toss'd and turn'd it almost all night long in my brains to no manner of purpose; and when I awoke in the morning, I found my spirit as much troubled with my *dreams*, as ever the king of Babylon had been with his; and I will not hesitate to affirm, it would have puzzled all the wise men of Paris, as much as those of Chaldea, to have given its interpretation.

LE DIMANCHE

PARIS

IT WAS Sunday; and when La Fleur came in, in the morning with my coffee and roll and butter, he had got himself so gallantly array'd, I scarce knew him.

I had covenanted at Montriul to give him a new hat with a silver button and loop, and four Louis d'ors *pour s'adoniser*, when we got to Paris; and the poor fellow, to do him justice, had done wonders with it.

He had bought a bright, clean, good scarlet coat and a pair of breeches of the same—They were not a crown worse, he said, for the wearing—I wish'd him hang'd for telling me—they look'd so fresh, that tho' I knew the thing could not be done, yet I would rather have imposed upon my fancy with thinking I had bought them new for the fellow, than that they had come out of the Rue de Friperie.

This is a nicety which makes not the heart sore at Paris.

He had purchased moreover a handsome blue sattin waistcoat, fancifully enough embroidered—this was indeed something the worse for the services it had done, but 'twas clean scour'd—the gold had been touch'd up, and upon the whole was rather showy than otherwise—and as the blue was not violent, it suited with the coat and breeches very well: he had squeez'd out ot the money, moreover, a new bag and a solitaire; and had insisted with the *fripier*, upon a gold pair of garters to his breeches knees—He had purchased muslin ruffles, *bien brodées*, with four livres of his own money—and a pair of white silk stockings for five more—and, to top all, nature had given him a handsome figure without costing him a sous.

He enter'd the room thus set off, with his hair dress'd in the first stile, and with a handsome *bouquet* in his breast—in a word, there was that look of festivity in every thing about him, which at once put me in mind it was Sunday—and by combining both together, it instantly struck me, that the favour he wish'd to ask of me the night before, was to spend the day as every body in Paris spent it besides. I had scarce made the conjecture, when La Fleur, with infinite humility, but with a look of trust, as if I should not refuse him, begg'd I would grant him the day, *pour faire le galant vis à vis de sa maitresse.*

Now it was the very thing I intended to do myself *vis a vis* Madame de R****—I had retain'd the *remise* on purpose for it, and it would not have mortified my vanity to have had a servant so well dress'd as La Fleur was to have got up behind it: I never could have worse spared him.

But we must *feel*, not argue in these embarrassments—the sons and daughters of service part with Liberty, but not with Nature, in their contracts; they are flesh and blood, and have their little vanities and wishes in the midst of the house of bondage, as well as their task-masters—no doubt they have set their self-denials at a price—and their expectations are so unreasonable, that I would often disappoint them, but that their condition puts it so much in my power to do it.

Behold!—Behold, I am thy servant—disarms me at once of the powers of a master—

—Thou shalt go, La Fleur! said I.—

—And what mistress, La Fleur, said I, canst thou have pick'd up in so little a time at Paris; La Fleur laid his hand upon his breast, and said 'twas a *petite demoiselle* at Monsieur le Count de B****'s.—La Fleur had a heart made for society; and, to speak the truth of him, let as few occasions slip him as his master —so that some how or other—but how heaven knows—he had connected himself with the *demoiselle* upon the landing of the stair-case, during the time I was taken up with my Passport; and as there was time enough for me to win the Count to my interest, La Fleur had contrived to make it do to win the maid to his—the family, it seems, was to be at Paris that day, and he had made a party with her, and two or three more of the Count's houshold, upon the *boulevards.*

Happy people! that once a week at least are sure to lay down all your cares together; and dance and sing and sport away the weights of grievance, which bow down the spirit of other nations to the earth.

THE FRAGMENT

PARIS

L A FLEUR had left me something to amuse myself with for the day more than I had bargain'd for, or could have enter'd either into his head or mine.

He had brought the little print of butter upon a currant leaf; and as the morning was warm, and he had a good step to bring it, he had begg'd a sheet of waste paper to put betwixt the currant leaf and his hand—As that was plate sufficient, I bad him lay it upon the table as it was, and as I resolved to stay within all day I ordered him to call upon the *traiteur* to bespeak my dinner, and leave me to breakfast by myself.

When I had finish'd the butter, I threw the currant leaf out of the window, and was going to do the same by the waste paper— but stopping to read a line first, and that drawing me on to a second and third—I thought it better worth; so I shut the window, and drawing a chair up to it, I sat down to read it.

It was in the old French of Rabelais's time, and for aught I know might have been wrote by him—it was moreover in a Gothic letter, and that so faded and gone off by damps and length of time, it cost me infinite trouble to make any thing of it— I threw it down; and then wrote a letter to Eugenius—then I took it up again, and embroiled my patience with it afresh—and then to cure that, I wrote a letter to Eliza.—Still it kept hold of me; and the difficulty of understanding it increased but the desire.

I got my dinner; and after I had enlightened my mind with a bottle of Burgundy, I at it again—and after two or three hours pouring upon it, with almost as deep attention as ever Gruter or Jacob Spon did upon a nonsensical inscription, I thought I made sense of it; but to make sure of it, the best way, I imagined, was to turn it into English, and see how it would look then—so I went on leisurely, as a trifling man does, sometimes writing a sentence —then taking a turn or two—and then looking how the world went, out of the window; so that it was nine o'clock at night before I had done it—I then begun and read it as follows.

THE FRAGMENT

PARIS

—NOW as the notary's wife disputed the point with the notary with too much heat—I wish, said the notary, throwing down the parchment, that there was another notary here only to set down and attest all this——

—And what would you do then, Monsieur? said she, rising hastily up—the notary's wife was a little fume of a woman, and the notary thought it well to avoid a hurricane by a mild reply—I would go, answer'd he, to bed.——You may go to the devil, answer'd the notary's wife.

Now there happening to be but one bed in the house, the other two rooms being unfurnish'd, as is the custom at Paris, and the notary not caring to lie in the same bed with a woman who had but that moment sent him pell-mell to the devil, went forth with his hat and cane and short cloak, the night being very windy, and walk'd out ill at ease towards the *pont neuf.*

Of all the bridges which ever were built, the whole world who have pass'd over the *pont neuf*, must own, that it is the noblest—the finest—the grandest—the lightest—the longest—the broadest that ever conjoin'd land and land together upon the face of the terraqueous globe——

By this, it seems, as if the author of the fragment had not been a Frenchman.

The worst fault which divines and the doctors of the Sorbonne can allege against it, is, that if there is but a cap full of wind in or about Paris, 'tis more blasphemously *sacre Dieu*'d there than in any other aperture of the whole city—and with reason, good and cogent Messieurs; for it comes against you without crying *garde d'eau*, and with such unpremeditable puffs, that of the few who cross it with their hats on, not one in fifty but hazards two livres and a half, which is its full worth.

The poor notary, just as he was passing by the sentry, instinctively clapp'd his cane to the side of it, but in raising it up the point of his cane catching hold of the loop of the sentinel's hat hoisted it over the spikes of the balustrade clear into the Seine—

—*'Tis an ill wind*, said a boatman, who catch'd it, *which blows no body any good.*

The sentry being a gascon incontinently twirl'd up his whiskers, and levell'd his harquebuss.

[612]

Harquebusses in those days went off with matches; and an old woman's paper lanthorn at the end of the bridge happening to be blown out, she had borrow'd the sentry's match to light it—it gave a moment's time for the gascon's blood to run cool, and turn the accident better to his advantage—*'Tis an ill wind*, said he, catching off the notary's castor, and legitimating the capture with the boatman's adage.

The poor notary cross'd the bridge, and passing along the Rue de Dauphine into the fauxbourgs of St. Germain, lamented himself as he walk'd along in this manner:

Luckless man! that I am, said the notary, to be the sport of hurricanes all my days——to be born to have the storm of ill language levell'd against me and my profession wherever I go—to be forced into marriage by the thunder of the church to a tempest of a woman—to be driven forth out of my house by domestic winds, and despoil'd of my castor by pontific ones—to be here, bare-headed, in a windy night, at the mercy of the ebbs and flows of accidents—where am I to lay my head?—miserable man! what wind in the two-and-thirty points of the whole compass can blow unto thee, as it does to the rest of thy fellow creatures, good!

As the notary was passing on by a dark passage, complaining in this sort, a voice call'd out to a girl, to bid her run for the next notary—now the notary being the next, and availing himself of his situation, walk'd up the passage to the door, and passing through an old sort of a saloon, was usher'd into a large chamber dismantled of every thing but a long military pike—a breast plate—a rusty old sword, and bandoleer, hung up equi-distant in four different places against the wall.

An old personage, who had heretofore been a gentleman, and unless decay of fortune taints the blood along with it was a gentleman at that time, lay supporting his head upon his hand in his bed; a little table with a taper burning was set close beside it, and close by the table was placed a chair—the notary sat him down in it; and pulling out his ink-horn and a sheet or two of paper which he had in his pocket, he placed them before him, and dipping his pen in his ink, and leaning his breast over the table, he disposed every thing to make the gentleman's last will and testament.

Alas! Monsieur le Notaire, said the gentleman, raising himself up a little, I have nothing to bequeath which will pay the expence of bequeathing, except the history of myself, which I could not die in peace unless I left it as a legacy to the world; the profits arising out of it, I bequeath to you for the pains of taking it from me—it is a story so uncommon, it must be read by all mankind—it will make the fortunes of your house—the notary dipp'd his pen into his ink-horn—Almighty director of every event in my life! said the old gentleman, looking up earnestly and raising his hands towards heaven—thou whose hand has led me on through such a labyrinth of strange passages down into this scene of desolation, assist the decaying memory of an old, infirm, and broken-hearted man, direct my tongue, by the spirit of thy eternal truth, that this stranger may set down naught but what is written in that Book, from whose records, said he, clasping his hands together, I am to be condemn'd or acquitted!—the notary held up the point of his pen betwixt the taper and his eye—

—It is a story, Monsieur le Notaire, said the gentleman, which will rouse up every affection in nature—it will kill the humane, and touch the heart of cruelty herself with pity—

—The notary was inflamed with a desire to begin, and put his pen a third time into his ink-horn—and the old gentleman turning a little more towards the notary, began to dictate his story in these words—

—And where is the rest of it, La Fleur? said I, as he just then enter'd the room.

THE FRAGMENT AND THE *BOUQUET

PARIS

WHEN La Fleur came up close to the table, and was made to comprehend what I wanted, he told me there were only two other sheets of it which he had wrapt round the stalks of a *bouquet* to keep it together, which he had presented to the *demoiselle* upon the *boulevards*—Then, prithee, La Fleur, said I, step back to her to the Count de B****'s hotel, and *see if you can get*—There is no doubt of it, said La Fleur—and away he flew.

In a very little time the poor fellow came back quite out of breath, with deeper marks of disappointment in his looks than could arise from the simple irreparability of the fragment—

* Nosegay.

[614]

Juste ciel! in less than two minutes that the poor fellow had taken his last tender farewel of her, his faithless mistress had given his *gage d'amour* to one of the Count's footmen—the footman to a young sempstress—and the sempstress to a fidler, with my fragment at the end of it—Our misfortunes were involved together— I gave a sigh—and La Fleur echo'd it back again to my ear—

—How perfidious! cried La Fleur—How unlucky! said I.—

—I should not have been mortified, Monsieur, quoth La Fleur, if she had lost it—Nor I, La Fleur, said I, had I found it.

Whether I did or no will be seen hereafter.

THE ACT OF CHARITY

PARIS

THE MAN who either disdains or fears to walk up a dark entry may be an excellent good man, and fit for a hundred things; but he will not do to make a good sentimental traveller. I count little of the many things I see pass at broad noon day in large and open streets.—Nature is shy, and hates to act before spectators; but in such an unobserved corner, you sometimes see a single short scene of her's worth all the sentiments of a dozen French plays compounded together—and yet they are *absolutely* fine;—and whenever I have a more brilliant affair upon my hands than common, as they suit a preacher just as well as a hero, I generally make my sermon out of 'em—and for the text —"Capadosia, Pontus and Asia, Phrygia and Pamphilia"—is as good as any one in the Bible.

There is a long dark passage issuing out from the opera comique into a narrow street; 'tis trod by a few who humbly wait for a *fiacre**, or wish to get off quietly o' foot when the opera is done. At the end of it, towards the theatre, 'tis lighted by a small candle, the light of which is almost lost before you get half-way down, but near the door—'tis more for ornament than use: you see it as a fix'd star of the least magnitude; it burns—but does little good to the world that we know of.

In returning along this passage, I discern'd, as I approach'd within five or six paces of the door, two ladies standing arm in arm, with their backs against the wall, waiting, as I imagined, for a *fiacre*—as they were next the door, I thought they had a prior

* Hackney-coach.

[615]

right; so edged myself up within a yard or little more of them, and quietly took my stand—I was in black, and scarce seen.

The lady next me was a tall lean figure of a woman of about thirty-six; the other of the same size and make, of about forty; there was no mark of wife or widow in any one part of either of them—they seem'd to be two upright vestal sisters, unsapp'd by caresses, unbroke in upon by tender salutations: I could have wish'd to have made them happy—their happiness was destin'd, that night, to come from another quarter.

A low voice, with a good turn of expression, and sweet cadence at the end of it, begg'd for a twelve-sous piece betwixt them, for the love of heaven. I thought it singular, that a beggar should fix the quota of an alms—and that the sum should be twelve times as much as what is usually given in the dark. They both seemed astonish'd at it as much as myself.—Twelve sous! said one— A twelve-sous piece! said the other—and made no reply.

The poor man said, He knew not how to ask less of ladies of their rank, and bow'd down his head to the ground.

Poo! said they, we have no money.

The beggar remained silent for a moment or two, and renew'd his supplication.

Do not, my fair young ladies, said he, stop your good ears against me—Upon my word, honest man! said the younger, we have no change—Then God bless you, said the poor man, and multiply those joys which you can give to others without change! —I observed the elder sister put her hand into her pocket—I'll see, said she, if I have a sous.—A sous! give twelve, said the supplicant; Nature has been bountiful to you, be bountiful to a poor man.

I would, friend, with all my heart, said the younger, if I had it.

My fair charitable! said he, addressing himself to the elder— What is it but your goodness and humanity which makes your bright eyes so sweet, that they outshine the morning even in this dark passage? and what was it which made the Marquis de Santerre and his brother say so much of you both as they just pass'd by?

The two ladies seemed much affected; and impulsively at the same time they both put their hands into their pocket, and each took out a twelve-sous piece.

The contest betwixt them and the poor supplicant was no more —it was continued betwixt themselves, which of the two should give the twelve-sous piece in charity—and to end the dispute, they both gave it together, and the man went away.

THE RIDDLE EXPLAINED

PARIS

I STEPP'D hastily after him: it was the very man whose success in asking charity of the women before the door of the hotel had so puzzled me—and I found at once his secret, or at least the basis of it—'twas flattery.

Delicious essence! how refreshing art thou to nature! how strongly are all its powers and all its weaknesses on thy side! how sweetly dost thou mix with the blood, and help it through the most difficult and tortuous passages to the heart!

The poor man, as he was not straighten'd for time, had given it here in a larger dose: 'tis certain he had a way of bringing it into less form, for the many sudden cases he had to do with in the streets; but how he contrived to correct, sweeten, concentre, and qualify it, I vex not my spirit with the inquiry—it is enough, the beggar gain'd two twelve-sous pieces—and they can best tell the rest, who have gain'd much greater matters by it.

PARIS

WE GET forwards in the world not so much by doing services, as receiving them: you take a withering twig, and put it in the ground; and then you water it, because you have planted it.

Monsieur le Count de B****, merely because he had done me one kindness in the affair of my Passport, would go on and do me another, the few days he was at Paris, in making me known to a few people of rank; and they were to present me to others, and so on.

I had got master of my *secret*, just in time to turn these honours to some little account; otherwise, as is commonly the case, I should have din'd or supp'd a single time or two round, and then by *translating* French looks and attitudes into plain English, I should presently have seen, that I had got hold of the *couvert**
of some more entertaining guest; and in course, should have resigned all my places one after another, merely upon the principle that I could not keep them.—As it was, things did not go much amiss.

* Plate, napkin, knife, fork, and spoon.

[617]

I had the honour of being introduced to the old Marquis de B****: in days of yore he had signaliz'd himself by some small feats of chivalry in the *Cour d'amour*, and had dress'd himself out to the idea of tilts and tournaments ever since—the Marquis de B**** wish'd to have it thought the affair was somewhere else than in his brain. "He could like to take a trip to England," and ask'd much of the English ladies. Stay where you are, I beseech you, Mons. le Marquis, said I—Les Messrs. Anglois can scarce get a kind look from them as it is.—The Marquis invited me to supper.

Mons. P****, the farmer general, was just as inquisitive about our taxes—They were very considerable, he heard—If we knew but how to collect them, said I, making him a low bow.

I could never have been invited to Mons. P****'s concerts upon any other terms.

I had been misrepresented to Madame de Q**** as an *esprit*—Madame de Q**** was an *esprit* herself; she burnt with impatience to see me, and hear me talk. I had not taken my seat, before I saw she did not care a sous whether I had any wit or no—I was let in, to be convinced she had.—I call heaven to witness I never once open'd the door of my lips.

Madame de Q**** vow'd to every creature she met, "She had never had a more improving conversation with a man in her life."

There are three epochas in the empire of a French-woman—She is coquette—then deist—then *devôte*: the empire during these is never lost—she only changes her subjects: when thirty-five years and more have unpeopled her dominions of the slaves of love, she re-peoples it with slaves of infidelity—and then with the slaves of the Church.

Madame de V*** was vibrating betwixt the first of these epochas: the colour of the rose was shading fast away—she ought to have been a deist five years before the time I had the honour to pay my first visit.

She placed me upon the same sopha with her, for the sake of disputing the point of religion more closely.—In short, Madame de V*** told me she believed nothing.

I told Madame de V*** it might be her principle; but I was sure it could not be her interest to level the outworks, without which I could not conceive how such a citadel as hers could be defended —that there was not a more dangerous thing in the world, than for a beauty to be a deist—that it was a debt I owed my creed, not to conceal it from her—that I had not been five minutes sat upon the sopha besides her, but I had begun to form designs—and what is it, but the sentiments of religion, and the persuasion they had existed in her breast, which could have check'd them as they rose up.

We are not adamant, said I, taking hold of her hand—and there is need of all restraints, till age in her own time steals in and lays them on us—but, my dear lady, said I, kissing her hand—'tis too—too soon—

I declare I had the credit all over Paris of unperverting Madame de V***.—She affirmed to Mons. D*** and the Abbe M***, that in one half hour I had said more for revealed religion, than all their Encyclopedia had said against it—I was listed directly into Madame de V***'s *Coterie*—and she put off the epocha of deism for two years.

I remember it was in this *Coterie*, in the middle of a discourse, in which I was shewing the necessity of a *first cause*, that the young Count de Faineant took me by the hand to the furthest corner of the room, to tell me my *solitaire* was pinn'd too strait about my neck—It should be *plus badinant*, said the Count, looking down upon his own—But a word, Mons. Yorick, to *the wise*—

—And from the wise, Mons. le Count, replied I, making him a bow—*is enough*.

The Count de Faineant embraced me with more ardour than ever I was embraced by mortal man.

For three weeks together, I was of every man's opinion I met.— *Pardi! ce Mons. Yorick a autant d'esprit que nous autres.——Il raisonne bien*, said another.—*C'est un bon enfant*, said a third.— And at this price I could have eaten and drank and been merry all the days of my life at Paris; but 'twas a dishonest *reckoning*— I grew ashamed of it—it was the gain of a slave—every sentiment of honour revolted against it—the higher I got, the more was I forced upon my *beggarly system*—the better the *Coterie*—the more children of Art—I languish'd for those of Nature: and one night, after a most vile prostitution of myself to half a dozen different people, I grew sick—went to bed—order'd La Fleur to get me horses in the morning to set out for Italy.

MARIA

MOULINES

I NEVER felt what the distress of plenty was in any one shape
till now—to travel it through the Bourbonnois, the sweetest
part of France—in the hey-day of the vintage, when Nature is
pouring her abundance into every one's lap, and every eye is lifted
up—a journey through each step of which music beats time to
Labour, and all her children are rejoicing as they carry in their
clusters—to pass through this with my affections flying out, and
kindling at every group before me—and every one of 'em was
pregnant with adventures.

Just heaven!—it would fill up twenty volumes—and alas! I
have but a few small pages left of this to croud it into—and half of
these must be taken up with the poor Maria my friend, Mr.
Shandy, met with near Moulines.

The story he had told of that disorder'd maid affect'd me not
a little in the reading; but when I got within the neighbourhood
where she lived, it returned so strong into my mind, that I could
not resist an impulse which prompted me to go half a league out
of the road to the village where her parents dwelt to enquire after
her.

'Tis going, I own, like the Knight of the Woeful Countenance,
in quest of melancholy adventures—but I know not how it is, but
I am never so perfectly conscious of the existence of a soul within
me, as when I am entangled in them.

The old mother came to the door, her looks told me the story
before she open'd her mouth—She had lost her husband; he had
died, she said, of anguish, for the loss of Maria's senses about
a month before.—She had feared at first, she added, that it would
have plunder'd her poor girl of what little understanding was left
—but, on the contrary, it had brought her more to herself—still
she could not rest—her poor daughter, she said, crying, was
wandering somewhere about the road—

—Why does my pulse beat languid as I write this? and what
made La Fleur, whose heart seem'd only to be tuned to joy, to
pass the back of his hand twice across his eyes, as the woman
stood and told it? I beckon'd to the postillion to turn back into the
road.

When we had got within half a league of Moulines, at a little
opening in the road leading to a thicket, I discovered poor Maria

sitting under a poplar—she was sitting with her elbow in her lap, and her head leaning on one side within her hand—a small brook ran at the foot of the tree.

I bid the postillion go on with the chaise to Moulines—and La Fleur to bespeak my supper—and that I would walk after him.

She was dress'd in white, and much as my friend described her, except that her hair hung loose, which before was twisted within a silk net.—She had, superadded likewise to her jacket, a pale green ribband which fell across her shoulder to the waist; at the end of which hung her pipe.—Her goat had been as faithless as her lover; and she had got a little dog in lieu of him, which she had kept tied by a string to her girdle; as I look'd at her dog, she drew him towards her with the string.—"Thou shalt not leave me, Sylvio," said she. I look'd in Maria's eyes, and saw she was thinking more of her father than of her lover or her little goat; for as she utter'd them the tears trickled down her cheeks.

I sat down close by her; and Maria let me wipe them away as they fell with my handkerchief.—I then steep'd it in my own—and then in hers—and then in mine—and then I wip'd hers again —and as I did it, I felt such undescribable emotions within me, as I am sure could not be accounted for from any combinations of matter and motion.

I am positive I have a soul; nor can all the books with which materialists have pester'd the world ever convince me of the contrary.

MARIA

WHEN Maria had come a little to herself, I ask'd her if she remember'd a pale thin person of a man who had sat down betwixt her and her goat about two years before? She said, she was unsettled much at that time, but remember'd it upon two accounts—that ill as she was she saw the person pitied her; and next, that her goat had stolen his handkerchief, and she had beat him for the theft—she had wash'd it, she said, in the brook, and kept it ever since in her pocket to restore it to him in case she should ever see him again, which, she added, he had half promised her. As she told me this she took the handkerchief out of her pocket to let me see it; she had folded it up neatly in a couple of vine leaves, tied round with a tendril—on opening it, I saw an S mark'd in one of the corners.

She had since that, she told me, stray'd as far as Rome, and walk'd round St. Peter's once—and return'd back—that she found her way alone across the Apennines—had travell'd over all Lombardy without money—and through the flinty roads of Savoy without shoes—how she had borne it, and how she had got supported, she could not tell—but *God tempers the wind*, said Maria, to the shorn lamb.

Shorn indeed! and to the quick, said I; and wast thou in my own land, where I have a cottage, I would take thee to it and shelter thee: thou shouldst eat of my own bread, and drink of my own cup—I would be kind to thy Sylvio—in all thy weaknesses and wanderings I would seek after thee and bring thee back— when the sun went down I would say my prayers, and when I had done thou shouldst play thy evening song upon thy pipe, nor would the incense of my sacrifice be worse accepted for entering heaven along with that of a broken heart.

Nature melted within me, as I utter'd this; and Maria observing, as I took out my handkerchief, that it was steep'd too much already to be of use, would needs go wash it in the stream.—And where will you dry it, Maria? said I—I'll dry it in my bosom, said she—'twill do me good.

And is your heart still so warm, Maria? said I.

I touch'd upon the string on which hung all her sorrows—she look'd with wistful disorder for some time in my face; and then, without saying any thing, took her pipe, and play'd her service to the Virgin—The string I had touch'd ceased to vibrate—in a moment or two Maria returned to herself—let her pipe fall—and rose up.

And where are you going, Maria? said I.—She said to Moulines. —Let us go, said I, together.—Maria put her arm within mine, and lengthening the string, to let the dog follow, in that order we entered Moulines.

MARIA

MOULINES

THO' I hate salutations and greetings in the market-place, yet when we got into the middle of this, I stopp'd to take my last look and last farewel of Maria.

Maria, tho' not tall, was nevertheless of the first order of fine forms—affliction had touch'd her looks with something that was scarce earthly—still she was feminine—and so much was there about her of all that the heart wishes, or the eye looks for in woman, that could the traces be ever worn out of her brain, and those of Eliza's out of mine, she should *not only eat of my bread and drink of my own cup,* but Maria should lay in my bosom, and be unto me as a daughter.

Adieu, poor luckless maiden!—imbibe the oil and wine which the compassion of a stranger, as he journieth on his way, now pours into thy wounds—the being who has twice bruised thee can only bind them up for ever.

THE BOURBONNOIS

THERE was nothing from which I had painted out for myself so joyous a riot of the affections, as in this journey in the vintage, through this part of France; but pressing through this gate of sorrow to it, my sufferings had totally unfitted me: in every scene of festivity I saw Maria in the background of the piece, sitting pensive under her poplar; and I had got almost to Lyons before I was able to cast a shade across her—

—Dear sensibility! source inexhausted of all that's precious in our joys, or costly in our sorrows! thou chainest thy martyr down upon his bed of straw—and 'tis thou who lifts him up to HEAVEN —eternal fountain of our feelings!—'tis here I trace thee—and this is thy divinity which stirs within me——not that, in some sad and sickening moments, *"my soul shrinks back upon herself, and startles at destruction"*—mere pomp of words!—but that I feel some generous joys and generous cares beyond myself—All comes from thee, great, great SENSORIUM of the world! which vibrates, if a hair of our heads but falls upon the ground, in the remotest desert of thy creation.—Touch'd with thee, Eugenius draws my curtain when I languish—hears my tale of symptoms, and blames the weather for the disorder of his nerves. Thou giv'st a portion of it sometimes to the roughest peasant who traverses the bleakest mountains—he finds the lacerated lamb of another's flock—This moment I behold him leaning with his head against his crook, with piteous inclination looking down upon it—Oh! had I come one moment sooner!—it bleeds to death—his gentle heart bleeds with it—

Peace to thee, generous swain!—I see thou walkest off with

anguish—but thy joys shall balance it—for happy is thy cottage—
and happy is the sharer of it—and happy are the lambs which
sport about you.

THE SUPPER

A SHOE coming loose from the fore-foot of the thill-horse,
at the beginning of the ascent of mount Taurira, the postillion dismounted, twisted the shoe off, and put it in his
pocket; as the ascent was of five or six miles, and that horse our
main dependence, I made a point of having the shoe fasten'd on
again, as well as we could; but the postillion had thrown away the
nails, and the hammer in the chaise-box, being of no great use
without them, I submitted to go on.

He had not mounted half a mile higher, when coming to
a flinty piece of road, the poor devil lost a second shoe, and from
off his other fore-foot; I then got out of the chaise in good earnest;
and seeing a house about a quarter of a mile to the left-hand, with
a great deal to do I prevailed upon the postillion to turn up to it.
The look of the house, and of every thing about it, as we drew
nearer, soon reconciled me to the disaster.—It was a little farmhouse surrounded with about twenty acres of vineyard, about as
much corn—and close to the house, on one side, was a *potagerie*
of an acre and a half, full of every thing which could make plenty
in a French peasant's house—and on the other side was a little
wood which furnished wherewithal to dress it. It was about eight
in the evening when I got to the house—so I left the postillion to
manage his point as he could—and for mine, I walk'd directly
into the house.

The family consisted of an old grey-headed man and his wife,
with five or six sons and sons-in-law and their several wives, and
a joyous genealogy out of 'em.

They were all sitting down together to their lentil-soup; a large
wheaten loaf was in the middle of the table; and a flaggon of wine
at each end of it promised joy thro' the stages of the repast—'twas
a feast of love.

The old man rose up to meet me, and with a respectful cordiality
would have me sit down at the table; my heart was sat down the
moment I enter'd the room; so I sat down at once like a son of the
family; and to invest myself in the character as speedily as I
could, I instantly borrowed the old man's knife, and taking up

the loaf cut myself a hearty luncheon; and as I did it I saw a testimony in every eye, not only of an honest welcome, but of a welcome mix'd with thanks that I had not seem'd to doubt it.

Was it this; or tell me, Nature, what else it was which made this morsel so sweet—and to what magick I owe it, that the draught I took of their flaggon was so delicious with it, that they remain upon my palate to this hour?

If the supper was to my taste—the grace which follow'd it was much more so.

THE GRACE

WHEN supper was over, the old man gave a knock upon the table with the haft of his knife—to bid them prepare for the dance: the moment the signal was given, the women and girls ran all together into a back apartment to tye up their hair—and the young men to the door to wash their faces, and change their sabots; and in three minutes every soul was ready upon a little esplanade before the house to begin—The old man and his wife came out last, and, placing me betwixt them, sat down upon a sopha of turf by the door.

The old man had some fifty years ago been no mean performer upon the vielle—and at the age he was then of, touch'd it well enough for the purpose. His wife sung now and then a little to the tune—then intermitted—and joined her old man again as their children and grand-children danced before them.

It was not till the middle of the second dance, when, from some pauses in the movement wherein they all seemed to look up, I fancied I could distinguish an elevation of spirit different from that which is the cause or the effect of simple jollity—In a word, I thought I beheld *Religion* mixing in the dance—but as I had never seen her so engaged, I should have look'd upon it now, as one of the illusions of an imagination which is eternally misleading me, had not the old man, as soon as the dance ended, said, that this was their constant way; and that all his life long he had made it a rule, after supper was over, to call out his family to dance and rejoice; believing, he said, that a chearful and contented mind was the best sort of thanks to heaven that an illiterate peasant could pay—

——Or a learned prelate either, said I.

[625]

THE CASE OF DELICACY

WHEN you have gained the top of mount Taurira, you run presently down to Lyons—adieu then to all rapid movements! 'Tis a journey of caution; and it fares better with sentiments, not to be in a hurry with them; so I contracted with a Voiturin to take his time with a couple of mules, and convey me in my own chaise safe to Turin through Savoy.

Poor, patient, quiet, honest people! fear not; your poverty, the treasury of your simple virtues, will not be envied you by the world, nor will your vallies be invaded by it.—Nature! in the midst of thy disorders, thou art still friendly to the scantiness thou hast created—with all thy great works about thee, little hast thou left to give, either to the scithe or to the sickle—but to that little, thou grantest safety and protection; and sweet are the dwellings which stand so shelter'd.

Let the way-worn traveller vent his complaints upon the sudden turns and dangers of your roads—your rocks—your precipices—the difficulties of getting up—the horrors of getting down—mountains impracticable—and cataracts, which roll down great stones from their summits, and block up his road.—The peasants had been all day at work in removing a fragment of this kind between St. Michael and Madane; and by the time my Voiturin got to the place, it wanted full two hours of compleating before a passage could any how be gain'd: there was nothing but to wait with patience—'twas a wet and tempestuous night; so that by the delay, and that together, the Voiturin found himself obliged to take up five miles short of his stage at a little decent kind of an inn by the road side.

I forthwith took possession of my bed-chamber—got a good fire—order'd supper; and was thanking heaven it was no worse—when a voiture arrived with a lady in it and her servant-maid.

As there was no other bed-chamber in the house, the hostess, without much nicety, led them into mine, telling them, as she usher'd them in, that there was no body in it but an English gentle-man—that there were two good beds in it, and a closet within the room which held another—the accent in which she spoke of this third bed did not say much for it—however, she said, there were three beds and but three people—and she durst say, the gentle-man would do any thing to accommodate matters.—I left not the lady a moment to make a conjecture about it—so instantly made a declaration I would do any thing in my power.

As this did not amount to an absolute surrender of my bed-chamber, I still felt myself so much the proprietor, as to have a right to do the honours of it—so I desired the lady to sit down—pressed her into the warmest seat—call'd for more wood—desired the hostess to enlarge the plan of the supper, and to favour us with the very best wine.

The lady had scarce warm'd herself five minutes at the fire, before she began to turn her head back, and give a look at the beds; and the oftener she cast her eyes that way, the more they return'd perplex'd—I felt for her—and for myself; for in a few minutes, what by her looks, and the case itself, I found myself as much embarrassed as it was possible the lady could be herself.

That the beds we were to lay in were in one and the same room, was enough simply by itself to have excited all this—but the position of them, for they stood parallel, and so very close to each other as only to allow space for a small wicker chair betwixt them, render'd the affair still more oppressive to us—they were fixed up moreover near the fire, and the projection of the chimney on one side, and a large beam which cross'd the room on the other, form'd a kind of recess for them that was no way favourable to the nicety of our sensations—if any thing could have added to it, it was, that the two beds were both of 'em so very small, as to cut us off from every idea of the lady and the maid lying together; which in either of them, could it have been feasible, my lying besides them, tho' a thing not to be wish'd, yet there was nothing in it so terrible which the imagination might not have pass'd over without torment.

As for the little room within, it offer'd little or no consolation to us; 'twas a damp cold closet, with a half dismantled window shutter, and with a window which had neither glass or oil paper in it to keep out the tempest of the night. I did not endeavour to stifle my cough when the lady gave a peep into it; so it reduced the case in course to this alternative—that the lady should sacrifice her health to her feelings, and take up with the closet herself, and abandon the bed next mine to her maid, or that the girl should take the closet, &c. &c.

The lady was a Piedmontese of about thirty, with a glow of health in her cheeks: the maid was a Lyonoise of twenty, and as brisk and lively a French girl as ever moved.—There were difficulties every way—and the obstacle of the stone in the road, which brought us into the distress, great as it appeared whilst the peasants were removing it, was but a pebble to what lay in our ways now—I have only to add, that it did not lessen the weight which hung upon our spirits, that we were both too delicate to communicate what we felt to each other upon the occasion.

We sat down to supper; and had we not had more generous wine to it than a little inn in Savoy could have furnish'd, our tongues had been tied up, till necessity herself had set them at liberty—but the lady having a few bottles of Burgundy in her voiture sent down her Fille de Chambre for a couple of them; so that by the time supper was over, and we were left alone, we felt ourselves inspired with a strength of mind sufficient to talk, at least, without reserve upon our situation. We turn'd it every way, and debated and considered it in all kind of lights in the course of a two hours negociation; at the end of which the articles were settled finally betwixt us, and stipulated for in form and manner of a treaty of peace—and I believe with as much religion and good faith on both sides, as in any treaty which as yet had the honour of being handed down to posterity. .

They were as follows:

First. As the right of the bed-chamber is in Monsieur, and he thinking the bed next to the fire to be the warmest, he insists upon the concession on the lady's side of taking up with it.

Granted, on the part of Madame; with a proviso, That as the curtains of that bed are of a flimsy transparent cotton, and appear likewise too scanty to draw close, that the Fille de Chambre, shall fasten up the opening, either by corking pins, or needle and thread, in such manner as shall be deemed a sufficient barrier on the side of Monsieur.

2dly. It is required on the part of Madame, that Monsieur shall lay the whole night through in his robe de chambre.

Rejected: inasmuch Monsieur is not worth a robe de chambre; he having nothing in his portmanteau but six shirts and a black silk pair of breeches.

The mentioning the silk pair of breeches made an entire change of the article—for the breeches were accepted as an equivalent for the robe de chambre; and so it was stipulated and agreed upon that I should lay in my black silk breeches all night.

3dly. It was insisted upon, and stipulated for by the lady, that after Monsieur was got to bed, and the candle and fire extinguished, that Monsieur should not speak one single word the whole night.

Granted; provided Monsieur's saying his prayers might not be deem'd an infraction of the treaty.

There was but one point forgot in this treaty, and that was the manner in which the lady and myself should be obliged to undress and get to bed—there was but one way of doing it, and that I leave to the reader to devise; protesting as I do it, that if it is not the most delicate in nature, 'tis the fault of his own imagination —against which this is not my first complaint.

Now, when we were got to bed, whether it was the novelty of the situation, or what it was, I know not, but so it was, I could not shut my eyes; I tried this side and that, and turn'd and turn'd again, till a full hour after midnight, when Nature and patience both wearing out—O my God! said I——

—You have broke the treaty, Monsieur, said the lady, who had no more slept than myself.—I begg'd a thousand pardons, but insisted it was no more than an ejaculation—she maintain'd 'twas an entire infraction of the treaty—I maintain'd it was provided for in the clause of the third article.

The lady would by no means give up her point, tho' she weakened her barrier by it; for in the warmth of the dispute, I could hear two or three corking pins fall out of the curtain to the ground.

Upon my word and honour, Madame, said I—stretching my arm out of bed, by way of asseveration—

—(I was going to have added, that I would not have trespass'd against the remotest idea of decorum for the world)—

—But the Fille de Chambre hearing there were words between us, and fearing that hostilities would ensue in course, had crept silently out of her closet, and it being totally dark, had stolen so close to our beds, that she had got herself into the narrow passage which separated them, and had advanc'd so far up as to be in a line betwixt her mistress and me—

So that when I stretch'd out my hand, I caught hold of the Fille de Chambre's

END OF VOLUME II

A Choice of the
SERMONS
of Mr. Yorick

Four volumes of *The Sermons of Mr. Yorick* were published during Sterne's lifetime (see Chronological Table), and a further three volumes, prepared for the press by his daughter, appeared in 1769. The text of the following seven sermons is that of the first editions.

Elijah and the Widow of Zarephath

A Charity Sermon

TO THE VERY REVEREND

Richard Osbaldeston, D.D.

DEAN OF YORK

SIR,

I *HAVE taken the liberty to inscribe this discourse to you, in testimony of the great respect which I owe to your character in general; and from a sense of what is due to it in particular from every member of the* Church of YORK.

I wish I had as good a reason for doing that, which has given me the opportunity of making so publick and just an acknowledgment; being afraid there can be little left to be said upon the subject of Charity, *which has not been often thought, and much better expressed by many who have gone before: and indeed, it seems so beaten and common a path, that it is not an easy matter for a newcomer to distinguish himself in it, by any thing except the novelty of his* Vehicle.

I beg, however, Sir, your kind acceptance of it, and of the motives which have induced me to address it to you; one of which, I cannot conceal in justice to myself, because it has proceeded from the sense of many favours and civilities which I have received from you. I am,

Reverend SIR,
Your most obliged,
and faithful
Humble Servant,
LAURENCE STERNE.

1 KINGS XVII 16

And the barrel of meal wasted not, neither did the cruse of oil fail, according to the word of the Lord which he spake by the prophet Elijah.

THE words of the text are the record of a miracle wrought in behalf of the widow of Zarephath, who had charitably taken Elijah under her roof, and administered unto him in a time of great scarcity and distress. There is something very interesting and affectionate in the manner this story is related in holy writ; and as it concludes with a second still more remarkable proof of GOD's favour to the same person, in the restoration of her dead son to life, one cannot but consider both miracles as rewards of that act of piety, wrought by infinite power, and left upon record in scripture, not merely as testimonies of the prophet's divine mission, but likewise as two encouraging instances of GOD Almighty's blessing upon works of charity and benevolence.

In this view I have made choice of this piece of sacred story, which I shall beg leave to make use of as the ground-work for an exhortation to charity in general: and that it may better answer the particular purpose of this solemnity, I will endeavour to enlarge upon it with such reflections, as, I trust in GOD, will excite some sentiments of compassion which may be profitable to so pious a design.

Elijah had fled from two dreadful evils, the approach of a famine, and the persecution of Ahab an enraged enemy: and in obedience to the command of GOD had hid himself by the brook Cherith, that is before Jordan. In this safe and peaceful solitude, blessed with daily marks of GOD's providence, the holy man dwelt free both from the cares and glories of the world: by miraculous impulse *the ravens brought him bread and flesh in the morning, and bread and flesh in the evening, and he drank of the brook;* till by continuance of drought, (the windows of heaven being shut up in those days for three years and six months, which was the natural cause likewise of the famine,) it came to pass after a while that the brook, the great fountain of his support, dried up; and he is again directed by the word of the Lord where to betake himself for shelter. He is commanded to arise and go to Zarephath, which belongeth to Zidon, with an assurance that he had disposed the heart of a widow-woman there to sustain him.

The prophet follows the call of his GOD:—the same hand which brought him to the gate of the city, had led also the poor widow out of her doors, oppressed with sorrow. She had come forth upon a melancholy errand, to make preparation to eat her last meal, and share it with her child.

No doubt, she had long fenced against this tragical event with all the thrifty management which self-preservation and parental love could inspire; full, no doubt, of cares and many tender apprehensions lest her tender stock should fail them before the return of plenty.

But as she was a widow, having lost the only faithful friend who would best have assisted her in this virtuous struggle, the present necessity of the times at length overcame her; and she was just falling down an easy prey to it, when Elijah came to the place where she was. *And he called unto her, and said, fetch me, I pray thee, a little water in a vessel that I may drink. And as she was going to fetch it, he called unto her and said, bring me, I pray thee, a morsel of bread in thine hand. And she said, as the Lord thy God liveth, I have not a cake, but a handful of meal in a barrel, and a little oil in a cruse, and behold I am gathering two sticks, that I may go in and dress it for me and my son, that we may eat it and die. And Elijah said unto her, fear not, but go, and do as thou hast said; but make me therefore a little cake first, and bring it unto me, and after make for thee and for thy son. For thus says the Lord God of Israel, the barrel of meal shall not waste, neither shall thy cruse of oil fail, until the day that the Lord sendeth rain upon the earth.*

True charity is always unwilling to find excuses—else here was a fair opportunity of pleading many: she might have insisted over again upon her situation, which necessarily tied up her hands;——she might have urged the unreasonableness of the request;——that she was reduced to the lowest extremity already;——and that it was contrary to ju·tice and the first law of nature, to rob herself and child of their last morsel, and give it to a stranger.

But, in generous spirits, compassion is sometimes more than a balance for self-preservation. For, as GOD certainly interwove that friendly softness in our nature to be a check upon too great a propensity towards self-love—so it seemed to operate here.— For it is observable, that though the prophet backed his request with the promise of an immediate recompence in multiplying her stock; yet it is not evident, she was influenced at all by that temptation. For if she had, doubtless it must have wrought such a mixture of self-interest into the motive of her compliance, as must greatly have allayed the merit of the action. But this I say, does not appear, but rather the contrary, from the reflection she makes upon the whole in the last verse of the chapter. *Now by this I know that thou art a man of God, and that the word of the Lord in thy mouth is truth.*

Besides as she was an inhabitant of Zarephath, (or, as it is called by St. Luke, Sarepta, subject to Sidon the metropolis of Phœnicia, without the bounds of GOD's people,) she had been brought up in gross darkness and idolatry, in utter ignorance of the LORD GOD of Israel: or, if she had heard of his name, which is all that seems probable, she had been taught to disbelieve the mighty wonders of his hand, and was still less likely to believe his prophet.

Moreover she might argue, if this man by some secret mystery of his own, or through the power of his GOD, is able to procure so preternatural a supply for me, whence comes it to pass, that he now stands in want himself, oppressed both with hunger and thirst?

It appears therefore, that she must have been wrought upon by an unmixed principle of humanity.———She looked upon him as a fellow-partner almost in the same affliction with herself.— She considered he had come a weary pilgrimage, in a sultry climate, through an exhausted country; where neither bread or water were to be had, but by acts of liberality.—That he had come an unknown traveller, and as a hard heart never wants a pretence, that this circumstance, which should rather have befriended, might have helped to oppress him.—She considered, for charity is ever fruitful in kind reasons, that he was now far from his own country, and had stayed out of the reach of the tender offices of some one who affectionately mourned his absence—her heart was touched with pity.———She turned in silence and *went and did according as he had said. And behold, both she and he and her house did eat many days;* or, as in the margin, one whole year. *And the barrel of meal wasted not, neither did the cruse of oil fail, until the day that God sent rain upon the earth.*

Though it may not seem necessary to raise conjectures here upon this event, yet it is natural to suppose, the danger of the famine being thus unexpectedly got over, that the mother began to look hopefully forwards upon the rest of her days. There were many widows in Israel at that time, when the heavens were shut up for three years and six months, yet, as St. Luke observes, *to none of them was the prophet sent, save to this widow of Sarepta:* in all likelihood, she would not be the last in making the same observation, and drawing from it some flattering conclusion in favour of her son.——Many a parent would build high, upon a worse foundation.——"Since the GOD of Israel has thus sent his own messenger to us in our distress, to pass by so many houses of his own people, and stop at mine, to save it in so miraculous a manner from destruction; doubtless, this is but an earnest of his future kind intentions to us: at least, his goodness has decreed to comfort my old age by the long life and health of my son:—— but perhaps, he has something greater still in store for him, and I shall live to see the same hand hereafter crown his head with glory and honour?" We may naturally suppose her innocently carried away with such thoughts, when she is called back by an unexpected distemper which surprises her son, and in one moment brings down all her hopes——*for his sickness was so sore that there was no breath left in him.*—

The expostulations of immoderate grief are seldom just—For, though Elijah had already preserved her son, as well as herself from immediate death, and was the last cause to be suspected of so sad an accident; yet the passionate mother in the first trans-port challenges him as the author of her misfortunes;——as if he had brought down sorrow upon a house, which had so hos-pitably sheltered him. The prophet was too full of compassion, to make reply to so unkind an accusation. He takes the dead child *out of his mother's bosom, and laid him upon his own bed; and he cried unto the Lord and said, O Lord my God! hast thou brought evil upon the widow with whom I sojourn, by slaying her son?* "Is this the reward of all her charity and goodness? thou hast before this robbed her of the dear partner of all her joys and all her cares; and now that she is a widow, and has most reason to expect thy protection; behold thou hast withdrawn her last prop: thou hast taken away her child, the only stay she had to rest on." —*And Elijah cried unto God, and said, O Lord my God, I pray thee, let this child's soul come into him again.*

The prayer was urgent, and bespoke the distress of a humane mind deeply suffering in the misfortunes of another;——more-over his heart was rent with other passions.—He was zealous for the name and honour of his GOD, and thought not only his omnipotence, but his glorious attribute of mercy concern'd in the event: for, oh! with what triumph would the prophets of Baal retort his own bitter taunt, and say, *his God was either talking, or he was pursuing, or was in a journey: or peradventure he slept and should have been awaked.*—He was moreover involved in the success of his prayer himself;——honest minds are most hurt by scandal.——And he was afraid, lest so foul a one, so unworthy of his character, might arise amongst the heathen, who would report with pleasure, "Lo! the widow of Zarephath took the messenger of the GOD of Israel under her roof, and kindly entertained him, and see how she is rewarded; surely the prophet was ungrateful, he wanted power, or what is worse, he wanted pity!"

Besides all this, he pleaded not only the cause of the widow; it was the cause of charity itself, which had received a deep wound already, and would suffer still more should GOD deny it this testimony of his favour. *So the Lord hearkned unto the voice of Elijah, and the soul of the child came into him again, and he revived. And Elijah took the child and brought him down out of the chamber into the house, and delivered him unto his mother; and Elijah said, see thy son liveth.*

It would be a pleasure to a good mind to stop here a moment, and figure to itself the picture of so joyful an event.—To behold on one hand the raptures of the parent, overcome with surprize and gratitude, and imagine how a sudden stroke of such impetuous joy must operate on a despairing countenance, long accustomed to sadness.—To conceive on the other side of the *piece*, the holy man approaching with the child in his arms—full of honest triumph in his looks, but sweetened with all the kind sympathy which a gentle nature could overflow with upon so happy an event. It is a subject one might recommend to the pencil of a great genius, and would even afford matter for description here; but that it would lead us too far from the particular purpose, for which I have enlarged upon thus much of the story already; the chief design of which is to illustrate by a fact, what is evident both in reason and scripture, that a charitable and good action is seldom cast away, but that even in this life it is more than probable, that what is so scattered shall be gathered again with increase. *Cast thy bread upon the waters, and thou shalt find it after many days. Be as a father unto the fatherless and instead of a husband unto their mother, so shalt thou be as the son of the Most High, and he will love thee more than thy mother doth. Be mindful of good turns, for thou knowest not what evil shall come upon the earth: and when thou fallest thou shalt find a stay. It shall preserve thee from all affliction, and fight for thee against thy enemies better than a mighty shield and a strong spear.*

The great instability of temporal affairs, and constant fluctuation of every thing in this world, afford perpetual occasions of taking refuge in such a security.

What by successive misfortunes; by failings and cross accidents in trade; by miscarriage of projects:—what by unsuitable expences of parents, extravagance of children, and the many other secret ways whereby riches make themselves wings and fly away; so many surprising revolutions do every day happen in families, that it may not seem strange to say, that the posterity of some of the most liberal contributors here, in the changes which one century may produce, may possibly find shelter under this very plant which they now so kindly water. Nay, so quickly sometimes has the wheel turned round, that many a man has lived to enjoy the benefit of that charity which his own piety projected.

But besides this, and exclusive of the right which GOD's promise gives it to protection hereafter, charity and benevolence, in the ordinary chain of effects, have a natural and more immediate tendency in themselves to rescue a man from the accidents of the world, by softening the hearts, and winning every man's wishes to its interest. When a compassionate man falls, who would not pity him? who, that had power to do it, would not befriend and raise him up? or could the most barbarous temper offer an insult to his distress without pain and reluctance? so that it is almost a wonder that covetousness, even in spite of itself, does not sometimes argue a man into charity, by its own principle of looking forwards, and the firm expectation it would delight in of receiving its own again with usury.—So evident is it in the course of GOD's providence and the natural stream of things, that a good office one time or other generally meets with a reward.— Generally, did I say——how can it ever fail?—when besides all this, so large a share of the recompence is so inseparable even from the action itself. Ask the man who has a tear of tenderness always ready to shed over the unfortunate; who, withal, is ready to distribute and willing to communicate: ask him if the best things, which wits have said of pleasure, have expressed what he has felt, when by a seasonable kindness, he has *made the heart of the widow sing for joy.* Mark then the expressions of unutterable pleasure and harmony in his looks; and say, whether Solomon has not fixed the point of true enjoyment in the right place, when he declares, "that he knew no good there was in any of the riches or honours of this world, *but for a man to do good with them in his life.*" Nor was it without reason he made this judgment.—Doubtless he had found and seen the insufficiency of all sensual pleasures; how unable to furnish either a rational or a lasting scheme of happiness: how soon the best of them vanished; the less exceptionable in vanity, but the guilty both *in vanity and vexation of spirit.* But that this was of so pure and refined a nature it burned without consuming: it was figuratively *the widow's barrel of meal which wasted not, and cruse of oil which never failed.*

It is not an easy matter to add weight to the testimony of *the wisest man,* upon the pleasure of doing good; or else the evidence of the philosopher Epicurus is very remarkable, whose word in this matter is the more to be trusted, because a professed sensualist; who amidst all the delicacies and improvements of pleasure which a luxuriant fancy might strike out, still maintained, that the best way of enlarging human happiness was, by a communication of it to others.

And if it was necessary here, or there was time to refine upon this doctrine, one might further maintain, exclusive of the happiness which the mind itself feels in the exercise of this virtue, that the very body of man is never in a better state than when he is most inclined to do good offices:—that as nothing more contributes to health than a benevolence of temper, so nothing generally was a stronger indication of it.

And what seems to confirm this opinion, is an observation, the truth of which must be submitted to every one's reflection—namely—that a disinclination and backwardness to do good, is often attended, if not produced, by an indisposition of the animal as well as rational part of us: So naturally do the soul and body, as in other cases so in this, mutually befriend, or prey upon each other. And indeed, setting aside all abstruser reasoning upon the point, I cannot conceive, but that the very *mechanical motions* which maintain life, must be performed with more equal vigour and freedom in that man whom a great and good soul perpetually inclines to shew mercy to the miserable, than they can be in a poor, sordid, selfish wretch, whose little, contracted heart, melts at no man's affliction; but sits brooding so intently over its own plots and concerns, as to see and feel nothing; and in truth, enjoy nothing beyond himself: and of whom one may say what that great master of nature has, speaking of a natural sense

of harmony, which I think, with more justice may be said of
compassion, that the man who had it not,—

> "——*Was fit for treasons, stratagems and spoils:*
> *The* MOTIONS *of his spirits are dull as night:*
> *And his affections dark as* EREBUS:
> *—Let no such man be trusted.*——"

What divines say of the mind, naturalists have observed of the
body; that there is no passion so natural to it as love, which is the
principle of doing good;—and though instances like this just
mentioned seem far from being proofs of it, yet it is not to be
doubted, but that every hard-hearted man has felt much inward
opposition before he could prevail upon himself to do aught to
fix and deserve the character: and that what we say of long habits
of vice, that they are hard to be subdued, may with equal truth
be said concerning the natural impressions of benevolence, that
a man must do much violence to himself, and suffer many a painful struggle, before he can tear away so great and noble a part of
his nature.—Of this antiquity has preserved a beautiful instance
in an anecdote of Alexander, the tyrant of Pheres, who though
he had so industriously hardened his heart, as to seem to take
delight in cruelty, insomuch as to murder many of his subjects
every day, without cause and without pity; yet, at the bare representation of a tragedy which related the misfortunes of Hecuba
and Andromache, he was so touched with the fictitious distress
which the poet had wrought up in it, that he burst out into a flood
of tears. The explication of which inconsistency is easy, and casts
as great a lustre upon human nature, as the man himself was a disgrace to it. The case seems to have been this: in *real* life he had
been blinded with passions, and thoughtlessly hurried on by
interest or resentment:—but here, there was no room for motives
of that kind; so that his attention being first caught hold of, and
all his vices laid asleep;—then NATURE awoke in triumph, and
shewed how deeply she had sown the seeds of compassion in
every man's breast; when tyrants, with vices most at enmity
with it, were not able entirely to root it out.

But this is painting an amiable virtue, and setting her off, with
shades which wickedness lends us, when one might safely trust
to the force of her own natural charms, and ask, whether any
thing under Heaven in its own nature, is more lovely and engaging?—To illustrate this the more, let us turn our thoughts within
ourselves; and for a moment, let any number of us here imagine
ourselves at this instant engaged in drawing the most perfect and

amiable character, such, as according to our conceptions of the Deity, we should think most acceptable to him, and most likely to be universally admired by all mankind.—I appeal to your own thoughts, whether the first idea which offered itself to most of our imaginations, would not be that of a compassionate benefactor, stretching forth his hand to raise up the helpless orphan? whatever other virtues we should give our hero, we should all agree in making him a generous friend, who thought the opportunities of doing good to be the only charm of his prosperity: we should paint him like the psalmist's *river of God* overflowing the thirsty parts of the earth, that he might enrich them, carrying plenty and gladness along with him. If this was not sufficient, and we were still desirous of adding a farther degree of perfection to so great a character; we should endeavour to think of some one, if human nature could furnish such a pattern, who, if occasion required, was willing to undergo all kinds of affliction, to sacrifice himself, to forget his dearest interests, and even lay down his life for the good of mankind.—And here,—O merciful SAVIOUR! how would the bright original of thy unbounded goodness break in upon our hearts? *Thou who becamest poor, that we might be rich— though Lord of all this world, yet hadst not where to lay thy head.* ——And though equal in power and glory to the great GOD of NATURE, *yet madest thyself of no reputation, tookest upon thee the form of a servant,*—submitting thyself, without opening thy mouth, to all the indignities which a thankless and undiscerning people could offer; and at length, to accomplish our salvation, *becamest obedient unto death,* suffering thyself, as on this day*, *to be led like a lamb to the slaughter!*

The consideration of this stupendous instance of compassion, in the Son of GOD, is the most unanswerable appeal that can be made to the heart of man, for the reasonableness of it in himself. —It is the great argument which the apostles use in almost all their exhortations to good works.—*Beloved, if Christ so loved us*—the inference is unavoidable; and gives strength and beauty to every thing else which can be urged upon the subject. And therefore I have reserved it for my last and warmest appeal, with which I would gladly finish this discourse, that at least for their sakes for whom it is preached, we might be left to the full impression of so exalted and so seasonable a motive.—That by reflecting upon the infinite labour of this day's love, in the instance of CHRIST's death, we may consider what an immense debt we owe each

* Preached on *Good-Friday.*

other: and by calling to mind the amiable pattern of his life, in doing good, we might learn in what manner we may best discharge it.

And indeed, of all the methods in which a good mind would be willing to do it, I believe there can be none more beneficial, or comprehensive in its effects, than that for which we are here met together.—The proper education of poor children being the ground-work of almost every other kind of charity, as that which makes every other subsequent act of it answer the pious expectation of the giver.

Without this foundation first laid, how much kindness in the progress of a benevolent man's life is unavoidably cast away? and sometimes where it is as senseless as the exposing a tender plant to all the inclemencies of a cruel season, and then going with sorrow to take it in, when the root is already dead. I said, therefore, this was the foundation of almost every kind of charity,— and might not one have added, of all policy too? since the many ill consequences which attend the want of it, though grievously felt by the parties themselves, are no less so by the community of which they are members; and moreover, of all mischiefs seem the hardest to be redressed.——Insomuch, that when one considers the disloyal seductions of popery on one hand, and on the other, that no bad man, whatever he professes, can be a good subject, one may venture to say, it had been cheaper and better for the nation to have bore the expence of instilling sound principles and good morals, into the neglected children of the lower sort, especially in some parts of Great-Britain, than to be obliged, so often as we have been within this last century, to rise up and arm ourselves against the rebellious effects which the want of them have brought down even to our doors. And in fact, if we are to trust antiquity, the truth of which in this case we have no reason to dispute, this matter has been looked upon of such vast importance to the civil happiness and peace of a people, that some commonwealths, the most eminent for political wisdom, have chose to make a publick concern of it; thinking it much safer to be entrusted to the prudence of the magistrate, than to the mistaken tenderness, or natural partiality of the parent.

It was consistent with this, and bespoke a very refined sense of policy in the Lacedæmonians, (though by the way, I believe, different from what more modern politics would have directed in like circumstances) when Antipater demanded of them fifty children, as hostages for the security of a distant engagement, they made this brave and wise answer, "They would not,—they could not consent:—they would rather give him double the number of their best up-grown men."—Intimating, that however they were distressed, they would chuse any inconvenience rather than suffer the loss of their country's education; and the opportunity (which if once lost can never be regained) of giving their youth an early tincture of religion, and bringing them up to a love of industry, and a love of the laws and constitution of their country.—If this shews the great importance of a proper education to children of all ranks and conditions, what shall we say then of those whom the providence of GOD has placed in the very lowest lot of life, utterly cast out of the *way* of knowledge, without a parent, —sometimes may be without a friend to guide and instruct them; but what common pity and the necessity of their sad situation engages:—where the dangers which surround them on every side are so great and many, that for one fortunate passenger in life, who makes his way well in the world with such early disadvantages, and so dismal a setting out, we may reckon thousands who every day suffer shipwreck, and are lost for ever.

If there is a case under Heaven which calls out aloud for the more immediate exercise of compassion, and which may be looked upon as the compendium of all charity, surely it is this: and I'm persuaded there would want nothing more to convince the greatest enemy to these kinds of charities that it is so, but a bare opportunity of taking a nearer view of some of the more distressful objects of it.

Let him go into the dwellings of the unfortunate, into some mournful cottage, where poverty and affliction reign together. There let him behold the disconsolate widow—sitting—steeped in tears;—thus sorrowing over the infant, she knows not how to succour.——"O my child, thou art now left exposed to a wide and a vicious world, too full of snares and temptations for thy tender and unpractised age. Perhaps a parent's love may magnify those dangers.—But when I consider thou art driven out naked into the midst of them, without friends, without fortune, without instruction, my heart bleeds beforehand for the evils which may come upon thee. GOD, in whom we trusted, is witness, so low had his providence placed us, that we never indulged one wish to have made thee rich,—virtuous we would have made thee;—for thy father, *my husband, was a good man and feared the Lord*, and though all the fruits of his care and industry were little enough for our support, yet he honestly had determined to have spared some portion of it, scanty as it was, to have placed thee safely in the way of knowledge and instruction.—But alas! he is gone from us, never to return more, and with him are fled the means of doing it:—For, *Behold the creditor is come upon us*, to take all that we have."—Grief is eloquent, and will not easily be imitated. —But let the man, who is the least friend to distresses of this nature, conceive some disconsolate widow uttering her complaint even in this manner, and then let him consider, *if there is any sorrow like* this *sorrow, wherewith the Lord has afflicted* her? or, whether there can be any charity like that, of taking *the child out of the mother's bosom*, and rescuing her from these apprehensions? Should a heathen, a stranger to our holy religion and the love it teaches, should be, *as he journey'd come to the place where* she lay, *when he saw, would he not have compassion on* her? GOD forbid, a christian should *this day* want it; or at any time *look upon* such a distress, *and pass by on the other side*.

Rather, let him do, as his Saviour taught him, *bind up the wounds, and pour* comfort into the heart of one, whom the hand of GOD has so bruised. Let him practise what it is, with Elijah's transport, to say to the afflicted widow——*See, thy son liveth!* ——liveth by my charity, and the bounty of this hour, to all the purposes which make life desirable,—to be made a good man, and a profitable subject: on one hand to be trained up to such a sense of his duty, as may secure him an interest in the world to come; and with regard to this world, to be so brought up in it, to a love of honest labour and industry, as all his life long to earn and eat his bread with joy and thankfulness.

"Much peace and happiness rest upon the head and heart of every one who thus brings children to CHRIST.——May the blessing of him that was ready to perish come seasonably upon him.—The Lord comfort him, *when he most wants it*, when he lays sick upon his bed; make thou, O GOD! all his bed in his sickness; and for what he now scatters, give him, then, that peace of thine which passeth all understanding, and which nothing in this world can either give or take away." Amen.

Philanthropy Recommended

LUKE X 36, 37

Which now of these three, thinkest thou, was neighbour unto him that fell amongst the thieves?—And he said, he that shewed mercy on him. Then said Jesus unto him—Go, and do thou likewise.

IN THE foregoing verses of this chapter, the Evangelist relâtes, that a certain lawyer stood up and tempted JESUS, saying, master, what shall I do to inherit eternal life?—To which enquiry, our SAVIOUR, as his manner was, when any ensnaring question was put to him, which he saw proceeded more from a design to entangle him, than an honest view of getting information—instead of giving a direct answer which might afford a handle to malice, or at best serve only to gratify an impertinent humour—he immediately retorts the question upon the man who asked it, and unavoidably puts him upon the necessity of answering himself; and as in the present case, the particular profession of the enquirer, and his supposed general knowledge of all other branches of learning, left no room to suspect, he could be ignorant of the true answer to his question, and especially of what every one knew was delivered upon that head by their great Legislator, our SAVIOUR therefore refers him to his own memory of what he had found there in the course of his studies—What is written in the law, how readest thou?—Upon which the inquirer reciting the general heads of our duty to GOD and MAN as delivered in the 18th of Leviticus and the 6th of Deuteronomy,—namely—*That we should worship the Lord our God with all our hearts, and love our neighbour as ourselves:* our blessed SAVIOUR tells him, he had answered right, and if he followed that lesson, he could not fail of the blessing he seemed desirous to inherit.—*This do and thou shalt live.*

But he, as the context tells us, willing to justify himself—willing possibly to gain more credit in the conference, or hoping perhaps to hear such a partial and narrow definition of the word *neighbour* as would suit his own principles, and justify some particular oppressions of his own or those of which his whole order lay

[646]

under an accusation—says unto JESUS in the 29th verse,—*And who is my neighbour?* Though the demand at first sight may seem utterly trifling, yet was it far from being so in fact. For according as you understood the term in a more or a less restrained sense— it produced many necessary variations in the duties you owed from that relation——Our blessed SAVIOUR, to rectify any partial and pernicious mistake in this matter, and place at once this duty of the love of our neighbour upon its true bottom of philan- thropy and universal kindness, makes answer to the proposed question, not by any far-fetched refinement from the schools of the Rabbis, which might have sooner silenced than convinced the man—but by a direct appeal to human nature in an instance he relates of a man falling among thieves, left in the greatest dis- tress imaginable, till by chance a Samaritan, an utter stranger, coming where he was, by an act of great goodness and com- passion, not only relieved him at present, but took him under his protection, and generously provided for his future safety.

On the close of which engaging account—our SAVIOUR appeals to the man's own heart in the first verse of the text—*Which now of these three thinkest thou was neighbour unto him that fell amongst the thieves?* and instead of drawing the inference himself, leaves him to decide in favour of so noble a principle so evidently founded in mercy.——The lawyer, struck with the truth and jus- tice of the doctrine, and frankly acknowledging the force of it, our blessed SAVIOUR concludes the debate with a short admoni- tion, that he would practise what he had approved—and go, and imitate that fair example of universal benevolence which it had set before him.

In the remaining part of the discourse I shall follow the same plan; and therefore shall beg leave to enlarge first upon the story itself, with such reflections as will rise from it; and conclude, as our SAVIOUR has done, with the same exhortation to kindness and humanity which so naturally falls from it.

A certain man, says our SAVIOUR, went down from Jerusalem to Jericho and fell among thieves, who stripped him of his ray- ment and departed, leaving him half dead. There is something in our nature which engages us to take part in every accident to which man is subject, from what cause soever it may have hap- pened; but in such calamities as a man has fallen into through mere misfortune, to be charged upon no fault or indiscretion of himself, there is something then so truly interesting, that at the first sight we generally make them our own, not altogether from a reflection that they might have been or may be so, but oftener from a certain generosity and tenderness of nature which disposes us for compassion, abstracted from all considerations of self. So that without any observable act of the will, we suffer with the unfortunate, and feel a weight upon our spirits we know not why, on seeing the most common instances of their distress. But where the spectacle is uncommonly tragical, and complicated with many circumstances of misery, the mind is then taken captive at once, and, *were* it inclined to it, has no power to make resistance, but surrenders itself to all the tender emotions of pity and deep concern. So that when one considers this friendly part of our nature without looking farther, one would think it impossible for man to look upon misery without finding himself in some measure attached to the interest of him who suffers it.—I say, one would think it impossible—for there are some tempers—how shall I describe them?—formed either of such impenetrable matter, or wrought up by habitual selfishness to such an utter insensibility of what becomes of the fortunes of their fellow-creatures, as if they were not partakers of the same nature, or had no lot or connection at all with the species.

Of this character, our SAVIOUR produces two disgraceful instances in the behaviour of a priest and a Levite, whom in this account he represents as coming to the place where the unhappy man was—both passing by without either stretching forth a hand to assist, or uttering a word to comfort him in his distress.

And by chance there came down a certain priest!—merciful GOD! that a teacher of thy religion should ever want humanity—or that a man whose head might be thought full of the one, should have a heart void of the other!—This however was the case before us—and though in theory one would scarce suspect that the least pretence to religion and an open disregard to so main a part of it, could ever meet together in one person—yet in fact it is no fictitious character.

Look into the world—how often do you behold a sordid wretch, whose straight heart is open to no man's affliction, taking shelter behind an appearance of piety, and putting on the garb of religion, which none but the merciful and compassionate have a title to wear. Take notice with what sanctity he goes to the end of his days, in the same selfish track in which he at first set out—turning neither to the right nor to the left—but plods on—pores all his life long upon the ground, as if afraid to look up, lest peradventure he should see aught which might turn him one moment out of that straight line where interest is carrying him— or if, by chance, he stumbles upon a hapless object of distress, which threatens such a disaster to him—like the man here represented, *devoutly* passing by on the other side, as if unwilling to trust himself to the impressions of nature, or hazard the inconveniencies which pity might lead him into upon the occasion.

There is but one stroke wanting in this picture of an unmerciful man to render the character utterly odious, and that our SAVIOUR gives it in the following instance he relates upon it. And likewise, says he, *a Levite, when he was at the place, came and looked at him.* It was not a transient oversight, the hasty or ill advised neglect of an unconsidering humour, with which the best disposed are sometimes overtaken, and led on beyond the point where otherwise they would have wished to stop.—No!—on the contrary, it had all the aggravation of a deliberate act of insensibility proceeding from a hard heart. When he was at the place, he came, and looked at him—considered his misfortunes, gave time for reason and nature to have awoke—saw the imminent danger he was in —and the pressing necessity of immediate help, which so violent a case called aloud for—and after all—turned aside and unmercifully left him to all the distresses of his condition.

In all unmerciful actions, the worst of men pay this compliment at least to humanity, as to endeavour to wear as much of the appearance of it, as the case will well let them—so that in the hardest acts a man shall be guilty of, he has some motives true or false always ready to offer, either to satisfy himself of the world, and, GOD knows, too often to impose both upon the one and the other. And therefore it would be no hard matter here to give a probable guess at what passed in the Levite's mind in the present case, and shew, was it necessary, by what kind of casuistry he settled the matter with his conscience as he passed by, and guarded all the passages to his heart against the inroads which pity might attempt to make upon the occasion.—But it is painful to dwell long upon this disagreeable part of the story; I therefore hasten to the concluding incident of it, which is so amiable that one cannot easily be too copious in reflections upon it.—And behold, says our SAVIOUR, a certain Samaritan as he journeyed came where he was; and when he saw him he had compassion on him—and went to him—bound up his wounds, pouring in oil and wine—set him upon his own beast, brought him to an inn and took care of him. I suppose, it will be scarce necessary here to remind you that the Jews had no dealings with the Samaritans—an old religious grudge—the worst of all grudges, had wrought such a dislike between both people, that they held themselves mutually discharged not only from all offices of friendship and kindness, but even from the most common acts of courtesy and good manners. This operated so strongly in our SAVIOUR'S time, that the woman of Samaria seemed astonished that he, being a Jew, should *ask* water of her who was a Samaritan——so that with such a prepossession, however distressful the case of the unfortunate man was, and how reasonably soever he might plead for pity from another man, there was little aid or consolation to be looked for from so unpromising a quarter. *Alas! after I have been twice passed by, neglected by men of my own nation and religion, bound by so many ties to assist me, left here friendless and unpitied both by a priest and a Levite, men whose profession and superior advantages of knowledge could not leave them in the dark in what manner they should discharge this debt which my condition claims—after this—what hopes? what expectations from a passenger, not only a stranger,—but a Samaritan released from all obligations to me, and by a national dislike inflamed by mutual ill offices, now made my enemy, and more likely to rejoice at the evils which have fallen upon me, than to stretch forth a hand to save me from them.*

'Tis no unnatural soliloquy to imagine; but the actions of generous and compassionate tempers baffle all little reasonings about them.—True charity, in the apostle's description, as it is kind, and is not easily provoked, so it manifested this character —for we find when he came where he was, and beheld his distress,—all the unfriendly passions, which at another time might have rose within him, now utterly forsook him and fled: when he saw his misfortunes—he forgot his enmity towards the man, ——dropped all the prejudices which education had planted against him, and in the room of them, all that was good and compassionate was suffered to speak in his behalf.

In benevolent natures the impulse to pity is so sudden, that like instruments of music which only obey the touch—the objects which are fitted to excite such impressions work so instantaneous an effect, that you would think the will was scarce concerned, and that the mind was altogether passive in the sympathy which her own goodness has excited. The truth is,—the soul is generally in such cases so busily taken up and wholly engrossed by the object of pity, that she does not attend to her own operations, or take

[650]

leisure to examine the principles upon which she acts. So that the Samaritan, though the moment he saw him he had compassion on him, yet sudden as the emotion is represented, you are not to imagine that it was mechanical, but that there was a settled principle of humanity and goodness which operated within him, and influenced not only the first impulse of kindness, but the continuation of it throughout the rest of so engaging a behaviour. And because it is a pleasure to look into a good mind, and trace out as far as one is able what passes within it on such occasions, I shall beg leave for a moment, to state an account of what was likely to pass in his, and in what manner so distressful a case would necessarily work upon such a disposition.

As he approached the place where the unfortunate man lay, the instant he beheld him, no doubt some such train of reflections as this would rise in his mind. "Good GOD! what a spectacle of misery do I behold—a man stripped of his raiment—wounded—lying languishing before me upon the ground just ready to expire,—without the comfort of a friend to support him in his last agonies, or the prospect of a hand to close his eyes when his pains are over. But perhaps my concern should lessen when I reflect on the relations in which we stand to each other—that he is a Jew and I a Samaritan.—But are we not still both men? partakers of the same nature—and subject to the same evils?—let me change conditions with him for a moment and consider, had his lot befallen me as I journeyed in the way, what measure I should have expected at his hand.—Should I wish when he beheld me wounded and half-dead, that he should shut up his bowels of compassion from me, and double the weight of my miseries by passing by and leaving them unpitied?—But I am a stranger to the man—be it so,—but I am no stranger to his condition——misfortunes are of no particular tribe or nation, but belong to us all, and have a general claim upon us, without distinction of climate, country or religion. Besides, though I am a stranger—'tis no fault of his that I do not know him, and therefore unequitable he should suffer by it:—Had I known him, possibly I should have had cause to love and pity him the more—for aught I know, he is some one of uncommon merit, whose life is rendered still more precious, as the lives and happiness of others may be involved in it: perhaps at this instant that he lies here forsaken, in all this misery, a whole virtuous family is joyfully looking for his return, and affectionately counting the hours of his delay. Oh! did they know what evil hath befallen him—how would they fly to succour him.—Let me then hasten to supply those tender offices of binding up his wounds, and carrying him to a place of safety——or if that assistance comes too late, I shall comfort him at least in his last hour—and, if I can do nothing else,—I shall soften his misfortunes by dropping a tear of pity over them."

'Tis almost necessary to imagine the good Samaritan was influenced by some such thoughts as these, from the uncommon generosity of his behaviour, which is represented by our SAVIOUR operating like the warm zeal of a brother, mixed with the affectionate discretion and care of a parent, who was not satisfied with taking him under his protection, and supplying his present wants, but in looking forwards for him, and taking care that his wants should be supplied when he should be gone, and no longer near to befriend him.

I think there needs no stronger argument to prove how universally and deeply the seeds of this virtue of compassion are planted in the heart of man, than in the pleasure we take in such representations of it: and though some men have represented human nature in other colours, (though to what end I know not) that the matter of fact is so strong against them, that from the general propensity to pity the unfortunate, we express that sensation by the word *humanity*, as if it was inseparable from our nature. That it is not *inseparable*, I have allowed in the former part of this discourse, from some reproachful instances of selfish tempers, which seem to take part in nothing beyond themselves; yet I am perswaded, and affirm 'tis still so great and noble a part of our nature, that a man must do great violence to himself, and suffer many a painful conflict, before he has brought himself to a different disposition.

'Tis observable in the foregoing account, that when the priest came to the place where he was, he passed by on the other side—he might have passed by, you will say, without turning aside.——No, there is a secret shame which attends every act of inhumanity not to be conquered in the hardest natures, so that, as in other cases, so especially in this, many a man will do a cruel act, who at the same time would blush to look you in the face, and is forced to turn aside before he can have a heart to execute his purpose.

Inconsistent creature that man is! who at that instant that he does what is wrong, is not able to withhold his testimony to what is good and praise-worthy.

[652]

I have now done with the parable, which was the first part proposed to be considered in this discourse; and should proceed to the second, which so naturally falls from it, of exhorting you, as our SAVIOUR did the lawyer upon it, *to go and do so likewise:* but I have been so copious in my reflections upon the story itself, that I find I have insensibly incorporated into them almost all that I should have said here in recommending so amiable an example; by which means I have unawares anticipated the task I proposed. I shall therefore detain you no longer than with a single remark upon the subject in general, which is this, 'Tis observable in many places of scripture, that our blessed SAVIOUR in describing the day of judgment does it in such a manner, as if the great enquiry then, was to relate principally to this one virtue of compassion—and as if our final sentence at that solemnity was to be pronounced exactly according to the degrees of it. I was a hungered, and ye gave me meat—thirsty and ye gave me drink—naked and ye cloathed me—I was sick and ye visited me—in prison and ye came unto me. Not that we are to imagine from thence, as if any other good or evil action should then be overlooked by the eye of the All-seeing Judge, but barely to intimate to us, that a charitable and benevolent disposition is so principal and ruling a part of a man's character, as to be a considerable test by itself of the whole frame and temper of his mind, with which all other virtues and vices respectively rise and fall, and will almost necessarily be connected.——Tell me therefore of a compassionate man, you represent to me a man of a thousand other good qualities—on whom I can depend—whom I may safely trust with my wife———my children, my fortune and reputation. 'Tis for this, as the apostle argues from the same principle—that he will not commit adultery—that he will not kill—that he will not steal—that he will not bear false witness. That is, the sorrows which are stirred up in men's hearts by such trespasses are so tenderly felt by a compassionate man, that it is not in his power or his nature to commit them.

So that well might he conclude, that chairty, by which he means, the love to your neighbour, was the end of the commandment, and that whosoever fulfilled it, had fulfilled the law.

Now to GOD, &c. Amen.

HEROD

MATTHEW II 17, 18

Then was fulfilled that which was spoken by Jeremy the prophet, saying,——In Rama was there a voice heard, lamentation, and weeping, and great mourning, Rachael weeping for her children, and would not be comforted because they are not.

THE words which St. Matthew cites here as fulfilled by the cruelty and ambition of Herod,—are in the 31st chapter of Jeremiah 15th verse. In the foregoing chapter, the prophet having declared GOD's intention of turning the mourning of his people into joy, by the restoration of the tribes which had been led away captive into Babylon; he proceeds in the beginning of this chapter, which contains this prophecy, to give a more particular description of the great joy and festivity of that promised day, when they were to return once more to their own land, to enter upon their ancient possessions, and enjoy again all the privileges they had lost, and amongst others, and what was above them all,—the favour and protection of GOD, and the continuation of his mercies to them and their posterity.

To make therefore the impression of this change the stronger upon their minds——he gives a very pathetic representation of the preceding sorrow on that day when they were first led away captive.

Thus saith the Lord, A voice was heard in Rama; lamentation and bitter weeping, Rachael weeping for her children, refusing to be comforted, because they were not.

To enter into the full sense and beauty of this description, it is to be remembered that the tomb of Rachael, Jacob's beloved wife, as we read in the 35th of Genesis, was situated near Rama, and betwixt that place and Bethlehem. Upon which circumstance, the prophet raises one of the most affecting scenes, that could be conceived; for as the tribes in their sorrowful journey betwixt Rama and Bethlehem in their way to Babylon, were supposed to pass by this monumental pillar of their ancestor Rachael, Jacob's wife, the prophet by a common liberty in rhetoric, introduces her as rising up out of her sepulchre, and as the common mother of two of their tribes, weeping for her children, bewailing the sad catastrophe of her posterity led away into a strange land—— refusing to be comforted because they were not,——lost and cut off from their country, and in all likelyhood, never to be restored back to her again.

The Jewish interpreters say upon this, that the patriarch Jacob buried Rachael in this very place, foreseeing by the spirit of prophecy, that his posterity should that way be led captive, that she might as they passed her, intercede to them.——

But this fanciful superstructure upon the passage, seems to be little else than a mere dream of some of the Jewish doctors; and indeed had they not dream't it when they did, 'tis great odds, but some of the Romish dreamers would have hit upon it before now. For as it favours the doctrine of intercessions—if there had not been undeniable vouchers for the real inventors of the conceit, one should much sooner have sought for it amongst the oral traditions of this church, than in the Talmud, where it is.

But this by the bye, There is still another interpretation of the words here cited by St. Matthew, which altogether excludes this scenecal representation I have given of them.——By which 'tis thought that the lamentation of Rachael, here described, has no immediate reference to Rachael, Jacob's wife, but that it simply alludes to the sorrows of her descendents, the distressed mothers of the tribes of Benjamin and Ephraim who might accompany their children, led into captivity as far as Rama, in their way to Babylon, who wept and wailed upon this sad occasion, and as the prophet describes them in the person of Rachael, refusing to be comforted for the loss of her children, looking upon their departure without hope or prospect of ever beholding a return.

Whichever of the two senses you give the words of the prophet, the application of them by the evangelist is equally just and faithful. For as the former scene he relates, was transacted upon the very same stage——in the same district of Bethlehem near Rama ——where so many mothers of the same tribe now suffered this second most affecting blow—the words of Jeremiah, as the evangelist observes, were literally accomplished, and no doubt, in that horrid day, a voice was heard again in Rama, lamentation and a bitter weeping—Rachael weeping for her children, and refusing to be comforted;—every Bethlemitish mother involved in this calamity, beholding it with hopeless sorrow—gave vent to it—each one, bewailing her children, and lamenting the hardness of their lot, with the anguish of a heart as incapable of consolation, as they were of redress. Monster!—could no consideration of all this tender sorrow, stay thy hands?—Could no reflection upon so much bitter lamentation throughout the coasts of Bethlehem, interpose and plead in behalf of so many wretched objects, as this tragedy would make?—Was there no way open to ambition but that thôu must trample upon the affections of nature? Could no pity for the innocence of childhood—no sympathy for the yearnings of parental love incline thee to some other measures for thy security—but thou must thus pitilessly rush in— take the victim by violence—tear it from the embraces of the mother—offer it up, before her eyes—leave her disconsolate for ever—broken-hearted with a loss—so affecting in itself——so circumstanced with horror, that no time, how friendly soever to the mournful——should ever be able to wear out the impression.

There is nothing in which the mind of man is more divided than in the accounts of this horrid nature.——For when we consider man as fashioned by his maker—innocent and upright—full of the tenderest dispositions—with a heart inclining him to kindness, and the love and protection of his species——this idea of him would almost shake the credit of such accounts;——so that to clear them—we are forced to take a second view of man—very different from this favourable one, in which we insensibly represent him to our imaginations——that is——we are obliged to consider him—not as he was made——but as he is——a creature by the violence and irregularity of his passions capable of being perverted from all these friendly and benevolent propensities, and sometimes hurried into excesses so opposite to them, as to render the most unnatural and horrid accounts of what he does but too probable.—The truth of this observation will be exemplyfied in the case before us. For next to the faith and character of the historian who reports such facts,——the particular character of the person who committed them is to be considered as a voucher for their truth and credibility;—and if upon enquiry, it appears, that the man acted but consistent with himself,—and just so as you would have expected from his principles,—the credit of the historian is restored,——and the fact related stands incontestable, from so strong and concurring an evidence on its side—

[656]

With this view, it may not be an unacceptable application of the remaining part of a discourse upon this day, to give you a sketch of the character of Herod, not as drawn from scripture, —for in general it furnishes us with few materials for such descriptions:—the sacred scripture cuts off in few words the history of the ungodly, how great soever they were in the eyes of the world,—and on the other hand dwells largely upon the smallest actions of the righteous.—We find all the circumstances of the lives of Abraham, Isaac, Jacob, and Joseph, recorded in the minutest manner.——The wicked seem only mentioned with regret; just brought upon the stage, on purpose to be condemned. The use and advantage of which conduct—is, I suppose, the reason,——as in general it enlarges on no character, but what is worthy of imitation. 'Tis however undeniable, that the lives of bad men are not without use,—and whenever such a one is drawn, not with a corrupt view to be admired,—but on purpose to be detested,—it must excite such an horror against vice, as will strike indirectly the same good impression. And though it is painful to the last degree to paint a man in the shades which his vices have cast upon him,—yet when it serves this end, and at the same time illustrates a point in sacred history—it carries its own excuse with it.

This Herod, therefore, of whom the evangelist speaks, if you take a superficial view of his life, you would say was a compound of good and evil,—that though he was certainly a bad man, —yet you would think the mass was tempered at the same time with a mixture of good qualities. So that, in course, as is not uncommon, he would appear with two characters very different from each other. If you looked on the more favourable side, you would see a man of great address—popular in his behaviour, —generous, prince-like in his entertainments and expences, and in a word set off with all such virtue and shewy properties, as bid high for the countenance and approbation of the world.

View him in another light, he was an ambitious, designing man,——suspicious of all the world,——rapacious,—implacable in his temper,—without sense of religion,—or feeling of humanity.——Now in all such complex characters as this,—the way the world usually judges, is—to sum up the good and the bad against each other,—deduct the lesser of these articles from the greater, and (as we do in passing other accounts) give credit to the man for what remains upon the ballance. Now, though this seems a fair,—yet I fear 'tis often a fallacious reckoning,—which though it may serve in many ordinary cases of private life, yet will not hold good in the more notorious instances of men's lives, especially when so complicated with good and bad, as to exceed all common bounds and proportions. Not to be deceived in such cases we must work by a different rule, which though it may appear less candid,—yet to make amends, I am persuaded will bring us in general much nearer to the thing we want,—which is truth. The way to which is—in all judgments of this kind, to distinguish and carry in your eye, the principal and ruling passion which leads the character—and separate that, from the other parts of it,—and then take notice, how far his other qualities, good and bad, are brought to serve and support that. For want of this distinction,—we often think ourselves inconsistent creatures, when we are the furthest from it, and all the variety of shapes and contradictory appearances we put on, are in truth but so many different attempts to gratify the same governing appetite.—

With this clew, let us endeavour to unravel this character of Herod as here given.

The first thing which strikes one in it is ambition, an immoderate thirst, as well as jealousy of power;——how inconsistent soever in other parts, his character appears invariable in this, and every action of his life was true to it.——From hence we may venture to conclude, that this was *his* ruling passion,——and that most, if not all the other wheels were put in motion by this first spring. Now let us consider how far this was the case in fact.

To begin with the worst part of him,——I said he was a man of no sense of religion, or at least no other sense of it, but that which served his turn—for he is recorded to have built temples in Judea, and erected images in them for idolatrous worship,—— not from a persuasion of doing right, for he was bred a Jew, and consequently taught to abhor all idolatry,—but he was in truth sacrificing all this time, to a greater idol of his own, his ruling passion; for if we may trust Josephus, his sole view in so gross a compliance was to ingratiate himself with Augustus and the great men of Rome from whom he held his power.——With this he was greedy and rapacious——how could he be otherwise with so devouring an appetite as ambition to provide for?—He was jealous in his nature, and suspicious of all the world.—Shew me an ambitious man, that is not so; for as such a man's hand, like Ishmael's, is against every man, he concludes, that every man's hand in course is against his.

Few men were ever guilty of more astonishing acts of cruelty

————and yet the particular instances of them in Herod were such as he was hurried into, by the alarms this waking passion perpetually gave him. He put the whole Sanadrim to the sword—sparing neither age, or wisdom, or merit——one cannot suppose, simply from an inclination to cruelty—no—they had opposed the establishment of his power at Jerusalem.

His own sons, two hopeful youths, he cut off by a public execution.—The worst men have natural affection—and such a stroke as this would run so contrary to the natural workings of it, that you are forced to suppose the impulse of some more violent inclination to overrule and conquer it.——And so it was, for the Jewish historian tells us, 'twas jealousy of power,—his darling object—of which he feared they would one day or other dispossess him—sufficient inducement to transport a man of such a temper into the bloodiest excesses.

Thus far this one fatal and extravagant passion, accounts for the dark side of Herod's character. This governing principle being first laid open—all his other bad actions follow in course, like so many symptomatic complaints from the same distemper.

Let us see, if this was not the case even of his virtues too.

At first sight it seems a mystery—how a man, so black as Herod has been thus far described—should be able to support himself, in the favor and friendship of so wise and penetrating a body of men, as the Roman senate, of whom he held his power. To counter-ballance the weight of so bad and detested a character —and be able to bear it up, as Herod did, one would think he must have been master of some great secret worth enquiring after—he was so. But that secret was no other than what appears on this reverse of his character. He was a person of great address —popular in his outward behavior.—He was generous, prince-like in his entertainments and expences. The world was then as corrupt at least, as now—and Herod understood it—knew at what price it was to be bought—and what qualities would bid the highest for its good word and approbation.

And in truth, he judged this matter so well——that notwithstanding the general odium and prepossession which arose against so hateful a character—in spight of all the ill impressions, from so many repeated complaints of his cruelties and oppressions—he yet stemmed the torrent—and by the specious display of these popular virtues bore himself up against it all his life. So that at length, when he was summoned to Rome to answer for his crimes——Josephus tells us,—that by the mere magnificence of his expences—and the apparent generosity of his behavior, he entirely confuted the whole charge—and so ingratiated himself with the Roman senate—and won the heart of Augustus——(as he had that of Anthony before) that he ever after had his favor and kindness; which I cannot mention without adding—that it is an eternal stain upon the character and memory of Augustus, that he sold his countenance and protection to so bad a man, for so mean and base a consideration.

From this point of view, if we look back upon Herod—his best qualities will shrink into little room, and how glittering soever in appearance, when brought to this ballance, are found wanting. And in truth, if we would not willingly be deceived in the value of any virtue or set of virtues in so complex a character——we must call them to this very account; examine whom they serve, what passion and what principle they have for their master. When this is understood, the whole clew is unravelled at once, and the character of Herod, as complicated as it is given us in history——when thus analysed, is summed up in three words—— *That he was a man of unbounded ambition,* who stuck at nothing to gratify it,——so that not only his vices were ministerial to his ruling passion, but his virtues too (if they deserve the name) were drawn in, and listed into the same service.

Thus much for the character of Herod——the critical review of which has many obvious uses, to which I may trust you, having time but to mention that particular one which first led me into this examination, namely, that all objections against the evangelist's account of this day's slaughter of the Bethlemitish infants ——from the incredibility of so horrid an account—are silenced by this account of the man; since in this, he acted but like himself, and just so as you would expect in the same circumstances, from every man of so ambitious a head——and so bad a heart.—— Consider, what havock ambition has made——how often the same tragedy has been acted upon larger theatres—where not only the innocence of childhood——or the grey hairs of the aged, have found no protection——but whole countries without distinction have been put to the sword, or what is as cruel, have been driven forth to nakedness and famine to make way for new comers under the guidance of this passion.——For a specimen of this, reflect upon the story related by Plutarch:——when by order of the Roman senate, seventy populous cities were unawares sacked and destroyed at one prefixed hour, by P. Æmilius —by whom one hundred and fifty thousand unhappy people were driven in one day into captivity——to be sold to the highest bidder to end their days in cruel labor and anguish. As astonishing as the account before us is, it vanishes into nothing from such views, since it is plain from all history, that there is no wickedness too great for so unbounded a cause, and that the most horrid accounts in history are, as I said above, but too probable effects of it.——

May GOD of his mercy defend mankind from future experiments of this kind——and grant we may make a proper use of them, for the sake of Jesus Christ, *Amen.*

THE CHARACTER OF

SHIMEI

---

2 SAMUEL XIX 21. 1st PART

But Abishai said, Shall not Shimei be put to death for this?—

—IT HAS not a good aspect—This is the second time Abisha has proposed Shimei's destruction; once in the 16th chapter, on a sudden transport of indignation, when Shimei cursed David,—"*Why should this dead dog, cried Abishai, curse my lord the king? let me go over, I pray thee, and cut off his head.*"—This had something at least of gallantry in it; for in doing it, he hazarded his own; and besides the offender was not otherwise to be come at: the second time, is in the text; when the offender was absolutely in their power—when the blood was cool; and the suppliant was holding up his hands for mercy.

—Shall not Shimei, answered Abishai, be put to death for this? So unrelenting a pursuit looks less like justice than revenge, which is so cowardly a passion, that it renders Abishai's first instance almost inconsistent with the second. I shall not endeavour to reconcile them; but confine the discourse simply to Shimei; and make such reflections upon his character as may be of use to society.

Upon the news of his son Absalom's conspiracy, David had fled from Jerusalem, and from his own house for safety: the representation given of the manner of it, is truly affecting:— never was a scene of sorrow so full of distress!

The king fled with all his houshold to save himself from the sword of the man he loved; he fled with all the marks of humble sorrow—"*with his head cover'd and barefoot*;" and as he went by the ascent of mount Olivet, the sacred historian says he wept —some gladsome scenes, perhaps, which there had pass'd—some hours of festivity he had shared with Absalom in better days, pressed tenderly upon nature,—he wept at this sad vicissitude of things:—and all the people that were with him, smitten with his affliction, *cover'd each* man *his head—weeping as he went* up.

It was on this occasion, when David had got to Bahurim, that

Shimei the son of Gera, as we read in the 5th verse, came out:—
was it with the choicest oils he could gather from mount Olivet,
to pour into his wounds?—Times and troubles had not done
enough; and thou camest out, Shimei, to add thy portion—

"*And as he came, he cursed David, and threw stones and cast
dust at him; and thus said Shimei, when he cursed: Go to, thou man
of Belial—thou hast sought blood,—and behold thou* art *caught
in thy own mischief:* for now hath the *Lord returned* upon thee all
the blood *of Saul and his house.*"

There is no small degree of malicious craft in fixing upon a season to give a mark of enmity and ill will: a word,—a look,
which at one time would make no impression——at another
time wounds the heart; and like a shaft flying with the wind,
pierces deep, which, with its own natural force, would scarce
have reached the object aimed at.

This seemed to have been Shimei's hopes: but excess of malice
makes men too quick-sighted even for their own purpose. Could
Shimei possibly have waited for the ebb of David's passions, and
till the first great conflict within him had been over—then the
reproach of being guilty of Saul's blood must have hurt him—his
heart was possessed with other feelings—it bled for the deadly
sting which Absalom had given him—he felt not the indignity of
a stranger—"*Behold, my son Absalom, who came out of my
bowels, seeketh my life—how much more may Shimei do it?—let
him alone; it may be the Lord may look upon my affliction, and
requite me good for this evil.*"

An injury unanswered in course grows weary of itself, and dies
away in a voluntary remorse.

In bad dispositions capable of no restraint but fear—it has
a different effect—the silent digestion of one wrong provokes
a second.—He pursues him with the same invective; *and as David
and his men went by the way, Shimei went along on the hill's side
over against him: and cursed as he went, and cast dust at him.*

The insolence of base minds in success is boundless; and would
scarce admit of a comparison, did not they themselves furnish us
with one in the degrees of their abjection when evil returns upon
them—The same poor heart which excites ungenerous tempers
to triumph over a fallen adversary, in some instances seems to
exalt them above the point of courage—sinks them, in others,
even below cowardice.—Not unlike some little particles of matter
struck off from the surface of the dirt by sunshine—dance and
sport there whilst it lasts—but the moment it is withdrawn—they

[663]

fall down—for dust they are—and unto dust they will return—whilst firmer and larger bodies preserve the stations which nature has assigned them, subjected to laws which no change of weather can alter.

This last, did not seem to be Shimei's case; in all David's prosperity, there is no mention made of him—he thrust himself forward into the circle, and possibly was number'd amongst friends and well-wishers.

When the scene changes, and David's troubles force him to leave his house in despair—Shimei is the first man we hear of, who comes out against him.

The wheel turns round once more; Absalom is cast down, and David returns in peace—Shimei suits his behaviour to the occasion, and is the first man also who hastes to greet him—and had the wheel turn'd round a hundred times, Shimei, I dare say, in every period of its rotation, would have been uppermost.

O Shimei! would to heaven when thou wast slain, that all thy family had been slain with thee; and not one of thy resemblance left! but ye have multiplied exceedingly and replenished the earth; and, if I prophesy rightly—Ye will in the end *subdue* it.

There is not a character in the world which has so bad an influence upon the affairs of it, as this of Shimei: whilst power meets with honest checks, and the evils of life with honest refuge, the world will never be undone: but thou, Shimei, hast sapp'd it at both extremes; for thou corruptest prosperity—and 'tis thou who hast broken the heart of poverty: and so long as worthless spirits can be ambitious ones, it is a character we shall never want. O! it infests the court—the camp—the cabinet—it infests the church—go where you will—in every quarter, in every profession, you see a Shimei following the wheels of the fortunate through thick mire and clay.—

—Haste, Shimei!——haste, or thou wilt be undone for ever—Shimei girdeth up his loins and speedeth after him—behold the hand which governs every thing,—takes the wheels from off his chariot, so that he who driveth, driveth on heavily—Shimei doubles his speed—but 'tis the contrary way; he flies like the wind o'er a sandy desart, and the place thereof shall know it no more ——stay, Shimei, 'tis your patron——your friend—your benefactor;—'tis the man who has raised you from the dunghill—'tis all one to Shimei: Shimei is the barometer of every man's fortune; marks the rise and fall of it, with all the variations from scorching hot to freezing cold upon his countenance, that the simile will admit of. Is a cloud upon thy affairs?—see—it hangs over Shimei's brow—hast *thou been* spoken for to the king or the captain of the host without success?—look not into the court-kalendar—the vacancy is fill'd up in Shimei's face—art thou in debt? tho' not to Shimei—no matter—the worst officer of the law shall not be more insolent.

What then, Shimei, is the guilt of poverty so black—is it of so general a concern, that thou and all thy family must rise up as one man to reproach it?—when it lost every thing—did it lose the right to pity too? or did he who maketh poor as well as maketh rich strip it of its natural powers to mollify the hearts and supple the temper of your race?—Trust me, ye have much to answer for; it is this treatment which it has ever met with from spirits like yours, which has gradually taught the world to look upon it as the greatest of evils, and shun it as the worst disgrace—and what is it, I beseech you—what is it that man will not do, to keep clear of so sore an imputation and punishment?—is it not, to fly from this, that *he rises early—late takes rest; and eats the bread of carefulness?*—that he plots, contrives—swears—lies—shuffles—puts on all shapes—tries all garments,——wears them, with this, or that side outward——just as it favours his escape.

They who have considered our nature, affirm, that shame and disgrace are two of the most insupportable evils of human life: the courage and spirits of many have master'd other misfortunes and born themselves up against them; but the wisest and best of souls have not been a match for these; and we have many a tragical instance on record, what greater evils have been run into, merely to avoid this one.

Without this tax of infamy, poverty, with all the burdens it lays upon our flesh—so long as it is virtuous, could never break the spirits of a man; all it's hunger, and pain and nakedness, are nothing to it—they have some counterpoise of good; and besides they are directed by providence, and must be submitted to: but those are afflictions not from the hand of GOD or nature——"*for they do come forth of the* DUST, and most properly may be said *to spring out of the* GROUND, and this is the reason they lay such stress upon our patience,—and in the end, create such a distrust of the world, as makes us look up—and pray, *Let me fall into thy hands. O God! but let me not fall into the hands of men.*"

Agreeable to this was the advice of Eliphas to Job in the day of his distress;——"*Acquaint thyself*, said he, NOW *with God:*"——Indeed his poverty seem'd to have left him no other friend: the swords of the Sabeans had frightened them away—all but a few; and of what kind they were, the very proverb, of *Job's comforters* —says enough.

It is an instance which gives one great concern for human nature, "That a man, *who always wept* for him who was in *trouble; —who never saw any perish for want of cloathing;—who never suffered the stranger to lodge in the street, but opened his door to the traveller;—that a man* of so good a character,——*that he never caused the eyes of the widow to fail,——or had eaten his morsel by himself alone, and the fatherless had not eaten thereof;"* ——that such a man, the moment he fell into poverty, should have occasion to cry out for quarter,——*Have mercy upon me, O my friends! for the hand of God has touched me.*——Gentleness and humanity (one would think) would melt the hardest heart and charm the fiercest spirit; bind up the most violent hand, and still the most abusive tongue:—but the experiment failed in a stronger instance of him, whose meat and drink it was to do us good; and in pursuit of which, whose whole life was a continued scene of kindness and of insults, for which we must go back to the same explanation with which we set out,—and that is, the scandal of poverty.—

"This fellow, we know not whence he is"—was the popular cry of one part; and with those who seemed to know better, the quere, did not lessen the disgrace:—Is not this the carpenter, the son of Mary?—of Mary!—great GOD of Israel! What!—of the meanest of thy people! (*for he had not regarded the low estate* of his hand-maiden)—and of the poorest too! (for she had not a lamb to offer, but was purified as Moses directed in such a case, by the oblation of a turtle dove.)—

That the SAVIOUR of their nation, could be poor, and not have where to lay his head,—was a crime never to be forgiven: and tho' the purity of his doctrine, and the works which he had done in its support, were stronger arguments on its side, than his humiliation could be against it,—yet the offence still remained;— they looked for the redemption of Israel; but they would have it only in those dreams of power which filled their imagination.—

Ye who weigh the worth of all things only in the gold-smith's balance!——was this religion for you?—a religion whose appearance was not great and splendid,—but looked thin and meagre, and whose principles and promises shewed more like the curses of the law, than its blessings:—for they called for sufferings and promised little but persecutions.

[666]

In truth it is not easy for tribulation or distress, for nakedness or famine, to make many converts out of pride; or reconcile a worldly heart to the scorn and reproaches, which were sure to be the portion of every one who believed a mystery so discredited by the world, and so unpalatable to all its passions and pleasures.

But to bring this sermon to its proper conclusion.

If Astrea or Justice never finally took her leave of the world, till the day that poverty first became ridiculous, it is matter of consolation, that the GOD of Justice is ever over us;—that whatever outrages the lowness of our condition may be exposed to, from a mean and undiscerning world,—that we walk in the presence of the greatest and most generous of Beings, who is infinitely removed from cruelty and straitness of mind, and all those little and illiberal passions, with which we hourly insult each other.

The worst part of mankind, are not always to be conquered— but if they are—'tis by the imitation of these qualities, which must do it:—'tis true—as I've shewn—they may fail; but still all is not lost,—for if we conquer not the world,—in the very attempts to do it, we shall at least conquer ourselves, and lay the foundation of our peace (where it ought to be) within our own hearts.

Hezekiah and the Messengers

---

2 KINGS XX 15

And he said, What have they seen in thine house? and Hezekiah answered, All the things that are in my house have they seen; there is nothing amongst all my treasures that I have not shewn them.

—AND where was the harm, you'll say, in all this?

An eastern prince, the son of Baladine, had sent messengers with presents as far as from Babylon, to congratulate Hezekiah upon the recovery from his sickness; and Hezekiah, who was a good prince, acted consistently with himself: *he received and entertained the men and hearkened unto them,* and before he sent them away, he courteously shewed them all that was worth a stranger's curiosity in his house and in his kingdom,——and in this, seemed only to have discharged himself of what urbanity or the *etiquette* of courts might require. Notwithstanding this, in the verse which immediately follows the text, we find he had done amiss; and as a punishment for it, that all his riches, which his forefathers had laid up in store unto that day, were threatened to be carried away in triumph to Babylon,—the very place from whence the messengers had come.

A hard return! and what his behaviour does not seem to have deserved. To set this matter in a clear light, it will be necessary to enlarge upon the whole story,—the reflections which will arise out of it, as we go along, may help us—at least, I hope they will be of use on their own account.

After the miraculous defeat of the Assyrians, we read in the beginning of this chapter, that Hezekiah was sick even unto death; and that GOD sends the prophet Isaiah, with the unwelcome message, *That he should set his house in order, for that he should die, and not live.*

There are many instances of men, who have received such news with the greatest ease of mind, and even entertained the thoughts of it with smiles upon their countenances,—and this, either from strength of spirits and the natural chearfulness of their temper,—or that, they knew the world,—and cared not for it,—or expected a better—yet, thousands of good men with all the helps of philosophy, and against all the assurances of a well spent life, that the change must be to their account,——upon the approach of death have still lean'd towards this world, and wanted spirits and resolution to bear the shock of a separation from it for ever.

This in some measure seemed to have been Hezekiah's case; for tho' he had walked before GOD in truth, and with a perfect heart, and had done that which was good in his sight,—yet we find that the hasty summons afflicted him greatly;—that upon the delivery of the message he wept sore;—that he turned his face towards the wall,—perhaps for the greater secrecy of his devotion, and that, by withdrawing himself thus from all external objects, he might offer up his prayer unto his GOD, with greater and more fervent attention.

——And he pray'd, and said, O LORD! I beseech thee remember—O Hezekiah! How couldst thou fear that GOD had forgotten thee? or, How couldst thou doubt of his remembrance of thy integrity, when he called thee to receive it's recompence?

But here it appears of what materials man is made: he pursues happiness——and yet is so content with misery, that he would wander for ever in this dark vale of it,—and say, "*It is good, Lord! to be here, and to build tabernacles of rest:*" and so long as we are cloathed with flesh, and nature has so great a share within us, it is no wonder if that part claims it's right, and pleads for the sweetness of life notwithstanding all it's care and disappointments.

This natural weakness, no doubt, had its weight in Hezekiah's earnest prayer for life: and yet from the success it met with, and the immediate change of GOD's purpose thereupon, it is hard to imagine, but that it must have been accompanied with some meritorious and more generous motive: and if we suppose, as some have done, that he turned his face towards the wall, because that part of his chamber looked towards the temple, the care of whose preservation lay next his heart, we may consistently enough give this sense to his prayer.

[669]

"O God! remember how I have walked before thee in truth;
——how much I have done to rescue thy religion from error and
falshood;——thou knowest that the eyes of the world are fixed
upon me, as one that hath forsaken their idolatry, and restored
thy worship;——that I stand in the midst of a crooked and corrupt generation, which looks thro' all my actions, and watches
all events which happen to me: if now they shall see me snatched
away in the midst of my days and service, How will thy great
name suffer in my extinction? Will not the heathen say, This it
is, to serve the God of Israel!—How faithfully did Hezekiah walk
before him?—What enemies did he bring upon himself, in too
warmly promoting his worship? and now when the hour of sickness and distress came upon him, and he most wanted the aid of
his God:—behold how he was forsaken!"

It is not unreasonable, to ascribe some such pious and more
disinterested motive to Hezekiah's desire of life, from the issue
and success of his prayer:—*for it came to pass before Isaiah had
gone out into the middle court, that the word of the Lord came to
him, saying, Turn again and tell Hezekiah I have heard his prayer,
I have seen his tears, and behold I will heal him.*

It was upon this occasion, as we read in the 12th verse of this
chapter, that Baradock-baladan, son of Baladine king of Babylon,
sent letters and a present unto Hezekiah: he had heard the fame
of his sickness and recovery; for as the Chaldeans were great
searchers into the secrets of nature, especially into the motions of
the celestial bodies, in all probability they had taken notice at
that distance, of the strange appearance of the shadow's returning
ten degrees backwards upon their dials, and had enquired and
learned upon what account, and in whose favour such a sign was
given; so that this astronomical miracle, besides the political
motive which it would suggest of courting such a favourite of
heaven, had been sufficient by itself to have led a curious people
as far as Jersualem, that they might see the man for whose sake
the sun had forsook his course.

And here we see how hard it is to stand the shock of prosperity,
—and how much truer a proof we give of our strength in that
extreme of life, than in the other.

In all the trials of adversity, we find that Hezekiah behaved
well,—nothing unman'd him: when besieged by the Assyrian
host, which shut him up in Jerusalem, and threaten'd his destruction,—he stood unshaken and depended upon God's succour.—
When cast down upon his bed of sickness, and threaten'd with

death, he meekly turn'd his face towards the wall,—wept and pray'd, and depended upon GOD's mercy:—but no sooner does prosperity return upon him, and the messengers from a far country come to pay the flattering homage due to his greatness, and the extraordinary felicity of his life, but he turns giddy, and sinks under the weight of his good fortune, and with a transport unbecoming a wise man upon it,—'tis said, he hearken'd unto the men, and shew'd them all the house of his precious things, the silver and the gold, the spices and the precious ointments, and all the house of his armour, and all that was found in his treasures; that there was nothing in his house, not in his dominions, that Hezekiah shew'd them not: for tho' it is not expressly said here, (tho' it is in the parallel passage in Chronicles)—nor is he charged by the prophet that, he did this out of vanity and a weak transport of ostentation;—yet as we are sure, GOD could not be offended but where there was a real crime, we might reasonably conclude that this was his, and that he who searches into the heart of man, beheld that his was corrupted with the blessings he had given him; and that it was just to make what was the occasion of his pride, become the instrument of his punishment, by decreeing, that all the riches he had laid up in store until that day, should be carried away in triumph to Babylon, the very place from whence the messengers had come who had been eye-witnesses of his folly.

"O Hezekiah! how couldst thou provoke GOD to bring this judgment upon thee? How could thy spirit, all meek and gentle as it was, have ever fallen into this snare? Were thy treasures rich as the earth—What! was thy heart so vain as to be lifted up therewith? Was not all that was valuable in the world—nay, was not heaven itself almost at thy command whilst thou wast humble? and, How was it, that thou couldst barter away all this, for what was lighter than a bubble, and desecrate an action so full of courtesy and kindness as thine appeared to be, by suffering it to take it's rise from so polluted a fountain?"

There is scarce any thing which the heart more unwillingly bears, than an analysis of this kind.

We are a strange compound; and something foreign from what charity would suspect, so eternally twists itself into what we do, that not only in momentous concerns, where interest lists under it all the powers of disguise,—but even in the most indifferent of our actions,—not worth a fallacy—by force of habit, we continue it: so that whatever a man is about,—observe him,—he stands arm'd inside and out with two motives; an ostensible one for the world, and another which he reserves for his own private use;—this, you may say, the world has no concern with: it might have been so; but by obtruding the wrong motive upon the world, and stealing from it a character, instead of winning one;—we give it a right and a temptation along with it, to enquire into the affair.

The motives of the one for doing it, are often little better than the others for deserving it. Let us see if some social virtue may not be extracted from the errors of both the one and the other.

VANITY bids all her sons to be generous and brave,—and her daughters to be chaste and courteous.—But why do we want her instructions?—Ask the comedian who is taught a part he feels not—

Is it that the principles of religion want strength, or that the real passion for what is good and worthy will not carry us high enough?—GOD! thou knowest they carry us too high—we want not *to be*—but *to seem*—

Look out of your door,——take notice of that man: see what disquieting, intriguing and shifting, he is content to go through, merely to be thought a man of plain dealing:——three grains of honesty would save him all this trouble:—alas! he has them not.——

Behold a second, under a shew of piety hiding the impurities of a debauched life:——he is just entering the house of GOD:—— would he was more pure—or less pious:—but then he could not gain his point.

Observe a third going on almost in the same track,——with what an inflexible sanctity of deportment, he sustains himself as he advances:——every line in his face writes abstinence;—— every stride looks like a check upon his desires: see, I beseech you, how he is cloak'd with up sermons, prayers and sacraments; and so bemuffled with the externals of religion, that he has not a hand to spare for a worldly purpose;—he has armour at least— Why does he put it on? Is there no serving GOD without all this? Must the garb of religion be extended so wide to the danger of it's rending?—Yes truly, or it will not hide the secret—and, What is that?

——That the saint has no religion at all.

——But here comes GENEROSITY; giving—not to a decayed artist—but to the arts and sciences themselves.——See,—he

[672]

builds not a chamber in the wall apart for the prophet: but whole
schools and colleges for those who come after. LORD! how they
will magnify his name!—'tis in capitals already; the first——the
highest, in the gilded rent-roll of every hospital and asylum—

—One honest tear shed in private over the unfortunate, is
worth it all.

What a problematic set of creatures does simulation make us!
Who would divine that all that anxiety and concern so visible in
the airs of one half of that great assembly should arise from
nothing else, but that the other half of it may think them to be
men of consequence, penetration, parts and conduct?—What
a noise amongst the claimants about it? Behold *Humility*, out of
mere pride,——and *Honesty* almost out of knavery:——*Chastity*,
never once in harm's way,—and *Courage*, like a Spanish soldier
upon an Italian stage——a bladder full of wind.—

—Hark! that, the sound of that trumpet,—let not my soldier
run, 'tis some good Christian giving alms. O, PITY, thou gentlest
of human passions! soft and tender are thy notes, and ill accord
they with so loud an instrument.

Thus something jars, and will for ever jar in these cases:
imposture is all dissonance, let what master soever of it, undertake the part; let him harmonize and modulate it as he may, one
tone will contradict another; and whilst we have ears to hear, we
shall distinguish it: 'tis truth only which is consistent and ever in
harmony with itself: it sits upon our lips, like the natural notes
of some melodies, ready to drop out, whether we will or no;—it
racks no invention to let ourselves alone,—and needs fear no
critick, to have the same excellency in the heart which appears in
the action.

It is a pleasing allusion the scripture makes use of in calling us
sometimes a house, and sometimes a temple, according to the
more or less exalted qualities of the spiritual guest which is lodged
within us: whether this is the precise ground of the distinction,
I will not affirm; but thus much may be said, that, if we are to be
temples, 'tis truth and singleness of heart which must make the
dedication: 'tis this which must first distinguish them from the
unhallowed pile, where dirty tricks and impositions are practised
by the host upon the traveller, who tarries but for a moment and
returns not again.

We all take notice, how close and reserved people are; but we
do not take notice at the same time, that every one may have
something to conceal, as well as ourselves; and that we are only

marking the distances, and taking the measures of self-defence from each other, in the very instances we complain of: this is so true, that there is scarce any character so rare, as a man of a real open and generous integrity,——who carries his heart in his hand,—who says the thing he thinks; and does the thing he pretends. Tho' no one can dislike the character,—yet, Discretion generally shakes her head,—and the world soon lets him into the reason.

"*O that I had in the wilderness a lodging of way-faring men! that I might leave such a people and go from them.*" Where is the man of a nice sense of truth and strong feelings, from whom the duplicity of the world, has not at one time or other wrung the same wish; and where lies the wilderness to which some one has not fled, from the same melancholy impulse?

Thus much for those who give occasion to be thought ill of:— let us say a word or two unto those who take it.

But to avoid all common-place cant, as much as I can on this head,—I will forbear to say, because I do not think it,—that 'tis a breach of Christian charity to think or speak evil of our neighbour, &c.

We cannot avoid it: our opinions must follow the evidence; and we are perpetually in such engagements and situations, that 'tis our duties to speak what our opinions are—but GOD forbid, that this ever should be done, but from its best motive—the sense of what is due to virtue, governed by discretion and the utmost fellow feeling: were we to go on otherwise, beginning with the great broad cloak of hypocrisy, and so down through all its little trimmings and facings, tearing away without mercy, all that look'd seemly,—we should leave but a tatter'd world of it.

But I confine what I have to say to a character less equivocal, and which takes up too much room in the world: it is that of those, who from a general distrust of all that looks disinterested, finding nothing to blame in an action, and perhaps much to admire in it,—immediately fall foul upon it's motives: *Does Job serve God for nought?* What a vile insinuation! besides, the question was not, whether Job was a rich man or a poor man;— but, whether he was a man of integrity or no? and the appearances were strong on his side: indeed it might have been otherwise; it was possible Job might be insincere, and the devil took the advantage of the die for it.

It is a bad picture, and done by a terrible master, and yet we are always copying it. Does a man from real conviction of heart forsake his vices?—the position is not to be allowed,—no, his vices have forsaken him.

Does a pure virgin fear GOD and say her prayers:—she is in her climacterick.

Does humanity cloath and educate the unknown orphan?—Poverty! thou hast no genealogies:—see! is he not the father of the child? Thus do we rob heroes of the best part of their glory—their virtue. Take away the motive of the act, you take away, all that is worth having in it;—wrest it to ungenerous ends, you load the virtuous man who did it, with infamy;—undo it all—I beseech you: give him back his honour—restore the jewel you have taken from him,—replace him in the eye of the world——it is too late.

It is painful to utter reproaches which should come in here.—I will trust them with yourselves: in coming from that quarter, they will more naturally produce such fruits as will not set your teeth on edge—for they will be the fruits of love and good will, to the praise of GOD and the happiness of the world, which I wish.

The Prodigal Son

And not many days after, the younger son gathered all he had together, and took his journey into a far country.—

I KNOW not whether the remark is to our honour or otherwise, that lessons of wisdom have never such power over us, as when they are wrought into the heart, through the groundwork of a story which engages the passions: Is it that we are like iron, and must first be heated before we can be wrought upon? or, Is the heart so in love with deceit, that where a true report will not reach it, we must cheat it with a fable, in order to come at truth?

Whether this parable of the prodigal (for so it is usually called)——is really such, or built upon some story known at that time in Jerusalem, is not much to the purpose; it is given us to enlarge upon, and turn to the best moral account we can.

"A certain man, says our SAVIOUR, had two sons, and the younger of them said to his father, Give me the portion of goods which falls to me: and he divided unto them his substance. And not many days after, the younger son gathered all together, and took his journey into a far country, and there wasted his substance with riotous living."

The account is short: the interesting and pathetic passages with which such a transaction would be necessarily connected, are left to be supplied by the heart:——the story is silent——but nature is not:——much kind advice, and many a tender expostulation would fall from the father's lips, no doubt, upon this occasion.

He would dissuade his son from the folly of so rash an enterprize, by shewing him the dangers of the journey,——the inexperience of his age,——the hazards his life, his fortune, his virtue would run, without a guide, without a friend: he would tell him of the many snares and temptations which he had to avoid, or encounter at every step,—the pleasures which would solicit him in every luxurious court,——the little knowledge he could gain—except that of evil: he would speak of the seductions of women,—their charms——their poisons:—what helpless indulgences he might give way to, when far from restraint, and the check of giving his father pain.

The dissuasive would but inflame his desire.——

He gathers all together.——

——I see the picture of his departure:——the camels and asses loaden with his substance, detached on one side of the piece, and already on their way:——the prodigal son standing on the foreground, with a forced sedateness, struggling against the fluttering movement of joy, upon his deliverance from restraint:——the elder brother holding his hand, as if unwilling to let it go:—the father,—sad moment! with a firm look, covering a prophetic sentiment, "that all would not go well with his child,"—— approaching to embrace him, and bid him adieu.——Poor inconsiderate youth! From whose arms art thou flying? From what a shelter art thou going forth into the storm? Art thou weary of a father's affection, of a father's care? or, Hopest thou to find a warmer interest, a truer counsellor, or a kinder friend, in a land of strangers, where youth is made a prey, and so many thousands are confederated to deceive them, and live by their spoils?

We will seek no further than this idea, for the extravagancies by which the prodigal son added one unhappy example to the number: his fortune wasted,——the followers of it fled in course, ——the wants of nature remain,—the hand of GOD gone forth against him,—"*For when he had spent all, a mighty famine arose in that country.*"—Heaven! have pity upon the youth, for he is in hunger and distress,——stray'd out of the reach of a parent, who counts every hour of his absence with anguish,—cut off from all his tender offices, by his folly,——and from relief and charity from others, by the calamity of the times.——

Nothing so powerfully calls home the mind as distress: the tense fibre then relaxes,——the soul retires to itself,——sits pensive and susceptible of right impressions: if we have a friend, 'tis then we think of him; if a benefactor, at that moment all his kindnesses press upon our mind.——Gracious and bountiful GOD! Is it not for this, that they who in their prosperity forget thee, do yet remember and return to thee in the hour of their sorrow? When our heart is in heaviness, upon whom can we think but thee, who knowest our necessities afar off,——puttest all our tears in thy bottle,——seest every careful thought,——hearest every sigh and melancholy groan we utter.——

Strange!——that we should only begin to think of GOD with

[677]

comfort,——when with joy and comfort we can think of nothing else.

Man surely is a compound of riddles and contradictions: by the law of his nature he avoids pain, and yet *unless he suffers in the flesh, he will not cease from sin* tho' it is sure to bring pain and misery upon his head for ever.

Whilst all went pleasurably on with the prodigal, we hear not one word concerning his father—no pang of remorse for the sufferings in which he had left him, or resolution of returning, to make up the account of his folly: his first hour of distress, seem'd to be his first hour of wisdom:——*When he came to himself, he said, How many hired servants of my father have bread enough and to spare, whilst I perish!*——

Of all the terrors of nature, that of one day or another dying by hunger, is the greatest, and it is wisely wove into our frame to awaken man to industry, and call forth his talents; and tho' we seem to go on carelessly, sporting with it as we do with other terrors——yet, he that sees this enemy fairly, and in his most frightful shape, will need no long remonstrance, to make him turn out of the way to avoid him.

It was the case of the prodigal—he arose to go unto his father.—

——Alas! How shall he tell his story? Ye who have trod this round, tell me in what words he shall give in to his father, the sad *Items* of his extravagance and folly?

——The feasts and banquets which he gave to whole cities in the east,——the costs of Asiatick rarities,——and of Asiatick cooks to dress them——the expences of singing men and singing women,——the flute, the harp, the sackbut, and of all kinds of musick—the dress of the Persian courts, how magnificent! their slaves how numerous——their chariots, their horses, their palaces, their furniture, what immense sums they had devoured!——what expectations from strangers of condition! what exactions!

How shall the youth make his father comprehend, that he was cheated at Damascus by one of the best men in the world;—— that he had lent a part of his substance to a friend at Nineveh, who had fled off with it to the Ganges;——that a whore of Babylon had swallowed his best pearl, and anointed the whole city with his balm of Gilead;——that he had been sold by a man of honour for twenty shekels of silver, to a worker in graven images; ——that the images he had purchased had profited him nothing; ——that they could not be transported across the wilderness, and had been burnt with fire at Shusan;——that the *apes and peacocks, which he had sent for from Tharsis, lay dead upon his hands; and that the mummies had not been dead long enough, which had been brought him out of Egypt:——that all had gone wrong since the day he forsook his father's house.

——Leave the story——it will be told more concisely.—— *When he was yet afar off, his father saw him,*———Compassion told it in three words—*he fell upon his neck and kissed him.*

Great is the power of eloquence: but never is it so great as when it pleads along with nature, and the culprit is a child strayed from his duty, and returned to it again with tears: Casuists may settle the point as they will: But what could a parent see more in the account, than the natural one, of an ingenuous heart too open for the world,——smitten with strong sensations of pleasures, and suffered to sally forth unarm'd into the midst of enemies stronger than himself?

Generosity sorrows as much for the over-matched, as pity herself does.

The idea of a son so ruin'd, would double the father's caresses: every effusion of his tenderness would add bitterness to his son's remorse.———"Gracious heaven! what a father have I rendered miserable!"

And he said, I have sinned against heaven, and in thy sight, and am no more worthy to be called thy son.

But the father said, Bring forth the best robe.——

O, ye affections! how fondly do you play at cross-purposes with each other?——'Tis the natural dialogue of true transport: joy is not methodical; and where an offender, beloved, over-charges itself in the offence,——words are too cold; and a conciliated heart replies by tokens of esteem.

And he said unto his servants, Bring forth the best robe and put it on him: and put a ring on his hand, and shoes on his feet, and bring hither the fatted calf, and let us eat and drink and be merry.

When the affections so kindly break loose, Joy, is another name for Religion.

We look up as we taste it: the cold Stoick without, when he hears the dancing and the musick, may ask sullenly, (with the elder brother) What it means; and refuse to enter: but the humane and compassionate all fly impetuously to the banquet, given *for a son who was dead and is alive again,—who was lost and is found.* Gentle spirits, light up the pavillion with a sacred fire;

* Vide 2 Chronicles ix. 21.

[679]

and parental love, and filial piety lead in the mask with riot and wild festivity!——Was it not for this that GOD gave man musick to strike upon the kindly passions; that nature taught the feet to dance to its movements, and as chief governess of the feast, poured forth wine into the goblet, to crown it with gladness?

The intention of this parable is so clear from the occasion of it, that it will not be necessary to perplex it with any tedious explanation: it was designed by way of indirect remonstrance to the Scribes and Pharisees, who animadverted upon our SAVIOUR's conduct, for entering so freely into conferences with sinners, in order to reclaim them. To that end, he proposes the parable of the shepherd, who left his ninety and nine sheep that were safe in the fold, to go and seek for one sheep that was gone astray,—telling them in other places, that they who were whole wanted not a physician,—but they that were sick:—and here, to carry on the same lesson, and to prove how acceptable such a recovery was to GOD, he relates this account of the prodigal son, and his welcome reception.

I know not whether it would be a subject of much edification to convince you here, that our SAVIOUR, by the prodigal son, particularly pointed at those who were *sinners of the Gentiles*, and were recovered by divine Grace to repentance;——and that by the elder brother, he intended as manifestly the more froward of the Jews, who envied their conversion, and thought it a kind of wrong to their primogeniture, in being made fellow-heirs with them of the promises of GOD.

These uses have been so ably set forth, in so many good sermons upon the prodigal son, that I shall turn aside from them at present, and content myself with some reflections upon that fatal passion which led him,—and so many thousands after the example, *to gather all he had together, and take his journey into a far country.*

The love of variety, or curiosity of seeing new things, which is the same, or at least a sister passion to it,—seems wove into the frame of every son and daughter of Adam; we usually speak of it as one of nature's levities, tho' planted within us for the solid purposes of carrying forwards the mind to fresh enquiry and knowledge: strip us of it, the mind (I fear) would doze for ever over the present page; and we should all of us rest at ease with such objects as presented themselves in the parish or province where we first drew our breath.

It is to this spur which is ever in our sides, that we owe the

impatience of this desire for travelling: the passion is no way bad,
—but as others are,—in it's mismanagement or excess;—order it
rightly the advantages are worth the pursuit; the chief of which
are——to learn the languages, the laws and customs, and understand the government and interest of other nations,—to acquire
an urbanity and confidence of behaviour, and fit the mind more
easily for conversation and discourse;—to take us out of the company of our aunts and grandmothers, and from the track of
nursery mistakes; and by shewing us new objects, or old ones in
new lights, to reform our judgments—by tasting perpetually the
varieties of nature, to know what *is good*——by observing the
address and arts of men, to conceive what *is sincere*,—and by
seeing the difference of so many various humours and manners,
——to look into ourselves and form our own.

This is some part of the cargo we might return with; but the
impulse of seeing new sights, augmented with that of getting clear
from all lessons both of wisdom and reproof at home—carries
our youth too early out, to turn this venture to much account; on
the contrary, if the scene painted of the prodigal in his travels,
looks more like a copy than an original,—will it not be well if
such an adventurer, with so unpromising a setting out,—without
carte,—without compass,—be not cast away for ever,—and may
he not be said to escape well—if he returns to his country, only as
naked, as he first left it?

But you will send an able pilot with your son—a scholar.—

If wisdom can speak in no other language but Greek or Latin,
—you do well—or if mathematicks will make a man a gentleman,—or natural philosophy but teach him to make a bow,—he
may be of some service in introducing your son into good
societies, and supporting him in them when he has done—but
the upshot will be generally this, that in the most pressing occasions of address,—if he is a mere man of reading, the unhappy
youth will have the tutor to carry,—and not the tutor to carry
him.

But you will avoid this extreme; he shall be escorted by one
who knows the world, not merely from books—but from his own
experience:—a man who has been employed on such services, and
thrice made the *tour of Europe, with success.*

—That is, without breaking his own, or his pupil's neck;—for
if he is such as my eyes have seen! some broken *Swiss valet de
chambre*,—some general undertaker, who will perform the journey in so many months "IF GOD PERMIT,"—much knowledge will

[681]

not accrue;—some profit at least,—he will learn the amount to a halfpenny, of every stage from Calais to Rome;—he will be carried to the best inns,—instructed where there is the best wine, and sup a livre cheaper than if the youth had been left to make the tour and the bargain himself.—Look at our governor! I beseech you:—see, he is an inch taller as he relates the advantages.—

—And here endeth his pride—his knowledge and his use.

But when your son gets abroad, he will be taken out of his hand, by his society with men of rank and letters, with whom he will pass the greatest part of his time.

Let me observe in the first place,—that company which is really good, is very rare—and very shy: but you have surmounted this difficulty; and procured him the best letters of recommendation to the most eminent and respectable in every capital.—

And I answer, that he will obtain all by them, which courtesy strictly stands obliged to pay on such occasions,—but no more.

There is nothing in which we are so much deceived, as in the advantages proposed from our connections and discourse with the literati, &c. in foreign parts; especially if the experiment is made before we are matured by years or study.

Conversation is a traffick; and if you enter into it, without some stock of knowledge, to balance the account perpetually betwixt you,—the trade drops at once: and this is the reason,——however it may be boasted to the contrary, why travellers have so little (especially good) conversation with natives,—owing to their suspicion,—or perhaps conviction, that there is nothing to be extracted from the conversation of young itinerants, worth the trouble of their bad language,—or the interruption of their visits.

The pain on these occasions is usually reciprocal; the consequence of which is, that the disappointed youth seeks an easier society; and as bad company is always ready,—and ever lying in wait,—the career is soon finished; and the poor prodigal returns the same object of pity, with the prodigal in the gospel.

PRIDE

LUKE XIV 10, 11

*But thou, when thou art bidden, go and sit down in the lowest room,
that when he that bad thee cometh, he may say to thee, Friend, go
up higher, then shalt thou have worship in the presence of them who
sit at meat with thee: for whosoever exalteth himself, shall be
abased; and he that humbleth himself, shall be exalted.*

IT is an exhortation of our SAVIOUR's to Humility, addressed
by way of inference from what he had said in the three
foregoing verses of the chapter; where, upon entering into
the house of one of the chief Pharisees to eat bread, and marking
how small a portion of this necessary virtue entered in with the
several guests, discovering itself from their choosing the chief
rooms, and most distinguished places of honour;——he takes
the occasion which such a behaviour offered, to caution them
against Pride;——states the inconvenience of the passion;—
shews the disappointments which attend it;——the disgrace in
which it generally ends; in being forced at last, to recede from
the pretensions to what is more than our due; which, by the
way, is the very thing the passion is eternally promoting us to
expect. When, therefore, thou art bidden to a wedding, says
our SAVIOUR, sit not down in the highest room, lest a more
honourable man than thou be bidden of him; and he that bad
thee and him, come and say to thee,—Give this man place:
and thou begin with shame to take the lowest room.
——But thou, when thou art bidden, go and sit down in the
lowest room:——hard lecture!—In the lowest room?—What,
——do I owe nothing to myself? Must I forget my station, my
character in life? Resign the precedence which my birth, my
fortune, my talents, have already placed me in possession of?
—give all up! and suffer inferiors to take my honour? Yes;—
for that, says our SAVIOUR, is the road to it: *For when he that
bad thee cometh, he will say to thee, Friend, go up higher; then
shalt thou have worship in the presence of them who sit at meat
with thee:—for whosoever exalteth himself, shall be abased; and
he that humbleth himself, shall be exalted.*

[683]

To make good the truth of which declaration, it is not necessary we should look beyond this life, and say, That in that day of retribution, wherein every high thing shall be brought low, and every irregular passion dealt with as it deserves;—that pride, amongst the rest, (considered as a vicious character) shall meet with it's proper punishment of being abased, and lying down for ever in shame and dishonour.——It is not necessary we should look so far forwards for the accomplishment of this: the words seem not so much to imply the threat of a distant punishment, the execution of which was to be respited to that day;—as the declaration of a plain truth depending upon the natural course of things, and evidently verified in every hour's commerce of the world; from whence, as well as from our reasoning upon the point, it is found, That Pride lays us open to so many mortifying encounters, which Humility in its own nature rests secure from,——that verily, each of them, in this world, have their reward faithfully dealt out by the natural workings of men's passions; which, tho' very bad executioners in general, yet are so far just ones in this, that they seldom suffer the exultations of an insolent temper to escape the abasement, or the deportment of a humble one to fail of the honour, which each of their characters do deserve.

In other vicious excesses which a man commits, the world (tho' it is not much to its credit) seems to stand pretty neuter: if you are extravagant or intemperate, you are looked upon as the greatest enemy to yourself;——or if an enemy to the public, ——at least, you are so remote a one to each individual, that no one feels himself immediately concerned in your punishment: but in the instances of pride, the attack is personal: for as this passion can only take its rise from a secret comparison, which the party has been making of himself to my disadvantage, every intimation he gives me of what he thinks of the matter, is so far a direct injury, either as it with-holds the respect which is my due,——or perhaps denies me to have any; or else, which presses equally hard, as it puts me in mind of the defects which I really have, and of which I am truly conscious, and consequently think myself the less deserving of an admonition: in every one of which cases, the proud man, in whatever language he speaks it, ——if it is expressive of this superiority over me, either in the gifts of fortune, the advantages of birth or improvements, as it has proceeded from a mean estimation and possibly a very unfair one of the like pretensions in myself,—the attack, I say, is personal; and has generally the fate to be felt and resented as such.

So that with regard to the present inconveniencies, there is scarce any vice bating such as are immediately punished by laws, which a man may not indulge with more safety to himself, than this one of pride;—the humblest of men, not being so entirely void of the passion themselves, but that they suffer so much from the overflowings of it in others, as to make the literal accomplishments of the text, a common interest and concern: in which they are generally successful,—the nature of the vice being such, as not only to tempt you to it, but to afford the occasions itself of its own humiliation.

The proud man,——see!—he is sore all over; touch him—— you put him to pain: and tho' of all others, he acts as if every mortal was void of all sense and feeling, yet is possessed with so nice and exquisite a one himself, that the slights, the little neglects and instances of disesteem, which would be scarce felt by another man, are perpetually wounding him, and oft times piercing him to his very heart.

I would not therefore be a proud man, was it only for this, that it should not be in the power of every one who thought fit—to chastise me;—my other infirmities, however unworthy of me, at least will not incommode me:—so little discountenance do I see given to them, that it is not the world's fault, if I suffer by them: ——but here——if I exalt myself, I have no prospect of escaping; ——with this vice I stand swoln up in every body's way, and must unavoidably be thrust back: whichever way I turn, whatever step I take under the direction of this passion, I press unkindly upon some one, and in return, must prepare myself for such mortifying repulses, as will bring me down, and make me go on my way sorrowing.

This is from the nature of things, and the experience of life as far back as Solomon, whose observation upon it was the same, —and it will ever hold good, *that before honour was humility, and a haughty spirit before a fall.—Put not therefore thyself forth in the presence of the king, and stand not in the place of great men:— for better is it——*(which by the way is the very dissuasive in the text)——*better is it, that it be said unto thee, Friend, come up higher, than that thou shouldst be put lower in the presence of the prince whom thine eyes have seen.*

Thus much for the illustration of this one argument of our SAVIOUR's, against Pride:—there are many other considerations which expose the weakness of it, which his knowledge of the heart of man might have suggested; but as the particular occasion which gave rise to this lecture of our SAVIOUR's against Pride, naturally led him to speak of the mortifications which attend such instances of it, as he then beheld:——for this reason the other arguments might be omitted, which perhaps in a set discourse would be doing injustice to the subject. I shall therefore, in the remaining part of this, beg leave to offer some other considerations of a moral as well as a religious nature upon this subject, as so many inducements to check this weak passion in man; which, tho' one of the most inconvenient of his infirmities,——the most painful and discourteous to society, yet by a sad fatality, so it is, that there are few vices, except such whose temptations are immediately seated in our natures, to which there is so general a propensity throughout the whole race.

This had led some satyrical pens to write, That all mankind at the bottom were proud alike;—that one man differed from another, not so much in the different portions which he possessed of it, as in the different art and address by which he excels in the management and disguise of it to the world. We trample, no doubt too often, upon the pride of Plato's mantle, with as great a pride of our own; yet on the whole the remark has more spleen than truth in it; there being thousands, (if any evidence is to be allowed) of the most unaffected humility, and truest poverty of spirit, which actions can give proof of. Notwithstanding this, so much may be allowed to the observation, That Pride is a vice which grows up in society so insensibly;—steals in unobserved upon the heart upon so many occasions;—forms itself upon such strange pretentions, and when it has done, veils itself under such a variety of unsuspected appearances,—sometimes even under that of Humility itself;—in all which cases, Self-love, like a false friend, instead of checking, most treacherously feeds this humour, ——points out some excellence in every soul to make him vain, and think more highly of himself, than he ought to think;—— that upon the whole, there is no one weakness into which the heart of man is more easily betray'd,——or which requires greater helps of good sense and good principles to guard against.

And first, the root from which it springs, is no inconsiderable discredit to the fruit.

If you look into the best moral writers, who have taken pains to search into the grounds of this passion,—they will tell you, That Pride is the vice of little and contracted souls;—that whatever affectation of greatness it generally wears and carries in the looks, there is always meanness in the heart of it:——a haughty and an abject temper, I believe, are much nearer a-kin than they will acknowledge;—like *poor* relations, they look a little shy at one another at first sight, but trace back their pedigree, they are but collateral branches from the same stem; and there is scarce any one who has not seen many such instances of it, as one of our poets alludes to, in that admirable stroke he has given of this affinity, in his description of a *Pride which licks the dust.*

As it has *meanness* at the bottom of it,—so it is justly charged with having *weakness* there too, of which it gives the strongest proof, in regard to the chief end it has in view, and the absurd means it takes to bring it about.

Consider a moment,—What is it the proud man aims at?—— Why,—such a measure of respect and deference, as is due to his superior merit, &c. &c.

Now, good sense and a knowledge of the world shew us, that how much soever of these are due to a man, allowing he has made a right calculation,—they are still dues of such a nature, that they are not to be insisted upon: Honour and Respect must be a *Free-will offering:* treat them otherwise, and claim them from the world as a tax,—they are sure to be withheld; the first discovery of such an expectation disappoints it, and prejudices your title to it for ever.

To this speculative argument of it's weakness, it has generally the ill fate to add another of a more substantial nature, which is matter of fact; that to turn giddy upon every little exaltation, is experienced to be no less a mark of a *weak brain* in the figurative, than it is in the literal sense of the expression—in sober truth, 'tis but a scurvy kind of a trick (*quoties voluit Fortuna jocari*)— when Fortune in one of her merry moods, takes a poor devil with this passion in his head, and mounts him up all at once as high as she can get him—for it is sure to make him play such phantastick tricks, as to become the very fool of the comedy; and was he not a general benefactor to the world in making it merry, I know not how Spleen could be pacified during the representation.

A third argument against Pride is the natural connection it has with vices of an unsocial aspect: the Scripture seldom introduces it alone—Anger, or Strife, or Revenge, or some inimical passion, is ever upon the stage with it; the proofs and reasons of which I have not time to enlarge on, and therefore shall say no more upon this argument than this,—that was there no other,—yet the bad company this vice is generally found in, would be sufficient by itself to engage a man to avoid it.

Thus much for the moral considerations upon this subject; a great part of which, as they illustrate chiefly the inconveniencies of Pride in a social light may seem to have a greater tendency to make men guard the appearances of it, than conquer the passion itself, and root it out of their nature: to do this effectually we must add the arguments of religion, without which, the best moral discourse may prove little better than a cold political lecture, taught merely to govern the passion so as not to be injurious to a man's present interest or quiet; all which a man may learn to practise well enough, and yet at the same time be a perfect stranger to the best part of humility, which implies not a concealment of Pride, but an absolute conquest over the first risings of it which are felt in the heart of man.

And first, one of the most persuasive arguments which religion offers to this end, is that which arises from the state and condition of ourselves, both as to our natural and moral imperfections. It is impossible to reflect a moment upon this hint, but with a heart full of the humble exclamation, *O God! what is man!— even a thing of nought*—a poor, infirm, miserable, short-lived creature, that passes away like a shadow, and is hastening off the stage where the theatrical titles and distinctions, and the whole mask of Pride which he has worn for a day will fall off, and leave him naked as a neglected slave. Send forth your imagination, I beseech you, to view the last scene of the greatest and proudest who ever awed and governed the world—see the empty vapour disappearing! one of the arrows of mortality this moment sticks fast within him: see—it forces out his life, and freezes his blood and spirits.

—Approach his bed of state—lift up the curtain—regard a moment with silence—

—are these cold hands and pale lips, all that is left of him who was canoniz'd by his own pride, or made a god of, by his flatterers?

O my soul! with what dreams hast thou been bewitched? how hast thou been deluded by the objects thou hast so eagerly grasped at?

If this reflection from the natural imperfection of man, which he cannot remedy, does nevertheless strike a damp upon human Pride, much more must the considerations do so, which arise from the wilful depravations of his nature.

Survey yourselves, my dear Christians, a few moments in this light—behold a disobedient, ungrateful, intractable and disorderly set of creatures, going wrong seven times in a day,—acting sometimes every hour of it against your own convictions—your own interests, and the intentions of your GOD, who wills and proposes nothing but your happiness and prosperity—what reason does this view furnish you for Pride? how many does it suggest to mortify and make you ashamed?—well might the son of Syrach say in that sarcastical remark of his upon it, *That* PRIDE *was not made for man*—for some purposes, and for some particular beings, the passion might have been shaped—but not for him—fancy it where you will, 'tis no where so improper—'tis in no creature so unbecoming—

—But why so cold an assent, to so incontested a truth?—Perhaps thou hast reasons to be proud:—for heaven's sake let us hear them.—Thou hast the advantages of birth and title to boast of—or thou standest in the sunshine of court favour—or thou hast a large fortune—or great talents—or much learning—or nature has bestowed her graces upon thy person——speak—on which of these foundations hast thou raised this fanciful structure?——Let us examine them.

Thou art well born;—then trust me, 'twill pollute no one drop of thy blood to be humble: humility calls no man down from his rank,—divests not princes of their titles; it is in life, what the *clear obscure* is in painting; it makes the hero step forth in the canvas, and detaches his figure from the group in which he would otherwise stand confounded for ever.

If thou art rich—then shew the greatness of thy fortune,—or what is better, the greatness of thy soul in the meekness of thy conversation; condescend to men of low estate,——support the distressed, and patronize the neglected.——Be great; but let it be in considering riches as they are; *as talents committed to an earthen vessel*—That thou art but the *receiver*,—and that to be obliged and be vain too,—is but the old solecism of pride and beggary, which, tho' they often meet,—yet ever make but an absurd society.

If thou art powerful in interest, and standest deified by a servile tribe of dependants,—why shouldst thou be proud,——because they are hungry?——Scourge me such sycophants; they have turned the heads of thousands as well as thine.—

—But 'tis thy own dexterity and strength which have gained thee this eminence:—allow it; but art thou proud, that thou

[689]

standest in a place where thou art the mark of one man's envy, another man's malice, or a third man's revenge,—where good men may be ready to suspect thee, and whence bad men will be ready to pull thee down. I would be proud of nothing that is uncertain: Haman was so, because he was admitted alone to queen Esther's banquet; and the distinction raised him,—but it was fifty cubits higher than he ever dream'd or thought of.

Let us pass on to the pretences of learning, &c. &c. If thou hast a little, thou wilt be proud of it in course: if thou hast much, and good sense along with it, there will be no reason to dispute against the passion: a beggarly parade of remnants is but a sorry object of Pride at the best;—but more so, when we can cry out upon it, as the poor man did of his hatchet,—* *Alas! Master,—for it was borrowed.*

It is treason to say the same of Beauty,—whatever we do of the arts and ornaments with which Pride is wont to set it off: the weakest minds are most caught with both; being ever glad to win attention and credit from small and slender accidents, thro' disability of purchasing them by better means. In truth, Beauty has so many charms, one knows not how to speak against it; and when it happens that a graceful figure is the habitation of a virtuous soul,—when the beauty of the face speaks out the modesty and humility of the mind, and the justness of the proportion raises our thoughts up to the art and wisdom of the great Creator,—something may be allowed it,—and something to the embellishments which set it off;—and yet, when the whole apology is read,—it will be found at last, that Beauty like Truth, never is so glorious as when it goes the plainest.

Simplicity is the great friend to nature, and if I would be proud of any thing in this silly world, it should be of this honest alliance.

Consider what has been said; and may the GOD of all mercies and kindness watch over your passions, and inspire you *with all humbleness of mind, meekness, patience, and long suffering.*—— Amen.

---

* 2 Kings vi. 7.

A Selection
FROM
THE LETTERS

Lydia de Medalle published three volumes of her father's letters, *Letters of the late Rev. Mr. Laurence Sterne, To his most intimate Friends*, 1775. This was the best and largest collection of Sterne's letters to appear in the period immediately following his death, and it has been mainly drawn upon in the following selection. Two years previously, in 1775, ten love-letters from Sterne to Mrs. Elizabeth Draper had been published under the title of *Letters from Yorick to Eliza*, and three of these have been selected. Numerous single letters, and several editions of the collected letters, appeared at various times throughout the following century; but most of these editions included many forgeries. The definitive edition is *The Letters of Laurence Sterne*, edited by L. P. Curtis, Clarendon Press, 1935. This text has been used for the present edition, for which thanks are due to Mr. Curtis and the Clarendon Press.

The authenticity of the letter opposite is suspect. Lydia de Medalle is the only authority for its text, which, as Mr. Curtis has shown, is very closely paralleled in Sterne's *Journal to Eliza* for 19–27 April, 1767. It therefore seems that either the *Journal* was a repetition of this much earlier letter, or, more likely, Lydia de Medalle extracted the letter from the *Journal* and published it as one of her father's letters to her mother.

To Elizabeth Lumley

[? *1739/40*]

YOU bid me tell you, my dear L. how I bore your departure
for S[taffordshire], and whether the valley where D'Estella
stands retains still its looks—or, if I think the roses or
jessamines smell as sweet, as when you left it—Alas! every thing
has now lost its relish, and look! The hour you left D'Estella
I took to my bed.—I was worn out with fevers of all kinds, but
most by that fever of the heart with which thou knowest well
I have been wasting these two years—and shall continue wasting
'till you quit S[taffordshire]. The good Miss S——, from the fore-
bodings of the best of hearts, thinking I was ill, insisted upon my
going to her.—What can be the cause, my dear L. that I never
have been able to see the face of this mutual friend, but I feel
myself rent to pieces? She made me stay an hour with her, and in
that short space I burst into tears a dozen different times—and in
such affectionate gusts of passion that she was constrained to
leave the room, and sympathize in her dressing room.—I have
been weeping for you both, said she, in a tone of the sweetest
pity—for poor L's heart I have long known it—her anguish is as
sharp as yours—her heart as tender—her constancy as great—
her virtues as heroic—Heaven brought you not together to be
tormented. I could only answer her with a kind look, and a heavy
sigh—and return'd home to your lodgings (which I have hired
'till your return) to resign myself to misery—Fanny had prepared
me a supper—she is all attention to me—but I sat over it with
tears; a bitter sauce, my L. but I could eat it with no other—for
the moment she began to spread my little table, my heart fainted
within me.—One solitary plate, one knife, one fork, one glass!—
I gave a thousand pensive, penetrating looks at the chair thou
hadst so often graced, in those quiet, and sentimental repasts—
then laid down my knife, and fork, and took out my handkerchief, and clapped it across my face, and wept like a child.—
I do so this very moment, my L. for as I take up my pen my poor
pulse quickens, my pale face glows, and tears are trickling down
upon the paper, as I trace the word L—. O thou! blessed in
thyself, and in thy virtues—blessed to all that know thee—to
me most so, because more do I know of thee than all thy sex.—
This is the philtre, my L. by which thou hast charmed me, and
by which thou wilt hold me thine whilst virtue and faith hold

[693]

this world together.—This, my friend, is the plain and simple magick by which I told Miss —— I have won a place in that heart of thine, on which I depend so satisfied, that time, or distance, or change of every thing which might alarm the hearts of little men, create no uneasy suspence in mine—Wast thou to stay in S[taffordshire] these seven years, thy friend, though he would grieve, scorns to doubt, or to be doubted—'tis the only exception where security is not the parent of danger.—I told you poor Fanny was all attention to me since your departure—contrives every day bringing in the name of L. She told me last night (upon giving me some hartshorn) she had observed my illness began the very day of your departure for S[taffordshire]; that I had never held up my head, had seldom, or scarce ever smiled, had fled from all society—that she verily believed I was broken-hearted, for she had never entered the room, or passed by the door, but she heard me sigh heavily—that I neither eat, or slept, or took pleasure in any thing as before;—judge then, my L. can the valley look so well—or the roses and jessamines smell so sweet as heretofore? Ah me!—But adieu—the vesper bell calls me from thee to my God!

L. STERNE

To Elizabeth Lumley

[? *1739/40*]

YES! I will steal from the world, and not a babbling tongue shall tell where I am—Echo shall not so much as whisper my hiding place—suffer thy imagination to paint it as a little sun-gilt cottage on the side of a romantic hill—dost thou think I will leave love and friendship behind me? No! they shall be my companions in solitude, for they will sit down, and rise up with me in the amiable form of my L.—we will be as merry, and as innocent as our first parents in Paradise, before the arch fiend entered that undescribable scene.

The kindest affections will have room to shoot and expand in our retirement, and produce such fruit, as madness, and envy, and ambition have always killed in the bud.—Let the human tempest and hurricane rage at a distance, the desolation is beyond the horizon of peace.—My L. has seen a Polyanthus blow in December—some friendly wall has sheltered it from the biting wind.—No planetary influence shall reach us, but that which presides and cherishes the sweetest flowers.—God preserve us, how delightful this prospect in idea! We will build, and we will plant, in our own way—simplicity shall not be tortured by art— we will learn of nature how to live—she shall be our alchymist, to mingle all the good of life into one salubrious draught.— The gloomy family of care and distrust shall be banished from our dwelling, guarded by thy kind and tutelar deity—we will sing our choral songs of gratitude, and rejoice to the end of our pilgrimage.

Adieu, my L. Return to one who languishes for thy society.

L. STERNE

To Elizabeth Lumley

[? *1739/40*]

BEFORE now my L. has lodged an indictment against me in the high court of Friendship—I plead guilty to the charge, and intirely submit to the mercy of that amiable tribunal.— Let this mitigate my punishment, if it will not expiate my transgression—do not say that I shall offend again in the same manner, though a too easy pardon sometimes occasions a repitition of the same fault.—A miser says, though I do no good with my money to-day, to-morrow shall be marked with some deed of beneficence—The Libertine says, let me enjoy this week in forbidden and luxurious pleasures, and the next I will dedicate to serious thought and reflection.—The Gamester says, let me have one more chance with the dice and I will never touch them more.— The Knave of every profession wishes to obtain but independency, and he will become an honest man.—The Female Coquette triumphs in tormenting her inamorato, for fear, after marriage, he should not pity her.

The apparition of the fifth instant, (for letters may almost be called so) proved more welcome as I did not expect it. Oh! my L—, thou art kind indeed to make an apology for me, and thou never wilt assuredly repent of one act of kindness—for being thy debtor, I will pay thee with interest.—Why does my L. complain of the desertion of friends?—Where does the human being live that will not join in this complaint?—It is a common observation, and perhaps too true, that married

people seldom extend their regards beyond their own fireside.—
There is such a thing as parsimony in esteem, as well as money—
yet as the one costs nothing, it might be bestowed with more
liberality.—We cannot gather grapes from thorns, so we must not
expect kind attachments from persons who are wholly folded up
in selfish schemes.—I do not know whether I most despise, or
pity such characters—nature never made an unkind creature—
ill usage, and bad habits, have deformed a fair and lovely
creation.

My L.!—thou art surrounded by all the melancholy gloom of
winter; wert thou alone, the retirement would be agreeable.—
Disappointed ambition might envy such a retreat, and disappointed love would seek it out.—Crouded towns, and busy
societies, may delight the unthinking, and the gay—but solitude
is the best nurse of wisdom.—Methinks I see my contemplative
girl now in the garden, watching the gradual approaches of
spring.—Do'st not thou mark with delight the first vernal buds?
the snow-drop, and primrose, these early and welcome visitors,
spring beneath thy feet.—Flora and Pomona already consider
thee as their handmaid; and in a little time will load thee with
their sweetest blessing.—The feathered race are all thy own, and
with them, untaught harmony will soon begin to cheer thy
morning and evening walks.—Sweet as this may be, return—
return—the birds of Yorkshire will tune their pipes, and sing as
melodiously as those of Staffordshire.

Adieu, my beloved L. thine too much for my *peace*,

L. STERNE

To Elizabeth Lumley

[? *1739/40*]

I HAVE offended her whom I so tenderly love!—what could
tempt me to it! but if a beggar was to knock at thy gate,
wouldst thou not open the door and be melted with compassion. —I know thou wouldst, for Pity has erected a temple in
thy bosom.—Sweetest, and best of all human passions! let thy
web of tenderness cover the pensive form of affliction, and soften
the darkest shades of misery! I have re-considered this apology,
and, alas! what will it accomplish? Arguments, however finely

spun, can never change the nature of things—very true—so a truce with them.

I have lost a very valuable friend by a sad accident, and what is worse, he has left a widow and five young children to lament this sudden stroke.—If real usefulness and integrity of heart, could have secured him from this, his friends would not now be mourning his untimely fate.—These dark and seemingly cruel dispensations of Providence, often make the best of human hearts complain.—Who can paint the distress of an affectionate mother, made a widow in a moment, weeping in bitterness over a numerous, helpless, and fatherless offspring?—God! these are thy chastisements, and require (hard task!) a pious acquiescence.

Forgive me this digression, and allow me to drop a tear over a departed friend; and what is more excellent, an honest man. My L! thou wilt feel all that kindness can inspire in the death of ———— The event was sudden, and thy gentle spirit would be more alarmed on that account.—But my L. thou hast less to lament, as old age was creeping on, and her period of doing good, and being useful, was nearly over.—At sixty years of age the tenement gets fast out of repair, and the lodger with anxiety thinks of a discharge.—In such a situation the poet might well say

"The soul uneasy, &c."

My L. talks of leaving the country—may a kind angel guide thy steps hither.—Solitude at length grows tiresome. Thou sayest thou wilt quit the place with regret—I think so too.— Does not something uneasy mingle with the very reflection of leaving it? It is like parting with an old friend, whose temper and company one has long been acquainted with.—I think I see you looking twenty times a day at the house—almost counting every brick and pane of glass, and telling them at the same time with a sigh, you are going to leave them.—Oh happy modification of matter! they will remain insensible of thy loss.—But how wilt thou be able to part with thy garden?—The recollection of so many pleasing walks must have endeared it to you. The trees, the shrubs, the flowers, which thou reared with thy own hands— will they not droop and fade away sooner upon thy departure. —Who will be the successor to nurse them in thy absence.— Thou wilt leave thy name upon the myrtle-tree.—If trees, and shrubs, and flowers, could compose an elegy, I should expect a very plaintive one upon this subject.

Adieu, adieu. Believe me ever, ever thine,

L. STERNE

[697]

To ——————

[*Summer, 1759*]

Dear Sir

I HAVE rec^d Your kind Letter of critical, and I will add of Paternal Advice too, which contrary to My Natural humour, set Me upon looking gravely & thinking gravely for half a day together. Sometimes I concluded You had Not spoke out, but had stronger grounds for Your hints & cautions, than what your good Nature knew well how to tell me—especially with regard to Prudence, as a divine;—and that You thought in your heart the vein of humour too free & gay for the solemn colour of My coat—A meditation upon Death had been a more suiting trimming to it (I own it)—but then it Could not have been set on by Me.

Mr Fothergil, whom I regard in the Class I do you, as My best of Criticks & well wishers—preaches daily to Me Upon Your Text—"get Your Preferment first Lory! he says—& then Write & Welcome" But suppose preferment is long acoming (& for aught I know I may not be preferr'd till the Resurrection of the Just) and am all that time in labour—how must I bear my Pains? —You both fright me with after-pains (like pious Divines) or rather like able Philosophers, knowing that One Passion is only to be combated by Another.

But to be serious if I can—I will use all reasonable caution— Only with this caution along with it, not to spoil My Book; —that is the air and originality of it, which must resemble the Author—& I fear 'tis a Number of these slighter touches which Mark this resemblance & Identify it from all Others of the [same] Stamp—Which this understrapping Virtue of Prudence woud Oblige Me to strike out.—A Very Able Critick & One of My Colour too—who has Read Over tristram—Made Answer Upon My saying I Would consider the colour of My Coat, as I corrected it—That that very Idea in My head would render My Book not worth a groat—still I promise to be Cautious—but I deny I have gone as farr as Swift—He keeps a due distance from Rabelais—& I keep a due distance from him—Swift has said a hundred things I durst Not Say—Unless I was Dean of St. Patricks—

I like Your Caution of the Ambitiosa recidet ornamenta—as I revise My book, I will shrive My conscience upon that sin &

What ever Ornaments are of that kind shall be defac'd Without Mercy.

Ovid is justly condemn'd in being Ingenij sui Amator—and it is a seasonable hint to Me, as I am Not sure I am clear of it—to Sport too Much with Your wit—or the Game that wit has pointed is surfeiting—like toying with a Mans Mistress—it may be a Very delightful Solacement to the Inamorato—tho little to the bystander.

Tho I plead guilty to a part of this Charge Yet twould greatly alleviate the Crime—If My Readers knew how Much I suppress'd of this desire—I have Burn'd More wit, then I have publish'd Upon that very Acc^t—since I began to Avoid the Very fault I fear I may have Yet given Proofs of. I will reconsider Slops fall & my too Minute Account of it—but in general I am perswaded that the happiness of the Cervantic humour arises from this very thing—of describing silly and trifling Events, with the Circumstatial Pomp of great Ones—perhaps this is Overloaded—& I can soon ease it—

I have a project of getting Tristram put into the ABishops hands, if he comes down this Autumn, Which will ease my conscience of all troubles Upon the Topick of Discretion—

I am, dear Sir Most trucly Y^r
Obliged
LAWRENCE STERNE

To Dr. * * * * *

[? *York*,] *Jan. 30, 1760*

Dear Sir,

—**D**E MORTUIS NIL NISI BONUM, is a maxim which you have so often of late urged in conversation, and in your letters, (but in your last especially) with such seriousness, and severity against me, as the supposed transgressor of the rule; —that you have made me at length as serious and severe as yourself:—but that the humours you have stirred up might not work too potently within me, I have waited four days to cool myself, before I would set pen to paper to answer you, "*de mortuis nil nisi bonum.*" I declare I have considered the wisdom, and foundation of it over and over again, as dispassionately and charitably as a good Christian can, and, after all, I can find nothing in it, or make more of it, than a nonsensical lullaby of some nurse, put into Latin by some pedant, to be chanted by some hypocrite to the end of the world, for the consolation of departing lechers.—'Tis, I own, Latin; and I think that is all the weight it has—for, in plain English, 'tis a loose and futile position below a dispute—"*you are not to speak any thing of the dead, but what is good.*" Why so?—Who says so?—neither reason or scripture. —Inspired authors have done otherwise—and reason and common sense tell me, that if the characters of past ages and men are to be drawn at all, they are to be drawn like themselves; that is, with their excellencies, and with their foibles—and it is as much a piece of justice to the world, and to virtue too, to do the one, as the other.—The ruleing passion *et les egarements du cœur*, are the very things which mark, and distinguish a man's character; —in which I would as soon leave out a man's head as his hobby-horse.—However, if like the poor devil of a painter, we must conform to this pious canon, *de mortuis*, &c. which I own has a spice of piety in the *sound* of it, and be obliged to paint both our angels and our devils out of the same pot—I then infer that our Sydenhams, and Sangrados, our Lucretias,—and Massalinas, our Sommers, and our Bolingbrokes—are alike entitled to statues, and all the historians, or satirists who have said otherwise since they departed this life, from Sallust, to S[tern]e, are guilty of the crimes you charge me with, "cowardice and injustice."

But why cowardice? "because 'tis not courage to attack a dead man who can't defend himself."—But why do you doctors of the faculty attack such a one with your incision knife? Oh! for the good of the living.—'Tis my plea.—But I have something more to say in my behalf—and it is this—I am not guilty of the charge —tho' defensible. I have not cut up Doctor Kunastrokius at all —I have just scratch'd him—and that scarce skin-deep. I do him first all honour—speak of Kunastrokius as a great man—(be he who he will) and then most distantly hint at a drole foible in his character—and that not first reported (to the few who can even understand the hint) by me—but known before by every chamber-maid and footman within the bills of mortality—but Kunastrokius, you say, was a great man—'tis that very circumstance which makes the pleasantry—for I could name at this instant a score of honest gentlemen who might have done the very thing which Kunastrokius did, and seen no joke in it at all—as to the failing of Kun[a]strokius, which you say can only be imputed to his friends as a misfortune—I see nothing like a misfortune in it to any friend or relation of Kunastrokius—that Kunastrokius upon occasions should sit with *** **** and *******—I have put these stars not *to hurt your worship's delicacy*—If Kunastrokius after all is too sacred a character to be even smiled at, (which is all I have done) he has had better luck than his betters:—In the same page (without imputation of cowardice) I have said as much of a man of twice his wisdom—and that is Solomon, of whom I have made the same remark "That they were both great men—and like all mortal men had each their ruling passion."

—The consolation you give me, "That my book however will be read enough to answer my design of raising a tax upon the public"—is very unconsolatory—to say nothing how very mortifying! by h[eave]n! an author is worse treated than a common ***** at this rate—"*You will get a penny by your sins, and that's enough.*"—Upon this chapter let me comment.—That I proposed laying the world under contribution when I set pen to paper—is what I own, and I suppose I may be allow'd to have that view in my head in common with every other writer, to make my labour of advantage to myself.

Do not you do the same? but I beg I may add, that whatever views I had of that kind, I had other views—the first of which was, the hopes of doing the world good by ridiculing what I thought deserving of it—or of disservice to sound learning, &c.—how I have succeeded my book must shew—and this I leave entirely to the world—but not to that little world *of your acquaintance*, whose opinion, and sentiments you call the general opinion of the best judges *without exception*, who all affirm (you say) that my book cannot be put into the hands of any woman of *character*. (I hope you except widows, doctor—for they are not *all* so squeamish—but I am told they are all really of my party in return for some good offices done their interests in the 176th page of my second volume) But for the chaste married, and chaste unmarried part of the sex—they must not read my book! Heaven forbid the stock of chastity should be lessen'd by the life and opinions of Tristram Shandy—yes, his opinions—it would certainly debauch 'em! God take them under his protection in this fiery trial, and send us plenty of Duenas to watch the workings of their humours, 'till they have safely got thro' the whole work.—If this will not be sufficient, may we have plenty of Sangrados to pour in plenty of cold water, till this terrible fermentation is over—as for the *nummum in loculo*, which you

mention to me a second time, I fear you think me very poor, or
in debt—I thank God tho' I don't abound—that I have enough for
a clean shirt every day—and a mutton chop—and my contentment with this, has thus far (and I hope ever will) put me above
stooping an inch for it, for—estate.—Curse on it, I like it not to
that degree, nor envy (*you may be sure*) any man who kneels in
the dirt for it—so that howsoever I may fall short of the ends
proposed in commencing author—I enter this *protest*, first that
my end was *honest*, and secondly, that I wrote not [to] be *fed*,
but to be *famous*. I am much obliged to Mr. Garrick for his
very favourable opinion—but why, dear Sir, had he done better
in finding fault with it than in commending it? to humble me? an
author is not so soon humbled as you imagine—no, but to make
the book better by castrations—that is still *sub judice*, and I can
assure you upon this chapter, that the very passages, and descriptions you propose, that I should sacrifice in my second edition,
are what are best relish'd by men of wit, and some others whom
I esteem as sound cricks—so that upon the whole, I am still
kept up, if not above fear, at least above despair, and have seen
enough to shew me the folly of an attempt of castrating my book
to the prudish humours of particulars. I believe the short cut
would be to publish this letter at the beginning of the third
volume, as an apology for the first and second. I was sorry to
find a censure upon the insincerity of some of my friends—
I have no reason myself to reproach any one man—my friends
have continued in the same opinions of my books which they
first gave me of it—many indeed have thought better of 'em,
by considering them more; few worse.

    I am, Sir,
     Your humble servant,
        LAURENCE STERNE

To My
Witty Widow, Mrs. F[enton]

Coxwould, Aug. 3, 1760

Madam,

WHEN a man's brains are as dry as a squeez'd Orange,—
and he feels he has no more conceit in him than a Mallet,
'tis in vain to think of sitting down, and writing a letter
to a lady of your wit, unless in the honest John-Trot-Style of,
yours of the 15th instant came safe to hand, &c. which by the by,
looks like a Letter of Business, and you know very well, from the
first letter I had the honour to write to you, I am a man of no
business at all. This vile plight I found my Genius in, was the
reason I have told Mr. Bains, I would not write to you, till the
next post—hoping by that time to get some small recruit, at least
of Vivacity, if not wit, to set out with;—but upon second thoughts,
thinking a bad letter in season—to be better than a good one out
of it—this scrawl is the consequence, which, if you will burn the
moment you get it—I promise to send you a fine set Essay in the
Stile of your female Epistolizers, cut and trim'd at all points.
—God defend me from such, who never yet knew what it was to
say or write one premeditated word in my whole life—for this
reason I send yours with pleasure, because wrote with the careless irregularity of an easy heart.—Who told you Garrick wrote
the medley for Baird?—'Twas wrote in his house, however, and
before I left town.—I deny it I was not lost two days before I left
town—I was lost all the time I was there, and never found till
I got to this Shandy-castle of mine.—Next winter I intend to
sojourn amongst you with more decorum, and will neither be
lost nor found any where.

Now I wish to God, I was at your elbow—I have just finished
one volume of Shandy, and I want to read it to some one who
I know can taste and rellish humour—this by the way, is a little
impudent in me—for I take the thing for granted, which their
high Mightinesses the World have yet to determine—but I mean
no such thing—I could wish only to have your opinion—shall I, in
truth, give you mine?—I dare not—but I will; provided you keep
it to yourself—know then, that I think there is more laughable
humour,—with equal degree of Cervantik Satyr—if not more than
in the last—but we are bad Judges of the merit of our Children.

I return you a thousand thanks for your friendly congratulations upon my habitation—and I will take care, you shall never wish me but well, for I am, Madam,

With great esteem and truth,

Your most obliged,

L. STERNE

P.S. I have wrote this so vily and so precipitately, I fear you must carry it to a decypherer—I beg you'll do me the honour to write—otherwise you draw *me* in, instead of Mr. Bains drawing *you* into a scrape—for I should sorrow to have a taste of so agreeable a Correspondent—and no more.

Adieu.

To John Hall-Stevenson

Coxwould, [*June*], 1761

Dear H[all],

I REJOICE you are in London—rest you there in peace; here 'tis the devil.—You was a good prophet.—I wish myself back again, as you told me I should—but not because a thin death-doing pestiferous north-east wind blows in a line directly from crazy-castle turret full upon me in this cuckoldly retreat, (for I value the north-east wind and all its powers not a straw) —but the transition from rapid motion to absolute rest was too violent.—I should have walked about the streets of York ten days, as a proper medium to have passed thro', before I entered upon my rest.—I staid but a moment, and I have been here but a few, to satisfy me I have not managed my miseries like a wise man—and if God, for my consolation under them, had not poured forth the spirit of Shandeism into me, which will not suffer me to think two moments upon any grave subject, I would else, just now lay down and die—die—and yet, in half an hour's time, I'll lay a guinea, I shall be as merry as a monkey—and as mischievous too, and forget it all—so that this is but a copy of the present train running cross my brain.—And so you think this cursed stupid—but that, my dear H[all] depends much upon the quotâ horâ of your shabby clock, if the pointer of it is in any quarter between ten in the morning or four in the afternoon— I give it up—or if the day is obscured by dark engendering clouds of either wet or dry weather, I am still lost—but who knows but it may be five—and the day as fine a day as ever shone upon the earth since the destruction of Sodom—and peradventure your honour may have got a good hearty dinner to-day, and eat and drank your intellectuals into a placidulish and a blandulish amalgama—to bear nonsense, so much for that.

'Tis as cold and churlish just now, as (if God had not pleased it to be so) it ought to have been in bleak December, and therefore I am glad you are where you are, and where (I repeat it again) I wish I was also—Curse of poverty, and absence from those we love!—they are two great evils which embitter all things —and yet with the first I am not haunted much.—As to matrimony, I should be a beast to rail at it, for my wife is easy—but the world is not—and had I staid from her a second longer it would have been a burning shame—else she declares herself happier without me—but not in anger is this declaration made— but in pure sober good-sense, built on sound experience—she hopes you will be able to strike a bargain for me before this time twelvemonth, to lead a bear round Europe: and from this hopes from you, I verily believe it is, that you are so high in her favour at present—She swears you are a fellow of wit, though humourous; a funny jolly soul, though somewhat splenetic; and (bating the love of women) as honest as *gold*—how do you like the simile?—Oh, Lord! now are you going to Ranelagh to-night, and I am sitting, sorrowful as the prophet was when the voice cried out to him and said, "What do'st thou here, Elijah?"-- 'Tis well the spirit does not make the same at Coxwold—for unless for the few sheep left me to take care of, in this wilderness, I might as well, nay better, be at Mecca—When we find we can by a shifting of places, run away from ourselves, what think you of a jaunt there, before we finally pay a visit to the *vale of Jehosophat*—As ill a fame as we have, I trust I shall one day or other see you face to face—so tell the two colonels, if they love good company, to live righteously and soberly as *you do*, and then they will have no doubts or dangers within, or without them —present my best and warmest wishes to them, and advise the eldest to prop up his spirits, and get a rich dowager before the conclusion of the peace—why will not the advice suit both, par nobile fratrum?

To-morrow morning, (if Heaven permit) I begin the fifth volume of Shandy—I care not a curse for the critics—I'll load my vehicle with what goods *he* sends me, and they may take 'em off my hands, or let them alone—I am very valourous—and 'tis in proportion as we retire from the world and see it in its true dimensions, that we despise it—no bad rant!—God above bless you! You know I am

Your affectionate Cousin,

LAURENCE STERNE

What few remain of the Demoniacs, greet—and write me a letter, if you are able, as foolish as this.

To Lady ———

Coxwold, Sept, 21, 1761

I RETURN to my new habitation, fully determined to write as hard as can be, and thank you most cordially, my dear lady, for your letter of congratulation upon my Lord Fauconberg's having presented me with the curacy of this place—though your congratulation comes somewhat of the latest, as I have been possessed of it some time.—I hope I have been of some service to his Lordship, and he has sufficiently requited me.—'Tis seventy guineas a year in my pocket, though worth a hundred—but it obliges me to have a curate to officiate at Sutton and Stillington.—'Tis within a mile of his Lordship's seat, and park. 'Tis a very agreeable ride out in the chaise, I purchased for my wife.—Lyd has a poney which she delights in.—Whilst they take these diversions, I am scribbling away at my Tristram. These two volumes are, I think, the best.—I shall write as long as I live, 'tis, in fact, my hobby-horse: and so much am I delighted with my uncle Toby's imaginary character, that I am become an enthusiast.—My Lydia helps to copy for me—and my wife knits and listens as I read her chapters.—The coronation of his Majesty (whom God preserve!) has cost me the value of an Ox, which is to be roasted whole in the middle of the town, and my parishioners will, I suppose, be very merry upon the occasion. —You will then be in town—and feast your eyes with a sight, which 'tis to be hoped will not be in either of our powers to see again—for in point of age we have about twenty years the start of his Majesty.—And now, my dear friend, I must finish this—and with every wish for your happiness conclude myself your most sincere well-wisher and friend,

L. STERNE

To Mrs. Sterne

Paris, March 17, 1762

My Dear,——

HAVING an opportunity of writing by a physician, who is posting off for London to-day, I would not omit doing it, though you will possibly receive a letter (which is gone from hence last post) at the very same time. I send to Mr. Foley's every mail-day, to inquire for a letter from you; and if I do not get one in a post or two, I shall be greatly surprised and disappointed. A terrible fire happened here last night, the whole fair of St. Germain's burned to the ground in a few hours; and hundreds of unhappy people are now going crying along the streets, ruined totally by it. This fair of St. Germain's is built upon a spot of ground covered and tiled, as large as the Minster Yard, entirely of wood, divided into shops, and formed into little streets, like a town in miniature. All the artizans in the kingdom come with their wares—jewellers, silversmiths,—and have free leave from all parts of the world to profit by a general licence from the Carnival to Easter. They compute the loss at six millions of livres, which these poor creatures have sustained, not one of which have saved a single shilling, and many fled out in their shirts, and have not only lost their goods and merchandize, but all the money they have been taking these six weeks. *Oh! ces moments de malheur sont terribles,* said my barber to me, as he was shaving me this morning; and the good-natured fellow uttered it with so moving an accent, that I could have found in my heart to have cried over the perishable and uncertain tenure of every good in this life.

I have been three mornings together to hear a celebrated pulpit orator near me, one Père Clement, who delights me much; the parish pays him 600 livres for a dozen sermons this Lent; he is K. Stanislas's preacher—most excellent indeed! his matter solid, and to the purpose; his manner, more than theatrical, and greater, both in his action and delivery, than Madame Clairon, who, you must know, is the Garrick of the stage here; he has infinite variety, and keeps up the attention by it wonderfully; his pulpit, oblong, with three seats in it, into which he occasionally casts himself; goes on, then rises, by a gradation of four steps, each of which he profits by, as his discourse inclines him: in short, 'tis a stage, and the variety of his tones would make you imagine there were no less than five or six actors on it together.

I was last night at Baron de Bagg's concert; it was very fine, both music and company; and to-night I go to the Prince of Conti's. There is Monsieur Popèlinière, who lives here like a sovereign prince; keeps a company of musicians always in his house, and a full set of players; and gives concerts and plays alternately to the grandees of this metropolis; he is the richest of all the farmer[s general]; he did me the honour last night to send me an invitation to his house, while I stayed here—that is, to his music and table.

I suppose you had terrible snows in Yorkshire, from the accounts I read in the London papers. There has been no snow here, but the weather has been sharp; and was I to be all the day in my room, I could not keep myself warm for a shilling a day. This is an expensive article to great houses here—'tis most pleasant and most healthy firing; I shall never bear coals I fear again; and if I can get wood at Coxwold, I will always have a little. I hope Lydia is better, and not worse, and that I shall hear the same account of you. I hope my Lydia goes on with her French; I speak it fast and fluent, but incorrect both in accent and phrase; but the French tell me I speak it most surprisingly well for the time. In six weeks I shall get over all difficulties, having got over one of the worst, which is to understand whatever is said by others, which I own I found much trouble in at first.

My love to my Lyd—. I have got a colour into my face now, though I came with no more than there is in a dishclout.

I am your affectionate

L. STERNE

For Mrs. Sterne at York.

To David Garrick

Paris, March 19, 1762

Dear G[arrick].

THIS will be put into your hands by Doctor Shippen, a physician, who has been here some time with Miss Poyntz, and is this moment setting off for your metropolis, so I snatch the opportunity of writing to you and my kind friend Mrs. G[arrick].—I see nothing like her here, and yet I have been

ntroduced to one half of their best Goddesses, and in a month
more shall be admitted to the shrines of the other half—but
I neither worship—or fall (much) upon my knees before them;
but on the contrary, have converted many unto Shandeism—for
be it known I Shandy it away fifty times more than I was ever
wont, talk more nonsense than ever you heard me talk in your
days—and to all sorts of people. *Qui le diable est ce homme là*—
said Choiseul, t'other day—ce Chevalier Shandy—You'll think
me as vain as a devil, was I to tell you the rest of the dialogue
—whether the bearer knows it or no, I know not—'Twill serve
up after supper, in Southampton-street, amongst other small
dishes, after the fatigues of Richard the IIId—O God! they have
nothing here, which gives the nerves so smart a blow, as those
great characters in the hands of G[arrick]! but I forgot I am
writing to the man himself—The devil take (as he will) these
transports of enthusiasm! apropos—the whole City of Paris is
bewitch'd with the comic opera, and if it was not for the affairs
of the Jesuits, which takes up one half of our talk, the comic
opera would have it all—It is a tragical nuisance in all companies
as it is, and was it not for some sudden starts and dashes—of
Shandeism, which now and then either breaks the thread, or
entangles it so, that the devil himself would be puzzled in winding
it off—I should die a martyr—this by the way I never will—

I send you over some of these comic operas by the bearer,
with the *Sallon*, a satire—The French comedy, I seldom visit
it—they act scarce any thing but tragedies—and the Clairon is
great, and Mad^lle. Dumesnil, in some places, still greater than
her—yet I cannot bear preaching—I fancy I got a surfeit of it in
my younger days. There is a tragedy to be damn'd to-night—
peace be with it, and the gentle brain which made it! I have ten
thousand things to tell you, I cannot write—I do a thousand
things which cut no figure, *but in the doing*—and as in London,
I have the honour of having done and said a thousand things
I never did or dream'd of—and yet I dream abundantly—If the
devil stood behind me in the shape of a courier, I could not write
faster than I do, having five letters more to dispatch by the same
Gentleman; he is going into another section of the globe, and
when he has seen you, he will depart in peace.

The Duke of Orleans has suffered my portrait to be added to
the number of some odd men in his collection; and a gentleman
who lives with him has taken it most expressively, at full length
—I purpose to obtain an etching of it, and to send it you—your

[709]

prayer for me of *rosy health*, is heard—If I stay here for three or four months, I shall return more than reinstated. My love to Mrs. G[arrick].

I am, my dear G[arrick]
Your most humble Servant,

L. STERNE

To Lord Fauconberg

Paris, Ap: 10. 1762

My Lord

MR. WILCOX the late Bishop of Rochester's Son, passing thro' this place, in his return from Italy, has given me an opportunity of troubling y^r Lordship with the Inclosed for Lady Catherine. I did myself the honour of writing a long Letter to Y^r Lordship dated the 11th of Feby from St Germains where I retired for a week w^h young Mr Fox; but I suppose that Letter never reach'd y^r Lordship, because 5 others sent by that post have all miscarried—thank God there was no Treason in any one of them. by all acc^{ts} you had a most dismal foggy winter in Town, had I continued there I had certainly been six weeks ago in my grave—the winter indeed has been extreamly severe here—but the air clear always & Elastick, & not one foggy day (which is not the Case, I believe, always) so that I have gradually been regaining my health, & on the mending hand ever since I came; this was so remarkable the first 3 Weeks that the Faculty advised me to stay where I was, & not go southwards, so long as I felt I gain'd ground where I was: by this, together with the great civilities I have met with from the french, I have been trail'd on till now in this metropolis, where I purposed to have continued till the end of May, & return'd home thro' Holland: I am told however by the Faculty here, I shall most certainly be where I was again, the next winter—If I do not give time for my Lungs to strengthen, by going down to Thoulouse & spending one winter free from coughs & colds; after wch they say, they shall look upon my Cure as compleat: this I should not regard on my own Account, but fear I shall be compell'd to it on my Girl's, who, my wife writes me word, & has done some time, is in a declining way with this vile Asthma of hers, which these last 3 winters has been growing worse & worse, & that unless something more

[710]

than bare Medecines can be done for her, she will be lost, & that the only chance for her is to try what one Winter in a warmer climate will do for her: this obliges me to wait here till they join me, & to go down & fix them at Toulouse where I have taken a little house w^h a large Garden, in the pleasantest part of the Town; & in case I find myself very well when I have fix'd them there, shall return—if not, stay the winter thro', & come back in may following.

I beg pardon, my Lord, for troubling you with this long & particular acc^t about myself & my affairs; but I thought it my duty to tell you my Situation—my family, my Lord, is a very small machine; but it has many wheels in it; & I am forced too often to turn them about,—not as I would—but as I can.

I could never have been in France at so critical a period, as this, when two of the greatest Concerns that ever affected the Interest of this kingdome are upon the Anvil together—the Affair of the Jesuists—& the War—for, much of this kingdoms future glory & wellfare seems to be depending upon these two great points—the first takes up the attention of the french, much more than the last—& well it may—for in this city alone, the Society have a rent of 95,000 pounds a year—what must their revenues be, from the whole Kingdome?—It will end, I trow, like our Henry y^e 8$^{th's}$, in a gen^l Resumption—

If y^t Lordship has not read *Le Compte rendu de Constitutions de Jusuists*, 'tis well worth y^r perusal; by this time I suppose it must have got to England. I hope y^r Lordship has had y^r health this winter; I wish it, as I do every other blessing to you & y^r family, with the zeal & truth wch becomes me.

   I am my Lord
    Y^r ever obliged & faithful Servt

        L. STERNE

To David Garrick

Paris, April [19], 1752

My dear G[arrick].

I SNATCH the occasion of Mr. Wilcox (the late Bishop of Rochester's son) leaving this place for England, to write to you, and I enclose it to Hall, who will put it into your hand, possibly behind the scenes. I hear no news of you, or your *empire*, I would have said *kingdom*—but here every thing is hyperbolized—and if a woman is but simply pleased—'tis *Je suis charmée*—and if she is charmed 'tis nothing less, than that she is *ravi*-sh'd—and when ravi-sh'd, (which may happen) there is nothing left for her but to fly to the other world for a metaphor, and swear, qu'elle etoit toute *extasiée*—which mode of speaking, is, by the bye, here creeping into use, and there is scarce a woman who understands the *bon ton*, but is seven times in a day in downright extasy—that is, the devil's in her—by a small mistake of one world for the other—Now, where am I got?

I have been these two days reading a tragedy, given me by a lady of talents, to read and conjecture if it would do for you— 'Tis from the plan of Diderot, and possibly half a translation of it—The Natural Son, or, the Triumph of Virtue, in five acts— It has too much sentiment in it, (at least for me) the speeches too long, and savour too much of *preaching*—this may be a second reason, it is not to my taste—'Tis all love, love, love, throughout, without much separation in the character; so I fear it would not do for your stage, and perhaps for the very reason which recommend[s] it to a French one.—After a vile suspension of three weeks—we are beginning with our comedies and operas again—yours I hear never flourished more—here the comic actors were never so low—the tragedians hold up their heads—in all senses. I have known *one little man* support the theatrical world, like a David Atlas, upon his shoulders, but Preville can't do half as much here, though Mad. Clairon stands by him, and sets her back to his—she is very great, however, and highly improved since you saw her—she also supports her dignity at table, and has her public day every Thursday, when she *gives to eat*, (as they say here) to all that are hungry and dry.

You are much talked of here, and much expected as soon as the peace will let you—these two last days you have happened to engross the whole conversation at two great houses where

TO DAVID GARRICK

I was at dinner—'Tis the greatest problem in nature, in this meridian, that one and the same man should possess such tragic and comic powers, and in such an equilibrio, as to divide the world for which of the two nature intended him.

Crebillion has made a convention with me, which, if he is not too lazy, will be no bad *persiflage*—as soon as I get to Thoulouse he has agreed to write me an expostulat[o]ry letter upon the indecorums of T. Shandy—which is to be answered by recrimination upon the liberties in his own works—these are to be printed together—Crebillion against Sterne—Sterne against Crebillion—the copy to be sold, and the money equally divided —This is good Swiss-policy.

I am recovered greatly, and if I could spend one whole winter at Toulouse, I should be fortified, in my inner man, beyond all danger of relapsing.—A sad asthma my daughter has been martyr'd with these three winters, but mostly this last, makes it, I fear, necessary she should try the last remedy of a warmer and softer air, so I am going this week to Versailles, to wait upon Count Choiseul to solicit passports for them—If this system takes place, they join me here—and after a month's stay we all decamp for the south of France—if not, I shall see you in June next. Mr. Fox, and Mr. Macartny, having left Paris, I live altogether in French families—I laugh 'till I cry, and in the same tender moments *cry 'till I laugh*. I Shandy it more than ever, and verily do believe, that by mere Shandeism sublimated by a laughter-loving people, I fence as much against infirmities, as I do by the benefit of air and climate. Adieu, dear G[arrick] present ten thousand of my best respects and wishes to and for my friend Mrs. G[arrick]—had she been last night upon the Tulleries, she would have annihilated a thousand French goddesses, *in one single turn*.

I am most truly,

my dear friend,

L. STERNE

To Mrs. Sterne

Paris, [May] 16th 1762

My Dear,

I T IS a thousand to one that this reaches you before you have set out—However I take the chance—you will receive one wrote last night, the moment you get to Mr. E[dmonds] and to wish you joy of your arrival in town—to that letter which you will find in town, I have nothing to add that I can think on—for I have almost drain'd my brains dry upon the subject.—For God sake rise early and gallop away in the cool—and always see that you have not forgot your baggage in changing post-chaises—You will find good tea upon the road from York to Dover—only bring a little to carry you from Calais to Paris—give the Custom-House officers what I told you —at Calais give more, if you have much Scotch snuff—but as tobacco is good here, you had best bring a Scotch mill and make it yourself, that is, order your valet to manufacture it—'twill keep him out of mischief.—I would advise you to take three days in coming up, for fear of heating yourselves—See that they do not give you a bad vehicle, when a better is in the yard, but you will look sharp—drink small Rhenish to keep you cool, (that is if you like it.) Live well and deny yourselves nothing your hearts wish. So God in heav'n prosper and go along with you—kiss my Lydia, and believe me both affectionately,

Yours,

L. STERNE

To Mrs. Sterne

Paris, [May] 31, 1762

My Dear,

T HERE have no mails arrived here 'till this morning, for three posts, so I expected with great impatience a letter from you and Lydia—and lo! it is arrived. You are as busy as Throp's wife, and by the time you receive this, you will be busier still—I have exhausted all my ideas about your journey— and what is needful for you to do before and during it—so I write only to tell you I am well—Mr. Colebrooks, the minister of Swisserland's secretary, I got this morning to write a letter for you to the governor of the Custom-House-Office, at Calais—

[714]

it shall be sent you next post.—You must be cautious about Scotch snuff—take half a pound in your pocket, and make Lyd do the same. 'Tis well I bought you a chaise—there is no getting one in Paris now, but at an enormous price—for they are all sent to the army, and such a one as yours we have not been able to match for forty guineas; for a friend of mine who is going from hence to Italy—the weather was never known to set in so hot, as it has done the latter end of this month, so he and his party are to get into his chaises by four in the morning, and travel 'till nine—and not stir out again till six; but I hope this severe heat will abate by the time you come here—however I beg of you once more to take special care of heating your blood in travelling and come *tout doucement*, when you find the heat too much— I shall look impatiently for intelligence from you, and hope to hear all goes well; that you conquer all difficulties, that you have received your pass-port, my picture, &c. Write and tell me something of every thing. I long to see you both, you may be assured, my dear wife and child, after so long a separation—and write me a line directly, that I may have all the notice you can give me, that I may have apartments ready and fit for you when you arrive. —For my own part I shall continue writing to you a fortnight longer—present my respects to all friends—you have bid Mr. C[roft] get my visitations at P[ickering] done for me, &c. &c. If any offers are made about the inclosure at Rascal, they must be enclosed to me—nothing that is fairly proposed shall stand still on my score. Do all for the best, as He who guides all things, will I hope do for us—so heav'n preserve you both—believe me

Your affectionate

L. STERNE

Love to my Lydia—I have bought her a gold watch to present to her when she comes.

To Mrs. Sterne

Paris, June 7, 1762

My Dear,

I KEEP my promise and write to you again—I am sorry the bureau must be open'd for the deeds—but you will see it done—I imagine you are convinced of the necessity of bringing three hundred pounds in your pocket—if you consider, Lydia must have two slight negligees—you will want a new gown or two—as for painted linens buy them in town, they will be more admired because English than French.—Mrs. H[odges] writes me word that I am mistaken about buying silk cheaper at Toulouse, than Paris, that she advises you to buy what you want here—where they are very beautiful and cheap, as well as blonds, gauzes, &c.—these I say will all cost you sixty guineas—and you must have them—for in this country nothing must be spared for the back—and if you dine on an onion, and lay in a garret seven stories high, you must not betray it in your cloaths, according to which you are well or ill look'd on. When we are got to Toulouse, we must begin to turn the penny, and we may, (if you do not game much) live very cheap—I think that expression will divert you—and now God knows I have not a wish but for your health, comfort, and safe arrival here—write to me every other post, that I may know how you go on—you will be in raptures with your chariot—Mr. R. a gentleman of fortune, who is going to Italy, and has seen it, has offered me thirty guineas for my bargain.—You will wonder all the way, how I am to find room in it for a third—to ease you of this wonder, 'tis by what the coach-makers here call a cave, which is a second bottom added to that you set your feet upon which lets the person (who sits over-against you) down with his knees to your ancles, and by which you have all more room—and what is more, less heat—because his head does not intercept the fore-glass little or nothing—Lyd and I will enjoy this by turns; sometimes I shall take a bidet—(a little post horse) and scamper before—at other times I shall sit in fresco upon the arm-chair without doors, and one way or other will do very well.—I am under infinite obligations to Mr. Thornhil, for accommodating me thus, and so genteely, for 'tis like making a present of it.—Mr. T[hornhill] will send you an order to receive it at Calais—and now, my dear girls, have I forgot any thing?

Adieu, adieu!

Yours most affectionately,

L. STERNE

A week or ten days will enable you to see every thing—and so long you must stay to rest your bones.

To Mrs. Sterne

Paris, June 14, 1762

My dearest,

HAVING an opportunity of writing by a friend who is setting out this morning for London, I write again, in case the two last letters I have wrote this week to you should be detained by contrary winds at Calais—I have wrote to Mr. E[dmonds], by the same hand, to thank him for his kindness to you in the handsomest manner I could—and have told him, his good heart, and his wife's, have made them overlook the trouble of having you at his house, but that if he takes you apartments near him they will have occasion still enough left to shew their friendship to us—I have begged him to assist you, and stand by you as if he was in my place with regard to the sale of the Shandys—and then the copy-right—Mark to keep these things distinct in your head—but Becket I have ever found to be a man of probity, and I dare say you will have very little trouble in finishing matters with him—and I would rather wish you to treat with him than with another man—but whoever buys the fifth and sixth volumes of Shandy's, must have the nay-say of the seventh and eighth.—I wish, when you come here, in case the weather is too hot to travel, you could think it pleasant to go to the Spaw for four or six weeks, where we should live for half the money we should spend at Paris—after that we should take the sweetest season of the vintage to go to the south of France—but we will put our heads together, and you shall just do as you please in this, and in every thing which depends on me—for I am a being perfectly contented, when others are pleased—to bear and forbear will ever be my maxim—only I fear the heats through a journey of five hundred miles for you, and my Lydia, more than for myself.—Do not forget the watch chains—bring a couple for a gentleman's watch likewise, we shall lie under great obligations to the Abbé M[acCarthy] and must make him such a small acknowledgement; according to my way of flourishing, 'twill be a present worth a kingdom to him—They have bad pins, and vile needles here—bring for yourself, and some for presents —as also a strong bottle-skrew, for whatever Scrub we may hire as butler, coachman, &c. to uncork us our Frontiniac—You will find a letter for you at the Lyon D'Argent—Send for your chaise into the court-yard, and see all is tight—Buy a chain at Calais

[717]

strong enough not to be cut off, and let your portmanteau be tied on the forepart of your chaise for fear of a dog's trick—so God bless you both, and remember me to my Lydia,

I am yours affectionately,

L. STERNE

To Mrs. Sterne

Paris, June [17], 1762

My dearest,

PROBABLY you will receive another letter with this, by the same post, if so read this the last—It will be the last you can possibly receive at York, for I hope it will catch you just as you are upon the wing—if that should happen, I suppose in course you have executed the contents of it, in all things which relate to pecuniary matters, and when these are settled to your mind, you will have got thro' your last difficulty—every thing else will be a step of pleasure, and by the time you have got half a dozen stages you will set up your pipes and sing Te Deum together, as you whisk it along.—Desire Mr. C[roft] to send me a proper letter of attorney by you, he will receive it back by return of post. You have done every thing well with regard to our Sutton and Stillington affairs, and left things in the best channel —if I was not sure you must have long since got my picture, garnets, &c. I would write and scold Mr. T[ollet] abominably —he put them in Becket's hands to be forwarded by the stage coach to you as soon as he got to town.—I long to hear from you, and that all my letters and things are come safe to you, and then you will say that I have not been a bad lad—for you will find I have been writing continually as I wished you to do—Bring your silver coffee-pot, 'twill serve both to give water, lemonade, and orjead—to say nothing of coffee and chocolate, which, by the bye, is both cheap and good at Toulouse, like other things— I had like to have forgot a most necessary thing, there are no copper tea-kettles to be had in France, and we shall find such a thing the most comfortable utensil in the house—buy a good strong one, which will hold two quarts—a dish of tea will be of comfort to us in our journey south—I have a bronze tea-pot, which we will carry also, as China cannot be brought over from England, we must make up a villainous party-coloured tea equipage to regale ourselves, and our English friends whilst we

[718]

are at Toulouse—I hope you have got your bill from Becket.—
There is a good natured kind of a trader I have just heard of,
at Mr. Foley's, who they think will be coming off from England
to France, with horses, the latter end of June. He happened to
come over with a lady, who is sister to Mr. Foley's partner, and
I have got her to write a letter to him in London, this post, to beg
he will seek you out at Mr. E[dmonds]'s, and in case a cartel ship
does not go off before he goes, to take you under his care. He
was infinitely friendly in the same office last year to the lady who
now writes to him, and nursed her on ship-board, and defended
her by land with great good-will.—Do not say I forget you, or
whatever can be conducive to your ease of mind, in this journey
—I wish I was with you to do these offices myself, and to strew
roses on your way—but I shall have time and occasion to shew
you I am not wanting—Now, my dears, once more pluck up
your spirits—trust in God—in me—and in yourselves—with this,
was you put to it, you would encounter all these difficulties ten
times told—Write instantly, and tell me you triumph over all
fears; tell me Lydia is better, and a helpmate to you—You say
she grows like me—let her shew me she does so in her contempt
of small dangers, and fighting against the apprehensions of them,
which is better still. As I will not have F.'s share of the books,
you will inform him so—Give my love to Mr. Fothergill, and to
those true friends which Envy has spared me—and for the rest,
laissés passer—You will find I speak French tolerably—but I only
wish to be understood.—You will soon speak better; a month's
play with a French Demoiselle will make Lyd chatter it like
a magpye. Mrs. [Hodges] understood not a word of it when she
got here, and writes me word she begins to prate a pace—you
will do the same in a fortnight—Dear Bess, I have a thousand
wishes, but have a hope for every one of them—You shall chant
the same *jubilate*, my dears, so God bless you. My duty to
Lydia, which implies my love too.

Adieu, believe me

Your affectionate,

L. STERNE

Memorandum: Bring watch-chains, tea-kettle, knives, cookery
book, &c.

You will smile at this last article—so adieu—At Dover the
Cross Keys, at Calais at the Lyon D'Argent—the master a Turk
in grain.

[719]

To Lady D.

Paris, July 9, 1762

I WILL not send your ladyship the trifles you bid me purchase without a line. I am very well pleased with Paris—indeed I meet with so many civilities amongst the people here that I must sing their praises—the French have a great deal of urbanity in their composition, and to stay a little time amongst them will be agreeable.—I splutter French so as to be understood—but I have had a droll adventure here in which my Latin was of some service to me—I had hired a chaise and a horse to go about seven miles into the country, but, *Shandean like*, did not take notice that the horse was almost dead when I took him—Before I got half way the poor animal dropp'd down dead—so I was forced to appear before the Police, and began to tell my story in French, which was, that the poor beast had to do with a worse beast than himself, namely *his master*, who had driven him all the day before (Jehu like) and that he had neither had corn, or hay, therefore I was not to pay for the horse—but I might as well have whistled, as have spoke French, and I believe my Latin was equal to my uncle Toby's Lilabulero—being not understood because of it's purity, but by dint of words I forced my judge to do me justice—no common thing by the way in France.— My wife and daughter are arrived—the latter does nothing but look out of the window, and complain of the torment of being frizled.—I wish she may ever remain a child of nature—I hate children of art.

I hope this will find your ladyship well—and that you will be kind enough to direct to me at Toulouse, which place I shall set out for very soon. I am, with truth and sincerity,

Your Ladyship's

Most faithful,

L. STERNE

To John Hall-Stevenson

Toulouse, August 12, 1762

My dear H[all].

B Y THE time you have got to the end of this long letter you will perceive that I have not been able to answer your last 'till now—I have had the intention of doing it almost as often as my prayers in my head—'tis thus we use our best friends —what an infamous story is that you have told me!—After some little remarks on it the rest of my letter will go on like silk. ****——is a good natured old easy fool and has been deceived by the most artful of her sex, and she must have abundance of impudence and charlatanery to have carried on such a farce. I pity the old man for being taken in for so much money—a man of sense I should have laughed at—My wife saw her when in town, and she had not the appearance of poverty, but when she wants to melt **** heart she put her gold watch and diamond rings in her drawer.—But he might have been aware of her. I could not have been mistaken in her character—and 'tis odd she should talk of her wealth to one, and tell another the reverse—so good night to her.—About a week or ten days before my wife arrived at Paris I had the same accident I had at Cambridge, of breaking a vessel in my lungs. It happen'd in the night, and I bled the bed full, and finding in the morning I was likely to bleed to death, I sent immediately for a surgeon to bleed me at both arms—this saved me, and with lying speechless three days I recovered upon my back in bed; the breach healed, and in a week after I got out —This with my weakness and hurrying about made me think it high time to haste to Toulouse.—We have had four months of such heats that the oldest Frenchman never remembers the like —'twas as hot as *Nebuchadnezzar's oven,* and never has relaxed one hour—in the height of this 'twas our destiny (or rather destruction) to set out by way of Lyons, Montpellier, &c. to shorten, I trow, our sufferings—Good God!—but tis over— and here I am in my own house, quite settled by M[acCarthy]'s aid, and good-natured offices, for which I owe him more than I can express or know how to pay at present—'Tis in the prettiest situation in Toulouse, with near two acres of garden—the house too good by half for us—well furnished, for which I pay thirty pounds a year.—I have got a good cook—my wife a decent *femme de chambre,* and a good looking *laquais*—The Abbé has planned our expences, and set us in such a train, we cannot easily go wrong—tho' by the bye the D[evil] is seldom found sleeping under a hedge. Mr. Trotter dined with me the day before I left Paris—I took care to see all executed according to your directions—but Trotter, I dare say, by this has wrote to you— I made him happy beyond expression with your crazy tales, and more so with its frontispiece.—I am in spirits, writing a crazy chapter—with my face turned towards thy turret—'Tis now I wish all warmer climates, countries, and every thing else at—that separates me from our paternal seat—*ce sera là où reposera ma cendre—et ce sera là où mon cousin viendra repandre les pleurs dues à notre amitié.*—I am taking asses milk three times a day, and cows milk as often—I long to see thy face again once more— greet the Col. kindly in my name, and thank him cordially from me for his many civilities to Madame and Mademoiselle Shandy at York, who send all due acknowledgments. The humour is over for France, and Frenchmen, but that is not enough for your affectionate cousin,

L. S.

(A year will tire us all out I trow) but thank heaven the post brings me a letter from my Anthony—I felicitate you upon what Messrs. the Reviewers allow you—they have too much judgement themselves not to allow you what you are actually possess'd of, "talents, wit and humour."—Well, write on my dear cousin, and be guided by thy own fancy.—Oh! how I envy you all at Crazy Castle!—I could like to spend a month with you—and should return back again for the vintage.—I honour the man that has given the world an idea of our parental seat—'tis well done—I look at it ten times a day with a *quando te aspiciam?*—Now farewell—remember me to my beloved Col.—greet Panty most lovingly on my behalf, and if Mrs. C[haloner] and Miss C[haloner] &c. are at G[uisborough], greet them likewise with a holy kiss—So God bless you.

To Robert Foley

Toulouse, August 14, 1762

My dear F[oley].

AFTER many turnings (*alias* digressions) to say nothing of downright overthrows, stops, and delays, we have arrived in three weeks at Toulouse, and are now settled in our houses with servants, &c. about us, and look as composed as if we had been here seven years.—In our journey we suffered so much from the heats, it gives me pain to remember it—I never saw a cloud from Paris to Nismes half as broad as a twenty-four sols piece.—Good God! we were toasted, roasted, grill'd, stew'd and carbonaded on one side or other all the way—and being all done enough (*assez cuits*) in the day, we were eat up at night by bugs, and other unswept out vermin, the legal inhabitants (if length of possession gives right) of every inn we lay at.— Can you conceive a worse accident than that in such a journey, in the hottest day and hour of it, four miles from either tree or shrub which could cast a shade of the size of one of Eve's fig leaves—that we should break a hind wheel into ten thousand pieces, and be obliged in consequence to sit five hours on a gravelly road, without one drop of water or possibility of getting any—To mend the matter, my two postillions were two dough-hearted fools, and fell a crying—Nothing was to be done! By heaven, quoth I, pulling off my coat and waistcoat, something shall be done, for I'll thrash you both within an inch of your lives — and then make you take each of you a horse, and ride like two devils to the next post for a cart to carry my baggage, and a wheel to carry ourselves—our luggage weighed ten quintals— 'twas the fair of Baucaire—all the world was going, or returning —we were ask'd by every soul who pass'd by us, if we were going to the fair of Baucaire—No wonder, quoth I, we have goods enough! *vous avez raison mes amis*—

Well! here we are after all, my dear friend—and most deliciously placed at the extremity of the town, in an excellent house well furnish'd, and elegant beyond any thing I look'd for —'Tis built in the form of a hotel, with a pretty court towards the town—and behind, the best gardens in Toulouse, laid out in serpentine walks, and so large that the company in our quarter usually come to walk there in the evenings, for which they have my consent—"the more the merrier."—The house

[723]

consists of a good *salle à manger* above stairs joining to the very great *salle à compagnie* as large as the Baron D'Holbach's; three handsome bed-chambers with dressing rooms to them—below stairs two very good rooms for myself, one to study in, the other to see company.—I have moreover cellars round the court, and all other offices—Of the same landlord I have bargained to have the use of a country-house which he has two miles out of town, so that myself and all my family have nothing more to do than to take our hats and remove from the one to the other—My landlord is moreover to keep the gardens in order—and what do you think I am to pay for all this? neither more or less than thirty pounds a year—all things are cheap in proportion—so we shall live for very verry little.—I dined yesterday with Mr. H[odges] —he is most pleasantly situated, and they are all well.—As for the books you have received for D[iderot], the bookseller was a fool not to send the bill along with them—I will write to him about it.—I wish you was with me for two months; it would cure you of all evils ghostly and bodily—but this, like many other wishes both for you and myself, must have its completion else where—Adieu my kind friend, and believe that I love you as much from inclination as reason, for

I am most truly yours,

L. STERNE

My wife and girl join in compliments to you—my best respects to my worthy Baron d'Holbach and all that society—remember me to my friend Mr. Panchaud.

To John Hall-Stevenson

Toulouse, Oct. 19, 1762

My dear H[all],

I RECEIVED your letter yesterday—so it has been travelling from Crazy Castle to Toulouse full eighteen days—If I had nothing to stop me I would engage to set out this morning, and knock at Crazy Castle gates in three days less time—by which time I should find you and the colonel, Panty, &c. all alone—the season I most wish and like to be with you—I rejoice from my heart, down to my reins, that you have snatch'd so many happy and sunshiny days out of the hands of the blue devils— If we live to meet and join our forces as heretofore we will give these gentry a drubbing—and turn them for ever out of their usurped citadel—some legions of them have been put to flight already by your operations this last campaign—and I hope to have a hand in dispersing the remainder the first time my dear cousin sets up his banners again under the square tower—But what art thou meditating with axes and hammers?—"*I know thy pride and the naughtiness of thy heart,*" and thou lovest the sweet visions of architraves, friezes and pediments with their tympanums, and thou hast found out a pretence, *à raison de cinq cent livres sterling* to be laid out in four years, &c. &c. (so as not to be felt, which is always added by the D[evil] as a bait) to justify thyself unto thyself—It may be very wise to do this—but 'tis wiser to keep one's money in one's pocket, whilst there are wars without and rumours of wars within.—St.——advises his disciples to sell both coat and waistcoat—and go rather without shirt or sword, than leave no money in their scrip, to go to Jerusalem with—Now those *quatres ans consecutifs,* my dear Anthony, are the most precious morsels of thy *life to come* (in this world) and thou wilt do well to enjoy that morsel without cares, calculations, and curses, and damns, and debts—for as sure as stone is stone, and mortar is mortar, &c. 'twill be one of the many works of thy repentance—But after all, if the Fates have decreed it, as you and I have some time supposed it on account of your generosity, "*that you are never to be a monied man,*" the decree will be fulfilled whether you adorn your castle and line it with cedar, and paint it within side and without side with vermilion, or not—*et cela etant* (having a bottle of Frontiniac and glass at my right hand) I drink, dear Anthony, to thy health and happiness, and to the final accomplishments of all thy lunary and sublunary projects.—For six weeks together, after I wrote my last letter to you, my projects were many stories higher, for I was all that time, as I thought, journeying on to the other world—I fell ill of an epidemic vile fever which killed hundreds about me—The physicians here are the errantest charlatans in Europe, or the most ignorant of all pretending fools —I withdrew what was left of me out of their hands, and recommended my affairs entirely to Dame Nature—She (dear goddess) has saved me in fifty different pinching bouts, and I begin to have a kind of enthusiasm now in her favour, and in my own, That one or two more escapes will make me believe I shall leave you all at last by translation, and not by fair death. I am now stout and foolish again as a happy man can wish to be—and am

busy playing the fool with my uncle Toby, who I have got soused
over head and ears in love.—I have many hints and projects
for other works; all will go on I trust as I wish in this matter.—
When I have reaped the benefit of this winter at Toulouse—
I cannot see I have any thing more to do with it, therefore after
having gone with my wife and girl to Bagnieres, I shall return
from whence I came—Now my wife wants to stay another year
to save money, and this opposition of wishes, tho' it will not be
as sour as lemon, yet 'twill not be as sweet as sugar candy.—
I wish T[ollot] would lead Sir Charles to Toulouse: 'tis as good as
any town in the South of France—for my own part, 'tis not to
my taste—but I believe, the ground work of my *ennui* is more to
the eternal platitude of the French characters—little variety, no
originality in it at all—than to any other cause—for they are very
civil—but civility itself, in that uniform, wearies and bodders one
to death—If I do not mind, I shall grow most stupid and sententious—Miss Shandy is hard at it with musick, dancing, and
French speaking, in the last of which she does *à marveille*, and
speaks it with an excellent accent, considering she practices within
sight of the Pyrenean Mountains.—If the snows will suffer me,
I propose to spend two or three months at Barege, or Bagnieres,
but my dear wife is against all schemes of additional expences—
which wicked propensity (tho' not of despotick power) yet I cannot suffer—tho' by the bye laudable enough—But she may talk—
I will do my own way, and she will acquiesce without a word of
debate on the subject.—Who can say so much in praise of his
wife? Few I trow.—M[acCarthy] is out of town vintaging—
so write to me, *Monsieur Sterne gentilhomme Anglois*—'twill
find me.—We are as much out of the road of all intelligence here
as at the Cape of Good Hope—so write a long nonsensical letter
like this, now and then to me—in which say nothing but what
may be shewn, (tho' I love every paragraph and spirited stroke
of your pen, others might not) for you must know a letter no
sooner arrives from England, but curiosity is upon her knees to
know the contents.—Adieu dear H[all] believe me,

Your affectionate,

L. STERNE

We have had bitter cold weather here these fourteen days—
which has obliged us to sit with whole pagells of wood lighted up to
our noses—'tis a dear article—but every thing else being extreme
cheap, Madame keeps an excellent good house, with *soupe, boulli,
roti*—&c. &c. for two hundred and fifty pounds a year.

To Robert Foley

Toulouse, Dec. 17, 1762

My dear F[oley]

THE post after I wrote last—I received yours with the inclosed draught upon the receiver, for which I return you all thanks—I have received this day likewise the box and tea all safe and sound—so we shall all of us be in our cups this Christmas, and drink without fear or stint—We begin to live extremely happy, and are all together every night—fiddling, laughing and singing, and cracking jokes. You will scarce believe the news I tell you—There are a company of English strollers arrived here, who are to act comedies all the Christmas, and are now busy in making dresses and preparing some of our best comedies—Your wonder will cease, when I inform you these strollers are your friends with the rest of our society, to whom I proposed this scheme [as a] *soulagement*—and I assure you we do well.—The next week, with a grand orchestra—we play the Busy Body—and the Journey to London the week after, but I have some thoughts of adapting it to our situation—and making it the Journey to Toulouse, which, with the change of half a dozen scenes, may be easily done.—Thus my dear F[oley] for want of something better we have recourse to ourselves, and strike out the best amusements we can from such materials.—My kind love and friendship to all my true friends—My service to the rest. H[odges]'s family have just left me, having been this last week with us—they will be with me all the holidays.—In summer we shall visit them, and so balance hospitalities.

Adieu,

Yours most truly,

L. STERNE

To the Archbishop of York

Toulouse, May 7, 1763

My Lord:

THOUGH there is little in this part of the world worth giving you an account of, and of myself, perhaps, the least of anything in it, yet bad as the subject is, it is my duty to say something about it, and your Grace, for that reason, I am sure will bear with the trouble.

It was this time twelve months that I thought myself so far recovered, that I was preparing to return home, when the attention to my daughter's health who had had an increase of an asthma under which she had lingered some time, determined my route otherwise; as an original weakness of lungs was her case as well as my own, I thought it just to give the daughter the same chance for her life which had saved her father's. Of this I wrote y^r Grace a letter, but had scarce sent it to the post, when (from what cause I know not, except the extreme weakness of the organ) I broke a vessel in my lungs, wch could not be closed till I had almost bled to death; so that to the motives of going with my daughter into the south of France, I had that superadded— my own immediate preservation; accordingly I have been fixed here with my family these ten months, and by God's blessing it has answered all I wished for, with regard to my daughter; I cannot say so much for myself, having since the first day of my arrival here been in a continual warfare with agues, fevers, and physicians—the 1st brought my blood to so poor a state, that the physicians found it necessary to enrich it with strong bouillons, and strong bouillons and soups a santé threw me into fevers, and fevers brought on loss of blood, and loss of blood agues—so that as *war begets poverty, poverty peace*, &c. &c.— has this miserable constitution made all its revolutions; how many more it may sustain, before its last and great one, God knows —like the rest of my species, I shall fence it off as long as I can. I am advised now to try the virtues of the waters of Banyars, and shall encamp like a patriarch w^h my whole household upon the side of the Pyreneans, this summer and winter at Nice; from whence in spring I shall return home, never, I fear, to be of service, at least as a preacher. I have preached too much, my Lord, already; and was my age to be computed either by the number of sermons I have preached, or the infirmities they have brought upon me, I might be truly said to have the claim of a *Miles emeritus,* and was there a Hotel des Invalides for the reception of such established upon any salutary plain betwixt here and Arabia Felix, I w^d beg your Grace's interest to help me into it—as it is, I rest fully assured in my heart of y^r Grace's indulgence to me in my endeavours to add a few quiet years to this fragment of my life—and with my wishes for a long and a happy one to y^r Grace, I am, from the truest veneration of y^r character,

Yours most dutiful servant,

L. STERNE

To Robert Foley

Montpellier, Jan. 5, 1764

My dear Friend,

YOU see I cannot pass over the fifth of the month without thinking of you, and writing to you—The last is a periodical habit—the first is from my heart, and I do it oftener than I remember—however, from both motives together I maintain I have a right to the pleasure of a single line—be it only to tell me how your watch goes—You know how much happier it would make me to know that all things belonging to you went on well.—You are going to have them all to yourself (I hear) and that Mr. S[elwin] is true to his first intention of leaving business—I hope this will enable you to accomplish yours in a shorter time, that you may get to your long wished for retreat of tranquillity and silence—When you have got to your fireside, and into your arm-chair (and by the by, have another to spare for a friend) and are so much a sovereign as to sit in your furr'd cap (if you like it, tho' I should not, for a man's ideas are at least the cleaner for being dress'd decently) why then it will be a miracle if I do not glide in like a ghost upon you—and in a very unghost-like fashion help you off with a bottle of your best wine.

January 15.—It does not happen every day that a letter begun in the most perfect health, should be concluded in the greatest weakness—I wish the vulgar high and low do not say it was a judgement upon me for taking all this liberty with *ghosts*—Be it as it may—I took a ride when the first part of this was wrote

towards Pezenas—and returned home in a shivering fit, tho'
I ought to have been in a fever, for I had tired my beast; and he
was as unmoveable as Don Quixote's wooden horse, and my arm
was half dislocated in whipping him—This quoth I is inhuman—
No, says a peasant on foot behind me, I'll drive him home—so
he laid on his posteriors, but 'twas needless—as his face was
turn'd towards Montpellier he began to trot.—But to return, this
fever has confined me ten days in my bed—I have suffered in
this scuffle with death terribly—but unless the spirit of prophecy
deceive me—I shall not die but live—in the mean time dear
F[oley] let us live as merrily but *as innocently* as we can—It has
ever been as good, if not better, than a bishoprick to me—and
I desire no other—Adieu my dear friend and believe me yours,

L. S.

Please to give the inclosed to Mr. T[hornhill]—and tell him
I thank him cordially from my heart for his great *good-will*.

To Mrs. F[enton]

Montpellier, Feb. 1, 1764

I AM preparing, my dear Mrs. F. to leave France, for I am
heartily tired of it—That insipidity there is in French
characters has disgusted your friend Yorick.—I have been
dangerously ill, and cannot think that the sharp air of Montpellier has been of service to me—and so my physicians told me
when they had me under their hands for above a month—if you
stay any longer here, Sir, it will be fatal to you—And why good
people were you not kind enough to tell me this sooner?—After
having discharged them, I told Mrs. S[terne] that I should set out
for England very soon, but as she chuses to remain in France for
two or three years, I have no objection, except that I wish my
girl in England.—The states of Languedoc are met—'tis a fine
raree-shew, with the usual accompanyments of fiddles, bears, and
puppet-shews.—I believe I shall step into my post-chaise with
more alacrity to fly from these sights, than a Frenchman would to
fly to them—and except a tear at parting with my little slut, I shall
be in high spirits, and every step I take that brings me nearer
England, will I think help to set this poor frame to rights. Now
pray write to me directed to Mr. F[oley] at Paris, and tell me
what I am to bring you over.—How do I long to greet all my

friends! few do I value more than yourself.—My wife chuses to go to Montauban, rather than stay here, in which I am truely passive.—If this should not find you at Bath, I hope it will be forwarded to you, as I wish to fulfill your commissions—and so adieu—Accept every warm wish for your health, and believe me ever yours,

L. STERNE

P.S. My physicians have almost poisoned me with what they call *bouillons refraichissants*—'tis a cock flead alive and boiled with poppy seeds, then pounded in a mortar, afterwards pass'd thro' a sieve—There is to be one crawfish in it, and I was gravely told it must be a male one—a female would do me more hurt than good.

To Lydia Sterne

Paris, May 15, 1764

My dear Lydia,

BY THIS time I suppose your mother and self are fixed at Montauban, and I therefore direct to your banker, to be delivered to you.—I acquiesced in your staying in France —likewise it was your mother's wish—but I must tell you both (that unless your health had not been a plea made use of) I should have wished you both to return with me.—I have sent you the Spectators, and other books, particularly Metastasio; but I beg my girl to read the former, and only make the latter her amusement.—I hope you have not forgot my last request, to make no friendships with the French-women—not that I think ill of them all, but sometimes women of the best principles are the most *insinuating*—nay I am so jealous of you that I should be miserable were I to see you had the least grain of coquettry in your composition.—You have enough to do—for I have also sent you a guittar—and as you have no genius for drawing, (tho' you never could be made to believe it) pray waste not your time about it—Remember to write to me as to a friend—in short whatever comes into your little head, and then it will be natural.—If your mother's rheumatism continues and she chooses to go to Bagnieres—tell her not to be stopped for want of money, for my purse shall be as open as my heart. I have preached at the ambassador's chapel—Hezekiah—(an odd subject your mother will say) There was a concourse of all nations, and religions too.

—I shall leave Paris in a few days—I am lodged in the same hotel with Mr. T[ollot] they are good and generous souls—Tell your mother that I hope she will write to me, and that when she does so, I may also receive a letter from my Lydia.

Kiss your mother from me, and believe me,

Your affectionate,

L. STERNE

To John Hall-Stevenson

[*Coxwold*,] *September 4, 1764*

NOW, my dear, dear Anthony—I do not think a week or ten days playing the good fellow (at this very time) at Scarborough so abominable a thing—but if a man could get there cleverly, and every soul in his house in the mind to try what could be done in furtherance thereof, I have no one to consult in this affair—therefore as a man may do worse things, the English of all which is this, that I am going to leave a few poor sheep here in the wilderness for fourteen days—and from pride and naughtiness of heart to go see what is doing at Scarborough —stedfastly meaning afterwards to lead a new life and strengthen my faith.—Now some folks say there is much company there— and some say not—and I believe there is neither the one or the other—but will be both, if the world will have but a month's patience or so.—No, my dear H[all] I did not delay sending your letter directly to the post—As there are critical times or rather turns and revolutions in *** humours, I knew not what the delay of an hour might hazard—I will answer for him, he has seventy times seven forgiven you—and as often wish'd you at the d[evi]l. —After many oscillations the pendulum will rest firm as ever.—

I send all kind compliments to Sir C[harles] D[avers] and G — s—I love them from my soul—If G[ilber]t is with you, him also.—I go on, not rapidly, but well enough with my uncle Toby's amours—There is no sitting, and cudgeling ones brains whilst the sun shines bright—'twill be all over in six or seven weeks, and there are dismal months enow after to endure suffocation by a brimstone fire-side.—If you can get to Scarborough, do.— A man who makes six tons of alum a week, may do any thing— Lord G[ranb]y is to be there—what a temptation!

Yours affectionately,

L. STERNE

[732]

To David Garrick

London, March 16, 1765

Dear G[arrick].

I THREATENED you with a letter in one I wrote a few weeks ago to Foley, but (to my shame be it spoken) I lead such a life of dissipation I have never had a moment to myself which has not been broke in upon, by one engagement or impertinence or another—and as plots thicken towards the latter end of a piece, I find, unless I take pen and ink just now, I shall not be able to do it, till either I am got into the country, or you to the city. You are teized and tormented too much by your correspondents, to return to us, and with accounts how much your friends, and how much your Theatre wants you—so that I will not magnify either our loss or yours—but hope cordially to see you soon.— Since I wrote last I have frequently stept into your house—that is, as frequently as I could take the whole party, where I dined, along with me—This was but justice to you, as I walk'd in as a wit—but with regard to myself, I balanced the account thus—I am sometimes in my friend [Garrick]'s house, but he is always in Tristram Shandy's —where my friends say he will continue (and I hope the prophecy true for my own immortality) even when he himself is no more.

I have had a lucrative winter's campaign here—Shandy sells well—I am taxing the publick with two more volumes of sermons, which will more than double the gains of Shandy—It goes into the world with a prancing list of *de toute la noblesse*—which will bring me in three hundred pounds, exclusive of the sale of the copy—so that with all the contempt of money which *ma façon de penser* has ever impress'd on me, I shall be rich in spite of myself: but I scorn you must know, in the high *ton* I take at present, to pocket all this trash—I set out to lay a portion of it in the service of the world, in a tour round Italy, where I shall spring game, or the duce is in the dice.—In the beginning of September I quit England, that I may avail myself of the time of vintage, when all nature is joyous, and so saunter philosophically for a year or so, on the other side the Alps.—I hope your pilgrimages have brought Mrs. G[arrick] and yourself back *à la fleur de jeunesse*—May you both long feel the sweets of it, and your friends with you.—Do, dear friend, make my kindest wishes and compliments acceptable to the best and wisest of the daughters of Eve—You shall ever believe and ever find me affectionately yours,   L. STERNE

To Lady Warkworth

Mount Coffee-house, Tuesday 3 o'Clock.
[23 April, 1765]

THERE is a strange mechanical effect produced in writing a billet-doux within a stone-cast of the lady who engrosses the heart and soul of an inamorato—for this cause (but mostly because I am to dine in this neighbourhood) have I, Tristram Shandy, come forth from my lodgings to a coffee-house the nearest I could find to my dear Lady [Warkworth]'s house, and have called for a sheet of gilt paper, to try the truth of this article of my creed—Now for it—

O my dear Lady—what a dishclout of a soul hast thou made of me?—I think, by the bye, this is a little too familiar an introduction, for so unfamiliar a situation as I stand in with you—where heaven knows, I am kept at a distance—and despair of getting one inch nearer you, with all the steps and windings I can think of to recommend myself to you—Would not any man in his senses run diametrically from you—and as far as his legs would carry him, rather than thus causelessly, foolishly, and fool-hardily expose himself afresh—and afresh, where his heart and his reason tells him he shall be sure to come off loser, if not totally undone?—Why would you tell me you would be glad to see me? —Does it give you pleasure to make me more unhappy—or does it add to your triumph, that your eyes and lips have turned a man into a fool, whom the rest of the town is courting as a wit?—I am a fool—the weakest, the most ductile, the most tender fool, that ever woman tried the weakness of—and the most unsettled in my purposes and resolutions of recovering my right mind. —It is but an hour ago, that I kneeled down and swore I never would come near you—and after saying my Lord's Prayer for the sake of the close, of not being led into temptation—out I sallied like any Christian hero, ready to take the field against the world, the flesh, and the devil; not doubting but I should finally trample them all down under my feet—and now am I got so near you— within this vile stone's cast of your house—I feel myself drawn into a vortex, that has turned my brain upside downwards, and though I had purchased a box ticket to carry me to Miss *******
benefit, yet I know very well, that was a single line directed to me, to let me know Lady [Warkworth] would be alone at seven, and suffer me to spend the evening with her, she would infallibly see

every thing verified I have told her.—I done at Mr. C——r's in Wigmore-street, in this neighbourhood, where I shall stay till seven, in hopes you purpose to put me to this proof. If I hear nothing by that time I shall conclude you are better disposed of— and shall take a sorry hack, and sorrily jogg on to the play— Curse on the word. I know nothing but sorrow—except this one thing, that I love you (perhaps foolishly, but)

most sincerely,

L. STERNE

To the Earl of Effingham

Coxwould, near Easingwould, May 29, 1765

My good Lord,

(FOR I believe you from my heart to be so,—or my pen would not have belied my opinion of you—and since I've begun with an article of belief—give me leave to add, that I *believe* you have power to be any thing—but no thanks to you—so I hope you render them to whom they are due—and so God prosper you) as all this is included in a parenthesis—your Lordship has a right to leave it out—it will not hurt the sense—I mean your own—for as for mine—the point has been some years ago settled by the world—tho' by the by—I intend to puzzle it—by some feeble Efforts in the work I am about—tho' was I to tell you the subject of the first sermon I've begun with—you would think it so truly Shandean, that no after-wit would bring me off—nothing venture nothing have—all which being duely perpended and consider'd by your Lordship, I return your Lordship thanks for your subscriptions—as I do to the *aimable Comtesse votre chere Mere*— for the honour of her name, &c.

Hall left me bleeding to death at York, of a small vessel in my lungs—the duce take these bellows of mine; I must get 'em stop'd, or I shall never live to *persifler* Lord Effingham again.— A propos! will you be at York races?—for next to the pleasure of getting my five and forty shillings out of your hands—I know nothing that will give me more delight than to see you in the *flesh*—who's? What? cura valetudinem tuam diligenter—as a means to which, keep your body in temperance, soberness and chastity—which is a quotation from the Church Catechism, which with all your good memory I fear your Lordship sometimes

[735]

forgets—Greet Scroope and Blaquiere in my name—present—
~~(not my brotherly love—but)~~ my fraternal pity to Dean ~~Wrotsly~~
—What should make ~~such a fool pop into my~~ head?—my own
vile passions, and ~~that's the truth~~ of the matter—~~and so I cross it
all out.~~

If the whole letter had been served the same way, it would not
have fared the worse with your Lordship—but I should have lost
the honour and satisfaction of saying

That I am

with the highest esteem

for your Character and Talents My Lord

Your most faithful

and obliged humble servant

L. STERNE

To ? John Wodehouse

Coxwould, [*? August*] *23, 1765*

A T THIS moment am I sitting in my summer house with my
head and heart full, not of my uncle Toby's amours with
the widow Wadman, but my sermons—and your letter
has drawn me out of a pensive mood—the spirit of it *pleaseth me*
—but in this solitude, what can I tell or write to you but about
myself—I am glad that you are in love—'twill cure you (at least)
of the spleen, which has a bad effect on both man and woman
—I myself must ever have some dulcinea in my head—it har-
monises the soul—and in those cases I first endeavour to make
the lady believe so, or rather I begin first to make myself believe
that I am in love—but I carry on my affairs quite in the French
way, sentimentally—"*l'amour*" (say they) "*n'est rien sans sentiment*"—Now notwithstanding they make such a pother about
the *word*, they have no precise idea annex'd to it—And so much
for that same subject called love—I must tell you how I have just
treated a French gentleman of fortune in France, who took
a liking to my daughter—Without any ceremony (having got my
direction from my wife's banker) he wrote me word that he was
in love with my daughter, and desired to know what *fortune*
I would give her at present, and how much at my *death*—by the
bye, I think there was very little *sentiment* on *his side*—My
answer was "Sir, I shall give her ten thousand pounds the day of

marriage—my calculation is as follows—she is not eighteen, you are sixty-two—there goes five thousand pounds—then Sir, you at least think her not ugly—she has many accomplishments, speaks Italian, French, plays upon the guittar, and as I fear you play upon no instrument whatever, I think you will be happy to take her at my terms, for here finishes the account of the ten thousand pounds"—I do not suppose but he will take this as I mean, that is—a flat refusal.—I have had a parsonage house burnt down by the carelessness of my curate's wife—as soon as I can I must rebuild it, I trow—but I lack the means at present—yet I am never happier than when I have not a shilling in my pocket—for when I have I can never call it my own. Adieu my dear friend— may you enjoy better health than me, tho' not better spirits, for that is impossible.

Yours sincerely,

L. STERNE

My compliments to the Col.

To ? John Wodehouse

Coxwould, [? September] 20, 1765

THANKS, my dear W. for your letter—I am just preparing to come and greet you and many other friends in town— I have drained my ink standish to the bottom, and after I have published, shall set my face, not towards Jerusalem, but towards the Alps—I find I must once more fly from death whilst I have strength—I shall go to Naples and see whether the air of that place will not set this poor frame to rights—As to the project of getting a bear to lead, I think I have enough to do to govern myself—and however profitable it might be (according to your opinion) I am sure it would be unpleasurable—Few are the minutes of life, and I do not think that I have any to throw away on any one being.—I shall spend nine or ten months in Italy, and call upon my wife and daughter in France at my return—so shall be back by the King's birth-day—what a project!—and now my dear friend am I going to York, not for the sake of society—nor to walk by the side of the muddy Ouse, but to recruit myself of the most violent spitting of blood that ever mortal man experienced; because I had rather (in case 'tis ordained so) die there, than in a post-chaise on the road.—If the amour of my uncle Toby do not

[737]

please you, I am mistaken—and so with a droll story I will finish this letter—A sensible friend of mine, with whom not long ago, I spent some hours in conversation, met an apothecary (an acquaintance of ours)—the latter asked him how he did? why, ill, very ill—I have been with Sterne, who has given me such a dose of *Attic salt* that I am in a fever—Attic salt, Sir, Attic salt! I have Glauber salt—I have Epsom salt in my shop, &c.—Oh! I suppose 'tis some French salt—I wonder you would trust his report of the medicine, he cares not what he takes himself—I fancy I see you smile—I long to be able to be in London, and embrace my friends there—and shall enjoy myself a week or ten days at Paris with my friends, particularly the Baron d'Holbach, and the rest of the joyous sett—As to the females—no I will not say a word about them—only I hate borrowed characters taken up (as a woman does her shift) for the purpose she intends to effectuate. Adieu, adieu—I am yours whilst

L. STERNE

To John Hall-Stevenson

May [24], near Dijon [1766]

Dear Antony,

MY DESIRE of seeing both my wife and girl has turn'd me out of my road towards a delicious Chateau of the Countess of M——, where I have been patriarching it these seven days with her ladyship, and half a dozen of very handsome and agreeable ladies—her ladyship has the best of hearts—a valuable present not given to every one.—Tomorrow, with regret, I shall quit this agreeable circle, and post it night and day to Paris, where I shall arrive in two days, and just wind myself up, when I am there, enough to roll on to Calais—so I hope to sup with you the king's birth day, according to a plan of sixteen days standing.—Never man has been such a wildgoose chace after a wife as I have been—after having sought her in five or six different towns, I found her at last in *Franche Comté*—Poor woman! she was very cordial, &c. and begs to stay another year or so—my Lydia pleases me much—I found her greatly improved in every thing I wish'd her—I am most unaccountably well, and most accountably nonsensical—'tis at least a proof of good spirits, which is a sign and token given me in these latter days that

[738]

I must take up again the pen.—In faith I think I shall die with it in my hand, but I shall live these ten years, my Antony, notwithstanding the fears of my wife, whom I left most melancholy on that account.—This is a delicious part of the world; most celestial weather, and we lie all day, without damps, upon the grass—and that is the whole of it, except the inner man (for her ladyship is not stingy of her wine) is inspired twice a day with the best Burgundy that grows upon the mountains, which terminate our lands here.—Surely you will not have decamp'd to Crazy Castle before I reach town.—The summer here is set in good earnest—'tis more than we can say for Yorkshire—I hope to hear a good tale of your alum works—have you no other works in hand? I do not expect to hear from you, so God prosper you —and all your undertakings.—

I am, my dear cousin,
Most affectionately yours,

L. STERNE

Remember me to Mr. G[?ilbert], Cardinal S[crope], the Col. &c. &c. &c.

To Lydia Sterne

Old Bond-street, February 23, 1767

AND SO, my Lydia! thy mother and thyself are returning back again from Marseilles to the banks of the Sorgue— and there thou wilt sit and fish for trouts—I envy you the sweet situation.—Petrarch's tomb I should like to pay a sentimental visit to—the Fountain of Vaucluse, by thy description, must be delightful—I am also much pleased with the account you give me of the Abbé de Sade—you find great comfort in such a neighbour—I am glad he is so good as to correct thy translation of my Sermons—dear girl go on, and make me a present of thy work—but why not the House of Mourning? 'tis one of the best. I long to receive the life of Petrarch, and his Laura, by your Abbé, but I am out of all patience with the answer the Marquis made the Abbé—'twas truly coarse, and I wonder he bore it with any christian patience—But to the subject of your letter—I do not wish to know who was the busy fool, who made your mother uneasy about Mrs. [Draper] 'tis true I have a friendship for her, but not to infatuation—I believe I have judgment enough to dis-

[739]

cern hers, and every woman's faults. I honour thy mother for her answer—"that she wished not to be informed, and begged him to drop the subject."—Why do you say that your mother wants money?—whilst I have a shilling, shall you not both have ninepence out of it?—I think, if I have my enjoyments, I ought not to grudge you yours.—I shall not begin my Sentimental Journey till I get to Coxwould—I have laid a plan for something new, quite out of the beaten track.—I wish I had you with me—and I would introduce you to one of the most amiable and gentlest of beings, whom I have just been with—not Mrs. [Draper], but a Mrs. J[ames] the wife of as worthy a man as I ever met with—I esteem them both. He possesses every manly virtue—honour and bravery are his characteristicks, which have distinguished him nobly in several instances—I shall make you better acquainted with his character, by sending Orme's History, with the books you desired—and it is well worth your reading; for Orme is an elegant writer, and a just one; he pays no man a compliment at the expence of truth.—Mrs. J[ames] is kind—and friendly—of a sentimental turn of mind— and so sweet a disposition, that she is too good for the world she lives in—Just God! if all were like her, what a life would this be! —Heaven, my Lydia, for some wise purpose has created different beings—I wish my dear child knew her—thou art worthy of her friendship, and she already loves thee; for I sometimes tell her what I feel for thee.—This is a long letter—write soon, and never let your letters be studied ones—write naturally, and then you will write well.—I hope your mother has got quite well of her ague—I have sent her some of Huxham's tincture of the Bark. I will order you a guittar since the other is broke. Believe me, my Lydia, that I am yours affectionately,

L. STERNE

To Mrs. Daniel Draper

[London, ? March 1767]

I GOT thy letter last night, Eliza, on my return from Lord Bathurst's, where I dined, and where I was heard (as I talked of thee an hour without intermission) with so much pleasure and attention, that the good old lord toasted your health three different times; and tho' he is now in his eighty-fifth year, says he hopes to live long enough to be introduced as a friend to my fair

Indian disciple, and to see her eclipse all other nabobesses as much in wealth, as she does already in exterior and (what is far better) in interior merit. I hope so too. This nobleman is an old friend of mine.—You know he was always the protector of men of wit and genius; and has had those of the last century, Addison, Steele, Pope, Swift, Prior, &c. &c. always at his table.—The manner in which his notice began of me, was as singular as it was polite.—He came up to me, one day, as I was at the Princess of Wales's court. "I want to know you, Mr. Sterne; but it is fit you should know, also, who it is that wishes this pleasure. You have heard, continued he, of an old Lord Bathurst, of whom your Popes, and Swifts, have sung and spoken so much: I have lived my life with geniuses of that cast; but have survived them; and, despairing ever to find their equals, it is some years since I have closed my accounts, and shut up my books, with thoughts of never opening them again: but you have kindled a desire in me of opening them once more before I die; which I now do; so go home and dine with me."—This nobleman I say, is a prodigy; for at eighty-five he has all the wit and promptness of a man of thirty. A disposition to be pleased, and a power to please others beyond whatever I knew: added to which, a man of learning, courtesy, and feeling.

He heard me talk of thee, Eliza, with uncommon satisfaction; for there was only a third person, and of sensibility, with us.— And a most sentimental afternoon, 'till nine o'clock, have we passed! But thou, Eliza, wert the star that conducted and enliven'd the discourse.—And when I talked not of thee, still didst thou fill my mind, and warmed every thought I uttered; for I am not ashamed to acknowledge I greatly miss thee.—Best of all good girls! the sufferings I have sustained the whole night on account of thine, Eliza, are beyond my power of words.—Assuredly does Heaven give strength proportioned to the weight he lays upon us! Thou hast been bowed down, my child, with every burden that sorrow of heart, and pain of body, could inflict upon a poor being; and still thou tellest me, thou art beginning to get ease;— thy fever gone, thy sickness, the pain in thy side vanishing also.— May every evil so vanish that thwarts Eliza's happiness, or but awakens thy fears for a moment!—Fear nothing, my dear!— Hope every thing; and the balm of this passion will shed its influence on thy health, and make thee enjoy a spring of youth and chearfulness, more than thou hast hardly yet tasted.

And so thou hast fixed thy Bramin's portrait over thy writing-desk; and will consult it in all doubts and difficulties.—Grateful and good girl! Yorick smiles contentedly over all thou dost; his picture does not do justice to his own complacency!

Thy sweet little plan and distribution of thy time—how worthy of thee! Indeed, Eliza, thou leavest me nothing to direct thee in; thou leavest me nothing to require, nothing to ask—but a continuation of that conduct which won my esteem, and has made me thy friend for ever.

May the roses come quick back to thy cheeks, and the rubies to thy lips! But trust my declaration, Eliza, that thy husband (if he is the good, feeling man I wish him) will press thee to him with more honest warmth and affection, and kiss thy pale, poor, dejected face, with more transport, than he would be able to do, in the best bloom of all thy beauty;—and so he ought, or I pity him. He must have strange feelings, if he knows not the value of such a creature as thou art!

I am glad Miss Light goes with you. She may relieve you from many anxious moments.—I am glad your ship-mates are friendly beings. You could least dispense with what is contrary to your own nature, which is soft and gentle, Eliza.—It would civilize savages.—Though pity were it thou should'st be tainted with the office! How canst thou make apologies for thy last letter? 'tis most delicious to me, for the very reason you excuse it. Write to me, my child, only such. Let them speak the easy carelessness of a heart that opens itself, any how, and every how, to a man you ought to esteem and trust. Such, Eliza, I write to thee,—and so I should ever live with thee, most artlessly, most affectionately, if Providence permitted thy residence in the same section of the globe; for I am, all that honour and affection can make me,

Thy BRAMIN

To Lydia Sterne

Bond Street, [*? 9 March,*] *1767*

THIS letter, my dear Lydia, will distress thy good heart, for from the beginning thou wilt perceive no entertaining strokes of humour in it—I cannot be chearful when a thousand melancholy ideas surround me—I have met with a loss of near fifty pounds, which I was taken in for in an extraordinary manner—but what is that loss in comparison of one I may experience?—Friendship is the balm and cordial of life, and without it, 'tis a heavy load not worth sustaining.—I am unhappy —thy mother and thyself at a distance from me, and what can compensate for such a destitution?—For God's sake persuade her to come and fix in England, for life is too short to waste in separation—and whilst she lives in one country, and I in another, many people will suppose it proceeds from choice—besides I want thee near me, thou child and darling of my heart!—I am in a melancholy mood, and my Lydia's eyes will smart with weeping when I tell her the cause that now affects me.—I am apprehensive the dear friend I mentioned in my last letter is going into a decline —I was with her two days ago, and I never beheld a being so alter'd—she has a tender frame, and looks like a drooping lily, for the roses are fled from her cheeks—I can never see or talk to this incomparable woman without bursting into tears—I have a thousand obligations to her, and I owe her more than her whole sex, if not all the world put together.—She has a delicacy in her way of thinking that few possess—our conversations are of the most interesting nature, and she talks to me of quitting this world with more composure than others think of living in it.— I have wrote an epitaph, of which I send thee a copy.—'Tis expressive of her modest worth—but may heav'n restore her! and may she live to write mine.

> Columns, and labour'd urns but vainly shew,
> An idle scene of decorated woe.
> The sweet companion, and the friend sincere,
> Need no mechanic help to force the tear.
> In heart felt numbers, never meant to shine
> 'Twill flow eternal o'er a hearse like thine;
> 'Twill flow, whilst gentle goodness has one friend,
> Or kindred tempers have a tear to lend.

Say all that is kind of me to thy mother, and believe me my Lydia, that I love thee most truly—So adieu—I am what I ever was, and hope ever shall be, thy

Affectionate Father,

L. S.

As to Mr. ——— by your description he is a fat fool. I beg you will not give up your time to such a being—Send me some *batons pour les dents*—there are none good here.

[743]

To Mrs. Daniel Draper

[*London, March 1767*]

My dearest Eliza!

I BEGAN a new journal this morning; you shall see it; for if I live not till your return to England, I will leave it you as a legacy. 'Tis a sorrowful page; but I will write chearful ones; and could I write letters to thee, they should be chearful ones too : but few, I fear, will reach thee! However, depend upon receiving something of the kind by every post; till then, [? when] thou wavest thy hand, and bid'st me write no more.

Tell me how you are; and what sort of fortitude Heaven inspires you with. How are you accommodated, my dear? Is all right? Scribble away, any thing, and every thing to me. Depend upon seeing me at Deal, with the James's, should you be detain'd there by contrary winds.—Indeed, Eliza, I should with pleasure fly to you, could I be the means of rendering you any service, or doing you kindness. Gracious and merciful God! consider the anguish of a poor girl.—Strengthen and preserve her in all the shocks her frame must be exposed to. She is now without a protector, but thee! Save her from all accidents of a dangerous element, and give her comfort at the last.

My prayer, Eliza, I hope, is heard; for the sky seems to smile upon me, as I look up to it. I am just returned from our dear Mrs. James's, where I have been talking of thee for three hours.— She has got your picture, and likes it: but Marriott, and some other judges, agree that mine is the better, and expressive of a sweeter character. But what is that to the original? yet I acknowledge that hers is a picture for the world; and mine is calculated only to please a very sincere friend, or sentimental philosopher.—In the one, you are dressed in smiles, with all the advantages of silks, pearls, and ermine;—in the other, simple as a vestal—appearing the good girl nature made you;—which, to me, conveys an idea of more unaffected sweetness, than Mrs. Draper, habited for conquest, in a birthday suit, with her countenance animated, and her dimples visible.—If I remember right, Eliza, you endeavoured to collect every charm of your person into your face, with more than *common* care, the day you sat for Mrs. James.—Your colour too, brightened; and your eyes shone with more than usual brilliancy. I then requested you to come simple and unadorned when you sat for me—knowing (as I see with *unprejudiced* eyes) that you could receive no addition from the silk-worm's aid, or jeweller's polish. Let me now tell you a truth, which, I believe, I have uttered before.—When I first saw you, I beheld you as an object of compassion, and as a very plain woman. The mode of your dress (tho' fashionable) disfigured you.—But nothing now could render you such, but the being solicitous to make yourself admired as a handsome one.— You are not handsome, Eliza, nor is yours a face that will please the tenth part of your beholders,—but are something more; for I scruple not to tell you, I never saw so intelligent, so animated, so good a countenance; nor was there, (nor ever will be), that man of sense, tenderness, and feeling, in your company three hours, that was not (or will not be) your admirer, or friend, in consequence of it; that is, if you assume, or assumed, no character foreign to your own, but appeared the artless being nature designed you for. A something in your eyes, and voice, you possess in a degree more persuasive than any woman I ever saw, read, or heard of. But it is that bewitching sort of nameless excellence, that men of nice sensibility alone can be touched with.

Were your husband in England, I would freely give him five hundred pounds (if money could purchase the acquisition) to let you only sit by me two hours in a day, while I wrote my Sentimental Journey. I am sure the work would sell so much the better for it, that I should be re-imbursed the sum more than seven times told.—I would not give nine pence for the picture of you, the Newnham's have got executed—It is the resemblance of a conceited, made-up coquette. Your eyes, and the shape of your face (the latter the most perfect oval I ever saw) which are perfections that must strike the most indifferent judge, because they are equal to any of God's works in a similar way, and finer than any I beheld in all my travels, are manifestly injured by the affected leer of the one, and strange appearance of the other; owing to the attitude of the head, which is a proof of the artist's, or your friend's false taste. The * * * * 's, who verify the character I once gave of teazing, or sticking like pitch, or bird-lime, sent a card that they would wait on Mrs. [James] on Friday.—She sent back, she was engaged.—Then to meet at Ranelagh, to-night.—She answered, she did not go.—She says, if she allows the least footing, she never shall get rid of the acquaintance; which she is resolved to drop at once. She knows them. She knows they are not her friends, nor yours; and the first use they would make of being with her, would be to sacrifice you to her (if they could) a second time. Let her not then; let her not, my dear, be a greater friend to thee, than thou art to thyself. She begs I will reiterate my request to you, that you will not write to them. It will give her, and thy Bramin, inexpressible pain. Be assured, all this is not without reason on her side. I have my reasons too; the first of which is, that I should grieve to excess, if Eliza wanted that fortitude her Yorick has built so high upon. I said I never more would mention the name to thee; and had I not received it, as a kind of charge, from a dear woman that loves you, I should not have broke my word. I will write again to morrow to thee, thou best and most endearing of girls! A peaceful night to thee. My spirit will be with thee through every watch of it.

Adieu

To Mrs. Daniel Draper

[London, ? 30 March 1767]

My dear Eliza!

I HAVE been within the verge of the gates of death.—I was ill the last time I wrote to you; and apprehensive of what would be the consequence.—My fears were but too well founded; for in ten minutes after I dispatched my letter, this poor, fine-spun frame of Yorick's gave way, and I broke a vessel in my breast, and could not stop the loss of blood till four this morning. I have filled all thy India handkerchiefs with it.—It came, I think, from my heart! I fell asleep through weakness. At six I woke, with the bosom of my shirt steeped in tears. I dreamt I was sitting under the canopy of Indolence, and that thou camest into the room, with a shaul in thy hand, and told me, my spirit had flown to thee in the Downs, with tidings of my fate; and that you were come to administer what consolation filial affection could bestow, and to receive my parting breath and blessing.— With that you folded the shaul about my waist, and, kneeling, supplicated my attention. I awoke; but in what a frame! Oh! my God! "But thou wilt number my tears, and put them all into thy bottle."—Dear girl! I see thee,—thou art for ever present to my fancy,—embracing my feeble knees, and raising thy fine eyes to bid me be of comfort: and when I talk to Lydia, the words of Esau, as uttered by thee, perpetually ring in my ears—"Bless *me* even also, my father!"—Blessing attend thee, thou child of my heart!

My bleeding is quite stopped, and I feel the principle of life strong within me; so be not alarmed, Eliza—I know I shall do well. I have eat my breakfast with hunger; and I write to thee with a pleasure arising from that prophetic impression in my imagination, that "all will terminate to our heart's content." Comfort thyself eternally with this persuasion, "that the best of beings (as thou hast sweetly expressed it) could not, by a combination of accidents, produce such a chain of events, merely to be the source of misery to the leading person engaged in them." The observation was very applicable, very good, and very elegantly expressed. I wish my memory did justice to the wording of it.—Who taught you the art of writing so sweetly, Eliza?— You have absolutely exalted it to a science! When I am in want of ready cash, and ill health will permit my genius to exert itself, I shall print your letters, as finished essays, "by an unfortunate Indian lady." The style is new; and would almost be a sufficient recommendation for their selling well, without merit —but their sense, natural ease, and spirit, is not to be equalled, I believe, in this section of the globe; nor, I will answer for it, by any of your country-women in yours.—I have shewed your letter to Mrs. B——, and to half the literati in town.—You shall not be angry with me for it, because I meant to do you honour by it. —You cannot imagine how many admirers your epistolary productions have gained you, that never viewed your external merits. I only wonder where thou could'st acquire thy graces, thy goodness, thy accomplishments—so connected! so educated! Nature has, surely, studied to make thee her peculiar care—for thou art (and not in my eyes alone) the best and fairest of all her works.—

And so, this is the last letter thou art to receive from me; because the Earl of Chatham (I read in the papers) is got to the Downs; and the wind, I find, is fair. If so—blessed woman! take my last, last farewell!—Cherish the remembrance of me; think how I esteem, nay, how affectionately I love thee, and what a price I set upon thee! Adieu, adieu! and with my adieu—let me give thee one streight rule of conduct, that thou hast heard from my lips in a thousand forms—but I concenter it in one word,

REVERENCE THYSELF.

Adieu, once more Eliza! May no anguish of heart plant a wrinkle upon thy face, till I behold it again! May no doubt or

[747]

misgivings disturb the serenity of thy mind, or awaken a painful thought about thy children—for they are Yorick's—and Yorick is thy friend for ever!—Adieu, adieu, adieu!

P.S. Remember, that Hope shortens all journies, by sweetening them—so sing my little stanza on the subject, with the devotion of an hymn, every morning when thou arisest, and thou wilt eat thy breakfast with more comfort for it.

Blessings, rest, and Hygeia go with thee! May'st thou soon return, in peace and affluence, to illumine my night! I am, and shall be, the last to deplore thy loss, and will be the first to congratulate, and hail thy return.—

FARE THEE WELL!

To A. L——e, Esq.

Coxwould, June 7, 1767

Dear L——e,

I HAD not been many days at this peaceful cottage before your letter greeted me with the seal of friendship, and most cordially do I thank you for so kind a proof of your good will—I was truly anxious to hear of the recovery of my sentimental friend—but I would not write to enquire after her, unless I could have sent her the testimony without the tax, for even how-d'yes to invalids, or those that have lately been so, either call to mind what is past or what may return—at least I find it so.—I am as happy as a prince, at Coxwould—and I wish you could see in how princely a manner I live—'tis a land of plenty. I sit down alone to venison, fish and wild fowl, or a couple of fowls or ducks, with curds, and strawberries, and cream, and all the simple plenty which a rich valley under (Hambleton Hills) can produce—with a clean cloth on my table—and a bottle of wine on my right hand to drink your health. I have a hundred hens and chickens about my yard—and not a parishioner catches a hare, or a rabbet, or a trout, but he brings it as an offering to me. If solitude would cure a love-sick heart, I would give you an invitation—but absence and time lessen no attachment which virtue inspires.—I am in high spirits—care never enters this cottage—I take the air every day in my post chaise, with my two long tail'd horses—they turn out good ones; and as to myself,

I think I am better upon the whole for the medicines, and regimen I submitted to in town—May you, dear L——, want neither the one, nor the other.

Yours truly,
L. STERNE

To Sir ? William Stanhope

[? Coxwold,] September 19, 1767

My dear Sir,

YOU are perhaps the drollest being in the universe—Why do you banter me so about what I wrote to you?—Tho' I told you, every morning I jump'd into Venus's lap (meaning thereby the sea) was you to infer from that, that I leap'd into the ladies beds afterwards?—The body guides you—the mind me.—I have wrote the most whimsical letter to a lady that was ever read, and talk'd of body and soul too—I said she had made me vain, by saying she was mine more than ever woman was——but she is not the lady of Bond-street nor—— square, nor the lady who supp'd with me in Bond-street on scollop'd oysters, and other such things—nor did she ever go *tete-a-tete* with me to Salt Hill.—Enough of such nonsense—The past is over—and I can justify myself unto myself—can you do as much?—No faith!—"You can feel!" Aye so can my cat, when he hears a female caterwauling on the house top—but caterwauling disgusts me. I had rather raise a gentle flame, than have a different one raised in me.—Now, I take heav'n to witness, after all this *badinage* my heart is innocent—and the sporting of my pen is equal, just equal, to what I did in my boyish days, when I got astride of a stick, and gallop'd away—The truth is this— that my pen governs me—not me my pen.—You are much to blame if you dig for marle, unless you are sure of it.—I was once such a puppy myself, as to pare, and burn, and had my labour for my pains, and two hundred pounds out of pocket.—Curse on farming (said I) I will try if the pen will not succeed better than the spade.—The following up of that affair (I mean farming) made me lose my temper, and a cart load of turneps was (I thought) very dear at two hundred pounds.—

In all your operations may your own good sense guide you— bought experience is the devil.—Adieu, adieu!—Believe me

Yours most truly,
L. STERNE

[749]

To the Earl of ————

My Lord,

'TIS WITH the greatest pleasure I take my pen to thank your Lordship for your letter of enquiry about Yorick—he has worn out both his spirits and body with the Sentimental Journey—'tis true that an author must feel himself, or his reader will not—but I have torn my whole frame into pieces by my feelings—I believe the brain stands as much in need of recruiting as the body—therefore I shall set out for town the twentieth of next month, after having recruited myself a week at York.— I might indeed solace myself with my wife, (who is come from France) but in fact I have long been a sentimental being—whatever your Lordship may think to the contrary.—The world has imagined, because I wrote Tristram Shandy, that I was myself more Shandean than I really ever was—'tis a good-natured world we live in, and we are often painted in divers colours according to the ideas each one frames in his head.— A very agreeable lady arrived three years ago at York, in her road to Scarborough—I had the honour of being acquainted with her, and was her *chaperon*—all the females were very inquisitive to know who she was—"Do not tell, ladies, 'tis a mistress my wife has recommended to me—nay moreover has sent her from France."—

I hope my book will please you, my Lord, and then my labour will not be totally in vain. If it is not thought a chaste book, mercy on them that read it, for they must have warm imaginations indeed!—Can your Lordship forgive my not making this a longer epistle?—In short I can but add this, which you already know— that I am with gratitude and friendship,

My Lord,

Your obedient faithful,

L. STERNE

If your Lordship is in town in Spring, I should be happy if you became acquainted with my friends in Gerrard-street—you would esteem the husband, and honour the wife—she is the reverse of most her sex—they have various pursuits—she but one—that of pleasing her husband.—

To A. L——e, Esq.

Coxwould, December 7, 1767

Dear L.

I SAID I would not perhaps write any more, but it would be unkind not to reply to so interesting a letter as yours—I am certain you may depend upon Lord ———'s promises—he will take care of you in the best manner he can, and your knowledge of the world, and of languages in particular, will make you useful in any department—If his Lordship's scheme does not succeed, leave the kingdom—go to the east, or the west, for travelling would be of infinite service to both your body and mind—But more of this when we meet—now to my own affairs. —I have had an offer of exchanging two pieces of preferment I hold here, for a living of three hundred and fifty pounds a year, in Surry, about thirty miles from London, and retaining Coxwould, and my prebendaryship—the country also is sweet—but I will not, cannot come to any determination, till I have consulted with you, and my other friends.—I have great offers too in Ireland—the bishops of C[ork], and R[oss], are both my friends—but I have rejected every proposal, unless Mrs. S[terne], and my Lydia could accompany me thither—I live for the sake of my girl, and with her sweet light burthen in my arms, I could get up fast the hill of preferment, if I chose it—but without my Lydia, if a mitre was offered me, it would sit uneasy upon my brow.—Mrs. S[terne]'s health is insupportable in England.—She must return to France, and justice and humanity forbid me to oppose it.—I will allow her enough to live comfortably, until she can rejoin me.—My heart bleeds, L——e, when I think of parting with my child—'twill be like the separation of soul and body—and equal to nothing but what passes at that tremendous moment; and like it in one respect, for she will be in one kingdom, whilst I am in another.—You will laugh at my weakness—but I cannot help it—for she is a dear, disinterested girl—As a proof of it—when she left Coxwould, and I bad her adieu, I pulled out my purse and offered her ten guineas for her private pleasures—her answer was pretty, and affected me too much. "No, my dear papa, our expences of coming from France may have straiten'd you—I would rather put an hundred guineas in your pocket than take ten out of it"—I burst into tears—but why do I practice on your feelings—by dwelling on a subject that will touch your

[751]

heart?—It is too much melted already by its own sufferings, L——e, for me to add a pang, or cause a single sigh.—God bless you—I shall hope to greet you by New-years-day in perfect health—Adieu my dear friend—I am most truly and cordially yours,

L. STERNE

To Mrs. William James

Tuesday. [London, ? 15 March, 1768]

YOUR poor friend is scarce able to write—he has been at death's door this week with a pleurisy—I was bled three times on Thursday, and blister'd on Friday—The physician says I am better—God knows, for I feel myself sadly wrong, and shall, if I recover, be a long while of gaining strength. —Before I have gone thro' half this letter, I must stop to rest my weak hand above a dozen times.—Mr. J[ames] was so good to call upon me yesterday. I felt emotions not to be described at the sight of him, and he overjoy'd me by talking a great deal of you. —Do, dear Mrs. J[ames], entreat him to come to-morrow, or next day, for perhaps I have not many days, or hours, to live— I want to ask a favour of him, if I find myself worse—that I shall beg of you, if in this wrestling I come off conqueror—my spirits are fled—'tis a bad omen—do not weep my dear Lady—your tears are too precious to shed for me—bottle them up, and may the cork never be drawn.—Dearest, kindest, gentlest, and best of women! may health, peace, and happiness prove your hand-maids.—If I die, cherish the remembrance of me, and forget the follies which you so often condemn'd—which my heart, not my head betray'd me into. Should my child, my Lydia want a mother, may I hope you will (if she is left parentless) take her to your bosom?—You are the only woman on earth I can depend upon for such a benevolent action.—I wrote to her a fortnight ago, and told her what I trust she will find in you.—Mr. J[ames] will be a father to her—he will protect her from every insult, for he wears a sword which he has served his country with, and which he would know how to draw out of the scabbard in defence of innocence—Commend me to him—as I now commend you to that Being who takes under his care the good and kind part of the world.—Adieu—all grateful thanks to you and Mr. J[ames].

Your poor affectionate friend,

L. STERNE

THE END